Child Psychology

SIXTH EDITION *Child*

Prentice-Hall, Inc., Englewood Cliffs, N. J.

Psychology

ARTHUR T. JERSILD *Teachers College, Columbia University*

To my grandchildren

Child Psychology, Sixth Edition, by Arthur T. Jersild

© *Copyright 1933, 1940, 1947, 1954, 1960, 1968, by Prentice-Hall, Inc., Englewood Cliffs, New Jersey. All rights reserved. No part of this book may be reproduced in any form without permission in writing from the publisher. Library of Congress Catalog Number 68–12376. Printed in the United States of America.*

Design by John J. Dunleavy

Photographs by George Zimbel, Monkmeyer Press Photo Service

PRENTICE-HALL INTERNATIONAL, INC., *London*
PRENTICE-HALL OF AUSTRALIA, PTY., LTD., *Sydney*
PRENTICE-HALL OF CANADA, LTD., *Toronto*
PRENTICE-HALL OF INDIA PVT. LTD., *New Delhi*
PRENTICE-HALL OF JAPAN, INC., *Tokyo*

Current printing (last digit)
10   9   8   7   6

C

Foreword

This sixth edition reflects impressive advances that have been made in developmental psychology since the fifth edition went to press. In chapters that have been added, and in other substantially revised sections of the book, I have incorporated new material from a number of sources.

I have expanded the treatment of children's thinking. In doing so I have taken account of the mounting interest in this subject and the large volume of research devoted to it, inspired by the continuing work of Jean Piaget, and stemming also from new lines of investigation. The treatment includes a new chapter on cognitive development in infancy; amplified sections on children's thinking at later age levels; and discussions of recent research on attention, perception, language development, and the development of moral concepts. I have extended also the account of dreaming to include findings precipitated by the spectacular breakthrough in dream research that occurred at about the time the fifth edition was published. In keeping with the recent upsurge of interest in behavior genetics, a separate chapter has replaced the previous treatment of heredity and further references to genetic factors appear throughout the book.

Other highlights of research in developmental psychology that have received special attention include: psychophysiological studies of the newborn child, which hold out some promise of detecting and predicting nuclear personality traits; evidence concerning the neonate's capacity for adaptation and learning; a continuous flow of striking findings on imprinting and on the role of stimulation and deprivation on development; findings which support earlier concepts regarding early-appearing individual differences in primary reaction tendencies; evidence regarding the dependability of parents' reports as sources of data; and new findings ranging through such varied topics as consistency and change in personality development, individual styles of thinking, the incidence and effects of brain damage, manifest anxiety, and the complex ramifications of a child's view of himself.

In this edition I continue to adhere to a position first announced in the fourth edition, namely, that in trying to understand children it is important to take account of both the subjective and objective dimensions of their lives, and that the concept of the self should be an essential consideration in the study of all aspects of developmental psychology.

I have received help from several colleagues. Millie Almy gave me valuable advice, notably in connection with chapters dealing with cognitive development. A number of persons kindly provided me with reprints and prepublication reports of investigations still in progress. I especially appreciate materials provided by Beverly M. Birns, Raymond B. Cattell, Dorothy Eichorn, John L. Fuller, Calvin Hall, Jerome Kagan, Lewis P. Lipsitt, George Rand, Howard P. Roffwarg, Joseph Schachter, Alexander Thomas, and Steven G. Vandenberg.

I am very thankful to Gerald Chiappa who combined forbearance with skill in converting my scribble into a legible manuscript and who accepted the responsibility of preparing and checking the bibliography.

With each new edition I have felt increasingly grateful to the members of the Prentice-Hall staff with whom I have worked. Through the years, Edgar P. Thomas has provided encouragement and friendly advice. Richard L. Roe has been especially helpful in connection with the present edition. I very much appreciate the imaginative and capable assistance of Nancy Hall, Helen Maertens, and John J. Dunleavy.

My wife has aided me in every way, as is her wont, by reading manuscript and proof, and, most helpfully, she has supported me with patience and good cheer throughout the book's ordeal of birth.

In preparing this edition, I am happy to have had the benefit of a pair of splendid new tutors, my grandchildren.

Arthur T. Jersild

Contents

PART ONE   *A Child Is Born*

1

Entering a Child's World   3

Stages in the Birth of a Personality. Two Approaches to the Understanding of Children.

2

Development in Perspective:
Principles and Theories of Development   9

Basic Concepts in Developmental Psychology. Critical Periods in Maturation and Learning. Motivations for Learning. Interplay between Heredity and Environment. Early Manifestations of Individuality. The Subjective and Objective Dimensions of the Child's World. Self-Development: "Conscious" and "Unconscious" Factors. The Impetus toward Health and Self-Repair. Persistence of Archaic Reaction Patterns.

3

Heredity and Development   25

The Physical Basis of Heredity. Variations in the Operation of Genes. Genotypes and Phenotypes. The Range of Genetic Variations. Genetic Factors in Intelligence. Heredity and Personality.

4   **Prenatal Development**   47

*Organization of Behavior. Fetal Activity and Later Development. Pre-
natal Influences. Hazards of Physical Growth before Birth. Psychology
of Pregnancy and Childbirth. The "Birth Ordeal." The World Surrounding the Newborn Child.*

5   **The Newborn Child**   59

*Generalized Movement. Reflex Action. Sensory Reactions. Other Sen-
sory Responses. Early Signs of Personality Differences. Emotions of
the Newborn Child. Personal Contacts and Child Care. The Premature child. Learning during the First Days and Weeks of Life.*

PART TWO   *Laying the Foundations*

6   **Infancy**   83

*Early Social Reactions. Friendly Beginnings. Interweaving of Perceptual,
Social, and Emotional Development. Individuality in Infancy. Learned
and Unlearned Forms of Behavior. Varieties of Learning Situations.
Learning by Way of Selective Attention and Habituation. Remembering.
Perception and Meaning. The Role of Environmental Stimulation.*

7   **The Origins of Intelligence in Infancy**   103

*Biological Roots of Intelligence. Beginnings of the Sensory-Motor Phase.
The World of Sound. A Many-Faceted World. Producing Effects on
the Environment. Intentional Behavior. Growing Awareness of an In-
dependently Existing Universe. Discovering New Means of Action
Through Experimentation. Substituting Mental Representations for
Overt Manipulation. Continuous Interaction of Assimilation and Ac-
commodation. Motivation Underlying Early Intellectual Development.
Imitation. Imitation and Early Intellectual Development. Imagery.
The Role of Play in Early Cognitive Development. Egocentricity.*

8   **Everyday Needs and Habit Formation
in Early Childhood**   119

*Psychological Meanings of Physical Care. Feeding and Behavior As-
sociated with the Oral Region. Sucking, Mouthing, and Sexuality. Additional Aspects of the Feeding Situation. Sleeping. Sleep Disturbances,
Restlessness, and "Bad" Dreams. Elimination. Sexual Aspects of the
Elimination Process. Further Aspects of Infantile Sexuality. Discipline.*

9   **Trends in Physical and Motor Development   141**

Physiological Functioning at Birth and Later Development. Trends in Physical Growth. Prehension: Use of Arms, Hands, and Fingers. Locomotion. The Impact of Walking. Developmental Impetus Underlying Early Motor Activities. Later Features of Motor Development. Interrelations in Motor Development. Heredity and Motor Performance. Relation of Physical and Motor Characteristics to Other Traits. Handedness.

PART THREE   *Self and Others*

10   **The Self:**
Structure, Origins, Functions   163

Structure of the Self. Beginnings of Self-Awareness. Overt Signs of Early Self-Awareness. Emotional Undertones of the Process of Self-Discovery. Other Evidences of Increasing Self-Awareness. Self-Assertion and Comparison of Self with Others. Factors Influencing the Child's View of Himself. Ascertaining Children's Ideas and Attitudes Regarding Themselves. Projection of Self into Future Roles and View of Self as an Achiever. Self-Regard and Regard for Others. Accuracy of Self-Perception as Determined by Objective Criteria. Self-Perception as Related to Social Acceptance. Stability of Self Ratings as Related to Age. Sex-Role Identification. Sex Differences and Developmental Traits. Sex-Role Preferences in Early and Later Childhood. Reflective Self-Awareness.

11   **Children and Their Parents   196**

Parents' Attitudes and Personality Trends. The "Psychological Parent." Deviations from Normal or Presumably Optimum Parental Care. Consequences of Rejection. Separation from Parents. The Institutionalized Child. Deprivation and Stimulation in Children and Laboratory Animals. Individual Differences in Response to Deprivation. Later Effects of Severe Deprivation. Multiple Mothering and Quasi-Institutional Care. Children of Working Mothers. Children and Divorce. Mixed Emotions. How Does a Child Perceive His Parents? Self-Assertion in a Child-Parent Relationship.

12   **Patterns of Parental Behavior   226**

Observational Procedures. Interview and Questionnaire Procedures. Responses of Children to Child-Rearing Attitudes and Practices. Problems Connected with the Assessment of Child-Rearing Procedures. Children's Temperamental Qualities and Child-Parental Interaction. Parents' Perception and Recall of Behavior. Differing Family Roles and Relationships. Influence of Others on the Child. Cultural Influences on Parental Practices.

13 **Children and Their Peers:**
First Steps in the Social World 243

Beginnings of Social Response. First Steps in Social World. "Natural"
and Acquired Aspects of Social Behavior. Beginnings of Cooperation.
Peer Preferences, Leadership and Friendships among Young Children.
Methods of Studying Social Interactions. Popularity and Self-Sufficiency.
Beginnings of Sympathy for Peers. Rivalry and the Beginnings of Com-
petition. Children's Aggressiveness, Fights, and Quarrels. Influence of
Skills on Social Behavior. Effects of Nursery School Experience.

14 **Peer Relationships in Later Childhood** 268

Off to School. Group Formation and Teamwork. Social Perception.
Social Perception as Related to Attitudes Toward Peers. Acceptance and
Rejection by Peers. Measurement of Social Acceptance. Rivalry, Coop-
eration, and Competition. Aggression in Older Children. Influence of
Socio-Economic Status on a Child's Social Development. Varieties of
Conditions Associated with Socio-economic Status. Boy-Girl Relation-
ships. Prejudice. Children's Games and Play Activities.

PART FOUR *Emotional Development*

15 **The Meaning of Emotion:**
Affection, Joy, Sexuality 305

Differences between Thoughts and Feelings. Early Emotional Reactions.
The Role of Needs, Drives, Motives, Goals. Concealment and Suppression of Feeling. Affection. Varieties of Affectional Attachments. Pleasures, Joys and Satisfactions. Boredom. Emotional Ramifications of
Sexual Development. The Concept of the "Latency Period." Laughter
and Humor.

16 **Fear and Anxiety** 327

The Role of Maturation. The Role of Learning. Age Changes and
Individual Differences in the Expression of Fear. Age Trends in "Fears."
Fears that Persist. Some Special Conditions of Fear. Factors Con-
tributing to Susceptibility to Fear. Children's Fears as Perceived by
Others. Helping Children to Deal with Fear. Anxiety. Perceptual,
Feeling, and Impulse Components in Anxiety and Fear. Theories of
Anxiety. Empirical Measures of Anxiety. Relationship between Tests of
Anxiety and Other Variables. Anxiety and Intelligence. Values of Fear
and Anxiety.

17

Anger and Hostility   366

*Sources and Expressions of Anger. Factors Contributing to Suscepti-
bility to Anger. Anger Outbursts as a "Problem." Losing Touch with
Anger. The Sway of Unresolved Anger. Dealing with Children's Anger.
Jealousy.*

PART FIVE   *The Growth of Understanding*

18

Fantasy and Dreams   383

*Early Manifestations. Changing Structure of Make-Believe. Motives
Underlying Imaginative Activity. Make-Believe Undercurrents in Seem-
ingly Unreasonable Behavior. Imaginative Activity and "Waiting Abil-
ity." Daydreams and Fantasies. Imaginary Companions. Needs Served
by Imaginary Companions. The Coming and Going of Imaginary
Companions. The Imaginary Companion as a Prophet. Other Forms
of Vivid Imagery and Association of Images. Projective Methods.
Children's Dreams. Laboratory Studies of Dreams and Dreaming. Sleep
Patterns, REM Periods, and Age. Laboratory Findings Regarding
Dreams and Dreaming. Differences between Sleeping and Waking
Thought. Motivation and Emotional Content of Dreams. Sex in
Dreams.*

19

Language Development, Perceptual Development   414

*The Development of Language. From Vocalization to Vocabulary.
The "First Word." The Development of Rudimentary Sentence Struc-
tures. Learning Syntax. Increased Understanding of Word Meanings.
Language and Mental and Social Orientation. "Nominal Realism."
Factors Related to Language Development. Children's Thinking as
Expressed by Their Questions. Language and Thought. Perceptual De-
velopment. Sensory Channels. Visual Perception of Pattern and Depth.
Recognition of Pictured Objects. Visual and Haptic Perception. Per-
ception of Graphic Symbols. Perceptual Development and Learning.
Effect of Desires and Motives on Perception.*

20

Conceptual Development   443

*"Operational" Thought. Conservation. From Reflex Action to Reflec-
tive Thought. Concepts of Number and Quantity. Tests of Piaget's
Theories. Other Aspects of Children's Thinking. The Growing World.
Children's Information. Factors Facilitating Conceptual Development.
The Influence of Training on Conceptual Development. "Cognitive
Style." Concrete and Abstract Cognitive Orientation. Intellectual De-
velopment as Related to Drive Level. Analytic vs. Thematic Approaches.
"Analytical-Global Field Approach." Reflectiveness and Impulsiveness.
Childhood Memories. Content of Early Memories.*

21   **Measuring and Predicting Intellectual Ability**   480

Intelligence Tests. Consistency and Reliability of Intelligence Ratings. Limits of Intellectual Growth. Components of Intelligence. Intelligence and School Achievement. Nature, Nurture, and Intellectual Ability. Effects of Schooling on Intellectual Development. Family and Socioeconomic Status and Intelligence. Exceptional Children. Creativity. Children with Below Average IQ's.

22   **Moral Development and Religion**   506

Trends and Directions in Moral Development. Moral Judgment as Related to Family Background. Relationship between Cognitive Ability and Moral Judgment. The Moral Conscience. Parents as Models of Morality. Resistance to Temptation. Relationship between "Maturity" of Moral Concepts and Behavior. Virtues Children Regard as Important. Children's Ideas Regarding What Is Wrong or Wicked. Moral Orientation as Revealed by Choices of "Heroes" and "Ideals." Religion.

PART SIX   *Personality Development*

23   **Personality:**
Normal, Deviant, Constant, Changing   527

Heredity, Environment, and Personality Development. Continuity and Change in Various Facets of Development. Early Display of Unique Personality Traits. Constancy and Change in Early and Middle Childhood. Long-Term Reaction Tendencies. Constancy and Resiliency. Children's Assets as Viewed by Themselves. Children's Shortcomings as Viewed by Themselves. Children's Problems as Viewed by Themselves and Others. Factors Underlying Problem Behavior. Antecedents of Behavior Problems. Knowledge of Self, Acceptance of Self, and Mental Health.

Bibliography   554

Author Index   590

Subject Index   599

Child Psychology

These pages illustrate some of the themes of change and development in the first two years of life.

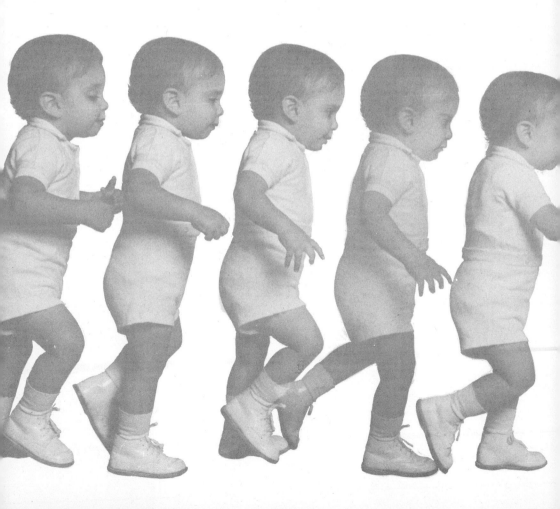

Plate 1

The permanence of objects

To a young infant, an object out of sight no longer exists. Later on, a child realizes that although the object is out of sight, it is still there and retrievable.

Out of sight, out of mind.

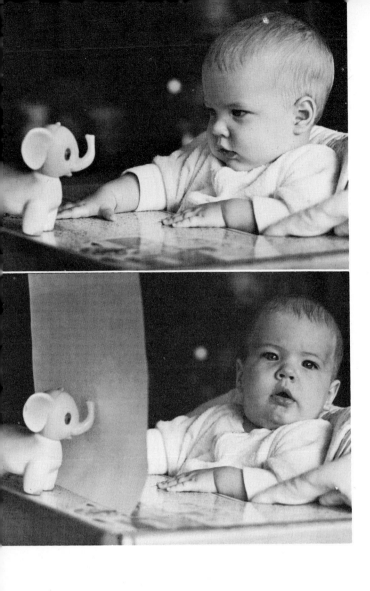

Out of sight, but still there.

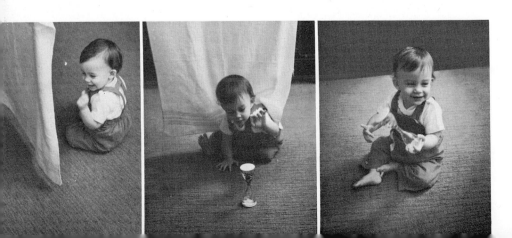

Plate 2   *Discovering a solution and applying it*

Toy will not fit through crib bars crosswise. By chance, the child discovers that it *will* go through endwise. When confronted later with a similar situation, the child applies previous successful solution to the new object.

Succeeds by chance.

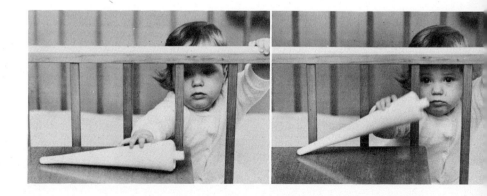

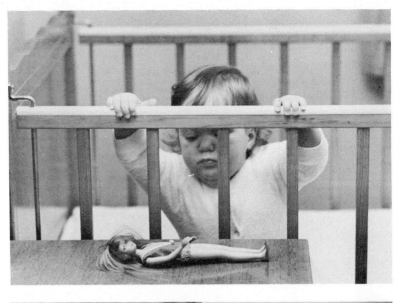

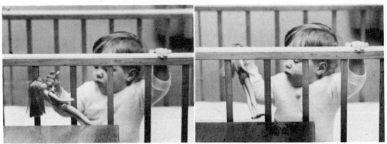

Previous solution applied to new object.

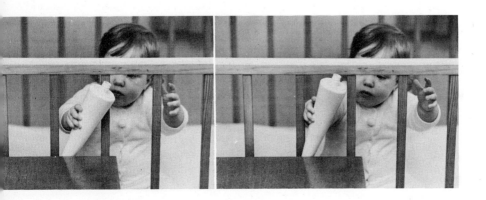

Plate 3 *Response to mirror image*

This is one of the early signs of self-awareness.

No recognition.

Recognition.

Plate 4   *Response to people*

When the baby first begins to smile, he will smile at any face. Later, he distinguishes between strangers and his own family.

A smile for everyone.

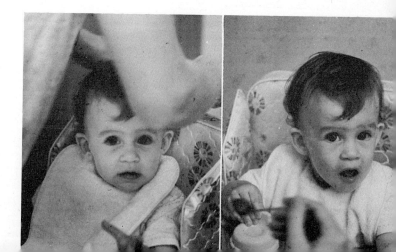

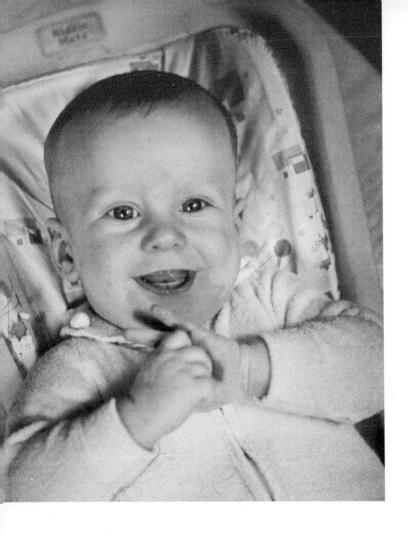

Distinguishes strangers from family.

Plate 5   *Postural control*

Holding the head erect is an important achievement in the development of locomotion and in mental development.

Sagging head, narrow field of vision.

Head erect, wider horizons.

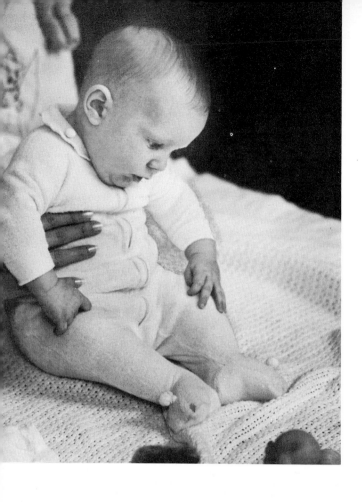

Creeping, a larger world to explore.

Plate 6 *Grasping*

A young infant closes in upon objects with a scooping or corraling movement of palm and fingers; there is almost no use of the thumb. In time, this yields to a well-aimed grasping with thumb and forefinger.

Corrals or scoops.

Grasping.

Plate 7 ## *Walking*

A child's ability to walk is the climax of a long series of developments. At first he walks for the thrill of walking. Later, he launches upon other skills that incorporate elements of walking into larger activity patterns.

For the thrill of walking.

To achieve a goal.

To achieve a goal.

A Child Is Born

1   *Entering*

a Child's World

Birth signals the arrival of a human being who forty weeks earlier was no more than a single cell. He looks helpless but he quickly comes to grips with life.

Soon his movements will be fashioned into countless skills. Within a few weeks or even hours he will display characteristics that set him off as a unique personality. In a year or two he will be able to speak. As a social creature he soon will be deeply involved in the fortunes of his fellows. While yet an infant he will feel the surge of most of the emotions that pervade the life of an adult.

Why should we study this child as he moves from infancy through childhood years? The answer is that to understand human beings we must study their beginnings. It is necessary to enter the child's world if we wish to understand others, or ourselves.

When we study the young child we must rely on what we can observe in his behavior. As he grows older we can observe him and also listen to what he says about himself, and, to a degree, participate in his experiences by drawing upon our own childhood memories. Recollections from our earlier years form a bridge between the child and us and establish a link between the persons we now are and the children we once were. However, the older child's recollections of his earliest experiences are dim and fragmentary. Much has happened in shaping his existence before he is able, through lasting memories, to pick up the threads that form the fabric of his mental life. Moreover, our remembrance of our own childhood experiences will be shaped not only by our own unique perception of happenings as they occurred but also by the ways in which later events in our lives influence our interpretation of what has gone before.

So, in a sense, we come as strangers when we seek to enter the world of a child or try to re-enter the world of our own childhood. But we do not come as complete strangers. We cannot read the child's mind but we can go far in judging the nature of his strivings, thoughts, and feelings as compared with our own. In the sphere of emotion, for example, the feelings expressed by a child when he is only a few weeks old are made of the same raw material as our own. Furthermore, the child each one of us once was still resides in us. Even if we try to abandon him by turning our minds to other things he will never abandon us. He is an essential part of *my* existence as I write, and of *your* existence as you read. And nothing comes closer to the essence of life than our own existence. For this reason it is a rewarding task to endeavor to understand the children we know in the light of the children we once were.

Stages in the Birth of a Personality

In the process by which a person comes into being, three steps are especially significant. The first is *conception,* the sparking of existence. The second is *the process of being born,* setting each one of us apart physically from others. *The development of selfhood* is the third step, involving all the experiences through which each of us becomes aware of his existence as a person, distinct from all others.

The Passive Phase

A baby, who in time will actively strive and plan to take the affairs of his life into his own hands, is at first passive. At the moment he was conceived a good part of what he might ever become was decided by the nature of his biological inheritance. His heredity was handed to him. He did not ask for it. He could not ask for it, nor could he ask to be conceived, or request that he might or might not be born. Life was thrust upon him. This is a simple fact and yet profoundly significant. The equipment a child will use as he faces the future is, to a large degree, determined in advance. There still is room, of course, for a tremendous range in the ways he may use this equipment and in the extent to which his environment helps or hinders him in realizing his potentialities. Yet there is something final about conception and birth. The main probabilities of existence have been laid down. There is no going back and the ultimate certainty is death.

Beginnings of the Active Phase

The third phase, during which a child begins to assert himself as a person, does not reflect this finality. This phase of his life is not completely predetermined. Neither is it fixed in point of time, for in the process of self-discovery we live not only in the present but also anticipate the future and incorporate the past. Even the past is not entirely unchangeable, for the effect of what has gone before may be changed by what now is and what is yet to be. Our past asserts itself, for example, when we discover that we can overcome a threat we once faced with fear.

In the development of the self there is no chance to be unborn, but there is, according to the experience of the person himself, a chance of being "reborn." As viewed from the standpoint of our own thoughts and feelings, we have some freedom to change and to choose. We are also aware that much unexplored and untried ground still lies ahead. In this phase of development there is, then, an added dimension; whereas the story of what is *probable* already has been told, the chronicle of what seems *possible* has only just begun.

Two Approaches to the Understanding of Children

There are two major approaches that can be used in studying children. One is to observe or to measure the *objective* dimensions of a child's make-up and conduct. The other is to inquire into the *subjective* aspects of his personal experience.

We use an objective approach when we measure a child's size, observe his abilities and overt behavior, record his language, and the like. We use the subjective approach when we not only take account of what can be seen and measured but also go on to ask: What is the nature of his personal experience? How does he regard the world? What are his private thoughts and feelings?

From an objective point of view we are interested in knowing that a three-year-old child is three feet tall. From the subjective point of view we are interested not solely in this statistic but in what it might mean to him.

Objectively, the child is near the average in height. He is a large child compared with his one-year-old brother and a small child compared with his ten-year-old sister. But the subjective dimension as viewed from the child's standpoint may be something else. He may regard himself as a rather large child if all his playmates are shorter than he, or he may be acutely aware of his smallness when he notices that bigger children have privileges that are denied him. A child's perception of his size and his feelings about his size are, from a psychological point of view, just as important as his physical stature as such.

The child's subjective view of his experience and of circumstances in the world about him may or may not be in keeping with views held by others. For example, a child may feel that his mother favors a younger brother. From the point of view of the mother, or from the point of view of a visitor, this may not be true at all. But this does not alter the significance of the fact that the child himself feels unfairly treated. Likewise, a youngster may be afraid of a rat in the cellar—a rat that actually isn't there. To him, the rat is a menace even though it is imaginary. The fear is real, even though the rat is unreal. If, in time, the youngster shakes off this fear, his relief also will be very real.

> Similarly, let us take three older boys who are running a race. Henry comes in first, Billy second, and Sammy third. Henry was the victor but he does not feel victorious; he knew in advance that he could win. Billy, although he came in second, has a feeling of triumph. He isn't as sure of himself as Henry and from his point of view it was an achievement to be in a race with Henry and to come in ahead of Sammy. And Sammy, too, although he came in last, and in that sense was a failure, may feel very good about the race for, although he did not win or place, the other boys at least let him race with them, and that, to him, is very gratifying.

We could multiply examples of this sort. Paralleling the external or objective facts about a child's development, his behavior, his ability as compared with others, or his emotions as viewed in the light of his reactions, are the child's private perceptions, feelings, and motives. These may or may not correspond to the objective happenings.

The sum total of all that is embraced in the subjective dimension of a child's experience constitutes what we call the *self*. The self begins to come into being in infancy, and it is in process of "becoming" as long as a person lives. The child's self includes all that he calls "I"; it is all that he calls "mine." It is his world as he experiences it.

The Spectator
and the Participant Observer

To understand children it is necessary to be concerned about both the objective and the subjective dimensions of their development. When we try to assess the meaning of a child's behavior at a given age, it is essential to view it in the perspective of development as revealed by impersonal data based on the study of many children. To understand a child it is necessary also to look into the personal aspects of his experience. To achieve this dual purpose it is necessary to be both a *spectator* and a *participant observer*.

A spectator observes or measures a child's characteristics in an impersonal way. A participant observer, on the other hand, endeavors to fathom the meaning of personal characteristics and conduct from the child's own point of view. A spectator simply notes a child's IQ as measured by standardized tests. A participant is interested in trying to understand what a particular youngster's IQ might mean in the realm of the child's own experience, his successes or failures, and how he assesses his own powers and limitations.

A participant observer also tries to appreciate the personal quality and implications of a child's joy, anger, fear, and other emotions, and of his social interactions with other persons. An observer who views a child in this fashion inevitably draws on his own personal experience—the meaning of success or failure, joy or grief, social acceptance or rejection in his life. While thus trying to understand the child, an observer is involved—he participates in what he observes through the medium of his own experience. He also however, runs the risk of becoming so involved that his powers of observation are blunted. This happens, for example, when parents are so moved by their child's distress that they are unable to take a thoughtful view of what the youngster's trouble might be. Furthermore, an observer's emotional leanings, his interests, worries, values, and moral standards may distort his perception. An observer is misled by his feelings, for example, if because of his own annoyance, he interprets a child's grin as a smirk.

In view of this danger of distortion, then, is it not better to avoid the role of a participant observer? The answer depends on many factors. It depends on the kind of information we seek when we study children. A vast amount of significant knowledge about children can be obtained without requiring a participant approach. The answer also depends in part on practical circumstances of the moment. No matter how much one might desire to appreciate the thoughts and feelings of children, his relationships with children in general, or with one particular child, will range from that of being an onlooker to one who is intensely absorbed. The answer also depends on the safeguards an observer employs when—by choice or necessity—he assumes the role of a participant observer.

The most useful safeguard against biased observation is to compare one observer's perception with that of others. In formal research, this is a standard procedure for detecting and guarding against errors of observation and biased judgment, and for establishing a method of observation that will be as reliable as possible. In the informal observations of everyday life, it is sometimes difficult to use this procedure, although many more opportunities arise for using it than people usually recognize.

An interesting and valuable by-product of testing one observer's account against another's is the light which such a comparison throws upon the observer himself. What a person sees in others is in part a reflection of himself, and he can learn a great deal from this mirror if he choses to do so, especially if his impressions differ from someone else's. If A and B both receive the same impression, we cannot be sure that both are right—both may be wrong. But if A sees one thing, or interprets what he sees in one light, while B makes an entirely different judgment, we can be pretty sure that both cannot be right. One or the other, or both, may be wrong. We now shift from observing the child to self-examination. If an observer is willing and able to learn from what he thus uncovers, he becomes not only a wiser observer of children, but also a wiser observer of himself.

Recommended Readings

Wayne Dennis' "Historical Beginnings of Child Psychology" (1949) gives a succinct, informative account of pioneer studies in developmental psychology. The *Handbook of Research Methods in Child Development*, edited by P. H. Mussen (1960), gives excellent expositions of a wide range of research procedures. Millie Almy's *Ways of Studying Children* (1959) contains clear descriptions of methods teachers and others in charge of groups of children can use to increase their understanding of children. The writer's book, *When Teachers Face Themselves* (1955), discusses the interplay between self-understanding and understanding of others. The annual volumes of *The Psychoanalytic Study of the Child*, edited by Ruth S. Eissler, Anna Freud, and others, presents a variety of studies based on a psychoanalytic approach to developmental psychology. Summaries of research and references to new developments in the psychology of childhood and adolescence appear regularly in chapters on "Developmental Psychology" in the *Annual Review of Psychology*, edited by Paul R. Farnsworth.

2

Development

in Perspective

The subject matter of developmental psychology falls into two main categories: (1) Writings that provide a factual description of aspects of development and behavior; (2) Writings that deal with theories, concepts, or principles of development. These categories often overlap. Factual accounts usually are based on certain theoretical assumptions, and theoretical writings usually are linked with real or assumed facts.

The most revealing portrayal of the sweep of a person's development is one that combines both fact and theory. Specific facts regarding any aspect of development become meaningful only when they are tied together in terms of a general concept, or are viewed in the light of underlying principles. Such principles constitute the theoretical structure of developmental psychology.

Ideally, such a theoretical structure should encompass a complete system of ideas regarding both the architecture and the dynamics, or governing forces, in human development. This ideal has not yet been achieved. There is not an all-encompassing set of developmental concepts on which all scholars agree. But, for that matter, no scientific discipline open to new findings and discoveries can offer a finished theoretical structure. Even the so-called "exact" sciences, such as chemistry and physics, undergo profound theoretical revision from time to time. However, any theoretical formulation is useful that (1) incorporates within a general principle all known factors that are at work in producing a result; or (2) provides a hypothesis, based on available knowledge, that can be tested by established research methods; or (3) offers an imaginative leap beyond what is generally known by questioning old assumptions, opening new areas of exploration, and providing the impetus for creating new research techniques.

Building theory in developmental psychology obviously is a rather complicated business. A student in this field deals with a system of events that is, to a large degree, open at both ends. At the time of conception a child has genetic potentialities that are partly predictable but also, to a large extent, unknown. Before him lies the almost infinite range of possibilities that are open to a living organism that is capable of growth, capable of learning, and able, in time, to build a vast superstructure of mental processes. A psychologist assumes a definite risk when he tries to formulate principles underlying this intricate spectacle of development.

When we inquire into theories in developmental psychology we encounter many controversial ideas. The controversy, however, is more superficial than real. With some exceptions, the difference between theories usually do not consist in a head-on collision between incompatible points of view (such as occurred when some geographers thought the earth was flat while others contended it was round). Controversies arise more often from what various theorists choose to emphasize and ignore, rather than from what they are able to deny.

Basic Concepts
in Developmental Psychology

The following pages will deal with considerations that are integral to the theoretical framework of developmental psychology. These considerations are not mutually exclusive, nor are they equally important; but they will receive separate attention for the sake of emphasis. Later sections in this chapter, and throughout the book, will deal with these ideas in more detail.

*The Biochemical Understructure
of Development*

The most rudimentary principle is that the development of behavior and all that transpires in the child's mental life is grounded on the biochemical structure of his organism. Everything that eventually emerges in the psychological sphere has a somatic base. Included in this somatic understructure are the substances that constitute the child's genetic endowment. These determine the course of his physical development and, directly or indirectly, influence all aspects of his psychological development.

Growth

The biological process of growth provides the structural foundation for the changes that occur in the course of a child's development. The impetus for growth is inherent within the organism. With proper nourishment and protection from harmful influences, growth proceeds in a lawful, progressive manner toward its mature state.

Maturation

New functions or capacities for action, made possible through growth, become established by a process of maturation. The terms "growth" and "maturation" are sometimes used interchangeably. In this text the term "maturation" will be used to denote the process by which underlying potential capacities of the organism reach a stage of functional readiness. This process involves both the changes in structure that come with growth and the progressive exercise of structures that provide groundwork for later performances.

Walking is an example. At the age of about one year, some children "learn" to walk almost overnight. This is a product of both growth and maturation. Growth provided the necessary bone, muscle, and nerve structures. But walking actually does not spring forth overnight. It is founded on earlier sequences of development in which the child progressively uses or exercises his emerging capacities. One of the first steps in walking occurred many months earlier when the child became able to hold his head erect.

Interplay between Maturation and Learning

The role of maturation can be observed most readily in early childhood in the development of the capacities underlying the basic coordinations involved in locomotion (such as creeping, standing, and walking) and in prehension (such as reaching, grasping, and opposition of thumb and fingers in handling an object). On the basis of motion picture recordings of infants' movements and manipulations, Ames (1940)[1] discovered that through a process of maturation, new and often complex behavior patterns can appear for the first time in a form so complete that several weeks—often several months—of subsequent exercise do not appreciably change either their form or speed. This does not mean that these accomplishments thrust themselves

---

[1] Writings cited in the text are listed in the bibliography at the end of the book. References are identified by date of publication.

upon a passive organism. But beyond providing an appropriate opportunity for a child to exercise his basic coordinations in his own way, there is little an adult can do to hasten these developments.

Maturation also plays an important role in language development, in intellectual development, and in determining the nature and range of a child's social and emotional behavior. To advance in his language development, for example, a child needs stimulation from his environment; but he will respond to such stimulation at his own pace (Strayer, 1930). Extra stimulation will not make a normal six-months-old child speak like a normal year-old child. Similarly, a child needs opportunities to interact with his environment in order to progress from one stage of thinking to the next, but given such opportunities he uses them at his own pace. It is not possible, at least by any presently known strategy of teaching or stimulation, to convert a normal two-year-old into a four- or six-year-old thinker.[2]

Learning

Although maturation is an essential factor in most aspects of development, it is not an all-sufficient factor. To use his capacities, a child needs not only to grow but also to learn.

Learning has been defined in many ways. According to one definition, learning consists of the establishment of an *acquired* response or, more generally, any acquired mode of behavior. This definition assumes a distinction between acquired behavior and behavior that is referred to as *native*, or inborn. The issue over what is acquired and what is native has long been a subject of debate. Much of the behavior that seems ready-made at birth has been "acquired," at least in the sense that it has emerged out of a compound of biological growth combined with active functioning prior to birth. It is possible, however, to distinguish between behavior that is inborn or "built in" at the time of birth and behavior which is "built into" the organism as a consequence of specific experiences after birth. Such a distinction can be made between *unconditioned* and *conditioned* responses which are described in Chapter 5.

Learning may also be defined as any form of behavior that is modified in any specific fashion as a result of experience. This definition would embrace behavior that becomes established through classical conditioning, through experiences initiated by the child himself, and through any kind of training instituted by others.

Nature and Quality of Learning as Related to Maturity Level. The child's level of maturity, in addition to affecting the extent to which he can profit from practice, will also affect the nature or quality of what he learns. A child who learns to climb while in the creeping stage will climb like a

---

[2] Findings in studies of the effects of training on stages in children's thinking as described by Piaget will be reviewed in a later chapter.

creeper (McGraw, 1935), pushing himself upward and forward by gripping with his toes. What he has gained may not be of much benefit to him when he has reached the "walking stage" and no longer grips with his toes but depends more on his arms.

At a certain maturity level children who make rapid strides in mastering one performance may make little or no progress in others. Their progress cannot be predicted on the basis of how an adult judges the difficulty of the task. This fact was illustrated in a study in which twins received "training" in riding a tricycle and in roller skating before they were two years old. An older child or adult usually can strike off on a tricycle much more easily than on roller skates, but it was easier for these youngsters to manage roller skating than riding a tricycle. It seems that the coordinations required in the clockwise motion of pedaling a tricycle, requiring forward pressure with one leg while releasing pressure with the other, is more difficult to master at an early age than later.

Some skills learned at one level of maturity may have to be relearned or re-adapted to the child's growth pattern at a later stage of maturity. This point was established in a study of the same pair of twins who had been exposed to roller skating, tricycling, and other activities before the age of two years and then were observed again at about the age of six years (McGraw, 1939). Both twins maintained their proficiency in riding a tricycle, although neither had ridden a tricycle in the meantime. Roller skating, which at first they had mastered more readily, was a different matter. Partly because of growth changes in their bodily proportions (including relatively longer legs, and a shift in the center of gravity), the twins, who had learned to roller skate when they were about two years old, had difficulty at the age of six in maintaining their balance on skates.

The fact that training at a certain age may produce remarkable results in one kind of performance and not in another was documented in studies by Jersild and Bienstock (1932, 1935). In a study of rhythm, children's ability to beat time with their hands in response to music was measured by an electrically timed apparatus. Although the youngsters responded to the music and to the task with considerable gusto, they showed little or no improvement with practice. On the other hand, youngsters of the same age who received practice in singing the tones struck on a piano made such spectacular gains that it was necessary, after the experiment was underway, to extend the range of tones at both ends of the scale used in the original tests.

Critical Periods in Maturation and Learning

In the discussion above we have pointed out that at a certain level of maturation a child is ready to profit from opportunities or experiences which were unfruitful at an earlier stage. Is there also a phase *during* which a child must acquire certain forms of behavior if he is to acquire them at all? Does the adage "Strike while the iron is hot" have implications for developmental psychology? The answer is yes, but the "yes" is not as resounding as we might wish, because the relevant evidence has been obtained mainly from work with lower animals.

The label "critical phase" has been used to denote a period in a creature's development *during* which it is possible to establish ways of behaving that may have life-long consequences and *beyond which* it is difficult, if not impossible, to achieve the same results. Lorenz (1935) has coined the word "imprinting" to describe ways of behaving that are established during the critical period. Anyone who has lived on a farm, especially in the good old days, has had an opportunity to observe imprinting on a somewhat crude scale. A "dairy" calf, removed at birth from his mother's udder and for a time brought up "by hand," becomes accustomed to human contacts at an early age and thereafter can be approached and petted in the pasture. But a "beef" calf, born and reared by his mother in the fields, will shy away from a human being. Many other creatures, such as chickens, ducklings, goslings, colts, pigs, and kids, if fed, handled, petted, and reared in frequent contact with human beings for a time during infancy, are likely to remain, as adults, more responsive to humans than will creatures who early in life had no such contacts.

Sometimes in a state of nature, but more probably under laboratory conditions, animals that are "natural enemies," or at least not "natural friends," may learn to live peaceably together. A kitten reared with mice may never become a mouser. A cockatoo brought up with puppies may become attached to puppies but indifferent or hostile when, at a later time, it meets members of its own species (Kuo, 1960).

According to Scott (1957) in every species of animal there is a short period in life, usually quite early, during which primary social bonds are formed. These bonds may be contrary to what we commonly regard as the animals' natural way of life. The period during which such behavior can be established varies with different species of animals.

In studies by Hess (1959) ducklings were imprinted by an artificial duck, a decoy equipped with a loudspeaker that emitted a sound produced by a human voice and moved about mechanically, on a circular runway. Some animals that have been imprinted not only "follow" the imprinting object but, in time, make sexual advances toward it.

Studies of the "critical phase" in the development of various species of animals raise many interesting speculations. If animals regarded as natural enemies, such as cats and mice, can be reared to live together in friendly fashion, what, we might ask, are the limits to which such a principle might be applied throughout the animal kingdom, and in the affairs of human beings? Would it be possible, for example, through proper management at critical periods, to rear a race of men whose aggressive impulses have been canceled? Unfortunately, the answer, if there is one, cannot be found in experimental work done with animals. In all such studies there have been interventions which cannot be duplicated on an appreciable scale in a state of nature. The cat who, as a kitten, learns in a laboratory to live with mice in a spirit of brotherly love does so with human help. But all the other unconfined cats and predators do not treat mice so kindly. In the meantime, the mouse-loving cats would still kill birds, unless trained not to do so. All we can infer from animal experiments in this area is that much of what we regard as "animal nature" is not as immutable as we ordinarily suppose. To translate this idea into practical human affairs would indeed be quite a challenging project.

Although the critical period has been studied mainly with lower animals the underlying concept has implications for the study of aspects of human development. We will explore some of these implications in later chapters.[3]

Motivations for Learning

The process of learning may be initiated accidentally, as when a child, having produced a clatter by inadvertently making an object fall to the floor, proceeds, with seeming intent, to produce more clatter. He has learned one way of making a noise. There is an underlying motive of some sort at work whenever a child deliberately pursues a line of action that leads to learning. The motives that come into play as time passes cover a vast range, including the desire to gratify a "primary" physical appetite, drive, or need; a desire to avoid or be rid of physical discomfort, or punishment; a desire to please or appease others; or to pursue various self-chosen goals.

In the past, accounts of learning placed considerable emphasis on rewards and punishment (including punishment flowing from others, or "punishment" in the form of discomfort arising as a consequence of an individual's own action). The label "reinforcement" currently is used with a variety of modifiers to denote incentives toward learning either to establish, or to avoid, or to abolish a given form of behavior. The reinforcement may be positive (rewarding), or negative (punishing, unpleasant); it may be "primary" in reducing or allaying a so-called primary drive (such as thirst), or it may be secondary, deriving its effectiveness from a learned, or conditioned, need or goal. (The need for social approval is sometimes cited as a need acquired through learning.) Reinforcements that promote or establish a certain learned response may be administered experimentally under controlled conditions, by teaching or training an individual under the conditions of everyday life, or as a consequence of an individual's own self-initiated actions.

In recent years, many psychologists have reiterated the concept, popular

---

[3] Issues and problems that arise in applying the concept of the critical period have been discussed by Caldwell (1962).

several generations ago, that a great deal of childhood learning results from activities which the child undertakes without the impetus of a "primary" need, without externally imposed rewards or punishments, and without any ulterior goal in mind. Such activity occurs when the child, as far as one can tell, undertakes an activity for its own sake, as when he repeatedly climbs up and down an incline, unsteadily at first, with nothing at the top to lure him, and with nothing at the bottom to entice him, and then, when he has mastered the act, abandons it and turns to other things. It occurs when he labors to put things together and then takes them apart, as though this were an undertaking sufficient in itself. Learning resulting from self-initiated activity also occurs when a child explores or experiments with no apparent intent other than to satisfy his curiosity.

In connection with such self-initiated activities, a child often manifests what Karl Bühler long ago spoke of as "function pleasure"—pleasure in doing, satisfaction derived from the sheer exercise of an activity that lies within his command, or that serves as a challenge to his powers and brings its own reward.

Extensions of self-initiated behavior that facilitate learning appear when children seek excitement, take risks as though playing with fear, or return again and again to an unfinished task that no one has imposed upon them. Frequently, when a child undertakes self-initiated activities, there is no distinction between means and ends—the means he employs seem to be ends in themselves.

Among recent writings, various proposals have been made for labeling the wide-ranging activities which cannot readily be explained by "primary" drives and which are not prompted by conventional laboratory rewards. Harlow and his associates (1950) speak of a drive to manipulate. Berlyne (1958) speaks of an exploratory or curiosity drive to account for the fact that animals (as well as children) spontaneously explore novel objects and then turn to other things when the novelty seems to have worn off. White (1959) uses the term "competence" to denote a variety of forms of exploratory behavior, manipulation, and behavior such as self-initiated grasping, walking, and paying attention, which form a part of a process whereby the individual learns to interact effectively with his environment. All these activities apparently are "motivated in their own right." He suggests that the motivation be termed "effectance" and that the experience produced be called a "feeling of efficacy."

Indigenous Motivation

Just as the impetus for growth is inherent within the organism, so also is the impetus for using the capacities that emerge in the process of growth. Inherent in the organism is an impulse to do what the organism is capable of doing. It is as though the eye seeks to see, the ear to hear. The child whose hunger has been appeased, whose thirst has been quenched, and who has no pain to distract him, busies himself with his own development. He exercises his muscles. He spontaneously undertakes a vast variety of activities. He practices his growing powers. He manipulates things with his hands. He creeps, even though there is no lure to attract him. He explores. He experiments with sounds. He "practices" speech sounds and when able to speak he "practices" his pronunciation and use of words. He inquires. He asks questions. He even toys with fear by taking risks, and he tempts an angry retort by testing the limits of his parents' or peers' forebearance.

The healthy child manifests an important principle of development; namely, the principle of *indigenous motivation*. Each healthy child has a tendency, spontaneously, to put his growing powers to use. Development is equipped with a self-starter, at least in its early stages. There is an elemental eagerness for action in every healthy infant and young child.

Pre-eminence, Wholeheartedness, and Gradation. At various periods of development there are strivings that are pre-eminent for a time in the child's preoccupations, and then recede. When a child begins to master a new activity he is likely to go "all out" for it. When he is ready, for example, to try to stand or walk, he concentrates on these performances. They take precedence over other occupations. He may be so absorbed that he neglects or resists other things; he may even refuse to be fed if his usual eagerly awaited feeding time happens to come at a moment when he is poised for a take-off. Then, as he becomes more accustomed to walking, his zeal subsides. Walking ceases to be a master, so to speak, and becomes a servant—a means of getting from one point to another.

Other instances of this phenomenon occur when a child, for a time, becomes passionately absorbed in feeding himself, in spite of messing and spilling; when he asserts himself by resisting every command or suggestion; when he goes on a questioning binge; when, in his social development, he plunges into common projects with his peers; and when, at adolescence, his striving for independence so absorbs him that he becomes rebellious and seems even to go out of his way to reject the parents on whom he once leaned for psychological support.

Developmental Revision of Habits. When a child becomes able, through the process of maturation, to accomplish feats that before were impossible, he supplants old ways of behaving with new ways. When such a change occurs it exemplifies an important principle—the *developmental revision of habits*.

This principle means that in the process of maturing, a child, of his own accord, if given proper opportunities and if spared from traumatic misfortunes, will change from a less to a more "mature" kind of behavior. It means also that in many areas of development the impetus of growth is stronger than the force of habit. According to the laws of learning, any response or performance tends to be perpetuated if it (1) is repeated again and again, and (2) is inherently satisfying or reinforced by desirable rewards. It becomes a habit that is hard to dislodge. However, the growing child's behavior frequently violates these laws. For example, at a certain stage a child devotes almost all his attention to creeping (the law of repetition is working overtime), and judging from his gusto and eagerness, his creeping is very rewarding. If he were simply a creature of habit, he would continue to creep his way through life. Instead, in due time, he tries to walk, even if there is no ulterior goal to tempt him and no external demand for swifter locomotion, and he will persist in walking in spite of tumbles and bruises.

There are numerous other modifications of behavior that conform to this principle. The child who once sucked for food begins to chew. The youngster who once wet his diapers acquires the "dry habit," oftentimes with a minimum of training, when, in the process of maturation, he becomes capable of controlling his bladder. In his daily routines, the youngster who once passively and contentedly allowed others to provide for him eventually insists on doing things for himself—feeding himself, dressing himself, using playthings, and embarking on countless other endeavors. His lauguage habits change: "muvver" eventually becomes "mother." In his intellectual development, he renounces one way of thinking and adopts another, as we will note in Chapters 6 and 20.

Interplay between Heredity and Environment

A child's development is a product of an interplay between his heredity and his environment. Often, in discussing these two factors, writers take sides, sometimes even using the phrasing, heredity *versus* environment. Actually, it is important to recognize both heredity and the environment, and the *interaction* between the two.

Most of the published works in developmental psychology place a heavy emphasis on the environment, and this emphasis also appears in this book. When we study children, we hope the knowledge we gain will help us to be more thoughtful and wise in dealing with them. Whenever we try to promote children's welfare, we do so by managing their environment. All child psychologists, and all parents, teachers, nurses, social workers, and others who are entrusted with the care of children are, in a sense, environmentalists by profession.

But when we thus try to provide a good environment, it is essential also to give heed to the child's original nature. Each child's development, obviously, is determined to an important degree by the seed from which he springs. To be alert to a child's welfare, it is necessary as far as possible to assess his inherent potentialities and limitations. It is essential also to be on guard against demands or hopes which require more of him than he can ever fulfill. It is also essential to consider the child's hereditary endowment when we try to understand interactions between him and others in his environment, particularly his parents. A child's inherent qualities play an important role in these interactions.

Over a span of several decades there has been a widespread tendency among psychologists to ignore or to minimize the role of genetic factors and to assume that if anything goes wrong in a child's development it is due to faulty upbringing by his parents or parent substitutes. Mothers especially have been singled out for blame by those who take a onesided environmentalist approach, but fathers, too, have received a goodly share of blame. Actually, a great deal of what influences a child's development, for better or for worse, is beyond parental control. Parents can, of course, choose whether or not to beget a child, but they have no choice in determining the genetic elements they transmit to their offspring. In assessing the interaction between heredity and the environment, it is necessary to recognize that there are also environmental forces over which parents have little or no control.

Fortunately, in recent years there has been an upsurge of interest in human behavior genetics which promises, as studies accumulate, to provide an increasingly thorough assessment both of genetic and environmental factors. Actually, as we have indicated, a child is both a creature and a creator of his environment.

In the physical sphere, a child obviously cannot thrive unless the environment provides shelter and food. The role of the environment is underscored by the fact that, in some parts of the world, children grow taller than their forebears, presumably because of better nutrition (see, e.g., Clements, 1953). But genetic factors also are at work. Given much the same diets, some children grow bigger and stronger than others. At adolescence, some reach puberty earlier than others. They differ in physique, physical attractiveness (in the eyes of others), in their tendency, with a given diet, to remain lean or to put on weight, and, when putting on weight, to accumulate fat in various parts of the body—some are "hippy," some have fat legs, etc.

There is an interplay of hereditary and environmental factors even before birth. Under favorable conditions, the course of an unborn child's development is determined primarily by heredity, but even the genetic elements that, so to speak, prescribe the course of development, reside in an organic environment and interact in various ways. Moreover, environmental misfortunes before birth may impair a child's development to a degree ranging from death to weaknessess that do not become apparent until several years after birth.

In the psychological sphere there is likewise an interplay between heredity and the environment. An adverse environment can impair or delay the normal course of development, no matter what a child's genetic potential might be. The most impressive evidence of such impairment comes from studies of institutionalized children who have been exposed to deprivation and neglect. However, under ordinary circumstances, similar environmental conditions do not produce equivalent developmental results, nor do variations in the environment produce corresponding variations in developmental results. This fact has been most impressively demonstrated through studies that compare identical twins and fraternal twins.[4]

The phenomenon of imprinting during the "critical" phase, as discussed earlier in this chapter, demonstrates dramatically the influence of the environment. The behavior induced through imprinting may be radically different from what ordinarily is regarded as an animal's predisposition. However, such artificially induced behavior also reflects the role of genetic factors. In the study by Hess and his associates (1959) cited earlier, it was found that some ducklings were highly imprintable while others showed very little imprinting response. When the "imprinters" were bred with other imprinters, and when the "non-imprinters" were mated, there was "a clear and significant difference in the imprinting behavior of the two groups, even in the first generation." The "imprinted" ducklings had "imprinting test scores more than three times higher than those of the 'non-imprinter' ducklings."

Other interesting findings concerning the complex interplay between heredity and the environment have come from studies of lower animals. On the one hand, such findings show that hereditary differences between individuals (such as a tendency to be active or passive) may become magnified through habit formation with the passage of time, even though the individuals are reared under environmental conditions that are controlled to make them as similar as possible (Scott, 1944; Scott and Charles, 1954). When a small initial genetic difference eventually makes a significant difference in the way in which an individual responds to his environment, it is difficult for an observer, if not impossible, to reconstruct or to detect the genetic factor unless he was on the spot from the beginning. Indeed, he very likely would be inclined to explain the characteristic entirely in environmental terms.

In every child's life, regardless of his heredity, there are environmental circumstances that are, so to speak, thrust upon him, leaving him no option to choose and no power to change, and oftentimes permitting no avenue of escape. But each child is also, to an important degree, the architect of his environment, at first inadvertently and later more deliberately. His environment is structured, in part, by his own unfolding powers: the active runabout child precipitates many restraints that were not imposed before he was able to get about. He also structures his environment by what he seeks, what he selects, and what he ignores.

The child's nature in many ways determines the nurture he receives. The frail child requires and, in a kindly home, will receive, a different kind of care than the child who is robust. The child with a cheerful disposition

---

[4] The role of genetic factors in development will be discussed more particularly in the chapter that follows.

evokes a smile. The child with mechanical aptitudes is likely, if his family has the means, to get tools for Christmas, while the one with aptitude and zest for reading receives books.

Early Manifestations of Individuality

When we seek to discover common developmental characteristics in children, we come upon a paradox. Each child is different from all the rest. As we will see in later sections of this chapter, signs of individuality appear in early infancy. Full-term, healthy babies manifest distinctive individual characteristics even during their first few days of life (see Chapter 5). Such characteristics are more likely to be consistent than to fluctuate from day to day. Soon after they are born, babies bear marks of individuality that cannot be traced to differences in post-natal care and treatment.

The Subjective and Objective Dimensions of the Child's World

Beginning in the first year of life, children's experiences have both an objective and a subjective dimension. The subjective dimension, as known to the child, is what we call the self. The concept of the self will be discussed in a later chapter, but it is so essential for understanding developmental psychology that it should have a place here.

The ideas, attitudes, and other mental states that constitute the self are a product of the child's experience, but they also impart structure to his experience. As time passes, the child's view of himself influences, to an important degree, his ideas concerning the doors of life that are open to him, or closed. For example, even at the kindergarten level children have attitudes which foreshadow how they will react to the tasks that lie ahead in school. One child sees himself as a person who can achieve; another child is less certain about his ability and less self-confident.

Ideas and attitudes regarding self also play an important role in a child's motivation. Having formed ideas about who and what he is, and about his worth as a person, he tends to maintain these ideas, to confirm and defend them.

His perception of himself influences how he will perceive others. If he regards himself as one whom other persons favor and respect, he is likely to perceive others accordingly. If he sees himself as one whom others treat unfairly, he is likely to interpret others in the light of this perception. This fact introduces one of the most profound but also one of the most baffling principles in developmental psychology: a child's perception of what others think about him, how they feel about him, what they do or intend to do with him is, for him, a reality. If, for example, he perceives a parent as one who admires him, or as one who is critical of him, then from the child's standpoint the parent *is* admiring or critical even though the perception may be erroneous from all standpoints other than his own. A child's perception is a subjective reality even if it is quite out of line with objective reality as perceived by everyone else.

The foregoing statement underscores the viewpoint set forth in the preceding chapter—namely, that it is necessary to study both the subjective and the objective dimensions of a child's world if we wish to understand him or to reach firm scientific conclusions about what causes children to be what they are and to do what they do.

Self-Development:
"Conscious" and "Unconscious" Factors

The currents flowing through every growing child's mental life range from events that he is quite clearly aware of to events that he does not even dimly grasp. An example appears in dreams and in other states of mind that occur during sleep. Recently developed techniques for detecting when a dream probably is occurring (discussed in a later chapter) have shown that persons who never can recall a dream, and who say they don't dream, actually can report a dream that was in progress when they were awakened in the act of dreaming. When a person has a dream but fails to recall it, it means that a vivid experience which held sway (as recorded, for example, in eye movements occurring during the dream) has not been brought into his stream of conscious awareness. Many other events are likewise lost. Few people can recall anything that occurred before they were about three years old, despite the early flood of experiences that probably shaped their later way of life.

Events that do not become part of a person's conscious record of experience include not only passing circumstances that are conveniently forgotten but also events that have left a mark which that person cannot explain. This happens, for example, in connection with troublesome fears and phobias, resentments, feelings of inferiority, and the like, which a person cannot trace to their source. It happens when a person is driven by motives he cannot understand and behaves in an irrational manner.

The labels "unconscious" and "unconsciousness" have been applied variously to events that have an impact on a person's way of life but do not lie within the purview of his conscious awareness. The concept of the unconscious, or something akin to it, has been discussed from ancient times, but in modern times it has been advocated most strongly by Freud and his followers. According to Freud, the unconscious includes not only primordial urges, the Id, which seeks gratification without thought or scruple, but also impulses that have been banished from a person's consciousness by a process of repression, but which continue to intrude upon a person's behavior, usually in disguised ways.

The concept of the unconscious has had a mixed reception among academic psychologists. The reason, in part, is that it has been clothed in rather imprecise language. But the importance of what has been referred to more or less loosely as unconsciousness, or the unconscious, is obvious to anyone who reflects upon himself, or examines his dreams and vagrant fantasies, or who contemplates behavior in others that cannot be explained on rational grounds.

The Impetus toward Health and Self-Repair

Generally speaking, the forces of normal development are arrayed on the side of good health and recovery from injury. From a genetic point of view, most children are well-born. Some do inherit bodily infirmities, or are fated to be mentally defective, or face the tragic prospect of mental illness, but far more are sound of body and mind, even though they vary greatly in their innate resources. In addition, children are usually blessed with an abundant capacity for self-repair. A child with a sound body has wonderful recuperative powers; his bruises soon vanish; his wounds heal quickly, unless vital structures have been destroyed. Many wounds not only heal but leave no lasting scars. Broken bones soon mend if properly set. The body's capacity to heal itself is generally stronger in childhood than in later years.

It is more difficult to observe and to measure the healing properties that are at work in the psychological sphere. Youngsters display what seems to be a remarkable degree of resiliency in facing the emotional upheavals of everyday life. But full recovery from emotional stress is hard to gauge; concealed wounds may remain. When a youngster's feelings are not openly displayed, or leave him vacant of feeling, we may suspect a deep hurt, and a slower process of healing. The reaches and limits of the capacity for self-repair in the psychological sphere have never been clearly defined.

Persistence of Archaic Reaction Patterns

The factors we have just discussed—developmental revision of habits and the organism's capacity for self-repair—have a benign influence on the course of development. Furthermore, as we have pointed out, heredity is usually a wholesome force; most human beings in spite of wide variations in genetic endowment are potentially sound of mind and body. Still another positive attribute is the growing individual's capacity for learning to cope with his environment.

However, to be most beneficial, the capacity to learn must include an ability not only to acquire but also to discard, an ability both to retain what is helpful and to cast off the residues of past problems.

Unfortunately, many persons, and probably all persons to some extent, carry over unresolved problems. Lingering fears, rivalries, grievances, or feelings of inadequacy from earlier days, may restrict a child's ability to deal with new situations. A youngster who harbored bitter feelings of rivalry toward a brother or sister may "transfer" these feelings to other persons later on in life. He does not start with a clean slate when he competes with schoolmates or, later on, with rival suitors or business associates. He may be hampered by persisting attitudes of hostility, or a need to vanquish, or feelings of inadequacy. An analogous situation prevails if he rebels against "authority figures," as once he rebelled against his father or mother. He then is unable to perceive people as they are or to take them as they come. Instead, he has a distorted perception of them; he sees them through a glass that has been darkened by his past experience.

Often when a person thus responds to new conditions with old reaction patterns he does so in an irrational manner: he is not aware of what is occurring; he is under the sway of what has been called unconscious influences.

Recommended Readings

The *Concept of Development*, edited by Dale Harris (1957), and *Theories of Child Development* by Alfred E. Baldwin (1967) discuss theories and concepts underlying approaches to the study of development.

3

Heredity

and Development

Genetic and environmental factors that shape the course of a child's development start to work at the moment he is conceived. Even the individual cell
containing the materials that constitute an individual's genetic endowment
represents a complex environment, with many interacting elements. The
complexity of this interaction proceeds apace in development before and
after birth.

The Physical Basis of Heredity

The germ cells of a child's parents normally contain forty-six structures
known as chromosomes, each of which contains countless substances known
as genes. It is the genes that contain the specifications for the child's inherited

characteristics. The genes represent what is sometimes referred to as the genetic "code." The forty-six chromosomes of each parent are arranged in twenty-three pairs. But only one member of each pair is contributed to the fertilized egg.

In ordinary cell division, through a process known as *mitosis*, each new cell contains a full complement of twenty-three pairs of chromosomes. However, each of the germ cells that unite to produce a fertilized egg has undergone a different type of cell division. Through a process known as *meiosis* two divisions occur, terminating in a germ cell which contains only one set of twenty-three chromosomes instead of the normal set of twenty-three pairs. The ovum and the sperm, each thus equipped, are known as *gametes*. When these unite at the time of fertilization, the fertilized egg, known as a *zygote*, contains a full complement of twenty-three pairs of chromosomes, one member of each pair contributed by the father and the other by the mother.[1]

Male and Female Chromosomes

The human male and female are alike in having twenty-three pairs of chromosomes, but they are unlike with respect to one of their pairs. In the female, this chromosome pair contains two corresponding members, known as XX. In the male, this pair includes an X chromosome and a Y chromosome. When the XX members of the female pair are segregated through meiosis each of the female gametes will contain an X chromosome. But a given male sperm, after meiosis, may contain an X chromosome or a Y. If the ovum is fertilized by a sperm with the X chromosome, the resulting pair (XX) will (if everything else is in good order) produce a female; but if the Y chromosome is transmitted by the male, the resulting pair (XY) will be a male.[2]

Possible Combinations of Chromosomes

In the process of fertilization, many different combinations of chromosomes are possible. Each parent, at the time of conception, received half of his or her chromosomes from the father and half from the mother. So, when the father's cells undergo meiosis, it is possible that all chromosomes in a certain sperm cell might have come from his mother's side, or all from

---

[1] The discussion of heredity in this text will not go into the intricate biochemical mechanisms underlying heredity. Many generations of scientists accumulated evidence regarding hereditary influences before much was known about the chemical nature of these mechanisms. A recent book by Beadle, (1964), with the appealing title: *The New Genetics: The Threads of Life*, gives an account of developments that have occurred in the biochemistry of genetics since DNA (deoxyribonucleic acid) was identified as the basic genetic material.

[2] Anomalous conditions in which the full complement of male or female physical characteristics is not produced, may be influenced not only by the action of X and Y chromosomes but by the presence or absence of unusual combinations of sex chromosomes and the interaction between sex chromosomes and other chromosomes.

his father's side, or all but one from his mother or from his father, and so on through other possible combinations. Moreover, the combinations that might occur are multiplied by the fact that the seminal fluid released by the father in the process of mating contains a vast number of spermatozoa, but (in the usual instance) only one of these will find its mark.

In the mother, the ripe egg that is waiting to be fertilized may also include any one of many combinations of the chromosomes transmitted to her by her parents. The combination lodged in a particular ovum that ripens at the time of menstruation may be different from the combination in the preceding menstrual cycle, or from the one that will ripen during the next cycle.[3]

Variations in the Operation of Genes

Genes should not be regarded as independent agents, each operating as though it were a separate craftsman. Rather, to varying degrees and in varying ways, they interact with one another and with the functioning organism of which they are a part. Moreover, according to Meissner (1965), we should think of them as "continually and dynamically operating to regulate the adaptation of the organism to its environment."

In the fertilized ovum, the genes in the paired sets of chromosomes may be identical in their arrangement and potential effects. Such would be the case, for example, if both sets of genes contain specifications for exactly the same eye-color. Genes in such a combination are known as *homozygous*. They represent, in effect, a double recipe for a given trait. The genes in a given arrangement may, on the other hand, be unlike in their effects, as would be the case if one set specifies dark and the other light eye-color. Such gene arrangements are known as *heterozygous*.

Because of the complicated action of genes, almost anything that might be said about their performance is likely to be an over-simplification. Yet, obviously, it is not an over-simplification to say that they do operate, producing genetic results that are visible to the naked eye. Moreover, it is possible to single out certain characteristics of genic action that help to account for the vast variety of genetic similarities and differences one can observe in everyday life or measure by objective tests.

A trait may arise primarily through the operation of a single gene, sometimes referred to as a *major* gene. Such an outcome is called a *single factor* mode of inheritance. Again, a characteristic may result from the action of several genes, producing what has been called the *multifactor* or *polygenic*

---

[3] In the reshuffling and redistribution of ancestral chromosomes during meiosis, a vast variety of combinations may occur. It has been estimated that the number of different types of combinations that a single pair of parents potentially might produce is larger than the number of human beings that ever have existed. (Fuller and Thompson, 1960). This means that the chances that two blood relatives (other than identical twins) might genetically duplicate one another are almost infinitesimal.

type of inheritance. Characteristics which show a normal range of variation, such as bodily size or intelligence, probably represent a polygenic form of inheritance (Dobzhansky, 1962; Kallman and Jarvik, 1959).

When the genes in a pair are unlike in their effects (*heterozygous*) one of the genes, called the *dominant* gene, may be more potent, overshadowing or suppressing the effect of the other, the *recessive* gene. Again, genes may be only partly or incompletely dominant.

When dominant genes prevail over their recessive counterparts, the offspring will exhibit the trait communicated by the dominant genes. But the recessive genes remain as part of the offspring's genetic endowment and may be transmitted to a later generation. They may remain as a latent hereditary factor, "skipping" several generations, and then, if both gametes contributed by a pair of parents contain corresponding recessive genes, the recessive trait will appear in the offspring. When this occurs, it means that a descendant possesses an inherited characteristic that has not been displayed by any of his immediate ancestors.

Hereditary impairments that occur through the operation of dominant genes are less likely to be perpetuated than impairments resulting from recessive genes. When dominant genes are at work, the impairment will be manifested. If the impairment appears prior to the time when an individual is able to reproduce, it is likely to reduce or even to nullify his chances for reproducing his kind. This self-limiting continuation of dominant genes is less likely to occur, of course, if the inherited trait or potential weakness is one that ordinarily does not appear until later in the life span (such as Huntington's chorea). On the other hand, defective genes will not similarly be manifest; they may be transmitted from one generation to the next with no sign that they are there until an offspring happens to receive similarly defective genes from both parents.

The fact that genes may operate in a dominant or recessive manner opens the way for many variations between members of the same family. The added fact that many traits are based on a *polygenic* type of inheritance opens the way for even wider variations.

Moreover, the outcome of polygenic inheritance is further complicated by the fact that the union between two different gametes may, in the first generation, produce what resembles a blend between the two. A union between a person with light skin color and one with dark color may result in an offspring with intermediate coloring. If one parent transmits genes for tallness and the other for short stature the offspring may be intermediate in height (Dobzhansky, 1962). But many other combinations are possible. (We should mention, of course, that body size is not determined by genes alone, but may be influenced also by ill health and by diet.)

The action of multiple genes may produce various outcomes in connection with other traits, such as intelligence, susceptibility to certain infectious diseases, and susceptibility to mental illness.

Genotypes and Phenotypes

The terms *genotype* and *phenotype* distinguish between what is manifest and what is inherent in an individual's make-up. The genotype consists of all the elements that pertain to an individual's inheritance—his total genetic endowment. The phenotype is the totality of an individual's manifest qualities and characteristics (*pheno* + type, as in phenomenon: that which shows, is visible or apparent) and represents the ways in which or the extent to which an individual's hereditary potentialities are realized or revealed. A person's phenotype is a product of (1) the particular chromosomes, genes, and genic patterns which happen to be combined in the fertilized cell when he is conceived; (2) the interaction between these elements such as occurs, for example, when dominant genes are ascendant over recessive ones, or when multiple factor genes are at work; and (3) the influence of his environment, before and after birth.

The genotype and the phenotype may correspond in varying degrees. Normal human beings invariably have two legs, for example, and in this respect the genotype and phenotype are identical. On the other hand, the two do not correspond if, for example, a person with a certain leg *length* has genes which might produce offspring with shorter or longer legs. The genotype and phenotype also are dissimilar when an individual displays a dominant trait but in his germ plasm carries recessive genes which can produce a different trait. Furthermore, the two are unlike if the environment has interfered with the development of an individual's genetic potentialities. This occurs, for example, if a child with an excellent hereditary background is unable to realize his potentialities because of damages or injuries he has sustained prior to, during, or after birth.

The more homogeneous the ancestral strains, the more likely that a particular individual's genotype and phenotype will be similar. Concordance between the genotype and phenotype can be increased by a process of "selective breeding," such as in "pure-bred" cattle or dogs. In experimental work with animals that have a short gestation period and that become sexually mature in a short period (such as fowl, mice and rats) it is possible by selective breeding to produce, within a relatively short period of time, strains that characteristically exhibit a given phenotype (such as a high activity level, "emotionality," aggressiveness, or a high or low level of ability to learn how to master a given task, such as running a particular maze).[4]

A human infant will, of course, usually have a far more diverse genetic background than prevails among inbred animals. Among humans there is, however, a considerable amount of selective breeding. The effects of such inbreeding are most noticeable in members of small social groups who remain

[4] See, e.g., Hall (1938), Tryon (1940), Hall and Klein (1942), Scott (1942) and Thompson (1953) and review of studies by Fuller and Thompson (1960) and by Fuller (1964, 1965).

aloof from the surrounding population and intermarry from one generation to the next and, to a degree, among persons of similar racial, ethnic, or national origins who intermarry. This kind of selection can establish a concordance between the phenotype and genotype in certain characteristics (such as skin color and facial features that are characteristic of Mongolians and Caucasians). Within a given group, other selective factors may also operate, such as a tendency to mate with a person of similar, rather than widely dissimilar, educational and socio-economic backgrounds.

However, such selective factors still leave room for tremendous diversity. It would be easier to estimate what a child's genotype and prospective phenotype might be if persons chose their mates on the basis of genetic considerations, such as would be the case if persons with an ancestral background of high intelligence chose mates with a similar background. But romance and genetics usually do not team up so neatly.[5]

Within the population at large there are defective genes that may flow, often unknown, from one generation to the next, but then manifest themselves in outcroppings of mental deficiency, mental disorder, or some other malady. As long as such genes exist, without being manifest, the genotypes and phenotypes of those who carry them will differ. According to Neel (1960), modern advances in medical science and medical care may increase this "pool" of defective genes by enabling more persons with genetic defects to survive and to reproduce. This view has not been advanced as a reason for withholding medical care. More optimistic is the view that the underprivileged (and seemingly "inferior") segments of the population contain countless persons who are genetically sound and who possess potentialities far beyond those they have had a chance to realize.

The Range of Genetic Variations

The range of individual differences due to genetic factors is stupendous. The difference becomes even more marked if an individual favored by nature is also favored by the fortunes of life, or if an individual who is ill-favored by nature is also visited by an unfavorable environment that exposes or augments his weaknesses and limitations.

Examples of differences within the "normal range," attributed to heredity, have been cited by Hardin (1962). According to Hardin, the individual with the highest concentration of Vitamin A in the blood may have a concentration as much as fifteen times that of the individual with the lowest. The concentration in the urine of the male hormone, androgen, may be eleven

---

[5] A correspondence between phenotypes and genotypes is perhaps more likely to appear in the offspring of persons who have a demonstrably poor genetic background, except in their ability to reproduce.

times higher in one person than in another. Minimum intoxicating percentage of alcohol in the blood may be eight times as high for a person who has the highest tolerance for alcohol as for a person who has the least tolerance. (This means that one person becomes as tipsy after drinking one ounce of liquor as another does after drinking eight ounces.)

Genetic Factors
and Physical Development

The influence of heredity is most noticeable among blood relatives who closely resemble each other. Identical twins may look so much alike that it is practically impossible for someone who does not know them intimately to tell them apart.

Findings regarding the resemblance in height between parents and children are given in Chapter 8. In the absence of illness, improper nutrition, or other damaging factors, heredity is the "great master" in determining physical growth (Krogman, 1962). Even when growth is seriously stunted for a time by malnutrition or illness, the organism has a "strong tendency to return to its natural growth curve" (Tanner, 1963).

According to Tanner, the organism's growth has a regulatory system, mainly genetically determined. It is as though it had a built-in "target-seeking" tendency. Tanner illustrates ways in which preadolescent children whose growth had been impeded for a time proceeded to "catch up" and return to their characteristic growth pattern when the restraining influences were removed.

One interesting (and highly fortunate) manifestation of the "target-seeking" and "catching up" phenomenon is seen in the relation between size at birth and later size. Most of the variation in relative body-length among adults is established by the age of two years. Tanner reports that the correlation between a child's body length at two years and his length as an adult is .80. Genetically determined differences in the time and intensity of the adolescent spurt, according to Tanner, account for most of the remainder of the adult variability.

However, a child who is big at two and who most likely will be big at twenty is not likely to be correspondingly big at birth. Tanner cites findings (Penrose, 1961) indicating that birth size is controlled by uterine factors. The correlation between birth length and adult length is only about .20, but during the first year, and continuing into the second year, the small child who has a genetic potential for being a large person "catches up." He gets "on target" and swings into a growth pattern that expresses his genetic potential.

The fact that birth size is restricted and does not reflect the ultimate size of one who genetically is destined to be a large person obviously has an important bearing on a child's and (his mother's) survival. If no such regulation occurred, the birth ordeal might be very severe for a child who had a large father and a small mother.[6]

Genetic factors that influence physical development have an important bearing on behavioral development. A physical impediment not only affects the range and scope of an individual's activity, but also the way he is able to respond to others, and the way others respond to him. The response he elicits from others obviously is environmental—it certainly is not part of his heredity—but it is shaped to an important degree by his heredity.

Genetically determined physical and physiological attributes may also play an important role in determining an individual's temperamental qualities and "personality" traits. This has been demonstrated most clearly in studies of animals selectively bred to produce strains that differ in activity level, "emotionality," aggressiveness, and the like (more regarding this in a later section).

In human beings, one of the most significant manifestations of the interplay between hereditary and environmental factors appears at adolescence. The early-maturing boy, for example, as a person, differs in many ways from the late-maturer (see, e.g., Jones, 1960, and Mussen and Jones, 1958). A difference that is generated largely from within appears when the early-maturer has an earlier growth spurt and stronger heterosexual interests, but the effect of this difference springs from the environment when his fellows esteem him because of his physique and athletic prowess. Such esteem may also enhance his own self-esteem. The esteem reflects the values that prevail in his social environment, but it is precipitated by his heredity.

Genetic Factors and Intelligence

Intelligence may be influenced by genetic factors in a variety of ways, some of which we will cover. Various forms of mental deficiency have been traced to the operation of recessive genes and to abnormalities in the chromosome structure, and it is believed that some may be due to anomalies in the cytoplasm (the substance surrounding the nucleus which contains the chromosomes).

The genetic mechanism governing the inheritance of intellectual potential within the "normal" range of intelligence, as distinguished from several forms of mental deficiency, has not been firmly established. In a review of theories in this area, Fuller and Thompson (1960) note that, according to one theory, intelligence within the middle range is determined by a dominant genetic factor, dependent on a single major gene, while high or low intelligence is

---

[6] Tanner mentions that a similar phenomenon has been observed in cattle: a calf born to a small cow that was mated with a large bull is smaller than a calf born to a large cow that was mated with a small bull. The two calves grow at different rates after birth so that by the time they reach adult size there no longer is any difference.

due to the operation of recessive genes. It seems more likely, however, that multiple genes are involved, although the genes in a multiple gene cluster "may not necessarily be equal or additive" (Fuller and Thompson, 1960, p. 225).

One prominent body of information regarding the role of heredity comes from studies of resemblances between children and parents who share the same homes and genetic background as compared with resemblances between children and foster parents who share the same environment but do not have the same genetic background. Another prominent source has been comparisons between siblings, *dizygotic* (fraternal) twins and *monozygotic* (identical) twins. Studies of twin groups have also included comparisons between twins reared together and twins who have been separated and reared in different environments.

Resemblances between "Own" and Adopted Children

Correlations between the intelligence of children and their fathers or mothers typically range around .50. If genetically there were a one-to-one correspondence between a child's ability and the ability of one or the other parent, the correlation should be much closer to 1.00 (but it probably would never reach exactly 1.00, for even in comparing test-retest scores of the same group of individuals, the correlation usually falls short of 1.00). From a genetic point of view (disregarding for the moment the influence the environment might have) a correlation of .50 is very substantial in view of the fact that (a) a child receives only half of his genetic endowment from one parent, and (b) there may be discrepancies between a parent's phenotype and genotype (he might transmit genetic potentials to his child that are not manifest in his own performance). In view of the complexity of the genetic apparatus, a child might have attributes that differ from those of his parents, but have a genetic base. However, the degree of resemblance between the mental abilities of parents and children does not, *per se*, measure the role of heredity, for the resemblance might be due to a common environment.

Studies of adopted children should help to clarify the role of environmental factors, although they are not likely to provide a sure test because of selective factors involved in adoption. One selective factor is that a child is not likely to be placed for adoption, but to be kept in an institution or to be placed under foster care without legal adoption, if he is obviously abnormal. When adoption agencies place a child for adoption they frequently try, if possible, to fit the child to his prospective home, such as assigning a child who seems most likely to be "college material" in the home of parents who probably, in time, will wish and be able to afford to send the child to college. There are, of course, frequent exceptions to "selective placement," for many prospective adoptive parents who are eager to have a youngster are likely simply to ask for a *child*, and not a child with certain specifications.

The most substantial long-term study of foster children has been conducted by Skeels and Skodak, who began their work with 180 children placed for adoption when under six months old. This study will be reviewed here in some detail because it touches in a significant manner on several important issues.

The children in the Skeels-Skodak study were placed in homes that were generally superior to the home background of their mothers. These children were tested periodically. In the latest complete published assessment (available as this is written) 100 of them were found and tested when between the ages of eleven and seventeen years, with an average age of thirteen years, six months (Skodak and Skeels, 1949). The children at this age had developed more favorably, and had a higher average level of intelligence than would have been predicted on the basis of the social background of their biological parents. According to preliminary indications in a later, incomplete (at this writing) assessment of these children sixteen years later, they continued, as adults, to achieve at a higher level than would have been predicted from the "intellectual, educational or socio-economic level of the biological parents" (Skeels, 1965).

The findings in the Skeels-Skodak study show impressively that children from an unpromising social background can thrive when placed in a better environment, and that many of them will attain above-average intelligence (their average IQ at an average age of thirteen and a half was 106).

But from a genetic point of view the findings are, in some respects, even more impressive. While the children, as a group, prospered in adoptive homes that were generally superior in educational level to the educational level of the biological parents they showed wide individual variation. There was little or no relationship between these variations in intelligence and variations in the educational level of the foster home. The education of the foster parents (in terms of highest grade completed) ranged from about the fourth grade through college. The correlation between educational level of the foster parents and the children's IQ's hovered near zero (ranging from − .03 to .10).[7]

By contrast, there was a substantial correlation between the intelligence scores of the children and the scores of their mothers, from whom they had been separated in early infancy. Intelligence test results were available for sixty-three of the true mothers, most of whom were tested after they had gone through the experience of having given birth to a child and giving him up for adoption, a time that probably would not be optimum for test purposes. The correlation between the intelligence scores obtained by the

---

[7] This is in contrast to correlations of about .50 or more between the intelligence scores of teenage children, reared in their natural homes, and the educational level of their parents, (Honzik, 1957).

true mothers and the scores of the children at an average age of thirteen and a half was .38 (on the basis of the 1916 edition of the Stanford-Binet test) and .44 on the basis of mothers' scores on the 1916 edition and children's scores on the 1936 revision of the Stanford-Binet test.

These are lower than the correlations of about .50 between children and parents who have spent their lives together, but the similarity between the coefficients is considerably more significant than the differences.

According to the findings in this study, we can conclude that while foster children can profit from good home environments, their IQ as they reach adolescence can be predicted much more effectively on the basis of the IQ's of the mothers from whom they were separated in infancy than on the basis of variations in the environments provided by the foster parents who rear them.

Intelligence of Identical Twins

The most impressive inquiries into the role of genetic factors in intelligence are studies that compare identical twins, fraternal twins and siblings. Fraternal, or dizygotic, twins spring from separate fertilized eggs and therefore their genetic endowment may be as diverse as that of brothers and sisters born a year or more apart.

Various criteria are applied to determine whether twins are identical or fraternal. Sex is one criterion (members of a brother and sister pair obviously are not identical). Almost "identical" appearance is another criterion used in everyday life, but it is not an adequate guide. Close resemblance may lead parents to regard a pair of twins as identical when actually they are not.[8] A standard procedure now used in identifying identical twins is to compare their blood type by laboratory analysis. In earlier studies, monozygosity was diagnosed on the basis of a variety of detailed physical features, such as eye color, iris pattern, and eyelash color and length; hair color, texture, and distribution on the forehead, temples and neck; characteristics of the skin, such as color, texture, and freckles; and a number of other detailed characteristics of the mouth, lips, teeth, form of nose, palm lines, and fingerprints.

Correlations between total intelligence scores of identical twins have varied somewhat from study to study.[9] But the typical finding has been that the resemblance between identical twins is substantially higher than the resemblance between fraternal twins or siblings.

Results from nine studies in this area have been assembled by Nichols

---

[8] Smith (1965) found that in numerous instances parents regarded twins as monozygotic when, according to blood-typing, they should be classified as dyzygotic.

[9] This variation may be due to the nature of the sampling, but it probably also is due to the nature of the tests employed. Different tests, to varying degrees, may tap abilities that, to varying degrees, are influenced by heredity or the environment.

(1965). Most of the correlations (eight of the nine) between the scores of identical twins ranged from .87 to .92. (This is about as high a resemblance as would be found between the two sets of scores obtained when the same individuals are measured by two forms of the same test). The corresponding correlations for fraternal twins ranged from .52 to .70. A lower correlation (.75) between identical twins was reported in one of the nine studies; this study also reported a lower correlation (.39) between fraternal twins. In all comparisons there was a substantially higher correspondence between the identical and non-identical groups.

In a study by Shields of British children (not included in the above summary) the correlations between intelligence test scores of identical twins reared together, and identical twins reared apart, were almost precisely the same (.76 and .77, respectively) as compared with a correlation of .51 for fraternal twins.

Findings from other studies (reviewed by Shields, 1962) indicate that when identical twins are reared apart they may resemble each other less than when reared together, but the results on this score are not consistent. Moreover, the resemblance between identical twins reared apart is likely to be considerably greater than between fraternal twins reared together. In the Shields study, variations that might stem from the environment were taken into account, but, according to Shields, "From an analysis of family structure, social background, and a number of other factors of possible importance psychologically, intelligence seems to be singularly little affected by the various differences in the environment" (Shields, 1962, p. 111). This statement should be qualified by the fact that where there is extreme deprivation, children's intelligence may be quite adversely affected.

Some of the earlier studies of smaller samplings of identical twins reared apart attribute a greater influence to the environment than appeared in Shields' investigation. (See, e.g., a study by Newman, Freeman and Holzinger, 1937.) In a review of studies in this area prior to 1960, Fuller and Thompson (1960) indicate that "the evidence on twins reared apart supports the hereditary hypothesis" but they also mention that differences in the environment can produce differences between monozygotic twins.

Although findings generally establish that identical twins are more alike in intelligence than fraternal twins, the latter, in most of the studies, resemble each other more than siblings. The correlations usually obtained in comparisons between siblings cluster around .50. In the nine studies reviewed by Nichols, the correlations between fraternal twins ranged from .39 to .64, with six of the correlations in the low .60's. On genetic grounds, fraternal twins should ordinarily not be more alike than siblings. When fraternal twins actually are somewhat more alike it seems reasonable to attribute this similarity to environmental rather than genetic factors (e.g., similar ordinal position within the family, similar schooling, simultaneous exposure to experiences that might affect intellectual development, and so on). However, greater similarity between fraternal twins might also be influenced to some degree by the fact that they probably have been tested under more nearly equivalent conditions that usually prevail in tests of siblings (both are likely to be tested at the same juncture of their development, probably by the same examiner). To obtain comparable results from siblings, it would be necessary to provide test conditions as nearly similar as possible, and at the same juncture in the siblings' development. This would, among other things, require that siblings be matched age-for-age by comparing, for example, the score obtained by a ten-year-old child with the score obtained by his older sibling when that sibling was ten years old.

In longitudinal studies (studies of the same children over an extended period of time) Olson and his associates (reviewed in Olson, 1959) have used this technique of comparing children of the same family in terms of test results obtained at the same chronological age despite different birth dates. In one such comparison, the correlation between the intelligence of siblings was .71. This is a higher coefficient than ordinarily is found when siblings have been compared. It approaches some of the highest correlations that have been obtained in comparisons of fraternal twins.

One reservation that can be raised concerning findings in studies of identical twins is that their high resemblance may be due to a similar environment. This reservation is obviated to a large degree by findings which have shown high resemblances between identical twins reared apart. But the similarity between the twins might be due in part to environmental influences prevailing prior to and during birth. Twins, both fraternal and identical, face more common hazards before and during birth than children born singly.

Actually, the environments of two identical twins may be quite dissimilar in important respects. One may be more favorably situated in the womb and one may have a more difficult birth. It is probably because of prenatal environmental influences that one twin at birth frequently is longer, heavier, and more robust than the other. Moreover, after birth, the twins themselves may, so to speak, create an environment that has a differential influence on the two members of the pair. This happens, for example, when one twin is more active and robust and demands and receives more attention. The fact that one twin (often the more sturdy of the two) frequently becomes the "leader" of the two is another indication that their environments are not the "same." To an observer it may appear that they live under equal conditions, have similar advantages or disadvantages; but there actually may be significant environmental inequalities within the small world in which they reside. This would be the case, for example, if a mother subtly or openly "takes sides" with the weaker of two twins, or responds more animatedly to the sturdier of the two.

Nichols (1965), in a study mentioned above, explored the role that the environment might play in producing similarities between twins. He excluded, from the groups he was comparing, twins who had dissimilar experiences, such as being separated for a period of time; pairs of twins in which one, but not the other, had suffered a major illness or disability; or had married at an early age; or had received some kind of special training. This led to the exclusion of 18 per cent of his identical and 25 per cent of his non-identical twin pairs. The correlations between the performance of the twins on mental tasks tended to be slightly higher when these twins were excluded, "indicating that differences in experience tend to produce differences in ability (or perhaps to reflect differences in ability rather than causing them)." But the changed correlations were about equal for both the identical and fraternal twins, "so that the conclusions regarding the effect of heredity were not affected" (Nichols, 1965, p. 241).

Heredity and "General" and "Specific" Intellectual Abilities

The complex ways in which genetic factors influencing intelligence may operate is indicated in recent studies dealing with specific intellectual abilities. "General intelligence," as measured by a comprehensive mental test, usually represents performance on a variety of tasks which tap a variety of abilities. Although these abilities tend to be positively correlated, a person may be quite uneven in his performance on the separate tasks represented in his total intelligence test score. Most of the findings dealing with heredity and intelligence have been based on total scores obtained on intelligence tests, rather than on the various sub-tests. (The sub-tests, each representing a smaller collection of tasks, usually give a less adequate and reliable assessment of intelligence than the composite of all sub-tests.)

Evidence presented by Nichols (1965) and Vandenberg (1965) supports the view that potentialities for specific intellectual abilities (such as verbal ability and arithmetical ability) may be independently inherited (Nichols, 1965, p. 241). Furthermore, there is evidence that the relative contribution of heredity and the environment varies in connection with different aspects of intellectual ability.

The fact that genetic factors may operate in quite specific ways is also indicated in studies of laboratory animals. In a well-known study by Tryon (1940), rats with lower error scores on a maze, and rats with higher error scores, were selectively mated to produce "maze-bright" and "maze-dull" strains. After several generations, the two strains of maze-runners were so distinct that the poorest performers in one group equaled or surpassed the best performers in the other. This study showed quite dramatically that learning ability, as measured by Tryon's maze, could be influenced by controlling the genetic factor.

However, a later study by Searle (1949) indicated that the "bright" maze runners were not characteristically superior in a variety of other situations. Animals from the twenty-second generation of Tryon's strains were tested in nine different situations, including among others, the original Tryon maze; a water tank arrangement (equipped with *culs-de-sac*, and requiring the rats to swim the length of the tank under water in order to escape); two mazes differing from the Tryon maze; and an apparatus which tested the rat's ability to learn to make the correct choice of a series of escape routes by responding to visual cues (black or white) or spatial cues (right or left).

The scoring system provided thirty measures on which the two groups could be compared. The scores of the "brights" (in the Tryon tests) tended to be slightly higher on the average than the "dulls." But the "dulls" were not generally inferior on measures of errors in learning. On three of five such measures, the "dulls" either equaled or did better than the "brights." The findings indicate that "maze-brightness," as determined in the original Tryon study, does not seem to represent what might be regarded as a "general intelligence" factor. The animals differed in characteristics such as hunger drive, "emotionality," sensitivity to the noise produced by the apparatus, spatial perception, and perception of visual cues.

Apparently the strain of rats that did so well on the original Tryon maze possessed the right combination of traits to manage this particular maze rather than a type of "cognitive" ability that would make them superior to other rats in a variety of tasks. This does not deny the significance of the fact that it was possible, through genetic control, to produce two remarkably different strains of animals in Tryon's study. It does, however, underscore the point that it is difficult to generalize about the operation of genetic factors on the basis of performance in a particular test. To produce new strains of animals that might possess the optimum combination of learning ability, perceptual ability, drive, and emotionality for dealing with the variety of tasks used in the Searle study would require a new (and probably very demanding and unpredictable) regime of selective mating.

Genetic Factors
in Certain Forms of Mental Deficiency

Genetic factors operate in many ways to produce intellectual deficiency. In this section we will discuss two of these ways.

One serious form of impairment, known as phenylketonuria, is attributed to the operation of a recessive gene. This condition, which appears early in infancy in the afflicted child, is due to a genetically determined metabolic disorder. If untreated, it produces intellectual impairment, with IQ's that may range from .30 to .70 (Fuller, 1964), which are likely to be accompanied by serious disorders in the social and emotional sphere. The consequences of this affliction can be ameliorated or remedied by diet control measures, if the condition is detected and treated very early in the child's life. (The cause and corrective for this condition have not been known long enough to follow the affected children through adolescence.) [10]

Other forms of mental deficiency have been traced to a variety of aberrations in the genetic apparatus. Various forms of a condition known as mongolism have been traced to an abnormality in the chromosome structure. In one of these forms, it appears that there is a flaw in the process of cell division (meiosis) that produces the ripe ovum. Normally, only one chromosome from each of the original pairs is present in the ovum that is prepared for fertilization; but in one form of mongolism this division or disjunction of the chromosomes fails to occur in one of the chromosome pairs. Thus the ovum will contain twenty-four instead of twenty-three chromosomes. When fertilized by a normal sperm, there will be an extra chromosome or three chromosomes (a condition known as trisomism) in this pair instead of the normal complement of two.

This particular type of mongolism is more likely to be transmitted by older than by younger mothers. Accordingly, a mother may give birth to this type of mongoloid offspring after having produced several normal children. In some other forms of mongolism, due to anomalies in the chromosome structure of the mother or father, this age difference does not appear.

Heredity and Personality

In her classic study of personality development during the first two years of life, Shirley (1933c) expressed the view that personality has its physiological basis in the structure and organization of the nervous system and of the physical-chemical constitution of the body as a whole. Gesell had earlier (1928) maintained that a person's basic developmental tempo, trend, and temperament are mainly inherent individual characteristics.

Neither of these statements implies that personality, viewed as a total gestalt, or that isolated personality traits, are directly inherited. Rather, the

---

[10] This is one example, of many, illustrating the significance of genetic knowledge for human welfare and for understanding psychological development. Evidence indicates that genetic factors play an important role in many forms of psychological disorder and lends support to the work of scientists who are seeking to discover what the biochemical basis for such disorders might be. If the physical basis is discovered, there is also a likelihood that a corrective might be found. Recent advances in behavior genetics suggest that there may be a genetic biochemical basis for many psychological misfortunes that formerly were believed by many to be primarily of psycho-social (environmental) origin.

statements imply that probably all personality manifestations are influenced, to a greater or lesser degree, by genetic factors. Whatever an individual's genetic constitution might be, he will not, of course, directly inherit a specific behavior pattern, such as becoming agitated or manifesting aggressive impulses when subjected to stress. Rather, he may inherit a predisposition to react in these or other ways. The influence of the genes in producing this predisposition is mediated through complex biochemical and metabolic processes.

For many years following the work of Shirley and Gesell, investigators paid relatively little attention to the role of heredity in human personality development, although striking findings did emerge from studies of temperamental and dispositional characteristics of laboratory animals. The relatively recent upsurge of interest in behavior genetics in human development promises to test the assumptions made by Gesell and Shirley even though, of course, it is more difficult to make definitive tests with human beings than with laboratory animals.

Findings concerning genetically influenced characteristics in infra-human animals obviously cannot be interpreted as applying to human beings. Yet they can lead to principles that may have wide general applications and that suggest leads for the study of man.

It is instructive to note some of these genetically determined characteristics in infra-human creatures. They range from organic weaknesses or impairments which, if present in man, would have profound psychological consequences, to behavior tendencies which, objectively, correspond to tendencies manifested by human beings.

Genetic differences among animal strains include differences in sexual behavior, maternal behavior, aggressiveness, and activity level. Genetically different strains of animals may also differ to a significant degree in emotional reactivity, although variations within each breed may be so broad that the most placid ones in a breed tending to be "emotional" may be less excitable than the most reactive individuals in a less "emotional" breed (findings dealing with the effects of selective breeding on a variety of characteristics have been reviewed by Fuller, 1965).

Differences in preference for alcohol have been found in inbred strains of mice, as well as differences in the rate of oxidation of alcohol and a tendency to prefer or to avoid alcohol. It seems that one individual, in whom alcohol is oxidized rapidly, may enjoy the effects more and acquire an appetite for alcohol while another, in whom the oxidation process is sluggish, apparently may get something resembling a hangover from a small amount of alcohol and develop a distaste for it.

The fact that there may be striking genetically determined differences among animal strains does not rule out the importance of the environment. This appears, for example, from studies of strains of guinea pigs possessing a comparatively high level of enterprise and vigor in their sexual behavior. When animals of a strain that characteristically showed a high level of sexual activity were separated from their kind and reared in isolation for a time while young, they were inferior in their sexual performance as adults. It appears that to be sexually effective at the adult level animals need to fraternize with their kind in a social environment during certain earlier periods of their development (Fuller and Thompson, 1960).

Some hereditary behavioral differences among strains of animals appear to be mediated through the endocrine glands, while others may be triggered not only by the presence of a large or small amount of hormones but also by the reactivity of appropriate nerve centers to such hormones.

In human personality development the operation of genetic factors appears most impressively in connection with certain forms of mental illness. In considering this point, we must remember that in any kind of disordered or normal personality manifestation that might be influenced by heredity there is an essential interplay between genetic factors and the environment.

Personality traits obviously are expressed through an individual's behavioral response to his environment. A particular response is likely to be influenced by (1) learning and (2) by the stresses or inducements in the environment that elicit it. For example, an individual with a tendency to "withdraw" when anxious is likely to learn how to withdraw most effectively and to learn how to seek ways of avoiding situations that aggravate his anxiety. Moreover, the extent to which he manifests this tendency to a seemingly normal or abnormal degree will be influenced by the severity of the demands and pressures within his environment.

Much of the evidence regarding genetic factors in mental disorders comes from studies of the incidence of mental illness among members of the same family. According to findings presented by Kallman, and findings from other studies reviewed by Kallman (1953), it is highly likely that if one member of an identical twin pair has an affliction diagnosed as schizophrenia, the other will be afflicted. (Various studies have indicated that the chances range from about 65 to 80 in 100.) Moreover, this degree of concordance is many times higher than the corresponding figure for fraternal twins or siblings. If, according to Kallman, one member of a fraternal twin pair is afflicted, the chances that the other member will also manifest the illness range from about 3 to about 17 in 100. Kallman (1954) and other investigators likewise have found a high degree of coincidence for another form of mental disorder, diagnosed as manic-depressive psychosis. (In monozygotic twins a coincidence of from 66.7 to 92.6 in 100 as compared with 16.4 and 23.6 in fraternal twins.)

There are three considerations in connection with the foregoing findings that should be noted. One rests on the possibility that identical twins may be subject to similar environmental stresses. Another is that when mental illness strikes one of two twins who are reared together, and who have had a close personal relationship, it is likely to have a profoundly disturbing effect on the other. The shock might conceivably be so severe as to produce a "nervous breakdown" in the other twin, even if he otherwise is very stable. If so, it would be environmental stress rather than a genic condition that would account for the affliction. (But this reservation must be weighed against the fact that the concordance rate in identical twins reared apart, and who presumably have not had an intimate relationship, or have not shared the same environments since childhood, is also many times higher than in blood relatives who are not identical twins.)

A third consideration is that even though the chances are high that when one of an identical twin pair suffers from a mental disorder the other will also display it, there are about twenty chances or more in a hundred that this will not be the case. This suggests that, in some manner or other, the environment has been more adverse for one of the two twins. It also suggests that a thorough inquiry into the interplay between environmental and genetic factors would require intensive longitudinal study, beginning preferably at the time of birth.

Although the weight of evidence indicates that a predisposition to schizophrenia and manic-depressive psychosis is hereditary, there are many questions pertaining to the subject that are still unsolved. Actually the diagnosis "schizophrenia" covers a wide range of symptoms. Even when two monozygotic twins are afflicted, they may manifest the disorder in different ways. Such variation may be due to environmental factors or to variations in the ways in which susceptibility to the disorder is genetically transmitted.

In earlier studies, geneticists have tended to explain the genetic mechanism underlying the disorder in terms of dominant or recessive genes. One theory is that the illness may be due to a major recessive gene. This gene does not directly produce the symptoms but causes a metabolic deficiency, which, in turn, impairs an individual's capacity to adjust to his environment. Another theory is that the genetic mechanism underlying the disorder is polygenic, leading to one or more metabolic defects which render the afflicted individual susceptible to "breakdown."

In assessing the interaction between hereditary and environmental factors in the sphere of personality development it is essential to take account of the fact that most of the characteristics falling under the heading of "personality" do not occur in an either-or fashion. Most of them fall on a continuum ranging from a very high level or degree of intensity to a low level or degree of intensity. Even traits which, in their extreme form, are regarded as pathological, may show gradations within the "normal" range and within the pathological range. A "normal" individual, for example, may to varying degrees show tendencies described as "manic." There are gradations also within the abnormal range. Moreover, there are gradations not only in the intensity of manifestation of a given type of behavior (such as excitability) but also in the degree of provocation necessary to activate the behavior. This suggests that in the interaction between an individual's hereditary equipment and his environment the manifestation of a given characteristic or weakness may be determined by the balance between his (1) hereditary tendency to be susceptible or immune to a given weakness and (2) the severity of the test his environment imposes on his inherent strength or weakness.

Moreover, as far as the genetic mechanism is concerned, Fuller and Thompson (1960) and others have suggested that certain traits which do not appear in an either-or fashion but which show considerable gradation and diversity can probably better be explained on the basis of a multiple-factor (polygenetic) mode of inheritance than on the basis of a single-factor mode of inheritance, by way of a major dominant or recessive gene.

Investigations relevant to this theory have been conducted by Fuller and his associates (1965) with mice. Some mice (and rats) display "audiogenic" seizures, seizures in response to high-pitched sounds, which may culminate in a severe convulsion. Inbred strains of mice vary in their susceptibility to audiogenic seizures. It appears that this genetic susceptibility can best be explained in terms of a cluster of genes. The elements in such a cluster may range from a high proportion of "susceptibility genes" to a high proportion of genes that render an individual resistant to stress. Whether or not an animal has a convulsive seizure will then depend on the relationship between (1) its inherent susceptibility and (2) the severity of the stress to which it is subjected (in the Fuller study, by varying the sound stimulus). One individual with a high level of susceptibility might never show it if always protected from stress while another, genetically more robust, might have a break-down if subjected to extreme stress.

There are several counterparts in the human sphere that seem to be in accord with the foregoing observations of mice. The course of development and, as it were, the fate of the particular individual, rests on a complex balance of genetic and environmental forces. Given a "weak" hereditary endowment, an individual may be overcome by stresses which leave a person with a more fortunate endowment unhurt.[11] Given a fortunate combination of genic attributes, a particular individual may triumph in spite of an unfortunate environment.[12] But even a richly endowed person may be broken, so to speak, by harsh environmental forces. And the child who is meagerly

---

[11] Prout and White (1956), in a study which made a comparison between siblings, one of whom became mentally ill while the other did not, found that the two groups did not differ so much in the severity of the adversities to which they had been exposed as in the way they reacted to these adversities.

[12] The late Professor Leta S. Hollingworth, one of the pioneers in the study of intellectually gifted children, often recounted how, in her search for gifted children, she would find youngsters who somehow had kept a brilliant intellectual spark alive even though they had been reared in a very unfortunate environment.

endowed by nature may, through a fortunate combination of circumstances, be shielded from stresses that might transform his potential weakness into an actual defeat in life.[13]

Studies dealing with the role of genetic factors in human personality development, on the basis of observation of behavior in early childhood and tests and ratings applied in later years, will be reviewed in a later chapter.

A thorough study of the role of genetics in personality development would require an exhaustive investigation into family backgrounds. It would require also a long-term study of individuals from the time of conception until late maturity, or even late old age, since some hereditary characteristics do not become apparent until late in life. Even a careful inquiry into the ancestral background might fail to uncover significant facts, since genetic elements may be masked or flow unnoticed through many generations. Moreover, to carry a longitudinal study into the end of the life span would almost necessarily require that at least two generations of scientists would have to participate in the same long-term study.

Available findings regarding genetic influences in personality development, while impressive, are still very meager. Most of the findings are based on individuals who have already undergone a long period of development, so that genetic and environmental factors are inextricably interwoven.

In future studies, investigators may be able to side-step some of these difficulties. In recent years there has been an upsurge in interest in several scientific areas that promise to yield a great deal of important evidence for developmental psychology: in behavior genetics, the biochemistry of heredity, and psychophysiology. Studies in the last named area, which combine psychological and physiological research, are likely to yield especially significant data about individual differences in behavior characteristics and tendencies from the time of birth, and perhaps even before birth. Findings in this area, some of which will be reviewed in the next chapter, indicate that it is possible to note distinct and relatively stable individual differences early in life in such phenomena as reactivity to stimulation, autonomic responses (such as heart-rate, skin resistance to the passage of an electric current), intensity of response, vigor of motor activity, the beginnings of what perhaps is a tendency toward "excitability," or a tendency to recover or "quiet down" quickly or slowly after having been aroused.

Through physiological measurements of tendencies early in life, it may be possible to detect the prototypes or nuclei of traits, strengths, and weaknesses which ordinarily are not measurable until expressed later in a child's overt behavior. Such early measurements will provide a basis for a clearer definition

---

[13] There are many intricacies in the interaction of genes, and in conditions that might damage them, and in the interplay between genetic and environmental forces which will not be discussed here. Readers who wish to pursue this topic are referred to Kallman (1953, 1962), Fuller and Thompson (1960), Dobzhansky (1962), Sturtevant and Beadle (1962), and Munn (1965).

of the role of genetic factors than can be obtained from measurements applied after a child's original tendencies have been overlaid, to an unknown degree, by environmental influences.

Recommended Readings

For discussions of the role of genetics, see J. L. Fuller and W. R. Thompson, *Behavior Genetics* (1960); S. G. Vandenberg (editor), *Methods and Goals in Human Behavior* (1965a); T. Dobzhansky, *Mankind Evolving* (1962); J. Shields, *Monozygotic Twins Brought Up Apart and Brought Up Together* (1962); G. W. Beadle, "The New Genetics: The Thread of Life" (1964); and F. J. Kallman, *Heredity in Health and Mental Disorder* (1953).

4 *Prenatal Development*

The development of behavior begins long before a child is born. At the end of the second month the child can be recognized as human in form. Prior to this time, some bodily activity has begun. The heart begins to beat by the end of the third week. At the twenty-fifth week the child is equipped with practically all the machinery necessary for him to survive as a separate creature, although most of this machinery requires further maturation.

A great deal of information regarding the beginnings of behavior has been obtained by studying fetuses that have been expelled or removed from the mother's body at various stages of development, due to accidents or other misfortunes.

At the age of about eight weeks an embryo responds to gentle stimulation in the region of the mouth (Hooker, 1952). Such stimulation elicits movement not only in the region of the mouth but also in the neck and upper trunk. As time passes, movement spreads in a gradually expanding pattern throughout the entire trunk and ultimately involves also the lower extremities. At about ten and a half weeks, gentle stroking the palm of the hands with a hair produces partial closing of the fingers. Soon thereafter, the embryo responds to stimulation of the inner and lateral surfaces of the upper arm and to stimuli applied to the upper eye-lid. As time goes on, more and more areas of the body respond to stimulation, with a gradual increase also in the spread of movement and integrated action of the musculature.

Before birth "the forehandedness of development" is strikingly illustrated. Many functions are established well in advance of the time when normally there is a need to use these functions. One result of this forehandedness is that even though babies normally are born about 280 days after conception, it is possible for a child to survive after having spent only about 180 days in the mother's body. According to some accounts, even younger fetuses have survived.

Direction of Early Development. Development before birth tends to proceed in a *cephalocaudal* direction (Scammon and Calkins, 1929)—that is, growth and differentiation progress from the head to the tail region. During the earlier stages of growth, development in the head region is far in advance of development in the posterior part of the body, although this does not mean that development is complete at one end before it begins at the other. Illustrating this tendency is the fact that the head is well developed before the legs assume their final form and that the arms are budding before leg buds appear. After a child is born, he can make good use of his arms and hands for reaching and grasping long before he can use his legs for standing and walking.

Development of segments of the body before birth is in a *proximodistal* direction: the structures that lie nearest the main axis of the body mature earlier than those that are more removed. After birth, this is illustrated by the fact that gross movements of the arms and forearms precede more refined movements of the wrists and fingers.

Organization of Behavior

The fact that an individual who begins life as a single cell becomes, in time, an organism with many parts, capable of many independent activities, raises this question: Does the development of behavior proceed originally as a totality, in which all parts are at first integrated with the whole? Or does the development of movements in separate segments of the body proceed in piecemeal fashion, with a considerable amount of independence? At first glance this seems like the equivalent to asking if a dog wags his tail or is the tail able to wag itself. The question has many ramifications. It has been raised not only in connection with early development but also in connection with theories of personality development, education, mental hygiene, and mental health. Is the primary state of the organism one of integration, which, if properly nurtured, will preserve a condition of unison and harmony in an individual's life?

One of the most persuasive answers to this question involves studies with a salamander. In studies of *amblystoma* (a salamander), Coghill (1929, 1936) reported that reactions of the total organism precede separate movements of parts of the body. The primary state is one of integration. Partial movements become *individuated* out of gross movements. Swimming movements in the salamander, for example, involve its whole body. The animal undertakes an S-like twist, with the right limb going up and the left down, and then reverses the movement. Before the limbs can move independently, their movement is tied in with, and is an integral feature of the movement of the entire body.

Coghill says that the act of seeing likewise involves at first a total bodily response. As an object moves from left to right through the salamander's field of vision, the animal does not merely sit rigidly and follow the object with his eyes. Instead, the young salamander's entire body participates in the act of seeing—the movement of the eyes is performed by movement of the head, and movement of the head is integrated with movement of the whole body. It is not until a later stage of development that the eyes can move more or less independently.

Coghill implies that his observations hold true for animals in general as well as for man. On this point, however, investigators are not in full agreement. In experiments by Carmichael and others [1] with the fetuses of mammals, specific movements have been detected that were not part of a larger movement complex. Moreover, even though individuation of specific movements out of formerly multiple activities accounts for much of the development of behavior, a full description would have to go many steps further. Various activities are differentiated at different rates. New relationships between some specific responses are established before specialization has proceeded very far in other activities.

After birth, behavior develops through a refinement and increasing specialization of specific movements, as well as through integration of movement systems that were not tied together at the start.

In human development after birth, there are parallels to what Coghill observed in the salamander. When, for example, an infant first thrashes with his arms his whole body more or less gets into the act. It is not until later that a youngster carries out a separate motion of one arm, still later that he can rotate his wrist in a relatively independent action, and still later that he can use his thumb and forefinger in a pincer-like movement to pick up an

---

[1] For a review of studies in this area see Carmichael's chapter in the *Manual of Child Psychology* (1954).

object while his arm and trunk remain stationary. However, as the elements in his behavior become more complex, it becomes more difficult to tell how each part is linked with a prior whole.

Fetal Activity and Later Development

Babies are not only active well before birth but they differ considerably in the amount of their activity. This poses the question as to what such differences might mean: does much or little activity foreshadow anything with respect to the child's development after he is born? The findings on this point are inconclusive. In a study by Richards and Newbery (1938) of a small number of cases, fetal activity, representing the number of minutes during which activity occurred as recorded by mothers, was compared with the performance of children after birth. The Gesell Developmental Schedule (1928), an inventory of behavior items that can be used as a test of development during early childhood, was used to measure and score the childrens' performance at about the age of six months and again at twelve months. There was a positive correlation between fetal activity and performance on the Gesell tests. However, later studies report conflicting results. Walters (1965), who, with the aid of mothers, studied the fetal movements of thirty-five children, obtained findings that were in keeping with those reported by Richards and Newbery. Bernard (1964) found a low positive correlation between fetal movements and performance on the Gesell tests of thirty-two children at six months, but varying and non-significant correlations between fetal movements and later test scores on the Gesell inventory and on other tests administered at the ages of twenty-four, thirty, and thirty-six months.

While findings suggest that a child who is more active before he is born will perhaps show a higher level of maturity than a less active fetus during the first few months of postnatal life, these findings need to be confirmed. They do, however, indicate as Walters points out, that to make a thorough study of the development of behavior it is necessary to begin even before a child is born.

Prenatal Influences

An unborn child is highly protected but he is not completely insulated from environmental events. One observer noted, for example, that kicking and other movements were exhibited by a child (thirty-one days before birth) when the sides of the bathtub in which its mother was lying was struck with a metal rod (Forbes and Forbes, 1927). During the late stages of pregnancy, mothers have reported that a musical concert may produce an increased amount of fetal activity.

Influence of the Mother's Condition. Conditions in a mother's life may lead to greater normal amounts of fetal activity (Sontag and Richards, 1938). Mothers have reported that they sense more fetal activity when they are fatigued than when they are rested, although this may be due to greater sensitivity on the mother's part. Changes have been noted also in the heart-rate of an unborn child. In some instances, the rate has been higher after the mother climbed a flight of stairs than some minutes later, and higher after she had smoked a cigarette than just before or some time later.[2]

Records of fetal activities reported by Harris and Harris (1946) showed that movements were more pronounced in strength and number at the close of the day, prior to a mother's retiring for the night, than in the morning before she got out of bed. The findings did not, however, show an unmistakable association between fetal activities and the mother's feelings of fatigue from day to day.

Can circumstances in a child's environment before birth, including the mental state of the mother, influence his character and disposition and the later course of his development? Actually, there is no medium through which the psychological state of the mother can be communicated directly to a child, but the effects of a mother's psychological condition might be communicated indirectly. When a mother is emotionally excited, for example, secretions from the ductless glands are released into her blood stream, and these hormone substances may be carried to the child in the fluid interchange between mother and infant. It is possible then that an unborn child might indirectly, through chemical means, be affected by conditions affecting its mother. Sontag and his associates (1935, 1944) have observed that fetuses show a greater than usual amount of activity when mothers are undergoing severe emotional stress.[3]

---

[2] For accounts of prenatal influences see Sontag and Wallace (1934, 1935), McMahon *et al.* (1959), and Ashley-Montagu (1962).

[3] In some instances, children of mothers who suffered from severe emotional disturbances during pregnancy have had difficulties after birth, such as trouble in feeding or retaining food. However, mothers have many emotional upsets that leave no marks on a child after he is born. This is fortunate, for there probably are few mothers who are free from emotional strain, especially when carrying their first child. Moreover, when serious emotional disturbances during pregnancy are followed by difficulties in a newborn child, it is possible that both mother and child have weaknesses that were aggravated but not caused by the mother's experiences during pregnancy.

Whatever the full story might be, the wisest rule for an expectant mother obviously is to be as careful as she can in watching her diet, her use of drugs, alcohol and nicotine, her rest and general health, and, with the aid of a kind providence, to avoid injury and illness. (This, of course, is a good rule for a prudent woman to follow at all times, whether or not she is pregnant.)

Hazards of Physical Growth before Birth

Fortunately, most children who are conceived develop satisfactorily as embryos and fetuses, and come lustily into the world at the time of birth. But in many instances the story is different. An unborn child and its mother face many hazards. There are limits to what a mother can give and what a child can take. Defective heredity or misfortunes that arise during pregnancy or childbirth result in many casualties and heartaches.

Some of these instances are starkly apparent. A fetus may be so lacking, or the mother so lacking, in what it takes to sustain healthy growth that the little creature is cast out stillborn, or dies at the time of birth. Unfortunate prenatal conditions may not be so radical as to cause death and yet produce impairments. Among the prenatal conditions that may impair the unborn child are infections, radiation energy, jaundice, asphyxia, and nutritional deficiency (McMahon, *et al.*, 1959) as well as incompatible maternal-fetal blood types, certain drugs, German measles, and perhaps also excessive cigarette smoking by the mother (Pasamanick and Knobloch, 1966).

Many investigations have shown that brain damage may be inflicted before or about the time of birth by toxins in the blood supply (toxemia of pregnancy), bleeding during pregnancy, an undersupply of oxygen (anoxia), and other conditions. The effects of such brain damage may be apparent at birth or may not be particularly noticeable until later when a child begins to have difficulty at school.

Notable among the investigations in this area are those of Pasamanick and his associates. Pasamanick's studies led him to postulate that there is a "continuum of reproductive casualty, consisting of brain damage incurred during the prenatal and paranatal periods as a result of abnormalities during these periods." Such damage may lead to a "gradient of injury" extending from death (during the fetal stage or at the time of birth) "through cerebral palsy, epilepsy, mental deficiency, reading disability, and behavioral disorder." [4]

Evidence of complications connected with pregnancy and prematurity have been obtained in studies of the medical histories of persons afflicted with the impairments just mentioned. Pasamanick and his associates found that the medical histories of children with behavior disorders showed significantly more complications of pregnancy and prematurity than their matched controls. Such disorders were less often associated with mechanical

---

[4] This quotation is from Pasamanick and Kawi, 1956. Other references to Kawi and Pasamanick (1959) and to Pasamanick are listed in the general bibliography. Reports by Pasamanick and Knobloch (1966) and by Knobloch and Pasamanick (1966) review earlier and more recent findings obtained by Pasamanick and his co-workers.

difficulties during labor than with non-mechanical abnormalities, such as toxemia. This was particularly evident in the case of children who were "hyperactive, confused and disorganized." (The investigators point out that there are obviously many factors in addition to abnormalities of pregnancy and childbirth that cause behavior disorders.) Other disorders that occur more often in children with a history of abnormalities of pregnancy and childbirth than in children with an uncomplicated history are hearing defects, strabismus (cross-eyes), school accidents, infantile autism (a condition in which a child is so lost in his fantasies that he is out of touch with reality), and juvenile delinquency (Pasamanick and Knobloch, 1966).

Any abnormality in a child's behavior after birth is likely to produce emotional tension in the mother. Such tensions are also likely to appear if an infant fails to thrive and grow in a healthy fashion. Writers in child psychology often tacitly assume that when a child is troubled and his mother is emotionally distressed it is the mother who caused the child's trouble. Knobloch and Pasamanick (1966) point out that a mother's distress may be a consequence rather than a cause.

Another factor that some writers have called attention to is the disturbing effect of hospitalization early in life. Here again a child's difficulties may not stem primarily from the experience of being hospitalized. But the disturbance and his need to be hospitalized may stem from a congenital disorder. In that event a child's distress during and following hospitalization may not simply be due to separation from the mother but to a complex set of circumstances in which the experience of being hospitalized aggravates already existing difficulties.

One very sober fact concerning children who have sustained injury before or during birth is that a large proportion of them are born to mothers of low socio-economic status. Such mothers, to a greater extent than mothers who are better situated economically, are likely to have poorer diets, to be subject to fatigue and harassment in providing and in caring for a large family, and to receive less careful medical supervision during pregnancy. Knobloch and Pasamanick (1966) report findings which indicate that pregnancy abnormalities occur more often in mothers who are underweight at the start of pregnancy and who remain underweight during pregnancy. They also report that the incidence of abnormal pregnancy can be reduced below the usual expectancy by supplementing the mother's diet with vitamins and by providing her with a considerably higher intake of proteins than commonly is found in the diet of low socio-economic groups. They add further that much might be done, at a cost an affluent society could well afford, to reduce the number of children who are crippled, to a greater or lesser degree, as a consequence of sub-standard maternal health care and diet.

Boys more often encounter difficulties in being born than girls. There are more stillbirths among boys than girls, more deaths following childbirth, more mental defectives, cerebral palsied, epileptics, and more boys who are hyperactive, confused, and disorganized (Rogers, Lilienfeld and Pasamanick, 1955). All the conditions which investigations have found to be associated with brain damage occur more often among males (Knobloch and Pasamanick, 1966).[5]

Psychology of Pregnancy and Childbirth

In an earlier section we touched upon the influence a mother's condition might have on her unborn child. The fact of bearing a child will also, of course, have an influence on the mother.

Down through the generations and in various cultures there have been many superstitions connected with pregnancy. Many of these are patently false, but one thing certain is that pregnancy and childbirth have profound emotional meanings to the mother. A mother is likely to respond to these experiences in her own individual way while showing a continuation of tendencies and traits that were established before her motherhood began.

Pregnancy, especially if it is the first one, binds a woman more firmly than before to the consequences of her earlier decisions—her choice of a mate, her decision to marry, her surrender, at least temporarily, of vocational plans. One price she must pay for having a child is added responsibility and a surrender of much of her previous freedom. Although the consequences of such choices are not entirely irrevocable, the coming of a child is one of the Rubicons, as it were, on life's journey which, when once crossed, cannot be re-crossed.

Pregnancy may give added intensity or a new emphasis to emotional tendencies that already exist.[6] A zestful woman may be in her element once she is pregnant. She exudes a glow and is exuberant in the knowledge of her fertility. If the pregnancy is her first, she may harbor a feeling of self-fulfillment and prepare herself to make a more or less placid transition from an old into a new state of existence.

But even if a woman is happily anticipating motherhood, and is a realistic person with healthy attitudes toward herself and others, her pregnancy will be quite a trial at times. If there are financial problems, heavy duties in the home, complications because other members of the family become "difficult,"

---

[5] Nature seems to have made it harder in some ways to be a boy. More boys than girls begin life with congenital defects. As babies they seem more vulnerable and dependent. At school, boys with reading difficulties far outnumber girls, and more boys are "problems." In times of hardship, such as occur in wartime, with lack of proper food, girls seem to show more stamina than boys. At adolescence there are about four times as many boys who become delinquents. As they enter adult life, boys face the prospect of a shorter life span than girls. One theory regarding the higher morbidity rate in boys during the prenatal, neonatal, and infancy stage is that it may in some way be linked with the chromosome structure. As mentioned in the preceding chapter, girls have an XX chromosome while the corresponding pair in boys is XY.

[6] See, e.g., Bibring, *et al.*, (1961); and Clifford (1962).

the test will be severe. Any venture that involves taking a chance with one's own role in life and with the destiny of other persons is likely to be accompanied by some struggle and apprehension. It is unlikely that any sensitive woman who is honest with herself could go into such a fateful undertaking without some fear. But as an antidote to this fear, there is also something challenging and rewarding in the experience and in the prospect.

A study by Hamilton (1955) offers a moving and enlightening account of the feelings mothers undergo during pregnancy and delivery, and after a child's birth. Hamilton had the cooperation of fourteen mothers of first-born children. These women confided intimate details of their experiences to her —their fears, their discomforts, their need for emotional support, and their reactions to superstitions and "old wives' tales" about the hazards of begetting a child. In Hamilton's study all but one of the mothers reported that there were times when they were afraid. Nine of the fourteen mothers feared that they might lose the child or that the child might be malformed.

If the expectant mother is one who ordinarily is subject to feelings of guilt, it is likely that she will have guilt feelings in connection with pregnancy. She may fear that she has not done the right thing.[7] She may dread that the child will be malformed because of something she has or has not done. Her misgivings about herself may lead her to imagine that disaster will strike her or her child as a kind of punishment. Such feelings of guilt are likely to be more intense if the mother actually has misgivings about having a child, even though she is already pregnant, and if she resists the idea of being a mother. Feelings of guilt might also lead her to be apprehensive about the prospect of taking anesthetics during the child's delivery for fear that she might, while in a drugged state, reveal carefully guarded secrets about herself.

Pregnancy brings added burdens if the mother is very prudish and squeamish about her body and if she shrinks from the prospect of being naked and exposed to doctors and nurses.

If she has difficulty in accepting herself as a female, or feels that, as a woman, she has been cheated by nature and not given her just rights, her protests against womanhood may take the form of a recognized or unrecognized (unconscious) protest against motherhood. But if the mother who bears a child is content with her role as a woman and accepts herself as a woman, the bearing of a child is a way of fulfilling her womanhood.

Pregnancy may add a happy quality to close relationships that already exist between husband and wife or aggravate difficulties that already prevail. According to one view, the period of a wife's pregnancy is a time when some husbands seem to think that they have the right to intimate relations with

---

[7] It seems that many parents find it easier to endure the consequences of what they regard as their misdeeds when these are visited on themselves than when they are visited on their children. Such persons can, for instance, more readily accept the fact that they themselves are crippled by an accident, which they blame on their own carelessness, than disabilities in their children for which (as they see it) they are to blame.

other women. The likelihood is that if a husband does stray it is not something brought about by the pregnancy. But, as we said, pregnancy can aggravate difficulties that already exist in the relations between husband and wife. According to Hamilton's study, if a wife normally enjoys sexual relations with her husband, she will probably continue to enjoy them during pregnancy. But if there is friction on this score, pregnancy may be used as an excuse for avoiding physical intimacy.

The "Birth Ordeal"

Poets, doctors, and psychologists have all speculated about the meaning of the birth process to a child. Obviously the fact of being born is a drastic upheaval and a tremendous change. A child is thrust from the warmth and protection of the womb, where nourishment flowed through him and where he was not even called upon to breathe. He now must exert effort to obtain food, draw his own breath, and, at times, gasp and cough and struggle to obtain it. He is exposed to changes in temperature, rays of light that strike his eyes, and sound waves that beat upon his ears. Instead of floating in a fluid within confines that are yielding yet firm, he now lies loose, naked, and unenclosed; free to move as his limbs thrash in empty space. His head sags if not supported. His body falls if not held. If a child who is being born had the ability to take note of the tremendous contrast between his previous and present state, we might expect that the process of moving from the womb into the world would have a staggering psychological effect.

There have been many conjectures about this situation. It has been said, for example, that the birth cry is not just a noise mechanically brought about by the first intake of air, but a cry of pain or protest or sorrow or fear. If has also been said that the process of being cast from the womb is a psychological shock which leaves a child, as long as he lives, with an unconscious yearning to return to the protection and security of the womb.

When viewed objectively, birth is a radical upheaval and, from a medical point of view, it involves many hazards. But when viewed from the standpoint of a child, the above theory of the drama of birth is, under ordinary circumstances, questionable. A child who is being born is a very immature and unfinished creature. His higher brain centers and the rest of his nervous system are not capable of functioning as those of an older person. His equipment for sensing and feeling is not fully developed. Moreover, the machinery with which the mother cares for a child as an embryo and fetus, providing oxygen, nourishment, and the room for a child's growing size, is not designed to care for him indefinitely. If we were to attribute wishes, hopes, and fears to a little child, we probably would have to assume that toward the end of pregnancy he hopes to be born even more than he desires not to be born. If we judged simply from what his mother says about his turning, squirming, jerking, wrenching, and kicking before he is born, we probably must assume that he is more eager to get out of the womb than he ever will be to get back in.

The theory of birth trauma is one of the many voices of doom to which parents are exposed. If taken literally, only a cruel adult would deliberately conceive a child who is headed for such a harsh fate. Actually, birth is part of a larger process by which a child comes into being, a process by which a child, in the fullness of time, moves from a womb which is no longer a suitable habitat. The process of coming into being reaches beyond birth, when a child, in the course of his development, continues to venture into the untried and unknown. In development from birth onward there are growing pains along the way. Among these are the pangs of giving birth which a newborn female child herself will undergo some years hence. But it is unlikely that a healthy person, in the process of development, will spontaneously seek to retreat into the past.

The World Surrounding the Newborn Child

Many environmental influences surrounding a newborn child are obvious to the eye, but there are also many that cannot be seen. An infant in his visible cradle is surrounded by an invisible environment consisting of the thoughts and feelings, attitudes, desires, hopes, and expectations of members of his family. If all is well, this composite of thoughts and feelings will offer the child a comfortable place. His mother will be drawn to him with feelings of pride in her role as one who has brought forth a child, and she will feel a strong impulse to protect him. His father will be drawn to him with sentiments he previously had not known.[8] Also, if all is favorable, older brothers and sisters will be prepared to welcome the newcomer, even though they may be disturbed by the events surrounding his birth and perplexed as to what it will mean in their own lives to have a new person in the household.

But this environment may not be so hospitable. A child may come unwanted into a troubled home. If so, he is soon likely to feel the effects of such unfriendly or conflicting emotions.

Although there are such differences in the setting into which a child is born, he is not entirely at the mercy of conditions as they are. From the beginning, he is not merely a creature of his environment; he helps to create his environment. Even in his weakness there is strength, for his helplessness draws others to him. Through his appearance and all his ways he commands attention, makes impressions, and, without so intending, influences the

---

[8] The blessed event of having a first-born child may also be a "crisis event" for parents because of the change they must make in their everyday lives (LeMasters, 1957). However, the blessing seems greater than the crisis, for most parents who want one child go on to want more.

attitudes of his elders, whatever they may have thought or felt beforehand. So, a woman who vowed that she could never become "crazy" about a baby may find when the baby comes that he has completely taken her over. A father who was secretly convinced that he could not love a second child as much as the first may discover that it is quite a different story when he holds the new youngster in his arms.

The tide may, of course, run in the other direction if the parents do not have the capacity to love a child or are over-burdened by tragedies in their own lives.

Recommended Readings

M. F. Ashley-Montagu, *Prenatal Influences* (1962); L. Carmichael, "The Onset and Early Development of Behavior" (1954) (chapter on prenatal development in Carmichael's *Manual of Child Development*); W. J. Hamilton, J. D. Boyd, and H. W. Mossman, *Human Embryology: Prenatal Development of Form and Function* (1962). B. Pasamanick and H. Knobloch, "Retrospective Studies on the Epidemiology of Reproductive Casualty: Old and New" (1966) have reviewed and discussed findings pertaining to brain damage prior to or during birth.

5 *The Newborn Child*

The newborn child looks like an unfinished and helpless little bundle of humanity even though he is capable of the functions essential for maintaining life. He continues after birth to manifest the characteristics of an unborn child: he maintains a fetal posture; he sleeps, or at least seems somnolent, much of the time.

Much of his activity, when he is awake and active, seems diffuse and aimless, yet he already possesses a large repertory of accomplishments. He can suck, salivate, excrete, defecate, vomit, hiccough, sneeze, yawn, stretch, kick, wave arms and legs, tremble, shiver, grimace, turn his head, blink, cry, grunt, sigh and respond to a large array of stimuli.

Generalized Movement

Even in connection with apparently simple reflex activities, or in response to stimuli applied to a limited area of the body, a newborn child is likely to show a variety of associated movements in other parts of the body. Some activities seemingly have little revelance to the conditions that produced them. One investigator found that infants made sucking movements when their hair was pulled, and when someone pinched their big toes (Jensen, 1932). However, even though a child exhibits a great deal of generalized movement, there is much specialization of behavior from the beginning. Offer a healthy child a nipple when he is hungry and he will do a fine job of sucking, regardless of other activities that may accompany it. Pinch his toe and his response is likely to be more pronounced in the limb that is pinched than in more remote areas of the body. Even when a newborn child sucks in response to having his hair pulled he shows he is ready for business, for sucking is one of his most essential accomplishments and it probably is better for him to overdo than underdo the act.

Reflex Action

Some involuntary reflex actions of a relatively specific and fixed character are less clearly defined when they are first exhibited by a newborn child than they become with the passage of time. Sucking, for example, is a response that a child is born with. As we have seen, sucking may be set off by events that have nothing to do with feeding. But this condition changes, and the act of sucking itself becomes more efficient during the days following birth (Gesell and Ilg, 1937).

Shortly after birth, babies commonly show what is known as the head orienting or "rooting" reflex. When a tactual stimulus (such as a gentle touch with a finger) is applied to the lips or to the cheek region near the lips, the child moves his head toward the stimulating object. If you place a finger on a child's cheek and move it toward his lips, he will move his head toward the approaching stimulus. Sometimes it is necessary to repeat the stimulus to elicit the response. When the stimulus is applied directly to the lips, a child may exhibit "searching" movements or other movements associated with the act of feeding, such as pursing the lips and opening the mouth. (For accounts of orienting and directed head turning responses see Prechtl, 1958, and Blauvelt, 1962.)

In the course of development some reflex activities wane, or are displaced by other forms of behavior. As a child's nervous system matures, he is able to check or inhibit some movements that were originally reflex actions. One reflex that follows an interesting course is the Moro *Umklammerungs* reflex, also called the clasping or embrace reflex (Freudenberg, 1921). This reflex may be elicited by striking a sharp blow on the surface on which a child is lying on his back. The infant throws out his arms and then brings them together as if in an embrace. At the same time, he throws out his legs and then flexes them. Freudenberg thought this reaction was an atavistic or primitive fright reaction in response to the jarring of the body. In a primate, such movements might enable a young creature to grasp his mother's body or the limb of a tree. Another investigator (Schaltenbrand, 1925) termed it a "readiness-to-jump reaction ensuring a safe landing." This reflex undergoes changes during the first months of life. McGraw (1937) found that at about three or four months the gross movements had diminished considerably. At about seven months, overt movements had further waned; the response consisted only of a weak body jerk and blinking. The changes from the grosser to the more refined and subdued response parallels certain developments in the infant's nervous system, according to McGraw. She states that the cerebral cortex is not functioning during the first phase of the response. As the cortex develops and comes into action, the primitive kind of movement over which the infant seems at first to have little or no control gives way to a more calculated act.

The grasp reflex is another involuntary act that changes. It occurs when an object is brought into contact with the palms of the infant's hands. His grasp may be so powerful at first that an infant, clinging to a bar, can support his own weight for many seconds. The act of involuntary grasping vanishes as the child matures and becomes increasingly capable of voluntarily controlling his hands.

Sensory Reactions

Sight. Almost from the time of birth an average infant gives signs of being able to see. When he fixes his eyes on an object and follows it as it moves through space, it is reasonable to assume that he is obtaining visual impressions of one sort or another, although we have no way of knowing just what kind of impression he receives. Infants vary considerably in their apparent ability to fix their eyes on an object. In some children, for a time after birth, movements of the eyes are not coordinated. Normally it is not until many weeks after birth that eye coordinations are fully established.

Soon after birth a child not only responds to visual stimuli but does so selectively. His aptitude goes beyond the mere ability to look at a beam of light or similarly to fix his gaze on any stimulus that is bright before his eyes. A study by Fantz (1963) has shown that during the first days of life babies vary the attention they give to visual stimuli of varying form and pattern. Fantz brought six different paper "targets" into the field of vision of infants ranging from ten hours to five days old. Among these targets, similar in shape, size, and gloss, there were three black-and-white patterns—a schematic face, concentric circles, and a section of newspaper containing print $\frac{1}{16}$ to $\frac{1}{4}$ inch high. The other three were unpatterned; one was white, and the other two fluorescent yellow and dark red.

The length of time the infants gazed at each target was recorded on a timer. The results showed that the infants gave about twice as much visual attention to the patterns as to the plain white, yellow, and red surfaces, even though two of these (the yellow and white) were more luminous. Both during the earliest period (under 48 hours) and later (2 to 5 days) the infants gave more heed to a schematic representation of a face than to any other stimulus. In so doing, they anticipated the behavior shown in an earlier study of babies aged two to six months who concentrated from about two to four times longer on a face than on other stimuli.

Fantz states that these results do not imply an "instinctive recognition" of the face, for there might be other patterns that would elicit as much or more prolonged attention. However, the longer fixation on the face suggests that "a pattern with certain similarities to social objects also has stimulus characteristics with considerable intrinsic interest or stimulating value. . . ."

In studying vision and response to other stimuli, one problem is how best to adjust observations of a child to his own ways. A newborn infant is unable to offer much cooperation, so it becomes the observer's job to cooperate with the infant. Suggestive in this connection is a study dealing with infants' ability to fix their gaze on an object and follow it with their eyes (Beasley, 1933). The experimenter tried to meet the infant at least halfway: he moved the stimulus (such as a light) into the child's line of vision until he found the point at which the child's eyes seemed to be fixed upon it. Only then did the experimenter proceed with the next step—finding how far and how long the infant would continue to keep his eyes on the object as it was moved about in his field of vision. When this procedure was followed, the children were more capable of following a visual stimulus than would be apparent if a more arbitrary procedure had been followed.

Hearing. Children sometimes respond to the physical vibrations that produce sound even before birth, but we cannot surmise from this whether the child actually "hears." Some investigators have claimed that infants are deaf at birth, but many studies show that a majority of babies respond to sounds within the first days of life, and show the beginning of ability to localize sound (by responding differently to a sound coming from the left or the right). They also show adaptation to sound by a decrease in response to a continuing sound (Leventhal, *et al.*, 1964). One rather complicated response that involves a rudimentary form of coordinating hearing and vision appears when a baby soon after birth turns his eyes toward the direction of a sound (Wertheimer, 1961).

Other Sensory Responses

The average infant responds positively to milk and to sweet solutions, and negatively to solutions that are strongly salt, sour, or bitter.[1]

Such odors as ammonia and acetic acid, which are powerful enough to

---

[1] For reviews of studies in this area, see Pratt (1954).

cause discomfort to adults (perhaps because of pain rather than olfactory stimulation) also produce reactions in newborn infants, while milder odors, which adults are able to detect, appear to have little effect.

Infants react to temperatures that are hotter or colder than the normal temperature of the body, and they appear to react more to extreme cold than to extreme heat (Pratt, *et al.*, 1930).[2]

From birth, infants are responsive to the stimulus of pressure or contact. During the first days of life infants also show a variety of responses to changes in their bodily positions. Righting responses of a sort that are eventually involved in maintaining an upright posture can be observed during the first days of life.

Pain

Infants seem relatively insensitive to certain forms of pain stimulation. We cannot determine how soon or how deeply an infant feels pain as compared with an adult, but it is undoubtedly true that many adult pains are more intense because of past experiences. If pain stimulation could be stripped of tensions and fears that grow out of past experiences, many agonies experienced by older people would, no doubt, be less severe.

It is interesting to observe how an infant's apparent insensibility to certain pains is reflected in medical practice. Infant boys undergo circumcision, for example, without anaesthetic and without marked signs of anguish. (Just the thought of a similar operation would make an adult wince.) However, this does not mean that the infant is impervious to pain. Some babies cry in seeming anguish when the unhealed wound is irritated by urine.

Early Signs of Personality Differences

From the standpoint of personality development, the most interesting reactions of newborn children are those that might throw light on the child's potential temperamental qualities and personality traits. To understand personality development it is important, as far as possible, to identify what might be the roots of personality tendencies. This is especially true in view of the fact that it is difficult, in an older child, to tell to what extent a given characteristic, such as one child's tendency to be very self-assertive and another child's tendency to be compliant, is due primarily to learning and to what extent it might be an outgrowth of a predisposition present at the time of birth.

During the first few days of life, infants show many distinctive differences

---

[2] For more studies of the responses of neonates (newborns) to various stimuli see Bridger (1961), Wertheimer (1961), Blauvelt (1962), Engen, *et al.* (1963), Kessen, *et al.* (1963), Lipsitt, *et al.* (1963).

in the way they overtly react to various stimuli, and they differ also in their physiological reactions when subjected to stress. Some of these reactions have a considerable degree of consistency and stability.

Perhaps it stretches the point a bit to discuss differences in reaction tendencies in neonates under the expansive title of "personality," for neither the origin of these differences nor what they might foretell about the child's future has been determined adequately. One thing is clear, however: newborn infants, who are healthy and apparently "well born," manifest many substantial and consistent individual characteristics. These appear while the infants are still under uniform and regulated hospital care and have not yet been exposed to the diversity of environmental influences they will encounter in their homes.

To obtain authentic measurements of early behavior tendencies it is necessary, of course, to guard against temporary dislocations or abnormalities in the neonate's behavior due to analgesic or anaesthetic administered to the mother during labor, the effects of complications of labor, distortions that might arise if the sampling included prematurely born infants, infants showing symptoms of neurological damage, or other disruptive influences. Essential safeguards include the selection of babies who, according to all available information, are full-term, and who have rated high on a number of criteria immediately after birth.[3]

Newborn children differ in the vigor of their reactions. Knop (1946) measured the muscular energy babies exerted to resist an applied force, such as the pull exerted when the experimenter, taking hold of the child's hands and forearms, raised the child from a reclining to a sitting position. The responses of the children were rated on a scale ranging from 1: passivity, no resistance, limpness and a sagging head, to a rating of 4: active resistance and strong muscular tensions. The infants varied considerably.

Newborn babies differ also in the intensity of their response to stimulation. In a study by Birns (1963) the stimuli were a loud noise, a moderately loud sound, and a cold metal disc applied to the infant's thighs. Characteristic differences appeared in children whether, at the time when the stimuli were applied, they were alert and active or rather quiescent. The differences in response showed a much higher degree of consistency from day to day than could be attributed to chance.

Other observations have shown that children differ in the vigor of their cries, and in their return to a normal state after an increase in the rate of heartbeat.

---

[3] What is known as the Apgar Scale provides widely-used criteria for judging the newborn child's functioning. The scale, designed to be used one minute and five minutes after birth, covers heart rate; respiratory effort (ranging from well-established breathing and lusty cries to breathing not established); color (ranging from pink to cyanotic); reflex irritability; and muscle tone. Each of these five are rated on a scale from 2 to 0, yielding a total possible rating of 10.

Excitability. According to Birns (1965) and Birns, *et al.* (1965), children differ at birth in their *excitability*—as shown by cries, bodily movement and heart-rate when they are subjected to stress, such as can be induced by flicking the soles of their feet. Although babies differ in their sensitivity to various forms of stimulation, they tend, if easily aroused by one form of stimulation, to be easily aroused also by other forms.

Whether a child is excitable or relatively unexcitable is likely to have an influence on the interaction between him and his mother. A baby who is excitable, who cries bitterly, may arouse anxiety in the mother. Moreover, a mother may be more gingerly and guarded, less spontaneous, when caring for a baby who is easily aroused than for one who is more serene.

Another characteristic in the newborn child that is likely to have an effect on mother-child interaction is the ease with which a child, once aroused, can be soothed. It is especially trying for a mother when a child keeps crying no matter what she does to calm him.

Soothability. Impressive individual differences in "soothability" were noted in a study by Birns and her associates (1965) of thirty-five normal, healthy, full-term babies, two to three days old. The babies were tested within an hour before a regular afternoon feeding, a time when most of the babies were moderately irritable. The babies were further aroused by flicking the soles of their feet, so that all would be in "a high state of arousal." Following this, on a timed schedule, efforts were made to soothe them with: a sweetened pacifier, a continuous tone, gentle rocking of the bassinette, and immersion of the neonate's foot in warmish water (108°F). Babies who served as controls were observed, following arousal, during a period when no soothing stimulus was applied.

All the conditions designed to soothe the babies were more effective than the control condition (no stimulation). None of the soothing methods was consistently more effective than the others for all the neonates, although some of the children were consistently more responsive to one stimulus than to another (e.g., one might be more responsive to the pacifier, another more responsive to being rocked).

Even with such variations, the babies tended to manifest an overall quality of *soothability*. The authors conclude that ". . . a neonate who is easily soothed by one stimulus tends to be easily soothed by all and conversely a baby difficult to soothe with one stimulus is relatively difficult to soothe with all stimuli" (p. 9).

It is interesting to note that sucking on a pacifier, which becomes the most common soothing activity of many babies as time goes on, was not, in this group of children, more effective than rocking, warmth, or a sound.

Studies such as the foregoing indicate that it is possible to obtain information at the neonatal level that might have much potential meaning, both from the standpoint of personality development and from the standpoint of factors influencing parent-child relationships. Such information would become especially significant if distinctive characteristics that mark one child as different from another remain consistent as time passes. Such information would also have great value if it could uncover characteristics early in life that foreshadow or represent the nucleus of personality traits that manifest themselves in differing ways as children grow older. What, if anything, at the neonatal stage, might be a forerunner or "predicter" of traits that appear, say, in a three- or six-year-old, in forms such as self-assertiveness, dependency, tolerance of stress, and so on? To answer this question would require long-term studies of groups of children from the time of birth. As time goes on, studies of neonates that carry into later stages of development probably will provide an increasing amount of basic information regarding behavioral forerunners of rather elusive temperamental qualities, personality traits, and emotional tendencies.

Physiological Reactions. One promising source of information is the study of the functioning of infants' autonomic response to stress as shown by physiological reactions, combined with records of overt activities such as crying, threshing of the limbs, and other overt responses. As time passes, the overt responses become more and more coordinated by the cerebral cortex. But physiological responses, such as respiration, heart rate, the digestive functions, glandular functions, and other responses do not. The autonomic nervous system plays an important role in the physiological changes that occur when an individual is emotionally aroused. Since emotional responses are associated with many personality traits (such as the anger experienced by an irascible person, the fear displayed by an individual who is easily frightened, the erotic desires and impulses of a "sexy" person), a study of autonomic reactions, as indicated by physiological functioning at or near the time of birth, provides a means of inquiring into children's predisposition to react mildly or intensely while the children still are impervious to many forms of emotional stimulation that become effective as they mature. It is also possible that early measures of the level of excitation of autonomic functions may indicate the extent to which a child is vulnerable to stress and has a predisposition to psychosomatic illnesses.

The physiological indicator of autonomic functioning that has most commonly been used with young children has been measurement of heart rate. Neonates vary in the degree to which their heart rate increases in response to stimulation. Moreover, although the change in heart rate may increase more in response to one type of stimulus than to another (such as a cold disc as compared with a loud sound), children who show a high level of excitation (as manifested by heart rate) to one type of stimulation are also likely to show a high level in response to other stimuli (Bridger, Birns, and Blank, 1965). Children in the Bridger, *et al.*, study who manifested a high level of autonomic excitation (as measured by heart rate) also tended to show a high level of excitability as measured by overt behavioral responses, but this is not uniformly characteristic, for behavioral and physiological responses may be relatively independent of one another (Bridger and Birns, 1963). Some children exhibit a relatively more intense overt response; some, a relatively more intense autonomic response.

A study by Schachter, et al. (1965) indicates that to get a measure of individual differences in reactivity in the newborn it is necessary to measure both his behavioral response (his observable activity level) and his physiological response. Moreover, measures of a variety of physiological responses are required, for these also may vary independently. In the Schachter, et al., study four physiological reactions were measured: heart rate, respiratory rate, frequency of changes in galvanic skin resistance [4] (above a minimum level), and magnitude of change in skin resistance (beyond that minimum level). Ratings were also made of overt behavior. The stimuli were loud tones and electric shocks. It was found, as in the studies reviewed above, that infants tended to remain highly consistent on repeated tests when ranked in terms of behavioral response or in terms of each of the separate physiological variables. In individual children, there was a positive relation between changes in overt behavior and in physiological response, but for the group as a whole, there was not a consistent or significant correlation between behavioral and physiological reactivity. Moreover, there was no consistent relationship between reactivity in terms of the individual physiological measures: for example, an infant showing relatively high reactivity in heart rate might or might not exhibit high reactivity in rate of breathing, or in galvanic skin resistance.

Findings which indicate that significant individual differences appear in neonates in a given type of physiological reactivity, and that such reactivity tends to be consistent in response to repeated tests, suggest that psychophysiological studies of newborn children offer a promising approach to the investigation of early indicators of personality development. However, the data now at hand are limited, and considerable work still remains to be done in interpreting what these data might predict regarding the future development of individual children.

Emotions of the Newborn Child

What capacity for feeling and emotion does an infant have during the first days and weeks of life? This is a difficult question, but an important one.

Most infants (even the serene ones) manifest what seems to be a great deal

---

[4] Measures of galvanic skin resistance show changes in the resistance of the skin to the passage of an electric current as determined by a galvanometer, with one electrode attached to one area of the body, such as the palm of one hand, and the other attached to another area. In a state of excitation there normally is a decline in resistance.

of emotion. They cry, squirm, wiggle, kick, and thrash about; they sigh, as though in relief; they settle down in what seems to be a state of contentment after a hearty meal. If an adult behaved in this fashion we would assume that he was experiencing a wide array of feelings.

Many opinions have been offered and much research has been done on a child's early emotions, but unfortunately both the opinions and the research leave large question marks. Freud set forth the view that a young infant is subject to profound emotional experiences, and Freud's followers have added to this point conjectures of their own. Freud spoke of the danger that confronts a child because of his helplessness, which gives rise to a need to be loved, a need that no human being ever outgrows. Isaacs (1936) maintained that wants and wishes, fear and anger, love and hate are there from birth. According to Despert (1946), a child comes into the world lonely, and afraid.

In assessing these views, it must be recognized that a child is helpless. He needs to be fed, sheltered, protected. When he gasps, cries, or gags, he obviously needs as much tender care as a parent can offer. Moreover, he can display a stirred-up state such as later would betoken a profound emotional experience. But it is also true that a child's higher brain centers, which play an important role in many of the emotional experiences of an older person (such as awareness or anticipation of danger), are not fully developed. To say that a newborn child is capable of feeling loneliness, love, and hate assumes a level of maturation that goes beyond what is known about the nervous system of a child at birth. This may seem to be an academic point; yet it is not, as far as the parents of a newborn child are concerned. Such parents are placed in a bewildering position if, beyond offering their child the most loving care they can provide, they must also face the challenge of dealing with a creature who is endowed with an emotional mystique, a creature who can feel bruised, abandoned, frightened, scorned, rejected in spite of all that the parents might do to provide loving care.

Personal Contacts and Child Care

Being hungry and being fed are relatively more prominent experiences in the life of a young infant than they are later on, and the same seems true of an infant's physical contacts with others when any of his wants are being cared for. These contacts are interwoven with his well-being and his survival from day to day. Within a few days after birth, he will cease his crying, at least for a time, if he is held in someone's arms, while earlier it required not only holding but also food to pacify him. Within a few weeks, he will cease fussing simply at the sight or sound of a person who is coming to him. Early in life there are times when he seems to want someone close to him even though he is comfortably warm and dry and well fed.

Soon after birth infants seek contacts beyond those required for feeding and other aspects of physical care. They seek companionship, and usually they receive it by being held in the arms, and by being spoken to, hummed to and sung to, and by being rocked, stroked, squeezed, patted and petted, nuzzled, cuddled, and fussed over in countless ways. Acts of this sort that involve affectionate comforting, tender, and playful contacts are known as "mothering." The typical infant soon after birth seems to crave mothering. We might argue that the desire for mothering is a "secondary" desire, derived from events associated with the "primary" need for food. Or we might claim that the infant's desire for mothering is something primary, representing a need that is just as primitive and unlearned as the need for food. Actually, it would not pay to debate this question. For whether this desire for contact with other human beings is inborn, or whether it is learned, it appears early and it is strong, and as time passes it is of great importance in the child's development as a person. From his crib in early infancy, a child's behavior proclaims that it is not good for man to be alone.

With the passage of time, the child welcomes contact with a friendly parent not only as a source of apparent satisfaction in itself but also as a help in stimulating his own efforts and in bearing the hurts and bruises of everyday life. Little children often exert themselves most—in their chatter, their handling of objects, their first articulation of a recognized word—when in contact with a loving person. As the child becomes older, pain from a fall, anger from the loss of a toy, rage from having been struck by another child becomes easier to bear if he is picked up and held in a parent's arms. He derives psychological support from such contacts, just as he derived life and physical well-being from the body of his mother before he was born.

In time, a youngster who welcomed physical evidences of tenderness also begins to bestow them. In time, also, the impulse toward physical communication of fellow-feeling is increasingly suppressed, oftentimes earlier in boys than in girls. A youngster who once eagerly crept into his parents' lap to cry, or just to nestle there, becomes more diffident about such behavior, especially when other persons are looking on. But a desire for psychological communication, by way of physical contact, is one of the attributes of early childhood which probably never is lost—no matter how overlaid it may be by cultural inhibitions. At the adult level there are moments (rare, it is true) when a man who has gone through an emotional crisis rests his head on another man's shoulder and weeps, as once he wept on a parent's shoulder when he was a child.

Crying

Crying is one of the most important accomplishments of a young child, and it has a complex set of functions and meanings. Through his crying a child expresses his needs, his wants, his discomfort, and, in time, his desire for company, his wish to be noticed, his hurts and bruises, his annoyances, his impatience, and his grief. Crying becomes not merely a sign of distress but also a kind of self-assertion. By crying, a child can call his friends to his side, and also very early in life (although not intentionally at first) can protest against those who ignore, neglect, or abuse him.

From an early age all healthy babies cry lustily, but even in this primitive means of expression there are marks of individuality. During the first few days of life, babies who are normal, healthy, and apparently not troubled by any internal distress differ considerably in their crying responses to mildly painful stimuli. The infant who cries most actively is not necessarily less robust or more "fussy" than the one who cries less readily.

Crying in response to a noxious external stimulus (as distinguished from whimpering and cries due to internal discomforts) may be a sign of alertness rather than weakness. A study by Karelitz and his associates (1964), bearing on this point, explored the relation between the crying of thirty-eight infants four to ten days old and the intelligence and speech development of the same babies at the age of three. The stimulus used to induce crying was a flick on the sole of the infant's foot with the experimenter's finger, or a snap on the foot with a rubber band, repeated a maximum of eight times in each of several experimental periods. There was a positive correlation between the number of experimental sessions in which children cried during the first days of life and their Stanford-Binet IQs at age three, as well as their speech ratings at age three. The correlation between number of early cries and later speech development was not statistically significant, but there was a significant difference between the average number of cries and the speech ratings of the ten children (roughly a fourth) who had the highest IQs and the ten with the lowest IQs. Further study would be necessary to confirm this finding and to explore its significance.

Crying and Colic

In young infants, notably during the first three months, "colic" is a frequent cause of crying. Medical books and journals offer many definitions and describe many forms of colic. As applied to infants, the term usually denotes a condition of loud, piercing cries combined with symptoms of acute distress in the digestive tract. In a study of infants who cried "excessively" as compared with other infants, the former showed "excessive" gas in the gastro-intestinal tract and a more rapid stomach emptying than babies in a low-crying group (Stewart, *et al.*, 1954).

Theories regarding the causes of colic range from the view that it arises mainly from the immaturity of the nervous system or some kind of inadequacy in the child's physical equipment to the idea that it might arise out of a disturbed psychological relationship between the mother and the baby.

Among those who have stressed the psychological effects of the mother is Harry Stack Sullivan. According to Sullivan, the mother-infant interaction is disturbed when a mother is highly anxious. A mother's anxiety induces anxiety in the infant and this interferes with an infant's normal functions. Others who have dealt with the effect a mother's emotional state might have on a child's physical well-being are Escalona (1945), Stewart and associates (1954), and Lakin (1957). In the last two studies, mothers of colicky babies, as compared with other mothers, seemed to be less accepting of their roles as mothers; they appeared more uncertain about themselves, and showed other evidences of being less secure and less in harmony with other people.

It seems reasonable to believe that conditions ranging from weaknesses in the make-up of the infant himself to stresses stemming from the emotional relationship between the mother and the child may cause some children to cry much more than others. In many instances the physical and psychological factors are probably interwoven. We cannot explain the situation simply by saying that if a crying, colicky baby has gas in his gut it is his bad mother who put it there. An infant's prolonged crying—whatever the cause—is bound to have a serious effect on the mother-child relationship. Even the best mother will become anxious and have doubts about her adequacy as a woman and as a mother if her child cries and cannot be consoled, no matter what she does.

Qualities of Children's Crying. Children vary not only in the extent but also in the manner and style of their crying. One baby's crying tends to be sharp and staccato while another's is characteristically more smooth and connected. Some babies cry loudly while others cry softly, like an adult might if he were weary or wishes to weep without calling too much attention to himself.

By the time he is a few months old, a child's crying acquires characteristic qualities of tone and rhythm and cadence.

We might gain a deep insight into this young person if we knew how to interpret his cries. For example, a motherless child who has been passed from hand to hand during a period of foster care, shifting again and again to strange cribs and to unfamiliar arms, might develop a bedtime cry which seems to express a protest against sleep and a fear of waking up once more in a strange place.

Adult Response to Crying. The crying of young infants is moving, but also fascinating and baffling. The baby's "birth-cry" is usually his first cry. Birth cries vary, but often they have a strident penetrating quality with a seeming blend of desperation, agony, and even anger.

The child's birth cry has many meanings to parents. In the days when maternity hospitals kept fathers outside the delivery room, as though they were germ-laden lepers, the birth cry had a special significance. To a father who loiters outside the delivery room door, the child's violent cry is a good sound, like the anthem proclaiming "the victory of life is won." But for such a waiting parent there is one thing more poignant than a cry, and that is silence—no cry at all—when all signs show that the child has been delivered, and the father eagerly waits for a signal that his child is alive. It takes time for this silence to sink in to tell the parent that his child, who did not cry at birth, perhaps is not destined to live, is destined never to cry.

Crying is disturbing to parents if it springs from distress which the parent cannot relieve, but a child's crying, even when "healthy," also is difficult for some adults to bear. A child's crying is threatening if, instead of arousing an impulse to succor and to comfort, it comes like an echo from the adult's past, activating old hurts, opening old wounds which his own childhood tears could not heal.

Absence of Clearly Defined
Emotional Responses

During the first weeks of life a child shows emotional excitement by crying and bodily activity, but his emotional reactions are more diffuse, less specific and defined than they will be later on. Even in an older person these patterns are none too clearly differentiated, but as a person grows older there are times when his expressions have unmistakable earmarks of anger, fear, or joy.

In studies of early emotional behavior, children have been observed when exposed to conditions that might produce pain, anger, or fear. To study "anger" such tactics as compressing the child's nostrils, restraining the use of his arms, and interfering with his head movements by pressing against his chin have been used. In a majority of instances, infants who have been treated in this way for brief periods during the first two or three weeks after birth have not shown anything resembling the classic pictures of rage. Indeed, many infants bear treatment of this sort as though it were meant in a friendly, or at least neutral spirit.

Before many weeks have passed the story will be different, of course. Physical restraint and thwarting of movement become quite effective in arousing anger. But even when a child is able to show anger, what constitutes restraint or interference will not depend solely on what another person does to him. If he is quiescent, or if he seems to be in the mood for a little horseplay, he will allow his arms to be held to his sides for a time and will even patiently accept the indignity of having his head pushed back by pressure on his chin. On the other hand, anger is likely to ensue if the thwarting is real from the standpoint of the child—if, for example, his arms are forcibly restrained just as he is in the act of using them, or if his feeding is delayed after he has seen the bottle and is all set to take his milk.

A sharp, shrill, or loud noise may cause an infant during the first days of life to start, kick, squirm, and perhaps cry, as though he were frightened. But other forms of stimulation, which a sympathetic adult would not regard as particularly fear-inspiring, may produce similar bodily movements and similar cries. On the other hand, infants sometimes do not seem frightened by rather drastic treatment. In one study (Irwin, 1932), each of twenty-four infants under one month of age was raised in a supine position above the experimenter's head, was dropped, and was caught after he had fallen a distance of two feet. In eighty-five trials of this sort, crying resulted only twice. In 12 per cent of the trials the infant made no detectable overt response. In half the number of instances in which the children did react to this treatment, they moved only their arms.

From the viewpoint of emotional expression, a child's reactions during the first two weeks of life group themselves roughly, on the one hand, as reactions of apparent withdrawal or rejection, such as squirms, twists, tension, movements of the trunk and the arms and extremities, turning of the head, and crying. On the other hand, there are reactions of apparent acceptance, quiescence, passivity, and a rudimentary form of pursuit, such as when a child turns his head and opens his mouth to suckle when an object is moved toward his lips.

The Premature Child

The average child is born approximately 280 days after he is conceived, but the period of gestation may vary widely, especially in the direction of prematurity. Precise records of the "age" of children at birth are difficult to obtain, but the age can be determined at least approximately. It is possible also to apply an objective criterion, such as weight at birth. For example (in order to have a fixed and arbitrary criterion), it has been assumed that a child weighing less than 5½ pounds at birth has been born before the full normal term of forty weeks (Scammon and Calkins, 1929).

Children at birth vary considerably in "maturity." Gesell and Amatruda (1945) have estimated that the range in age of newborn babies who are capable of living is as wide as from twenty-six to forty-six weeks. These figures indicate the vast leeway of chance and possibility within which life proceeds. Although the average birth weight is a little above seven pounds for girls, and about seven and a half for boys, babies have survived who weighed less than two pounds. However, it is unlikely that a child weighing less than about two and a half pounds will survive, and the chances of survival increase with added weight up to four or five pounds.

Children who are born well before full term are usually known as "premature" babies. This label is a useful one, but it is somewhat imprecise. Actually, two children may be born at exactly the same fetal age, yet one may be more "mature"—more fully developed—than the other (Blatz and Millichamp, 1937). Or a child may be "premature" in the sense of being born in advance of the average of forty weeks and yet be more "mature" in the sense of being more advanced in his development than another child who has been born at full term. Differences in rate of growth, which are so conspicuous after birth, appear also in growth before birth.

The "premature" child has the characteristics of an "immature" child. The growth patterns that usually occur between the period of his untimely delivery and the period when babies normally are born have not developed fully. The more immature he is, the less he is equipped to carry on the business of living an independent life. The premature child has less chance than the full-term baby to live, and if he does survive he is more subject to weakness and impairments of many kinds.[5] These may be an outgrowth of the conditions that caused him to be born prematurely or they may arise from the hazards he faces after birth. One hazard faced by the incubator-reared premature child is a form of blindness, a condition known as retrolental fibroplasia. This hazard is being minimized by improved knowledge in regulating the baby's oxygen supply.

A premature child looks like a tired, little old man. He often has a cadaverous appearance with a huge head out of proportion to the size of his body. He is so near life's beginning yet he looks as though he were near its end. He obviously requires special attention. Care must be taken to keep him warm, partly because he lacks the deposits of fat that normally accumulate during the later stages of fetal growth. It may be necessary to aid his respiration by feeding him oxygen. He may need help in taking nourishment because of weak sucking or swallowing reflexes, or inadequacies in his digestive organs. If not artificially cared for, his temperature will fall, breathing will cease, and his heart, which has been beating steadily from the time he was about one month old, will stop.

So this child who came too soon into the world is placed in an incubator, and continues to grow and to mature. It is almost as though he were still in his mother's womb. The incubator in which he is kept alive is a mechanical thing, but it provides a kind of motherly care, one step removed. Only in a civilization that values the life of every human being could it have been contrived.[6]

Development of the Premature Child. Being born prematurely does not mean that a child "skips a grade" in his development. If he is born at six months, he has the characteristics of a six-month fetus. "He remains faithful to his fetality, even when birth has made him an infant" (Gesell and Amatruda, 1945). However, even though he does not leap into a later phase of

---

[5] See studies by Rogers, Lilienfeld, and Pasamanick (1956); Rossier (1962); Lubchenco, *et al.* (1963); and Caplan, *et al.* (1963).

[6] The care shown for a premature child, and usually for newborn children in general, is inspiring. Yet it is depressing to note that human beings whose sympathies are so readily aroused by the obvious physical helplessness of an infant often are quite impervious to the less obvious signs of psychological helplessness in the same child when he is older.

development, he is likely, unless burdened with persisting organic impairments associated with his prematurity, to set a faster pace in many aspects of his development, from the time of his birth until the time when he normally would have been born, than the pace set by the child who is spending this same period in his mother's womb. A healthy child who is born six months after conception is likely to be more competent and alert to his environment three months later than a full-term baby who is newly born nine months after conception. However, the full-term baby, three months from the time of his birth (or almost twelve months from the time of conception) is likely to be further advanced in his development than a six-month premature child born at the same date as he.

When age is calculated from time of birth, the average premature child is likely, at the start, to be backward in his development as compared with full-term children. As time passes, the premature child tends to "catch up" (although there are exceptions, especially if the child also suffers from organic defects). Investigators differ in their estimate of when an organically unimpaired premature child is likely to have caught up; indeed, the estimates have varied from a matter of months to a matter of several years. Prematurely born children, in common with full-term babies, eventually show an enormous range of individual differences in mental and physical characteristics and in temperament and personality traits.

Some investigators have maintained that certain mannerisms and characteristics are peculiar to prematurely born youngsters during the first years of life and perhaps even later. For example, prematurely born children in one study were found to be relatively more advanced in "personal-social" behavior (smiling, noticing people, and so on) than in motor ability (Shirley, 1938). In another study, prematurely born children proved to be relatively more alert in the use of their senses than in coordinated use of their muscles; they were sensitive to sights, colors, moving objects, and sounds, while remaining somewhat backward in such motor performances as sitting upright or manipulating objects (Shirley, 1939).

Apart from factors in his heredity and prenatal environment there are special factors in the environment after birth that may influence the development of the premature child. Since he begins life even more helpless than the normal child, he must have extra care and attention. His parents may be overanxious at first, look even more eagerly than other parents for signs of progress in the child's development, while also anxiously protecting him. Later, according to Shirley (1938), parents may shift from a policy of shielding the child to one of urging him on, in order to accelerate his development. In this way the lot of the premature child can be less easy-going and "natural" than that of a baby born at full term. In dealing with a young premature child, parents face, to a more pressing degree, an issue that confronts parents of all children—namely, the need to protect a child without over-protecting him and encouraging him without "pushing" him.

Learning during the First Days
and Weeks of Life

As soon as a child is born the stage is set for him to begin learning. How early does this process of learning begin? Probably from the time of birth, if not before.

Mothers report signs of learning soon after birth when a hungry, crying baby ceases crying as soon as he is picked up and held in his mother's arms. Formerly, he became quiet only when actually fed. It is as though the child accepts the picking up and holding as a signal of feeding. When the child thus responds to a signal, where previously he actually had to have a sip, it seems that he has "learned." However, observations such as these do not necessarily prove that learning has occurred. The experience of being picked up and held would probably, in time, have a quieting effect in itself, even if it were not previously associated with the experience of being fed. Evidence of learning becomes more convincing if the child resumes his crying, more vigorously than ever, if there is a longer than usual delay between the time when he is picked up and the moment he is fed.

Many studies have raised the question as to how early in life it is possible to establish a conditioned response. In these, as in other classical conditioning studies, the procedure is to present an originally neutral or ineffective stimulus (known as the conditioned stimulus, or CS) in conjunction with an originally effective stimulus (the unconditioned stimulus, or UCS) and then to note whether the former, after a succession of trials, will elicit the response made to the latter. Studies have been made of *aversive* responses, such as the withdrawal of a limb in response to an electric shock that is administered in conjunction with the sounding of a buzzer (Wickens and Wickens, 1940) and of *appetitional* responses, such as sucking in response to the insertion of a nipple into the child's mouth, accompanied by the sounding of a buzzer. In one experiment (Marquis, 1931), eight infants were bottle-fed from the time of birth, and at each feeding a buzzer was sounded. After three to six days, seven of the eight infants showed an increase in sucking and mouth-opening and a lessening of general activity and crying in response to the buzzer alone. Since an infant's response to any sort of stimulus may be quite generalized, some of these effects might possibly have occurred even if feeding had not been used as a "conditioning" stimulus.

A clearer picture emerges in a study (Kantrow, 1937) of sixteen infants whose ages when the experiment first began ranged from one month and fourteen days to three months and twenty-seven days. In this study a buzzer was sounded for five seconds, and then continued to sound during fifteen additional seconds as the nipple of a milk bottle was inserted in the infant's mouth and the infant proceeded to feed. Here it was found that sucking in response to the buzzer alone was established in from three to nine feedings (during the course of which the buzzer and the bottle had been presented together from sixteen to fifty-three times).

The infants responded to the buzzer by sucking when they were hungry but not when they were sated. Even though a connection had been established between sucking and the buzzer, it required the motive of hunger to call it forth. The infants apparently used what they had learned only when there was good use for it. In addition, the conditioned response to the buzzer disappeared when, in a second part of the experiment, the buzzer was sounded repeatedly without the accompaniment of feeding after the infants were partially sated. While still less than four months old, these infants were thus demonstrating the beginnings of "intelligent" behavior in two ways: (1) They learned to respond to significant signals (buzzing as a signal of food) and, (2) they learned to discard false signals (buzzing that no longer betokened food).[7]

Infants who were only three and four days old and were subjects in a conditioning experiment by Lipsitt, *et al.* (See Lipsitt, 1963), which combined the insertion of a nipple with a sound. In reporting this study, and in a review of numerous other studies, Lipsitt states that the data ". . . indicate strongly that a classical appetitional conditioning phenomenon can be observed during the first few days of human life" (1964, p. 167).

Other findings reported by Lipsitt and his associates (for a review, see Lipsitt, 1966) indicate that neonates manifest the kind of habituation which occurs when an individual ceases to respond to repeated stimulation of a kind that initially evoked a response.

Lipsitt and his associate (Engen) made tests to find whether such seeming habituation to stimulation might be a kind of negative adaptation or "sensory fatigue" (such as occurs when a person after a time no longer smells an odor that at first produced a clear olfactory sensation). They presented infants with a mixture of two odors, and, after several trials, there was a decline in response to this mixture. Then, while continuing the timing of stimulus presentation without interruption, they presented a substance containing only one component of this odorous mixture. The infants now renewed their responses to this odor as though it were a different or novel stimulus.

In another experiment, Lipsitt and Kaye (1965) noted effects which might be regarded as a form of early learning and remembering. They used two stimuli, one an ordinary bottle nipple and the other a flat piece of rubber tubing. The nipple was more effective than the tube in evoking a sucking response when inserted into the infant's mouth. In response to the nipple alone, there was an upward trend and in response to the tube alone there was a downward trend in amount of sucking when each was presented five

---

[7] See also Wenger (1936), and Wickens and Wickens (1940).

times in succession. But an interesting result occurred when infants were alternately presented with the nipple and the tube (each five times in succession). When shifting from the nipple to the tube, there was a carry-over of the high response from the nipple to the tube, followed by a decline in response to the tube. When the shift was made from the tube to the nipple, there was low response to the nipple at first and then a rise in response. It was as though the infants, taken off guard so to speak, continued a former response to a changed stimulus and then quickly corrected themselves.

To discover whether and when an infant is able, at a given time after birth, to acquire a conditioned response it is important not only to choose an effective unconditioned stimulus but also to make a proper choice of the conditioned stimulus. The former is easier than the latter. We can be quite sure that the unconditioned stimulus is effective when, for example, the child invariably recoils from an electric shock administered to the sole of his foot. But when, after many trials, he fails to withdraw his foot to a stimulus that has been paired with this stimulus, such as a light or a tone or buzzer, it is not certain that he cannot be "conditioned." The conditioned stimulus may be one that ordinarily would not capture his attention, or he may have become habituated to the stimulus so that he no longer notices it, in much the same manner that many other recurring stimuli in his environment go unnoticed.

It is necessary also to take account of maturation. As the days go by, a healthy neonate normally responds to a widening range of stimuli. As a consequence, the infant might respond, in time, to a seemingly conditioned stimulus even if it had not previously been paired with an unconditioned stimulus.

Another approach to the subject of learning in early infancy was made in an investigation of whether infants adapt to (that is, "learn") a feeding schedule within the first ten days of life (Marquis, 1941). A record was obtained of the general bodily activity of sixteen babies who were fed on a three-hour schedule until they were eight days old and then, on the ninth day, were changed to a four-hour schedule. A record was also made of the activity of another group of newborns who were on a four-hour schedule, and of a third group fed on a self-demand schedule—that is, fed whenever they seemed hungry. Activity was recorded mechanically by a device that supported the bassinets in which the infants lay.

Records of the three-hour and four-hour groups through the eighth day showed a falling off in activity after a feeding, as though the infants were gradually settling down. At the end of three hours, the three-hour group was relatively quiet, while the four-hour infants showed a rising rate of activity between the third and fourth hour. When the three-hour group was shifted to a four-hour feeding schedule, the activity of the infants increased abruptly at the end of the third hour and by the end of the fourth hour it reached a level higher than at any previous time. The activity level, during the fourth hour for children previously fed every third hour, exceeded the level shown by the children who had been fed on a four-hour schedule from the beginning. This high level of activity was frequently accompanied by crying. Moreover, the increased rate of activity continued even after the infants had been fed. It might have been expected that the infants, when changed from a three-hour to a four-hour schedule, would have become so fatigued by the extra activity during the extra hour's wait that they would settle down after at last having been fed and would go to sleep sooner than before. Not so. During the first part of the four-hour period the infants continued to be more active than usual and then, at the end of the third hour, there was a further abrupt rise in activity.

These observations indicate that the infants on the three-hour schedule seemed to have "learned" to expect food at the end of three hours.

In this same study, there was evidence, although not unmistakable, that the infants on a four-hour schedule were "learning" to wait four hours. As noted, they showed an increase in activity between the third and fourth hours, but as the days went on, this activity tended to lessen rather than to increase. They apparently were accustoming themselves to a longer wait between feedings than they would have preferred. Their preferred period would probably be nearer to three than to four hours, as indicated by the fact that the children in the group fed whenever they showed signs of wanting to be fed showed an average wait between feedings of about three hours.

Findings in studies of newborn children, as reviewed above, indicate that these children have a considerable capacity for modifying their behavior and a considerable degree of resiliency, a capacity to adapt to what the environment demands or affords.

Recommended Readings

K. C. Pratt's "The Neonate" (1954) gives a comprehensive review of findings pertaining to the newborn child into the early 1950's. Many of the recent studies referred to in the text have not been compiled in a single review.

PART TWO

Laying the Foundations

6   *Infancy*

Each person who observes the development of an infant is impressed in his own way by what he sees. And each baby puts on his own show, so to speak. But there are some features that are especially impressive.

One of these is the speedy emergence of the infant as a distinct individual. No two are the same, not even "identical" twins. Linked with this is the rapid development of the child's responsiveness to his environment, and notably to people in his environment. The resources of an infant's humanity are rich even when he is only a few weeks old.

In his response to people and to things, the reach of an infant's senses soon goes beyond the reach of his body, particularly in the way he uses his eyes. Among the muscle systems that quickly come into service in early infancy are those involved in the use of the eyes.

Shirley (1933a), in a study of the development of twenty-five infants, noted the following achievements by 50 per cent or more of the babies during the first weeks of life: following a light with the eyes at five days; watching an object one or two times at three weeks; following an object (a tape) moved in a horizontal direction at five weeks, and in a vertical direction at nine weeks.

Gesell and Ilg (1943), in speaking of an infant at about sixteen weeks, comment that "he can 'pick up' a small object with his eyes long before he can pick it up with his fingers."

In her discussion of the rapid development of visual ability, Shirley concludes that a two-year-old child can probably see with his naked eye anything an adult can see. He will, of course, see things from a different angle, and he will be unable to impart as many meanings to what he sees as an adult does.

Although an infant's sensory ability in some ways outruns his motor ability, these two abilities very early in life work together as a team. Among the important early developments that expedite this team-work is the establishment of postural control. For a time after birth a baby continues to assume the curled-up posture of the fetus. When he is lifted, his head—large in proportion to the rest of his body—will sag if not supported. At about the age of three weeks, while lying on his stomach, he is able to lift his head and raise his chin clear of the surface which supports him. Further postural control appears within a few weeks, including the ability to hold his head erect, to balance and turn it, and to sit, at first with support and later without support. Such postural control, combined with a steady increase in motor coordination, greatly expands the child's psychological field. He can sweep the surrounding scene. He can coordinate different sense modalities, such as when he turns his head and eyes toward the source of a sound or brings an object that he sees into contact with his mouth. Through the combined use of his sensory and motor abilities, particularly his arms and hands, the child can proceed actively to explore the world in which he lives.

Early Social Reactions

From the time when infants are able to take notice of their surroundings they are likely especially to pay attention to other persons. This might have been interpreted, in the earlier days of psychology, as a manifestation of a gregarious or social instinct. However, it might also be interpreted as a learned response, induced and reinforced by the fact that human beings, through their movements, contacts, sounds, and ministrations, provide a child with a more varied and satisfying source of stimulation than anything else in his environment.

Whatever might be the reason, a child begins very early in life to reserve a distinctive response for other human beings—he smiles. The physical act of smiling appears before it can be regarded as a social response. During the first month of life infants frequently smile in the absence of any external stimulus that might account for the smiles. Such smiles are likely to occur when an infant is sated, has his eyes closed, and seems to be falling asleep (Freedman, 1965). In the second month, the smiling is more likely to occur if there is an external stimulus. This need not be a visual stimulus (such as sight of the mother's face) for smiling might occur in response to being touched or hearing a voice or some other sound. Babies who are blind will smile when petted and spoken to in an endearing way. According to Freedman, however, the first distinctly social smile of a seeing child is likely to be preceded by a period of several days during which the infant fixes his gaze on the mother's face, without smiling. When once the smiling in response to a human being has become established, smiling thereafter is likely to appear as a distinctive social reaction.

According to one view, the muscular activities involved in smiling originally represented a reaction of surprise, almost a primitive response of being on guard. Moreover, the parting of the lips and of the teeth are among movements involved in sucking. But a youngster's smile is not merely a way of getting set for trouble or for a meal. Babies at the smiling stage will smile when they seem to have no fear or no desire for food. They will smile at the sight of a human face when they offer no smile on seeing a bottle held out to them by a person whose face is not within view. Babies will greet persons with a smile even though they have had a minimum of attention. In addition to smiles in response to persons, some babies during the first year frequently smile in connection with their own self-initiated activities.

Friendly Beginnings

If an infant could speak, he might well say: "I begin my life as a friend." In their reactions to adults, infants show far more "positive" than "negative" behavior, as indicated in an early study by Bühler (1930) and confirmed in a later study by Rheingold (1956). The same note is struck in a later study of sixteen infants who lived in an institution and who were given a series of tests at weekly intervals for eight weeks, beginning when they were about six months old. A record was kept of "negative" responses—such as frowning, or a worried look, whimpering, crying, turning the head away, rolling or crawling away from the adult—and of "positive" responses—such as smiling, laughing, and rolling or reaching toward the adult. In their response to a total of 527 social contacts, the infants reacted negatively in only 65 instances. Even some of these reactions were debatable, for in many instances an infant would exhibit the "negative" response of rolling away from the experimenter but would also smile and laugh and promptly roll back.

Interweaving of Perceptual, Social and Emotional Development

In their earliest social reactions, babies tend to be quite undiscriminating. At first, in the smiling-in-response-to-persons stage, they smile at all comers. At about six months (sometimes earlier, sometimes later) they are likely to be more selective. Following this period, there appears in many children an interesting three-dimensional change in behavior: (1) discrimination between strange and familiar persons; (2) first signs of fear of strangers; and (3) the beginning of selective emotional attachment to one or more persons.

The ability to distinguish between strange and familiar persons represents a landmark in a child's perceptual development. This ability emerges through the combined factors of maturation and learning. Maturation sometimes appears quite dramatically. Almost overnight, with no known intervening experience, a child who responded cheerfully to all who came along will, for the first time, show fear when approached by someone who is not a regular member of the family. The role of learning obviously is important, too, for it is only through past experience that a child can distinguish between the strange and the familiar.

While all normal children sooner or later manifest an ability to discriminate between strange and familiar persons, they differ very much in their manner of showing this ability. Some youngsters exhibit marked signs of fear at the approach of a "stranger" (who might have been a visitor in the home many times). Others just seem to be a bit cautious or guarded and then, sooner or later, seem to take strangers in their stride. It is likely that a child who has been held close to the nest by a solicitous and possessive mother will, at a given juncture of his development, fear the intrusion of a stranger more than one who has freely been shared with others and has, so to speak, been passed from one friendly hand to another. But some youngsters appear to be more inclined than others to accept or to fear unfamiliar persons regardless of their experience prior to the development of their ability to discriminate between the familiar and unfamiliar. (Differences in this respect, which may be due to genetic factors, have been described by Freedman, 1965.)

Along with the development of the ability to discriminate between strange and familiar persons, and temporary or more enduring fear of the strange, there comes another development—selective preferences for, or emotional attachments to, particular individuals. This topic, embroiled in varying views regarding the importance of a "primary love object" in a child's early life, will be discussed in a later section.

Individuality in Infancy

The marks of individuality children show soon after birth become more conspicuous as they move into the infancy period. As children become able to undertake an increasing variety of activities and social interactions, they vary the ways in which they display their distinctive qualities.

From time immemorial parents have observed that children have their own distinctive qualities. The same discovery is also made by substitute parents, as indicated in a study by Berezin (1959). These substitute parents were "boarding mothers" of infants who were awaiting adoption. The mothers not only noticed unique characteristics in the children under their care but also found, in spite of their own personal leanings, that they had to vary their mothering practices with different babies. What worked well with one child did not work well with another.

The fact that children have their distinctive individual traits has also been documented by authorities in child psychology—particularly by those who recognize, as axiomatic, the fact that conditions are not the "same" just because objective conditions in the environment or in a laboratory have been "controlled." The more a student of child behavior seeks to learn what a child can teach him (as distinguished from what he can teach *it*), the more likely he is to perceive and deeply respect each child's unique characteristics as a person.

Many students of child development were profoundly aware of this fact back in the 1920's and 1930's, when there was a strong upsurge of interest in the study of children as children rather than as laboratory animals. These investigators, such as Gesell (1928), Bühler (1933), Shirley (1933), and many others, stood out against pronouncements by the behaviorist John B. Watson (1928) to the effect that the course and outcome of a child's development was almost entirely determined by those who reared him. Watson proclaimed, but prudently did not try to prove, that he could take any well-born child and fashion the child in any way that he desired.

The fact that babies have their own individual qualities has been re-emphasized in a recent longitudinal study, still in progress, by Thomas and Chess and their associates (Thomas, *et al.*, 1963; Chess, *et al.*, 1965). On the basis of observation and details of overt behavior described by mothers, these investigators classified infants according to their "primary reaction patterns," in terms of nine categories. They were rated on a scale representing, for example, at one extreme, a tendency to be preponderantly *active*, and, at the other extreme, a tendency to be *inactive* or passive.

As of 1966, 141 children had been included in the study, and over a ten-year period, 136, or 96 per cent, continued to be actively observed. The children first came under investigation in early infancy, and follow-up studies were made at regular intervals thereafter. The first rounds of information concerning each child's behavior were obtained by interviews with the mothers, and only reactions that were described in objective terms were used as data. Mothers' reports were checked against information obtained by two members of the research staff who independently observed a randomly selected sampling of the children in their homes.

The nine categories of primary reaction patterns as set forth by Chess represent only one of many formulations that have been applied in studying young human beings, yet most of them represent an attempt to describe basic tendencies, as distinguished from other categories that apply to later behavior and often carry an implied adult evaluation (such as "dependency").

1. *Activity level.* The motor component present in a given child's functioning, and the diurnal proportion of active and inactive periods; motility during bathing, eating, playing, dressing, and handling, reaching, crawling, and walking.

2. *Rhythmicity.* Predictability and rhythmicity or unpredictability and arrythmicity in relation to the sleep-wake cycle, hunger, appetite and elimination.

3. *Approach or withdrawal.* The nature of the response (approaching and accepting or withdrawing) to a new stimulus, be it a new food, new toy, new person, new routines.

4. *Adaptability.* Also refers to responses to new or altered situations—not to the nature of the initial responses, but the ease with which they are modified.

5. *Intensity of reaction.* The energy level of response, irrespective of its quality or direction.

6. *Threshold of responsiveness.* The intensity level of stimulation necessary to evoke a discernible response, irrespective of the specific form that the response might take or the sensory modality affected; reactions to sensory stimuli, environmental objects, and social contacts.

7. *Quality of mood.* The amount of pleasant, joyful, and friendly behavior, as contrasted with unpleasant, crying, and unfriendly behavior.

8. *Distractibility.* The effectiveness of extraneous environmental stimuli in interfering with, or in altering the direction of, the ongoing behavior.

9. *Attention span and persistence.* These two categories are related. Attention span is the length of time a particular activity is pursued by the child. Persistence refers to the continuation of an activity in the face of obstacles to the maintenance of the activity.

Babies in the Chess-Thomas study were first rated according to the categories above in the age-range from about a month to a bit over four months.
(This means, unfortunately, that the data do not go back to the first days
of life.) Repeated ratings at intervals during the first two years showed that
the children tended to display a high degree of consistency in the prepon-
derant pattern of their behavior. The correspondence between successive
ratings, although considerably less than perfect, was considerably higher than
could be expected by chance.[1]

As we have mentioned, the observations in this study regarding the individual bent of each child are in keeping with earlier views. In biographical
studies of development, Gesell, *et al.*, (1939) tried to guard against the
exercise of hindsight and the bias that might infect a biographer's observations. Such bias would occur if an investigator, having formed an impression
of a given child, later encounters behavior that confirms this impression.
Gesell and his associates obtained movies of five children at the ages of one
and five and then asked an observer, who was unacquainted with the children, independently to rank the one-year-olds (as depicted in the movies)
and the same children at five years on fifteen traits, such as dependence,
social responsiveness, and amount of energy displayed. The ranks accorded
the children at one age level as compared with the other corresponded to a
degree far beyond what could be attributed to chance.[2] According to Gesell,
the results "clearly show prophetic characters in behavior traits in the first
year." Shirley (1933c), in a study of twenty-five babies during their first two
years of life, also found early and persisting marks of individuality. In a later
investigation Shirley (1941) followed the development of two boys (whose
mothers differed quite strikingly in their procedures) during their first six
years. On the basis of the latter study, coupled with her earlier investigation,
Shirley (1941) states that each child has a "tough core" of temperamental
qualities that prevents him ever from becoming a complete puppet in the
hands of others. Bühler also found that infants differ in ways that cannot
be explained by the environment in which they live (1933) and pointed out
that there are children with backgrounds that are not promising but who
develop unexpectedly well, while others, "in spite of their mothers' devotion"
founder along the way.

Investigators agree that there are wide individual differences in children
from the time of birth. There is not like agreement however, concerning the
extent to which such differences represent basic and tenacious tendencies,
what might be called a "germinal layer" of personality development.

To qualify as a basic mark of a child's individuality, a given characteristic
should, ideally, meet certain conditions. First, it should appear early, not

---

[1] Findings obtained in later stages of this study will be discussed in later chapters.

[2] There were 75 rankings—fifteen traits, five children—at the two age levels that could
be compared. Out of 75, 48 coincided, 21 were displaced by one rank order, five were displaced by two rank orders, and one was displaced by three rank orders.

necessarily soon after birth, but at the level of maturity when children can begin to manifest a given quality (such as a tendency to be sociable, or a tendency to be shy in the presence of strangers). Second, a characteristic that distinguishes one child from another should appear in a manner that cannot be explained by any known, specific prior circumstances in the environment (including the prenatal environment). Third, it should represent a characteristic way of responding in various situations rather than just a specific response to a specific circumstance. Fourth, it should remain stable during the infancy period as the child's repertory of activities expands. Fifth, it should be prophetic of later trends in personality development.

To discover what might be prophetic it is necessary to take account of the fact that behavior tendencies manifest themselves in varying ways as children grow older. For example, a certain young child may have a tendency to be fearful, or to cry easily. But, falling in with the course of development, at a later age he checks his tears and conceals his fears. One child, at an early age, may be irascible and aggressive, but, as he grows older, he displays his anger and aggressiveness much less openly. Moreover, there may be sex differences in this regard. An older girl may be more free than an older boy to cry, but less free openly to show her aggressiveness. Due to influences of this sort, consistency or change in a given characteristic cannot be assessed simply in terms of obvious manifestations. It is necessary to ask, What, at age ten, or sixteen or twenty-two is the *psychological equivalent* of behavior manifested at a younger age even though the overt behavior is quite different?

Learned and Unlearned Forms of Behavior

Learning consists of any acquired or modified form of behavior that comes about as a consequence of past experience. It is difficult early in the child's life to distinguish between behavior that is learned or *acquired*, on the one hand, and behavior that is *native* or inherent. It is also difficult to distinguish between behavior that emerges primarily through the process of maturation and behavior that is structured primarily through the child's experience with specific environmental stimuli. Within a given category of behavior, responses may range from those requiring no prior opportunities to learn, or a minimum of such opportunity, to those which could not possibly be established without prior learning. When, at about five months or later a child recognizes the difference between a strange and familiar person, he is manifesting a learned response. Yet, as we pointed out in the preceding chapter, he is able almost from the time of birth, and with a minimum of prior experience, to respond selectively to a patterned visual stimulus. It is only through learning that children become able to speak a given language. But early in life they come forth with a similar variety of vocalizations, including crying and cooing sounds, even though they have had no obvious opportunity to "learn" them. This was noted in a study by Lenneberg, *et al.* (1965), which compared the vocalizations of infants born to congenitally deaf parents (including one infant who was himself born deaf) with infants born to normally hearing and speaking parents.

It is only through observing and learning from what he observes that a child can imitate the wide range of expressive reactions shown by a mature person who is emotionally aroused. But some of the earliest expressive reactions seem to appear with a minimum of prior opportunity to learn. There are strong similarities, for example, between the facial expressions of a young blind-deaf child and those of a seeing and hearing child when they are emotionally aroused (Goodenough, 1932). A vast amount of the behavior of the neonate and infant is not "learned" in the manner, say, that a child in a laboratory study learns to obtain a reward by choosing the middle-sized object in an array of three.

Varieties of Learning Situations

Experimental work on children's learning has employed a variety of designs. One is the classical conditioned reflex or conditioned response design, discussed in the preceding chapter (pp. 76–79). Another type of experimental learning situation investigates what some writers refer to as "operant" learning. As in the conditioned response situation, the procedure rests on a process of association. But operant learning does not depend on the association between what might be called a coercive or inherently effective stimulus (such as an electric shock) and a neutral stimulus (such as a buzzer) but more on chance or manipulated coincidence. Operant learning would occur, for example, if a hungry child, in due time, always turned his head to the right for food when previously he has been given a bottle only when he turned to the right and had had his cheek pricked with a pin when he turned to the left. The bottle for a right turn, and the pin prick for a left turn, are positive and negative "reinforcers."

In experimental studies, a variety of procedures have been used to study learning that involves positive or negative reinforcement. For example, the child may have before him a number of levers, each of which activates an electric current. If he pushes one lever, a green light appears, and that is all, but another lever may produce a red light accompanied by a reward. Or, in a more complex set-up, he may have to press a number of levers in a certain sequence in order to gain a reward. It is possible to vary experimental conditions through an almost endless range of choices and to introduce other variables such as delayed rewards, distractions, and the like.

Experimental studies of learning in young children have not, to date, provided a major breakthrough into what and how and why children learn.

An adequate study of learning must involve more than simply recording what children do in an experimental situation in which all variables are presumably "controlled." Experimental controls may be determined by the experimenter's preconceptions. For example, what an experimenter regards as a reinforcing reward, similar for all his subjects, may not at all be similar for all the subjects. The reward may be alluring to some children but have little or no appeal to others. Furthermore, a given learning task may capture and hold one child's attention but to another child it may simply be something he is assigned to do. To assess learning it is also necessary to take account of the role of maturation.

In everyday life, as distinct from a controlled experiment, most of a child's learning occurs through his own spontaneous discovery. A child's "laboratory" consists of the whole world within reach of his limbs and within the purview of his senses. Anything and everything in this laboratory can, in one way or another, provide the conditions from which learning ensues: objects with varying shapes, textures, sizes, colors; everything that can be manipulated, put together or torn asunder or taken apart, separated or piled into a heap; every sound, taste, smell; everything that is light or heavy, soft or hard, liquid or solid, cold or warm, sharp or blunt, translucent or opaque; everything that produces pleasure or pain as a consequence of the child's own activities or rewards and punishments from other persons; everything that provides the child with a model to imitate; and so on, indefinitely.

One of the important tasks confronting a young learner is to bring some kind of order into the scatter of things and conditions he encounters. Some such order is achieved when, for example, he dimly perceives that certain actions have predictable consequences, such as winning approval or reproof; that things will fall out of reach if pushed too far out on the edge of the tray on his high-chair; that round objects will roll and square objects won't; that soap, even though it looks edible, has an unpleasant taste.

Learning by Way of Selective Attention and Habituation

A child learns not only through a process of giving active attention to and exploring the new or unfamiliar but also through a cumulative increase in the number of events he ignores. Countless sights, sounds, and other things that once caught his attention are, so to speak, "laid by." At a given time he will stop, look, and listen when a shade is drawn, or when the clock strikes, or when the refrigerator motor goes on; and then, with time, he scarcely notices these happenings, if at all.

In the daily life of a child, as of an adult, there is a tremendous amount of what might be called "selective inattention." The extent of this selective inattention during the day's routine is sometimes brought out sharply by what a person notices at night. During the day, a shift in temperature may produce unnoticed creaking noises in the wood-work or on the stair-way and in the radiators. But these same noises may seem strange and ominous in the stillness of the night. Even a drowsy adult may have the impression that someone is walking up the stairs when, as the heat comes on, there is a succession of creaking noises on the stairway.[3]

Selective Attention

Attentional behavior occurs when a child selectively gives heed to a particular thing or happening (including any activity of his own) and seeks, as it seems, to hold on to it.

A child's ability to fix his attention is most readily observed in the visual field, where it is possible to observe his eye movements and to note how long he fixes his gaze on a given scene.

The process of paying attention is a rather complex mental activity. When a child fixes his gaze upon a particular thing, it means that this thing has priority over other things that lie within his field of vision. When a child selectively and actively gives heed to one thing, it probably means that he notices a difference between this and other things he chooses to ignore.

Many informative observations regarding the development of attentional behavior in infants have emerged from studies by Lewis, Kagan and Campbell (1965). They worked with two independent samplings of children, each consisting of sixteen boys and sixteen girls. When first studied, the children were twenty-four weeks old (or within four days of being twenty-four weeks old). The stimuli, presented under standardized experimental conditions, included pictures of human faces, a bull's-eye, a nursing bottle and a panda bear, patterns of blinking lights, and a variety of sound recordings. The stimuli were repeated several times, in a different order, with brief rest periods between each presentation.

Measures of attention included the total time the infant oriented his eyes toward the visual stimuli, records of arm movements, vocalizations, respiration rate, and rate of heart beat. The latter record was taken because earlier work had shown that there is a temporary slowing of the heart-beat when an otherwise physically inactive person attends to a visual or auditory stimulus.

Among the findings were the following: at first, the child's attention is caught by what is presented, and then, as the stimulus continues or is repeated, he seems to become habituated to it and his attention wanes. However, this waning of attention, as though the novelty has worn off, varies in

---

[3] It is quite likely that many of the "irrational" fears of the uncanny or mysterious which children and their parents report so often (Jersild and Holmes, 1935a) arise out of a difference in what is noticed and what is ignored during the bustle of the day and the quiet of the night. A child may become so habituated to sounds occurring during the day that he never singles them out for special attention. Consequently, when these sounds burst out in the quiet darkness, they seem unfamiliar and mysterious.

response to the different things. To measure attention it is necessary not only to note what initially seems to attract the infant's interest but also the pattern of responses that follows—whether, for example, a stimulus quickly loses its holding power, or continues to catch and hold the child's attention when presented several times.

The children gave more attention to representations of a human face, or to something resembling a human face (such as the panda bear) than to other forms, such as the bull's eye or nursing bottle. This is in keeping with many observations, dating back through the years.[4]

The attention an infant pays to events that pass before him depends not simply on the objective intensity or eye-fetching quality of what is presented but on the meanings the stimuli apparently have acquired in the infant's past experience.

As time passes, many sights that draw the attention of a child at a given age do not attract his notice when he is older. This point appeared in a second study at thirteen months of thirty children who had participated in the study of children aged twenty-four weeks (Kagan and Lewis, 1965). An infant who fixed his attention on a photograph of a human face at an earlier age may be more attentive, later on, to a line drawing which is not just an obvious reproduction but requires, as it were, to be "figured out." In other words, a child's alertness cannot be determined simply by finding whether he pays heed to this or that but must be considered in terms of what has gone before. What is attention-getting for a child at an early age may have lost its drawing power when he is older. Kagan and Lewis found that the more attentive a child is at about six months the more likely he is, at one year, to prefer a novel to a familiar pattern (as shown by giving more attention to the schematic drawing of a face than to the photograph of a face).

A child who is *not* attentive to a given phenomenon at a certain age may actually be more advanced, intellectually, than one who is attentive. The former child's inattentiveness may mean that he has, so to speak, "laid by" this phenomenon and is turning his attention to other things. Similarly, an alert child's attention at a given age may be arrested by something which seems to make little impression on a less alert child.[5]

Remembering

A child shows evidence of some kind of retention or "memory" whenever his behavior is modified or influenced by a past experience. Infants manifest such retention practically from the time of birth. We cannot assume that

---

[4] The evidence suggests that infant girls are likely to pay more attention to human-like representations than infant boys, and more attention to the female face than to the male.

[5] An example of this is given in a later chapter dealing with children's fears. A bright two-year-old may manifest fear of animals and novel happenings which do not frighten less intelligent children until they are older.

an infant remembers in the sense that he can consciously recall a past event and dwell upon it. In time, however, the ability to "store" past impressions, to act upon them, to reconstruct and reflect upon them, plays a crucial role in thinking. The role of memory becomes especially pronounced when a person not only can revive images of concrete happenings but is able to use a "store-house of ideas."

A milestone in the development of the memory function appears when a young child is able to act upon an impression when the source of this impression is no longer within reach of his sense organs. This happens when a child looks searchingly in the direction of a sound he no longer can hear, or pursues an object he no longer can see.

During the first few months, an object "out of sight is out of mind." If a toy with which a child is playing is covered with a towel, it is as though the toy ceased to exist. But at six months, more or less, he will go after the toy as though it still were there, uncover and retrieve it. Such behavior is more than a chance occurrence, particularly if a child does not recapture the toy immediately and must overcome obstacles and experience some delay before he does.

This response is one of many that enables a child increasingly to internalize, within his own grasp of things, the objective realities of the world in which he lives. When, for a child, an object out of sight is no longer out of mind, he has begun, in Piaget's terms, to be aware of the *permanence* of things. The world is no longer constituted simply by the things that impinge on his senses. Stated in terms more sophisticated than the child yet can formulate, there is something lawful, constant, and invariant that exists apart from the flow of the child's sensations and his perception of things.

Perception and Meaning

The term "perception" has many connotations and, in the history of theoretical psychology, it has been the focus of controversy. Traditionally, perception has been defined as a complex type of mental activity which has been derived from previous experience, as distinguished from sensation, which was regarded as a simpler and prior component of experience. Actually, there are unresolved questions as to what might be regarded as the simplest, irreducible unit of direct experience.[6] However this may be, it is clear that there are developments in the area of perception that arise through time as a result of learning. One such development appears when a child is able to respond increasingly to a part of a past stimulus situation as though it represented the whole. For example, he need see only the edge of a toy to

---

[6] As indicated in Chapter 5, Fantz (1963) found that newborn children, with a minimum of previous experience, respond selectively to a complex patterned visual stimulus, as distinguished from a simple monochromatic stimulus.

reach for it, as though he knows the whole toy is there. He may even, in time, respond similarly to the contours of a toy that is completely covered by his blanket.

In the course of everyday experience there are countless situations in which a small detail of a total stimulus context will cue a response as though the total stimulus were there.

This phenomenon of "cue reduction"—enabling a child to respond, as it were, to a shorthand type of message—appears when, without having to test things out, he reacts appropriately to things that are hard and soft, movable and immovable, rollable, mountable, bounceable, edible, reachable, and so on. It occurs in his reactions to persons, pets, and all the paraphernalia of his environment.

Depth Perception. An important aspect of a child's perception of the space in which he moves is his ability to recognize depth—the difference in downward depth, for example, between the edge of an unscreened porch and the ground beneath, or between one step on a stairway and the step below it.

To study this aspect of perception, Gibson and Walk (1960) and Walk and Gibson (1961) designed an apparatus which they called the "visual cliff." The apparatus resembles a large table, with walls around the edges. The surface of the table is made of heavy plate glass. In the center is a platform, one inch higher than the surrounding surface, where the child who is being observed is placed. Beneath the glass is a patterned mat of linoleum that can be placed at varying distances below the surface of the table. The apparatus is so contrived that the distance between the glass surface and the underlying linoleum looks like depth, so that if the child moves from where he is to the area next to him, he would have to fall or descend to a corresponding depth.

In their experiments, Gibson and Walk used an arrangement that, to the eye, offered a shallow drop on one side and a deep drop on the other. Infants aged six and a half to fourteen months were placed on the center platform and were urged by their mothers to come to them, from the "deep" and from the "shallow" sides. Eighty-nine per cent of the infants who responded to their mother's urging did so on the shallow side, but refused to come when she called from the deep side. Many of those who refused to venture over the seeming cliff on the "deep" side actually felt and patted the even surface with their hands but apparently trusted the visual appearance of depth more than their sense of touch.

From studies with this apparatus, the investigators concluded that normal infants from the time when they are capable of locomotion can perceive the difference between a shallow and deep drop-off.

In various supplementary experiments the investigators found that a child's tendency to avoid moving from the level he is occupying to one that seems deeper increases as the depth between the two, as seen by the eye, increases.

When infants avoid the deep side, it is difficult to establish to what extent they are prompted by inherent capacity for depth perception or by learning. Human infants, tested with the visual cliff when able to crawl, have had many experiences from which they might possibly learn to discriminate depth even though they have never fallen. The evidence from further studies suggests, however, that the depth perception is innate.

Gibson and her associates (1963) used the visual cliff apparatus in tests of young animals of various species. They found that young animals avoided the deep side as soon as they were able to walk, before they had had any experiences from which they might have learned to avoid it, such as falling, climbing, or walking into things. Goats and chickens avoided the deep side before they were twenty-four hours old. When first exposed to the apparatus, rats avoided the deep side, whether they had been reared in the dark (precluding an opportunity to learn to respond to visual stimulation) or under normal conditions of light and darkness. Kittens reared in the dark were impaired both in their locomotion and depth-perception. But even the kittens, when restored to a normal environment, began to avoid one side and to choose the other in a manner that seemed to rule out learning as the causal factor. Gibson concludes that depth discrimination matures, when normal conditions of development are provided, without benefit of reward or punishment or associative learning.

The Role of Environmental Stimulation

Nearly everything that can be said about a growing infant portrays him as an active infant. Much of this activity is self-initiated. The fact that infants display an orderly sequence in the emergence of the new activities described in this and other chapters indicates that maturation plays an important role in the process of development. However, the factor of maturation cannot be divorced from the factor of experience, for whenever anything appearing at a later stage builds upon and incorporates activities that have gone before, it is apparent that experience plays an essential role.

The infant obviously needs the opportunity to try out his growing powers. For example, to combine vision with reaching and grasping, a child, at a given stage, needs an opportunity to exercise the postural control required for sitting upright. A sitting position gives a far greater range to a child's activities than a recumbent position does. If deprived, at the appropriate juncture, of opportunities to use the muscles used in sitting his intellectual activities will be curtailed. As shown in a study by Dennis (1960) of institutionalized children, an infant who is backward in his ability to sit upright may, on a baby test, give the appearance of being mentally retarded. He has not acquired the postural coordination necessary for handling the materials used in a baby test.

The nature and consequences of environmental deprivation, as revealed mainly by studies of institutionalized children, will be discussed in a later chapter. At this point, it is timely, however, to call attention briefly to effects of stimulation and lack of stimulation as shown by studies of laboratory animals.

Studies by Levine and his associates have precipitated a fascinating line of investigations of the effects of experimental stimulation (and lack of stimulation) on growth and later development (Levine, *et al.*, 1954; Levine, 1956, 1957, 1960).

Findings in these investigations have varied. Some studies have reported spectacular results while in others the effects of stimulation have been negligible.[7] It seems that some inbred strains of white rats are particularly susceptible to stimulation (or deprivation) while other strains are not. It is instructive first, however, to review some of the procedures that have been used, with positive results.

In their original investigations, Levine and his associates studied the effects of early painful experience by subjecting infant rats to mild electric shock on a regular schedule. A second group of rats, serving as controls, were placed in the shock cage on the same schedule but received no shock. Rats in a third group, also serving as controls, were left in their nests and not handled at all. It was expected that the shocked rats would be unfavorably affected by their experience and show signs of emotional disorder at adulthood. On the contrary, it was the group that was not handled at all that "behaved in a peculiar manner," while those that had been handled (with or without shock) developed more favorably. It appeared that stimulation, even painful stimulation (combined with handling) was far better than no stimulation at all.

In later studies, rats subjected to varying degrees of stress and amount of handling were compared with non-manipulated animals, and again it was the latter who later showed deviations of behavior and development. The behavior differences between the stimulated and non-stimulated groups appeared particularly in response to stress. One test consisted of observing the animals in an "open field"—a square-box area marked off into smaller squares. In this situation the previously manipulated animals were active and freely explored their surroundings. The non-manipulated ones tended to cower in a corner or to creep timidly about. Moreover, they showed further reactivity to stress by tending to defecate and urinate frequently (these functions are controlled by the division of the autonomic nervous system which is thrown into action by stress).

If the outcomes were judged only by the behavioral terms, we might maintain that rats accustomed to human handling as infants should be ex-

---

[7] Such vagaries in laboratory rats may spring in part from selective breeding and their artificial man-controlled conditions of life. Laboratory rats, according to Piaget, "are a degenerate strain which has lost almost all of its rodent instincts." (P. IV of Foreword, Almy, 1966).

pected to respond more favorably than unhandled rats to a man-controlled situation as adults. However, other tests revealed that the effects of early stimulation were more profound than simply the behavioral reactions.

Animals stimulated as infants, as well as previously non-stimulated animals, when subjected to shock displayed an increase in the release of certain hormones (steroids) into the blood stream. This is a physiological reaction to stress. However, there was a difference in the manner in which this release occurred. Animals previously exposed to stress increased their output of these substances more promptly, but for a shorter period of time, than non-stimulated animals. Non-stimulated animals were slower in increasing the release of their stress-induced hormones, but they maintained an increased output for a longer period of time. A prompt response, followed by relatively speedy recovery, is biologically more adaptive in time of temporary stress than slow response and a prolonged high level of stress-induced hormone content.

In addition, animals stimulated in infancy, as compared with non-stimulated animals, showed evidence of a more rapid maturation of the central nervous system; they opened their eyes earlier; achieved motor coordination sooner. They also had a heavier coat of hair at weaning time; and gained weight more rapidly (apparently through better utilization of food rather than from greater food intake).

Other studies of laboratory animals indicate that stimulation can produce both behavioral and physical effects. Rosenzweig (1966) compared rats reared after weaning in "enriched" environments with rats kept in an "impoverished" environment. The enrichment consisted of providing the animals with a variety of "toys" such as ladders, wheels, boxes, platforms, and varying patterns of barriers in the cages. It also involved training in a series of mazes. The rats in the impoverished environment were confined to individual, unfurnished cages where they were unable to see or to touch one another. At the termination of the experiment, measurements of the cerebral cortexes of those that had lived in an enriched environment showed an overall weight 4 per cent higher than the weight of the cortexes of the animals that had lived in the restricted environment.

Evidence of the profound effect experiences in infancy might have on later behavior comes from a series of studies by Dennenberg (reviewed in Dennenberg, 1963). In these studies, as in the Levine studies just cited, rats reared under varying laboratory conditions were, as adults, given "open field" tests to measure the extent to which they were active, flexible in their behavior, free to explore (or the opposite), and displayed emotional disturbance by involuntary defecation and urination when placed in an unfamiliar situation. When a normal and "an emotionally" disturbed mother gave birth the same day, the mothers were switched so that the mother of one litter fostered the offspring of the other. In these experiments it was found that, while "the genetic constitution is not without influence on later emotional behavior," interaction with a normal or disturbed mother between the time of birth and weaning "brings about a relatively permanent change in the emotional behavior of the offspring" (1963, p. 3). In yet another variation, infants subjected to handling, as in the Levine study cited above, or to isolation, were placed in various infant-mother combinations. One aim behind this approach was to study what effect the rearing of a normal or unstable infant might have on the mother. On open field tests conducted twenty-five days after birth, emotionally stable mothers that had reared emotionally stable infants scored highest in emotional stability. Disturbed mothers that had reared disturbed infants scored lowest. In between were the disturbed mothers who had reared normal infants and normal mothers who had reared disturbed infants. These results showed, in general, that significant changes in the emotional behavior of both the mothers and the infants occurred in mother-infant interactions between birth and weaning.

Animal studies of the influence of experiences in infancy have also indicated that an infant's development can be profoundly influenced by the presence or absence of age-mates. One well-known investigation of this influence was conducted by Harlow and his associates (see, e.g., Harlow and Harlow, 1962). Monkeys reared with artificial mothers, and with no contact with their kind, did not, as young adults, exhibit normal social behavior, and their sexual behavior was noticeably impaired.

Dennenberg (and some other investigators) also studied the effect of an "enriched" environment as compared with a relatively barren cage environment. The enriched "free environment" provided more space and was equipped with ramps, tunnels, and platforms. On later tests, rats that had been reared in this environment for a time and, in addition, had been handled, scored higher than unhandled rats reared in this environment. Both of these groups scored higher than unhandled infants reared in laboratory cages.

The findings just cited indicate that stimulation in infancy may have important effects on development and later behavior, at least in some species or strains. Not all of the investigations, however, have produced impressive results such as those cited above (see e.g., Ader, 1957; Griffiths and Stringer, 1952; Hunt and Otis, 1955). In a study by Goldman (1964) groups of rats that had received varying kinds of treatment in infancy were compared as adults on a variety of measures (open field activity, drinking behavior, reaction to shock and survival under stress). "Sociological litters" of four were formed; each of these contained a mother with one of her own offspring and one offspring from each of three other mothers. The experimental groups that were formed included nest controls, animals that were picked up, animals that were handled, and animals that received shock. All were placed on an experimental time schedule. Rats that had received shock in infancy and rats that had been handled showed less resistance as adults to being picked up than rats in the control group. In earlier work, such resistance to being picked up had been regarded as a sign of "emotionality." Goldman did not find, however, as had been found in some earlier studies, that rats handled in infancy weighed more or survived stress better or were more effective in their adaptive behavior than rats that were not handled.

The effect of stimulation apparently varies for different families of animals, and within one family it may vary considerably in one breed or strain as compared with another. This appears in studies of the effects of isolation which (in studies of rats and monkeys, among other creatures) has been found to have a deleterious effect on development and may be regarded as a form of lack of stimulation. In a study of dogs, Fuller (1966) found that some dogs will tolerate what would seem to be rather severe isolation without apparently suffering from it.

Fuller exposed beagle and terrier puppies to varying experimental conditions including complete isolation, isolation with only small breaks, isolation in a double-sized cage with one litter mate companion, and being reared as pets. During isolation the puppies had no visual or physical contact with a human being. Their cages were dimly lighted and were ventilated by a blower which masked some external sounds. Effects of deprivation in infancy were measured by means of an "Arena Test" which permitted the experimenters to observe the animal's initial response when transported to the arena; its ensuing responses to the apparatus; and its response to human handling, to toys, and to another puppy. The responses were tallied in terms of the animals' readiness to enter and explore, their activity level, and their emotional behavior (tail wagging, making friendly advances to the experimenter, and so on). As compared with the completely isolated puppies, puppies whose isolation had been interrupted for short intervals developed almost normally, and some of the isolated puppies rapidly adapted themselves to the new situation presented by the arena test, indicating that "the sensitive or critical period for socialization had an elastic upper age boundary" (1966, p. 4). Beagles and wire-haired terriers characteristically responded differently. Isolated terriers were consistently more active in the arena test and were more responsive to some of the stimuli. Terriers, normally more active than beagles, were consistently more active than the beagles after similar "dosages" of isolation. Even when first confronted with the arena test, terriers were more active and, in later tests, terriers with an isolation history were even more active than pet-reared beagles. In all tests following various types of experimental treatment the least active individual among the terriers showed more activity than the most active individual beagles. In other words, a treatment as drastic as complete social and partial sensory isolation, and various gradations of such isolation, during a critical period of development produced widely different effects in beagles and terriers. Fuller concludes that "there is no reasonable doubt that hereditary factors play a major role in determining the vulnerability of puppies to rearing in a severely restricted environment" (p. 8).

Studies of laboratory animals (and studies of human beings to be discussed in another context) confirm the axiomatic view that an organism cannot thrive in an empty environment. However, whether a certain environment will be stimulating or empty at a given period of development seems to depend not only on the character of the environment but also on the nature of the organism. Many studies show that for some creatures, under certain conditions, what seems to be a rather moderate degree of added stimulation can produce spectacular results. Other studies indicate that what seems to be a radical lack of stimulation during a given period of time has little or no demonstrable effect.

The studies of the effects of deprivation and stimulation in the laboratory have opened up exciting vistas that potentially hold great significance for developmental psychology. As far as the child is concerned, more information is needed concerning what is optimal, what is minimal, what is damaging. Probably, as evidence accumulates, it will be found that there is an irreducible minimum and an unproductive maximum of stimulation, that this varies at different levels of development, and that it varies also with the individual's genetic constitution.[8]

---

[8] Findings reviewed in a later section dealing with the development of institutionalized and home-reared children suggest that among children, as among laboratory animals, there are inherent differences in response to environmental stimulation and deprivation.

Recommended Readings

Revealing accounts of the development of behavior after birth and the emergence of distinct individual characteristics in babies can be found in the following books written a number of years ago: Charlotte Bühler, *The First Year of Life* (1930); W. Preyer, *The Mind of the Child* (1888); Arnold Gesell and Helen Thompson, *Infant Behavior* (1934); Mary M. Shirley, *The First Two Years*, Volumes I-III (1933); and W. E. Blatz, *et al.*, *Collected Studies on the Dionne Quintuplets* (1937). More recent recommended readings include Dorothy Burlingham's *Twins: A Study of Three Pairs of Identical Twins* (1952); A. Thomas, S. Chess, *et al.*, *Behavioral Individuality in Early Childhood* (1963); and L. P. Lipsitt and C. C. Spiker (editors), *Advances in Child Development and Behavior in First Year of Life* (1964).

7

The Origins

of Intelligence in Infancy

The most systematic account of early intellectual development has been offered by the renowned Swiss scholar, Jean Piaget. His studies of children's thinking are fortified by a versatile array of interests, including zoology, epistemology, and logic. He has combined these interests with a capacity for astute observation of children and what seems to be an inexhaustible store of energy.[1]

This sketch of early intellectual development is based primarily on the work of Piaget, although the writer has taken some liberties in phrasing and emphasis. It is set off in a separate chapter, for several reasons, the main one being that Piaget's distinctive ideas cannot readily be woven into a fabric with the miscellany of ideas from others. But, equally important, along with

---

[1] Unfortunately, as even his admirers ruefully acknowledge, some of his ideas are phrased in language that is not easy to understand.

his original concepts, he incorporates into his system many concepts that long have held a crucial place in developmental psychology. He recognizes (without making much to-do about it) the important role of maturation. He emphasizes the role of active interchange between the child and his environment, recognizing that maturation is a necessary but not sufficient condition for the drama of development. He incorporates into his system the concept of self-initiated activity as an essential driving force in a child's progress from less to more mature modes of behavior. And he recognizes that a child, acting on his environment in his own way and at his own pace, can reveal truths that cannot be gleaned from artificial laboratory situations.

Although Piaget's ideas are presented here in the context of development during infancy, they are relevant to all stages and ages. The intellectual processes displayed by an infant play an essential role in the thinking of the most sophisticated adult.

Biological Roots of Intelligence

According to Piaget, intelligence is rooted in two biological attributes that invariably are found in all living creatures. One is an underlying *organization;* the other is a capacity for *adaptation.*[2]

Organization

Every living organism has a biological organization so constituted that it can carry on the activities characteristic of its mode of life. In multicellular animals, these activities may be a function of organs or structures that are more or less separate in function but are all essential to the life of the organism. The structural organization is determined by genetic factors, but the manner of functioning is determined by (a) interaction with the environment, and (b) the level of maturation an organism has reached at a given stage of growth.

Among the activities provided for in a child's biological organization are those involved in the functioning of the intellect. A normal child is biologically so organized that he is destined to become a knowing organism. He does not possess innate ideas. But he is so constituted that he reacts to the environment through inborn channels of experience in a manner which eventually leads to an elaborate mental organization. At first he responds in a rather piecemeal fashion, mostly by way of the reflexes he is born with. Then, in the process of development, reflex reactions give way to responses that are controlled by the cerebral cortex. There is an expansion of response

---

[2] This account of Piaget's work draws largely on two of his writings, *The Origins of Intelligence in Children* (translated paperback edition, 1963) and *Play, Dreams and Imitation in Childhood* (translated paperback edition, 1962).

patterns within any given area of experience (such as in the sphere of vision) and there is a merger and coordination of experiences from various avenues of experience (such as a pattern that combines seeing with grasping).

A child's mental processes become increasingly organized and coordinated through a lawful sequence of developments, each stage of which provides the foundation for the next. At first he responds only in overt fashion and in response to immediate and direct stimulation. In time his mental processes become self-sustaining and self-generating. He becomes able to build, as it were, an internal world. Eventually he can detach himself from the concrete and think abstractly. He moves from sod to symbols. He becomes transformed from a creature governed largely by reflexes into a creature who can reflect on his own thoughts.

Adaptation

Another fundamental biological attribute of the organism is a capacity for adapting to the environment. Adaptation consists not simply in yielding to external demands. It is a process through which, in interaction with the environment, the organism becomes more effective in dealing with the environment. It is through progressive and increasingly complex adaptations that a child becomes more and more able to gain an intellectual grasp of the nature of the world in which he lives.

Assimilation and Accommodation. The capacity for adaptation, as described by Piaget, includes two complementary processes: *assimilation* and *accommodation.*

In the physical sphere, an organism ingests nutriments which, when assimilated, provide for physical survival, physical growth, and activity. Food is transformed into bone, muscle, and nerve structure in a manner that is in keeping with the genetic constitution of the particular organism.

Assimilation of nutriments from the environment also occurs in the intellectual sphere. Just as a child's physical structures are nourished by food received through the alimentary tract, so his mental structures are nourished by way of all his inborn channels for receiving and acting upon stimuli from his environment.

But adaptation involves more than merely taking in what the environment offers and fitting it into an already existing structure. It also involves a process of accommodation—a modified way of reacting to anything new or different that will not fit into an already established reaction pattern. Such a modification is required, for example, when a person, expecting everything that looks like sugar to taste like sugar, for the first time puts salt in his mouth. An accommodation also is required when a child, accustomed to drawing nearby small objects through the bars of his crib, fails when he tries to bring a ruler cross-wise into his crib and then, perhaps by chance at first, succeeds in bringing it in length-wise. He shows that he has assimilated this modified way of doing things when later he applies it to all other long objects within his reach.

The complementary processes of assimilation and accommodation, according to Piaget, continue as fundamental factors in intellectual functioning as a child moves from the early stages of cognition into later more complex levels. A sophisticated scientist, faced with a puzzling phenomenon, brings to bear on it the explanatory principles he already is familiar with. He tries to assimilate the new into the old. But when this won't work—when he cannot establish harmony or equilibrium between the new phenomenon or question and formerly established modes of thought, he must (if he desires to find out) go through a process of accommodation.

Beginnings of the Sensory-Motor Phase

Piaget has called the first phase of intellectual development the *sensory-motor* phase. It lasts from birth to about eighteen to twenty-four months.

Knowing through Sucking

In Piaget's account, the process of adaptation in the infant begins on a humble scale. Pre-eminent among a child's first reaction patterns are those involved in sucking. At first, some babies suck in a faltering way. But a healthy child soon sucks eagerly when a nipple is brought in contact with his mouth. Then, in time, the sucking configuration or *schema*, as Piaget calls it, expands. True to his inherent biological nature, the child makes *adaptations* of the sucking response. Instead of fumbling, he goes directly to the target. But more is added. He uses and varies the sucking pattern even when he is sated. The activity of the reflex becomes augmented through its own use (Piaget, 1963, p. 33).

Concurrent with his early sucking behavior, a child makes independent prehensory movements with his arms and hands. At first these movements appear to be diffuse and undirected. In time, perhaps by chance, his hand "finds" his mouth or his mouth "finds" his hands. In due time a child seizes upon this random combination of movements and repeats it again and again. He sucks his hand or fingers, seemingly merely for the sake of sucking. Sucking has moved beyond its primitive biological purpose and has become an important avenue of contact with the world of things.

The combined sucking and hand-to-mouth configuration enlarges the scope of the child's potential cognitive field. By a process which Piaget calls "generalizing assimilation" the child incorporates increasingly varied objects into the sucking schema. During the first weeks of life he sucks his own fingers, fingers extended to him by others, materials that come into contact with his mouth—his pillow, quilt, bedclothes, and other available materials. In so doing, "he assimilates these objects into the activity of the (sucking) reflex." (Piaget, 1963, p. 34.)

Coordination of Visual, Auditory, and Prehensory Modes of Experience

In the areas of vision, hearing, and prehension (involving motor activity and tactile and kinaesthetic experiences in use of arms and hands) there likewise is an expanding range of encounters with the environment through the child's active and repetitive use of these facilities.

Expansion in the Visual Sphere. In his visual activity a child moves from relatively passive looking to increasingly active and varied ways of looking. Lights and objects brought into his field of vision provide the original functional "aliments" (nutriments) for visual activity. At first a child responds relatively passively to visual stimuli, but within a few days he is actively adapting himself to the visual world. At about one month he directs his glance toward an object and follows it with his eyes. He looks at more and more objects, thereby assimilating a variety of sights into his visual sphere. When a visual object passes out of sight, he seeks to recover it. In doing so, he is not simply taking in a visual impression by a process of assimilation; he is adapting to his environment by means of an accommodation. At this early period, his preoccupation seems to be primarily sensory rather than perceptual in character: he feeds upon what his vision offers, without being aware of the meaning of the objects themselves.

As time passes, he directs his glance at one object, then at another—gazing at the face of one person near his crib, then at the face of another, as though he were beginning to make comparisons. His responses become more selective and differentiated. The rudimentary beginnings of *recognition*, perceiving a given sight as having a differentiated meaning of its own, appears when he characteristically smiles at the sight of a human face. At first, as we mentioned earlier, this perception seems to be global in the sense that any face can elicit a smile. A more particularized sign of recognition appears when he smiles at a familiar person but not at an unfamiliar visitor. Another sign of recognition appears when a child at three or four months perceives his bib as a sign that he will be fed.

Combining Vision with Prehension. The child has a greatly enriched source of experience when vision is combined with prehension. At first, a child's hand movements seem relatively independent of his vision—he moves his hands randomly and unnoticed, in and out of sight. But, in time, he catches his hands with his eyes, and, through repetition, is able to keep them in sight. In so doing he has made an important rudimentary discovery—he can to some extent control the visual world (the sight of his hands) by his own actions. Soon something more is added. Through a movement, which might be quite accidental, he displaces an object, such as a toy dog, with his hand. In time, he seizes upon this response, and repeats it. With further development, he becomes able to grasp objects within view, at first when his hand and the object are both within his field of vision and later if only the object is within view. This further extends his command over his environment.

The World of Sound

Meanwhile the scope of a child's encounter with his environment is increased by differentiation in his response to sounds, and the coordination of hearing with vision. During the first few weeks of life, a child's own vocalizations consist largely of crying, seemingly from hunger or bodily discomfort. Hunger cries may be quieted, at first by food; later by the sight of the bottle, only to be resumed if feeding is delayed. However, during the first two months or so, a child begins to manipulate his vocalizations—he prolongs or repeats a cry. In the act of crying, the child may produce a certain sound which somehow catches his attention. He seizes upon the sound, repeats it and with time, varies it. It is as though vocalization which originally, like sucking, served a primitive need early in life, becomes a source of experience in its own right.

In his response to sounds, a child at first, according to Piaget, listens for the sake of listening, but then begins to be more discriminating, producing and repeating a variety of sounds. He also begins to show signs of distinguishing between (recognizing) sounds.

Listening to What is Seen, Looking at What is Heard. Hearing becomes an especially fruitful aid to a child's grasp of his environment when it is coordinated with seeing. Piaget places this development at about three months. When this coordination occurs, a child does not merely see what he sees, or hear what he hears, as though these were independent sources of experience. Instead, a child tries, in a sense, to listen to what he sees and to look at what he hears. (In Piaget's terms, there is reciprocal assimilation of the visual and auditory schemata.)

A Many-Faceted World

The developments so far discussed largely appear in what Piaget calls the second stage of the sensory-motor period, lasting from one to four months. (The first stage, during which behavior is limited largely to the repertoire of activities present at birth, lasts, according to Piaget, from birth to one month.)[3]

During this second stage, as can be seen, a child has become increasingly flexible in his use of response patterns present at birth or soon thereafter, and he combines various experiences and performances into larger constellations. This "world," to be sure, is still closely confined to what is immediately before him. But already during this early period the world is beginning to be shaped in a manner that goes beyond this or that isolated impression. Piaget states that when various schemata which at first were more or less independent (sucking, seeing, hearing, prehensory activity) are simultaneously coordinated into a larger schema, a child is making progress toward *objectifying* things about him—viewing them as having external attributes of their own. When an object can be sucked, looked at, grasped, and apprehended as a source of sound, it begins to acquire "an ensemble of meanings and consequently a consistency which endow it with interest" (Piaget, 1963, p. 121).

Producing Effects on the Environment

During the next stage (the stage of secondary circular reactions, as described by Piaget), ranging from four to eight months, a child continues activities established during the preceding stage, but he is now more interested in the effects he can produce on his environment. Instead of hearing for the sake of hearing, he now produces sounds, often by banging. He happens, by chance, to produce a banging noise, and then repeats the banging.

In this stage, according to Piaget, a child employs procedures for making interesting sights last—similarly, procedures to repeat and preserve other experiences that he has stumbled upon. In the process, he begins to make distinctions between the ways in which objects in his environment may be handled—a ribbon or string can be pulled, for example; a rattle can be shaken to produce a noise; and a spoon, when shaken, produces no sound but does produce a sound when it is banged. A discriminating response of this sort appears to be a rudimentary form of classifying objects in the environment.

During this phase, when a child repeats activities that appear to have unforeseen but interesting consequences, his behavior is intentional in the sense that he desires to repeat an effect he has produced, but not in the sense that he foresees and works toward an outcome that has not yet occurred.

---

[3] This second stage (in a sequence of six in the sensory-motor period) is, in Piaget's words, the stage of "the first acquired adaptations and primary circular reactions." The designation "circular reaction" was adopted by Piaget from Baldwin (1925). Baldwin used it to denote the process by which infants discover, select, and conserve responses which originally may have occurred by chance but which, in Piaget's terms, have "advantageous results" (1963, p. 138).

Intentional Behavior

In stage four, from about eight to twelve months, a child exhibits behavior more clearly intentional in character. He now uses various means of activity in a means-end, goal-oriented manner.

According to Piaget, we cannot assume that a child has an intention or a conscious purpose if he responds simply and directly to what lies before him. We probably can assume the presence of a conscious desire if a child persists in an activity of his own choosing in spite of encountering obstacles and delays, or when there are intermediate activities between the initial act and the end result, or when a child seems to have a prevision of an outcome that has not yet been achieved. At an earlier period a child grasps for the sake of grasping. The activity is, so to speak, self-contained, and has no ulterior or extrinsic goal. In moving into what Piaget calls the stage of "secondary circular reactions," a further dimension is added: the child now uses means to produce effects on his environment.

At first the means-end combination may be fortuitous, with no intention or understanding of the cause and effect relationship between the act and the outcome. For example, Piaget's children (variously from about the third into the sixth or seventh month), discovered that they could produce a rattling noise by pulling at a string attached to a rattle and that they could produce a movement of the hood overhanging their cribs by pulling at a doll suspended from the hood. These effects at first were produced without seeming intention or foresight. Then they were repeated (through "procedures to make interesting sights last"). Later the outcome was anticipated —the child first looked at the hood while grasping the doll. The doll, which had been solely an object to be grasped or sucked, now became a means of producing an external result. When the child understands this phenomenon, he is making strides toward (a) the use of intermediate means to produce an end result, (b) prevision or expectation of an outcome that is not, initially, within view.

Growing Awareness
of an Independently Existing Universe

When a child, capable of intentional behavior, has a prevision of an outcome that does not yet exist, his universe has expanded beyond what lies immediately before him. He has made yet another stride when, at about the same time, he becomes aware of the *permanence* of objects. He reaches for an object that has disappeared from view. This means that something that is out of sight has not ceased to exist—it has an independent existence, apart from him. The universe is becoming objectified, "detached from the self" (1963, p. 211).

Discovering New Means of Action
Through Experimentation

In the fifth stage, from twelve to eighteen months, the child discovers new methods of active experimentation. (Piaget refers to this also as the stage of tertiary circular reactions.) He now gives the impression of deliberately exploring the world about him. He not only "submits to" and repeats results he has produced but varies his approaches to discover how he might change the results. He uses "the experiment in order to see." He distinguishes between his acts and objects in his environment instead of using only already familiar reaction patterns to achieve an intended result; he tries out new or varied methods. For example, he uses a stick to bring an object within his reach—to do so he must manipulate the stick until he finds the right approach; he discovers, after some fumbling efforts, how to bring a stick through the horizontal bars of his crib. If he grasps the center of the stick and holds it upright, the bars will not budge, but if he draws it in lengthwise or at a proper angle, he evades the bars.

Substituting Mental Representations
for Overt Manipulation

In the sixth stage (eighteen months and on) there is "the invention of new means through mental combinations." During this stage, instead of discovering new ways of achieving a result by visible, overt experimentation, the child employs "inner" or mental combinations. He now employs representations of acts or means that are not tangibly before his eyes. One of Piaget's children, for example, confronted the problem of recovering a small chain from a match-box. Hitherto, she had learned to reach into the match box, only partially closed, to extract the chain, or to tip the box upside down, so the chain would fall out. In the example in question, however, the match box was nearly closed, so the child had to devise new ways of retrieving the chain. The child looked at what remained of the slit attentively, then, several times in succession, opened and closed her mouth, as though representing to herself by a motor signal or image, that the aperture should be enlarged. Soon thereafter, she put her finger in the slit, widened it, and took hold of the chain.

The ability to use mental representations of things in the last stage of the sensory-motor period adds to the child's "practical intelligence," which also at the end of this period encompasses coordination of perception and action; the notion that objects are permanent—that they exist independently of the perceiver—is established, as is the notion that space is constant, and that there are constants in form and dimension.

Continuous Interaction of Assimilation and Accommodation

Through the complementary action of assimulation and accommodation, the child progressively *interiorizes* the world about him, constructing an inner world of cognition which increasingly corresponds to outer reality.

When he encounters something new that fits readily into an already existing scheme of things, the scheme is enlarged. This happens, for example, when, in his first experience with hard candy he finds that, in keeping with his earlier experience with hard lumps of sugar, it yields to sucking and is sweet to the taste.

But when a marble, which resembles a hard piece of colored candy, does not yield to sucking, and is tasteless, he must accommodate himself to the fact that objects which look alike do not taste alike, and that some things which look alike are not similarly soluble. He must modify his view of the marble. But this modified view may involve assimilating of the marble into another scheme of things—such as one he has established in his dealings with round beads. Moreover, a concurrent act of assimilation may also occur when he sees that the marble, like a hard round piece of candy, will roll when pushed.

Motivation Underlying Early Intellectual Development

What impels a child to undertake adaptations such as those we have just described? Some of his behavior is, of course, prompted by hunger and other "primary" needs, and, in time, by "secondary" needs derived from the primary ones. According to Piaget, a child has inherent needs for taking up activities that further his intellectual development. At the beginning, he has a built-in need for repeating the response patterns he is born with. The tendency of the reflex is to "reproduce itself"; a tendency toward repetition is a primitive and elementary fact of psychic life (1963, p. 33). At the outset, "he tries to assimilate the real, impelled by an invincible and vital tendency" (1963, p. 275). A child not only is impelled to repeat experiences that are assimilated into an already established pattern but also tends to repeat experiences that have required a revised approach or modified view of things (accommodation).

The mind, according to Piaget, does not develop through a process of passive accretion or enforced habit formation. Habits become a form of automatic repetition, but mental development goes beyond repetition to innovation. It does not occur by a process of reinforced association, such as might be induced in a laboratory experiment in which a child learns to push the right button to get a piece of candy. Instead, a child, with his inherent drive to use what he has, is equipped with his own supply of internal reinforcers. Early in life he sucks for the sake of sucking, looks for the sake of looking. In time, he reaches a stage when sheer repetition no longer suffices, and he then seeks novelty. Then "the more objects a child sees, the more new ones he wishes to see" (1963, p. 277).

Whether functioning on a low or high level of behavior, a child "tries to reproduce every experience he has lived" (1963, p. 43). Why? Because such activity has a functional meaning; it represents something of value for the individual who undertakes the activity. "But whence comes the value? From functioning as such" (Piaget, 1963, p. 43). According to Piaget, the organism has a "fundamental need which is that of organism's development" (Piaget, 1963, p. 170). This need operates in both the physical and the psychological sphere. "The need sets in motion the act and its functioning, but this functioning itself engenders a greater need which from the very first goes beyond the pure satisfaction of the initial need" (p. 170). The organs of the body are subordinated to this chief tendency (the organism's development) "which defines life itself" (p. 170).

Imitation

In Piaget's account, the imitation displayed by a child during the preverbal sensory-motor period of development is "one of the manifestations of his intelligence" (1962, p. 5). Imitation is not a passive process by which a ready-made mode of conduct is grafted to a child's behavior repertoire. Rather, according to Piaget, it involves an active process of accommodation to reality.

In his imitative activities, a child passes through sequences of development corresponding to those noted in the evolution of intelligent behavior. It is questionable whether true imitation occurs during the first (reflex) stage of sensory-motor development. It is questionable, for example, whether "contagious" crying in the hospital nursery can be regarded as imitation. But when an infant's crying is triggered, or intensified, by a crying baby in a nearby crib, he is apparently incorporating external elements into his crying or vocalization schema. When a child is able to do this, the beginnings of imitation are possible, according to Piaget.

More distinct evidence of imitation occurs when a child reproduces a sound made by someone else, or captures and repeats a sound he happens to have produced himself. He does not, however, early in life, imitate external sounds that he has not already differentiated in his own vocalizations. In other words, to imitate a sound, a child must already have produced it.

Nor does his imitation of other behavioral models at first go beyond the scope of his own self-initiated activities. He does not, for example, imitate hand movements made by someone else unless these movements are already part of his repertoire. Moreover, in the early stages he will not imitate a visible movement made by another person unless he has seen himself perform the same movement. One of Piaget's subjects, for example, at about six months, did not imitate her father when he opened and closed his hands: she had not seen herself open and close her own hands. She did, however, imitate her father when he separated his hands and brought them together again, for she had watched herself do the same thing. Another child, who had watched herself opening and closing her hand but had not yet seen herself placing her hands together and spreading them apart, imitated the former action but not the latter.

According to Piaget, with the passage of time, and as a child's ways of responding became increasingly coordinated and elaborate, it becomes possible for him to imitate movements that he is familiar with but are not visible to him. For example, at about eight months, Piaget imitated mouth movements made by one of his children and then, an hour later, the child imitated his imitation, even though her own mouth movements were not visible. Earlier, she had not imitated him. This act of imitation came at a time when she was actively interested in producing sounds with her mouth.

Piaget offers interesting examples of how an infant, at later stages, may translate the action of a model into an already familiar behavior pattern. While watching Piaget open and close his eyes, his children at about nine to eleven months variously opened and closed their mouths, or opened and closed their hands. They imitated the act of "opening and closing," but only through the medium of well-established actions. Piaget refers to this mistake as ". . . intelligent confusion" (1962, p. 44).

Imitation and Early Intellectual Development

When children are able to imitate movements that are familiar but not visible to them, they also, according to Piaget, begin to imitate new auditory and visual models. This development corresponds, in time, with the evolution of a child's ability to perceive things as having a distinct, independent reality rather than as a continuation of their own activity. At first, such imitations are confined to actions which are already familiar, even though the model is new. Later, corresponding to the period when children are able, in their own self-initiated behavior to discover "new tools through active experimentations" and to use systematic trial-and-error procedures, they will employ exploratory movements to imitate actions involving invisible parts of the body. (Piaget offers the example of a one-year old child who touched her forehead in imitation of her father. She combined a visual perception of her father's forehead and groping contacts with her own face, starting with the eye and eventually touching her forehead, apparently convinced that she had located the right spot. On following days, she moved her hand directly to her forehead.) Still later (the sixth stage of what Piaget speaks of as the period of sensory-motor intelligence), a child becomes capable of "internal" imitation. He can manipulate models by means of mental images (as distinguished from direct, objective action). Imitation now becomes a function of "representation" and can be immediate or deferred. This development transpires during the second year.

Imagery

The ability to form a mental image of things is important in the development of thinking. According to Piaget, the first images consist of "interiorized imitation" (p. 74) but in time the image acquires "a life of its own." Images break loose from their moorings, as it were, and they can be combined, re-shuffled and organized into a synthesis that transcends the objective realities which they originally reflect. Eventually, the images become not simply a mimic of reality but mental structures which a child, in turn, can imitate. Such takes place when, in make-believe play, a child imitates an imaginary creature.

The Role of Play
in Early Cognitive Development

According to Piaget, play serves an important function in early cognitive development.[4] Play he describes as a form of adaptation through *assimilation* (as distinguished from imitation which, as we mentioned, he described as a form of *accommodation*). In play there is a relaxation of effort; a child exercises, solidifies, and extends reaction patterns that have emerged during the course of his development. During the early stages of the sensory-motor period a child engages in "practice games" when he looks for the sake of

---

[4] This account is based on *Play, Dreams and Imitation*, 1962, paperback edition.

looking and handles for the sake of handling. These actions are not forced upon him by external pressures. They have no ulterior aim.

In his account of the motivation underlying the beginnings of play, Piaget invokes Karl Bühler's classical concept of "function pleasure" (*Funktionslust*)—satisfaction derived from sheer unimpeded activity. For example, a child, in repeating sounds he himself has made, "plays" with his voice, laughs and evidently is pleased

As a child matures and becomes capable of producing intentional effects, "pleasure in being the cause" is added to the pleasure gained from sheer repetition. The action of producing effects becomes a game (play) only when the procedure is successful and, for the time being, no further adaptive effort is demanded.

The dimensions of play are further enlarged according to Piaget's account when a child becomes able to apply known reaction patterns to new situations. Here, as in the earlier stages, the game does not consist in an initial discovery but in the repetition of action involved in the discovery.

Piaget distinguishes between what he calls intelligent adaptation and play. Intelligent adaptation occurs, for example, when a child through his own efforts acquires a new response, such as learning that he can remove obstacles from a desired objective (pushing aside an adult's hand to reach a toy). On the other hand, when thereafter he fixes his interest on the action itself, seemingly gaining delight from pushing aside an obstacle, the activity is play. Likewise, a previous intelligent adaptation becomes a game when a child repeats in a variety of contexts a procedure he has learned. He has learned, for example, that he is able, with his right hand, to retrieve a block which he has pushed to the right out of reach of his left hand. He now makes a game of repeating this procedure with other objects.

The scope of play is extended further when a child begins to be able to manipulate things subjectively, to use images (interiorized imitation) without being bound to the concrete, objective situation, and to make one thing represent another. This marks the beginning of pretense or "make-believe." Now the child can make a game with symbols. He "drinks" from a box; he "eats" paper and other objects as though they were food; a towel serves as a blanket; in preparing "dinner," a clothes-pin, shaken well, serves as a pepper-shaker, and simply the motion of ladling things into a coffee-tin will provide the gravy.

According to Piaget, every symbolic game (such as when a child takes the role of a mother in doll play) is both imitative and imaginative. Piaget classifies games into three stages from the point of view of their "mental structure" (p. 113). In what he designates as the sensory-motor period, games are "practice" games: these involve playful repetition of activities with concrete materials. Symbolic play, play that involves symbolic representation or make-believe, comes in the next stage. (In the third stage, usually considerably later, games with rules appear. These may involve practice or symbolism, but their distinguishing characteristic is that they are governed by rules, often handed down from one generation of children to the next with little or no adult intervention.)

Egocentricity

In Piaget's account, a significant characteristic of a young child's mentality is its egocentricity. The child is ego-centered, even before he has what might be called an ego or any distinct awareness of himself as a separate entity. The only universe that exists is the one that flows through the channels of his experience. He does not discriminate between himself and the external environment. He does not, at first, seem to have any awareness of the boundaries and properties of his physical being. Even when he shows a growing awareness of himself as one who produces effects on the environment, he does not seem for a time to have any clear notion that this environment has a separate existence. For a time, for example, a toy that he has been using no longer seems to exist if it rolls out of sight or is covered by another object. In Piaget's account, as pointed out above, a child has made an important advance when he views the world as having an existence apart from him by showing a growing awareness of the *permanence* of objects. Such awareness may at first appear when he retrieves a toy that is momentarily out of sight. It is more solidly established when he reaches for an object which not only is out of sight but which he has not seen for days or weeks. Other signs that he is finding himself in a universe that has a stable structure of its own appear when he acts toward objects as though they had constant and predictable characteristics—round objects will roll; hard objects, but not soft ones, can be banged to produce a noise. A child's external world is further established as a separate entity when a youngster views the larger dimensions of his environment as permanent—when, for example, he seems to have a mental map of his surroundings and knows which way to turn in going from one place to another.

Even after a child seems to have a clear notion of a world separate from himself this world is still structured by his own perceptions. The only universe that exists is the one he apprehends from his own point of view. He is unable, for some time, to view things from the standpoint of another, or to comprehend how another person's desires, thoughts, and perception of things might be different from his own.

The fact that a child's view of things will at first be ego-centered is, of course, no more than could be expected. He obviously sees things through his own eyes and cannot, so to speak, borrow someone else's eyes and perceptual apparatus. To appreciate another's point of view, it would be necessary for a child not only to understand that physical phenomena have an existence independent from him but also that there are psychological phenomena separate from and independent of his own. It would also require an ability to translate phenomena in relationship to perspectives other than his own. Such an ability would be needed, for example, for a child correctly to recognize that the right hand of a person directly facing him is not the hand on his own right side.

According to Piaget, children remain primarily egocentric in their thinking well beyond the period we have considered in this chapter, up to the age of six or seven.[5] There is, however, some question about how pervasively children of preschool years are bound to an egocentric orientation. (This topic will be touched upon in later sections.)

---

[5] Even then, of course, a considerable amount of egocentricity remains, as is true throughout life. Even brilliant individuals have difficulty in seeing things from the viewpoint of another, especially when their own views are rooted in their emotions.

Recommended Readings

J. Piaget, *The Origins of Intelligence in Children* (1963) and *Play, Dreams and Imitation in Childhood* (1962).

8

Everyday Needs

and Habit Formation

in Early Childhood

This chapter will center, in part, on developments associated with three aspects of everyday life: feeding, elimination, and sleeping. These activities are sometimes prosaically called "routine habits." Actually, they are neither prosaic nor routine, for they emerge from a confluence of significant forces in the child and his environment. This chapter will also deal with early aspects of sexual development; the subject of discipline; the child's need for mothering; and issues connected with provisions for appropriate maternal care.

Psychological Meanings of Physical Care

A child's contacts with his mother and others who care for him, when counted one by one, run into the tens of thousands. It would be quite a job to keep a tally of the number of times, within a year, that a young child is picked up, held, fed, patted, burped, changed, washed, dried, rubbed, and powdered. Each event of this sort involves more than physical manipulation. In her actions the mothering person may be gentle or abrupt, patient or impatient, skillful or rather inept. Due to conditions in her life that have no direct connection with her child, she may be happy or unhappy, serene or anxious. If her lot has been difficult she may harbor resentments, sorrows, and apprehensions. When a mother goes to her child she carries with her all that she embodies as a person. This obviously is the only thing she can do, no matter how strong or weak her devotion to her child may be.

In the past, some writings in developmental psychology have emphasized practical techniques in caring for a child's physical needs. Other writings have maintained that a mother's underlying attitude is the most important factor.

In recent years much attention has been centered on Harry Stack Sullivan's views regarding the attitudes of a mother (or mothering person—who may be any woman, man, or older child who fulfills a mother's role). Sullivan stresses the *interpersonal* aspects of the give-and-take of a mother's dealings with her child. A helpless child has tensions linked with the process of survival, such as those occurring when he is hungry or cold. These tensions can be relieved only by a mothering person—a mother who can provide solicitous, tender care. In Sullivan's account, mothering means tenderness. Relief of a child's tensions provides security for the child. But if the mothering person is anxious, the infant's tensions will not be relieved. According to Sullivan, a mother's anxiety is contagious—it is induced in the child through a process of empathy, a kind of communication which occurs before a child is able, through his own awareness, to sense or perceive what is transpiring between himself and his mother. An infant's anxiety can be relieved only by the tenderness of a mothering person. The degree to which a mother is able to provide tenderness, the degree to which she is in the grip of anxiety, will influence an infant's well-being—his tendency, say, to be a good feeder, or to be finicky and to suffer from digestive upsets.

This concept that there is a kind of emotional communication between an adult and an infant through cues that are different from those older people usually recognize squares with the fact that babies seem more at ease, or more fretful, with some persons than with others. Hospital personnel report, for example, that some nurses have a soothing effect, while the same babies are "fussy" when in the care of other nurses.

It is plausible to assume that a mother's emotional state affects her child. However, to make a conclusive test it would be necessary not only to study the characteristics of mothers but also of children, since some babies are more serene or cry more than others no matter who is caring for them.

While Sullivan's account emphasizes the child's need for mothering, and the mother's role as a person rather than just as a technician, it leaves several questions unanswered. Unfortunately, Sullivan did not supplement his theoretical views with empirical studies. He does not clearly define the difference between individual anxiety which may be mild or acute, and anxiety as an inherent and universal element in human existence. Although emphasizing the concept of an *interpersonal* relationship, he gives only meager attention to the child's role at the beginning of this relationship.

Child Care
and the Process of Self-Discovery

To the extent that the practices a person uses with children are an expression of his own inner tendencies, he has something like a mirror of himself in his dealings with children. If he has the courage to look and the insight to see, he may be able to learn something profoundly significant about himself. It is not, of course, merely in the parent-child situation, but in all interpersonal situations, that a person might catch a glimpse of himself. (People are often astonished when, for example, they view a sound-film of themselves.) To profit from an effort at self-scrutiny it usually is necessary to get help, such as can be provided by an independent observer whose notes or perceptions could be compared with a parent's own perception of how he fulfills the parental role.

Feeding and Behavior
Associated with the Oral Region

Behavior associated with feeding should be the simplest of all aspects of a child's development. He is hungry, he is fed, his stomach takes on from there, and that should be that. But it isn't. The feeding situation is the rallying ground for a variety of forces that operate in a child's relationship with his parents. But there are complications even when a youngster eats heartily and his delighted parents ply him with the right foodstuffs. It takes more than milk or bread to satisfy the impulses and needs associated with the feeding process.

Sucking and Impulses
Connected with Sucking

As we mentioned earlier, the ability to suck is one of a newborn child's finest accomplishments. He not only is able to suck but he seeks, as it were, to lay hold of something to suck. He is responsive to tactual stimuli in the region near the mouth and orients himself toward such stimuli. His sucking mechanism may be thrown into gear even by stimuli that promise no satisfaction, such as having his hair pulled. Moreover, as Feldman (1920) has pointed out, the mechanism involved in sucking is well protected. The suction cushion in each cheek, composed of a pad of fat, remains even in emaciated babies from whom all other bodily fat has disappeared.

Sucking Apart from Food-Getting

Sucking activities appear apart from the process of feeding (technically known as nutritive sucking) at an early age. A baby sucks, even though his appetite is sated. Many babies do a certain amount of sucking, apart from nursing, from birth. It seems that an infant may suck his thumb even before he is born (Gesell and Ilg, 1937). One baby's thumb was swollen on delivery, and soon after the birth cry he placed the swollen thumb in his mouth.

All babies are likely to suck their fists, fingers, thumbs, or other handy objects at some time during infancy and early childhood, especially during teething—but this is not the only occasion. Many children, as we all know, continue the finger or thumb-sucking habit for several years. And many continue into adult life with sucking, biting, and mouthing habits. Someone, like a beaver, gnaws at pencils; another is a lip biter; still another sucks on a dry pipe; someone else's tongue and lips caress a juicy cigar.

Adults are often disturbed by a child's thumb-sucking, for they think there is something unbecoming about it; and some worry about the possibility that such sucking, if continued, will cause the jaw and teeth to become malformed.[1]

There is an interesting sex difference in thumb-sucking. Several studies have pointed out that girls do more thumb-sucking than boys (Honzik, 1959).

Many theories have been proposed to account for finger-sucking. The most obvious, of course, is that a child sucks his fingers because he wants to, but there are other more learned theories.

Sucking as a Response to an Oral Drive

One view is that a child sucks his thumb or fingers because his need for exercising the sucking mechanism is not satisfied while sucking to obtain food (Levy, 1937). According to this theory, a bottle-fed child is more likely to continue to suck if the nipple hole is large, permitting the milk to flow

---

[1] Many children who suck persistently for extended periods and then drop the habit show no harmful dental defects. Moreover, in some cases where malformation has occurred, it appears that the deformity may be corrected in the process of growth after the sucking is stopped. Apparently, the chances of malformation are greater if the practice is continued vigorously after the child has his secondary teeth (Lewis, 1937) and if a child already has a poor bite (Sillman, 1951).

freely, than if the aperture is small, thus requiring him to work harder and longer to obtain the same amount of milk.

By way of analogy, Levy gives the example, familiar to anyone who has been raised on a farm, of the behavior of young calves. A dairy calf who is not allowed to suckle his mother but is taught from the start to feed from a pail is likely, for some time after his first feedings, to suck an accommodating finger or the ear or tail of another calf or any other thing that is handy. Such sucking may be inspired by the fact that the pail-fed calf probably gets smaller rations than a calf who has a whole cow as a source of supply. But, at any rate, the pail-fed calf continues to suck when even he must realize there is not much nourishment in it. Such sucking by the calf seems to correspond, at least in some respects, to thumb-sucking in the child, although the child's sucking is likely to continue long beyond the time when a calf stops sucking and turns his attention to other things.

Lack of sufficient sucking exercise in connection with food-getting probably accounts for some finger-sucking, but this theory alone cannot account for all finger-sucking in childhood (Blau and Blau, 1955). Some children suck their fingers even though they are allowed to nurse at their mother's breast as much as they wish (Simsarian, 1948).

Exploratory Functions of Mouth and Lips

A child's use of his tongue, lips, and mouth play a very important part in his early ventures in life, representing not simply a means of food-getting, or a kind of striving for sensuous pleasure, but a device through which he explores the world in which he lives. This fact has been emphasized by many observers, including Piaget as noted in the preceding chapter. A young child's lips, tongue, and mouth serve much the same function as his eyes and ears. When we interfere with the child's oral activities we are depriving him, to some degree, in the same way we would deprive him if we put blinders on his eyes or sound-plugs in his ears. Even after a child is using sight and hearing as his main sources of information he continues for a long time to use his mouth and lips to investigate the world about him. An infant explores contours and surfaces, tests the taste, temperature, hardness, and softness of things with his lips and teeth. This exploration may include cramming a block into his mouth, and mouthing balls of lint, bits of earth, crayons, and even morsels of food that he discovers on the floor, after he has refused what remains on his plate.

Sucking, Mouthing, Sexuality, and Primary Interpersonal Relationships

The foregoing observations, coupled with the fact that sucking is an essential adjunct to the gratifying experience of relieving hunger, affirm the extreme importance of sucking in a child's life.

The importance of sucking and mouthing receives added emphasis in views set forth by Freud and Sullivan. Freud regarded the inner membranes of the mouth region as an erotogenic area, a source of "organ pleasure." Stimulation of this zone, according to Freud, provides a child's first erotic gratification. According to this view, the oral area is involved not in one, but in two primitive drives: the life-preserving hunger instinct and race-preserving libidinal instincts.

Freud's views regarding a relation between oral behavior and sexual behavior has received support from an interesting quarter—namely, experimental studies that have grown out of the discovery that there are recurring stages in the sleeping cycle when dreaming is most likely to occur, as manifested by rapid eye movements (REM) and brain wave patterns. As indicated in a review of this work in Chapter 18, there apparently is a pervasive activation of the sexual apparatus during dreams. Some animals, when deprived of REM sleep, not only show a sharp increase in overt sexual activity but also a sharp increase in oral activity.

In Sullivan's account, the oral area is an avenue for interpersonal contacts that are of supreme importance in the child's early life. In embracing the nipple, a sucking child achieves an intimate—and, for him essential—contact with a mothering person. An infant's early interpersonal contacts may be satisfying, and tension-relieving in a context of tenderness; or they may occur in a context of tension and anxiety.[2]

Oral Drives, Feeding Practices, and Personality Development

The foregoing account suggests that the management of a child's early feeding and oral activities is indeed a serious business. According to Sullivan's account, a child's experiences connected with his oral activities, and the tenderness or lack of it in the interpersonal context of the feeding situations, have a profound influence on the substratum of security or anxiety that determines his emerging attitudes regarding himself. Freudian writers have emphasized the role that frustrations a child encounters in connection with his oral drives may form the basis for character traits that are carried over into later years.

Among other matters, some writers have attributed great significance to the weaning process—its timing and the practices used in weaning the child. According to Fenichel (1945), the deprivation of oral satisfaction, stemming from early weaning, may create a craving for such satisfaction, resulting in a pessimistic or sadistic character. On the other hand, late weaning, which

---

[2] Sullivan tells, in terms probably meant to be both literal and figurative, of how a child may have access to a "good nipple" (the milky, juicy, satisfying nipple of a tender mother) or an unsatisfactory nipple (hard to hang on to and to manage, not yielding a rich flow; or an "evil nipple" (the nipple of an anxious mother, offered in an aura of tension).

denotes fuller and longer satisfaction of oral drives, may result in self-assurance and optimism (Fenichel, 1945).[3]

One issue in this connection concerns the merits of breast-feeding and bottle-feeding. Some years ago, from time to time, writers have stressed the value of breast-feeding. In the same vein, bottle-feeding has been deplored as a way of rejecting a child and as a sign that the mother lacks warmth and is renouncing her biological role as a woman and her emotional role as a mother. According to this view, the breast-fed child has a great advantage over the bottle-fed youngster.

Actually, research data do not support any conclusion so simple and categorical. It has not been established, for example, that the earlier the weaning occurs the greater will be the evidence of a drive to meet unfulfilled needs for oral satisfaction. As a matter of fact, there is some evidence that a child's desire for oral activity, rather than diminishing, increases the longer he is allowed to go unweaned and suck freely at the bottle or breast during his first year or so (Sears and Wise, 1950).[4] Neither has it been established that breast-feeding, as such, is a boon or bottle-feeding a bane.

Although theory has far outstripped research in this area of development, there are some reasonably firm generalizations that can be made.

Since feeding and oral activities occupy a prominent role in the child's early life, it is axiomatic that adult ways of dealing with these activities also occupy a prominent role in the child's upbringing.

Attitudes that pervade the total relationship between a parent and a child are likely to be more important than the practical management of this or that detail of feeding or weaning.

Observations by Newton (1951) suggest that breast-feeding or a flexible or rigid handling of the feeding schedule are not *per se* the important factors. A mother's attitude toward her child as expressed in the total feeding situation is more important than any one isolated factor in the manner of feeding. Similar overt procedures in feeding can have psychologically different meanings, depending on a mother's attitude. Findings in a large-scale longitudinal study by Heinstein (1963) showed no conclusive differences between the long-term effects of bottle- or breast-feeding. Boys who were breast fed for a long period by "cold" mothers seemed to be more likely than any other group to experience adjustment problems.

Two passing notes should be added to the foregoing. One pertains to

---

[3] For pronouncements, critiques of pronouncements, and reviews of research dealing with this and other aspects of early child care see Ribble (1943), Orlansky (1949), Pinneau (1950), and Stone (1954).

[4] In a study by Sewall and Mussen (1952), in which information was obtained from mothers and personality tests were administered to children, the results did not show a significant relationship between abrupt or gradual weaning and personality adjustment. In another study (Thurston and Mussen 1951), questionnaires and the Thematic Apperception Test (described in Chapter 18) were used with college students to explore the relationship between early oral gratification and later traits. The results were conflicting and no clear relationship was found.

thumb-sucking. A tolerant attitude toward thumb-sucking is likely to be far better than stern disapproval or brusque efforts to curtail it. A youngster who is permitted to suck his thumb is likely to be more serene emotionally than one who tries to suck his thumb and is forcibly restrained. The other point pertains to the fact that practices in child feeding may properly vary a great deal because of individual differences among children. The manner of bottle-feeding is an example. According to one view, a really accepting and "warm" mother cuddles her child while holding and tilting the bottle for him. It is supposed to be bad form to prop the bottle on a pillow and let a child tilt it himself.[5] Actually, some babies when only a few months old insist on holding the bottle themselves.

Additional Aspects
of the Feeding Situation

Chewing

A child usually does not bite until about the fourth month, although some infants bite considerably earlier. Gesell and Ilg (1937) observed that occasionally children show "surprising strength of bite" even at the time of birth and add that "this strength is not only unseasonable but unsuitable to normal sucking." Likewise, chewing movements may appear even before a child has any teeth and may precede by a considerable time the actual chewing of food.

Many children go through the motions of chewing before they have a practical need for it in feeding. They "chew" on milk, applesauce, and puréed vegetables as though they were practicing for the future. This is another illustration of the developmental principle of anticipation as set forth in Chapter 2.

Spontaneous Food Demands

When babies are placed on a "self-demand" breast- or bottle-feeding schedule (fed whenever and as much as they want), there are fluctuations in the number of feedings they demand per day yet also a considerable degree of consistency (Simsarian and McLendon, 1942). As an infant grows older, he reduces the number of feedings he demands per day. Furthermore, the amount he eats varies widely from day to day and from feeding to feeding. A child might, on one occasion, demand a large meal and on another,

---

[5] In an unpublished study of twins, Lazar (1963) noted that this view had caused distress for some mothers. When both twins simultaneously cried for the bottle, the mothers could not cuddle and tilt the bottle for both at the same time—so they would prop the bottle, now for one, now for the other—but they felt guilty about doing so.

when his mother expects him to be quite hungry, take only a sip. But in his day-to-day and week-to-week demands he is likely to be more consistent if he is in good health.

Most infants seem to be well nourished when on a feeding schedule geared to their own demands.[6] Some mothers maintain that the self-demand schedule is, if anything, psychologically more satisfying both to the infant and to the mother than is a fixed schedule. In this area, as in others, it is necessary, however, to guard against sweeping rules that do not consider a child's own individual bent.

A self-demand schedule may be well-suited to a child who has a good appetite and who lustily lets his needs be known. On the other hand, it is poorly suited to a child who is not vigorous in asserting his hunger.

Self-Selection of Formulas in Early Infancy. Infants have shown a wisdom and logic of their own, not only when allowed to choose when and how much they should eat, but also when given a choice of food.

In one experiment (Davis, 1935) three infants, beginning at or before the tenth day of life, were offered, in rotation, four different formulas at each feeding and were permitted to take as much of each as they wished. The children showed unmistakable preferences almost from the beginning. As the children grew older (the experiment was continued until they were about eight months old), they would sometimes reject the bottle with the unfavored formula without even tasting it—apparently responding to odor, appearance, or some other cue. There were considerable differences among the babies in patterns of choice. At the end of the experiment the nutritional status of the infants was reported to be "excellent in every way."

Spontaneous Food Selection and Consumption in Later Infancy. When a child's diet includes solids, his feeding increasingly involves questions of what he should be fed as well as when and how much. To what extent can a child now be trusted to make sound choices?

Davis (1928, 1933) observed children who were free to select their own diets. The children had several choices at each meal, but all the items in the total menu were not presented at any single meal. At a particular feeding, a tray consisting of twelve items (selected from a list of thirty which were variously combined at different meals) was placed before each child. It included, among other things, whole milk and lactic milk, raw and cooked meat, raw and cooked vegetables. Each child was free to choose; food was not offered to him or suggested; a nurse sat nearby and helped the child to get what he wanted, as he indicated his wants by pointing, and in other ways. So far as they desired or were able, the children were permitted to feed themselves by means of their fingers and to wield their own spoons.

---

[6] Studies of infants on self-demand schedules have been reported by Gesell and Ilg (1937), Trainham, *et al.* (1945), and Simsarian (1948).

There were wide variations in the self-selected menus of the same child from time to time and in the menus selected by different children. But physical examinations and measurements seemed to show that the children made wholesome choices and thrived.

When the experiment was begun—with three newly weaned infants who had had no experience with solid foods—each infant at first chose some foods which he spat out. After the first few meals, however, the infants chose foods promptly without regard to their position on the tray, and there was no more spitting out. A youngster would often select a bizarre diet, including as many as seven eggs at a single sitting (in another series of observations, a two-and-a-half-year-old ate ten eggs at one meal) or as many as four bananas. Salt was taken only occasionally, and then often the infant would sputter, choke, and even cry, but would keep it in his mouth and swallow it.

The infants frequently ate certain foods in waves. After eating moderate amounts of fruits, eggs, or cereal, there would be a period when they would eat "astonishingly large" amounts, followed by a decline to the previous level. Symptoms of overeating did not appear in connection with such "jags," nor were they followed by periods of disgust. The children were omnivorous. They showed no consistent preferences for cooked or raw food, but some items were definitely preferred cooked and others raw. They dunked hard crackers in milk or water, especially at periods when a new tooth was erupting. They tended to take their foods "straight" rather than to mix them or even to pour milk over cereals. One infant who had rickets when the study began spontaneously consumed large quantities of cod-liver oil, and then later left it untouched, when blood tests and x-ray examinations proved that they had been cured.

In another study of fourteen children in a hospital ward (Davis (1931), the findings conformed to those mentioned above, and the children, for all the vagaries of their appetites, and occasional grotesque selections, seemed to choose wisely as far as could be determined by records of their digestive balance, health, energy, and growth. Less food was wasted than under the usual system.

Davis' study, as well as others, indicates that a young child has more sense about eating what is good for him than he often is credited with, granted that he has wholesome articles of diet from which to choose. However, here again it is best not to over-generalize. It is apparent from the Davis study that there were sharp individual differences among children. Moreover, a self-selection program in the average home would involve many complications and, to be properly safeguarded, would require some knowledge about nutrition. In view of the vast variety of conditions and circumstances that affect the feeding situation at home, the findings with regard to self-demand (in timing and amount of feedings) and self-selection (in choice of foods after the child can begin to choose) should not be, and cannot be, adopted too literally. But the findings so support an attitude of respect for a child's wants and underscore the point that "mother knows best" only if what she "knows" takes account of what she can learn from her child.

Self-Help in Eating

Many of a child's earliest efforts to try out his abilities are expressed as he tries to feed himself with his fingers. Later, some of his sturdiest battles for self-determination are fought with a fork and a spoon. In his efforts to feed himself, a child shows a progression from crude and gross forms of manipulation to more refined control, such as appears in other aspects of his motor development.

The period during which a child is learning to handle table utensils is trying for many parents. Even if a parent is not finicky or squeamish, he is likely to become impatient at times with the spilling and messing, the tipping of food containers, and a child's insistence on doing some things for himself when it is obvious he cannot succeed. A child has quite a job also; not only must he practice new skills, but he must struggle for permission to try them out. A youngster's endeavors, before he has become skilled, are complicated by the fact that he does a great amount of free wheeling on the side: he pours food from one container to another less appropriate one; if given a chance, he mixes the meat and the pudding and makes finger-paintings with the gravy.

Feeding Problems

Many so-called "behavior problems" are feeding problems. In one study in which five hundred parents took part (Jersild, *et al.* 1949), the most frequently mentioned problems under the heading of "routine care" had to do with food. Concern over feeding is frequently expressed by mothers when they consult their pediatrician (Blum, 1950).

In one study by Macfarlane and her associates (1954), over half the children in the age range from twenty-one months to six years displayed varying degrees of "food finickiness," according to their mothers. Fewer children were reported as being finicky in the age range from seven to fourteen years. "Finickiness," denoting an active aversion for many or several specific articles of food, was reported as a problem considerably more often than insufficient appetite for food in general.

Parental concern over a child's feeding behavior is complicated by the fact that some children who had voracious appetites at the age of one or two seem to want proportionately less food at the age of three or four.

Moreover, as a child grows older he may revise the timing of his food intake. A child who is just beginning to go to school, for example, may take very little breakfast but eat heartily at suppertime.

In dealing with a "feeding problem" it is wise first to ask whether there really is a problem. To answer this question it is necessary to take account of the child's level of development. Some youngsters resist for a time when they are introduced to solid foods. Furthermore, if a child seems to be finicky about his food, it is well to remember that children differ greatly in the strength of their appetites, their food preferences, and food intake. A child's finickiness may be a harmless idiosyncrasy.

If a feeding problem really exists it is important to inquire into its nature and meaning. The difficulties may arise from physiological factors (such as specific allergies, digestive weaknesses). Or they may spring from psychological factors and indicate a variety of concerns in a child's life. If so, the difficulties cannot be remedied simply by trying to correct specific food habits.

Food and the process of eating have many psychological meanings. Food is a symbol of intimacy and sharing. It can be used to satisfy cravings that run deeper than mere physical hunger. According to observations by Bruch (1947), some persons use food as a means of satisfying unfulfilled needs for security and other yearnings. Overeating and undereating also at times may be symptoms of anxiety.

A child's feeding difficulties may be an expression of anger (when he takes revenge by refusing to eat); or of fear (when he dreads the thought of going to school and has no appetite for breakfast). A child's feeding problems may also serve as a means by which he asserts himself or calls attention to his needs. Macfarlane and her associates, in the study we cited earlier, found that food-finickiness in boys may be linked with their "dependence-independence struggle."

Sleeping

In a newborn child, periods of complete wakefulness are considerably briefer than they are later on. As time passes, periods of wakefulness increase, especially during the daytime hours, and periods of uninterrupted sleep likewise increase. The total amount of time spent in sleep also diminishes, although with many fluctuations. If placed on a fixed feeding schedule, a child often must be awakened to be fed; sometimes a child will refuse to nurse or take the bottle, or will do so while remaining drowsy.

Table 1 shows the average amount of time spent in sleep by a number of children at various age levels from one month to eight years as reported by their parents. The averages are based on results for all seasons combined and are therefore approximate, since the amount of sleep varies with the seasons, being greater in winter and smaller in summer.

The values represent averages for all seasons combined

Age	Hours	Minutes
1-6 months	15	3
6-12 months	14	9
12-18 months	13	23
1½-2 years	13	6
2-3 years	12	42
3-4 years	12	7
4-5 years	11	43
5-6 years	11	19
6-7 years	11	4
7-8 years	10	58

From J. C. Foster, F. L. Goodenough, and J. E. Anderson, *The Sleep of Young Children* (Minneapolis: University of Minnesota, Institute of Child Welfare, 1930), Circular No. 4, 11 pp. Reproduced by permission.

Children differ considerably in the amount of time they spend sleeping. Below the age of one year, there was a difference of more than three hours between the 10 per cent of children represented in Table 1 who slept most and the 10 per cent who slept least. Up to the age of four years, the corresponding difference was more than two hours; from four to eight years, the difference was more than one hour. The differences between individual children at the two extremes were decidedly greater. As young children become more active, it is difficult to tell what might be the optimum amount of sleep for a particular youngster.

Some children apparently are prevailed upon to stay in bed longer than is necessary, but it is no simple matter to let the runabout child control his sleep schedule according to his own demands. Many elements in his environment (such as boisterous play and excitement) may keep a child awake when he normally would become drowsy and to wake him before he becomes "slept out" (such as the bustle of the household in the morning). The difficulties of regulating sleep are even greater in children whose equilibrium is disturbed by malnutrition, illness, digestive difficulties, or other disorders. Such disturbances may make a child wakeful even when he badly needs sleep.

Lacking full information about a given child's natural sleep needs, conscientious parents generally feel that the more sleep a child can conveniently get the better it is for him. Parents of young children, however, sometimes invite trouble. If they insist that a child go to bed early, they may simply be depriving themselves of sleep, for the earlier a child goes to sleep the earlier he is likely to awaken them in the morning.

Studies of children's sleep demands have yielded results that parallel their spontaneous food demands in some respects. Children who stayed in a nursery school for several weeks showed wide variations in sleep from day to day (Reynolds and Mallay, 1933). However, there was a much higher degree of constancy in their total amount of sleep over longer stretches of time, such as one two-week period compared with the next. This corresponds to children's eating patterns—a child may show wide short-term fluctuations in food intake and yet show a high degree of stability when intake is measured in terms of weeks rather than hours or days.

Daytime Naps. The total amount of sleep a child takes during a twenty-four hour span is reduced, even during the first weeks after birth, mainly by his cutting the amount of time he spends in sleep during the daytime hours. Many children merge an early morning nap and a late evening nap with nighttime sleep.

An afternoon nap is usually a part of a two-year-old's daily schedule. Many children continue this practice during the next year or two; others become more and more wakeful during part or all of it, but remain in bed. As described by Sherman (1930), "The child learns to stay in bed a certain amount of time." Reynolds and Mallay (1933) found that many children abruptly drop the daytime nap instead of gradually tapering off.

Sleep Disturbances, Restlessness, and "Bad" Dreams

Early in life (as in the years to come) sleep is not simply a peaceful sanctuary. Frequently "the cares that infest the day" do not "silently steal away," but spill over into the night.

Restlessness in the form of tossing and turning, kicking off the covers, waking at a light noise, is common. Such restlessness is manifested from time to time by all children, but in many youngsters it is so pronounced that parents regard it as a problem. In a long-term study that followed children from the age of twenty-one months to fourteen years, Macfarlane and her associates (1954) found that restlessness was regarded as a problem most often at the youngest level (38 per cent of boys, 27 per cent of girls); it was less common at three years (18 and 22 per cent).

"Disturbing" dreams also are quite common. Such dreams, including nightmares with screams of panic, or "trouble dreams," occurring almost every night, and less violent, distressing dreams, were reported (in the study named above) as "problems" at the earliest level (16 per cent of boys, 13 per cent of girls) and then increased (29 and 29 per cent, respectively, at age three, and with frequencies ranging from 20 to 47 per cent in ages three and a half through eleven). The percentage of youngsters who had occasional disturbing dreams, but not to an extent regarded as a "problem," would probably come close to a hundred.

The fact that so many children, from so early an age, have "bad" dreams lends impressive testimony of the tensions prevailing in a child's life. Such dreams are, of course, frequently aggravated by upsets, frights, mistreatment, and other difficulties. But it is not simply a child labeled as "emotionally disturbed" who has troublesome dreams. These dreams occur in all children, to a greater or lesser degree. When unusually severe they probably signify that a particular youngster is over-burdened with difficulties. But there is reason to believe that any enterprising child who seizes what life has to offer will have troubled dreams at times (and that there may be something wrong with a child who doesn't). Moreover, recent studies indicate that dreams, instead of having a sinister connotation, serve a benign and healing function. Studies dealing with the serious consequences of *not* dreaming, as disclosed by experiments with artificial "dream deprivation," will be reviewed in a later section.

Bedtime as a Time of Communion. Bedtime for many children is quite a ritual. There are stories that must be told; songs that must be sung; verses that must be recited. A child may demand not one but several drinks of water; the shade must be adjusted just so; dolls or other possessions must be settled in the right place; for good measure, a child may demand "a little more scratching." When all this has been done, a parent may be called back for another round on the plea that a detail has been forgotten or that the youngster has a new bit of information to relay or a new question to ask. Some children have a fertile supply of ideas that require discussion just when bedtime arrives.

Even though the day is over, and a child (so the parents think) should be weary, bedtime can become the most important period of the day. A child and parent may be most warmly and comfortably responsive to each other at bedtime. If a child is troubled, the bedtime ritual may bring comfort and assurance of the companionship and friendliness of his parent. If there are several children in the family, and each is tucked in separately, bedtime may be the only occasion when a child feels he has the parent all to himself. Sometimes confidences are shared, sins are confessed, fears are revealed, pains which have worried the child are described, and much else that has been hidden is brought to light. No lullaby a parent might sing could be more soothing than for him to sit there and listen while saying just a comforting word or two. At the end, a bedtime prayer—if it is a family custom —may come as a benediction, even though the young child has only a hazy idea about what the prayer means.[7]

---

[7] Many children continue to cherish childhood prayers after they put aside other childish things. In later years these echoes of childhood may recur when adults are deeply moved, or about to undergo a critical experience, such as a serious operation.

Elimination

It would be nice if infants were housebroken at birth. The fact is that bladder and bowel control develops relatively slowly, entailing labor on the parents' part and frequently some emotional complications for a child.

To control elimination it is necessary to inhibit processes that are completely involuntary at birth. An infant lacks the nervous mechanism for voluntary control of his urination or bowel movements, even if by some freak of nature he had a desire to do so. So the infant freely empties his bladder and his bowels. But, in the course of maturation there is a change in this natural flow of events. When training in bladder and bowel control is timed and adapted to the growth pattern, some children require hardly any "training." Unless other complications arise (such as illness, or chronic emotional disturbances), a child is eager, in his own good time, not to wet or soil himself.

Progress in the Control
of Elimination

Gesell and Ilg (1937) draw an interesting parallel between control of bladder and bowel and the development of voluntary control of other movements. They point out that a child acquires rather slowly the power deliberately to release an object held in his hand. In early infancy a child is not able, at will, to release his grasp and let go of an object. They also point out that an equivalent control of the bladder sphincter muscles is in some respects more difficult.

A child is likely to exhibit several signs when he is approaching the stage of being able to assume voluntary bladder control (McGraw, 1940). He may notice the tinkle, seem to realize that the sound effects originate with him, show interest in puddles, and begin to learn a word or sound for the act of urination. "Even a glint in his eye may reveal his awareness of the act" (although the glint is more likely to be found in the eyes of his parents).

But the first flush of success does not necessarily mean that the triumph is complete. There may be regressions arising from other circumstances that are not connected with the bladder. Even if he heeds the call of nature, a child may wet himself because he does not allow himself enough time. He may be so absorbed in trying out his motor skills that he cannot be bothered with other things.

Children vary in the timing of their ability to assume control, due, apparently, to their rate of maturation and also to the kind of encouragement they receive. Some do not achieve full control until the age of three or even four or five. The "norms" for bladder control vary considerably. Daytime control usually precedes nighttime control.

After the child has established control, it may be some time before he is capable of self-help in going to the toilet and in managing his clothes. This is especially true if the fixtures and his clothing are not suited to his limited abilities.

Control of the bowel usually is established more readily. In a healthy child, bowel movements are more regular and considerably less frequent; they can be anticipated more accurately and at an earlier age than can voidance of the bladder, and this helps the learning process.

Lapses in bladder control are so common that they should be regarded as a normal feature of development. A child's performance is affected by such factors as teething, illness, temperature, and consumption of liquids. Even after several years of consistent control a child may relapse under trying conditions. Some children, for example, again wet their beds when they begin to go to school, apparently as a symptom of emotional strain. Some "regress" when a new sibling comes into the household, as though they were demanding once more to be treated as infants. The fact that stresses in a child's life may produce incontinence was noted in British children who were evacuated from city to country places during World War II (Burt, 1940). According to one observer, bed-wetting so impressed some of the hosts of these children that it seemed as though "a virtual Niagara" was flooding the British hinterlands.

Parents sometimes become discouraged when a child who seems well on the way to complete control of elimination backslides. The child himself may feel ashamed, try to conceal what he has done, lie, or blame the mess on others, such as Grandma or the family dog.

Attitudes with Regard to Elimination and Genital Organs

In our culture, the process and the organs of elimination become enveloped in furtiveness, secrecy, and shame. To an older person, the excrements are unpleasant, and wetting and soiling are uncomfortable. A young child is not squeamish about contact with his urine and feces, but in time he also shows distaste. He probably would acquire this distaste even if not vigorously taught by others. (Many animals, whose manners are not too refined in other respects, become quite fastidious about contact with their own waste products. A pig carefully deposits his in a separate part of his pen; a grazing calf leaves a little ring of uncropped grass around droppings in the pasture—unless grass is quite sparse.)

It is seldom, however, that the child is left unaided in acquiring an aversion to waste products or an attitude of modesty toward the processes of elimination. Adults and older children usually are very alert to hasten the development of such attitudes. The processes of elimination become associated with uncleanness, with the shame which in many families is connected with nakedness, and with the guilt feelings associated with sex. The tendency to regard the process of elimination and the organs connected with elimination as obscene is so strong that even children whose parents are least prudish and rather free and outspoken at home pick up attitudes prevailing in the community. As they become older, such children sometimes admonish their parents not to use "dirty" words, not to be so shameless about nakedness, and not to go to the bathroom so openly.

Elimination Processes
and Attitudes toward Self

The attitudes parents show toward the process of elimination and express during a child's toilet-training are bound to have an important influence on the attitudes a child acquires concerning his own bodily functions. Moreover, a parent's views concerning toilet-training are likely to reflect attitudes he has regarding himself and his child. If he is harsh in dealing with a child who is in the process of establishing bladder and bowel control, he probably also will be harsh in other ways. If he is strongly competitive in his approach to child rearing, he is likely to be impatient for the child to acquire the dry habit and prove himself to be better than the next fellow even in this humble enterprise. On the other hand, if he is able to abide the demands of his own nature, without deploring the "lower" part of his nature, he is likely to view the operations of his child's bladder and bowels in the same light.

Bladder and bowel activities are a channel of significant communication between a parent and a child. To punish a child for wetting or soiling is a way of rejecting him. To call him dirty and smelly and view his excrements with abhorrence is, in effect, a way of telling a child that *he* is a shameful character.

Bladder control and soiling are frequently mentioned by parents as "problems" when children are quite young (Macfarlane, *et al.*, 1954). To regard a child under the age of two as a "problem" if he wets or soils himself when he is still too immature to control his elimination is much the same as viewing a child in the creeping or babbling stage as a "problem" because he is still too immature to walk or talk.

When parents thus regard a child as a problem and try to "train" him out of it, the youngster is bound to feel the pressure. If the pressure is severe he will feel that his parents disapprove of him and, in his own way, he may feel that *he* has failed and should disapprove of himself. A child who feels disapproved of by others and then disapproves of himself *for not achieving something which he does not have the power to achieve,* is measuring himself against an impossible standard. He is measuring himself *as he is* (one who is unable to control his bladder at times) against an ideal of *what he should be* (one who ought always to be able to control his bladder).

Freud's theory that sensations connected with voiding the bladder and bowel are erotic in nature and play an important role in the child's sexual development has important implications for the upbringing of children. According to Freudian theory, unfavorable character traits will result if a child's efforts to satisfy his anal interests are severely frustrated, as when parents put severe pressure on a child, try to hurry him, treat him coercively while he is in the process of developing voluntary control, or shame him. It has been claimed that a child who has been frustrated in this way may acquire a tendency to limit all his primitive pleasure-seeking activities; he may be tight-lipped and stingy as an adult; in extreme cases he may lose spontaneity and regard freedom as dangerous; or he may become saddled with restrictive character traits, such as acquisitiveness, or a tendency to be meticulous and to assume a punitive attitude toward himself or toward others.[8]

In this writer's opinion, the theory of "anal eroticism" should be viewed according to the position taken earlier in this chapter in the discussion of "oral eroticism." Anything which occupies a child's attention and absorbs his interest and energies and affords satisfaction is significant in his development. A youngster who goes through a phase of intense absorption in oral activities also goes through periods when he is intensely interested in the process and products of elimination. He undoubtedly derives pleasure from voiding himself. When we ask whether this pleasure should be regarded as erotic, linked to the development of sexuality, it should be noted that the linings of the mouth, rectum, and sex organs have grown from the same primitive tissue. That there is an association between rectal and genital response is seen in the fact that rectal sphincter contractions occur simultaneously with an orgasm (Masters and Johnson, 1966).

Further Aspects of Infantile Sexuality

A child's sexual development begins before birth and his sexual behavior begins soon after birth. The view that sexuality appears in infancy was emphasized by Freud in his classic theories of the role of sex in human development. Many investigators have found that children display sex activities and interests at an early age, although investigators disagree on whether a child's sexual development conforms to the stages described by Freud. (We have already, in preceding pages, discussed Freudian theories regarding oral and anal aspects of sexuality.)

[8] For a discussion of this subject, see Freud (1930, 1938b), Fenichel (1945), Despert (1944), Huschka (1942), Fries (1947), and Orlansky (1949).

In a study by Halverson (1940) of nine male infants aged three to twenty weeks, tumescence (erection of the penis) occurred at least once daily in at least seven of the nine; in individual children it occurred from four to over thirty times during an eight-hour period. Tumescence was accompanied by restlessness while detumescence was associated with a more relaxed state. This does not necessarily mean that a young boy has erotic sensations similar to those of an older person, but it does mean that the genital organ is active at an early age. Spitz (1949) observed that some kind of genital play occurred quite generally during the first fifteen months in children living in a normal home environment. Genital play in the first year of life is one of the normal activities of a young child. Manipulation of the genitals at the infancy level, and similar behavior—sometimes accompanied by other signs of interest in sex, at the preschool level (Issacs, 1933; Koch, 1935; Levy, 1928)—may be transitory, or it may persist for an extended period of time; it may occupy a child many times during a day, or it may occur at widespread intervals. In this behavior, as in all other aspects of development, there are wide individual differences among normal children.

Some parents become unduly alarmed by failing to recognize that interest in sex and sex play are common and normal features of development. Severe restraint or punishment, or an obvious show of squeamishness or revulsion by parents, may have a very unwholesome effect on a child. By their own irrational attitudes, parents may stimulate a child's interest or induce unwholesome feelings of anxiety, and impulses which the parents deplore may become stronger rather than weaker.

Discipline

Infancy and early childhood have been called the period of domestication. This is a dour way of looking at the dramatic tasks of development during the early years of life, yet it is true that an important aspect of a child's early development consists in acquiring skills, habits, and manners that are characteristic of a more or less polite civilized human being. Some of the change comes about in the process of growth. But a young child soon is under pressure to conform to certain external standards of conduct. These pressures may be imposed with a heavy hand or through gentle nudges. They constitute the beginnings of discipline.

The Nature of Discipline

Discipline arises from the need to bring about a balance between what an individual wants to do, what he wants of others, and the limitations and restrictions demanded by society or by the hazards in the physical environment. What a child does and abstains from doing by virtue of the discipline he receives is something he would not at first do of his own accord. He spontaneously will try to feed himself, but usually it is due to discipline that he acquires table manners.

The Need for Discipline

The aim in discipline is not to curtail freedom but to give a child freedom within manageable limits. A parent must be both permissive and restrictive, and a failure to strike a fairly good balance between the two or, better yet, an integration of the two, will have unfortunate effects. A child who has more freedom than he can handle will get into trouble. A child needs freedom to grow and to learn in his own way, but he cannot thrive on unlimited freedom. He needs discipline. This is one of many paradoxes in development. A child cannot fully enjoy the fruits of freedom without surrendering some of it. A parent cannot help a child to learn how to enjoy his freedom fully without in some ways curtailing that freedom.

Without discipline it would be hard for a child to survive and, if he did survive, he probably would be a wreck. Through restrictions and controls, a child is spared from many dangers while he is still too young to perceive the consequences of his actions, as when he plays with fire, or runs into street traffic, or ventures into deep water before he can swim.

Other circumstances that require discipline are regulations tied to the public interest, convenience and necessity, traffic regulations, time schedules, everyday amenities of life, and cleanliness.

The necessity of sharing limited goods is one form of discipline. Rationing continually occurs in the home: one child does not get all the steak while another gets nothing but spinach; mother and father avoid giving all their attention to the one most demanding child in the family.

In a sense, discipline must be imposed upon a person either by others or by himself as long as he lives. As a young person grows up, he must learn to accept many rules and regulations even if they seem meaningless to him. He must learn to bow to some of the facts of life or he will wear himself out in futile resistance.

Children who have not learned to curb their expectations are due for some hard jolts. Their vague notions of omnipotence and illusions concerning their own rights will clash with the realities of life. Even the most angelic parent eventually will be tried beyond endurance if his child, in growing older, continues to make such demands as we usually allow only a young child to make or expects such privileges as only an older person can win by his own efforts.

Discipline as such is neither good nor bad. Its value depends on its appropriateness. Good discipline is scaled to a child's maturity level. It protects him from his own imprudence. It relieves him of the responsibility for deciding matters over which he has no choice and thus frees his energies for action where he does have a choice. Good discipline provides the child with a foundation for healthy self-discipline.

Recommended Readings

Benjamin M. Spock's *The Common Sense Book of Baby and Child Care* (1946) and *Infant and Child in the Culture of Today* (1943) by Arnold Gesell and Frances L. Ilg are helpful books for parents and others who have young children in their care. The United States Children's Bureau regularly issues excellent booklets on child-rearing.

9

Trends in Physical

and Motor Development

Before going into additional aspects of psychological development, it is instructive to examine developments in a child's physical structure and functions. These physical attributes provide a vehicle for a child's expanding feats in the psychological sphere.

Physiological Functioning
at Birth and Later Development

In an earlier chapter (Chapter 5) we mentioned that newborn children differ in their display of muscular energy and in their physiological response to stimulation (heart rate, respiratory rate, galvanic skin reflex). We noted that to gauge the significance of these early manifestations it would be necessary to study the later development of these children. A study by Edwards (1967) offers interesting information on this point. One hundred and forty-seven babies for whom "Apgar Scores" were obtained at the time of birth (at one minute and five minutes after delivery) were tested at four years on the following: Stanford-Binet intelligence; concept formation (tested by means of a sorting task); fine motor coordination (tested by means of a maze, a pegboard, and copying a circle, cross, and square); gross motor coordination (walking on a line, hopping on right and left foot, catching a ball). Total five-minute Apgar Scores (heart rate, respiratory effort, color, muscle tone, and reflex irritability) five minutes after birth correlated with later measures as follows: with intelligence, .25; concept formation, .32; fine motor coordination, .46; gross motor coordination, .48. Although all of these coefficients were statistically significant,[1] the first two indicate only a low degree of prediction of later performance on the basis of the ratings at birth. The correlations between ratings at birth and fine and gross motor performance at four years are, however, quite impressive.

Trends in Physical Growth

The average newborn child is about 20½ inches long. During the first year, his length increases by over a third, and by the age of five he will be about twice as tall as he was at birth.

The average birth-weight of boys is about seven and a half pounds, and of girls a little over seven pounds. These averages are meaningful only for rough comparative purposes. As stated in Chapter 3, Tanner (1963) and others have found that weight at birth gives little indication of what an infant's weight might be at six months or a year. Moreover, there is a large spread in the weight of healthy well-born children. Birth-weights substantially below average have, in general, more meaning than birth-weights above average. A weight of under five and a half pounds has been regarded as a probable sign of prematurity. In the study by Edwards (1967), mentioned above, there were low positive correlations between weight at birth and (1) performance in fine motor activities at age four and (2) performance in gross motor performance. But functioning at birth as measured by Apgar scores, was much more significantly related to later performance than weight at birth.

During the period of physical growth, there are continuing changes in the proportions of the body. The head, for example, is comparatively very large at birth and does not increase nearly as much in size as other parts of the

---

[1] At the .001 level.

body. There is a considerably greater increase in the length of the trunk and an even greater increase in the length of the arms. When full stature is attained, there is a still greater increase in the length of the legs. These trends are generally in keeping with the cephalocaudal (head-tail) direction of development.

The parts of the body grow at different rates and reach their maximum size at different times during the period from early childhood to maturity. This is also true of the internal organs. Not only is there a differential course of growth for the various parts of the body, but the pattern of growth differs from individual to individual.

*Influence of Heredity
and Environment on Physical Growth*

There is a high degree of correspondence between the height of children and their parents. This correspondence in relative height is likely to be more prominent during the second year and beyond than during the first year. Table 2 is based on a long-term study by Bayley of a group of children who were measured at intervals over a period of years. "Mid-parent" heights were computed by means of a formula which expressed, is one figure, the heights of both parents. The table includes separate father-child and mother-child correlations at the eighteen-year level.[2]

---

[2] The paper from which this table is adapted gives more detailed comparisons and an account of the formula used in computing "mid-parent" height.

Table 2   **Correlation Between Mid-Parent Heights and Heights of Their Children**

Age	Boys		Girls	
	Number	Correlation	Number	Correlation
6 months	32	.35	29	.61
2 years	27	.36	23	.66
10 years	24	.60	24	.59
18 years	21	.58	17	.76
18 years	21		17	
	(father-sons)	.52	(father-daughters)	.64
	(mother-sons)	.44	(mother-daughters)	.52

Adapted in abridged form from Nancy Bayley, "Some Increasing Parent-Child Similarities During the Growth of Children." *Journal of Educational Psychology*, 1954, 45, 1-21. Reproduced by permission.

Table 3, based on a study by Eichorn (1959), supplies information of a kind that is rare in writings on development and is therefore especially interesting. It shows comparisons between height measurements of children and of the children's parents when they were children. It also shows comparisons between the adult height of the parents and their children's height, and the height of the parents as children and as adults.[3]

Eichorn's study shows that there is a far higher than chance resemblance between a person's adult height and his height as a young child (correlations ranged from .61 to .83; the correlation would be zero if the two measurements were completely unrelated).

Bayley's and Eichorn's studies both indicate that heredity is an important

---

[3] Table 3, and Table 2 from Dr. Bayley's study, are based on a long-term investigation at the Institute of Child Welfare, University of California. Table 3 includes a combination of father-child and mother-child pairs. The measurements of the two sexes were converted into "standard scores" based on measurements of a large population. (This meant, for example, that a woman of average height received the same height score as a man of average height even though the man is taller than the woman.) Because of a number of considerations mentioned by Dr. Eichorn it is difficult to tell to what degree her findings would hold for children in general. The number of persons represented in Table 3 is small (although large when viewed against the difficulty of getting repeated measurements of two generations). Members of the first generation were more homogeneous in height (taller, on the average) than adults in the population at large. Statistically this would tend to lower the parent-child correlations, but genetically it might raise them, since people do not mate entirely at random (there is more than a chance likelihood that a tall woman would select a tall man). Moreover, the second generation, in most instances, contained several children from one family.

Table 3   **Two-Generation Similarities in Height During the First Five Years**

Age in Months	Number	Correlation: Children and Parents as Children	Correlation: Children and Parents as Adults	Correlation: Parents as Children and as Adults
3-8	30	.18	.29	.61
9-14	29	.19	.12	.66
15-20	17	.52	.49	.69
21-30	24	.31	.40	.65
31-42	27	.27	.40	.66
43-53	18	.22	.39	.68
55-66	18	.67	.67	.83

Adapted from Dorothy H. Eichorn, "Two-Generation Similarities in Weight, Height and Weight/Height During the First Five Years." Reported at Twenty-fifth Anniversary Meeting, Society for Research in Child Development, National Institutes of Health, Bethesda, Md., March 10, 1959. Reproduced by permission.

factor in determining height. But physical characteristics are also influenced by the environment. In the United States and several other countries, recent generations of children are taller than their forebears, presumably because of improved nutrition. Significant increases in both height and weight have occurred during the past decades. The increases have been greater in the lower- than in the upper-income groups, suggesting that the lower-income groups have most to gain in physical growth from a generally improved standard of living. According to reports from Japan, the population there has undergone a significant increase in height even within one generation following World War II.

Prehension:
Use of Arms, Hands, and Fingers

When an adult at a gay party picks up a peanut and puts it in his mouth no one watching him is likely to admire his fine coordination. But back of this act lies a long story of development.

At first a child's reaching consists of crude shoulder and elbow movements (illustrating the proximo-distal direction of development described in Chapter 3). His aim is poor and his approach is clumsy. At first, if he made a pass at a pile of peanuts, he would probably brush them hither and yon, and fail to snare a single one.

In time, a youngster becomes able to make selective movements with his wrist, to aim more accurately, to rotate his hands, and to make voluntary grasping movements with his hands.

In his first attempts at grasping, he makes practically no use of his thumb. He closes in upon the object with a scooping or corralling movement of palm and fingers. This, in time, yields to a deft grasping with the thumb and the tip of the forefinger. Until he is about twenty-four weeks old, an infant's approach seems to consist of three distinct acts: raising his hand, a circuitous and forward thrust of his hand, and then lowering his hand. Finally, at about forty weeks, the act is coordinated into a single performance, bearing little trace of the separate acts (Halverson, 1931).

These observations illustrate just a few of the steps involved in the seemingly simple act of reaching, grasping, and handling an object. The age at which children achieve the performances described above varies, of course, with different individuals.

Table 4 shows the median age at which various performances with arms, wrists, and fingers were achieved by infants in a study by Bayley (1935). The items in this table have been selected from a larger list.[4]

---

[4] Studies dealing with motor activities that are reviewed in Chapter 2 in the discussion of the role of learning and growth in development will not be reintroduced here.

Table 4 Advances in Prehension

Motor Performance	Age Placement in Months
Retains red ring (retains a ring, designed for the test, when placed in his hand)	0.7
Arm thrust in play (when lying in a dorsal position, makes vertical arm thrusts in random play)	1.7
Hands predominantly open (hands predominantly open even though not grasping an object)	3.6
Beginning thumb opposition (beginning evidence of use of thumb in opposed manner in grasping a cube)	4.1
Partial thumb opposition (opposes thumb to fingers in a partial, but not complete, manner, using the palm of the hand, as well as thumb and fingers in picking up the cube)	5.1
Unilateral reaching (tends to reach and manipulate with one hand more often than bimanually)	6.4
Rotates wrist (rotates wrist in manipulating toys)	6.7
Complete thumb opposition (picks up the cube with thumb and fingers completely opposed, and without the use of the palm)	7.6
Partial finger prehension (picks up a small pellet with several fingers opposed to thumb and not with a scooping into the palm with the fingers)	7.8
Fine prehension with pellet (picks up a small pellet precisely with thumb and forefinger)	9.3

Adapted from Nancy Bayley, *The Development of Motor Abilities During the First Three Years,* Monographs of the Society for Research in Child Development (1935), No. 1, 2 pp. Reproduced by permission.

Locomotion

A child's ability to walk is the climax of a long series of developments. The groundwork for the ability to walk is being laid many months before the child is able to stand or walk alone. Locomotion begins not with the legs, but with the muscles of the upper trunk and arms.

Although children differ considerably in the *rate* at which they learn to walk, they usually are quite similar in the *order* in which various accomplishments appear. Shirley (1931) describes several stages that lead to walking: First, postural control in the upper regions of the body, including the ability to lift the head, and then the chest; control of head movements; and ability to sit on a lap, with some support. Later skills include the ability to sit alone for a moment, and then for a longer interval. A child is likely to achieve the power of moving his body forward or backward by hitching, pulling or pushing, or "swimming" motions, many weeks before he can creep. In Shirley's study, the median child was able to stand while holding on to furniture at forty-two weeks, to creep at forty-four and a half weeks, to walk when led at forty-five weeks, to stand alone at sixty-two weeks, and to walk alone at sixty-four weeks.

Ordinarily, when children have an opportunity to practice in their own way, there is a good deal of uniformity in the phases through which young-sters pass as they progress from a recumbent position to the act of walking alone. However, before they are able to walk, children are very ingenious when seized by an urge to move about. Some are able to cover ground at a fine rate by wiggling forward, almost in snake-like fashion. Some are able to move backward before they can move forward, as though the reverse gear in their motor were in better working order than the forward gears. Some move from a sitting position—pushing with the arms and pulling with their legs.[5]

A youngster with strong arms and a lot of determination can overcome many obstacles. He may hoist himself over the bars of his crib and reach the floor without injury, and then come clattering downstairs, with whoops of triumph, surprising his mother who thought he was quietly napping.

As soon as a child is able to walk, he launches upon other skills that incorporate elements of walking into larger activity patterns, as we will note later in this chapter.

The Impact of Walking

Walking affects all other aspects of a child's development. He is able now to expand his contacts with other people and with things. But while able to walk into new areas of interest, exploration, and adventure, he is also able to walk into mischief and danger. It is harder now for his parents to keep an eye on him. The beginning of walking ushers in a period which for a year or two is strenuous for a child and strenuous also for parents. A child's ability to get about and to get into things far exceeds his judgment and awareness of danger. It is delightful to watch a child during this period and to stroll along with him; but on some days he looks most charming to his tired mother when he finally closes his eyes in sleep at the end of the day. If not carefully watched, he will pull books off shelves; make off with scissors and knives; lay hold of cigarette butts; jerk the tablecloth off the table; make his way upstairs and then come tumbling down; discover and drain the last dregs from a beer can; eat from the dog's food-bowl; drink from the bird-bath; stroll off into brambles and poison ivy; creep under parked cars; toddle

---

[5] Youngsters in a study by Dennis (1961), earlier referred to, made amends for lack of proper opportunities to practice creeping by progressing by means of what Dennis refers to as a "scooting" way of locomotion.

into the path of traffic; raid the ice box; make forays on medicine cabinets and the garbage pail.

Many clashes of purpose are in store for the walk-about child—he is not only testing his legs but also trying out his ability to do things with his hands, to assert himself, and to pursue matters in his own way. Many parents experience considerable anxiety when a child enters the run-about stage, especially if they already have a tendency to be anxious. But the anxiety is not just of a "nervous Nellie" sort, for many children at this age do get into serious accidents. In many neighborhoods adults have vivid memories of hearing or reading about two-year-olds who wandered off into traffic or into woods and swamps. Parents fear for the safety of their children far more often than danger actually strikes, but parents' apprehensions are not relieved by knowledge of the actual statistical probabilities. And it would be rather rough on children if the ratio between fears and fatalities were reversed.

Developmental Impetus
Underlying Early Motor Activities

A young child's motor development underscores principles we already have covered. It illustrates the role of maturation: when organically "ready," a child will proceed (unless sharply curtailed) from one phase to the next in his development. In due time he will reach, grasp, and use the hand and finger coordinations described earlier in this section. Special opportunities, and efforts to "train" him before he is ready, have little effect (Gesell and Thompson, 1929). Likewise, when organically ready, he will undertake the activities that lead to his ability to walk. These activities may be hampered by confinement and restraint, but they cannot be hastened materially by efforts to coach him or lure him on.

Early motor developments also emphasize the role of "indigenous motivation"—a child's spontaneous effort to exercise his growing powers. A child's self-generated zeal in physical activities is one of his most conspicuous characteristics. His passion for creeping cannot be attributed to hunger or thirst, or a need to avoid pain or extremes of heat or cold, or to maintain a state of equilibrium; and it would be ridiculous to assume that it is a sexual urge that makes him lunge off into a walking spree. Nor does he (at least in his first ventures) walk to gain social approval, for often he strides forth in spite of his parents' wishes. Neither is he impelled by a need for security; he is, if anything, taking risks rather than playing safe.

Shifts from a lack of interest to eager interest, followed by boredom, were noted in a study by Damann (1941), who observed the responses of a child who was given an opportunity to climb an inclined board. The first observations were made at eight months, when the youngster had just begun to creep. This apparently was not well timed in terms of his own maturity level. The child had to be lured to the board by means of a toy. His attention span was short and he was easily distracted, so he would pause to examine a knot in the wood, a speck of dust, or a scratch in the varnish. Later, the act of climbing the board became satisfying in itself. The youngster frequently went up and down the slide several times, even though there was no lure. Then when he had mastered the skill of climbing, the inclined board no longer seemed to offer a challenge in itself. To make things more interesting he would vary his methods of climbing.

Later Features of Motor Development

After a child has achieved the ability to walk alone, his progress in specific motor skills depends more on special opportunities than it did earlier. However, within broad limits, children reared in similar environments exhibit a good deal of uniformity in their progression from one level of performance to the next and in adding new skills to their repertory. Studies show that children who have not had the opportunity to acquire a certain skill will tend to pass through stages similar to those exhibited by children who acquire the same skill at an earlier age. However, when an older child does get an opportunity, he is likely to pass through the preliminary stages more rapidly.

Walking, Running, and Jumping. Table 5 on page 150 summarizes children's progress in certain locomotor skills after they have learned to walk.

Use of Wheel Toys. An account by Jones (1939) of the development of children's uses of wheel toys (doll carriage, wagon, dump truck, kiddie car, and tricycle) offers many insights into changing motor reactions as children become older. The study involved observation of twenty-four children from the age of twenty-one to forty-eight months. The following account illustrates a change in the uses made of vehicles, and shifts in interests as the child's ability increases.

At ten months, David crept to a small doll carriage which was in the room. He looked inside it, then held on to the side as he raised himself a little, and ran his finger along the rough surface. He started to creep away, but turned and gave the carriage a slight push. His interest span was thirty-five seconds.

At twelve months, Barbara, who could walk only a few steps alone, saw her older brother, aged thirty months, climb into a large doll carriage. She rose to her feet and pushed the carriage with her brother in it across the floor. At other times she was unable to push it because it slipped away from her. (This item illustrates the fact that small children will often, at first, try to make use of a carriage as a support in walking; a relatively heavy, sturdy carriage, which has a low center of gravity and which does not move at a light touch, is more suited to the child's purposes at this age than is a flimsy or easily pushed vehicle.)

At later ages, as would be expected, the children became more adept at using the doll carriage for pulling and pushing on the level floor or up an incline or under an arch. At twenty-one months, 15 per cent of the children used the carriage as a conveyance for other materials; at thirty-six months, 55 per cent of them did this.

The following statements describe the use made of a wagon at successive age levels; the records are much abridged:

Twenty-one months: Starts to climb in; walks away; returns and looks at wagon; pushes it forward from behind; leaves; examines other material in the room; manipulates a light fixture on the wagon; pushes wagon back and forth; plays with other material in the room, and so on. (During ten minutes, he has gone to the wagon and left it again three times.)

Twenty-four months: Gets into wagon with right knee in and left foot on floor; leans over and examines light; sits and shakes handle (note that

Table 5   Advances in Locomotion

Motor Performance	Age Placement in Months
Walks sideways	16.5
Walks backward	16.9
Stands on one foot with help	19.9
Walks upstairs with help	20.3
Walks downstairs with help	20.5
Walks upstairs alone, marks time	24.3
Walks downstairs alone, marks time	24.5
Jumps off floor; both feet	28.0
Stands on left foot alone	29.2
Stands on right foot alone	29.3
Walks on tiptoe	30.1
Stands on walking board with both feet	31.0
Walks on line; general direction	31.3
Jumps from chair	32.1
Walks upstairs, alternating forward foot	35.5
Walks tiptoe three meters	36.2
Jumps from height of 30 cm.	37.1
Distance jump—36 to 60 cm.	39.7
Jumps over rope less than 20 cm. high	41.5
Distance jump—60 to 85 cm.	48.4
Hops on right foot less than 2 meters	49.3
Walks downstairs—alternating forward foot	50.0

Adapted from Nancy Bayley, *The Development of Motor Abilities During the First Three Years,* Society for Research in Child Development Monographs (1935), No. 1, 26 pp. Reproduced by permission.

there is no propelling, although he is in a position to propel); touches trade-mark on side; he examines wheels, touches various parts, makes one attempt to pull handle up, lays the handle down and says: "I want to go home and see Charlie" (this after five minutes spent entirely in or with the wagon); observer suggests that he use the wagon; he makes a few passes at the wagon, pulls it briefly, then wanders about.

Thirty months: Gets into wagon with right knee, with left foot on floor, and propels the wagon, first forward and then backward; gets out and asks for doll carriage (apparently desires to combine other materials with wagon, for when asked to continue to use wagon, he gets a small wagon and puts it into the larger one); pushes and pulls; sits astride and tries to propel with both feet, but cannot reach the floor, then propels with one leg as before; continues pushing, pulling and the like.

Thirty-six months: Propelling with one foot now established; a new performance is to pull wagon empty to the top of an incline and coast down; the child also hauls dirt with the wagon.

Forty-eight months: Pulling, pushing, propelling, coasting, and use of wagon to haul things continues, with two notable additions: (1) uses in make-believe game ("I'm playing moving van"); and (2) stands up in wagon, steering it by means of the handle, as his sister pushes him on request, saying, "Look everybody, I'm standin' up riding," and later telling another boy "Did you ever stand. . . ? It's lots of fun. . . . Can you hold your balance?"

When a child had mastered an activity so well that it did not require his full attention, he often proceeded to merge it with another performance. In other words, the progress was from work with a separate movement toward a combination of several movements into one activity. But later, at about forty-eight months the children centered their attention mainly on predominating ideas which they were attempting to put into practice. As a result, the performance of any one skilled movement was usually secondary to the project as a whole.

Increase in Speed and Strength. Changes in speed, accuracy, and power in certain athletic performances are shown in Table 6. This table is based upon findings obtained by Jenkins (1930) in measurements of fifty boys and fifty girls at each level from five to seven years. The original study should be consulted for information concerning the children who were tested and concerning the spread of scores at each age level.

Integration of Skills With Social and Intellectual Enterprises. As motor skills become established, they tend more and more to be incorporated into larger projects and enterprises that combine physical activities with social or intellectual activities. In her study of the development of children's uses of wheel toys, Jones found that children would concentrate all their attention

Table 6 Average Scores Obtained by Five-, Six-, and Seven-Year-Old Children in Various Motor Performances

| Activity and Measure Used in Scoring | Age Groups | | | | | |
| | 5-year-olds | | 6-year-olds | | 7-year-olds | |
	Boys	Girls	Boys	Girls	Boys	Girls
35-yard dash—timed in seconds	9.30	9.70	8.52	8.84	7.92	8.02
Hop 50 feet without error—timed in seconds	10.82	10.33	9.20	8.89	8.81	7.59
Baseball throw at target—10-foot distance—error in inches	8.87	16.90	5.40	13.17	4.20	8.50
Baseball throw—distance in feet	23.60	14.50	32.80	17.80	41.40	24.40
Soccer kick—distance in feet	11.50	8.00	18.40	10.10	25.40	15.00
Standing broad jump—distance in inches	33.70	31.60	39.30	38.00	42.20	41.00
Running broad jump—distance in inches	34.40	28.60	45.20	40.00	58.80	50.80
Jump and reach—vertical distance in inches	2.52	2.22	4.02	3.48	4.98	4.28

Adapted from L. M. Jenkins, *A Comparative Study of Motor Achievements of Children at Five, Six, and Seven Years of Age*, Contributions to Education (New York: Teachers College, Columbia University, 1930), No. 414, 54 pp. Reproduced by permission.

on a certain motor performance as a project sufficient in itself while they were still in the process of mastering the performance (Jones, 1939). But once the children had mastered the basic operations (such as riding the tricycle, propelling the Kiddie Kar with good control of direction), they tended to spend less time on the activity as an occupation in itself and merged it with a more extensive enterprise, such as a make-believe game of transportation.

The fact that a child has become skillful in a performance does not mean, however, that the performance no longer has any appeal in its own right, for the child may go on to perfect and enlarge his skill, to add hazards and "embroideries" to his performance, as when he takes his tricycle over the bumps or rides it along ledges or down steep grades, or when he goes down the slide backward, or endeavors to make a one-hand or running catch after he has become adept at catching a ball with both hands while standing still. Some skills that can be used satisfactorily even by a small child still afford almost limitless opportunity for further refinement and improvement as he grows older. Examples are such activities as playing marbles, roller skating, swimming, bicycling, and ball play of various sorts. Ball play is a good illustration of an activity which offers so wide a range of possibilities that it is challenging to a clumsy beginner and to a major leaguer.

Interrelations in Motor Development

From early childhood into adult years, motor achievement represents a combination of many factors. Among the more obvious of these are strength and speed, size, and anatomical build. Among the more elusive factors that influence motor performance are interest, self-confidence, a tendency to be intrepid or fearful, willingness to take a chance, and self-consciousness and its opposite.

A child may be quite unskilled at one performance and still do well in others. Studies show relatively little correlation between ability in various specific motor performances (Gates and Scott, 1931; Wellman, 1937). Low correlations, usually ranging below 0.30, have been found between scores in separate activities, such as throwing, climbing, and jumping. While correlations between various tests of strength tend to be considerably higher (ranging from 0.40 to above 0.80), there may be relatively little relationship between strength and speed. Because of this lack of interrelation, Wellman (1937) concluded that we should be hesitant in speaking about "the motor ability" of a child. Rather, we should, according to her, regard motor abilities as a series of skills that are not closely related. Further study is necessary, however, to determine to what extent this apparent lack of interrelation is due to variable opportunities to acquire various skills.

Heredity and Motor Performance

Since motor performances are executed by bodily structures that have a genetic base, we might expect that heredity would have an important bearing on these performances. On the other hand, practically all motor skills are learned, and to that extent they should reflect environmental influences. Actually, in the more elementary motor activities, such as those involving speed of movement and brute strength, most children, with proper diets and space in which to move, have fairly equal environmental opportunities to cultivate their capacities. Even in the more skilled athletic activities (as the next section will indicate) children who vary in cultural advantages that might produce a difference in intellectual performance do not, as a group, differ significantly in their motor activities. Yet, as is apparent to any observer, children in all groups differ in their motor abilities. To what extent might this be due to genetic factors?

Information bearing on this question was offered in a study by McNemar back in 1933. McNemar's study deals with pairs of boy-twins, of junior high school age, located through a search in several cities. This group included forty-six fraternal pairs and forty-seven pairs judged to be identical on the basis of a wide range of criteria.

The tests that were used, and the correlations between the performances of fraternal and identical twins, are shown in Table 7. These cofficients represent values obtained with age held constant and after correction for attenuation. The "raw" r's, uncorrected for age differences or attenuation, show a substantially similar magnitude of differences between the two groups.

McNemar cites findings from other studies which indicate that the difference between identical as compared with fraternal twin coefficients "are of the same order of magnitude for motor abilities as for physical traits" (including height, weight, head length, and head width).

McNemar raises the question whether the higher resemblance between identical pairs might be due to more nearly equal opportunity for previous practice. (In considering this question it should be noted that while the measurements dealt with types of coordinated movement common in everyday life, it is unlikely that junior high school children in either of the two groups could have had prior experience with the specific tests that were used). After a period of practice with two of the tests (pursuit rotor and spool packing) the correlations between the scores of the fraternal twins were higher than on the initial tests, but, viewing the results as a whole, McNemar concludes that "the hereditary hypothesis is the most plausible explanation of individual differences in motor skills" in an environment which offers children an opportunity for the development of motor coordination.

Table 7   Twin Resemblances in Motor Skills

Motor Skill	46 Fraternal Pairs	47 Identical Pairs
1. Accuracy of eye-hand coordination in following a target moving rapidly in a circular path (Koerth pursuit rotor)	.51	.95
2. Steadiness of motor control of arm, hand and fingers (measured by the Whipple steadiness tester)	.43	.83
3. Speed of rotary arm, wrist and finger movement in turning a small hand drill (Mile's speed drill)	.56	.82
4. Speed and accuracy in coordinated movement of both hands (measured by the Brown spool packer)	.44	.71
5. Speed of card sorting	.39	.73

Adapted, by permission, from Quinn McNemar, "Twin Resemblances in Motor Skills and the Effects of Practice Thereon." *Pedagogical Seminary and Journal of Psychology,* 1933, 42, 60–99.

**Relation of Physical
and Motor Characteristics to Other Traits**

The general finding has been that there is a low positive correlation between the mental and the physical status of children.

In a study of young children, Bayley (1933a) found a relatively high correlation (0.50) between "motor" and "mental" abilities, as far as these could be differentiated and separately measured. Success in one sphere seemed to be associated with success in the other. After the age of fifteen months the correlations were low, although positive. This suggests that the operations labeled as mental and motor during early infancy were not well differentiated. Other investigators, working with older children, have found a low or near zero relationship between intelligence and motor performance (see, e.g., Jones, 1949).

The low correspondence between mental and motor abilities means that many children who have a hard time in intellectual tasks may be able to do very well in practical arts and crafts and in several athletic activities. If a school program calls for only one kind of ability, there will be many children in that school who will be doomed to failure or humiliation or boredom. Where the program calls for, and honors, varied abilities in children, more children will have a chance for achievement in some field. The personal satisfaction that a child derives from being able to do something well is an important factor in his growing conception of himself. In other words, motor development—as well as mental development—is vital from the standpoint of mental health. In the opinion of the writer, the people in the school and in the community who prescribe how schools are to be equipped and what the curriculum shall be have greatly underrated the role of motor development.

Motor Ability in Relation to Socio-Economic Status

Ability in the common athletic skills (and probably also in common mechanical skills) is not tied to socio-economic status or what some authors refer to as social class. In studies of adolescents and near-adolescents, Jones (1949) found little or no correlation between children's performance in various physical feats and their socio-economic status. This differs from measurements of intelligence and scholastic achievements, in which children of higher socio-economic status usually tend to have an advantage.

So here is an additional facet of the role of motor abilities in the larger affairs of life. They provide, to a degree, a democratizing influence. A child who might be discriminated against when appraised in terms of his intelligence quotient or academic grades, may be able to make the grade in other important matters if he is given a chance to develop his motor potentialities. It does not follow, of course, that a poorer child will be the better performer in mechanics or sports—that is not the nature of the relationship. But it does follow that children who do not "rate" on the basis of IQ or school grades or family background are about as likely as their brighter and more affluent playmates to possess athletic competence that has a high value in the eyes of their peers. This finding emphasizes the importance of viewing a child's motor abilities in the light of the total perspective of his development and in the light of the assets and limitations he brings to his relationships with his peers.

Motor Performance as a Personality Manifestation. A child's motor activity often seems congruent with other features of his makeup (Frauquier, 1940). While the factors of maturation and opportunities to practice are important, as we have seen, something more is involved, for children of the same maturity level and with equal opportunities for practice differ very widely in their choice of activities and the way in which they pursue them. For example, a child who is aggressive and competitive in his day-to-day conduct is likely to display these characteristics in his motor activities. Again, a child who is intrepid and enterprising is likely to reveal these qualities also in his choice of games and sports. Many other personality traits may appear in a child's actions. One child persists in a motor activity in spite of difficulties and failure while another gives up quickly. One child braces himself to catch a hard-hit baseball or risks a rough tackle in football, while another shrinks from being hurt, yet has his own favorite list of less rugged sports. One child does not hesitate to try his hand at a competitive sport, even if he is not good at it; it doesn't seem to bother him that he is inept and that he probably cuts a poor figure in the eyes of the spectators. Another has a higher standard for himself, is less able to let himself go or to run the risk of looking foolish.

When one youngster shrinks from a sport or a game or test of skill because he fears ridicule and the possibility of making a poor showing, while another is uninhibited, each reveals traits that go beyond the sphere of motor development. Something more pervasive is involved, something tied to a child's attitude regarding himself and others and the role he should play.

Handedness

Handedness exemplifies the way in which a given form of behavior may represent an interplay of many factors, including conditions within the organism, circumstances in the environment, a child's relationships with others, and his views concerning himself.

It has been variously assumed that handedness is inherited; that it is linked to physical differences between the two sides of the body, such as dominance of one hemisphere of the brain or of one eye over the other; that it arises through chance; that it is due to direct or indirect training imposed by others who have grown up in a traditionally right-handed world.[6] It seems most likely that hand preference is an outcome of a combination of genetic factors and a child's early training (Falek, 1959).

Children vary considerably in their display of a distinct hand preference, and the emergence of hand preference is related to other aspects of their development. In a study by Cohen (1966) 52 of 100 babies aged seven-and-a-half months (46 boys and 54 girls) showed a hand preference. Most of the remaining 48 would, presumably, reveal a preference later. The developmental status of these children was assessed by means of revised forms of the Bayley Mental Development and Motor Development Scales (for earlier reports of tests of mental and motor development, see Bayley, 1933a, 1933b, and 1935). On the basis of these tests, the children in Cohen's study were classed as "advanced" (performing at a level substantially above what was normal for their age-level) "normal," "suspect," and "abnormal" (performing somewhat or considerably below the norm for eight-months-old children). Practically all of the children in the "advanced" group (24 of 26) showed a hand preference, as compared with less than half of the "normal" group (28 of 62), and half of the small "suspect" group (6-12). In other words, children who were advanced in their over-all development as indicated by a battery of mental and motor tests tended also to be advanced in the emergence of hand preference.

A large majority of children in both the "advanced" and "normal" groups who displayed a preference showed a preference for the right hand. But the proportion was smaller (40 of 52 in the two groups combined) than in the adult population at large or in the group of mothers (about 90 per cent of the mothers were righthanded). Since there was no reason to view this sampling of children as atypical with regard to hand preference, many of the youngsters who preferred the left hand at about eight months probably would shift to the right hand in time. It is likely that learning would play an important role in such a shift. But it is interesting that early development of a *specific* hand preference is more closely related to general development

---

[6] A preference for the right hand apparently goes back to antiquity. Dennis (1958) noted a marked preference for the right hand in reproductions of Egyptian decorations of about the year 2500 B.C., depicting workers engaged in various daily activities. The Hebrew Scriptures portray God as emphatically right-handed, and a large array of references give an honored place to the right hand of Biblical characters. Left-handedness is also noted, however. According to Judges 20:16, the Benjamite army included "seven hundred chosen men lefthanded; every one could sling stones at a hair breadth, and not miss."

than is a preference for either the right or the left hand. (Actually, there was a somewhat higher proportion of preferences for the left hand in the "advanced" group.) In other words, early hand preference gives a more significant indication of a child's developmental status than early preference for the right hand, which for most children will ultimately be the "preferred" hand. The findings in this and other studies also suggest that if children were not reared in a predominantly right-handed world more of them, by choice or chance, would become left-handed than now is the case.

Even when apparently well established, hand preference may be less clear-cut than it seems. A person may use his left hand in writing, throwing, and eating, but use a right-handed approach to some other performances, like batting a ball or digging with a spade; and he may perform additional acts equally well with both hands.

Practical Considerations

There are three major questions that can be raised when we seek to understand left-handedness as it affects the individual child. First, how did he get that way? If his own natural bent toward left-handedness was so strong that it won out against the pressures of a right-handed world, it is a good thing for him that he is left-handed. There probably are many such "naturals" among left-handers. The situation may not be so favorable, however, if he is left-handed by reason of neglect or if he had to put up a sharp struggle to remain left-handed. Moreover, it appears that in some instances left-handedness—or lack of clear hand preference—may be the symptom of an impairment. Pasamanick and Knobloch (1966) report a relatively higher than expected proportion of persons without a clear hand preference among children whose medical history indicated that they might have sustained brain damage preceding or during birth.

Second, what practical handicaps, if any, does a child's left-handedness impose on him? There are bound to be some inconveniences even if no busybodies point a finger at him. There may be a subtle psychological effect that operates when an adult and a child have different hand preferences: one or the other may become discouraged because the model set by the adult cannot be followed precisely by the child. Many performances are difficult for a right-handed person to demonstrate to a left-handed child—drawing, knitting, tying a necktie, tying a bow, managing a musical instrument. The left-handed child may learn to write in a crab-like fashion, holding his hand so that it smudges what he already has written; this often means that his schoolwork has an untidy look. He may be handicapped in using sports equipment—for example, he cannot share the baseball gloves other boys use (at least not without some awkwardness).

Third, apart from any important practical handicaps that might go with it, how does the left-handed person himself feel about his handedness? He is bound to feel a bit "different" if others call attention to his handedness, and there usually are people who will. He might feel a bit ashamed so that he makes a special effort not to be conspicuous. For example, he may be self-conscious when there is company at mealtime, trying to avoid a collision between his left elbow and the right elbow of the hearty feeder next to him.

These details are small in themselves and may not mean much, but anything that hinders communication between the child and others will, at least to a small degree, curtail his spontaneity and freedom. However, handedness *as such* is likely to have a very small impact on the child's personality and his view of himself if other circumstances in his life and in his relationships with others are favorable. The difficulties faced by a child who might have been a right-hander but turns out to be a left-hander are likely to be minor compared with the plight of the child who has a strong natural bent toward left-handedness, or who gets a long start in learning to prefer the left hand, and then is compelled to shift to the right hand.

Other Practical Considerations. That children who have been compelled to change from the left to the right hand may show a tendency to stutter, at least for some time, has been observed in some cases, but the cause-and-effect relationship here is not entirely clear. It is difficult to determine whether the stuttering is directly due to the change in handedness or whether it is due primarily to the methods that are used and the atmosphere that prevails when a child is being forced into using his right hand. The stuttering, in other words, may be a symptom of the tension and confusion produced by the pressures that are brought to bear rather than a direct result of the change itself. If a child shows confusion in his hand preference, along with stuttering, it is possible that both conditions might be due to a common factor, such as brain damage.

Stuttering by no means occurs in all cases in which a child is prevailed upon to change to the right hand; in addition, stuttering appears in cases in which there is no clear evidence of difficulty with regard to hand preference. To sum up, a change in hand preference as the result of pressure from others may, in individual cases, have unwholesome consequences. Risking such consequences is certainly not advisable.

Considerably more frequent than efforts to change an established preference for the left hand are the efforts parents exert while hand preference is still in its formative stages. In a great many cases, youngsters seem spontaneously to develop a preference for the right hand, without parental intervention. But many parents take pains to cultivate right handedness—favoring a child's right side in placing toys and tools within his reach; placing the spoon, cup, or pencil always in his right hand; and gently transferring operations to the right hand if the child seems in a random way to have started with the left. There are numerous little things parents can do to encourage the use of the right hand, and in most cases a child turns out to be the fine little right-hander his parents intended him to be.

The left-hander is bound to face inconveniences in a right-handed world. To some extent these inconveniences may be offset by the greater degree of ambidexterity some left-handers acquire. There is room for more systematic study in this area. Handedness is important enough to deserve the attention of parents when a child is developing hand preference. But right-handedness is not so important in itself that parents should interfere if the child shows a strong inclination to lead with his left as he squares off for the battle of life.

Recommended Readings

For interesting accounts of human growth see J. M. Tanner, "Growth and Constitution," in G. A. Harrison, J. M. Tanner, *et al.*, *Human Biology* (1964); and J. M. Tanner, "The Regulation of Human Growth," in *Child Development*, 1963, 34, 817–847.

Accounts of early motor development are given in Volume I of Mary M. Shirley's *The First Two Years* (1931) (excerpts from this volume are reproduced in Jerome M. Seidman's book of readings, 1958), and in Nancy Bayley's "The Development of Motor Abilities During the First Three Years," *Monographs of the Society for Research in Child Development* (1935). "Physical Growth" by Helen Thompson (1954) reviews a wide range of studies dealing with physical development from the fetal stage through adolescence. Many aspects of motor development as reflected by children's play are described by Ruth E. Hartley and Robert M. Goldenson in *The Complete Book of Children's Play* (1963).

PART THREE

Self and Others

10   *The Self*

A person's self comprises his experience of his identity as a distinct individual. The ideas and attitudes which constitute a person's awareness of his own existence take shape as a child, with all that is inherent in his make-up, sets forth on his career as a living creature. Some time early in life—just when we cannot exactly tell—he recognizes that he is a participant in, and yet someone apart from, events in the physical and social world in which he lives. He experiences as his own the sensations arising from within his own body, and he becomes aware of the properties and boundaries of his body. As time passes, he comes to know himself as one who can perceive, as the author of his own thoughts, as one who harbors feelings and desires, as one who can weigh alternatives and make decisions.

Cognitive Component

Eventually, a child's self embodies a combination of many mental states. It includes cognitive components through which he is aware of himself as one who knows and is able to think. These cognitive elements include his perception of his physical attributes and his conception of himself—of who and what he is, of his qualities as a person, his abilities, the purposes, beliefs, moral commitments and values which he knowingly embraces. His conception of himself incorporates not only his view of his present situation but also, eventually, his view of himself in the perspective of time—as one who, while living in the present, also has roots in the past and is able to project himself into the future.

Toward the end of childhood, the cognitive component of the self includes not only a state of knowing but a capacity for reflection, which enables a person to make his ideas, feelings, impulses, and choices the objects of his own thought. This capacity for reflection represents the most supreme attribute of the human mind and the most sophisticated preoccupation within the functioning of the self. When this capacity is cultivated a person becomes able to disengage himself, so to speak, from the unpremeditated flow of his feeling and thought and to examine this flow, to question his ideas, to inquire into his motives, to scrutinize the very perceptual and conceptual fabric of his self.

Affective States. The self also includes *affective* states, embracing the full range of human feelings, sentiments, and moods. The affective sphere not only includes awareness of feelings that are directly precipitated by conditions that impinge upon a person but also feelings pertaining to himself, sometimes described as positive or negative self feelings, such as pride and shame.

Self-Evaluative and Attitudinal Components. These cognitive and affective states are often linked with another property of the self—namely, a capacity for *self-evaluation*—a capacity for viewing oneself, or a facet of oneself, with approval or disapproval.

When affective states of approval or disapproval, combined with the knowledge of what is approved or disapproved, become relatively stable and constant, they constitute another component of the self, the *attitudinal* component. A person's favorable or unfavorable attitudes regarding himself may center upon a particular characteristic or facet of his make-up, as when he is pleased with his ability to learn and displeased with his freckles. Attitudes toward self may also be more global and pervasive, falling on a continuum ranging from serene "self-acceptance" to bitter "self-rejection."

The self has many other characteristics, embodying, in various ways, cognitive, affective, evaluative, and attitudinal processes. When once a view or attitude regarding self has been established, there is a tendency to preserve and to defend it. Thus it is that a person who has taken the position, "this is me," "this is what I am" (whether, from the standpoint of any criterion other than his own, it is true or false), will mobilize all the resources of his mind to preserve this position. In the process, he may use his cognitive capacities to rationalize his position; and affective states, such as anger, or fear, or pleasure arise if his position is threatened or strengthened. This tendency represents what might be called a stubborn streak within the self. It reflects what seems to be a universal need to maintain a degree of stability, a conviction of certainty regarding who and what one is. A person's craving for certainty is often stronger than his craving for truth.

But there is a paradox here. For while a person strives to preserve a cherished view of himself he is never, as long as he retains his vitality, completely immune to circumstances of life, pressures from within and reminders from without, that challenge this view and threaten to modify or dislodge it. When these occur, the machinery for rationalizing and shutting off the threat may be thrown into gear. But there always remains the possibility that a person will use his reflective capacities and take stock of himself.

Beginnings of Self-Awareness

When does the child become aware of himself as a distinct individual? Many conjectures have been made about this; one estimate is that it is sometime during the first year that the infant "discovers himself" and "finds a place in, yet apartness from, the outside world" (Ames, 1952).

The development of self-awareness does not occur in an all-or-none fashion which would enable us to state that up to this point the child does not possess it but beyond this point he does. It is more likely that a child comprehends different aspects of what he eventually calls himself with varying degrees of clarity at different times (Sarbin, 1952). His awareness of his distinctness from others seems to take place while he still has not gone very far in his perception and conception of many of the characteristics that eventually comprise what he calls himself. Moreover, the process of self-discovery is actively going on at least as long as the child is developing or discovering new potentialities, and in a healthy person the discovery of self continues as long as he lives.

The development of the self involves, among other things, a process of differentiation. The child begins life as though he were part of his mother's body. For some time after birth he continues to be helpless and dependent.

But sooner or later (we cannot tell just when) he begins to note ways in which he functions as a creature in his own right. Among the factors in the emergence of self-awareness we may conjecture the following:

The Sentient Self. Sooner or later he becomes aware of himself as a seat of sensations. At first, so it seems, he acts unthinkingly as his biological nature decrees. He breathes and gasps for breath; he cries when his stomach is empty, when he experiences wetness and coldness and encounters sharp objects. He probably does not have any distinct presentiment, at first, that it is he who is responding to stimulation, it is he who breathes, seeks nourishment. But, in time, he makes this discovery. At the beginning he does not seem to be aware of the parts and contours of his body, nor is he able clearly to recognize the area of his body from which sensations arise. In time, he recognizes the boundaries of his body and distinguishes between sensations arising from various areas of the body.

Separateness from Others. As a child grows older, he has experiences that eventually will make him aware that he is a unique individual. This growing awareness, it seems, requires, in part, a condition of frustration. As a fetus, his needs were satisfied by the natural flow of vegetative processes. After birth, his bodily wants trigger his ability to cry and squirm. If his cries automatically produce satisfaction, he is still, in a sense, floating in a prenatal order of things. But something else becomes involved when he cries and there is no automatic and prompt assuagement of his discomfort and desires. He then is confronted with the fact that there is a difference between the promptings of his body and the relief his body craves. Sooner or later in his dawning awareness, there is a reminder of a condition that will be impressed upon him more clearly as time goes on: his needs are not automatically supplied; there is a difference between him as a wanting entity and the conditions that minister to his wants; he is the seat of desire, but desire does not hold within itself the promise of fulfillment. This compels him, as time passes, to become aware that to achieve what he wants he cannot just sit passively by, but must actively assert his wishes and strive for their fulfillment.

Awareness of Self as a Doer

The embryonic self thus emerges not merely from one's growing awareness of himself as an individual who is separate from the rest of the world but as someone who requires, and also is capable of, action. So, added to a child's growing awareness of himself as a seat of sensation goes an awareness of himself as a doer—as one who can produce an effect. At first, a child probably experiences his role as a doer in the effect he has on other persons. One of his first opportunities to realize that he can achieve an effect is to note that he can summon another person with his cries. But in time he realizes he can be an agent in producing effects on things. He is one who not only is able to grasp objects within his reach but also to release them, to push them aside, to assemble them, to toss them aside, and to retrieve them. He is no longer a passive vessel, he is an activator, with a power of his own.

An account by Preyer (1888, 1890) illustrates a child's role as an active agent. Preyer noted that his five-month-old child seemed to discover, while tearing a page from a journal, that it was he who produced the sound and the severing. He then patiently proceeded to tear page after page as though gaining satisfaction from being a cause of change and from seeing ". . . that the remarkable alteration of an entire journal into little scraps (was) due to his own activity."

The Expanding "Inner World"

This dawning sense of power is greatly enhanced when the maturation of a child's mental capacities joins forces with his improving muscular coordination. At first, when he casts an object out of his field of vision, it is gone—as though it no longer existed. But, in time, he is able, so to speak, to maintain his mastery even of the unseen, as he acquires the capacity to keep an object in mind, and later to retrieve it, even though it is out of sight. As a child grows in his ability to retain and to act in terms of impressions he has received not only from the visual but from all sensory modalities, his role as a doer expands apace. His "inner world," as we might call it, embraces more and more of the outer world. He also increasingly becomes a master of time. He can begin to form intentions that extend beyond the present; he can harbor expectations built on his recollections from the past; and, as his development proceeds, he can borrow from the future in making plans and anticipating eventualities.

The Self as a Chooser

As time passes, a child not only perceives himself as one who can initiate action but also as one who can choose. He is able to recognize alternatives and has the power to select one and reject the other. This further extends the dimensions of his "inner world." As his awareness of ability to choose expands, a child not only is confronted with alternatives in the present, and possibilities relating to the future, but also with the consequences of choices he has made in the past. Through his own discoveries and reminders from others he considers what might have been. A child's view of himself as one who can make choices carries with it, to a greater or lesser degree, the experience of being personally *responsible* for choices made in the past and for choices yet to be made. When a child thus regards himself as a responsible agent, two further ingredients are added to his view of himself—regret or self-congratulation regarding past decisions, and a condition of inner conflict when he is confronted with competing present and future alternatives. Eventually, for some persons, the experience of being responsible for themselves becomes a source of pride ("I am the captain of my fate!"). To others, it becomes an awesome thing shrouded by a guilt-ridden past and shadowed by dread of the future.

Overt Signs of Early Self-Awareness

Children are likely to show signs that betoken some degree of self-awareness during the first year, and increasingly thereafter. It is possible, of course, for an adult to read more meaning into these early manifestations than actually is there, but it is wiser (so the author believes) to be alert to them, and to risk an error on the side of over-interpretation, than to ignore them.

Hurt Feelings

One such sign is a show of "hurt feelings." To an adult observer, these appear to differ from a simple display of anger. For example, a child puckers his facial muscles, seems close to tears, but does not cry out or strike out. This may occur when a child's outstretched hand is peremptorily brushed aside or when an adult brusquely snatches away a toy the youngster is reaching for. The child responds (as seen by an adult) as though he had been insulted.

Self-Consciousness

Other signs of self-awareness occur when a child seems to be self-conscious: looks up to see if he is noticed, calls attention to himself, averts his eyes or head as though embarrassed. Indications of self-consciousness also appear when a child, who previously was quite uninhibited, seems to check his cries, as though aware of the sound of his crying and as though not wishing to call attention to himself.[1]

Whenever a child, responding in the presence of others, seems deliberately to check himself, or to put on an "act," (such as crying out loudly when his parents leave him in the care of another, and then quickly subsiding and seeming to be cheerful when they are out of ear-shot) we can suspect he has a considerable degree of self-awareness.

Response to Mirror Image. One approach to the study of self-awareness is to observe the way infants respond to a mirror image of themselves. Children recognize others (such as their mothers) in a mirror and in pictures before they recognize themselves.

---

[1] Interesting changes in the nuances of infants' emotional reactions, suggesting the beginning of what may be regarded as a kind of self-control, have been described by Meili (1957).

Five children who took part in a study by Dixon (1957) of the development of "self-recognition" showed distinct changes with age in response to a mirror and the order of these changes was remarkably similar in all five infants. At first, the infants regarded their reflections "briefly and soberly" but showed no sustained interest, even though, at this stage, they readily recognized their mothers' reflection in the mirror (this was also observed by Zazzo, 1948). Later on, the children became more sociable with their images, smiling, talking, and trying to make contact with the reflection in the mirror. Dixon calls this the "playmate stage"—the child reacts to the mirror image in much the same way as he reacts when placed before another infant. Then came what Dixon calls the "Who dat? Who do dat when I do dat?" stage, in which the child seems to be connecting the mirror image with himself—keeping his eye fixed on the changing image, the child repeats certain acts (such as opening and closing his mouth, raising his arm and moving his fingers) as though he were trying to ". . . master and work his new-found puzzling discovery." At the "who dat?" stage, ". . . an apparent attempt at conversation-testing, as though expecting an echo. . . ," was observed a few times but soon died out, as did pointing at the image while asking a portentous question such as "Dah?".

Sometime between the age of twelve and eighteen months the children entered what Dixon calls the "coy" stage. When confronted with his mirror image, the child now ". . . instead of basking in reflected vanity . . ." might turn his head away, or cry, or smile coyly, or kiss the image after refusing for some time to approach it. Such coyness also has been observed by others.

Emotional Undertones
of the Process of Self-Discovery

A child's growing awareness of himself has emotional overtones. When he first recognizes himself in a mirror, for example, it is not as though he were merely eyeing a portrait. Some children show a great deal of animation in connection with this discovery. One investigator was especially impressed by the emotional coloring of this development, noting the "jubilant interest" shown by an infant at the sight of his own image in a mirror, and of the child's ecstasy when he saw that the movements in the mirror corresponded to his own movements. There appeared to be a real affective value in a child's seeing a reflection of his whole body rather than parts of it (Lacan, 1953).

A display of emotion also often occurs in connection with other forms of self-discovery. A child lets forth a jubilant cry, for example, when he discovers how to ring a bell or how to take the lid off a box. A detailed record of joyful episodes in the life of a young child would probably show that a large proportion of these are connected with experiences in which he tries himself out and realizes, in a new way, the reaches of his own strength and ability. If we grant this, the question still remains: Why, then, do some babies not only show an eager interest but also grow coy, as though they were embarrassed when they first seem to realize that the image in the mirror is their own? And why should a child cry? Perhaps a child who cries is somewhat apprehensive, as though this new-found creature were both a stranger and a familiar figure.

Other Evidences
of Increasing Self-Awareness

Another approach to the subject of early self-identification has been to study how children think of themselves with reference to their bodies. In one study (Horowitz, 1935), two-, three-, and four-year-olds, and students in psychology were asked to "localize" themselves (e.g., the experimenter would ask, while pointing to a leg, head, and so forth: "Is this Joan?"). One child located herself in the abdomen and lower thorax; another localized herself in her lower right jaw; another in the mouth region of the face. The students mentioned a variety of localization points, including the head, brain, eyes, face, heart, and, (probably with tongue in cheek), the genitals.

An important step in children's self-awareness occurs when they recognize bodily differences between boys and girls and clearly identify the sex to which they belong. (The subject of sex-role identification will be discussed in a later section.)

After a child has learned to talk, signs of self-awareness become increasingly apparent, as when, for example, he correctly distinguishes between "I" and "you" and "mine" and "yours"; or is able to distinguish between dreams and actual happenings; is able to acknowledge feelings as his own, saying (as one four-year-old did) "Don't bother me, I'm in a bad mood"; or when he takes pains to conceal his feelings, saying, "I'm not scared," in spite of signs to the contrary.

Self-Assertion and Comparison
of Self with Others

A significant phase in the development of the self occurs when a child begins to assert himself in opposition to others. As we will see more particularly in a later chapter, many children go through a phase when they are especially obstinate or "negativistic," beginning at about the age of two. During this phase a youngster seems to be testing his powers of self-assertion in his relationship with others.

Another important phase in the development of a child's view of himself appears when he is able to compare himself with his peers and to test his powers in competition with them. When a child knowingly competes, he is using others as a standard against which to measure himself. Still another significant sign of self-scrutiny occurs when a child is openly critical of his own work.

Self and Ethnic or Social Awareness

Sometime during childhood a youngster is likely to form a more or less clear conception of his family's socio-economic status or social class. He also becomes aware, in time, of his religious affiliation, the nationality of his parents, and the ethnic stock from which he came. Children's awareness of social class differences does not usually appear to be established until they are well along in the elementary school years (Stendler, 1949).

The age at which children realize the ethnic group to which they belong (whether Negro or white, for example) depends in part on circumstances in the environment in which they live. A child who associates only with his own ethnic group early in life does not have any particular reason to be aware of his ethnic identity. On the other hand, a youngster in a community which includes a mixture of ethnic groups or nationalities is likely to be reminded of his background while he is still quite young. This will especially hold true if there are distinct cleavages within the community or if he is a member of a minority group against which there is prejudice. Among the most moving accounts of childhood are those given by older children and adults of their first-remembered encounter with prejudice. A child who is abused because of his ethnic origins bears an extra burden in the process of forming ideas and attitudes pertaining to himself, especially if he is made to feel ashamed of his background.

In a study in which Negro children aged three to five were asked to identify themselves by pointing to pictures they regarded as most nearly like themselves (Clark and Clark, 1940), light-skinned Negro children chose a white child as being most like themselves more often than did Negro children with darker skins, suggesting that children identify themselves in terms of skin color, which is to them a "concrete reality," before they identify themselves in terms of "race," which is a more sophisticated concept. Pictures were also used in a study by Horowitz (1940) who found that a child who seemed to be aware of being a member of a minority group might still choose a picture of a majority group member as being most like himself.

According to various studies, most children between the ages of three and five become aware of differences between "white" and "colored." Children are likely to recognize this distinction in response to pictures before they apply the label of white or colored to themselves. "White" children identify themselves as white more readily than Negro children identify themselves as Negro. (For a review and discussion of this condition, see Clausen and Williams, 1963.)

When children of preschool age first begin to recognize differences between "white" and "colored" they are likely to do so in a more matter-of-fact manner than at a later age. But the fact that Negro children tend to be slower and more confused in acknowledging their identity suggests that children even at the preschool level are being affected by the prejudices in the larger society in which they live.

Factors Influencing
the Child's View of Himself

A growing person's view of himself is shaped by everything that affects the sweep of his development, ranging from his genetic makeup to obvious and subtle social influences in the society in which he lives. One widely accepted theory pertaining to the development of the self is that a child's self evaluation is profoundly influenced by "significant" persons, particularly his parents. This view has been especially emphasized by Harry Stack Sullivan, who claimed that a young child's "self system" comes into being through a process of "reflected appraisals." As a child is appraised by "significant others," so he in time appraises himself. Approval by others who are significant in his life, especially his mother, instills the beginnings of self-approval, and disapproval by significant persons leads to self-disapproval.

Some empirical studies have indicated that there is likely to be a considerable degree of correspondence between a child's self-evaluation and the way he is regarded by his parents (see, e.g., Khon, 1961). The fact that such correspondence exists does not in itself, however, indicate what is the nature of the cause-and-effect relationship. It is practically axiomatic that a child who is disapproved or rejected by his parents will find it more difficult to view himself in a favorable light than a child who is approved and loved. A child who is predominantly disapproved faces many hard alternatives. If he passively accepts the disapproval as a measure of his own worth, he automatically becomes self-disapproving. If he resists and resents disapproval, he is trying to cope with figures more powerful than himself. If he tries to protect himself from disapproval by being a good child, he may be driven into a state of self-surrender, curbing his impulse to assert himself as a healthy child and sacrificing his ability to become a person in his own right.

But as we have already pointed out in an earlier chapter, the interplay between a child and his parents does not consist simply of a process by which a strong parent imposes his attitudes upon a helpless youngster. Unless the parent is a harsh and unrelenting bully, the child's own qualities and characteristics influence the way he is perceived by his parents, influence the affinity that can exist between him and them, and the nature of the discipline, approval, and disapproval his parents manifest in their dealings with him. Moreover, as we will note more particularly in the next chapter, the impact the parents have on a child depends not only on what they actually feel or think or do but on the child's perception of what they think, feel, or do. This is an aspect of development that is extremely important but which has received little systematic attention in research studies. The clearest, but certainly not the most conclusive, testimony regarding this facet of children's experiences comes from adults who in retrospect describe how their attitudes toward themselves were influenced by what they later regarded as a misperception of their parent's attitudes and intentions.

Another important influence affecting a youngster's evaluation of himself is provided by his peers. Indeed, it appears that in connection with some aspects of self-appraisal, a youngster's evaluation may be influenced by peers as much as by parents.

Ascertaining Children's Ideas and Attitudes Regarding Themselves

Children's ideas and attitudes regarding themselves have been studied by a variety of methods, including records of what young children say about themselves when performing an assigned task, informal interviews, projective procedures, brief written compositions, and elaborate inventories or tests. Most of the information regarding self-assessment has been obtained from persons who are old enough to read and write. Tests used to measure childrens' and older persons' perceptions of themselves have usually been built on lists of personality traits or lists of adjectives or descriptive items pertaining to attitudes, emotional tendencies, abilities, and tempermental qualities that a person might use in characterizing himself or others. A descripitve item such as "cheerful" preceded by phrasing such as "I am" may be followed by modifiers (such as never, sometimes, usually, always) to enable the child to mark the term that he thinks most aptly describes him.

A child's response to a list of such items presumably indicates how he appraises himself, or at least how he would like to have others think he appraises himself. This appraisal has sometimes been referred to as an assessment of a child as he is, or his "actual" self. In a further version of such a test, the words "I would like to be," or "I think I ought to be" can be substituted for "I am," allowing a child to express what he thinks he should be, or wishes he might be. This assessment has been called a measure of a person's "ideal" self.

By substituting other phrasings such as "other people are" (or a succession of names known to the child, such as "John is" "Peter is") a youngster can indicate his appraisal of others as he claims they are. And when, in this version, the terms "ought to be" are used, he can report what others ideally should be. Other phrasings, such as "others think I am" (or, in the singular, "John thinks I am"), or "others think they are" ("John thinks he is") permit a child to express his judgment as to how others will appraise him, or how he thinks they will appraise themselves.

Another procedure has been to put the descriptive items on separate cards and then instruct the subject being tested to sort these items into piles ranging from items that he regards as most descriptive to those he regards as least descriptive of himself (or others). In a procedure known as the Q-sort, an individual is given a pack of cards, each with a descriptive item, and told to sort these cards according to a prearranged distribution which approximates a normal distribution.

Still another procedure is to require the respondent to rank items on a list or on separate cards in an order from the most to the least descriptive.[2]

Results from instruments such as these can be used to determine the extent to which there is concordance or discrepancy between a child's "real" and "ideal" self; the extent of agreement between his self-rating and his ratings of others; the degree of agreement between his self-ratings and the way he is rated by others, and so on. Moreover, it is possible to use these instruments to determine the degree to which self ratings remain stable or fluctuate with the passage of time and the changes, if any, that occur when self ratings are repeated after an intervening experience, such as success or failure in school.

Instruments for self-assessment and assessment of others and by others have yielded some interesting findings, even though these instruments have many short-comings. Obviously, in responding to such an instrument, a person is applying his own subjective standards, and these may vary from person to person. This in itself is not a flaw, since the avowed aim in administering the test is to obtain a picture of an individual's view of himself regardless of how "correct" this view is as judged by standards other than his own. If a person, for example, describes himself as very popular and actually believes that he is popular, this is an important item of information about him, whether or not he actually is rated popular by his peers.

A serious shortcoming of this manner of assessment is that the results do not in themselves reveal how candid or forthright persons are when rating themselves. One person might deliberately set out to give himself favorable ratings, while another tries to assess himself as honestly as he can. Another serious shortcoming is that these tests, even when the respondent answers as honestly as he can, do not in themselves measure his degree of insight into himself, or his perceptiveness and insight in judging others. As a consequence, a person who harbors hostility and is aware of it and freely

---

[2] The Q-sort was introduced by Stephenson (1935). Other self-assessment instruments have been prepared by Berger (1952); Bills, Vance, and McLean (1951); Spivack (1956); Jervis (1958); Phillips (1951); and Fey (1955). Wattenberg and Clifford (1964) have described a method for eliciting children's statements about themselves at the kindergarten level.

acknowledges it may seem to be less self-accepting, more critical of himself, than a person who has a hostile streak but is quite unaware of it and rates himself as one who is free of hostility.

"Real" and "Ideal" Self

Most children who are old enough to understand will report discrepancies between what they are, as perceived by themselves, and what they would like, or think they ought, to be.[3]

Some discrepancy between what a youngster thinks he is and what he thinks he would like to be or ought to be is probably inevitable, and healthy. Even if he receives no reminders from others he is likely, within the framework of his own experience, to become aware of his limitations. There is a discrepancy between the "real" and the "ideal" when his reach exceeds his grasp, when he aspires to a degree of ability and self-sufficiency that he knows he falls short of achieving, or when the roles he plays in his fantasies are more heroic than anything he actually can accomplish.

Apart from their own discoveries, children are repeatedly made aware of their limitations by other children and adults. Such awareness arises both from example and exhortation. Children begin to compare themselves with others and to compete with others while still at the preschool level. A child who is sensitive to competitive standards obviously is bound, in one way or another, to fail to measure up; even if he could outdo all others of his own age, he will be outdone by older children, such as older siblings.

In early childhood, it is likely to be the parents who provide the most important sources of a child's awareness of the gap between what he is and what he thinks he ought to be. The fact that parents, as a matter of duty and necessity, must restrain, admonish, and discipline a child, almost forces them into the position of reminding a child of discrepancies between what he is and ought to be.

But it is not merely open and avowed reminders from parents that will affect a child's self-evaluation. Parental influence flows through many channels. Varying degrees of discrepancy between what a child is, as he sees himself, and what he more or less clearly thinks he ought to be, will arise when a youngster tries to emulate the example set by his parents, even if the parents do not demand that he use them as his models. A child's self-appraisal will also be influenced by his perception of his parent's attitudes

---

[3] In a study by the writer (1952) about 2,000 persons in the fourth grade and beyond, responded anonymously, in brief compositions, to the question, "What I dislike about myself." About 94 per cent named characteristics they claimed they did not approve of. The rest said, "nothing," or refused to answer, or gave unintelligible replies. Approximately the same percentage failed or refused to respond to the question, "What I like about myself." There were more refusals to respond at the senior high school level than at lower grade levels.

or demands—how they judge him—what they expect of him—whether or not this perception is realistic. In addition, a child's self-evaluation may be influenced by his parent's evaluation of him, whether or not this evaluation is directly communicated to him in so many words. Parents' evaluations of their children may be based on attitudes which parents themselves are not aware of (as would be the case if an ambitious father unknowingly resents a son for not being at the top of his class) or they may be based on standards which the parents clearly recognize.

It seems that most parents—probably all of them—are consciously aware of discrepancies between their "real" child, as they perceive him, and their child as he ideally might be. In a study by Medinnus (1961), the fathers and mothers in a small community gave Q-sort[4] descriptions of their five-year-old children, and of what they regarded as an ideal five-year old. The results showed that parents differed considerably in the degree to which the description of their children corresponded to their description of an ideal child, but the degree of correspondence between the "real" and the "ideal" in the total group was rather small (the average correlations between the various "real" and "ideal" sorts by fathers and mothers for boys and girls combined ranged from .26 to .36).

According to Medinnus, there is only "moderate acceptance" of a child's behavior *if* these real-ideal coefficients can be interpreted as ". . . the degree to which the parent accepts the child's behavior." The *if* in this statement is, of course, a large *if*, for in describing an "ideal" that differs from the "real" a parent is not necessarily rejecting his child. He may simply be noting characteristics which, in his judgment, might make life more serene and happy for his offspring. A parent might even relish and admire traits in his children which are not, in themselves, generally regarded as admirable or advantageous but which give flavor to the individuality to a particular youngster (Jersild, *et al.*, 1949). In other words, a parent may admire and prefer hot-tempered Johnny to any other boy in all the world even though, from an ideal standpoint, he realizes that Johnny might have an easier time in life if he were more even-tempered. Even so, a youngster whose "real" identity as perceived by his parent differs from the parent's image of an "ideal" child is more likely, in the course of time, to regard this discrepancy as a reproach rather than as a source of admiration.

A discrepancy between the "real" and "ideal" self is usually not only inevitable, but probably, on balance, a healthy state of affairs in the normal course of life. There will always be a gap between what is and what might

---

[4] Forty-two descriptions of positive traits or characteristics (e.g., can take disappointments calmly) and 42 descriptions of negative characteristics (e.g., gets mad easily) were typed on separate cards. In the "real" sort, each parent sorted each of the two sets of cards into seven piles, ranging from "most characteristic of my child" to "least characteristic of my child," with six cards in each pile. In the "ideal" sort, positive traits were arranged from those most valued to those comparatively least valued and the negative traits from those "least bad" to those "worst for the ideal 5-year old to possess."

be in a youngster who is seeking and striving to realize his potentials. However, the discrepancy ceases to be a mark of healthy striving and becomes a symptom of disorder when a youngster reaches for the impossible, or is unable to gain satisfaction from what he in reality has achieved. A wide divergence between self as is and an ideal version of self is especially unfortunate if a child blames himself for limitations which he does not have the power to surmount. Such self-blame often arises from a stigma of failure imposed by others.

Varying Meanings of Discrepancies Between "Real" and "Ideal" Self. Some writers have regarded the degree of correspondence or disparity between the "real" self and the "ideal" self (as indicated by self-ratings) as a measure of a child's self-esteem, self-acceptance, or self-rejection. This is a dubious measure, however, in view of all that remains unrevealed when youngsters respond to a self-assessment instrument. There are two shortcomings of this measure that should especially be pointed out. One is that in the typical procedure, items on a test are regarded as numerically equivalent. For example, a person might say he is very poor in musical ability but wishes he were very good; on this item he reveals a maximum degree of discrepancy. He might also say that he is a very poor reader and wishes he were a top-notch reader: again, a maximum discrepancy. The discrepancy on the reading item may, however, be vastly more important to him than the music item. But both, in the usual quantitative treatment of test results, are treated as equivalent.

An even more serious shortcoming resides in the different personal meanings the markings regarding the "ideal" self may have. One youngster, may name, as ideal, qualities that are quite unrealistic and ephemeral, while another may report solid aspirations which he is actively striving to attain. Actually, when a person names an ideal which he has not attained but which he actively pursues, and confidently hopes to attain, he may express a far higher degree of self-acceptance than one who names ideals that he neither strives to realize, nor hopes ever to achieve.

Projection of Self Into Future Roles and View of Self as an Achiever

One of the most elusive but important facets of the self is a growing child's view of himself with reference to the future. In late childhood and adolescence, most normal children nourish expectations that only the future can fulfill and many actively strive toward goals not yet within their grasp. Others are more bound to the present. Such differences appear in connection with attitudes toward school and in more or less clearly formulated plans for a future vocation.

Some children, as they approach their teens, take it for granted that they will continue their schooling through high school, and perhaps beyond, and expect to make the grade. Others are neither so forward-looking nor confident. A critical time for the latter youngsters often comes when they drop out of school about midway through high school, but this step very likely has been in the making for several years.

There are, of course, many factors that influence a youngster's view of himself as one who should and can, or should not and cannot, look forward to continued schooling. Much attention has been centered in recent years on high school dropouts who come from poor socio-economic backgrounds and are socially and culturally "disadvantaged." Many such children are at a disadvantage in coping with school, due, in part, to lack of "achievement motivation," and sometimes a different approach to learning and concept formation than prevails among children reared in middle-class homes.[5] Whatever might be the nature of a child's initial disadvantages, his attitudes toward school and his ability to cope with school are likely to be further impaired if he faces continued failure.

However, environmental factors associated with socio-economic status, such as those noted above, do not alone explain why some children have low aspirations and display poor achievement. There are youngsters from sub-standard social environments who do well, and some who do remarkably well in school and in building firm expectations for the future (just as some slum children in "delinquency areas" become delinquents while others do not). Something more than just the more or less obvious factors in the social environment must also be taken into account to explain why some children who are culturally "disadvantaged" are "upward mobile" in their aspirations when they reach adolescence, while others seem bound, as though by fate, to remain in the circumstances in which they are reared.

A decisive factor in determining a youngster's approach to the future seems to reside in attitudes he has regarding himself. While these attitudes have not been studied systematically, it is not difficult, in theory, to describe them. It is more difficult to explain how they became established.

In a thought-provoking paper, Shumsky (1964) has described the self-picture of a child in school who copes with his present circumstances in a way that builds effectively for the future. He behaves as one who believes in his capacity for taking an active part in shaping his own "life chances." He proceeds as one who can effect a change in his life situation. He is assertive rather than passive in his approach to intellectual tasks. His way of coping bespeaks an undercurrent of self-reliance and optimism.

As Shumsky points out, it is an uphill struggle for children reared in culturally deprived circumstances to acquire such a view of themselves. They

---

[5] For studies bearing on this subject, see Eels, *et al.* (1951); Haggard (1954); Douvan (1956); Siller (1957); Bernstein (1959); Deutch (1960); Barker (1961); and Riesman (1962).

have less opportunity and receive less encouragement; the immediate concrete needs for day-to-day survival in an adverse environment hampers their freedom to formulate abstract goals or long-range expectations. Rousselet (1962), in a study of adolescents who had quit school, found that these youngsters, preoccupied with obtaining immediate financial gains, were unable "even in dreams" to project themselves beyond the narrow limits of their immediate environment. Levine (1962), in a study of children's self-awareness in the age range from six to twelve years, likewise notes that children who were socio-economically underprivileged and poor students differed from good students in their self-concepts and in their view of the future.

In a study which compared boys who were "upward" and "downward" mobile in their professed plans for future work, Douvan (1956) found that the "upward" boys relied more on their own ideas and more often set goals that could be realized only in a distant future.

All of the foregoing statements emphasize that there is a link between a growing person's contemporary ideas and attitudes regarding himself and his ability to project himself into the future. Findings have also indicated that adverse socio-economic circumstances create obstacles in the way of achieving self-reliance in the present and setting goals for self-fulfillment in the future, particularly in the academic area. The findings do not, unfortunately, tell why and how some youngsters, in spite of adverse circumstances, are able to establish long-range goals and to pursue them, while others are not.

There probably is no adverse external circumstance in the lives of children who do poorly at school that does not also prevail among many children who do well. The conditions which mold a child's view of himself are apparently a crucial factor. Several studies have indicated that pupils who do not achieve well at school have less favorable views of themselves than successful pupils (Bruck, 1957; Coopersmith, 1959; Hamachek, 1960).

Apparently, an unfavorable view of self that goes with poor achievement is already established in many children before they enter the first grade, according to a study by Wattenberg and Clifford (1964). These investigators assessed the self-concepts of kindergarten children by compiling records of what the children said with reference to themselves, while drawing pictures of their families and responding to incomplete sentences. The findings, in the authors' words, indicated that ". . . measures of self-concept and of ego strength taken at the kindergarten were predictive of reading achievement two and one-half years later."

What is there in the life of one child who at an early age has a favorable view of his competence and personal worth, and, in another's life that leads to an unfavorable view of self? Unfortunately, this is an unanswered question. According to the Wattenberg and Clifford study, the factor of intelligence does not, to a decisive degree, account for the difference. But perhaps an answer is in the making. An aim in some of the current programs designed to forestall or to remedy self-defeating attitudes is to provide experiences at the preschool level that might help a child to view himself as one who can achieve and as one whose achievement is worthy of notice.

Conscious and Unconscious Processes
and Self-Awareness

The foregoing sections have dealt with various aspects of *self-awareness* and with the characteristics which a person clearly *recognizes* or *claims* to be part of his make-up. These constitute a person's *phenomenal self* (the self which, as a *phenomenon*, appears, shows, is perceptible). There also are facets of a person's make-up which influence his ideas and attitudes about himself but which are *unconscious* in the sense that he does not consciously recognize them.

The term *unconscious* has a vast variety of meanings and interpretations which we do not here need to explore. But it is necessary to take account of some of the meanings of the concept of the unconscious when we seek to understand children. There are many currents in a child's life which he does not comprehend. A child does not comprehend the roots of his experience, when, for example, he harbors fears springing from happenings which he has forgotten or has a phobia arising from conflicts he does not understand. Likewise, a child is not conscious of what is occurring when, for example, he warms up to a teacher without realizing that he does so because the teacher touches off sentiments he has for his mother, or if he is deeply wounded by a mild criticism without realizing that the criticism triggers feelings of self-reproach springing from earlier experiences in his life.

What is referred to as "the unconscious" is also at work if a child who has learned to suppress his anger gamely grins and feels no rage when someone abuses him but then later, for no apparent reason, experiences a pain in his stomach and throws up his dinner. In later sections, notably those dealing with emotion and the devices a child uses to defend his pride, there will be other illustrations of the way in which motives which a youngster does not recognize influence his actions and his endeavor to maintain a cherished view of himself.

A condition which a person is not consciously aware of occurs when he has an "idealized image" of himself that is not in keeping with the realities of his life. An idealized self image containing elements which a person does not knowingly perceive occurs when he adopts a pose or façade and then somehow loses sight of the fact that he is posing. Such a condition occurs, for example, if an adult sees himself as a cold-hearted cynic when actually his cynicism is only a veneer, covering warm-hearted impulses. It occurs if an older child, with a powerful, competitive drive, views himself as a disinterested scholar, eager to learn for the sake of learning, without recognizing that he is using his scholarly efforts as a vehicle for competing with others.

The "idealized self" is discussed again in later sections of this book dealing with anxiety and personality problems. For a more complete discussion of the concept of the idealized image, the reader is referred to the writings of Horney (1937, 1939, 1945, 1950). Horney describes the idealized self as a kind of pseudo-identity. The "idealized self," containing elements which a person is not consciously aware of, has a different meaning from the "ideal self" which a person describes when he knowingly tells about his aspirations. The idealized self is not, from a person's own point of view, an ideal toward which he is striving but something he actually has attained—it is his "real self" as he sees it.

When we use an inventory to measure a person's ideas about himself as he thinks he really is, or to measure his ideas concerning his ideal self—the kind of person he thinks he ought to be—we cannot be sure to what extent one or the other account reflects unrecognized elements of an idealized self image.

Self-Regard and Regard for Others

In several studies it has been found that persons who give themselves a favorable rating also tend to give a favorable rating to others. This has been interpreted to mean that a self-accepting person is also accepting of others and that a person who rejects himself also tends to reject others. There is some empirical evidence to support this interpretation. Trent (1953) found that Negro children who expressed positive feelings about themselves also expressed more positive feelings toward other Negroes and whites than did children who were less positive in their attitudes about themselves. In a study by Tabachnick (1962) it was likewise found that children who were more satisfied with themselves tended to be less prejudiced than those who were less satisfied with themselves.

One of the key concepts in the lore of the self is the concept that love of self incorporates love of others, and that ability to love others requires an ability to love oneself. This concept probably expresses one of the verities of human existence. But the empirical devices psychologists have used to test the concept have, so far, been rather superficial.

It is reasonable to expect, simply on theoretical grounds, that there will be a positive relationship between self-acceptance and acceptance of others. Unfortunately, the typical instrument for assessing regard for self and regard for others does not adequately assess this relationship. Some items are, in effect, tautologous and practically demand a similarity in ratings of self and ratings of others. If a person, for example, says he is charitable, he is almost compelled, in rating "others" or "most people" to say that they, too, are charitable. To do otherwise would, in effect, negate his own claim of being charitable.

A positive relation between the acceptance of self and acceptance of others in older children and adults might be expected, not only on theoretical but also on empirical grounds. In its profoundest sense, self-acceptance is built upon a frank and realistic view of self. Thus appraised, a self-accepting person sees himself as less than perfect. He acknowledges his limitations without self-blame. He is aware of a discrepancy between what is and what might be. He recognizes his weaknesses. He is able to feel regret and even remorse without saddling himself with the burden of guilt. He is not the slave of an unrelenting conscience. He can perceive ways in which others might be more gifted, more serene, more able than he without being compelled to try to outdo them or to feel inferior. He does not need to pretend to be what he is not or to deny what he is. Such a person is likely within the dimensions of his own private life, to be more at ease, more free to take things as they come, more able to accept himself as he is and others as they are.

Accuracy of Self-Perception as Determined by Objective Criteria

Many of the ideas and attitudes youngsters have with regard to themselves are beyond the reach of measures that might tell how true or how realistic these attitudes are. However, when youngsters rate themselves on abilities that can be measured, or with respect to the attitudes they think others have regarding them, it is possible to get an indication of how their views correspond to independent tests and ratings.

In a study by Brandt (1958) sixth graders and eleventh graders rated themselves on a number of performances including arithmetic, spelling, reading, vocabulary, strength of grip, distance they could throw a softball, and distance they could jump from a standing position. The students were given the names of class members and were asked to record in connection with each name whether they could do better than, or not as well as, this person in each of the performances. The students also marked themselves and others on a social reputation test.

Some students were highly accurate in assessing their abilities in all areas, as judged by external criteria, while others were not. On the whole, students overrated themselves more than they underrated themselves, a tendency toward overestimation that has also been apparent in other studies. However, in spite of this general tendency to overrate, some of the youngsters consistently underestimated themselves.

The tendency to overestimate or underestimate appeared to be more related to the total framework of a person's view of himself than to vary widely in terms of specific performances or specific characteristics.

The older children in Brandt's study were more accurate (as judged by the criteria that were used) in their self-estimates than the younger ones. The likelihood that there is an increase with age in correspondence between self-estimates and ratings by others was further shown in a study by Phillips (1963), who compared the ratings third- and sixth-grade children assigned to themselves on a personality test with the ratings they received when judged by their teachers and their peers.

It appears that realistic self-perception is not only related to a child's social acceptance (as noted in an earlier section) but also to his personal adjustment. Sixth-grade children in a study by Taylor and Combs (1952), whose adjustment had been assessed by means of a personality test, were asked to respond to statements describing faults that are common to most children (e.g., "I sometimes disobey my parents"; "I sometimes say bad words or swear"). Youngsters rated as least well adjusted less frequently admitted an awareness of such faults than did children rated as well adjusted. Similar statements were presented to fourth-grade children in a later study by Perry (1961). Well-adjusted children were selected on the basis of judgments by teachers and principals, and maladjusted children were selected on the basis of diagnoses by clinicians and a small battery of tests. The well-adjusted children (thirty-one in number) admitted a cumulative total of 205 faults, and the maladjusted (thirty-two in number) admitted 149 faults.

The findings in the two studies just cited support the view that well-adjusted persons have less need to distort reality or to defend themselves against making what might be regarded as self-incriminating admissions about themselves. Further findings bearing on this topic have been reported by Weiner (1964) in a study of four-year-old children. Weiner set out to test the hypothesis that ". . . accuracy of self-appraisal is inversely related to the need for defensiveness." In individual interviews, the children were asked questions such as "Do you like to play with (name of a school-mate)"? "Does (name of a school-mate) like to play with you or doesn't he like to play with you"? "Are you better than (name of a school-mate) in (name of an activity—drawing, dressing self, climbing) or is (name of school-mate) better than you"? The children were also rated by their teachers. Most of the children gave themselves high ratings. This meant that there would be more than a chance likelihood that those who were rated high by classmates and teachers would have a high "accuracy" score. In spite of this complication, however, the over-all results indicated that children who were most accurate in their self-ratings (as judged by the ratings they received from other children and teachers) were popular, and rated as well adjusted by teachers, while those who were least accurate were rated as being poorly adjusted, dependent, passive, and lacking in self-confidence.

Self Perception
as Related to Social Acceptance

The youngsters in the study by Brandt cited above who were most favorably regarded by their peers were, on the whole, more accurate in their self-estimates than those who were less favorably regarded. A study by Goslin (1962) underscores the likelihood that children who have a relatively accurate and realistic perception of themselves will be more popular with their peers than children whose view of themselves differs substantially from the way they are viewed by others. Goslin (1962) used sociometric tests in several seventh- and eighth-grade classes to assess the degree to which youngsters were accepted or rejected by their classmates. In each class the five youngsters who were most accepted and the five who were least accepted were singled out for separate study. They were given a list of traits (modest-immodest, bad tempered-cheerful, honest-dishonest, etc.) and each of the subjects was asked (1) to rate himself, (2) to indicate how "most of the others" in his class would rate him. In addition, ten other members in each class rated the five most accepted and the five least accepted classmates on the twenty traits.

Rejected students showed a higher disparity between the ratings they gave themselves and the ratings assigned to them by others in nearly all of the groups studied. Furthermore, they showed a higher disparity between their estimate of how others would rate them and the ratings they actually received than did the more popular pupils.

In most of the groups in Goslin's study, the rejected students more often predicted that their classmates would rate them higher, rather than lower, than actually proved to be the case. Some rejected pupils, however, conspicuously underestimated the way in which others would describe them.

The foregoing findings raise these questions: Is a child rejected because he misperceives how others regard him? Or does he misperceive how others react to him because others reject him? It would require further study to answer these questions. However, the fact that rejected children are less realistic than accepted children in assessing how they are regarded by others suggests two practical questions: Can a child be helped to perceive himself more realistically? If so, might there be an improvement in the regard others have for him?

According to a study by Staines (1958), it is possible for a perceptive and sensitive teacher to help children to take a more thoughtful view of themselves. In classroom observations, Staines noted that some teachers, much more than others, used opportunities to help children gain a clearer picture of themselves. Staines obtained information about pupils in two classes, one taught by a teacher who tried in connection with regular teaching procedures to help children to assess themselves. The other class was taught by a teacher who stressed the conventional academic subject matter, without any effort to use the learning situation as a means whereby children might learn about themselves. Staines reports that, at the end of a twelve-week teaching period, youngsters in the former group were more discriminating in their self esti-mates, they were more moderate, less rigid in describing themselves, more sure and accepting of what they were like, more certain of what they wanted to be like.

To explore the full ramifications of teaching designed to promote realistic self-perception, and whether the results of such teaching might improve a child's acceptability in the eyes of others, would, of course, require an investi-gation on a considerably larger scale. In the present context it is interesting, however, that the youngsters in this limited study who received instruction designed to promote self-understanding became more aware of how they thought others would judge them. The study does not indicate whether this greater awareness, in turn, might influence the extent to which they were approved by others, but it does suggest that unrealistic self perceptions and unrealistic perceptions of how one is regarded by others, such as were mani-fested by rejected children in the Goslin study, need not be regarded as fixed and unchangeable characteristics. In passing it may be noted that gains children in the Staines study made in understanding themselves were not achieved at the expense of academic performance. The children who had received instruction which sharpened their self-perception made at least as much progress in learning academic subject matter as children who had not received such instruction.

Stability of Self Ratings as Related to Age

Unfortunately, no thorough longitudinal studies have been made of stable and changing features of the view individuals have of themselves from early childhood into adolescence and beyond. As indicated in a preceding section, older children seem to form a more accurate picture of themselves (as judged against other criteria) as they grow older. Furthermore, children's assessments of themselves also tend to become more stable as they become older. In a comparison between 4th- and 6th-grade children, Perkins (1958) found that children's self estimates were more stable when tested and retested within a short space of time at the 6th-grade level than when tested and retested at the 4th-grade level. Perkins also found that there was more congruence between children's ratings of themselves as they are and as they said they ideally would like to be at the 6th- than at the 4th-grade level. Perkins notes, however, that more research is needed to establish the relationship between increased maturity and the stability of children's concepts regarding them-selves.

Children whose views regarding themselves were first assessed at age twelve were examined again at age sixteen in a study by Reckless and Dinitz (reviewed by Lively, *et al.* 1962). At age 12, these youngsters were subjects in an investigation, using many sources of information, designed to find to what extent future delinquency and non-delinquency could be predicted at the pre-adolescent level. At twelve the boys judged to be potential delinquents had a less favorable view of themselves than those judged to be non-delinquent. Scales and indices used to measure "self-concepts" at age sixteen indicated that the boys who at twelve had been judged as probably not heading toward delinquency had retained "a positive or favorable image" of themselves, as well as of their fathers, mothers, friends, and teachers. The same scales indicated that the boys judged to be potential delinquents at twelve continued to hold a less favorable image of themselves and others at sixteen. "No significant change in the concepts of self and others had occurred in the interim" (p. 166). According to the authors, ". . . once internalized in preadolescence, these images or orientations tend, in the absence of major external modifications, to be resistive to change" (p. 166–167).

Sex-Role Identification

An important facet of selfhood is a child's awareness of being a boy or a girl. By the end of the third year, children are likely to recognize anatomical differences between the sexes. There are conflicting views concerning the effect this discovery has on a child. There are those who maintain that a child's discovery of genital differences comes as a shock, particularly to girls. According to one theory, girls will have a tendency to acquire what is known as "penis envy," involving a disposition, at a conscious or unconscious level, to regard their genitalia and their identity as females as inferior to the male's equipment and status. Other observers, however, dispute the view that the discovery of sex differences is typically charged with emotion, or the view that the typical girls become envious of males. For differing interpretations, see Levy (1940) and Conn (1940).

As time goes on, awareness of anatomical sex differences constitutes, of course, only one of a host of details that are incorporated into children's ideas concerning what it means to be a boy or a girl and what may be regarded as appropriate masculine and feminine behavior.

In discussions of sex-role identification, it has often been assumed in Western societies that males are more valued than females; that the tasks assigned to males have more prestige; that male children are more prized than female children; and that girls, sensing that boys are preferred, have less incentive than boys for accepting their sex roles.

The assumption that children perceive their parents as preferring boys has been questioned in a study by Hartley, *et al.* (1962), who asked eight and eleven-year-old children to complete a story in which a childless couple seeking to adopt a child had to choose between a boy and a girl. The children were then asked, Which do you think they chose?. Which do you think the husband wanted?. Which do you think the wife wanted? Most of the boys and the girls perceived the hypothetical man as preferring a boy and the hypothetical woman as preferring a girl. When children who, in response to questioning, said they planned to have families in adult life were asked to name their preferences, a number of children expressed no preference, but in both sex groups a majority expressed a preference for a child of the same sex as themselves.

Adults who, to a significant degree, provide children with sex-role models, more or less take for granted that some characteristics are typically masculine and other characteristics are typically feminine. Women, in general, are quite commonly thought of as more emotional than men, warmer, softer, more tender and delicate. Men are viewed as stronger than women, less emotional, more dominant, braver and more rugged. Such differences, along with many others, constitute the stereotyped view in our culture of what is masculine and feminine.

However, apart from inherent biological differences between the sexes, a wide range of characteristics that presumably distinguish the masculine and feminine role are not exhibited in an either/or fashion. In connection with many of them, it can be said that the more rounded a person is, whether male or female, the more this person is likely to possess qualities that supposedly are typical of the other sex. For example, even though a woman, according to the popular view, might be regarded as more sensitive, tender-hearted, and emotional than the typical man, it is likely that a man who is free to draw on his resources will also be sensitive and tender-hearted and will not feel a compulsion to hide his emotions under a façade of manliness. The fact still remains, however, that at a given time and in a given culture there are traits which a large proportion of the population would regard as more characteristically masculine or feminine.

It is necessary to inject the reservation "at a given time," since styles change with regard to what is considered as uniquely appropriate for one sex or the other. A survey would probably show that today far more young fathers do "womanly" work, such as washing the dishes or changing the baby's diapers, than was true some generations ago.

Sex Differences and Developmental Traits

Before going further into sex-role preferences it is instructive to point out some developmental differences between boys and girls in addition to differences in primary physical sex characteristics.

On the biological side, during the formative years, girls are in many respects more hardy, robust, and "mature" than boys. The birth rate for white boys is higher than for girls (in a ratio of about 105–100), but the mortality rate for boys is higher during infancy, childhood, and adolescence. Boys appear to be more susceptible to disease, especially during infancy.[6] More boys than girls suffer from impairments attributed to brain damage.[7] With the approach of puberty, girls seem to be less susceptible than boys to adverse circumstances (such as malnutrition or wartime hardships) that might retard their physical growth (Greulich, 1951; Tanner, 1963).

From an early age, the bone structure of the average girl is more "mature" than that of the average boy. According to one study (Flory, 1936), x-ray pictures showing the degree of ossification—hard and brittle bone formation characteristic of older persons compared with the softer and more cartilaginous structure of the young—indicate that at the time of entering school girls are about one year ahead of boys in "skeletal age," and that at the time of entering high school they are about two years ahead of boys.

Although these differences are interesting, it has not been established just what differential influence, if any, they might have on boys' and girls' perception of themselves or their sex roles. A more pronounced effect probably is exerted by an additional important difference in the physical sphere—namely, in the onset of puberty, as indicated by the onset of the first menstrual period, and a corresponding stage of development in boys. Girls mature sexually at an earlier age than boys, and, correlated with this, a girl's adolescent "growth spurt" comes at an earlier age. From a physical standpoint, the transition from viewing themselves as children to viewing themselves as young women comes earlier in the average girl's life than the corresponding transition from childhood to the beginnings of manhood in boys.

With the onset of puberty, several physical sex differences begin to disappear or are reversed. The average boy "catches up" in skeletal maturity and sexual maturity and moves ahead of girls in height and weight. Moreover, while boys during childhood, in many respects, lag behind girls in bodily development they are, if anything, more enterprising in using their bodily properties.

In the sphere of sexual functioning, the typical near-teenage and teenage boy is sexually much more active (as measured by sexual "outlets") than the typical girl (Ramsey, 1943; Kinsey, 1948, 1953). The difference between boys and girls is perhaps influenced by more severe cultural restraints against premarital sex activity that are placed on girls. But the difference is probably influenced by biological factors as well. Kinsey's findings suggest that even

[6] For references dealing with these topics see Dublin (1965); Washburn, *et al.* (1965); and Donaldson and Kohl (1965).

[7] One explanation offered for this is that the boy's head circumference at birth is greater than the girl's, with consequent greater difficulty in labor. Another explanation (less flattering to males) is that the girl's complement of chromosomes (including a double chromosome designated as X, and lacking what is known as the Y chromosome in boys) makes her genetically more hardy.

when girls seem not to be bound by restraints, they are sexually less active than boys.

In the motor sphere, many differences between boys and girls, especially after the preschool years, are so conspicuous that they scarcely need to be reviewed. There is evidence which suggests, although not conclusively, that newborn boys are more "dynamic" than girls in the muscular activity (Knop, 1946). As time passes, boys' play and games are, on the whole, more active and vigorous, and usually cover more ground, and range farther afield. With the approach of adolescence, boys excel girls in tests of gross strength and speed, and in the more robust common athletic activities.

With the onset of adolescence, boys continue for several years to gain in some gross physical performances (such as throwing a ball and running speed), while girls tend to level off or even to show a decline (Espenschade, 1940). At the preadolescent years and beyond, the ascendancy of boys in the sports which attract most public acclaim is so great in the typical school that girls are practically assigned to the subservient position of sitting on the sidelines, admiring and cheering the male athletes. To be sure, a large proportion of boys who are not "varsity material" also sit on the sidelines, but the value system both among boys and girls assigns high prestige to the athletic, muscular, masculine boy. There is no single attribute that can be counted on to win similar acclaim for girls. Moreover, it seems to be easier for an adolescent boy to capitalize on his "masculine" physical qualities than it is for a girl to capitalize on her "feminine" qualities. A superior physical endowment which makes a boy popular with other boys is also likely to make him popular with girls. On the other hand, the qualities that make a girl popular with girls are not so likely to make her popular with boys. It appears that boys are judged to a greater extent than girls by a single standard (Tryon, 1939).

There are many differences between boys and girls in the spheres of intellectual performance and social behavior that variously might influence, or be influenced by, their views regarding their masculine and feminine roles. Girls tend to be somewhat superior to boys in early language development. From the time they begin their schooling, girls have fewer academic problems than boys. The proportion of boys who have difficulty in learning to read or who encounter continuing reading problems, far exceeds the proportion of girls. Apart from reading problems, boys also far outnumber girls as "problem pupils" at school. This is linked, in part, with the fact that girls tend more than boys to be conforming, while boys tend to be more rebellious.

From an early age, girls are relatively more interested than boys in persons, while boys are relatively more interested in things. Even as infants, girls seem to fix their attention more on persons than boys do. At the elementary school level and beyond, girls more often than boys mention other people when describing their interests and in recounting their past experiences (Jersild and Tasch, 1949).

Along with a greater concern about people, girls also, as we mentioned, tend to be more conforming in their social relationships. A girl's tendency to conform seems to operate as a two-edged sword in the development of her views regarding herself. On the one hand, by conforming she is likely to win approval from others, or at least to encounter less disapproval, punishment, and failure at school, and fewer negative evaluations by others which might impair her own self-evaluation. But the more important approval from others becomes to her, the more she places her fate in the hands of others. She is more dependent on the admiration and good will of her elders and peers than the youngster who goes his own way with less concern about the impression he makes on others.

Several studies indicate that as youngsters move into the high school and college years, girls become more vulnerable than boys to the opinions of others. As described in a study by Carlson (1963), with the approach of adolescence, girls exhibit a stronger "social orientation" than boys, while boys display more of a "personal orientation." The socially oriented person's conception of himself is, to an important degree, dependent on the nature of his relationships with others; he is concerned about how he is appraised by others. The self-esteem of a personally oriented individual is less dependent on the attitudes of other persons.

In a longitudinal study, Carlson found that during a six-year period beginning in preadolescence, a substantial percentage of girls shifted from a personal to a social orientation, while most of the boys either maintained, or shifted toward, a personal orientation. Results in other studies at the adolescent and adult levels are in keeping with the idea that males are more likely than females to evaluate themselves according to independent, autonomous standards, as distinguished from social standards (Hovland and Janis, 1953; Douvan, 1960). At the college level Jameson (1941) found that inability to be popular with men was a source of unhappiness for many girls.

Several studies at the high-school and college-age levels indicate that it is easier for a boy to capitalize on his assets than it is for a girl, due, in part, to the girl's social orientation, as mentioned above, and to traditional notions of what is appropriate to the masculine and feminine roles. Boys have more freedom (or allow themselves more freedom) to assert themselves, to assume a dominant stance in relations with the opposite sex, and to be aggressively competitive. To the extent that this is true, girls must, to a degree, repudiate themselves. In high school it has been observed that the brightest girls frequently do not assert their brightness to the full for fear of jeopardizing their popularity (Coleman, 1961). Later on, many girls report that, to remain properly "feminine" in the eyes of the traditional "masculine" man, they "play dumb," pretend to be inferior in skills, tastes, talents, and intellectual ability (Komarovsky, 1946, Wallin, 1950).

One might expect from this that there would be more instability in girls' than in boys' professed self-esteem as they move from childhood into adolescent years. However, this has not been demonstrated conclusively. Unfortunately, the findings dealing with the constancy of self-regard through childhood and adolescence are rather meager.

Sex-Role Preferences
in Early and Later Childhood

Studies dealing with sex-roles have been based on a variety of methods, ranging from direct observation of play-activities to paper-and-pencil check lists. In work with children, tests using picture materials, toys, and checklists of preferred interests and activities have been employed to discover differences between boys' and girls' choices and the extent to which a given child selects "masculine" or "feminine" items.

Several studies of children have used what is known as the IT Scale (Brown, 1956, 1957). The IT scale contains a child-figure referred to as "IT," intentionally drawn so that it is ambiguous and not structured to represent a male or female, and a set of picture cards of objects and figures designed to represent things ". . . socially defined and identified with the masculine or feminine roles in our culture." A child is presented with sets of pictures and is asked to make choices for IT. For example, in one set the choice could be a picture of a rifle (selected as representing a "male" object) or a picture of doll and dishes (representing a "female" item). In another section, pairs of pictures representing male and female alternatives are presented (e.g., Indian chief and Indian princess, cosmetic articles and shaving articles) and the child is asked, in behalf of IT, to choose one from each pair.

In work with adolescents and adults, one procedure has been to submit a list of activities, interests, occupations, and descriptions of personality traits to members of a jury who are instructed to rate each item on the list on a scale with gradations such as MM (most masculine), M (masculine), M-F (neither distinctly masculine or feminine), F (feminine) and FF (most feminine). According to one group of raters, an MM item was "Take a trip through wild jungles." An FF item was "Select slip covers and drapes for my home." In ratings adjectives descriptive of personal traits, "delicate," for example, was judged to be considerably more feminine than masculine, as contrasted with "rugged," which was rated high as a masculine trait. Similarly, "dominant" was rated as distinctly more masculine and "submissive" as distinctly more feminine (Robinson, 1964).

In work with the IT Scale referred to above, Brown (1956, 1957) found that girls do not show nearly the same degree of preference for pictures representing the feminine role that boys show for the symbols of the masculine role. This characteristic is in keeping with some other findings. It has been found, for example, that only a small proportion of males say that they have ever wished to be a girl, while a larger proportion of females have at one time or another wished to be a boy. In a study by the author and his associates (1933) 200 boys and 200 girls in the age range from five through twelve years were asked "Would you rather be a boy or a girl (girl or a boy)?" Only one boy said he preferred to be a girl, while about 12 per cent of the girls said they would prefer to be boys, primarily because boys have more freedom and opportunities.

Findings obtained by means of the IT Scale with children between the ages of three and five indicate that some facets of sex-role differentiation appear at least as early as age three (Hartup, 1960). Findings in this study, as compared with findings obtained with older children, indicate also that girls are likely to express more feminine sex-role preferences (as determined by the IT test) at the preschool level than they will at any later stage of childhood. But even at this early level, the boys' preference for the masculine role was stronger than the girls' preference for the feminine role.

Not only do boys have stronger preferences than girls when faced with the alternative of making choices presumed to be appropriate for their sex, but they also seem to manifest clear-cut patterns of preference earlier than girls. This tendency emerged was in the course of a study in which children were asked to state their preferences from a set of toys, some representing those that conventionally are regarded as appropriate for boys and others as appropriate for girls (Rabban, 1950).[8]

Findings such as the foregoing are open to various interpretations. They may represent remnants of masculinity-femininity stereotypes that are in process of change. Lansky and McKay (1963) have presented findings which suggest that boys are becoming more variable in their choices and that today's parents are perhaps less likely than were their elders to apply pressures in keeping with traditional views regarding sex roles.

One interpretation of the above findings has been that pressures on boys to be masculine, and to eschew anything that might smack of femininity, is stronger than corresponding pressures on girls. Another assumption might be that males (both father and son) are more rigid and stereotype-bound than females, and that young girls are more versatile in determining what their preferences should be.

Informal observations suggest that boys are more guarded than girls in maintaining their sex role, as though it were a greater fault for a boy to be regarded as feminine than for a girl to be regarded as masculine. It is more shameful for a boy to be called a sissy than for a girl to be called a tomboy. (Apparently, however, girls undergo a change in this respect as they enter adolescence.)

Studies employing the concepts of masculinity and femininity have given

---

[8] Rabban also found that preferences for toys conventionally regarded as appropriate for either sex appeared earlier in his groups among lower-class children than among middle-class children.

considerably more attention to the more superficial social aspects and symbols of male and female roles than to an inquiry into what might be deeper-lying factors. Many of the earmarks of the masculine as contrasted with the feminine role seem to be rather trivial. But some of these earmarks probably have a more profound meaning than others. The question as to which "masculine" and "feminine" characteristics might be an outgrowth of capricious social customs and which might reflect a genetic difference between the sexes is almost entirely unanswered. In this area of child psychology, as in many others, questions regarding genetic origins have seldom been raised, much less answered.

Reflective Self-Awareness

Some time in the course of their development, as we saw early in this chapter, children become able, more or less, to reflect upon their own states of mind. They become able to detach themselves, as it were, from the unpremeditated flow of their experience, and to view it objectively. When they have achieved this level, they are able, to a degree, to begin to heed the ancient admonition, "Know Thyself."

Self-awareness or knowledge of self rests on a continuum ranging from little or no awareness at all to a sophisticated and profound form of self-inquiry. Take fear as an example. At the level of least self-awareness, a person is simply immersed in his fear, and swept by it. Something is added if a person can reflect, "Now I am really scared." He goes a step further, after the acute phase of fright has passed, when he asks himself, "Why am I afraid, why does this scare me?" Going still further (further than an unassisted child probably would go), he might inquire "What is there in me that makes me susceptible to this fear?" This inquiry might, in turn, have almost endless ramifications as he tries to delve into the past history of his fear, seeks to discover why he is vulnerable, examines his fear in the light of other concerns, recalls and mulls over dreams in which a similar fear has occurred, and so on.

Available findings offer no final answer concerning when children might begin to reflect about their feelings and motives. The most relevant answer comes from Piaget's studies, which center primarily on childrens' ability to examine the logical and impersonal aspects of their thinking.

According to Piaget, a young child's thinking is *egocentric,* as we noted in Chapter 7. His reasoning has a primitive quality which renders him unable to recognize that there are points of view other than his own. Egocentric thought is naive and unreflective. An egocentric person cannot, as an onlooker, take note of and examine his states of mind, or consider that there is any perspective other than that which appears within the spontaneous course of his own thinking. He is incapable of introspection, ". . . unable to uncenter himself . . ." (1959, p. 270) or to turn toward himself ". . . as a subject of knowledge" (1959, p. 273). He lacks both self-perception and objectivity (1954). To overcome egocentrism, according to Piaget, a child must become ". . . aware of what is subjective within himself" (p. 271).

According to Piaget, children's thinking is dominated by egocentrism until about the age of six or seven. However, he has also pointed out that the age at which children move from one stage to another in the development of thinking varies in any culture, and in one culture as compared with another (1964).

Piaget's description of egocentrism is offered primarily in the context of his account of children's ability to understand logical relationships and to grasp concepts of quantity, time, space, number, and other properties in the physical world. He does not dwell much upon the question whether the limitations in children's thinking when dealing with impersonal logical relationships also holds in connection with their thinking about more personal affairs, such as their feelings and motives, although he implies as much when he speaks of a child's lack of self-perception and inability to be introspective.

As a first step in an effort to explore the development of childrens' and adolescents' perception of and insight into their own and others' feelings and motives, the author and an associate (Jersild and Flapan, 1965) collected, with the help of parents, teachers and others, anecdotal accounts of situations in which children seemed to display a degree of self-perception. Such accounts cannot, of course, be regarded as solid research data, yet in the aggregate they suggest that at least some children at a rather early age are capable of some awareness of their states of mind. Following are a few examples:

> Wanda, aged three, was in a bad mood. Her mother tried to comfort her. Wanda said, "I don't want to be talkin to. I don't want to be holdened. I'll be back when I do." It seemed that Wanda was aware of her state of feeling and also was able to anticipate that her feelings might change.

> Someone had just called attention to Mabel, aged four, and everyone was looking at her. In this strained situation Mabel began to laugh, and then she said, "Sometimes people laugh when they don't know what else to do." It seemed that Mabel was able to recognize her own embarrassment and that she was aware of her way of coping with it.

> One day Carol's strict teacher asked Carol, aged six, a rather shy child, why a child as bright as she refused to take part in the reading group. Carol said, "I can't learn to read when I am nervous. Please be patient with me and let me read at my own fastness." Here it seems that Carol was aware of a state of mind and was making a plea to be understood.

Other records in this study describe instances in which children warned others about how they felt; predicted how they might feel in the future; identified a feeling and explained why they had it; and criticized themselves. Such expressions suggest that a more systematic study might reveal that young children are more capable of viewing themselves objectively than would be predicted from Piaget's account of egocentrism.

However, even if an inquiry into this dimension of children's thinking revealed trends similar to those described by Piaget, his account of childrens' thinking has significant implications in the present context. When Piaget noted that egocentrism is on the wane by the age of seven or so, he opened the door to possibilities in the realm of children's thinking which his followers have almost completely ignored. Investigations and interpretations inspired by Piaget's work have centered almost exclusively on children's ability to think logically in dealing with impersonal issues. If, however, as Piaget indicates, children after the age of seven, having passed beyond the first egocentric stage, are becoming able to introspect, to "uncenter themselves," to become aware of their own subjectivity, to turn to themselves as a subject of knowledge, we must assume that they possess some of the basic tools not only for understanding the rules of logic and the laws of natural science, but also for gaining an understanding of themselves.

Recommended Readings

William James' chapter on "The Consciousness of Self" in Volume I, *Principles of Psychology*, published in 1890, is a classic, interesting both from an historical and a contemporary point of view.

Many of the important writings on the subjective dimensions of experience reflect, to a large degree, an endeavor to reconstruct childhood experiences from the thought and theories of adults rather than from first-hand study of children. The literature includes writings on ego psychology, influenced largely by Freud, several of whose writings are listed in the bibliography at the end of this book, and writings that use the terminology of the self. Important books on the theory of the self include Carl Rogers, *Counseling and Psychotherapy: New Concepts in Practice* (1942); Prescott Lecky, *Self Consistency: A Theory of Personality* (1945); Arthur W. Combs and Donald Syngg, *Individual Behavior: A Perceptual Approach* (1959); George H. Mead, *Mind, Self and Society* (1934); Karen Horney, *Our Inner Conflicts* (1945) and *Neurosis and Human Growth* (1950); and Harry Stack Sullivan, *Conceptions of Modern Psychiatry* (1947).

Don E. Hamachek has compiled selected readings in *The Self In Growth, Teaching and Learning* (1965).

11

Children

and Their Parents

When we consider the role of parents in a child's life, there are a few facts and a few elementary principles that should be kept in mind. One simple fact is that a child and his parents are thrown together for better or for worse. A child has no choice and the parents have relatively little choice, at the outset, in determining what their child's make-up will be. They can choose to conceive a planned baby, but they cannot prescribe the combination of genes they will transmit to him. Barring an unsuspected genetic misfortune (that might produce abnormalities such as are noted in Chapter 3), they can be quite certain that their offspring, genetically, will resemble one or both of them to a degree far greater than chance. But the genetic apparatus works in such complicated ways that no parent can predict his child's genotype.[1]

---

[1] According to a well-known story, Isadora Duncan suggested that she and George Bernard Shaw together produce a child having his brains and her beauty. Shaw asked, what if the child should get his looks and her brains?

A further fact is that each child, from early infancy, has his individual temperamental and behavioral style. Other things being equal, a child who from the time of birth is inclined to be genial and adaptable, and who readily establishes a predictable rhythm in the routines of daily life will be easier to rear than one who is inclined in the opposite direction. Indeed, the surest way to be a good parent is to be fortunate enough to beget a child who is easy to rear. But even though their offspring has many qualities that are beyond their control, parents still have a vast leeway for exercising judgment and good will.

Parents' Attitudes and Personality Trends

A great deal has been written to advise parents regarding the countless practical details and decisions of everyday child care. Such advice may be helpful, but it may be rather futile. Any advice that prescribes one correct way of dealing with children is likely to be poor advice. No prescription for child-rearing can be equally appropriate for all children in view of their great individual differences. Moreover, such a prescription is likely to be doctrinaire, representing the "experts'" personal preconceptions or the prevailing fads. Notions about the right way to bring up children change with time, so that what is "right" in one generation may be "wrong" in the next.[2]

The underlying philosophy of child-rearing also undergoes change (see, e.g., Bronfenbrenner, 1961). For some time, at least until quite recently, the general drift was toward a "permissive" rather than authoritarian type of child-rearing. The idea of permissiveness also infiltrated many schools. Lately it seems that in the school, at least, the drift has been in the other direction, especially with an increased emphasis on conventional academic subjects. Pressures in school, increased emphasis on the competitive advantages of a college education, and the difficulty of getting into a chosen college, indirectly have induced a tightening of the reins on children in many homes, particularly in connection with homework.

The role of a parent obviously involves more than a succession of separate acts. His qualities and characteristics as a person will have an important bearing on his performance as a parent. Shirley (1941) has maintained that the attitudes and the personality of the mother determine the manner in which she administers each phase of child care, even in such matters as

---

[2] For an account of changes in emphases in recommended child-rearing practices see Wolfenstein (1953). In a book titled *Don't Be Afraid of Your Child*, Bruch (1952) writes sympathetically about modern parents who "have been exposed to a flood of advice on how to be 'good' parents." This advice comes to them through mass communication media "whether they ask for it or not." But despite all these instructions, according to Bruch, "modern parents are beset with the most amazing number of questions and worries" and it is they who take the blame if the child falls short of fulfilling all the expectations placed upon them.

bathing and dressing her child. From a study of twenty-five mothers, Behrens (1954) concluded that a child's upbringing is influenced more by the quality of the mother's "character structure" and its effect on the "total mother-child interaction" than by specific child-rearing practices and techniques. But it is not the mother's personality alone that is decisive. The father's personality is also an important part of the picture.

The child's own characteristics also influence the behavior of parents. As we have seen, in earlier chapters, children show marked individual traits almost from birth. Even one of a pair of identical infant twins may be, from the beginning, more hungry, robust, and demanding than the other (Burlingham, 1952). Regardless of a mother's personality or character structure, she is likely to deal differently with a rugged baby than with a very fragile and sensitive baby. In discussing this point, Coleman, Kris, and Provence (1953) point out, for example, that a child who readily accepts cuddling will elicit a different response from the mother than a child who does not. The fact that the parent-child relationship is interpersonal, and cannot be fathomed simply by viewing parental behavior as a cause and a child's personality as an effect, has been overlooked in much of the published research.

The "Psychological Parent"

In her treatise on the psychology of women, Helene Deutsch (1944–45) makes a distinction between a biological mother and a psychological mother. This distinction might be extended to include not just a psychological mother but a psychological parent. A biological parent, as the term implies, is one who has borne fruit by begetting a child. A psychological parent is one who, whether fruitful or childless, has the qualities of a fatherly or motherly person.

The concept of the psychological parent has wide implications, for practically all adults (and even many adolescents and children) are cast in a parental role. This is not confined to the family circle. Nor is it confined to persons who obviously function, continually or now and then, as surrogate parents such as a teacher, nurse, pastor, and doctor. A voter who cares about child welfare is a psychological parent; so is a janitor who is solicitous about the comfort of children in his building. A psychological parent might be defined as anyone whose attitude toward children, or childishness, is tempered by compassion.

The attributes of a fatherly or motherly person are likely to have their roots in early years while a growing child learns to accept and bestow affection. All other things being well, they are enhanced at the time of puberty and early adulthood when, according to H. S. Sullivan (1953), the biological capacity to reproduce is joined with a capacity for tenderness.

The concept of the psychological parent has been approached only obliquely in systematic research. But it is possible, in theory at least, to give a sketch of one who might qualify as a psychological parent. He must be able to bestow affection; to appreciate and respect a child as a person and derive some enjoyment from the child as a companion; recognize and make allowance for the kinds of childishness a youngster manifests because he is still a child; allow a child to lean on him for support, while not fostering dependency. A parent must also be able to exercise patience; (although not unlimited patience); and when necessary, to give a child's needs priority over his own comfort, and to endure fatigue and inconvenience. He must be able to tolerate a good deal of stubbornness, apparent stupidity, and seeming rejection.[3]

A psychological parent tries, as far as he is able, to understand before he passes judgment or punishes. He seeks, as far as his own emotional hardihood permits, to fathom his child's grievances, anger, discouragement, and disappointment. He is especially fortunate (and so are those in his care) if he is able, without undue self-reproach, to admit his mistakes; to accept himself as one who is considerably less than a perfect parent; to stand out against those who would stamp him as a "rejecting" parent when things go wrong; to see himself as one who, in the course of being a parent, will inevitably at times be angry, impatient, cranky, perplexed, unreasonable, confused and uncertain of what is right. A parent with such attitudes will admit to himself that there are times when he wishes his youngsters would get out of his hair, and he may allow himself to be skeptical now and then as to whether he ever should have become a parent.

All will probably agree that the most important ingredient in a psychological parent's make-up is the ability to love. But what is love? It is commonly thought of as a tender sentiment that enables a person to give another's well-being as high a rank, and perhaps a higher rank, than his own. But love is not all soft. Sometimes it is tough. It is tough when a parent endures a child's displeasure and anger even though the easiest way at the moment would be to over-indulge the child (and thereby, himself). It is tough when a sentimental heart says yes, but a considered judgment says no, and the no stands.

Nor is the harvest of love necessarily a harvest of sweet sentiment. It may be, and is, when a father exults and a mother's bosom swells in an overwhelming realization that their child has reached, for the time being, a height of happiness. But love's reward quite often is more somber. The price of love quite often is a price of pain. The outcome of love's labor quite often is sorrow, rather than joy. But to a parent who has loved a child—his own or a child who was his to care for—it is better, as the saying goes, to have loved and lost than never to have loved at all. In the ledger of a psychological parent, it is better to feel sorrow than never to have cared enough to grieve.

---

[3] Ability to tolerate rejection is especially helpful in a teacher serving as a surrogate parent for troubled pupils who are surly, angry, unwilling to learn, and who do not respond to intended kindness.

The "Accepting" Parent

A great deal has been written about an accepting parent as contrasted with a rejecting parent. An accepting parent is usually described as a loving parent. But love is likely to be most effective when a parent not only accepts his child but can also accept himself. A self-accepting parent will not simply be an easy mark, a pushover, unable to draw a line between a child's wishes and his own, or unable to distinguish between a child's wishes and the rights and duties of an older person. While granting his child the right to be himself, he remains convinced of his own rights—the right to say yes or no, the right to have and to assert his own beliefs, the right to be devoted to his child without becoming the child's slave. This aspect of the parent-child relationship presents difficulties to many parents. Frequently it is easier to shower a child with gifts and to indulge him (until his demands become unbearable) than to set limits, to deny the child something when, in the long run, it would be best to do so.

To be wisely accepting a parent needs to be realistic. Our culture cherishes the belief that if a parent really wills it he can be loving, patient, thoughtful, and wise enough to solve all problems. There probably is no human being who can be *that* loving, patient, thoughtful, and wise.

One mark of realism is to recognize that, no matter how glorious it is to have children, parents often have feelings and thoughts about them that are quite inglorious. This point is brought out in a study by Le Masters (1957) who interviewed forty-six young couples about their experiences with their first child. Thirty-eight (83 per cent) reported that they had faced an "extensive" or "severe" crisis in adjusting to their first child. Some of the experiences that made adjustment difficult (as reported by mothers) were loss of sleep, chronic fatigue, confinement to the home, having to give up social contacts and income from outside employment, guilt at not being a "better" mother, and worry over changes in appearance. Fathers echoed most of what the mothers said and added items of their own, such as a decline in the wife's sexual response, worry about a second pregnancy, and a "general disenchantment with the parental role." According to Le Masters, the crisis was not a result of not wanting children. Moreover, it occurred in a large number of marriages which were rated "good" both by the couples themselves and their close friends. Most of the couples also said that they were able to work out a sound adjustment as parents, although the transition was difficult.[4]

---

[4] When parents report difficulties in getting used to their first child, this does not necessarily mean that the first child has a rougher time than children born later. Lasko (1954) found that some mothers are less warm emotionally and more restrictive with their second-born than with their first-born children.

Another mark of realism is to recognize that there are limits to what a loving parent can do. He cannot spread his love over the entire landscape. He cannot always be there to assuage a child who falls into the hands of cruel playmates, or unfeeling teachers, or adults who have no love for children.

Consequences of Being Accepted. A child who has been reared in a climate of acceptance has many advantages. While still helpless and weak, the child can count on protection. He does not have to fight battles he is not strong enough to win. In an atmosphere of affection a child has an opportunity to acquire an attitude of confidence and trust in those who rear him. As he grows older he will be in a better position to develop his own capacity for affection for others. In a climate of affection and understanding he will have a kind of freedom—freedom to grow, to venture, to try and fail and then to try again, without always having to prove his worth or defend himself. He will be freer to express his feelings.

Probably the greatest advantage of being an accepted child is that the growing youngster will have a better chance to learn to accept himself.

Deviations From Normal
or Presumably Optimum Parental Care

It is generally believed that the best nurture for a child is provided (1) in the home; (2) with one person primarily serving as the mother; (3) in an intact family, consisting of an unseparated father and mother, providing (4) continuity in the child's upbringing in an atmosphere of loving acceptance. There are many deviations from this model.

Among the deviations, as described in the literature are: (1) homes in which one or both parents reject the child; (2) a home in which the continuity of mothering is broken by temporary separation, as when a mother, or a child, is hospitalized for a time; (3) a matriarchic home, where an unmarried mother presides; (4) a home broken by separation or divorce; (5) a fatherless home due to death or long absence of the father; (6) a partially motherless home marked by the absence during many hours a day of a working mother; (7) a home or substitute home in which there are multiple mothers; (8) no home, in the usual sense, as in the case of a child who is in an institution.

These conditions overlap. The institutionalized child, for example, frequently never has had a home with an intact family; if he has, he has been separated; and usually he is under the care of multiple mothers. There are many other deviations, such as those represented by an adopted child, stepchild, or orphan who is cared for by his parents' relatives.

The literature on child psychology frequently mentions "parental rejection" and "the rejecting parent." When used judiciously, these labels refer poignantly to the plight of children who are unwanted and unloved and subject to unkindness, ranging from constant disapproval or neglect to harsh abuse. Such children clearly have a hard lot. A truly "rejecting" parent is also a pitiable creature. His rejection, which may bring misfortune and tragedy into the lives of his children, springs from misfortunes and tragedies in his own life.

It is good to be cautious before labeling a parent as "rejecting." Accepting and rejecting attitudes are often intermingled. A parent may seem to be rejecting even if he is deeply devoted to his child. Moreover, the press of everyday life, and the need for setting limits on what a child can expect or be allowed to do, inevitably means that every parent is quite often regarded by a child as a rejecting parent. According to Anna Freud (1955) the concept of the rejecting mother has been used too loosely. She distinguishes between various types of rejecting behavior and points out that no matter how devoted a mother might be she cannot meet all the boundless demands made on her by her child.

Among the more extreme signs that a parent is rejecting his child, as described by one of the earlier writers on this subject (Fitz-Simons, 1935) are the following: A parent deserts a child or puts him into an institution (such as reform school or military school) to discipline him or avoid being bothered by him; the parent is able to see only the child's faults, and uses very severe punishment. Other items listed as signifying rejection are frequent criticism, threats to evict, locking the child up (in closet or basement), or deliberately frightening him. Still other signs of rejection, rated as somewhat less severe, include nagging, spanking, paying no attention to the child, failing to provide him with money or toys or advantages, comparing him unfavorably with others, making no effort to improve his condition through the help of doctors, teachers, and other trained adults.

One of these milder items by itself does not mark a parent as "rejecting," but if a parent habitually resorts to many of them, with no off-setting friendly ways, it seems highly probable that he not only lacks affection for his child but actually feels hostile toward him.

There are many other ways of rejecting a child. One can reject him by ignoring signs that he is afraid or is being mistreated at school. One can reject a child by promising to love him only if he is good or if he keeps clean or does superior work. One can reject a child by over-indulging him, giving in to him and giving him almost everything he desires in order to quiet him and be rid of him.

Over-indulgence may appear to be a form of over-protection, which on the surface looks very different from rejection. But over-protection is in many respects a way of rejecting a child by not giving him the opportunity to develop his own strength and ability to fend for himself. To develop his own potentials, as he grows older, a child must act for himself, think for himself, and assume some of the risks of everyday life.

Behavior such as the following has been regarded as a sign of an "over-protecting" attitude, as contrasted with a "rejecting" attitude: excessive contact of mother with child (sleeping in same bed, continually keeping within sight); infantile care prolonged far beyond infancy; lack or excess of parental control; indulging the child or caring for his physical needs to an excessive degree.

Consequences of Rejection

A child who is reared without affection faces a hard struggle. While young and weak he cannot count on the protection and help he needs. He is thrown on his own resources when his resources are very limited. He may be left for long periods, hungry, uncomfortable, angry, frightened, friendless, and alone.

A child who is not only ignored but actively abused (as some children are, even in infancy) does not have the strength to defend himself. His main weapon is crying. But when he cries in anger, grief, or fear his cries are likely to evoke complaint instead of sympathy. Under conditions of severe rejection a child is like a warrior who is wounded even before he has a chance to fight.

An older child carries a heavy burden if there is no friendly adult at home to blunt the edge of assaults which he receives from unkind playmates or teachers, or other members of the community who have a cruel streak. He is constantly driven back on his own defenses. If he withdraws within himself, he cuts himself off from the friendliness he might somewhere find. If he fights back, he is likely to meet further rejection.

A child whose faults are noticed while his merits are ignored is constantly failing in the eyes of others, and no one can thrive on a diet of complete failure. A child who receives no love will have difficulty learning how to bestow it. He will lack a model of love and good will that would help him to trust others, to count on their mercy, and to acquire love for others. Having received no affection, he learns not to expect it. He learns to expect nothing, or to expect the worst, and having learned that, his guard is up against everyone he encounters. But the more he guards himself the more he erects a wall between himself and those who might befriend him. The flow of fellow-feeling, so important in healthy relationships with others, is cut off. There is a rift between him and other people. But more, there is a rift also within him. Under a regimen of rejection and failure it will be hard for him to develop confidence in his own worth. If no one esteems him it will be difficult for him to learn to esteem himself.

In spite of all his handicaps, the plight of a rejected child is not necessarily without hope. In one of his studies of the effects of privation in early child-hood, Goldfarb (1945) gives a thoughtful account of ways in which a *rejected* child may have advantages over a *neglected* child. Although a rejected child is exposed to hostility, the chances are that parental feelings are mixed rather than completely rejecting. Moreover, he is less likely than a neglected child to lack stimulation. Indeed he may, if anything, receive too much harsh stimulation, but unkind handling may be better than no handling at all. He is at least in contact. He experiences the give and take of life which can foster his capacity and desire for entering into human relationships even though the "give" is cruel and the "take" is bitter. Moreover, the necessity for defending himself against unkindness can become a stimulus to his intellectual development. At any rate, he must devise such weapons as he can to fight back, and anger is a better tonic for growth than the apathy sometimes found in a child whose life has been a story of neglect.

Separation from Parents

In the normal course of development, many children exhibit fear and other forms of distress when separated from their parents. The cries of a child who is "lost" in a department store or at the fair grounds reveal this distress in acute form. Many children, old enough to understand what is afoot, cry and protest violently when their parents take off for an outing and leave a baby-sitter in charge. Often it seems that a child is not particularly afraid but is protesting against not being included in the outing, for his cries subside as soon as the parents are out of hearing, and he joins the baby-sitter as though no upset had occurred. Some children are distressed when their mothers leave home to be hospitalized, or when they themselves are hospitalized. Some children also appear upset when their mothers, for the first time after an extended stay at home, leave home to go to work.

Probably all children, at a given juncture in their development, would be frightened if accidentally separated from their parents in a strange place. Youngsters differ greatly in their response to separation of a more deliberate sort, however, such as the temporary absence of their parents, hospitalization, and the day-time absence of a working mother. When such separation is deeply rather than momentarily disturbing, it probably aggravates emotional difficulties that already exist.

The Institutionalized Child

Youngsters placed in institutions have been particular objects of research attention. Pronouncements regarding the institutionalized child at one extreme, paint him as one who is, of necessity, a blighted, tragic figure.

Judging from some accounts, any kind of institution is worse than a poor home. At the other extreme he is pictured as one who, in spite of his bereavement, can manage to do quite well.

The fate of institutionalized children has great significance from a developmental and social point of view. They are worthy of solicitude in their own right. And a study of their development can throw light on conditions that help or hinder the development of children in general. Their fate is particularly pertinent in view of the fact that many home-reared children in the lower rungs of the socio-economic system live in conditions that foster delinquency and are a threat to society at large.

Before reviewing findings regarding the effects of institutional life, it is well to consider who these children are. Children placed in an institution by reason of necessity (as distinguished from deliberate policy, as in the *kibbutz* in Israel) are children of misfortune. Due to bad luck, or poor heredity, or a combination of both, they are outcasts. Their parents either could not or would not care for them, or place them with solicitous relatives. Thus a selective process has been at work before they are placed in an institution and, in many instances, it continues after they are there. The most promising children, and those with the most endearing ways, are most likely to be selected for adoption. This leaves behind children who have twice been screened and twice rejected. Their parents would not or could not establish a home for them and potential foster parents have chosen someone else. The further development of these children will be determined, in the main, by their native endowment and by the attention they receive in the institution to which they have been consigned.[5]

Although some researchers have painted these children as facing a gloomy future, others have found a brighter side.

Among the studies that report the most damaging effects of being torn from the mother and placed in an institution are those of Spitz (see Spitz, 1951, and references in this study to earlier reports). Spitz describes dire consequences of loss of the mother in terms of such symptoms as emotional shock, apathy, anxiety, and *marasmus,* a form of wasting and withering away which cannot be explained in physical terms but is attributed to emotional starvation. Spitz's account is very moving, and even more moving are his motion pictures of the toll of *grief* in a child bereft of his mother. The impact of a child's tragedy, as portrayed by Spitz, remains even when one considers that he did not give an adequate account of the child's heredity or of the kind of institution to which the child was assigned. These factors must be taken into account, although they do not lessen the poignancy of the plight of suffering children.

---

[5] Many of the findings regarding the development of children in sub-standard institutions tell a melancholy story. Such findings do not, of course, tell what the condition of these unfortunate children might be if they had faced neglect and deprivation in a sub-standard home.

The effects of institutionalization cannot be assessed simply on the *a priori* assumption that the loss of love of a child's mother is bound to be damaging. It is necessary to ask, what is there in institutional life that differs from home life? How do institutions differ in what they provide and what are the effects, if any, of different types of care?

In a study by Rheingold (1959) careful techniques were applied to measure the attention five infants received from their mothers at home and the attention five babies received from caretakers in an institution. The babies ranged in age from 3.2 to 3.8 months. Very impressive differences were noted between the number of contacts home-reared babies had with their mothers and the contacts institutional children had with their caretakers. In terms of units of time, home infants received attention four and a half times more often than the institutional children. In terms of specific types of attention, the home-reared children were many times more frequently looked at, fed, held, talked to, patted, played with, rocked, and shown other forms of affection. On the other hand, the institutional children spent less time alone in their room, and frequently there were two or more adults in the room, as compared with usually one adult (the mother at home).

The infants in each group differed widely in their activities, as measured and recorded in this study, but as a group the home-reared infants did not differ materially from the institution-reared infants. According to Rheingold, "That no differences of statistical significance were found in the infant activities recorded suggests the possibility that wide as the differences in caretaking were, they were still not wide enough to produce differences in infant behavior." (There is still the possibility, Rheingold suggests, that differences in the behavior of the babies might show up if they were older, or that there might have been differences in forms of behavior that were not measured in her study.) One significant finding was that the attention individual children received at home varied far more than the amount of attention individual children received in the institution. But such variation did not produce corresponding differences in the activities of the infants.

Dennis and Najarian (1957) compared babies reared in an institution in which "mothering" and all other forms of adult-child interaction were at a minimum because the institution was seriously understaffed, with home-reared children who were brought to a clinic. The institutional children's average "developmental quotient," as determined by standardized tests, was approximately 100 (normal) at two months, but between the ages of three and twelve months the average was about 63. Dennis and Najarian conclude that ". . . the retardation prevailing between three and twelve months seems to be due to lack of learning opportunities in situations comparable to the test situations." The babies spent most of their time on their backs during this period, with little opportunity, in a sitting position, to practice various skills, such as following objects with their eyes or manipulating them with their hands. However, on tests at the 4½- to 6-year levels, the average developmental scores were about 90, leading to the conclusion that "Retardation in the last nine months of the first year . . . does not result in a generally poor performance at 4½ to 6 years, even when a child remains in a relatively restricted environment."

From their observations of the children's emotional reactions (such as crying, smiling, friendliness, tendency to show fear) Dennis and Najarian found ". . . nothing to suggest that emotional shock, or lack of mothering or other emotion-arousing conditions, were responsible for behavioral retardation." They believe that their findings pertaining to the retarding effects of being reared in an institution which provides a minimum of individual care ". . . can be interpreted in terms of specific kinds of restrictions on infant learning."

Rheingold and Bayley (1959) made a study of sixteen babies living in an institution during approximately the first nine months of their lives. From the sixth through the eighth month half of them, known as the experimental group, were cared for by one person during seven-and-a-half hours a day. These children received a considerable amount of personal attention. They became more socially responsive than the children in the control group who were cared for under the usual institutional routine. The two groups did not differ significantly, however, on various standardized tests while the experiment was under way. Fourteen of the babies were tested again at the age of nineteen months, after they had returned to their homes or had been placed in boarding or adoptive homes. On the retests, the children who had received special mothering while in the institution were more vocal than members of the control group, but apart from this the two groups did not differ significantly in their developmental progress or social responsiveness. The children in both groups were friendly, and they did not resemble the emotionally disturbed and mentally retarded children described in some of the studies that have been made of the effects of institutional life or separation from the mother.

The findings just mentioned and other investigations,[6] indicate that institutionalization *per se* does not necessarily have a traumatic emotional effect and that an institutionalized child may or may not show impairment in other aspects of his development. As Yarrow (1961) has pointed out, to assess the effects of institutionalization it is necessary to give careful attention to a wide range of circumstances including the child's developmental stage when he is first placed in an institution, the length of time he is kept there, and the conditions of life preceding and following this experience.

It is generally agreed, however, that lack of sensory stimulation in infancy and restrictions on self-initiated activity can seriously retard early development. Such retardation may be temporary, but to test what kinds of deprivation lead to remediable or irreversible impairment would require a long-term

---

[6] See e.g., Gavrin and Sachs (1963), Casler (1961), and Yarrow (1961).

study. As a child moves from infancy into early childhood, he obviously needs proper nurturing for normal emotional, social, and intellectual development. Such nurture, is of course, essential whether he is reared at home or in an institution. To find whether it is impossible in an institution to supply what is offered in a happy home would require more rigorously controlled studies than now are available.

Dramatic findings regarding what might be done to arrest or remedy the harm done to children in an inferior institution have been reported by Skeels, Updegraf, and associates (1938). The children in this study lived in an orphanage where the provisions for child care were grossly inadequate. The children were more on the defensive, less free to reach out for friendly care than normal children who had been cared for at home. They were backward in nearly all aspects of their development—in ability to handle the physical environment, in language ability, in ability to enter into the give and take of social interaction.

A special nursery school was set up in the orphanage. The children did not at first respond as nursery children normally do. Although they had been left to shift for themselves, they were less able to care for their physical needs than normal children. They did not know how to use equipment, such as blocks and wheel toys; they destroyed a good deal of property; their attention span was short; they tended to lose control of themselves when thwarted or frustrated by others. Behavior such as this, particularly destructiveness, poor impulse control, and aggressiveness, has been observed in other studies of neglected children.

One of the first necessities was to help each of these children to develop "consciousness of himself as an individual"—to become capable of achievement and able to receive consideration from others. It took about six months to bring them to the point where they were able to profit from the educational opportunities the nursery school provided but which had been lacking in their previous orphanage environment. But as a cheerful note, it should be added that the children who were placed in the nursery school, in the hands of devoted teachers, improved substantially after a time in their motor, social, and emotional behavior. Furthermore, the children in the nursery school maintained their level of intelligence while children in a control group within the same orphanage showed losses in IQ.

Findings in studies of young institutionalized children have varied so much, and, in most instances, background information about the children has been so meager, that no general conclusions can be made as to whether, and in what specific ways, institutional life *per se* will reduce a child's realization of his developmental potentials. There are some generalizations, however, that can be made. Childrens' development is likely to be retarded in an impoverished institutional environment. This retardation is likely to be most manifest, as time passes, in various forms of behavior which, in an appropriate environment, normally emerge at a given juncture of a child's development.

A child who has reached what normally would be the creeping stage will be retarded in creeping (and may never creep at all) if kept on his back on a soft mattress which does not permit him to roll over on a firm surface and gradually exercise and perfect his ability to creep (Dennis, 1960). Such a child is likely also to be retarded in his postural development, such as his ability to sit alone without support. This, in turn, combined with lack of opportunity and material for exercising manipulative abilities, may lead to retardation (and seeming impairment) in the intellectual sphere. A child who is deficient in postural control and in his eye-hand coordinations will be at a great disadvantage in performing the tasks included in a baby test. This will lower his score and give the impression that he is mentally retarded. Later, when the child is better able to exercise the coordinations involved through the impetus of his growth and his own effort, he may overcome such a deficiency. Dennis and Najarian (1957) found that children in an institution were retarded on a baby test during the first year but children in the same institution at about age five showed no signs of similar retardation on a performance test (the Goodenough Draw-A-Man Test). However, continued stay in an impoverished environment will cause widespread retardation in the development of normal motor skills (Skeels, Updegraf, *et al.* 1938). Likewise, children in such an environment will be retarded in language development, intelligence, and in their social and emotional development.

The evidence does not conclusively prove that institutionalization *per se* will impair a child's emotional development. To this a supplementary statement must be added—namely, that the timing of institutionalization may influence the emotional effects (according to findings reviewed by Casler, 1961). It appears that a child who has reached the stage at which he becomes discriminating in his affectional behavior, showing a definite attachment to one or more persons, may be more disturbed if institutionalized at this juncture than a child who is placed in an institution earlier in infancy. The development of affectional attachments was discussed in Chapter 6. We mentioned there that it occurs quite commonly in the third quarter of the first year, that it is often accompanied by fear of strangers, and apparently is linked with significant developments in the cognitive sphere. We stated also that children vary greatly in their tendency to show fear of strangers and in their versatility and resiliency in forming affectional attachments. Wide differences between children in these and other aspects of development probably account in part for the fact that even in inadequate institutions there are some children who seem to thrive.

Deprivation and Stimulation in Children and Laboratory Animals

The effects of severe deprivation on children parallel the effects recorded in several of the studies of laboratory animals. Both lines of study underscore the importance of stimulation. Both indicate that deprivation may have pervasive unfavorable effects in adaptive (or intellectual), social and emotional spheres. Both also reveal variable effects, indicating that there is no precise yardstick for measuring the point at which stimulation is inadequate and a state of harmful deprivation exists.

The parallels that can be drawn between studies of children and laboratory animals are limited, since it is neither possible nor desirable to expose children to the variety of experimental conditions that have been used with animals. Neither is it possible nor desirable to control the sampling of human subjects in investigations of severe deprivation. Human beings in such investigations have been pre-selected, as it were, by an unfortunate fate rather than by experimental design. Nor is it possible to control or precisely to equate the time factor. As compared with human infants, the "childhood" of animals most commonly used in laboratory experiments is so highly condensed that weeks, days, or even hours in their lives may correspond to a child's "formative years."

Although there are humane restrictions against deliberately giving human subjects less stimulation than they need, there is no restriction against giving them more stimulation than they normally would receive.

Findings regarding the effects of giving children an extra ration of stimulation have varied. In a long-term study, Gesell and his associates (1929) offered one of two identical twins (Twin *T*) a succession of special opportunities for learning beginning in infancy. In describing the characteristics of these two twins at the time of adolescence, Gesell (1941) states: "Twin *T* has been subjected to hundreds of hours of preferred and specialized training designed to improve her motor coordinations, her neatness, her constructiveness, her span of attention, her vocabulary,—a considerable variety of behavior attainments which have been recounted. There is no evidence that all these systematized experiences added either a cubit to her mental stature or a basic component to her individuality. . . . We should like to think that her present prowess in the 50-yard dash is in some lawful manner the full flower of her systematic training in stair climbing at the tender age of 46 weeks; but we cannot make the claim" (p. 118). This study, and several similar studies, do not provide a crucial test of long-continued deprivation. They do underscore the fact that the benefits a child might derive from extra stimulation (in the form of special opportunities to learn and coaching) are relative to his level of maturation. Other studies (referred to in Chapter 2) indicate that children at a given maturity level who seem to derive no benefit from efforts to stimulate their performance in one area may respond with remarkable gains in another area. Given a normal and an adequate environment, the effects of special attention a child receives will not depend on the amount of such attention but on its timeliness.

An experiment by Ourth and Brown (1961) with newborn children offers an interesting theoretical and practical approach to the question as to the timeliness of stimulation. These investigators took note of the fact that birth means an abrupt and radical change in a child's environment. But instead of assuming (as some have assumed), that a newborn child's environment might be somewhat overwhelming because of an over-supply of new forms of stimulation, they assumed the opposite—namely, that a newborn child is, relative to his preceding state, deprived of stimulation. Before birth he is firmly held within the womb, but this is a very stimulating environment, judging from what is known about the development of the nervous system before birth, the motility of the fetus during the later stages of pregnancy, and a child's ability at birth to respond to a wide range of stimuli. The fetus is constantly exposed to changing pressures and positional stimuli connected with the mother's movements; it responds to external sounds late in pregnancy and conceivably it might even dimly hear the mother's heart-beat. When expelled from the womb, lying with closed eyes in a nursery crib, a child is bereft of much of this stimulation. With this in mind, Ourth and Brown tried to simulate, after birth, the type of stimulation prevailing before birth. Each baby in an experimental group was given special mothering several times a day at feeding time. The mother held the baby, firmly wrapped in blankets, in close contact with her body, and gently rocked him. Babies in a control group were handled no more than was necessary in the course of routine hospital care. The babies who received the mothering prescribed by the experiment cried less than the babies in the control group, notably between feeding periods as distinguished from the period immediately preceding feeding. The authors of this study point out that more definitive research is needed to determine what the relation might be between a child's pre-natal condition and his post-natal mothering needs. A follow-up study would be also necessary to determine what effect stimulation of the pre-natal environment after birth has on a child's eventual adaptation to a normal post-natal environment.

Individual Differences
in Response to Deprivation

Although deprivation and stimulation may produce radical results, a given amount of deprivation or stimulation will not have similar effects on all children. Children vary in what might be the minimum amount of deprivation they can tolerate or the maximum amount of stimulation that will benefit them. Some findings from studies of infants are in accord with findings with laboratory animals reviewed in Chapter 6: dogs from genetically different strains showed a marked difference in their response to varying degrees of isolation as distinguished from being reared as pets (Fuller, 1966).

In a study of two pairs of infants, Escalona (1963) found that similar attention from the mother may produce varying effects on different children. A child's own self-initiated activity level makes a difference in his response to stimulation, or lack of it. A study by Schaffer (1966) confirms this finding. Schaffer's infants included a group of children who had been hospitalized for periods of from seven to thirty-one weeks and then discharged as fully recovered, and a baby-home group. The hospitalized infants lived under conditions of less variety and experienced considerably less social stimulation than the children in the baby-home. It appeared that hospitalization had a retarding effect on some children but little or no effect on others as measured by performance on a baby test. The amount of retardation was not related to the length of hospital stay. It was, however, related to the children's activity level. Tests administered at the end of hospitalization and again after the children had been under home care for a time indicated that the most active children were least affected by the restricted hospital environment. It appears that a highly active infant is better able than the inactive child to maintain a high level of stimulation. His activity maintains a stream of excitation within the nervous system. He is also able to add variety to his environment. By changing his position, he changes the array of visual stimulation he receives from his surroundings, thus decreasing what Schaffer refers to as the perceptual monotony that besets the non-active child. The study supports the point, made earlier in this text, that an important feature of a child's environment is what the child himself brings to this environment.

Later Effects of Severe Deprivation

The effects of severe deprivation, as recorded, for example, in the study by Skeels, *et al.*, are likely to become more marked if continued over time.

Findings regarding the long-term effects of deprivation in an institution do not yield a clear conclusion because of unknown elements that enter the case, such as prior background and the factors which decide whether a child will be taken into an adoptive home or kept under institutional care. For this reason, it is not possible to disentangle what is cause and what is effect in the plight of those who remain for long periods in a state of neglect under institutional care. But whatever the cause and effect factors might be, the story of such children is a sad one.

According to Goldfarb (1945), a child residing in an institution that is depriving, lives within narrow horizons of experience. There is no one with whom a child can identify; no one in whom to place his trust; no model he is moved to emulate; no stimulus that impels him to foster his individual resources. He is likely to be restless, unable to concentrate. Having had no emotional anchorage, it will be difficult for him to become genuinely affectionate toward anyone. He will be stunted in his capacity for fellow-feeling and in his ability to adapt to the pressures of ordinary social give-and-take.

Here we see a child, who, having been abandoned, abandons others, and even abandons things through which he might strive to reclaim his birthright.

One characteristic of a deprived child, as described by Goldfarb, is his inability, as he grows older, to think in sweeping, conceptual terms. Unlike a normal child, he is tied to perceptual details and is unable to free himself from the concrete. He cannot think big thoughts or let his mind rise from the practical and particular into the abstract world where what is possible, conceivable, and imaginable resides. A neglected and deprived child, according to Goldfarb, unlike a rejected child, is left empty-handed; he has no weapons for retaliation, no substance on which to build, except a bleak tenement of emptiness.

Long-term effects of deprivation have been reported in a further study by Skeels (1966). After a lapse of twenty-one years a follow-up study was made of thirteen children who had been transferred from a regular orphanage environment to a more stimulating environment within the orphanage; eleven of these were later placed for adoption. These were compared with children in a "contrast group" who had remained in a non-stimulating orphanage environment over a long period of time. At the beginning of the investigation, the children in the "contrast group" had a somewhat higher level of intelligence than those in the experimental group.

As young adults the children who had received special attention in the orphange, and most of whom had later been adopted, showed a favorable history of development. All were self-supporting or functioning as housewives. None was a ward in an institution. Half of them had completed the twelfth grade, and four had gone on to one or more years of college. The picture of the "contrast group" was rather grim. One of the members had died in adolescence following prolonged residence in a state institution for the mentally retarded; four were still wards of institutions, one in a mental hospital and three in institutions for the mentally retarded. Half of the group had not gone beyond the third grade. Those who were employed, with one exception, held rather menial jobs.

The difference between these two groups indicates that a stimulating environment and the nurture offered by devoted mother-surrogates can produce a radical change for the better in orphans who, in early childhood, have been reared for periods ranging from seven months to somewhat over two years in a sub-standard environment.

The implications of this study are that a planned program of intervention with an enriched environment might have almost incalculable value for children who are born into poverty and a condition of maternal, social, and cultural deprivation. This is the human side of the picture. There also is a social and economic side. Skeels estimates that the cost to the state of rearing children who remained under what was essentially custodial care was about five times greater than the cost of the provisions made for the experimental group in his study. Moreover, the costs to the state, in caring for the "contrast group," will continue to be high in years to come for at least four of the twelve original members of this group.

**Multiple Mothering
and Quasi-Institutional Care**

In addition to studies made in the usual orphanage, there are several other sources of information about the effects of maternal deprivation and multiple mothering. Prominent among these is the center for training in home-management provided here and there by university departments of home economics. Another prominent source is the *kibbutz* in Israel.

The later development of children who as infants had been residents in a university home-management house was studied by Gardner, *et al.* (1961). These children, subsequently adopted and available for study, were compared with continuously home-reared classmates in the age range from eight to seventeen years. The home-management children were recruited from an agency in charge of children awaiting adoption. Since it was impossible to go back and match these children, as infants, with home-reared infants, the matching in the follow-up study was made primarily on the basis of IQ, age, age of parents, and socio-economic status.

Babies in the home-management house had been admitted at an average age of five months, had resided in the house an average of a little over five months, and had been placed for adoption at about the age of one year. This means that most of them had spanned the period regarded by some investigators as crucial in an infant's life (the period during the third quarter of the first year when affectional attachments are formed and fear of strangers is most likely to appear). Furthermore, the children from the home-management group had experienced several presumably unfavorable conditions. They had been removed from their own mothers, placed with an agency, then placed in a home-management house, and later placed in an adoptive home. While in the home-management house they had both multiple and discontinuous mothering, as one squad of students after another successively took charge of them. In other words, their history differed radically from that of the usual home-reared child and from what, theoretically, is the best kind of rearing.

When compared in later years with a control group, one personality test favored the children who had not been exposed to unusual upbringing, although not quite to a statistically signfiicant degree; and there was no significant difference between the two groups in school achievement, personal and social adjustment, anxiety level (as measured by the children's response to a manifest anxiety scale) or response to frustration.

Findings such as these might be questioned. How typical of disinherited infants were those selected for residence in a home management house? How much of the difference between these and regularly reared children might be washed out by matching them according to the matching criteria that were used? As against this, the findings are likely to carry a ring of truth to anyone who has personally observed the great range of resiliency infants show in adapting to the vicissitudes of life and to anyone who has personally known the type student who elects to be a "mother" in a home-management house.

The Israeli *kibbutz* offers a fascinating field for study, equally alluring to those who have an earthy concern about children and those who come with a batch of theories.

The *kibbutz* is a voluntary type of settlement, with a collective form of economic and social life, and with communal provisions for rearing children. According to Rabin (1965) the adults in *kibbutzim* (plural for *kibbutz*) vary in their political ideology, but more or less typical provisions prevail. The children reside in their own separate quarters at first, in an infant house, and later in shared quarters, apart from the domiciles of their parents. At first the mother comes to feed (preferably breast-feed) her newborn child, but later the contacts between parents and their children occur at arranged periods —such as after working hours and other times when the parents are free.

The *kibbutz* offers the child conditions that, theoretically, have been regarded as unfavorable to child-rearing. There is partial "maternal deprivation," in the sense that the mother is not physically in continuous attendance, and there is multiple mothering, in that during most hours of the day a mother's place is taken by a surrogate mother, a nurse called a *metaplete*—one who takes care. The details of child-care in the *kibbutz* have, it seems, been influenced with the passage of time by the fashions and winds of change that blow through all child-rearing theories in the world at large.

Although findings have varied (probably, in part, because procedures in the *kibbutz* and the preconceptions of researchers have varied), it appears in the main that there is some retardation during infancy in the children's intellectual and social-emotional behavior; a reversal of such retardation later on; a picture, at the age of late adolescence, of a person who has developed into a rather well-balanced individual, and who, compared with other young people, is less given to sibling rivalry, has a greater concern for the social good, less pressure of long-term ambitious goals, and somewhat less equanimity, and more conflict, with regard to sex.

There are interesting sidelights in published reports about *kibbutzim* children. The classical Freudian Oedipus triangle apparently is blurred in the *kibbutz*. Boys and girls who share the same sleeping quarters and bathroom facilities to the age of about eighteen do not apparently become promiscuous, as some might have feared. Strict taboos on sexual intimacy, combined with, or producing a degree of modesty and desire for privacy among girls, apparently makes this situation less provocative than it might be under other circumstances.[7]

---

[7] For studies of *kibbutz*-reared children, see Rabin (1965), Golan (1961), Fried (1960), Arnon (1961), and Kaffman (1961).

Children of Working Mothers

In several studies it has been found that children of working mothers develop in much the same fashion as children whose mothers remain at home. A mother's outside employment apparently is not likely, *per se*, to have unfavorable effects. When children of working mothers do have difficulties, these are likely to arise from factors which also have an adverse effect on the children of home-bound mothers (factors such as poverty, marital discord, a broken home).[8]

Children and Divorce

It is difficult to trace the effects of divorce on children since divorce is usually an outgrowth of a complicated family situation. The divorce may come as a shattering experience. It may represent a formality, legally acknowledging the dissolution of a marriage in which the partners have, psychologically, been divorced for some time. It may come as a great relief.

Over a thousand parents participated in a study by Burchinal (1961) of the effects of divorce on children of adolescent age. The findings indicated that children in homes broken by divorce do not fall into a class by themselves, with certain common characteristics that distinguish them from other children. They are as heterogeneous as children at large. It does appear, however, that children who formerly had perceived their home as a happy place are more disturbed by divorce than children who viewed their home as unhappily torn by dissension (Landis, 1960).

Since remarriage is a frequent sequel to divorce, many children must adapt themselves to step-parents. As in other circumstances, children can be expected to respond to a step-parent in their own diverse, individual ways. It is likely, however, that a step-mother's role is more difficult than a step-father's role. This point appeared in a study by Bowerman and Irish (1962) who compared information obtained from over two thousand seventh to twelfth grade step-children with similar information drawn from several thousand children of unseparated parents. Children with step-parents tended to report more stress, ambivalence, and less cohesiveness in the home than children living with their natural parents. As a group, daughters reacted more strongly than sons to the presence of a step-parent.

---

[8] For studies and reviews, see Nye (1959), Stolz (1960), Peterson (1961), Thomas, *et al.* (1961), Burchinal and Rossman (1961), Perry (1961), Radke-Yarrow (1963), and Siegel, *et al.* (1963).

Mixed Emotions

The full range of human emotions—anger, fear, and sorrow, as well as love and joy—enters into the parent-child relationship. When all goes well, the predominant feeling is affection. But frequently the feelings of children for their parents and of parents for their children are mixed. When children and parents have strong feelings that clash, they face a conflict within themselves. The label "ambivalence" or "ambivalent feelings" has been used to identify opposing feelings, such as anger and love or fear and love.

Ambivalence as Revealed by Children's Fantasies. Ambivalent feelings toward parents often appear in children's make-believe. In doll-play, for example, a girl, acting the part of a mother, spanks one of the babies unmercifully, or pets one baby while pushing another aside, or "feeds" one baby while letting the other go hungry. Here, on a make-believe level, mother is portrayed as punitive and unfair. The actual mother, observing this behavior, may dismiss it as childish play. Or (as the writer has learned in discussions with some mothers) she may secretly feel hurt, and perhaps openly protest against what the child is doing. One mother asked, for example, "Why does my daughter treat her dolls so brutally? She beats them. I have never given her that kind of beating."

In assessing the meaning of such make-believe play three things must be borne in mind. First, a child's make-believe does not just happen—it probably reflects something very significant in his experience. Second, a child's make-believe often, from an adult point of view, seems exaggerated. In spanking a doll a girl perhaps administers a more severe kind of physical punishment than she herself has received. But spanking may be the child's way of acting out, in a crude way, punishments which she has received (or might wish to administer) in a more subtle way. Third, a youngster who acts out his aggressive impulses is not necessarily more hostile or browbeaten than one who doesn't. Without additional information we cannot tell whether the mother of a child who spanks a doll is a more punishing kind of person than the mother of a child who never spanks a doll.

Many illustrations of the way in which children, in their make-believe and fantasies, seem to express mixed or ambivalent feelings toward parents and other members of the family were recorded in a study by Griffiths (1935) which remains one of the classics in its field. In her work with five-year old children in London and Brisbane, Griffiths obtained her data by means of stories, drawings, an "imagery test," accounts of dreams, and an ink-blot test. She states that children's ". . . daydreams and subjective ideas" differ from the ". . . objective crust of current thought . . ." and reveal significant insights into their emotional life.

Children's imagery and make-believe relating to parents express both negative and positive attitudes. "Crude and brutal imagery occurred not only in the records of children from poor and overcrowded homes but also in those of children from better homes." According to Griffiths, ambivalence is expressed not only toward the least-liked member of the family (such as a rival sister) but ". . . usually towards the most beloved individual . . . the ambivalence is most strikingly expressed."

As an illustration Griffiths describes a London boy who greatly admired his father (a carter skillful with horses), but also feared him. The boy spoke of an ". . . old man—some old man, any old man what's gonna catch me—he takes yer to his house and cooks yer and eats yer up. If he did that to me I would push the pot up and hit him and run away. . . . It is a bit like my dad when he gonna hit me . . . (but) my dad not really like that." Another boy was devoted to two babies in his home, but he also had many images such as ". . . a baby fell downstairs . . . a baby got killed by the soldiers." Yet another boy, a "gentle" child, apparently well cared for in a superior home, played happily at "mothers and fathers" yet also displayed antagonism, as, for example, in telling a story about a man who ". . . fell out of a window and was dead. And a 'copper' came along, and got a big pail o' crabs, and he dropped it on the man, and they eatin' the man all up."

Discomforts of Mixed Emotions

Parents and children alike commonly try to evade the meaning that underlies the raw and unpleasant emotions that enter into their relationships with one another. One way of dealing with uncomfortable emotions is to pretend they don't exist, or at least to play them down. If we ask a parent, "Does your child love you?" he is likely to say, "Yes, I think so, at least I hope so." But when asked, "Does your child hate you or fear you?" the typical parent is tempted to side-step the question or to say that while his youngster does get angry at times and may even be afraid at times, these feelings are merely transient ripples. It would, of course, be easier if all concerned could face the fact that unpleasant as well as pleasant emotions are intermingled in parent-child relationships, and frankly acknowledge this condition not as a glaring fault but as one of the simple facts of life.

How Does a Child Perceive His Parents?

To probe the meaning of the parent-child relationship we need to ask not only what the parents do and what they intend but also how the child perceives the situation. The child's view, of course, may be very different from what the parents have in mind. Ausubel and his associates (1954) have expressed this matter in the following assumption: ". . . although parent behavior is an objective event in the real world, it affects the child's ego development only to the extent and in the form in which he perceives it. Hence, perceived parent behavior is in reality a more direct, relevant and proximate determinant of personality development than the actual stimulus context to which it refers." [9]

Children's views regarding the characteristics of their parents can roughly be grouped into two classes: those that seem to reflect a rather generalized picture of what one or the other parent is like, and those of a more specific or particularized nature.

In several studies it has been found that children tend, in general, more often to view fathers as more dominant, more powerful, more inclined to punish, and more to be feared than mothers. Such views, to a considerable extent, resemble stereotyped sex-role expectations—the notion that it is masculine to be somewhat hard and feminine to be on the softer side. If such views are strongly held they will make a difference in how a child interprets his parent's actions and intentions in the give-and-take of daily life. In a given situation, a child may perceive his father as being angry, while in a similar situation he may regard his mother as tolerant and forgiving. If a youngster sees his father as severe and his mother as gentle (or the other way around) he is likely to run into experiences that will help to polish his mother's halo and to sharpen his father's horns. This is in keeping with the general observation that anyone with a strong belief is likely to seize upon evidence to support that belief.[10]

In daily life children's perceptions of their parents are more likely to be focused on particular aspects of the parents' actions and attitudes than to take the form of viewing one as more or less preferable to the other. A child may, for example, regard one or both parents as more critical of him than

---

[9] Other studies dealing with the ways in which children and parents perceive one another have been reported by Davidson, *et al.* (1958), Henry (1957), Jackson (1956), Kagan (1956, 1960, 1961), Emmerich (1961), and Matsumoto, *et al.* (1961).

[10] The tendency to react to parental behavior in terms of a preconceived notion is illustrated by the following account. During childhood a son (now adult) had viewed his father as rather harsh and unloving and his mother as an angelic, loving person. Once while recounting his grievances against his father he happened to have a vivid recollection of a daily occurrence in his home. Each evening he went to kiss his father goodnight, but to the boy this was not a pleasant thing for the father's cheek, unshaved since morning, when pressed against the boy's cheek, had a grating effect. Then something else occurred to the reminiscing son which he had not thought of before. As far as he could recall, his mother had never kissed him goodnight. He recalled also that sometimes, when saying goodnight, the father would inquire, "You are not angry, are you?" as though asking forgiveness for any harsh thing he might have done. Then other recollections of events that the boy, so to speak, had pushed aside emerged. Among other things he recalled an occasion when a family cow, which the boy was very fond of, was sold and as it was led away the father did a very unusual thing: he gave the boy a dime. Out of such thoughts emerged a new view of things. Perhaps, in spite of a lifetime of thinking to the contrary, it was his father, not his mother, who had been the tender one.

they are or ever intended to be. Another frequent misperception (as viewed by the parents) occurs when a child thinks his parents favor or admire a sibling more than they favor or admire him.

A child's perception of his parents in a particular situation may be a projection of his own feelings: if, for example, he feels self-reproachful about something he has done, he may picture his parents as being more reproachful than they are.

The pictures children form of their parents may be quite different from an objective assessment of them. Jenny's mother is away from home, at work, every day. Janet's mother is absent only for a half-day once a week doing volunteer work in a hospital. But Janet, being dependent and demanding, may protest that her mother is always away from home, while Jenny, more self-sufficient says that her mother is always available when she needs her.

If parents had the courage and interest to inquire and children the freedom to respond frankly, most parents would probably be quite surprised by the pictures their children paint of them. In one instance a father asked his adolescent boy, "When you think back, what's the worst thing I ever did to you?" The father, remembering times when he, as a thought, had been too severe or too impatient, thought the boy would speak of one of these episodes. But the boy's reply was, "When I started school the teacher was strict, but at home you would talk things over with me, and in school the teacher wouldn't. So it was very hard for me to get used to school. And that is the worst thing you have done to me."

The Idealized Parent

A child may think that his parents are worse than they really are, but he may also regard them as being much more noble, saintly, and reasonable than they are. In either event, the misperception makes it difficult for parents and children to communicate with one another. In one of the writer's studies, a boy confessed to his mother that his teacher had punished him that day. Why? He had used bad words. "What words?" The boy shrank back, "I can't tell those words to you—they are not fit for a woman's ears!" The words apparently were not unfit for the coarse ears of the woman who was his teacher, but they could not be spoken before his mother, who he regarded as too pure to listen to such words.

The more idealized a child's picture of his parents, the more difficult it may be for him to go to them with some of his problems. If he pictures his parents as being especially virtuous, he may prefer to remain silent, unwilling to confess his faults to parents who seem so perfect. Here we have an interesting paradox. In theory, parents should set a good moral example for their children. But when parents set such an example, they may create a barrier between themselves and their children. Probably every child has committed at least a small theft or had an impulse to steal. But his parents—they are not thieves! If they ever stole or had an impulse to steal, he will not realize it. So he is psychologically separated from them. He cannot openly go to them, as one thief might go to another. Probably every healthy child even while quite young, has been involved in sex play, or has had fantasies about forbidden sex behavior. But if he regards his parents as being sexually pure, not only in their actions but also in their thoughts, he is separated from them.

Keeping the Image Alive. A child will perceive his parents' behavior as something to admire or rebel against depending on his interests and desires at the moment and also—as time passes—on his need, once he has taken a position, to cling to it and even to justify it. Consequently, an older child or an adult in telling about the kind of treatment he received from his father or mother may be consistent with the view that he has taken but not consistent with the incidents that occurred, as another person might interpret them. At the adult level it appears that many persons find it very important to protect and defend an image they have of their father or mother. A father who was harsh may be pictured as a virtual Olympian character, or as one much harsher or much less considerate than he really was. Similarly, a mother may be seen in a glowing idealistic light or in distinctly unflattering terms.

The image we retain of our parents, as we grow older, will not only color our memories of childhood but also is likely to influence our perception of others who are father and mother figures, such as teachers. Partly because of perceptions carried over from childhood, a certain instructor is a wonderful person in the eyes of one student while another student regards the same person as a lout.

Perceptions carried over from childhood and a desire to preserve these perceptions are likely to influence the meaning individuals derive from studying child psychology and even the studies on which child psychology is based. When, for example, scholars advocate differing theories about parent-child relationships or report conflicting research findings, the main reason probably is that conflicting forces actually are at work and the relationship is hard to untangle. But part of the reason may be that each scholar is influenced by his individual preferences or prejudices as he theorizes, defines the nature of his problem, sets up the design for his study, and interprets his results.

Self-Assertion in a Child-Parent Relationship

In striving for independence many young children go through a phase when they are especially resistant or "negativistic."

In many children, resistance in relationships with their elders becomes most noticeable at about eighteen months and peaks at about the age of four (Reynolds, 1928). This is the time when many children are busy acquiring and asserting what we call "a will of their own."

Resistant Behavior as Related to the Larger Context of Growth. Some children, while going through a "negative" or "resistant" phase, seem to be stubborn just for the sake of being stubborn. Resistant behavior, however, is related to the larger sweep of a child's development. When a child begins to be especially obdurate, at about the age of two, he is experiencing a phase of growth in which significant things are happening to him. His "life-space," the world in which he lives, has expanded greatly beyond that of infancy. He is able to walk and has far more ability to explore and discover. He is able to understand a great deal of what others say and he can judge, better than before, what they expect of him, and what they intend for him to do or not to do. He has begun to talk, is advancing rapidly in his language development. One word he uses frequently is "I" (or "me" or "mine") and he also often uses the word "no." These words mark him as one who is strongly preoccupied with his own undertakings.

The "negativistic" child is, in many ways, a little baby, yet his sphere of action is very broad. Many paths of self-assertion are open to him. He lives in a big kingdom, but as a child he is still a little king, bound by many restraints. He not only resists many of these restraints but also is testing the limits, testing his ability and right to have a say of his own. Viewed in this perspective, the "resistant phase," while trying to his elders, can also be a fascinating expression of a child's impulse to venture into life.

Some Effects of Resistance on Parents. A child's resistance is in many ways a threat to the self-esteem of those who care for him. A parent who likes to think of himself as a reasonable person faces quite a test when his child rejects his tidy reasoning. Similarly, if an adult likes to think of himself as unusually generous and forbearing, his child's sturdy stubbornness will threaten this cherished self-image, and such a threat is tough on any parent. On the other hand, a child's resistance, although not in itself easy to take, may give parents a great deal of satisfaction. If they are not unduly hampered by a compulsion always to be right and to appear right, they can get quite a thrill out of their child's self-assertiveness.

Forms of Resistance

In a young child, resistance frequently takes the form of failure to carry out a request he quite apparently understands, or seeming not to hear or understand a request, or being stubborn about eating and the entire daily routine, or many other small acts of self-assertion. Children sometimes carry their resistance to the extreme of refusing to urinate until they no longer can control the urge, or refusing to take food or to swallow, or vomiting, or holding their breath until they become blue in the face.

Resistance may also take the form of bickering and argumentativeness and continuous questioning after an answer has been given. An example was the case of a two-and-a-half-year-old child who had become extremely disputatious. One day his father was telling this boy and two other children about a chicken farm once owned by the boy's grandfather. Some of the chickens on this farm, the father related, were black and some were white. The boy interrupted to say: "Naw, they were not black and white, they were blue." This form of bickering shortly disappeared, almost as suddenly as it had arisen.

Varying Degrees and Areas of Resistance. In a study by Reynolds (1928), "negativism" (resistance), defined as refusal to comply with understood requests, was approached from several angles. Children were rated by their parents and by nursery-school teachers and were also observed under experimental conditions. The experimental situations afforded thirteen opportunities to be resistant (such as refusing to repeat numbers and continuing to play with blocks when asked not to). In this situation "resistance" scores ranged from zero (compliance with every request) to 12 (resistance to all but one of the requests). The average score was 4.38.

There was no significant resemblance between the negativism scores in the experimental situations and negativism at home or in nursery school as rated by parents or teachers of the same children. Everyday examples confirm this point. A child may be very stubborn with one person and cooperate fully with another, obliging in one situation and balky in another. A child who is stubborn and headstrong at home may be quite compliant and cooperative at school, or when visiting a neighbor. Accordingly, a parent and a teacher might have quite different views concerning a child's tendency to be compliant or resistant. What sometimes seems to happen is that a child discovers where and when and with whom he can safely assert himself.

The fact that youngsters are quite resistant in some situations and not in others sometimes leads to erroneous conclusions. If a child behaves like a little angel with a teacher or relative, and like a little devil with his own father or mother, the relative and teacher may feel that the youngster is a fine character, that they really know how to get along with him and that there must be something wrong with the parents. If, however, the child were theirs, and the person who is now the parent came and took over (without the protection of being an occasional visitor or operating within the bulwark of the school), it might be the parent who would look "good." [11] It is interesting to observe changes in a child's response to adults who shift their roles, as

---

[11] The fact that children in struggling to assert themselves often choose their own battleground can also be observed at later age levels. One result is that a child's "adjustment" may be viewed very differently by different adults. In a long-term study of school children (Kraus, 1956), it was found that a rather large proportion of children who were rated as not well-adjusted at home were rated as well-adjusted at school and a large proportion of those rated as not well-adjusted at school were rated as well-adjusted at home. Some children, of course, have difficulty both at home and at school, but many of them, it appears, choose where they will assert themselves or act out their problems.

when Grandma no longer is an occasional visitor but takes over during mamma's absence. The little angel who could not do too much to please a visiting Grandma soon shows a different face when Grandma begins to take charge.

Some Contributing Factors. There are, of course, many conditions that influence resistance aside from a child's own endeavors to assert himself. He is likely to resist if he is often needlessly interfered with, if he is prodded or pushed abruptly while already trying to obey a command, if he is frequently caressed and fondled against his wishes, if he is frequently teased or given contradictory commands, or if he is coerced in any way, whether roughly or by a person who is an expert at gentle coercion.

Resistant behavior is sometimes aggravated by the fact that people do not take proper account of a child's limited capacity for concentration. In playing with a child, adults often are tempted to overextend their attentions. If a child is just beginning to talk, for example, an adult may be tempted to coax him to repeat words or to speak new words. Such urging soon becomes tedious. Sometimes, too, resistance is a bid for attention.

Even in the best of homes a young child is subject to numberless "no's" and "don'ts," many of them spoken, many of them expressed through restraining gestures and other techniques that keep a child from forbidden ground. If these could be tallied, it no doubt would be found that the "no's" and "don'ts" to which a child is exposed are far more frequent than the "no's" and "I won'ts" with which he retorts. When we consider the amount of regimentation to which children are inescapably exposed at home and at school the remarkable thing is not that they resist but that they resist so little.

Resistance at Later Ages. As children grow older they usually show less resistance in the somewhat crude forms described above; but there are exceptions, particularly as they approach or enter adolescence. Open resistance may decline because an older child understands more clearly what is expected of him, is better able to circumvent or comply, or has learned that stubbornness does not pay. Or, resistance may decline because parents learn to be more astute in handling situations that are likely to provoke resistance.

Continuing Symptoms of Rebellion. Although overt resistance usually declines after the fourth year, it persists in one form or another throughout life. As a child grows older, his methods of resisting become more subtle. He pretends not to hear or understand, refuses to see the point, persists in referring to a topic that has been closed, carelessly executes commands, teases, resorts to indirect recriminations, and employs a number of other devices. At adolescence, many youngsters show a new upsurge of resistance, sometimes called the "second negative phase" and sometimes referred to as just plain mutiny. The "resisting" adolescent, like the child of two or three, is waging his own struggle for independence, sometimes in a way that gets him into serious trouble.

Resistant tendencies resembling those of children often appear in otherwise normal adults. A certain person may consistently "rise" against suggestions, go out of his way to eat or to wear what he has been advised against, or persist in mannerisms for no apparent reason other than that he has been urged not to.

Recommended Readings

Readings in the Psychology of Parent-Child Relations, edited by Gene R. Medinnus (1965), gives a compilation of original studies by various authors.

Behavioral Individuality in Early Childhood by Alexander Thomas and his associates (1963) and *Your Child is a Person: A Psychological Approach to Parenthood Without Guilt* by Stella Chess and her associates (1966) provide a previously much needed emphasis on the importance of taking account of a child's individuality in assessing parent-child relationships. *The Happy Family* by John Levy and Ruth Monroe, published in 1938, continues to be a timely, earthy, readable account of the satisfactions and frictions that arise in relationships between parents and children.

12

Patterns

of Parental Behavior

In this chapter we will examine some patterns of child-rearing and findings and viewpoints regarding the relationship between parental behavior and the personality development of children.

Much of our information about the interaction between parents and children has been obtained by directly observing parents and children, but most information has been obtained from parents' descriptions and claims in response to questionnaires, interviews, check-lists, and self-rating scales regarding their attitudes and practices. All these procedures have definite shortcomings, as we will see a bit later. But it is instructive first to examine some of the approaches that have been taken and some of the findings that have emerged.

Observational Procedures

When the method of direct observation is used, an investigator goes to the home and notes what the parents and children do and say as they interact with one another. The observer may simply go with pencil and paper and, during set periods of time, write down details as they occur, later classifying these under various headings—such as "coerces," "scolds," "praises," "shows affection," "answers questions." Or he may record what he hears and sees on a form or check-list, prepared after preliminary study. He may also, as a separate entry, rate or evaluate the behavior he observes.

Parental behavior in the home has been studied by Champney (1941) and Baldwin and his associates (1945, 1949), who devised and applied a form for evaluating the interaction between parents and children. Their findings showed syndromes or clusters of behavior in the ways in which parents dealt with their children. Some parents, for example, showed a preference for "democratic" practices. Other parents could be classed as "indulgent"— parents who seemingly were unable to separate their own personalities from the personalities of their children and who tended to give them too much care and protection. Parents were evaluated also in terms of their warmth, and their tendency to be rejecting. In a later study, Crandall and Preston (1955) used this same instrument and added a new category—"coercive control."

Evidence that the way an adult deals with children reflects certain motifs also comes from observation of teachers (H. H. Anderson, *et al.* 1937a, 1937b, 1945). Some teachers used what the investigators called "dominative" approaches to children while others used "socially integrative" approaches. The characteristics of the teachers seemed to persist from one year to the next, even though the teachers were dealing with different groups of children. In other words, whether a teacher is peremptory and bossy, or whether she enters into a relationship with an attitude of thoughtful give and take, depends not only on the characteristics of the pupils but also upon tendencies within the teacher herself.

Twenty-one mothers obligingly invited one investigator (Lafore, 1945) into their homes where she recorded the practices the parents used and the behavior of their children. No parent consistently used a single approach, but Lafore was able, on the basis of tallies of practices used by parents, to classify them into four groups as follows:

"*Dictators.*" Parents who usually followed a dictatorial approach and emphasized authority and obedience.

"*Cooperators.*" Parents who were predominantly friendly, who seemed to deal with children on a basis of mutual respect and who appeared to feel that if things could be explained, and if there could be joint action, unquestioning obedience was not necessary.

"*Temporizers.*" Parents whose approach seemed to be preponderantly "situational." These parents followed no consistent pattern of behavior, but seemed to fall into one situation after another. If the situation was pleasant they were pleasant; if the situation got out of hand, they became confused, without seeming to know what they should do, what they had done, or what they would do.

"*Appeasers.*" Parents whose approach was predominantly conciliatory and who seemed somewhat afraid of the child, as though he was in control. These parents tended to avoid issues and tried to circumvent problems that arose. Their apparent aim was to prevent trouble rather than to face an issue.

When we call a parent a "dictator" or an "appeaser," we are fixing him with an unpleasant name, and if the parents in Lafore's study read her account it is likely that some of them would recognize themselves and not feel particularly complimented. Yet all the parents in this study were concerned about their children and they definitely were cooperative parents; they were interested enough to allow an investigator to come into their homes and to see them as they were. Lafore speaks feelingly about these parents and their children, recognizing the strains and perplexities that arise in every family. In her visits to the homes she became convinced that each parent and each child was trying his best, yet she also noted ("with a feeling of pity") that they often worked at cross purposes.

Interview and Questionnaire Procedures

In a study of patterns of child-rearing, Sears and his associates (1957) used a carefully developed interview form to obtain information regarding the way in which parents dealt with aspects of child care such as cleanliness, aggressiveness, sex behavior, care of property, noisiness, and toilet-training. Comparisons were made between parents differing in socio-economic status.[1]

Sears and his associates found that mothers tended to express similar attitudes in dealing with various aspects of child care. Mothers who reported a permissive attitude toward aggressiveness, for example, also were more likely to express a permissive rather than a severe approach to such matters as sex, cleanliness, care of property, noisiness, toilet-training, and use of physical punishment as a means of discipline. The correlations between ratings of attitudes shown in various aspects of child care were not high but most of them were positive. An exception to this occurred in attitudes toward quarreling and other forms of aggression directed against others and directed against

---

[1] For other instruments that have been developed for assessing parental attitudes, see Shoben (1949), Schaefer and Bell (1955), and Markley (1958).

the mother herself. There was "virtually no correlation between permissiveness of aggression toward them (the mothers) and toward other siblings or other children." Many mothers applied one set of standards to interaction between children and another to interaction between children and themselves.

While the Sears study (in common with others cited here) demonstrates certain prevailing trends in the attitudes of parents, we cannot conclude that knowledge of one facet of a parent's personality will enable us safely to infer what another facet might be. Sears and his associates found, for example, that a permissive mother "was not necessarily a warm and affectionate one."

In a study of the way in which parents carry out their roles, G. B. Watson (1957) undertook to locate parents who were "permissive" and parents who were "strict" in their discipline with a view to examining the effects of such discipline on the personalities of children. Watson and his associates worked in a suburban community in which most of the parents were above average in income and education; they selected only parents of "normal" children living in "good" homes where children were "wanted, loved, and well cared for." Watson used a questionnaire designed to find how parents managed each of thirty-five fairly common situations, such as feeding, sleeping, dressing, toilet-training, and cleanliness. To each situation the questionnaire provided three possible responses, ranging from clearly permissive to strict standards. Weights were assigned to the responses so that the total possible score ranged from 35 (meaning the choice of the "strict" response to every one of the thirty-five items) to 175 (meaning the choice of the "permissive" response in every instance).

No parent according to his or her own report was consistently either "strict" or "permissive." The range in scores was from 55 to 158.

Watson then undertook to make a special study of parents who were distinctly permissive as compared with others who were not. This part of the undertaking was not easy, for, as Watson says, "the first surprise of the study was our difficulty in finding parents who were fairly consistently permissive."

Responses of Children
to Child-Rearing Attitudes and Practices

How do children respond when their parents show certain predominant trends in their behavior? This question can best be answered if treated as two: What day to day relationship, if any, exists between parental behavior and the behavior of their children? What answers can be found when we try to establish a long-term cause-and-effect relationship between parental behavior and a child's personality development?

Baldwin and his associates obtained ratings, by teachers and observers, of the nursery school behavior of children whose parents' behavior at home had been observed and evaluated. In the study by Watson, children from permissive and strict homes were rated by their teachers.

The findings in these two inquiries did not lead to any sweeping conclusion that a given mode of parental behavior can be counted on to produce a given type of child. On the whole, however, it appears likely that children from permissive or democratic homes will be more active in their relations with their peers, show more initiative, produce creative ideas, and tend to be more enterprising, freer to express their feelings, and less conforming. Children subjected to more rigid control are likely to be more restricted in asserting or expressing themselves through playfulness, disobedience, or aggressive behavior. Children whose homes combine warm acceptance with democratic procedures tend to be most active, free, and effective in asserting themselves in relations with their peers.

In Watson's study, children reared permissively did not differ significantly in a number of other personality traits that were explored. When rated with respect to a tendency toward happiness or sadness, there was a slightly larger proportion of children from permissive homes in both the "happy" and the "unhappy" categories, but the differences were unreliable. When rated with respect to "security-anxiety," there were no clearly distinct differences between the two groups. Half a dozen children from strict homes and half a dozen children from permissive homes showed "marked evidence of anxiety," while another half dozen from each category seemed to be easy and secure. Watson states that what makes for anxiety in a child must be something other than usually strict or unusually lax parental control.

In summing up his results, Watson points out that none of the personality differences found in this study appeared in all cases. "Some children from strict and some from permissive homes may be found at every level on every characteristic tested." Watson also states, however, that no clear personality advantage was associated in general with strict discipline in a good home, and, where differences did appear, these were more consistently to the credit of the more permissive upbringing.

Watson points out the complicated interplay of factors in the development of personality as related to parental practices. In his own words: "This study cannot distinguish the extent to which the advantages associated with permissiveness are due to that procedure alone and the extent to which more permissive parents may convey hereditary or cultural assets with which the permissive attitudes happen to be correlated. . . . Perhaps the kind of parents who choose the permissive role transmit, via heredity or via associated cultural influences, a different temperament or pattern of living. It should not be assumed that if parents who have heretofore practiced strict discipline were simply to change over to great permissiveness, their children would thereby become more independent or cooperative. They might or might not. A correlational study cannot satisfactorily answer questions of causation" (Watson, 1957).

Lafore's study established that parents who frequently dictated to and interfered with their children received the largest number of expressions of hostility from their children. Parents who showed numerous instances of blaming, hurrying, punishing, threatening, and interfering had children who often cried. Children who were frequently threatened tended to show a good deal of fearfulness. Children who were cautioned most often tended to be low in resourcefulness.

Lafore describes Michael, an enterprising child of three years whose mother was labeled a "cooperator" but whose father was more of a "dictator." First we see Michael and his father:

> Michael and a friend are playing happily, sitting at a small table talking about eggs. Michael says "Eggs are pink." Tom, the friend, adds "Eggs are purple." Michael continues "Eggs are green." Michael's father interrupts. "Since when is an egg green? Michael, what is the color of an egg?" Tom says "Eggs are green, blue, and red." Michael's father says "No, Michael, what *is* the color of an egg?" At this point the father notes Michael's face and interrupts himself to say, "Did you get paint on your lips? Come here and let me see. Stand up. Did you put this in your mouth? Open your mouth." Michael says "No," but allows his father to pull him to his feet and wash out his mouth. When he is released, the situation is changed. Michael begins to nag and to ask plaintive questions, and after he and his friend sit down to painting once more the father again interrupts with instructions not to use so much water, not to get the paper wet, not to use a cup but a jar, not to take so much water, not to use a certain brush but another. When Michael calls attention to a painting the father scolds him for the "mess" he has made. . . . The record continues to show repeated interruption, interference, and commands, and after a time the two boys begin to throw clay at each other and the father orders the visiting boy to go home. Michael cries. Michael and his father argue, first about putting some blocks away, then about closing a door, and then about the father's order that Michael should play with blocks. Following this the father tries to undress Michael who kicks and scratches. The family cat approaches the bed on which they are sitting and the father pushes it away. Michael says to his father "I don't like you any more." His father replies, "I don't like *you* any more."

Another record shows Michael with his mother:

> The mother gave few commands, offered no interference, and instead entered into a good deal of give and take. Michael several times wanted to do things his own way but at no time did he say, "No, I won't." An example of how the two worked things out together appears in the following excerpt: His mother says, "Now let's see. How are the hands? I would wash them." Michael (who insists on doing things for himself) says, "I want to wash." His mother replies, "All right and try not to soil your clothes. Just wash the hands and that's all." Michael says, "I can do it myself." His mother says, "Of course you can. Now rinse them off. That's a very good job."

During the periods when Michael and his parents were together, the father *interfered* with the boy thirteen times; the mother three times. The father *dictated* fourteen times; the mother once. The father *praised* twice; the mother six times. The father *hurried* the child three times; the mother not at all. The father *blamed* three times; the mother never blamed Michael. The father *offered a reason* four times; the mother seven times. Both father and mother resorted to a number of other practices in which they were more alike than different in their treatment of the child.

Sears and his associates found that mothers who were anxious about how successful they were in child-rearing tended to have more aggressive children than mothers who did not worry unduly about the job they were doing. Similarly, there was some tendency for children to be more aggressive if mothers were dissatisfied with the way in which child-rearing interfered with their free time, if they held their husbands in low esteem, or if they disagreed considerably with their husbands about child-rearing.

So far in our discussion we have seen that it is possible, to some degree, to detect certain prevailing attitudes and tendencies in the way in which parents deal with their children, and some relationships between the behavior patterns of parents and characteristics of their children. The relationships between parental attitudes and personality traits of children, as measured by ratings and statistical computations are not, however, outstanding or consistently in one direction or the other.

In a large batch of other studies dealing with the effects of parents' attitudes and child-rearing practices on the personality development of children, the findings have varied greatly. Apparently, within a reasonably "good" home, there is considerable leeway in what parents can do without giving children a marked advantage or disadvantage that can be disclosed by the methods of study that generally have been used. (If more exacting methods were used, the story might be quite different; this subject will be discussed shortly.) When studies are made of an atypical group—such as delinquents—the evidence regarding a relationship between home conditions and children's behavior is likely to be more emphatic. The histories of many of these unfortunate youngsters show a record of broken homes, neglect, rejection, and other unfavorable conditions (Koppitz, 1957).

Histories of persons who become mentally ill also frequently give evidence of very unfavorable parent-child relationships, but findings dealing with the relation of parental practices and attitudes to mental illness in the offspring are conflicting and inconclusive (Frank, 1965).

Problems Connected with the Assessment of Child-Rearing Procedures

We face many questions when we try to assess a parent's influence on his child. What does a parent actually do? A record of his behavior supplies a partial answer, but such a record does not always answer the question: What were his intentions and underlying attitudes?

How does a child perceive what the parent is doing? In the preceding chapter we noted that the actions of the parent *as perceived by the child* may be more decisive than the actions themselves, as regarded objectively by someone else.

How does a parent perceive himself in his dealings with his child? We can ask parents to tell us, through interviews or in response to questionnaires and check-lists such as those mentioned earlier in this chapter, but how does a parent's perception of his actions and attitudes compare with the judgment someone else would make about him? In one study (Crandall and Preston, 1955) mothers rated themselves and were rated by a clinical psychologist who observed them in their homes. There was "only moderate agreement between mothers' self-ratings and the Home Visitor's ratings of the mothers' overt behavior." Correlations computed for twenty-two characteristics that were rated ranged from .59 to −.16 (half of the correlations ranged from .23 to −.16 and half of them from .26 to .59).

When a parent and an outside observer show little agreement regarding many aspects of a parent's behavior, we cannot be sure whose judgment to accept. A parent (in common with others) may conceal as much as he reveals, and both parent and observer may be misled. In the handling of anger and hostility, for example, one parent may "let himself go" when angry, openly showing his feelings, while another angry parent may remain smooth and unruffled. A parent who "lets go" may see and describe himself as a rather cantankerous person and an outside observer may put him down as a punitive parent. A parent who cloaks his hostility may look on himself as forbearing and patient, and an observer may also see him in that light. But a parent who shows anger may, in the long run, be a more comfortable person to live with than the one who works hard to conceal it. Similarly, a parent who seems fretful and freely admits it may produce less tension in the home than a parent who uses a great store of energy to keep his anxiety concealed from himself and from others.

Likewise, a parent who always seems to be unaggressive may be very aggressive but in ways that will not show on a self-rating instrument or in the records of an occasional observer in the home. His aggressiveness may be expressed, for example, in an "I can top that" approach. Before his son can finish telling about playing in a close baseball game, the father begins to tell about games *he* played as a child. He may also seem to be very permissive. He does not beat or scold his son for neglecting to mow the lawn, but at supper-time he tells about the large lawn he so faithfully mowed when he was a boy. Similarly, a parent may be anxious in ways that a self-rating form or the records of an occasional observer will not reveal. The parent's anxiety may be aroused when a troubled child makes a brave attempt to tell about his fears or his bitterness toward a teacher, but the record may only show a breezy, "Cheer up, things will get better."

Other questions arise, especially when we try to determine what is cause and what is effect in the interplay between parents and children. When parents and children exhibit similar excellent characteristics is this due to a common heredity or a common environment? When they do not fare so well, is this due to a common heredity or a common environment?

Differences among children in response to similar types of parental care have been noted in studies by Escalona (1963), who writes: ". . . very different actions on the part of mothers (or over environmental variations) may have very similar consequences in terms of their impact on the child's experience as reflected in behavior; and conversely, . . . similar or identical external stimulation may have varying and opposite consequences—in terms of the directions in which they alter behavior." (p. 242).

Due to variations in children's response to the same or different kinds of care, it is fallacious to take for granted that if a child is developing in fine fashion he must have had good mothering, and that if there are deficiencies in his development he must have had poor mothering. Escalona points out that a given child may fail to respond to others in a normal way because he has not had a mother who responded to him as normal mothers do. If so, his impairment is due to an environmental deficiency. But a child may fail to respond normally even though his mother has tried to give him all that mothers usually give to their children. He may be so constituted that he cannot respond with normal patterns of interaction. This may be due to an inborn defect. Such a child ". . . is just as motherless . . ." according to Escalona, as a normally equipped child without a mother.

Children's Temperamental Qualities and Child-Parental Interaction

Some children are by temperament easy and others are difficult to rear. This point is brought out in the studies by Thomas, *et al.*, referred to in Chapter 7, dealing with children's "primary reaction patterns" or "temperamental style."

One combination of characteristics found quite commonly in a youngster called an *easy child* to rear (who is "usually a joy to his parents, pediatricians, and teachers") is regularity in his physical rhythms, such as sleeping, elimination, and desire for food; a positive approach to new conditions when these are first introduced, such as a new food or any change in daily routines; high adaptability to such changes as time goes on; and a tendency to show predominantly a positive mood of mild or moderate intensity, such as a ready smile and genial acceptance of attention, without a tendency to be fussy or cranky (Thomas, 1966).

At the opposite end of the continuum is a youngster called *the difficult child*—irregular in his bodily functions; a predominant tendency to withdraw from anything new; low or slow adaptability to change; frequent negative moods and predominantly intense reactions (including both loud laughter and loud and frequent crying). These children are not easy to feed, to put to sleep, or to bathe or dress, and tend to protest or cry when confronted with new foods, faces, activities, or other novel events. Being less adaptable and spontaneous and less resilient in facing changes in their environments, they are subject to frustration where another child would take things in stride. There are, of course, children with constellations of qualities varying from those described above.

Thomas and his associates ". . . found no evidence that the parents of difficult children are essentially different from the other parents." Nor do the studies ". . . suggest that the temperamental characteristics of the children are caused by the parents." It is apparent, however, that children with a "difficult" constellation of temperamental characteristics require patient and wise management if they are to be spared from stresses leading to behavior problems.[2] The outcome, for better or for worse, will depend on the nature of the interaction between a child and his parents. Thomas points out that the same parents who are relaxed and consistent with an easy child may become resentful, guilty, or helpless with a difficult child, depending in part on their own individual reactions to stress.

Parents' Perception and Recall of Behavior

Many studies of the behavior of children as related to the attitudes and practices of parents are based on information obtained from parents orally or in writing. The procedures in eliciting information have included interviews which more or less permit the parent to tell his story in his own way. Frequently the information has been obtained by presenting a parent with a detailed set of questions or statements, offering a choice of answers, such as *yes* or *no* to questions of fact, and *I agree* or *I disagree* to statements pertaining to attitudes or opinion.

What is the meaning of information so obtained? How authentic is it? These questions are rather crucial from a research point of view when we try to evaluate the influence of parents. They are crucial also from a personal and practical point of view, particularly when information obtained from parents is used as a basis of "expert" advice, or for diagnosing difficulties and for counseling, and so on.

Assuming that parents are replying as forthrightly as possible (in itself a

---

[2] A study by Friedman (1964) gives interesting case-study illustrations of how various mothers dealt with children who, according to predictions from their primary reaction patterns in infancy, would be easy or difficult to manage. One child, for example, who seemed destined to be "difficult," was led over the shoals of routine habit formation with a minimum of stress by an exceptionally patient, resourceful, and intelligent mother. Another child, who was predicted "easy," unfortunately had a less able and serene mother and ran into difficulties.

questionable assumption), the information they supply does not necessarily present an adequate picture of their attitudes and practices and their children's behavior. Their replies might reflect their present attitudes and procedures, but do not tell to what extent these may have changed. It has been found that parents' child-rearing procedures sometimes change with time, as more children come into the home. If so, the answers they now give with, say, their three-year-old child in mind, may not represent what they did in rearing older children in the family.

Even when parents are trying to be as truthful as possible, how much and what part of the truth do they single out to tell? An interesting study by Ingraham and Videbeck (1965) bears on this issue. Records were made of the activities of ten families, with one to three children, during a family meal. As the families ate, remotely controlled video cameras and microphones recorded what happened and what was said. In addition, an observer watched each family from behind a one-way mirror that overlooked the dining room table. Such records were kept during two meals. Eight of the ten families reported that they felt quite at ease in this situation and the tapes indicated that as the meal progressed little attention was paid to the cameras. (The presence of the equipment may still have had some effect.)

At intervals of three and six weeks after the second meals, the fathers and mothers were interviewed, at first through questions that offered as few reminders as possible of what might have taken place and then with two lists of more specific questions. One list included questions asked about feeding behavior in an interview form prepared by Sears, *et al.* (1957), referred to earlier in this chapter. The questions were adapted by having them center on the two family meals. (Questions in this list covered items such as table manners and problems about eating enough or eating the right foods.) The parents in the study were also given a list of fifty descriptions of behavior which could have occurred and did occur in the experiment but not necessarily in all families during the meals (such as a child stuffing too much food in his mouth).

A comparison between items of behavior that occurred (as shown by the recordings) and items correctly recalled indicated that 56.5 per cent of the incidents were not recalled by the parents (even with the aid of a list of items that might help remind them). Along with this, 22 per cent of the behavior the parents "recalled" as having occurred actually did not occur.[3] Accurate recall also was low when separate computations were made of behavior commonly regarded as "problem behavior."

These findings indicate that parents' memory for events occurring in a family situation is fallible, to say the least. It would be interesting to compare these results with adult recall in a comparable situation that did not involve their own children. There probably would be a great discrepancy between

---

[3] If the parents' responses were scored according to the right minus wrong formula commonly used in grading true-false test items, their score would have been almost zero.

details that occurred and details recalled. However, the findings in this study are quite consistent with other studies of parents' recall of events in the lives of their children. Thomas, *et al.* (1963), point out that there is a wide discrepancy between what parents report when interviewed about their children's behavior and what they will report later when asked to give retrospective accounts of their children's behavior.

An impressively well-conducted study of parents' retrospective accounts over an extended period of time has been reported by Radke-Yarrow (1963). The children of the mothers in this study had attended nursery school where systematic records were kept of psychological and medical examinations, teacher ratings, and interviews with mothers. These children were from 6 to 32 years old when retrospective interview reports were obtained from their mothers. Approximately eighty variables or aspects of maternal care and childhood behavior were singled out for study.

The findings indicate that retrospective accounts given by mothers were, on the whole, quite undependable, both when they described the childrearing practices they had used and when they described the characteristics manifested by their children at an earlier age.

The percentage of agreement between the "baseline" data (at the nursery school level) and later recall was under 40 in connection with such matters as maternal warmth, parental strictness, parental agreement, and use of reasoning. There was a higher agreement—63 per cent—in recalling resort to physical punishment. Correlations between baseline ratings and later ratings based on parental recall of such child characteristics as aggressiveness, independence, and ability to establish relationships with others ranged from .38 to .25. Only one comparison (with respect to shyness) showed a correlation above .40.

Other studies of parents' retrospective accounts of their own practices and of the characteristics of their children reveal much the same trend. Robbins (1963) found that retrospective accounts obtained from parents of three-year-olds, compared with accounts they gave earlier in the course of a longitudinal study, were quite inaccurate. When questioned about their earlier child-rearing procedures, the parents tended to depict them as being in accord with the recommendations of experts in child rearing.[4] Wenar and Coulter (1962) likewise found that a large proportion of mothers, when re-interviewed three to six years after an earlier interview, gave different information about their children. Forty-three per cent of their statements were judged as differing from previous statements, and a sizable proportion of these (40 per cent) represented a rather extremely different version.

It is interesting that there is a considerable degree of similarity in the findings dealing with the dependability or accuracy of parents' retrospective accounts of their own and their children's behavior whether these accounts

[4] When mothers today are questioned, it appears that many claim that they have reared their children according to the earthy advice offered by **Benjamin Spock**.

pertain to past or quite recent periods. The average is somewhere in the range from 35 to 60 per cent. This average would be considerably reduced, if it were possible, statistically, to incorporate into it not only the historical details that are omitted, but details that are altered (from previous accounts) or distorted (as compared with objective evidence).

It is also interesting, and rather disconcerting, to note that a vast superstructure of pronouncements about child-rearing has been built upon the feeble foundation of retrospective reports.

The authenticity of information based on retrospective accounts becomes even more dubious when the information is obtained at a time of crisis. Most of the information concerning families that have been struck by mental illness, failure of a child at school, delinquency, and other misfortunes, is obtained after a tragedy has occurred. It is likely that retrospective accounts from persons who are in a state of turmoil will be even less dependable than accounts given under ordinary circumstances. What the afflicted parents and children say is likely to be colored by remorse, guilt, sorrow, anger, defensiveness, and the like. To assign blame in such a situation, as often is done directly or by implication, is bad enough; but it is even worse when the blame is based on highly questionable information. When trouble occurs in a child's life, it may be due to his parents' shortcomings, or it may be due to his own weaknesses, or it may be that both he and his parents have been caught in the same web of misfortune. But it is unlikely that retrospective accounts can reveal how this web was spun.

Differing Family Roles and Relationships

An illustration of how a child influences relationships within the family was given in an earlier reference to a study of identical twins (Burlingham, 1952), and it is pertinent, in the present connection, to consider a few additional details from this study. Burlingham noted that the twin who emerged from the prenatal environment as the more robust and healthy of the two demanded food ". . . more impatiently and with greater energy . . ." than the other twin. In a pair of twin boys, the hungrier of the two became the more aggressive. In a pair of twin girls, Bessie and Jessie, it was Bessie who ". . . screamed for her food hungrily . . ." and ". . . became the more passionate twin from then onwards." Moreover, ". . . the difference in behavior, which was initiated in the feeding situation . . ." continued to express itself in her relationship with her mother and with her twin sister and in her stubbornness. According to Burlingham, in the case of Jessie and Bessie it was possible to observe the mother-relationship in minute detail and to be assured that the behavior of the mother towards the children was equal except when the greater demandingness of Bessie enforced differences.

Within a family consisting of two or more children, each child has a role of his own which will be influenced by, and also will have an influence on, the role played by each of the other members of the family. Even identical twins (as we have noted) are not likely to play identical roles. One may be a bit more enterprising than the other, and this slight edge will make a considerable difference in determining who leads and who follows, who yields and who resists. The effects of such a difference may be so subtle that a visitor does not detect it. The twins look and act so much alike that he cannot tell them apart.

In a large family there may be a very complicated network of roles and relationships. An older brother who is a bitter rival of the brother next in line may "adopt" a younger brother and with him play the part of a kind, big brother. The last-born child, if considerably younger than his brothers and sisters, may be treated in a parental way by his brothers and sisters so that instead of having two parents he has a whole houseful of parents.

Within a large family there may be differences even in the names children give one another. The youngest girl, for example, is called Ann by everyone except her oldest sister, to whom she is "Baby" or "Honey." Little Sam may be Sammy to everyone except an older brother who affectionately calls him "Tootsie"—until "Tootsie" gets older and begins to object.

The varying roles that might be played by children in a family have been discussed by Bossard and Boll (1957). One may take the part of a responsible child, taking life seriously and being somewhat bossy with the other siblings. According to Bossard and Boll, such a youngster is often the first child, especially if a boy. Another role is that of the sociable, well-liked child—who may be the second child. Some of the other roles children may assume are: the social butterfly, the isolate, the irresponsible child, the sickly one, or the spoiled one.

No parent can predict the effect a second child will have on the first child or on the total family situation, or what effect a third child will have on the fourth, and so on. What parents do with one sibling will be influenced by the presence of other siblings. The way they perceive each child in the family, and the way the parents are perceived, will be inflenced by each of the other children.

Influence of Others on the Child

The influence a parent can exert is modified, as the child grows older, by the influence of peers, teachers, and other members of the community. A study by McGuire (1953) is one of several which discuss this aspect of personality development.

A child and his parents face an especially complicated situation if the standards established in the home strongly conflict with those of other parents and children in the community. In dealing with this situation, children sometimes adopt one line of conduct at home and another when with their peers. One boy who had learned to use "correct" English at home acquired a second set of speech habits (he called it his "dialect") when he went to school in a community where most of the families used poor grammar. For example, the expression "I don't have any" was changed to "I ain't got none" when he talked to his pals.

A child's teachers may also influence him in ways that are largely beyond the control of parents. Amatora and her associates (1954) rated teachers and pupils on twenty-two elements of personality such as kindness, sympathy, dependability, and thoughtfulness of others, and found a positive correlation between the personality ratings of teachers and of children on all the scales that were used. Amatora concludes that while a similarity between the personality of teachers and children does not prove that the teachers have caused the traits children display, the findings at least indicate that care should be taken to employ teachers with well-adjusted personalities. The interplay between the personalities of teachers and the behavior of children has also been brought out in a study by H. H. Anderson and his associates (1946), and by Herrick (1945); they observed, for example, that when a teacher is peremptory, or uses a cooperative approach, pupils are likely to respond in kind.

Cultural Influences on Parental Practices

Regardless of their own personal leanings, parents are bound to be influenced by the customs of their community. Various sections of society use somewhat different child-rearing practices, and even within a particular social group there may be changes from one generation to the next—or even from one decade to the next—in ideas about the right way to bring up children.

Changing Fashions and Philosophies

These changes may occur so swiftly that parents face one set of pressures in rearing their first-born child and a different set in rearing a later child.

Parents are sometimes swayed by fads and fashions in child-rearing and then regret it. Among a group of mothers interviewed in a study by the author and his associates (1949), there were some who had their first children when pronouncements made by the behaviorist, J. B. Watson (1928), were still very much in the air. (Watson had warned parents against the dangers of too much love. He admonished parents not to be demonstrative with their children.) Two parents stated regretfully that they had taken these pronouncements to heart in bringing up their first baby. Because of changing fads and their own spontaneous impulses, they used a different philosophy in bringing up their second child.

Varying child-rearing procedures in different cultures have led some writers to maintain that there are characteristics of temperament and personality which distinguish members of one culture from those of another. Such observations raise this question: Are the characteristics shown by children in any particular group "natural" or are they a product of the particular culture in which the children are reared? When we observe that most of the children in a typical American community are rather competitive and show a good deal of aggressiveness, it is easy to conclude that these common characteristics are a natural and inevitable feature of development. But when anthropologists maintain that children in some other cultures do not display these characteristics, we may wonder whether these simply reflect the way of life prevailing in a particular culture.[5]

In assessing the influence of cultures that seem quite different, it is necessary to inquire whether the difference (in the display of friendliness, competition, aggressiveness) is genuine or real. People in various cultures probably differ considerably more in their customs and overt actions than in their underlying attitudes. A person who visits another culture can easily be misled by the surface appearances. An example of cultural differences that are more apparent than real is offered by Hallowell, who observed Indians of the Saulteaux society living in a region east of Lake Winnipeg (1940). According to Hallowell ". . . to the casual observer, cooperation, laughter, harmony, patience, and self-control appear to be the key notes as described a couple of decades ago, of Saulteaux interpersonal relations." These people seldom showed anger, seldom fought, showed a spirit of mutual helpfulness, and on the surface everything seemed almost idyllic. Yet, Hallowell pointed out, this picture ". . . does not expose the deeper psychological realities . . ." of Saulteaux life. On closer acquaintanceship, Hallowell found powerful currents of hostility and aggressiveness in this society, but these were expressed indirectly in ways that often seemed more vicious and harmful than an open show of hostility. For example, the Saulteaux resorted to gossip (such as saying scandalous things behind a person's back). They also used covert insults instead of direct assault. Another indirect expression of hostility was by way of sorcery and magic. Hallowell points out that while there were no *official* records of murder among the Saulteaux, murderous intentions had been and were expressed through sorcery and magic.

The position that an outsider can be led into faulty generalizations about the character of people in a certain culture from a superficial evaluation of child-rearing practices in that culture is also set forth by Kerlinger (1953), who takes issue with generalizations that have been made by several an-

---

[5] Among anthropologists whose studies of cultural differences have received a great deal of attention are Mead, Benedict, Gorer, and Kluckhohn. Studies in this area have been discussed by Whiting and Child (1953), and Kerlinger (1953). A symposium under the chairmanship of H. H. Anderson (1960) discusses outcomes of similar studies conducted in a number of different countries. A collection of studies of child-rearing in six cultures has been published under the editorship of B. B. Whiting (1963).

thropologists regarding characteristics of the Japanese. The writer's own observations while residing in Japan similarly led him, as time passed, to question the validity of much he read in books about the differences between the character of Japanese and Americans. On the surface, people in various cultures may differ considerably, but the closer we come to the underlying currents of human experience the more they turn out to be alike.

Recommended Readings

The readings listed at the end of Chapter 11 are again recommended.
Patterns of Child Rearing by Robert R. Sears, Eleanor E. Maccoby, and Harry Levin (1957) combines a wealth of research findings obtained from parent interviews with an interpretation of these findings from a practical and theoretical point of view. John W. Whiting and Irvin L. Child in *Child Training and Personality: A cross-cultural Study* (1953) and Beatrice B. Whiting in *Six Cultures* (1963) have compiled findings and studies dealing with practices in various cultural groups. David P. Ausubel's *Theory and Problems of Child Development* (1958) discusses many facets of the parent-child relationship, emphasizing the principle that to understand this relationship it is necessary not only to examine the parent's conduct and attitudes but also to consider the characteristics and perceptions of the child.
G. H. Frank, in a review of literature on "The Role of the Family in Psychopathology" (1965) has ably shown that generalizations regarding the role of parents must be viewed with considerable caution.

13

Children

and Their Peers

FIRST STEPS

IN THE SOCIAL WORLD

Most children are skillful in dealing with older persons before they learn to play a role with children their own age. Even after establishing comfortable relations with his age-mates, a youngster frequently comes to adults, as though using them as a base from which to make excursions into the world of his peers. He is likely to step out among his age-mates with more assurance if he feels secure about his relationships with adults.

Beginnings of Social Response

As set forth in an earlier chapter, one of the most noteworthy aspects of an infant's early social development is his smile in response to other persons. During the first two months of life, infants begin to fix their eyes upon their mothers' faces and smile. For a time, infants who are "smilers" will smile at any face, whether familiar or strange. Then, at about half a year or within one or two months thereafter, they become more discriminating.[1]

When babies first begin to smile in response to a person, they tend to respond indiscriminately whether the person is smiling or shows an angry expression. Likewise, they do not discriminate between a friendly and an angry tone of voice (unless the angry tone is loud and startling). Changes in an infant's behavior in this regard were studied in an experiment by Bühler and Hetzer (1928) and reviewed in Bühler (1933). The experimenter bent over a child and first smiled then broke into an angry expression; she spoke kindly to the child and then used scolding words and tones. She made inviting and then threatening gestures with her hands. At three and four months, babies reacted positively to the angry as well as the kind word and look. At five to seven months the babies tended to reject the assumed expression and to cry at the sound of the scolding voice and threatening gesture. At about eight to twelve months the babies began to revise their reaction to the un-friendly expressions—apparently realizing that the expressions were assumed and did not really denote anger or unfriendliness. At this age the children would begin again to smile—sometimes after several seconds of hesitation. The babies were able to view the seemingly disapproving expressions as a kind of play.

Response to Other Children

A child begins to notice another child his own age at about the age of six months, and during the following months his interest in other children becomes more active. Before the age of one year, many children pay brief attention when another child cries. Some babble to gain attention, or actively attempt to exclude another child from their sphere of activity. It usually is not until considerably later that cooperative play with another child occurs.

When Babies Meet

A "baby-party" technique, consisting of placing two or more children together, has been used to investigate young children's reactions to one another. In one such study (Maudry and Nekula, 1939) children showed relatively little social interchange or response to one another up to the age of about nine months. From nine to fourteen months, the children continued

---

[1] This shift, as we saw in Chapter 6, is part of a larger complex of developments, in-cluding increased perceptiveness in the cognitive sphere, fear (or wariness) in response to strangers, and the beginning of selective affectionate attachments to one or more persons.

to give more attention to their surroundings and to play materials than to one another, and when they did interact they frequently pushed one another aside.

From fourteen to eighteen months, there was a gradual transition to a more positive sort of social response. By the age of twenty-five months, social responses and interest in play materials became more closely integrated. At this time, also, friendly and cooperative interchanges predominated over negative responses.

At about the age of two years, some youngsters are quite sensitive in their dealings with other children. In Maudry and Nekula's study, some children were especially sensitive if others excluded them. There also were some who showed a distinct preference for particular children. After children become active group members they are likely to show strong affinities, but it is instructive to note that even before the age of two a youngster may be drawn to one child and not to another. This aspect of human relationships has not been thoroughly explored, yet in the life of an older person, and probably also in the life of a young child, it is very important. The qualities that make a congenial relationship seem far more subtle than the gross features we commonly measure in tests of social adjustment or popularity.

Beginnings of Group Behavior

At about the age of two, normal children are definitely sociable with other children, but the give-and-take exchanges between two or more children are likely to be brief. When several children of this age occupy the same play space they take notice of one another, tend to gather in the same place a good deal of the time, and make contacts with one another. Much of the time, however, the children's activities will be *parallel* and adjacent—with occasional interchanges—rather than merged into a joint, continuing activity (Parten, 1932).[2]

After the age of three there is an increase in group activities, and such activities stretch over longer periods of time. By the age of five or six, children will sometimes play in groups of five or six members or more, but they usually prefer groups no larger than three (Green, 1933b). At this age, children will sometimes play with youngsters they don't particularly like in preference to spending all their time alone; they would rather have an uncongenial companion than no companion at all. The six-year-old undertakes a wide range of social behavior, including cooperation, friendliness, sympathy, competition, fighting, and quarreling.

---

[2] Many of the studies cited in this chapter go back to the 1930's and 1940's. During this period a great amount of research on early social development was conducted by the method of direct observation in settings in which children were free to select their companions and to choose and follow their own pursuits, such as on a nursery school playground.

As a child progresses from relatively little social interchange to participation with more and more children, lapses into earlier forms of behavior are likely now and then to occur. He may be a participator in one group and an on-looker in another. At any stage of growth, when a child faces a new social situation, his first tentative approaches may roughly reproduce the sequence in his early behavior (such as watching, parallel play, brief contacts with a few children) until he begins to feel at home.

"Natural" and Acquired Aspects of Social Behavior

The new forms of social behavior that emerge in early childhood are influenced both by learning and changes that take place within the child in the process of growth. Bühler (1933), in noting the emergence of smiling at about six weeks, observes that such smiling may have many antecedents, yet she considers it likely that the smile is an ". . . original and primary reaction to the human voice and look." A pair of infant twins in a study by Dennis (1938) were reared in a restricted environment until they were seven months old. They were well cared for, but in a stolid way: no one smiled at them or cuddled or fondled or played with them. But when they reached the age when babies usually begin to smile at adults, these babies smiled too. When they reached the age when babies usually laugh, they laughed, and they also showed signs of affection for their attendants. Such observations do not, of course, prove that these forms of behavior will occur without stimulation from the environment, but they do indicate that a child has a potentiality for being responsive to human contacts at an early age and that he will attempt to make contact with others even though he receives little specific stimulation or encouragement.

On the basis of continuing observations and tests of infants during the first two years of life, Shirley (1933a) concluded that children show a sequence of development in the sphere of social behavior just as they do in the sphere of motor development. She reports, for example, that manifestations of shyness and self-consciousness during the second year of life appeared consistently enough to suggest that they were not due to learning alone but were a normal outcome of growth. Observations such as these do not, of course, mean that social responses spring forth full-fledged, apart from environmental influences. But when, within a relatively uniform environment, a form of response emerges quite typically at a given juncture in a child's career it seems likely that it represents a new turn in the process of development rather than simply an additional bit of learning. It is interesting to note that the onset of self-consciousness in children in the presence of other persons, roughly corresponds in timing with a child's first signs of being able self-consciously to recognize his own image in a mirror.

Beginnings of Cooperation

Young children are likely to be more cooperative and friendly than competitive and hostile. The proportion between friendly and unfriendly responses will vary, of course, with different children and in different situations, but it is significant that in studies of young children the balance has run strongly in favor of the friendly forms of behavior.

After a child has begun to mingle actively with members of his own age group, friendly contacts are likely to be more frequent than unfriendly ones. (As mentioned in Chapter 6, children prior to this exhibit far more positive than negative responses in their reactions to adults.) In a study of two-year-olds, Mengert (1931) found that friendly actions outnumbered unfriendly ones by over four to one. In a later study of three-, four-, and five-year-olds, Walters and his associates (1957) noted that at all of these levels children were more affectionate than aggressive in their dealings with one another. In an observational study of preschool children, Stith and Connor (1962) found an interesting parallel between independence and helpfulness. With an increase in age there was a decrease in children's dependent contacts with adults and an increase in the helpful contacts they made with both children and adults.

These findings suggest that the potentialities for friendly, cooperative behavior are as strong as, and probably stronger than, the potentialities for self-assertive behavior at the expense of others. It might, of course, be maintained that the rather high level of cooperative behavior in young children is deceptive because they are urged and trained to act cooperatively and politely. However, as we will see in the next section, even when young children are left to work out their relationships with one another, with a minimum of exhortation from adults, they are able to achieve a remarkable amount of cooperation.

Group Loyalties

A fascinating account of the way in which children at an early age can form a social structure of their own is given by Freud and Dann (1951). They describe six young German-Jewish orphans whose parents had been killed during the Hitler regime. These youngsters, after being passed from hand to hand during the first year of their lives, lived together as a group (instead of being placed with families) in a reception center and later in a refuge called Bulldogs Bank in England during their second and third years.

These children, according to Freud and Dann, were without parents in the fullest sense of the word, not merely orphaned at the time of observation, but most of them without an early mother or father image even in their unconscious minds. Instead of having parents as objects of love, their companions of the same age were their real love objects. At first, when moved to a settled refuge, they centered their attention on one another, treating the adult staff members with cold indifference or with active hostility. They insisted on being together and became upset when separated, even for short moments. Although members of the group had individual preferences, they spontaneously shared and took turns. They were ". . . a closely knit group of members with equal status, no child assuming leadership for any length of time, but each one exerting a strong influence on the others." After several weeks in the refuge they began to show individual personal attachments to adults, but during their stay at Bulldogs Bank the ties of these children to the adults ". . . in no way reached the strength of their ties to each other."

These children, ". . . bypassing as it were the parent relationship which is the normal way to social attitudes . . . ," apparently found nurture in their relationships with one another. There was some impairment in their development (although distinct improvements were evident when, in time, adults began to play an important part in their lives) but, as described by Freud and Dann, they were neither deficient, delinquent, nor psychotic. Originally they spoke German with an admixture of Czech words, but in the new environment they learned English. According to Freud and Dann, their ability to acquire a new language in the midst of their upheavals bears witness to a ". . . basically unharmed contact with their environment."

The "experiment" into which fate thrust the children in the study by Freud and Dann is different from most of the psychological experiments conducted with children. The things we contrive in our studies usually are not made of such stern stuff.[3]

Other observations of ways in which children respond when their upbringing is, so to speak, left in the hands of their age-mates at a very early age are reported by Freud and Burlingham (1944). These children were uprooted from their families and lived together in an institution, where, for a time, they received only routine attention from adults. At an age when most children have become firmly anchored to the home, these youngsters were thrown into a world consisting mainly of their own age group. They had to "become social" at an age "when it is normal to be antisocial." According to the authors, "Under pressure of these circumstances they developed a surprising range of reactions: love, hate, jealousy, rivalry, competition, protectiveness, pity, generosity, sympathy, and even understanding." After a time, these children were divided into small units and placed in artificial families under the care of one adult acting as a foster mother. In this situation, their behavior changed. The adult rather than the peer group became the center of attention. The family arrangement had a very positive effect on the children's development, but for a time it introduced "disturbing and complicating elements" into their lives.

---

[3] In a paper privately communicated to the writer, Alice Goldberger describes these children as young adults. The total picture of these young persons' adjustment to life—including adoption, employment and marriage—is, so it seems, as favorable as one might find if six children, chosen at random, were followed from early childhood into adult years.

"Children who have shown themselves adaptable and accommodating under group conditions suddenly become insufferably demanding and unreasonable." Their jealousy, and, above all, their possessiveness of the beloved grown-up seemed to be boundless.

The studies we have just reviewed, dealing with children who were not living under typical conditions, definitely do not imply that a fatherless and mother-less child can obtain from his own age group all that he demands and all that he receives from a parent or a parent substitute. They do, however, reveal that children, even when very young, have a great capacity for supporting one an-other, and for influencing and being influenced by their peers.

Peer Preferences, Leadership, and Friendships among Young Children

Before the age of two, a child is likely, if there is occasion, to begin to show that he has preferences among the children with whom he has a chance to play, and by the age of three or four years strong attachments between two children often occur. Such attachments may last only a few days or weeks, but sometimes close friendships persist over a period of months and even years, although in the meantime each child has dealings with many others. One of the greatest fortunes of childhood is to have a close friend in whom to confide; one of the greatest sorrows is to lose such a friend.

In connection with one of his studies the writer had occasion to observe two boys who had a warm friendship, which had begun when they were two years old. At the age of six, one of the boys moved with his family to another locality, and the two saw each other only once in a long while. When they met after periods of separation there were no effusive greetings; they scarcely even smiled; yet they slid at once into an effortless kind of companionship, as though they had been together all the time.

Friendships among young children are influenced by such obvious factors as similarity in age, intelligence, sociability and interests, resemblance of one child to a previous companion or a sibling of the other, and resourcefulness in enlisting cooperation. But each friendship or apparent friendship has its own characteristics and may represent a wide range of relationships. A friendship may be based on real affinity between two people or it may be based on a more opportunistic relationship. One of the friends may be dominant, the other submissive. One may be the leader and the other a follower.

Leadership among young children takes many forms. One child may be a leader partly because he is voluble, mobile, and able to cover much ground. Another child may select and dominate the play activities of a group by virtue of aggressive methods and coercion. Still another child leads because he is re-sourceful in seeing new and original possibilities and in establishing friendly relations with other children.

Perhaps the most warmly accepted leader is the one who makes it pleasant to be a follower. Here is an example of resourceful leadership: Kirk had the knack of making another child feel important, while he himself was running things. On one occasion, he initiated a make-believe game of running a boat, using a big box. Kirk approached another child and asked him to be the captain, saying, "The captain is the big boss, you be the captain. I'll be the engineer." When the "captain" was installed in all his glory on the deck, the humble engineer, from below, ran both the captain and the ship.

The Friendless One

Occasionally we can observe a young child who seems to have no particular friends. This child may behave in a manner that makes others reject him. He may be ill at ease with other children and seek rather to associate with adults. He may be interested for the time being in following his own solitary pursuits. Or he may have interests that others do not share.

One such solitary child, observed in one of the writer's studies, was precocious in his language development; he used words other children could not understand. When he approached other children, they did not actively rebuff him but merely gave him an uncomprehending look and went their own way.

Sometimes, of course, a child is friendless because he has characteristics that other children find unpleasant. For example, a boy spent two years in a nursery school without ever, as far as could be ascertained, being warmly received by any other member of the group. This boy had a habit of poking about, edging up now to one group, now to another, and always announcing his presence by asking, in a somewhat whiney tone, such questions as: "What's that you're making?" "Why do you do that?" "What's that for?" He was not an alluring playmate, but he was trying in his own way to be accepted by others.

Methods of Studying Social Interactions

Before proceeding further, it is appropriate to take note of some of the many techniques that have been used to assess the social behavior and competence of young children.

One method is the method of direct observation. When this is used, an observer notes and records the behavior of children in their interactions with one another. This method, when applied systematically, includes a "time-sampling" procedure which insures that each child will be under observation during a uniform period of time, spread over a uniform number of intervals (such as being observed through twelve separate ten-minute intervals, on separate days with an intervening stretch of time, during the early, middle, and later periods of the nursery-school day).

The method of direct observation can be used in a free or structured situation. In a free situation, such as a nursery school or kindergarten playground, the children move about as usual and the observer adapts his movements and stance to them. In a structured situation, conditions may be manipulated in a variety of ways, such as "planting" things in the play space to elicit curiosity and questioning, or bringing children two by two into a staged setting, equipped with interesting things that might precipitate various types of behavior, such as sharing, competition, cooperation, dominant or submissive behavior, and the like.[4]

During recent years, equipment for tape recording sound and motion has greatly improved, greatly extending the "observer's" accuracy and reach. An ingenious method for multiple track recording of sound, with wireless transmitters, has been described by Herbert and Swayze (1964).

Another frequently used method is to obtain teacher ratings of members of a group of young children. Yet another method (among several) is to get children to rate or evaluate one another. In one such procedure, known as the sociometric technique, a child is asked, for example, to name the youngster (or youngsters) whom he would like most to have as a playmate, or for whom he would like to do a favor, or whom he would most want as a friend. The sociometric test can be administered in a variety of ways, ranging from simply asking a child to name his choice (or choices) to a more systematic procedure, such as asking a child to make a succession of choices when he is presented with pictures of his classmates, two at a time, so arranged that each classmate is paired with each of the others.[5]

Popularity and Self-Sufficiency

A young child who is most effective in social relations, and most popular, is likely to be one who combines sensitivity to the desires of others with a confident reliance on his own resources. This is underscored in a series of studies by McCandless and his associates (1961) and by Moore and Updegraff (1964). According to these studies, preschool children who depend heavily on adults are not likely to be popular. But the kind of dependency makes a difference. A child who is dependent on adults for *emotional* support (seeking reassurance, leaning on the adult as a helpless child might lean on his mother) is less likely to be popular than a child who leans on an adult for "instrumental" support—that is, seeks out an adult for practical help in carrying on his own designs. Moreover, it seems that a child who seeks help and support from his peers is likely to be more popular than the one who continues, as he grows older, to depend on adults.

---

[4] For an excellent account of methods of direct observation and the safeguards required in the use of observational techniques see Wright (1960).

[5] For a description of sociometric procedures with nursery school children see Starkweather (1962).

Beginnings of Sympathy for Peers

An important element in the social relationships of older children and adults is the capacity for sympathy and fellow-feeling. Unless a person eventually becomes sensitive to the joys and sorrows, hurts and satisfactions of others, he will be unable to enter into any degree of close communication with them.

When a child actively sympathizes with another, the experience combines *perception, feeling*, and *action* (or an impulse to act). The child must be able to perceive the signs of another's distress. He must be able to allow his own feelings to come into play. And he must be able to communicate his feelings through what he does or says.

A child's ability to perceive the misfortunes of others expands as his mind matures and as he learns, through his own experience, to appreciate the meaning of misfortune. In a study of nursery-school children aged two to four years, Murphy (1937) observed that the older children responded to a wide range of distress situations: they noted, for example, that another child had a bruised hand even though he did not wear a bandage. The older ones also more often actively tried to comfort, help, or defend a troubled child while the younger children were more inclined to stare or to ask anxiously about the distress of others.

A child's ability to feel sympathetic depends on many factors (Murphy, 1937). If he is deeply absorbed in his own concerns he may not be able to respond to those of others. If he is frightened by another's distress (as when another child is crying because of ill-treatment from a person whom the youngster himself is afraid of) he may be so absorbed in his own need to defend himself that he is unable to sympathize with the one who cries.

In observations of pairs of sisters, McFarland (1938) noted that a child's tendency to sympathize with another youngster depended not simply on the degree of distress shown by the sufferer, but upon the child's relation to this distress. For example, a child would sympathize with her sister if the sister herself got into trouble or if her distress was caused by someone else, but would fail to sympathize when she herself was the cause of distress. Children who were responsive to the misfortunes of their sisters tended also to be sympathetic toward others who were in trouble.

A child's sympathies are likely to vary, depending on what he has at stake. He may have a strong streak of sympathy but show just the opposite response if the other child's demands conflict with his own desires. Again, if a child's effort to be sympathetic is rebuffed, he may switch from a friendly to a hostile approach. (This change in attitude may also be seen in a child's dealings with animals: If a child tries to befriend a hungry kitten, the youngster's mood may change to anger when the kitten won't take the milk the child offered.) One child may be sympathetic when he himself is somewhat afraid and insecure and then grow less sympathetic as he gains in confidence, while another child may show the reverse tendency.

Expressions of sympathy in young children cover a wide range (Murphy,

1937), such as helping, removing or attempting to remove causes of distress, comforting, punishing the cause of distress, protecting and defending the distressed person, warning, telling an adult that another child is having trouble, questioning to discover the cause of trouble, suggesting or effecting a solution. When children are conscious of another's distress but don't quite know what to do about it they sometimes show their concern by disorganized responses such as watching anxiously, head shaking, frowning, compressing the lips, and crying and whimpering.

When two groups of nursery-school children were observed by Murphy (1937), the following frequencies of sympathetic response were recorded:

	Hours of Observation	Number of Sympathetic Responses	Number of Unsympathetic Responses
Group A	188	318	195
Group B	234	398	60

The children in Group B represented a wider age range and a higher average age than the children in Group A. The B Group also had a larger playground than the A Group. The ratio of sympathetic to unsympathetic responses, initiated and received, varied considerably from child to child. In the older group some children, when faced with another child's distress, almost always sympathized, while others of the same age seldom did so. Likewise, although intellectual ability contributes to the quality of sympathetic responses and to the insight a child might have into another's distress, the factor of intelligence was less influential than other factors, such as a child's interests and responsiveness to other children.

Youngsters who are active socially tend to show a larger number of both "positive" (friendly, cooperative) and "negative" (quarrelsome, rivalry) forms of behavior. This interesting aspect of social behavior has been observed in many studies. When the children in Murphy's study were rated with respect to sympathy and aggressiveness, the scores showed a positive relationship. The children who most often sympathized tended also most often to be aggressive. There were notable exceptions to this trend, however; one child, for example, stood near the bottom in his tendency to be sympathetic and near the top in his tendency to be aggressive.

Rivalry and the Beginnings of Competition

A child's first experience with competition usually occurs within the home. He may be the rival of one or both of his parents, demanding that he receive the affection and attention of one or both at the other's expense. If there are two or more children in the home, it is inevitable that some sibling rivalry will occur. Rivalry between siblings can be relatively mild or can attain an almost shattering degree of intensity and bitterness.

When a condition of intensive rivalry exists, it is sometimes openly displayed, sometimes not. It shows directly when a youngster tries to harm a baby brother or sister by smothering him, or by pushing him down the stairs, or by giving him a sharp knife to play with. It may appear indirectly as when a child in make-believe play with a "baby" doll sticks pins into the doll or threatens to put it on the stove and burn it. Sometimes, however, children suppress feelings toward a sibling rival and even convince themselves that no rivalry exists. There are adults who will say, for example, that they had no inkling of the intensity of their bitter feelings toward a brother or sister until they reached adult years. An adult who has acknowledged only a mild rivalry situation in his childhood may, in discussing early experiences (as in the course of therapy), come forth with an outburst of rage and a flood of tears.

If parents (or other adults) are obviously unfair or openly favor and admire one child more than another, it is quite understandable that the unfavored child might feel hurt. However, sibling rivalry illustrates the fact that we cannot understand what will happen in a *social* situation simply by studying the separate characteristics of each *individual* involved in the situation. Nor can the rivalry situation be averted simply by manipulating the environment. In a study of relationships between pairs of sisters, McFarland (1938) found, for example, that a policy of providing "two of everything" (two swings, two sand-boxes, two tricycles, two pairs of similar galoshes) did not prevent rivalry. Such things may not touch on the real sources of rivalry. The tricycle or swing may be the battleground but not the cause of conflict.

Rivalry becomes an especially acute problem if one or all the siblings in a family happen to have a strong streak of possessiveness, or if the children are especially demanding. Some youngsters seem much more inclined than others to want to establish a monopoly—to have everything for themselves, all the attention, all the care, all the favors. Others, even at an early age, seem to find it easier to share.

The *proportion* a child receives may to him be far more important than the *amount*. The same is true of adults. A person with sharp eyes and a keen appetite for pie is likely to be more contented if he gets a small but equal piece of a little pie than if he gets a much larger but unequal piece of a big pie. This tendency in childhood to demand a fair proportion has many ramifications in later life. We see this when an heir has inherited a fortune, which would leave most people gasping for joy, feels nothing but bitterness because, as he sees it, he did not get his fair share.

Early Manifestations of Competition

Competition for prestige and accomplishment usually comes later than competition for the affections of parents, but many children at the age of two, and more thereafter, show awareness of what another child is doing, and of their own showing compared with that of another. Such expressions as "I am older," "I am bigger," "Mine's nicer" are among the milder signs. One nursery school child, on learning that today was the birthday of a playmate, proceeded not only to claim that today was *his* birthday, too, but also to go the rounds inviting children to his birthday party.

In verbal "I-am-better-than-you" battles, the child with a superior vocabulary may have an advantage, as illustrated in the following encounter between two children:

> JOHN: I can count up to a hundred.
> FRANK: I can count up to a thousand.
> JOHN: I can count up to a million.
> FRANK: I can count up to a billion.
> JOHN: I can count up to a trillion.
> FRANK: I can count up to infinity.

Competition among peers is likely to be more prominent at the age of four and thereafter than at the age of three. In a study by Leuba (1933), children aged two to six were observed in an experimental room, singly and then in pairs, where they had an opportunity to play with a peg board. In the two-year-old group, the presence of another child did not seem to have much influence on what a child did or said. The children did not compete but were interested mainly in the materials before them. Three-year-old children showed they were aware of what the other child was doing. At four to six years, a majority of children revealed a desire to excel and an increased understanding of the idea of excelling. At six years, some of the children were also more critical in judging their own work than they had been before.

A similar increase in competition was found in a study by Greenberg (1932) of children aged two to seven years, observed while playing with blocks. Children aged two to four usually picked up blocks as they needed them, but four- to seven-year-olds more often cornered a supply. There was an increase with age in children's favorable remarks about their own work and a steady increase from one year to the next in the percentage of children who showed signs of competition (the percentages at three, four, five, and six years were, respectively, 42.6, 69.2, 75.4, and 86.5).

Competition at the kindergarten level has been in evidence when children are faced with a difficult task (Wolf, 1938). The children stayed longer with a task, on the average, when competing than when working alone. Some children, however, responded much less to competition than others.

Many instances of rivalry were noted in a study by McFarland (1938) of twenty pairs of sisters. Individual children were stirred to rivalry by different types of situations. An interesting finding was that pairs of sisters who exhibited rivalry most frequently were about as companionable as those who showed less rivalry. From this study, as we will note more particularly in dealing with cooperation and competition in older children, it is apparent that competition—while it may take the form of "going against" others—may be a part of a larger cooperative relationship.

Children's Aggressiveness, Fights, and Quarrels

The healthy preschool child not only cooperates, sympathizes, and establishes friendly relationships, but also bickers, quarrels, and fights. Children's fights and quarrels usually attract a good deal of attention from adults, especially if a youngster is in danger, or is very combative, or is a helpless target of the aggressiveness of other children.

Adult Attitudes toward Aggressiveness in Children and Their Own Aggressiveness. When a child fights (or cringes when attacked), he is likely to touch off feelings adults harbor regarding their own aggressiveness. Adults differ greatly in the way they handle their own aggressive impulses. Some openly attack (occasionally with fists but more often with the tongue) when in a fighting mood; others carefully control their aggressiveness, and among these there are some who have succeeded in persuading themselves that they really don't have aggressive tendencies; some cringe under the assault of aggressive persons and then go off with hurt feelings, muttering in their beards; some manage to divert or detour their aggressiveness into socially acceptable channels, such as intense competition. The reaction of adults to children's aggressiveness ranges from a rather tolerant view to a very determined and even anxious attitude of demanding that the child squelch it or at least hide it from the public eye.

Overt and Covert Aggressiveness

Usually we judge a child's aggressiveness or lack of aggressiveness by his actions. When a child comes out fighting, clawing, or breathing fire, it is obvious that his intentions are not very peaceable. Such a youngster may not, however, be basically more aggressive than one who, at an early age, has learned to smother his anger. In understanding aggressiveness in children, we must also consider the child who seldom fights openly, but who engages covertly in rather polite but hostile forms of make-believe play or in savage fantasies that he keeps to himself. Even at the nursery-school age (as Fite, 1940, has shown) there may be a vast difference in the extent to which children display and express their aggressive impulses. In educating children, we are likely to "do something" about the youngster whose anger takes the form of a clenched fist. But we are likely to ignore the child whose anger turns inward (unless he is obviously timid, anxious, and withdrawn). Here we have another illustration of the difference between overt behavior and what a child might be hiding in his feelings and thoughts.

Aggressiveness may be a sign of healthy enterprise or of distress. This is illustrated by the records of two nursery-school children whose conflicts increased significantly during the course of the school year (Jersild and Fite, 1939). The first child, at the beginning of the school year, had spent much of his time with a companion whom he dominated; but with the help of the teachers, the dominated child was able to establish ties with other children. When the boy discovered that his hold over his companion had been broken, he tried to find new associates. Partly because of his aggressive techniques and his small size, he met rebuffs from the other children whom he tried to approach. They would tell him to go away; he would then tell them to shut up, and they would tell him to shut up; he would strike out and they would strike out. This boy resorted to fighting as a means of meeting his difficulties, but his fighting actually increased his difficulties, at least for a time.

The second child whose conflicts increased was a girl who, at the beginning of the year, was dominated by a playmate. As the weeks went by, this girl became more and more sociable in her relations with other children, but in the process she had to fight off her dominating companion. In this case, an increase in conflicts was connected with an improvement in the child's social relationships within the group as a whole.

Definitions of Overt Aggression

In a study of children's conflicts with one another, Debus (1953) defined aggressiveness as ". . . the directed expression of hostile feeling." To supplement this definition, the investigator adopted one used in a study of children's fights and quarrels by the writer and Markey (1935). An act of aggressiveness was defined as occurring in any situation in which one child ". . . attacks another person, or by word or deed interferes with another, or threatens by word or gesture to do so, or tries by force or spoken demands to direct another's activities or to possess another's things in opposition to the apparent desires of the person against whom the aggression is made."

Conflicts Arising
in the General Course of Give and Take

The more a child "gets around" and the more contacts he makes, the more he is likely to collide with others. Quarrels are likely to be frequent among children who spend much of their time together. According to one study (Green, 1933a) ". . . mutual friends are more quarrelsome, and mutual quarrelers are more friendly than the average," and ". . . quarreling is part of friendly, social intercourse at these ages." (This is in keeping with the positive correlation between aggressive and sympathetic behavior mentioned on an earlier page.) Children who are most sociable are likelier than the inactive ones to get into situations where they notice another's hurt and sympathize with him, or bump into another and fight with him. But there are, of course, many exceptions to this.

Among the circumstances that give rise to fights and quarrels are: a desire for possessions, intrusions by an unwanted playmate, a desire to be the boss, and disagreement about what should be done and how it should be done. As we have seen, conflicts also sometimes arise from a seemingly unprovoked attack by one child upon another. Many feelings flow into such attacks, including jealousy, ill-will carried over from an earlier time, a desire to annoy, or resentment aroused by others and now displaced on a handy victim.

Sometimes children get into a tussle for no apparent cause and with no obvious sign of resentment. On the surface, at least, it seems that the children are merely experimenting and testing out their strength. The participants in such a fracas seemingly had no initial intention either of stirring up a fight or of gaining anything in particular by it.

Frequencies and Forms
of Combative Behavior

At the preschool level there is a wide range in the extent to which children are openly involved in fights, quarrels or disputes. In the study by the writer and Markey (1935) mentioned above, fifty-four children, two to four years old, were observed over a period of time, during ten-minute intervals, for a total of two hours. Conflicts occurred, on the average, once every five minutes, although most of the conflicts were brief (lasting less than half a minute).

At one extreme was a child who engaged in 141 conflicts during the course of the observations, while at the other extreme was a child who took part in only 17. One child made a personal attack on another (hitting, pushing, throwing things, holding, making threatening gestures) 87 times; another child did not lay hands on anyone or threaten to do so at all.

In a somewhat similar study of Australian children (Debus, 1953) found that a conflict occurred every six or seven minutes, but most of these, also, were quite brief. One child in this study took part in 132 aggressive situations; two children took part in only 6. One child was the aggressor 59 times during the period of observation while, at the other extreme, there were three children who were never observed starting a squabble.

The two studies just cited yield similar findings on the frequency of encounters and the differences between the most aggressive and least aggressive children. This similarity may be a coincidence (in the study by the writer and Markey, far less aggressive behavior was observed in two of the groups than in the third). The exact frequencies are not so important as the fact that children differ markedly in how much initiative they take in aggressively opposing one another.

Between the ages of two and four, the most significant change in children's aggressive behavior is in the techniques they use. In the groups cited above, there was a decline in screaming, weeping, and cries for help, and in hitting and other forms of physical attack. There was an increase in the use of language during conflicts. As children grow older they become more adept at using language as a weapon, and in many adults such use of language has been developed into a fine art. It would make quite a spectacle if a polite verbal battle between two dinner guests could suddenly be transformed into a hitting and biting pair of three-year-olds.

As children grow older their conflicts tend to last longer. In one study it was noted that when two-year-olds fought with one another, only 40 per cent of their conflicts extended beyond one stage or "round," while 67 per cent of conflicts between four-year-olds went two rounds or more (Appel, 1942).

Sex Differences in Aggressiveness. The common finding (and expectation) is that boys are, on the whole, more openly aggressive than girls. This difference, however, is more likely to appear when children are older than when they first begin to join in group activities. At the age of two, for example, boys and girls in the study cited above (Jersild and Markey, 1935) were quite similar in the frequency of their screaming and crying. But as they grew older, the boys cried relatively less, hit relatively more, and were aggressive more often than the girls. In an investigation in which a doll-play situation was used, Sears (1951) found that boys were more aggressive than girls and that girls were more likely to inflict psychological harm than to resort to physical attack.

Conflicts between Children as Related to Background. Children in a day nursery, representing a somewhat underprivileged economic and educational background, entered into more conflicts than did children in a nursery school, representing a relatively higher socio-economic background.[6] Group differences were noted also in the study by Appel cited above. Children representing homes of relatively low socio-economic status showed more conflicts over possession of material objects than did children of higher socio-eocnomic status.

---

[6] At the adult level we likewise can observe that people in some groups of low socio-economic status are quite free to use their fists when they fight, while in more highly educated circles people are expected to fight it out with words. Feelings of anger may run just as high in the latter group as in the former, however, and the aftereffects of bitterness and resentment may be just as intense.

Adults differ considerably in the methods they use when dealing with children's fracases. Some nursery school teachers repeatedly use what Appel called "ending" techniques, while others more often used "teaching" techniques. Those who used the latter were not trying merely to stop a fight but to help children learn to get along together.

Adults can do a great deal to help children to learn socially approved ways of getting along with one another. In one study (Chittenden, 1942), domineering children who were inclined to use force, threats, commands, and criticism in dealing with other children were singled out for special attention. Play situations (in which dolls were used to represent preschool children in typical social situations) were arranged to help the children understand and interpret social situations and to learn cooperative techniques. The children in the group studied were able to learn more effective ways of dealing with others.

We cannot assume that young children will learn to use more socially acceptable ways of handling their difficulties simply by being restrained from bickering or told not to fight. In one group studied by the writer and Markey (1935), the teachers interfered more than did teachers in another group. In addition, there was more passive interference, since three or four teachers were usually in charge, as compared with only one or two in the other group. During the year, when these conditions prevailed, the restricted children fought less often than did the children who had more freedom to settle their disputes in their own way. But the following year, when children from both groups moved on to two kindergartens, in both of which the teachers interfered relatively little with the children, the reverse was true. The children whose fighting had been restricted doubled the frequency of their conflicts (despite the fact that normally, if anything, there is a decline with age in open aggressiveness). On the other hand, the previously less restricted, more openly aggressive children, instead of fighting even more when allowed a greater degree of freedom, actually did slightly less fighting than during the preceding year. It seems that this group of children had profited from an opportunity, in their own way, to acquire improved social techniques.

Influence of Skills on Social Behavior

Whether a child is young or old, his ability to take part in the games and other activities favored by his group will greatly affect his social relationships.

The way in which increased ability in handling situations can influence a child's dealings with others is shown in an investigation by Jack (1934). A number of children were first studied to note their tendency to be ascendant or non-ascendant in their relations with others—the extent to which they asserted themselves or failed to assert themselves in securing play materials, in defending their possessions, and in directing others or taking directions from others.

Then five children who were least ascendant were given special help in certain performances, including fitting mosaic blocks into a frame, fitting together the parts of a picture puzzle, and repeating a story that was read to them. After the children had mastered these performances, each of the five was observed when paired with another child and confronted by these tasks. As a result of the special help, the five children now more often showed a tendency to lead, to assert themselves, to direct the other child, and to exhibit "ascendant" behavior than in the initial series of observations.

When an adult helps a child to improve his practical skills, something more than just a mechanical operation is involved. The experience of working with a friendly adult, tasting companionship with the adult, and succeeding in the relationship apparently can help a child to acquire increased confidence in himself.

Effects of Nursery School Experience

A child who goes to nursery school has a splendid opportunity to further his own growth. At the beginning of the nursery school period, a youngster is ready to make some of his first ventures into work and play with his peers. By the end of this period, a typical youngster has the capacity for a wide range of social activities, including cooperative play with small groups, showing sympathy, and competing, and he has at his command a wide variety of techniques to use in dealing with other children.

Theoretically, a child has a great deal to gain from attending nursery school. This experience comes at an important juncture in a child's life. The foundations have been laid for him to advance on many fronts. He can talk and is on the brink of a rapid increase in his language ability. He possesses basic coordinations that will enable him to develop a wide range of motor skills. All being well, he is in the midst of a program of self-assertion and is striving for a degree of independence. He is ready to be initiated into the society of his peers and to enter into the give and take of social interaction. It is through this social interaction that he eventually will learn the acts of cooperation, teamwork, competition, friendliness, sympathy, and the strategies for protecting his own rights while respecting the rights of others. He is ready to begin to dilute his former almost exclusive ties to his parents with the establishment of ties with his peers. Above all, without being conscious of the fact, he is in the process of building the content and structure which constitute his noumenal self: an unspoken reliance on self, or the opposite; an implicit confidence in his competence, or a lack of it; an undefined conviction of being worthy, or the germs of an attitude of self-rejection.

The nursery school is the cradle of planned, supervised education outside the home. On the theory that an individual is most malleable—and vulnerable —when the process of personality development is in its nascent or formative phases, the potential benefits of nursery school education should be regarded as more significant—and the failure to realize those potentials (whatever they might be) should be regarded as more fateful—than anything that can be offered in a child's later educational career. If this theory were accepted there would be quite a revolution in the educational system. Many current values, and systems of remuneration, would be turned upside down. The nursery school teacher would be accorded a higher place of honor in society than the typical college professor. She (the teacher almost invariably is a she) would be selected with better care, trained more thoroughly, and paid a higher salary than instructors at higher levels. There would still have to be some sort of leadership, of course, so the highest distinction would probably have to go to those who through their knowledge, insight, and articulate devotion are best able to teach and prepare those who go out to teach the young.

The above line of thought is not, of course, as logic-tight as it might be. It assumes that there is a wisdom of the mind and heart that a nursery school teacher can bring to his or her vocation, with greater potential results than those produced by teachers in the upper grades.[7]

At any rate, in the usual nursery school (usual at least until quite recently) a child works and plays with children of his own age under adult supervision. The nursery school teacher is frequently a woman who has chosen to work with young children even though she could earn more teaching older children. In a well-planned nursery school the physical equipment (ranging from sandboxes, blocks, wheel-toys, and painting materials to child-sized chairs and small toilets) is especially designed for young children. Many of the restraints imposed at later levels are missing; there are no mid-year examinations, no demands from above that all pupils meet certain academic requirements. Here is a small world that seems made to order for a small child.

Group Trends

Many studies have been undertaken to assess what children gain from nursery school. Among the trends indicated by studies [8] in this area are the following: an increase in participation in group activities, and a decrease in

---

[7] Ideally, perhaps, there is such wisdom, but no one yet seems to have found it. Currently there is a scramble to *conceptualize* the training of young children, with an effort to convert young children into logically minded intellectuals almost as soon as they are out of their diapers. It is too soon to judge how much good—or how much damage—the advocates of a cognitively-oriented curriculum for young children are able to achieve.

[8] Among the studies that deal directly or indirectly with this problem are investigations by Hattwick (1936), Kawin and Hoefer (1931), Murphy (1937), Thompson (1944), Bonney and Nicholson (1958), and Brown and Hunt (1961).

"onlooker" behavior; an increase in poise and spontaneity in social participation, and a decrease in fear of other people, attempts to shrink from notice and to hover near adults; an improvement in self-help in eating, dressing, toileting, with resulting increases in freedom of action and diminished dependence upon adults.

Nursery-school attendance can help to dilute tensions between a child and others in the home environment. Indeed, one very important, although little publicized, function of the nursery school is to free a mother for a little while from a child's continuing demands. Although no study has been made of whether the respite helps the mother to put more verve and patience into her dealings with the child during the rest of the day, the likelihood is that it does.

Gains have been noted, as we might expect, in children's skill and resourcefulness in using the play materials and equipment provided by the school. Some of these gains may be only temporary, to be sure, or restricted largely to the nursery school environment.

One significant finding is that when a child shows a gain in sociability in nursery school it does not mean that his personality is being submerged more and more by the group. Rather, along with an increase in sociability, it is likely that a child will increase his tendency to exercise independence, to assert himself as an individual, to stand up for his interest and his rights as he sees them. In one study, for example, children's scores on "resistance" (the number of times they refused by word or deed to carry out the demands of others, to yield ground to another, and so on) were somewhat more closely related to the length of time they had spent in nursery school than to their chronological age (Caille, 1933). In another study, Ezekiel (1931) observed that children who were rather unaggressive at the beginning of the school year showed an increasing tendency to make themselves the center of activity. On the other hand, children who had been aggressive when the school term first began continued to retain this characteristic with the passage of time.

Results such as these seem all to the good, but what difference, if any, do they produce in a child's later behavior? And, if changes carry over to a later time, do they help a child or hinder him? The answer seems to be that a nursery school graduate does not necessarily have an advantage later on. In a study by Brown and Hunt (1961) it appeared that kindergarten children who had attended nursery school were, if anything, according to their teachers, less comfortably adjusted than those who had not. Brown and Hunt wisely point out that this finding cannot be taken at face value. It is possible that the children who were sent to nursery school were not, initially, as well adjusted as those who were not enrolled in nursery schools. There may have been selective factors. The children sent to nursery school may have been initially more difficult, more inclined toward poor adjustment of one sort or another. If so, nursery school experience would be only one factor, and perhaps a small one, in the total complex of factors that influenced the lives of these children.

There is, however, another angle to consider. Children who move from nursery school to higher rungs on the educational ladder may, in the process, be subjected to quite different types of evaluation. The qualities of spontaneity and free pursuit of personal interests which a particular nursery school encourages may conflict with the social conformity a kindergarten or first-grade teacher regards as important. The qualities which are applauded in the nursery school may be the very ones that are deplored later on in school.

In another study (Bonney and Nicholson, 1958), elementary school children who had had preschool experience (nursery school or kindergarten or both) did not have a decisive advantage over non-preschoolers when rated by teachers and tested by sociometric techniques. Here again it should be noted that a youngster might receive benefits from preschool experiences which cannot be measured by elementary school standards. To throw light on this question, we need a deeper appraisal of the child than the usual rating methods provide and also we need to look critically at the values by which children are judged in the elementary school.

To judge the long-term effects of nursery school experiences, it would be necessary also to study more intensively just what the nursery school teachers intend to accomplish for individual children and to what extent these intentions are achieved. As noted by Fite and the writer (1939), we cannot assume that children will benefit simply from being thrown together as a group in a nursery school.

Individual Variations. The study just cited revealed also that while a nursery school group as a whole showed a sharp increase in the frequency of social contacts, some children showed relatively little change, and two children seemed to retrogress. To appraise the value of nursery school experiences would require an intensive study of each individual child. From such a study we would probably discover that experience in a nursery school group is better suited to some children than to others.

Children respond in their own individual way to nursery school. Table 8 is based on a study of a group of children who were observed individually in the fall, soon after the beginning of the school term, and again in the spring, near the end of the school year. Some of the children (labeled "old" children) had formerly attended nursery school while others (labeled "new" children) were attending for the first time. A count was made of "social contacts"; the child received a tally of one for each half-minute period during part or all of which he engaged in social interchanges with other children.

The "old" children entered into more than twice as many social contacts, on the average, at the beginning of the school year as did "new" children. But by spring, the two groups were practically equal. Indeed, computations not shown in the table indicated that "new" children began to gain rapidly on the "old" ones during the first few weeks of school.[9]

---

[9] It is not here taken for granted that the more "social contacts" a child exhibits the better off he is, although an increase in sociability, as measured by the present techniques, usually represents a wholesome trend.

The "old" children did not have a lasting advantage over the newcomers. Even though not attending nursery school, the "new" children had been maturing and gaining experience and, when given a chance, they quickly made up for lost time.

Children have their own way of responding to a nursery school, just as they have their own individual way of responding to what is offered to them from the moment of birth. One child is actively aggressive, another is seldom, if ever, aggressive. One child is almost constantly involved in social activity (see, for example, Nancy and Alice in Table 8) while other youngsters seem to be involved only because they are placed in the same space as other children (see, for example, Sammy and Bernard in Table 8).

As seen from the pupil's standpoint, we cannot speak of *the* nursery-school situation as though it were the same environment for all the pupils. Although all the youngsters go to the same school, the school represents about as many different situations as there are children.

Influence of Type of Nursery School Program. Even so, a school that has clearly formulated educational objectives may have quite a different effect on a child's behavior than a school which lacks well-defined policies. This

Table 8 **Percentage of Intervals during which Social Contacts Occurred**

Chronological ages in years and months, in the fall, are shown in parentheses

"New" Children (without previous nursery-school experience)			"Old" Children (with one or more preceding years of nursery-school experience)		
Name	Fall	Spring	Name	Fall	Spring
Alice (3–6)	42.0	82.5	Holden (2–11)	67.3	45.0
Thelma (3–8)	25.7	58.8	Dennison (3–0)	64.0	81.3
Dick (3–9)	25.7	64.5	Nancy (3–6)	58.3	83.8
Sally (2–10)	25.7	43.8	Evan (3–6)	53.3	71.3
Morris (3–10)	14.0	47.5	Kirk (3–5)	46.3	71.3
Nell (3–1)	10.0	61.3	Joyce (2–10)	21.7	42.5
Sammy (2–10)	6.0	21.3	Bernard (3–8)	19.3	12.5
Average	21.3	54.2	Average	47.2	58.2

Children "new" to the group but with one year of previous experience in other, separate, schools:

Jerry (2-10)	50.3	73.8
Carter (3–6)	36.7	71.3

Adapted from Jersild and Fite, *The Influence of Nursery-School Experience on Children's Social Adjustments*, Child Development Monographs (New York: Teachers College, Columbia University, 1939), No. 25, 112 pp. Reproduced by permission.

was brought out impressively in a study of children in two nursery school groups with differing policies (Thompson, 1944). In both schools (designated A and B) the teachers were instructed to be responsive to the children, but in school A the teacher was told to make only minimal contacts with the children on her own initiative and to let them work out their own plans and activities, assisting only when asked. In school B the teacher was told to participate more actively, to try to become a warm friend of each child, to guide the children's thinking and activities into productive channels *not* by telling the children what to do but by her own interested participation and willingness to supply information, to cooperate, to supply and arrange materials in the most constructive manner. At the beginning of the experiment the children in groups A and B were equivalent in various measurements of their behavior. At the end of the experiment (eight months later) they differed in many ways. Group B, in which the children received teacher guidance, excelled group A, which had little teacher guidance, in *constructiveness* when faced with possible failure, in *ascendant behavior*, in *social participation*, and in *leadership*. Group B also showed fewer *nervous habits*, but the difference between the groups in this respect was not statistically significant. There was no significant difference between the two groups in IQ.

Further studies of these children would be needed to discover how much of the benefit they appeared to have gained carried over into their out-of-school conduct or into their later lives. This is significant in light of the fact that children's attitudes toward learning and their confidence in their ability to achieve apparently are established to an important degree before they enter first grade. Moreover, a child's progress in the first grade is likely to foreshadow, to an important degree, how he will fare in later grades.

Influence of the Nursery School Teacher. The benefits children derive from nursery school will probably be influenced to a large degree by the personality and competence of the teacher.

A revealing account of what a nursery-school teacher does in her moment-to-moment and hour-to-hour contacts with children has been given by Rigney (1952). A record was made of all the practices used by several experienced and several less experienced teachers. The most conspicuous finding was the vast amount of attention given to "routines"—helping children with wraps, picking up, arranging materials, and so forth. These duties constituted about a third of all practices. The second largest emphasis was on duties and rules governing the use, care, and protection of materials and property. In other words, considerable attention was given to the external aspects of the environment and external characteristics of behavior as distinguished from helping children to gain in understanding others or to become more aware of their own interests, purposes, and feelings. Rigney questions whether this emphasis is inevitable: "In wiping noses, buttoning pants, everlastingly washing, tidying, 'resting,' keeping objects in their place and handling them just so, are we evading rather than meeting up with realities in the lives of children? In coming closer to children's physical and material needs, do we, whatever the reason may be, leave little time and emotional energy for deeper psychological involvement with children?" [10]

---

[10] Recently what is known as a "Head Start" program has been designed to help underprivileged preschool children to gain in competence and self-confidence. Conclusive results from this program are not yet available.

Recommended Readings

The study by Anna Freud and Sophie Dann, referred to in this chapter, entitled "An Experiment in Group Upbringing," was originally published in *The Psychoanalytic Study of the Child*, Vol. VI (1951). It has been reproduced in the Bobbs-Merrill Reprint Series in the Social Sciences, p. 119. It is also reprinted in *Readings in Child Behavior and Development*, Second Edition, edited by Celia Stendler (1964). Stendler's volume also contains reproductions of other studies of social behavior. As noted in an earlier footnote, many of the investigations designed to study the social behavior of young children in "free" or "naturalistic" situations were conducted in the 1930's and 1940's.

Harold H. and Gladys L. Anderson's "Social Development" (1954) is a thoughtful review of studies on social development, sprinkled with refreshing Andersonian observations. Charlotte Bühler, one of the pioneers in the study of early social development, has a chapter in Carl Murchison's *Handbook of Child Psychology* (1933), which offers many insights and poses many questions that still remain unanswered. Susan Isaac's *Social Development in Young Children* (1933) discusses the socialization of the child from a psychoanalytic point of view.

14

Peer Relationships

in Later Childhood

In this chapter we will consider children's social development from the late preschool years into adolescence. During this time a child's life becomes less centered in the home and he comes more and more under the influence of his age-mates and social forces in the community at large.

A growing child encounters a tremendous variety of social situations. The range is shown vividly in a study by Barker and Wright (1954) of the "psychological habitat" of children in a town of about 700 inhabitants (designated as "Midwest, U.S.A."). Barker and Wright identified a total of 2030 "behavior settings" that were open to some or all of the children. Of these, 1445 were home situations (these were "family behavior settings" such as meals, festive occasions) and 585 were found in the town community (such as school classes, clubs, grocery stores, service stations, churches, the movies). Even the children of preschool age covered a wide territory. When one of the observers expressed astonishment at seeing a four-year-old boy "on his own so far from home" the boy said, "I go over the whole world." Wright (1956) reports that "something like this was true for Midwest children of every age."

Off to School

For many children, the beginning of their school career in the first grade or kindergarten marks a radical departure from their previous way of life. A youngster is now legally and psychologically in the custody of someone outside the home several hours of the day. All children are probably deeply impressed with the important step they are taking. Some children move eagerly into this new phase of existence; some have looked forward to school for a long time; but for many children it is a time of stress. Quite a few show the strain openly through an increase in "behavior problems" (Macfarlane, *et al.* 1954), or by clinging to their parents, crying, or making a scene, during the first day or even during the first few weeks of school. We cannot, however, judge a child's feelings, whether of joy or of distress, at this juncture of his life simply by noting his smiles or his tears.

In one investigation in which the same children were studied as they moved from kindergarten into the elementary-school grades, the children who were most explosive in showing their feelings about entering school made as good an adjustment and, if anything, a better adjustment to school in the long run than those who seemed to take the venture calmly (Kraus, 1956). This finding may have other meanings, but it suggests that children who seem distressed when entering school may be no more deeply stirred than those who remain outwardly calm; the difference may be that some youngsters freely express their emotions while others keep them hidden. As we have noted in several sections of this book, it is quite common for children to feel deeply moved when they enter a new phase in their careers. And it is not the children alone who are moved, for many parents also feel a surge of emotion. When a child sets off for school, his departure is a symbol of a larger undertaking. The child is taking an important step on a long road; at the end of the road, if all goes well, he will no longer be a child but an independent adult. It is no wonder, therefore, that many parents, while pleased that their child is growing up, also feel a tightening at the throat as they watch him leave home for his first day at school.

Group Formation and Teamwork

At the age of six, a child's capacity for work with groups is still quite limited, but he is beginning to show an interest in games that involve several children. The games in which he joins are likely to be loosely organized, or to involve make-believe themes that allow for a good deal of individual freedom.

A typical class of twenty or thirty six-year-old first-graders is a *group* only in the formal sense that they are kept together in the same room. When they work as a unit on a common project it is not by virtue of a cohesive group organization of their own but by virtue of the teacher's leadership.

At the first-grade level, the children who are leaders are likely to lead small groups rather than the entire class. It is not until about the fourth grade or later that a class is likely to act as a whole, united under a common leader, on a common project, originated and directed by the children themselves. When the older children operate as a cohesive unit it is often because one or two or more youngsters are able to take the lead (Bühler, 1933).

At the beginning of the elementary-school years, children are not only limited in their ability to act as a total group but also in their intellectual comprehension of the group situation in which they find themselves. If asked to describe his classmates as persons, a first-grader is likely to show that he has a distinct impression of some members of his class but a rather vague and indistinct notion about some of the others. According to one investigator (Reininger, as reported by Bühler, 1933), at age ten children are able to rank all their classmates in order of their importance (as perceived by the child who is doing the rating). Younger children cannot do this so successfully. Even the ten-year-old is likely to have a more distinct picture of the youngsters he ranks high and low than of those he ranks in the middle.

Development of Teamwork and Group Rules

As children grow older, they are increasingly able to identify themselves with the fortunes of a team or club, and they show increased ability in following complex rules of action. In their own activities, children in time establish complicated regulations governing procedure, the roles of individual members, taking turns, and the like. Rules governing many games are handed down from one generation to the next without adult influence. However, when children of a wide age range play together, they frequently will adapt their procedures to the varying capacities of the players. Thus, when ten-year-old boys play ball, each is expected to take a regular position and to follow a definite order in batting. But, if a six-year-old is in the game he may be given a roving commission as backstop for both teams, with freedom to drop in and out of the game; he may even be indulged with irregular turns at bat; he and other less able players may be allowed four strikes instead of three; and the poorer team may be allowed more than three "outs" before losing its turn at bat. Similarly, in a game of "cops and robbers," the older child is expected to stay "dead" when he is shot until the rules of the game permit him to revive, while a younger child may be permitted to peek when he is supposed to be dead.

Increase in Intellectual Teamwork

During the elementary-school period a child develops increasing ability to exchange ideas with other persons. Social interaction through the sharing of ideas has a bearing on, and is influenced by, developments in the intellectual sphere. To communicate with others he must so formulate and phrase his thoughts that others can understand them. He must also assume a frame of mind that enables him to understand what others are trying to communicate to him. This means an effort to understand things from the viewpoint of another—quite different from his earlier egocentric orientation as described by Piaget. Table 9 is based on a study of children's contributions during class discussions in school. In the second grade only 12 per cent of the contributions made by the children in their class discussions continued a line of thought that had been introduced by a previous speaker. At the sixth grade, in contrast, three-fourths (77 per cent) of the contributions dealt with an idea that someone else had previously introduced. Conversely, most of the contributions at the second-grade level represented "new topics"—that is, the child was simply giving voice to something that happened to occur to him. He made no effort to link his statement to what had been said before or to merge it into the treatment of a common topic.

Social Perception

An important aspect of a child's social development is his growing perception or awareness of the feelings, moods, and intentions of others. Awareness of others may take the form of a clearly defined perception, such as occurs

Table 9 Percentage of Children's Contributions in Class Discussions in Elementary School that Continued an Earlier Topic or Brought in a New Topic

Contribution	Grade 2 (62 pupils)	Grade 4 (54 pupils)	Grade 6 (45 pupils)
New Topic, not obviously related to what earlier speaker had said	87%	33%	23%
New Topic, but apparently suggested by something said by a previous contributor	8	24	33
Logical Continuation of a topic previously introduced	4	43	44

Adapted from H. V. Baker, *Children's Contributions in Elementary-School Discussion,* Child Development Monographs, No. 29. (New York: Teachers College, Columbia University, 1942.) Reproduced by permission.

when a child correctly concludes that a playmate is enjoying himself or is ill at ease. A child can also be responsive to the moods of others even though he is not able, at a moment's notice, to formulate in words the cues on which his response is based.

Awareness of Expressions of Emotion. In a study by Gates (1923, 1925), children ranging in age from three to fourteen years were shown photographs of an actress expressing joy, anger, surprise, fear, scorn, and pain. Adults are usually able to identify the emotions these pictures are intended to show. At the kindergarten level 70 per cent of the children recognized laughter but less than half of them recognized expressions of pain, anger, and fear. None of the children of kindergarten age could interpret the pictures showing surprise and scorn. In tests of older children it was found that more than half of them could identify anger at the age of seven, fear at ten, and surprise at eleven. In daily life, with familiar, living faces before them, these children undoubtedly would recognize moods which they could not identify in a photograph of a stranger, but it is nonetheless instructive to note how far some children lag behind adults in recognizing the conventional signs of emotion.

A somber picture of children's perceptions of the feelings and moods of others emerges from a study by Dimitrovsky (1964). It seems that children are more inclined to give a negative rather than a positive interpretation to the emotions expressed by adults. Dimitrovsky's study is one in a series, undertaken by Davitz and his associates (1964), of children's interpretations of the simulation of emotion through tone of voice, music, and graphic art.

Dimitrovsky studied children's ability to identify recordings of a voice intended to express anger, happiness, love, and sadness. The children ranged from five through twelve years (to facilitate the responses of the younger children a set of stick figure drawings designed to depict the various emotions was used. The emotions these figures were intended to express were readily identified). Each of the four emotions was expressed vocally three times by a male voice and three times by a female voice in random order.

There was an increase with age in the average number of presentations correctly identified (from 8.07 at five to 15.68 at twelve; the maximum possible score was 24).

Table 10 shows the average number of correct identifications of each of the four emotions at each age level. As can be seen, the "sad" items were identified correctly most often, followed, in order, by "angry," "happy" and "loving" items. It should be noted, in interpreting the table, that when children have a stronger tendency to name any vocal expression as "sad" or "angry" than as "happy" or "loving" they are likely, by chance, to make more "correct" identifications of the former than of the latter (if they are not penalized for incorrect responses).

Dimitrovsky shows, in a separate tabulation, the number of times each expressed emotion was identified as the experimenter had intended, or identified as one of the other three emotions. Expressions designed to represent love were identified as sadness 600 times, whereas sadness was interpreted as love only 155 times. "Happiness" was identified as "anger" 458 times, while "anger" was identified as "happiness" 217 times. Dimitrovsky reviews other findings which indicate that the tendency to give a negative interpretation to vocal expressions of emotion is considerably more characteristic of children than of adults.

It would require a separate study to tell whether children in daily life, with more cues to guide them, likewise tend more readily to attribute anger or grief to others than to perceive others as happy or affectionate. This question becomes very meaningful when considered alongside the view (set forth in Chapter 12) that a child's *perception* of what others think, feel, or intend may, to him, be a more potent "reality" than what others actually do think, feel, or intend.[1]

A study by Flapan (1965) goes beyond the procedures described above by offering children an opportunity to react to two dramatic sound-motion pic-

---

[1] From informal observations and talks with parents, the writer has come across several instances in which children perceived their parents as being angry when the parents maintained they were not. A "worried" parent may, for example, be seen as an angry parent.

Table 10 Average Number of Correct Identifications of Vocally Expressed Emotions at Various Age Levels

The maximum possible score for any emotion was 6. (For ease of comparison the averages and the standard deviations are separated.)

Age	Averages				Standard Deviations			
	Happy	Sad	Angry	Loving	Happy	Sad	Angry	Loving
5	1.36	3.00	2.14	1.57	0.83	1.44	1.56	1.40
6	1.61	4.46	2.68	1.25	1.47	1.45	1.33	1.55
7	1.93	4.64	3.39	1.57	1.09	1.10	1.71	1.32
8	2.14	4.82	4.14	1.71	1.08	0.72	1.08	1.54
9	2.82	5.07	3.93	2.39	1.12	0.77	1.30	1.59
10	2.93	5.21	4.36	2.61	1.41	0.74	1.16	1.13
11	3.04	5.32	4.04	2.68	1.40	0.61	0.84	1.36
12	2.93	5.14	4.39	3.21	1.54	0.71	1.20	1.64

Adapted from Lilly Dimitrovsky, "The Ability to Identify the Emotional Meaning of Vocal Expressions at Successive Age Levels." In J. R. Davitz, *The Communication of Emotional Meaning*. (N. Y.: McGraw-Hill, 1964.)

tures of human interaction. One of the films opens by showing a girl practicing on her new roller-skates while a visiting boy is demanding a turn. There
is conflict between the two. The parents intervene (each trying to shift responsibility for a decision for disciplining the girl on to the other), followed
by a peremptory decision by the father to take the skates away from his
daughter and to send her to bed without supper, contrary to what she had
understood would happen; followed by scenes in which the father regrets the
punishment he imposed, and the daughter is troubled and further scenes in
which the father makes amends for his injustice by taking his daughter to see
a circus that is passing through—arranging for her to see an elephant which
picks her up with its trunk. In the other film sequence, the girl, competing
with the boy, throws a stone and unintentionally kills a squirrel. Her father
appears, notices her distress, and "gives" her a newborn calf to make her feel
better. Later, the mother, not knowing what has happened, practically takes
the calf away from the girl; the girl is deeply disappointed; then it is decided
that the calf belongs to the whole family.

Three groups of middle-class girls of about average intelligence, aged, respectively, six, nine, and twelve years, took part in the study. Children's own
accounts of what they had witnessed were analyzed in terms of a set of
categories ranging from literal statements about what happened, what was
said, and what was obviously expressed emotion to statements imputing feelings, thoughts, intentions, or giving "psychological explanations" which the
viewer could glean only through a process of inference or interpretation (for
example, inferring from the father's restlessness that he felt sorry about having
punished his daughter as he did, or inferring that the mother tells the father
that a circus will be moving through because she thinks maybe he would take
the girl to see it; or explaining that the father said his hands were too big
because he wanted an excuse for not slapping her).

The children's responses to a series of questions which followed children's
own accounts of what they had seen were rated on a three-point scale (0, 1
and 2) ranging from literal, descriptive answers to answers that imputed
complex feelings, thoughts, or intentions to the characters in the movie.

The findings in Table 11 indicate that there is an increase with age in
interpretations and inferences regarding the feelings and thoughts of others.
The scores at age nine and twelve are not wide apart and the differences
between the six-year-olds and the nine-year-olds suggests that there is a
transition period, somewhere between age six and nine, when children shift
from a relatively literal to a more psychological way of viewing the behavior
of others. It appears also, however, that a few children at six spontaneously make rather sophisticated interpretations of other person's states
of mind.

Part A of Table 11 tells more concerning the kind of interpretations children are able to make spontaneously concerning the thoughts, feelings, and

intentions of others than about their tendency to single out and to emphasize these psychological states. One of the two films used in Flapan's study was quite moving. Several children cried at one point in the movie (as did some adult viewers). Moreover, when children in one group (not included among those represented in the table), discussed the movie after viewing it, they spoke with a great deal of animation. Yet, in Flapan's study, the typical child gave predominantly a factual, objective account of most of what transpired even though she now and then did slip in a reference to underlying feelings. It seems that children, at least in a school setting, are rather prosaic and matter-of-fact even when giving their version of an emotional scene. Whether this reticence about feeling is "natural" or has been induced by the training they receive, the study mentioned above does not tell, but it seems fair to

Table 11   Children's Descriptions and Interpretations of Sound-Motion Picture Films Portraying Interpersonal Interactions

The values in part *A* show the number of girls at each age level (20 in each group) who once or oftener gave responses in various categories when telling about the movies in their own way. Part *B* shows average scores at each age level, based on ratings of the psychological content of their responses to a set of questions.

		Age level	
Response	6	9	12
PART A			
Description and reporting			
Describing the objective situation and action	20	20	20
Reporting what the characters said	20	20	20
Describing expressive reactions (e.g. crying)	16	17	17
Describing feelings quite obviously expressed (e.g., angry attack)	19	19	20
Describing obvious intentions	13	20	20
Interpretation and Inference			
Imputing feelings not obviously expressed	0	13	18
Inferring thoughts or expectations	2	13	15
Inferring intentions or motives	2	6	10
Explaining in psychological terms	3	12	14
PART B			
Scores on ratings of response to specific questions (maximum possible score = 106) mean	36.5	61.0	73.7
SD	10.2	12.2	10.7

Adapted from Dorothy Flapan, *Children's Understanding of Social Interaction.* (N.Y.: Teachers College Press. In press, 1967.) Reproduced by permission.

say that the school is a rather cold-blooded institution. A show of emotion, except polite laughter, is not encouraged, and any discussion of the many emotions that arise in the lives of all pupils is usually avoided.

Social Perception as Related to Attitudes Toward Peers

A child's own characteristics and the way he views himself are likely to influence what he sees in others (Trent, 1953; Tabachnick, 1962). As he grows older, he is more likely to have a preference for individuals whom he perceives to be similar to himself than for those perceived as less similar whether or not, by criteria other than his own, there really is a greater similarity (for studies bearing on this, see Fiedler and his associates, 1952, 1954).

Children in a camp were subjects in a study by Davitz (1955) of the relation between a child's perception of other children and his preferences among these children. Preferences were measured by means of sociometric techniques (whom would the child like to have as a cabin-mate; whom would he like to invite to a party). Perception of others was measured in terms of what each child regarded as the preferred activities of other children. An instrument with twenty items, each of which named two camp activities (such as ping pong and dodge ball) was used to elicit from each child, in connection with each pair of activities, what he thought would be the choice of children who stood highest, and those who stood lowest, in his sociometric preference list. The child also indicated his own preferred activities. It was possible then to determine (1) how closely the activity choices he attributed to others (others as he perceived them) corresponded to (2) the choices of activity these others actually made and (3) to the choices the child himself had made. Children who were preferred on the sociometric test were perceived as more similar to the child himself than those who were unpreferred, and preferred children were perceived as being more similar to the child himself than they actually were.

Davitz introduces the concept of identification to account for the finding that children perceive those whom they prefer as more similar to themselves than they really are. According to one theory of identification, a child at first tries, consciously or unconsciously, to emulate persons whom he values—a loving father or mother, or some other hero. He thereby, presumably, incorporates these persons into himself.[2] Later on, identification with an admired person may be achieved by viewing this person as similar to oneself, if need be, by a process of distorted perception.

---

[2] The concept of identification, notably at first with parents, has frequently been invoked as an explanatory principle in developmental psychology. The concept of identification is discussed in Chapter 22.

Acceptance and Rejection by Peers

A child's desire to be noticed and accepted, which first appeared in his relations with his parents, follows him as he moves into the larger social world. Some children go to great lengths to attract notice by clowning or "showing off," or by misbehaving.

Behavior that is baffling to adults often is motivated by the child's desire to please his peers or to gain their attention. His feelings when rebuffed or ridiculed by his peers may range from grief and despair to intense rage. It is difficult for a youngster to express such feelings, and the reasons for them, to adults, for to do so he must admit to himself the bitter fact that persons whose good will he desires actually do not like him. Instead of directly expressing his feelings he may reveal them through symptoms such as fault finding, fighting back, complaining, and other responses of the "sour-grapes" variety. As a consequence, his elders may not realize that when he is telling how much he detests certain children he actually may be expressing how much he would like to be liked by these same children, or how deeply he feels contempt of himself.

The following account shows how one child reacted to rejection by her peers and how her parents tried to help her:

> Isabel was six years old and in the first grade. On two occasions her parents, while driving past the school during recess, happened to notice that the girl stood by herself while the other children were playing. This was puzzling, for she was quite gregarious. A few days later Isabel happened to mention that she had played that day with some "big boys from the third grade." Some days later she again mentioned that she had played with one of the big boys and had pulled his shirttails out of his pants. That evening, as though troubled, she asked her mother at bedtime, "Have I been a good girl today?" In answer to this unusual question the mother said yes, and then added rather lightly that she thought it would be better if Isabel did not pull shirttails out of boys' pants. At this she burst into tears. She sobbingly asked, "Then who shall I play with? When I eat lunch I sit alone, and out on the playground the other girls don't play with me." The difficulty, in part, was that Isabel was a newcomer among girls who had been playmates before coming to school.
>
> Isabel's parents now tried to help. Two schoolmates chosen by Isabel were invited to the home by the mother and this may or may not have been partly responsible for the fact that the girl soon became accepted by the group.

When children have troubles of this sort and do not reveal them, it is difficult, of course, for adults to understand or to try to help. Through lack of understanding the adult may even make things harder for the child. In the instance above, for example, it might have made matters worse if the mother through ignorance of the situation had scolded the child for rough play with older boys when actually this play, from the child's point of view, was a poor substitute for play with girls her own age.

Measurement of Social Acceptance

Sociometric techniques for measuring children's acceptance by their peers were briefly introduced in the preceding chapter.[3] The most common procedure is to phrase the sociometric questions in positive terms—whom does he prefer as a friend, seat-mate, and so on. Negative opinions may be obtained by asking youngsters to name persons whom they do not care to have as friends, or as seat-mates, or as study companions. This approach has not been used as often as the positive approach, for there are children who are reluctant to speak unfavorably about others. Some negative information can be inferred from the positive approach. For example, if a child is not named by anyone when children choose their seat-mates, it is evident that he is not especially popular. It does not follow, however, that he is actively rejected.

A simple example of results obtained by means of a sociometric method applied to fourteen boys in a fourth-grade group is shown in Table 12 on page 279. The children were asked to name the person or persons in their class whom they would like best to have as a friend. They were also asked to name the person or persons in the class whom they did not especially care to be friends with. The diagram on page 280 is a simple illustration of a *sociogram*; it portrays only the positive responses represented in Table 12. As shown in Table 12, the children named more persons when choosing whom they liked than when naming whom they disliked.

The information obtained by sociometric methods answers a variety of questions: Who is chosen most? Who is chosen least or not at all? Who is chosen by whom, but does not reciprocate? To what extent are choices associated with various factors such as age, sex, socio-economic status, and nationality? Some findings obtained with this technique may simply confirm what is already known from observation of the group; but the findings may also yield important new information, and sometimes the findings with respect to individual children are quite surprising.

The sociometric technique yields results that are interesting from a research point of view and also impressive from a personal point of view. In Table 12 there is one boy (Harper) whom five classmates pointedly named as one

---

[3] Research in this area received a great impetus from studies published in 1934 by Moreno. For an account of "old and new trends in sociometry" see Moreno (1954). A study by Cunningham in collaboration with a number of classroom teachers (1951) gives revealing findings obtained when teachers use sociometric techniques as a first step in an effort to understand their pupils. A widely used booklet by Cunningham (1947), "How to Construct a Sociogram," offers time-saving suggestions on how to compile the results of sociometric ratings.

whom they did not care to have as a friend, and no one in the group named him as a friend. As far as we can tell from the sociometric results, Harper is an outcast (in the language of sociometry, Harper is called an "isolate"), but it would require a more personal kind of inquiry to discover how vigorously he is rejected by the boys who name him as one they don't care for, or why he is unchosen by anyone else, and what all this means to Harper.

Stability of Sociometric Ratings

While the sociometric method is simple to apply and sometimes requires only that children, on the spur of the moment, write or check the names of youngsters whom they prefer (or don't prefer), it usually provides information that is reliable and significant, as far as it goes. Even at the preschool level, it was observed in one study (Biehler, 1954) that children's choices of companions were very similar when measured by records of their actual behavior and when measured by a sociometric technique (children indicated their choices by means of photographs). In studies of older children, it has been found (in most instances) that children's choices show a high degree of stability, when a sociometric test is applied and again after a year or more.[4]

[4] For studies dealing with this subject, see Laughlin (1953), and a review by Witryol and Thompson (1953).

Table 12 **Distribution of Choices and Rejections Among Boys—Made by Fourteen Boys in a Fourth-Grade Class**

Name and Number	Sex	Age	Chooses	Chosen by	Rejects	Rejected by	Mutual Choices
1. Don	B	10	2, 8, 12	—	4	5	—
2. Duval	B	9	6, 8, 12, 13	1, 3, 5, 6, 8, 12	—	—	8, 12
3. Henry	B	10	2, 8, 12	5	10	—	—
4. Harper	B	9	—	—	—	1, 6, 7, 8, 10	—
5. James	B	10	2, 3, 11, 12	11	1, 7	—	11
6. Jasper	B	9	2, 8, 13	2, 11, 12	4	—	2
7. Jacob	B	9	10, 11	11	4	5, 9	11
8. Luke	B	8	2	1, 2, 3, 6	4	—	2
9. Matthew	B	9	14	11	7	—	—
10. Porter	B	9	12	7, 11	4	3	—
11. Philip	B	9	5, 6, 7, 9, 10	5, 7	12	—	5, 7
12. Ramos	B	9	2, 6, 13	1, 2, 3, 5, 10	—	11	2
13. Tom*	B	—	—	2, 6, 12	—	—	—
14. Fritz*	B	—	—	9	—	11	—

In this group there was no instance in which two children mutually rejected each other, or in which a child chose a youngster who had rejected him, or in which a child rejected a youngster who had chosen him.
*Absent but either chosen or rejected.

In some studies it has been found that children's "social acceptance scores" remain almost as constant from year to year as their scores on intelligence tests. An investigation of children who were first tested in various elementary schools showed a high degree of stability in their sociometric ratings when re-tested after they had moved on to a junior high school, with a considerable reshuffling of the population (Laughlin, 1953).

Qualities Associated with Acceptance and Non-Acceptance

Numerous qualities make a child appealing or unappealing in the eyes of one or more of his fellows, but certain qualities have been found in several studies to stand out.[5] Children who win a high degree of acceptance have been described by their associates as active and alert and interested (but not restless

---

[5] For studies dealing with this subject, see Laughlin (1953); Dunnington (1957); Trent (1957), and VanKrevelen (1962).

Figure 1 Sociogram showing choices (but not rejections) by boys represented in Table 12.

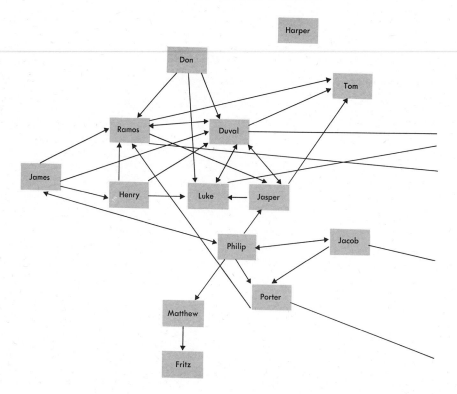

or obviously out to get attention), good natured, peppy, cheerful, and friendly. Popular children tend, if anything, to be above average (but not necessarily a great deal above the average) in intelligence, scholastic standing, and health, more dependent on themselves and less dependent on adults, sensitive to the thoughts and interests of others. Children who are accepted by others are likely to have a more realistic perception of themselves than children who are not accepted (Goslin, 1962).

The factors associated with unpopularity are also quite varied. Among children who are low in acceptance there are some who have no apparent interest in the general environment and little interest in other persons, or who are quiet or shy, or "socially ineffective," or who are noisy, rebellious, boastful, or obviously seeking attention. Children who appear to be anxious, as shown by restlessness and other signs, are frequently in the non-accepted group.

The child who is deeply preoccupied with problems of his own is not likely to be appealing to others. Troubled children who have benefited from therapy have shown an improvement in their social relationships along with an improvement in their emotional state (Cox, 1953).

Children who are most accepted by their peers possess qualities such as those we have just noted, but there are many undisclosed nuances of need, self-interest, and interest in others which influence the choice of one child by another particular child. To be accepted socially a youngster must, in general, have certain qualities but not to excess: he is interested in others, but does not too obviously seek attention; he is active, but not hyper-active; he is confident but not boastful.

If we could look more deeply into social acceptance "scores" we would probably find that they have many different meanings. When a certain youngster names three children as his favorites, one of these may be a child whom he intensely likes while the other two may be "also-rans." One youngster may choose another because he genuinely likes him and another because he stands high in prestige in the group and belongs to the proper set. A youngster may be chosen because he has prestige rather than because he is especially liked (Keislar, 1953).

The preferences and affinities children reveal in their relationships with one another show that the factor of IQ has less weight when school children are appraised by each other than when they are appraised by the school (Laughlin, 1953). At the adolescent level, H. E. Jones (1949) also found little correlation between intelligence test scores and popularity.

Beneath the Sociogram

A sociogram (as illustrated on page 280) is revealing as far as it goes but it provides only the first step in an endeavor to understand the children whose position it records. When we ask, "What does it mean from the standpoint of the individual child?" we raise a host of questions. As a general proposition, it seems obvious that the youngster who stands high in social acceptance is well off and the child who stands low, or is actively rejected, is certainly not in a comfortable spot. However, to assess the situation of an individual child we need more than a sociogram. We must look both at the child and at the group standards by which he is being judged. A child who is not accepted by his peers may have qualities which, in a larger view, are admirable. He may have qualities that children in one group will reject but which, in another group, would be admired. An example of this is given in an account by Hollingworth (1926) of a child who was unusually bright. When in a class consisting mainly of children of average intelligence, this boy was practically cut off from the social life of the group. But when transferred to a class which included bright children, he was warmly appreciated. The rejected "Perfessor" in one social set became an accepted pal in another.

In considering this case we might ask: If the boy was as bright as all that why wasn't he sensitive to the social climate in the average class and smart enough to pass himself off as a "regular guy"? The answer may be that he was unwilling or unable to change his ways in order to become popular.

Some youngsters (and adults) do have a knack for tailoring their behavior to the standards of the group. In one instance, a bright boy who had "skipped a grade" was able to blunt the sharp edge of rejection in his new group by pretending to be like the rest. Occasionally, for example, he would deliberately misspell a word after two or three of the bigger children had failed to spell it. He would rather receive a reproof from the teacher than hostile glances from his classmates. Similar tactics were used by a boy (mentioned in Chapter 10) who adopted a "dialect" of poor grammar to conform to the speech habits of other children in the community. In knuckling down to the standards of his peer group, this boy, like the one who deliberately misspelled words, knowingly paid a price in order to avoid the discomfort of being a social misfit. In many instances, of course, children are not able or willing to pay such a price, especially if it involves a severe conflict of values.

If we could look beneath the surface of group behavior into the lives of the individual children we probably, in every instance, would find a complicated drama. At the high end of the scale of social acceptance, there are youngsters who are comfortable with the group and also comfortable within themselves. But a high standing in the group may be bought at great cost. Wittenberg and Berg (1952), in a moving account, have pointed out how a youngster can achieve popularity by surrendering personal integrity. If such a surrender is not made knowingly (as in the two illustrations above) but in a blind effort to win approval, the child who stands high in the sociometric scale may be in a sorrier plight than the one who stands low.

A child with strong interests of his own and with a sturdy regard for his own rights will not be as concerned about the impression he makes on others as a youngster who has little confidence in himself and whose sense of his own worth is completely at the mercy of what others think of him. So if a child with independent interests is relatively low on the scale of acceptance over a period of time this may simply mean that he has the strength as time passes, to follow his own bent. However, there probably are few who are so strong as to be unaffected by disapproval from the group.

Rivalry, Cooperation, and Competition

Cooperation and competition have many elements in common, and activities which outwardly appear to be competitive or cooperative may spring from a variety of motives. Competition usually denotes a struggle or contest in which one individual seeks to equal or excel another, or to secure objects, recognition, prestige, attainments, or honors also sought by others. Cooperation involves mutual action on a common enterprise toward a common goal.

Competition and cooperation are in some respects opposites, but often both are parts of a larger project. Many competitive games involve a great deal of cooperation just as many cooperative ventures entail a good deal of competition. Children compete vigorously in a game of baseball, for example, but without a great deal of cooperation they would not come together in the same place for the same purpose or follow the rules of the game.

Competition and cooperation both provide the growing child with opportunities to discover his resources and to test his abilities. When he races another child he is not necessarily just trying to assert his superiority—he is perhaps also testing himself.

Competition

When they enter elementary school most children in our culture are launched on a competitive career, although they differ greatly in the intensity of their competitiveness. They differ also in their choice of competition. In an unpublished study the writer and his associates recorded the number of times each child in several classrooms took part in "free" class discussion. In every class there were several children who competed for a chance to be heard and each class contained one or two highly competitive youngsters who monopolized a large share of the discussion consistently from day to day. In several classes, one or two children managed regularly to be heard as often as all the other class members combined. Some children were choosy in selecting their competitors. In one class, two boys consistently out-talked all others in the room. One day, one boy was absent and the research team expected that the other—now having the field to himself—would really have a talk-fest. Instead, he was strangely silent. On the next day, when the classmate was back in school, both sounded forth again. It appeared that these two boys were not competing with the rest of the class or the teacher by demanding so much attention; they were using the class situation to compete with each other.

While the school is not the primary source or cause of competitiveness, it is apparent that most schools encourage and exploit competition, notably in connection with assignments which need "extraneous" motivation—assignments which in themselves are uninteresting and rather meaningless to many of the pupils. In most schools, academic learning and competition are joined as though "you can't have one without the other." This combination is fortunate when it produces a zest for learning but not when it places a higher premium on the amount than on the meaning of what is learned. Competitiveness also strongly emphasizes the speed with which intellectual operations can be performed, as though education were preparing students for an intellectual horse race. Competitiveness in school sometimes approaches the ridiculous. The writer witnessed an exhibition of sharp competitiveness in an avowedly progressive school: The youngsters were competing with each other in a discussion of the evils of competition!

Children face conflicting pressures bearing on cooperation and competition: They are urged to cooperate, and some schools have an entry in the report card for marking the child's cooperativeness. Yet in the same schools they are also under great pressure to compete. All children to some degree face the problem of how to be cooperative within a competitive structure and how to assert their competitiveness within a cooperative structure.

Selection of Areas of Competition. A child's competitiveness is influenced by many conditions in the social situation and, as time goes on, by his need to measure himself against others, to support his self-evaluation by equalling or excelling others.

Some children seem to compete in almost every sphere of their lives while others specialize, staking out areas in which they will vie with others; still others seem to resign from competition. After being reminded again and again that he cannot successfully compete with others in reading or spelling a youngster may give up his efforts to compete in these subjects. He may seem lacking in the desire to excel, and his report card may even include such statements as "Is not well-motivated," "Does not work up to capacity." Such a youngster, however, may at the beginning have felt the competitive pressure just as keenly as those who were successful and his sting of defeat may have been just as intense as the others' glow of victory. Evidence of a tendency to select only certain areas in which to compete appears in findings at the adolescent level that show low or zero correlations between academic grades and success in athletics. While a low correlation may mean there is little basic relationship between potential academic and athletic ability, it probably also means that individual youngsters have chosen to center their efforts in one field and not the other.

The values of cooperation are obvious. An atmosphere of genuine cooperation is likely to be more relaxed, friendly and pleasant than an atmosphere of intense competition. In a cooperative setting a child can express and enjoy the strong potentialities for "positive" human feelings that he and all children possess.

Competition affects a child as a member of a competitive society and as an individual. As a member of society, a child benefits from the competitiveness of others when, for example, under the spur of competitive drives, scientists discover new medicines, or inventors develop useful products, or industrial enterprises open up new resources of wealth and employment. A person's competitive efforts may bring advantages to others even if he himself is more bent on achieving individual glory than on serving the general welfare.

In countless practical situations the competing child serves as a pacemaker, an aid to the process of self-discovery. The pace and performance of others often set a standard which the youngster can achieve and enjoy. He may, for example, discover that he can get his homework out of the way more effectively than he had thought, get dressed in less time than was his custom, endure and enjoy the water of a cold stream which otherwise he would not plunge into, draw upon reserves of strength in his work and play.

In competing with others outside the home a youngster may get a truer view of some of his qualities than he previously had. This is especially valuable if a youngster has previously underrated himself in comparison with an older sibling, or if ambitious parents have set before him a standard that he could never live up to.

Moreover, competition (especially in a cooperative setting) can give zest to many enterprises which are useful (or at least required) but which, in themselves, would be rather boring. Whether we like it or not, competition is one of the main props, and in some cases *the* major prop, in our educational system.

Competition also has its unhealthy side. Very often, the competitiveness of older children has a driven quality.

Competition is unhealthy if the child's self-regard depends on his ability to outdo others. It is unhealthy if the child has a tendency to regard himself as inferior unless he can prove his superiority to all comers. Competitiveness has a sick quality if the child is vindictive, gloating over his rivals and relishing their defeat. It also has a morbid quality if the child, when he fails to win, feels bitter toward himself (or others), has vengeful fantasies, or feels that he has to grit his teeth and train hard solely to prove he can win, even though the contest itself has little or no value to him. This would be the case, for example, if a child seeks to be elected to a class office, or to head a committee, not because he likes the job or feels he can contribute something, but simply to show that he can win the job.

Competitive pressures at school are unhealthy if they force a judgment of failure on those who do not, of their own accord, have a compulsion to compete, or if the standards used in evaluating the students are narrow, arbitrary, and favorable only to a few.

The results of a narrow competitive standard are strikingly shown at graduation time in some schools when a few selected children march self-consciously again and again to the stage to receive prizes and awards while the other children are expected to applaud politely.

In the academic program of most schools, the road to competitive success (or defeat) is largely verbal. Even the child who has an outstanding aptitude for painting, music, or mechanics is likely to get a low mark if he does not know the right *words*.

> A boy who had outstanding mechanical ability got poor grades in a mechanics course because his reading and spelling abilities were below average. No one in the class surpassed him in taking generators and carburetors apart, repairing them, and putting them together again. But this didn't count in his favor because in the written examination he misspelled "generator" and "carburetor."

When children are judged according to narrow competitive standards, they are not respected for their basic humanity. Competitive standards give little, if any, recognition to the child who—though not the first to cross the finish line—entered the race under a great handicap. Yet if gameness were the criterion, he should get the prize. Competitive standards give a medal to the winner of the oratorical contest but they ignore the one who, in joining the contest, scored a magnificent triumph over his shyness, even though he did not surpass someone else's skill.

If, on Commencement Day, it were possible to show a film depicting the struggle each student had gone through, the heights each had scaled, and the difficulties each had overcome, and a jury, viewing it were asked to draw up an honor roll, the jury would probably select many names that are not among those listed on the printed program. Many names would appear which, by ordinary competitive standards, would go "unwept, unhonored, and unsung." It is perhaps even more likely that as the members of the jury came to know the drama of each child's life they would refuse to single out any one for mention above the rest. According to this view, the more fully we appreciate another's struggle the less desire we have to triumph over him or to profit (through taking first place) from the fact that he was in the second or last place. John Greenleaf Whittier caught some of this spirit in the poem, "In School Days," when the girl says to the boy ("As if a fault confessing"):

> "I'm sorry that I spelt the word:
> I hate to go above you,
> Because,"—the brown eyes lower fell,—
> "Because, you see, I love you!"

Aggression in Older Children

Open fighting and squabbling usually decline from the preschool period into the elementary-school years, although most children continue to have occasional battles and some children continue to feud. Many factors, both inherent in the child and in his environment, contribute to a decline in open combat. A child's increased understanding of property rights eliminates many conflicts on that score. With time, the child also gains more understanding of other children, what he can expect from them, what they will tolerate from him.

The labels "aggression" and "aggressiveness" are used in a variety of contexts with a number of meanings. In its most primitive form, an aggressive act is one that inflicts harm or injury on someone against whom it is directed. "Aggressiveness" is also used, however, to connotate vigor, forcefulness, and determination—when we say, for example, that a person is aggressive in asserting his opinions or aggressive in his "attack" on an intellectual problem, or stands up and "fights" verbally for his rights.

As most commonly used in describing children, the term "aggression" pertains to active belligerence which can be observed and measured in terms of overt behavior.

When thus defined, aggression and aggressiveness are useful labels as far as they go. Certainly they denote behavior which prevails among children, sometimes to a very troublesome degree. But this definition also has obvious limitations. It does not adequately take account of covert, as distinguished from overt, aggression; aggression that appears in fantasies; aggression that is rife in children's and adults' dreams; aggression that springs from impulse or calculated intention; aggression that might serve as a rather triumphant form of self-assertion or aggression that is a symptom of weakness, vulnerability, defeat, and despair.[6]

Overt aggression is expressed in a variety of ways. It may be frequent or infrequent; violent or mild; impulsive or controlled; eruptive or deliberate; sporadic or pervasive; provoked or seemingly without cause. Aggressive behavior may be "immature," after the manner of a small angry child, or it may be linked with a "mature" set of principles and convictions.

Overt aggression varies also in its object or target. It may be centered primarily on persons within the home, or directed primarily against persons outside the home. It may be directed against specific individuals or rather indiscriminately against people in general. It may be expressed through personal attack, or more impersonally through the violation of rules (at school) or through destructiveness, thievery, and vandalism.

---

[6] Ways in which aggressiveness may represent a variety of meanings, interests, and motives in adolescent boys and girls has been described by Lansky, *et al.* (1961).

An account of the origins, scope, and meaning of aggressiveness in children could be one of the most significant chapters in child psychology. But a definitive account cannot be written on the basis of present evidence. To assess the origins and role of aggressiveness it is necessary to take account of what is overt and what is covert. To account for individual differences in aggression it is necessary to consider environmental factors but also, as far as possible, to take account of hereditary factors.

In Chapter 3 we noted that animal strains of the same species manifest genetic differences in aggressiveness. To ascertain the role of genetic factors in human beings would be difficult, to say the least, for data regarding a child's ancestry usually is inadequate. However, when it is observed, for example, that aggressive children frequently have aggressive parents we cannot assume, as a foregone conclusion, that the children have acquired their aggressiveness by using their parents as models. The similarity between the parents and children may be due, at least in part, to genetic factors. To interpret findings which seem to show a connection between aggressiveness in children and their parent's child-rearing procedures it is necessary to obtain information more substantial than has commonly been obtained through interviews and retrospective reports.

It has generally been found that boys are overtly more aggressive than girls. It is possible that inherent physical differences between boys and girls might, in part, account for this, but the more usual explanation is that parents are more tolerant of aggressiveness in boys (unless it is directed against the parents themselves). To make a thorough assessment of sex differences it would be necessary to inquire not only into the more obvious signs of aggressiveness but also to take account of aggressiveness that is covert and elusive.

It has also generally been found that children of lower socio-economic status are more aggressive than children in the higher socio-economic brackets. This seems to be due, in part, to greater toleration of fighting at the lower levels, and also to the fact that children at the lower levels are subject to more provocation by living conditions, such as crowding and other discomforts. The difference probably also is related to the fact that middle-class children are, on the average, somewhat more verbal. Even at the preschool level, children make a substantial shift from the use of physical force to the use of words in resolving conflicts of interest. Other things being equal, the more verbal a child is the more resources he has for solving or forestalling difficulties that might provoke overt aggression.

Two reservations should be mentioned regarding aggressiveness in persons of low socio-economic status. First, there are wide individual differences. Many of the children of low status are less aggressive than many of the children of high status. Second, many of the differences that do appear may be due to a difference in freedom openly to express aggressive impulses.

There is, as everyone probably will concede, a great amount of restrained or hidden or contained aggressiveness in children and in adults at all social levels. Most children learn to suppress their aggressive impulses, or at least to direct them at "safe" targets, for the usual adult response to aggression is to reprimand or to punish it. This helps to keep things in a fairly peaceful state, at least during the day. During the night, when asleep, a child is even more peaceful—except within himself. As we will note in a later chapter, there is a great amount of aggression in children's dreams and in the dreams of adults. Latent aggressiveness has been described as a ticking time-bomb. Sometimes it explodes in lynchings, riots, and warfare. More often it explodes by way of acts of aggression in dreams. It is conceivable that society might be torn apart with strife if aggressive impulses did not so often find an outlet in dreams.

Adults usually look favorably on a child who keeps his aggressiveness in check. But it seems that, for some childern, the price that must be paid for this favor is high.

The view that nonaggression may carry a penalty comes from studies of the childhood histories of persons who eventually succumb to schizophrenia. Several investigators have reported that a person with a history of overt aggressiveness *prior to* his hospitalization has a better chance of recovering from schizophrenia than one who did not "act out" his aggressiveness (Schofield, *et al.*, 1961; Nameche, *et al.*, 1964; Grossman, 1967).

According to these findings there may be conditions under which distressed parents of a troubled child should welcome rather than deplore childhood aggressiveness which, considered simply in its own right, is quite unfortunate (such as fighting with siblings, poor deportment at school, and aggressive acts outside the home and school).

The findings that the prospects are somewhat brighter for a schizophrenic patient if he had a history of aggressiveness prior to the onset of acute symptoms of illness can perhaps best be understood when we consider the clinical picture of schizophrenia. One of the chief symptoms is a tendency to withdraw from the give and take of everyday life. An aggressive child is not a withdrawn child—at least not in his overt behavior. His brighter prospects for recovery when he does become ill may mean that he started out in life with less of a predisposition to withdraw than the person with a history of nonaggression prior to his breakdown.

The findings mentioned above do not mean that a prior history of aggressiveness may be taken *per se* as a hopeful sign in persons who are vulnerable to the stresses of life. It seems that a youngster heading for delinquency, for example, is more likely to continue as an offender in later years if his history shows that he acted out against others.[7]

---

[7] For studies dealing with the relation between recovery from psychiatric disorders in relation to various types of aggression, and the period in the life span when aggression was manifested, see Feldman, et al., 1954; Albee, 1950; Robins and O'Neal, 1958.

Studies of hospitalized mental patients indicate that a prior history of various types of aggression may have a variety of meanings, ranging from favorable to very unfavorable. The same no doubt holds true also in the lives of children heading toward a normal adulthood. Even at the nursery school level, one child may use aggression in a constructive manner, such as fighting against domination by another child. Another youngster may use aggression in a self-defeating way—as when his fighting to be included in the play of other children makes them all the more determined to exclude him.

Response to Frustration

The view that frustration leads to aggression was regarded some years ago as virtually axiomatic. A less tidy but more correct statement is that frustration *may* lead to aggression, or it may produce any one or more of several other types of response, or no noticeable response at all.[8]

In experiments with frustration, a common procedure has been to expose laboratory subjects to presumably vexing treatment, such as delay or failure to present a promised reward, blocking the child's effort to get a deserved toy, taking away a reward he already has received, interfering with his activity, arbitrarily requiring him to repeat an activity, and so on. In a controlled experiment, aimed at yielding quantitative results, it is necessary to assume that the "frustrating" event is a constant variable. This, of course, is a questionable assumption, for the effectiveness of any intended frustration depends not simply on what is done to the subject, but also on what it means to him. To withhold a promised gift may be a serious affront to one child who is eager to have the gift while it may be merely a passing event to a child who doesn't care whether he gets it or not.

Reactions to frustrating conditions may range from apathy (sometimes seen in institutionalized children whose needs are denied) to increased vigor of response, to overt attack.

Another response to a frustrating condition is to show a decline in quality of performance. An example of this, from a study by Seashore and Bavelas (1942), is given in Chapter 17.

Influence of Socio-Economic Status on a Child's Social Development

The bearing of socio-economic status on children's upbringing is discussed in several contexts in this book, so only a brief overview will be offered in this section.

---

[8] For a review and discussion of studies of frustration, see Bandura and Walters (1963).

Children of low socio-economic status who live in crowded quarters in a poor neighborhood feel the pinch in many ways. Crowding creates many frictions from which children in more spacious quarters are spared. Children in crowded homes are less likely than those in more affluent homes to be shielded from the raw facts of life. With less privacy they are more likely to come in contact with the processes of birth, illness, death, family worries, and quarrels. If the family is large, or if both parents are working, children may also be required to assume responsibility for their own care and safety at an early age.

In one study (Jersild, *et al.*, 1949) parents in poor economic circumstances, in describing their relationships with their children, gave more emphasis to the physical aspects of child care (such as physical discomforts, physical health) than did parents of higher status. Wealthier parents gave more emphasis to psychological aspects of child care (such as personality traits).

In the past, parents of low socio-economic status had more children, on the average, than parents of higher status (in recent years the difference has narrowed).

Even if the father and mother of a large family are devoted to their children they will have less time to give to each. There will be more distractions, more calls upon their energy, less money for baby-sitters or vacations which might provide the children with an outing and the parents with some respite. When older children tell about their earliest memories, those of low socio-economic status are likely to mention recollections of angry feelings and aggressive and sexual behavior, while those of middle socio-economic status have relatively more pleasant memories (Epstein, 1963).

In comparisons between children of lower and higher socio-economic status it has been found that those of lower status are, on the average, more openly aggressive and more punitive in their moral attitudes, more likely to become delinquent, more likely to have fears of a superstitious nature and also fears of certain concrete dangers (such as beatings, drunks, "bad guys," rats, illness without money to pay doctors' bills).

It has generally been found that children of low socio-economic status have a lower average intelligence than those of a higher status, but there are, of course, great variations in intelligence in both the low and high groups. In a study of a community in which children had a similar general cultural background Haller and Thomas (1962) computed correlations between a number of personality variables and socio-economic status. Only the correlation between socio-economic status and intelligence was "moderately large." In a longitudinal study of culturally heterogenous groups of children in New York City, Almy and her associates (1966) found that middle-class children at the

291

kindergarten level performed almost as well as lower-class second-grade children in tests of thinking.[9]

Children of low socio-economic status tend to be more "motoric" in expressing emotion (striking when angry, jumping when joyful) than middle-class children (McNeil, 1956).

In some poor neighborhoods a child may be encouraged to be a fighter, although subject to certain rules (Davis, 1944). However, various segments of the population differ in this respect and it cannot be said that, as a general rule, parents of low socio-economic status tolerate aggressiveness more than parents of higher socio-economic status (Sears, *et al.*, 1957; Markley, 1958).

In weighing the meaning of conduct in relation to socio-economic status it is necessary to consider both the overt behavior and the emotional undertones. The difference between people in the lower and middle social ranks may be more a difference in mode of expression than in intensity of feeling. In some areas, for example, "lower-class" boys, until prohibited, have been found to carry knives with them to school, presumably as weapons. To a middle-class teacher this is a horrible practice. The wound that might be inflicted by a lower-class boy can be severe, but the hurts inflicted by the sarcasm of a middle-class teacher (who would not think of using a knife) can also be very severe.

Child-Rearing Practices and Attitudes. In many of the earlier studies dealing with child-rearing practices and attitudes it was concluded that middle-class parents were, on the whole, more demanding, more ambitious, and less easy-going than lower-class parents. For many years it was accepted as a truism that middle-class parents insisted more on cleanliness, were more rigid in the handling of children's weaning and toilet training, more intolerant of aggressiveness, more prudish about sex, and allowed children less freedom to roam about in the community. Many writers, while describing the "lower-class" child as one who, in many ways, has a rough time, have also portrayed him as enjoying more freedom than his peers in the middle-class. This picture has not been confirmed in recent studies. Sears and his associates (1957) found, for example, that middle-class mothers were generally more permissive and less punitive in dealing with their children than were working-class mothers. Working-class mothers were, if anything, more severe in toilet training and they pushed the child to complete his training more than did the middle-class mothers. Working-class mothers were less likely to allow their young children to wander about the community without supervision. They were less lenient toward sex behavior and toward aggression. Other studies, which dispute the view that the child of low socio-economic status is under

---

[9] Those tests are described in Chapter 20.

less pressure, include investigations by Maccoby and Gibbs (1954) and by Markley (1958). Markley makes the reservation, however, that middle-class parents perhaps apply subtle pressures which they themselves do not recognize or report.

In a discussion of differing findings in this area, Havighurst and Davis (1955) state that as we learn more about social conditions in the United States "it becomes clear that one should not attempt to generalize concerning child-rearing to an entire social class in one part of the country, even if it is a representative sample."

Attitudes toward Education. Parents in high socio-economic groups more often than those in lower groups expect that their children will continue their education through high school and go on to college. According to one point of view (Hollingshead, 1949) parents of middle or higher socio-economic status are also more in favor of the sort of education schools usually provide and more sympathetic toward the overall idea of schooling than parents of lower status. However, more recent research casts some doubt on this theory. Sears and his associates (1957) noted that while middle-class, better educated families took it for granted that their children would go to college this did not mean that they were putting more pressure on the school achievement in the earlier grades than did the working-class families. How pressures of this sort affect the ideas an individual child acquires about what he *should* do as a child and what he might look forward to as an older person would require a study of the youngsters themselves.

Delinquency and Socio-Economic Status. The delinquency rate is higher in the lower than in the higher socio-economic groups. One reservation with regard to the meaning of this statistic is that youngsters of higher socio-economic status who perform delinquent acts are more likely to be protected and less likely to be brought to court than children of lower income groups. However this may be, a youngster living in a community in which the delinquency rate is high certainly faces a different social situation than one living in a community where the rate is low. The former is more exposed to the influence of delinquent companions. He cannot count on the protection of his parents or of the community when he does something wrong. He may even develop a cynical attitude toward policemen and toward the idea of law and justice. In one class which the writer visited in a school in a "delinquency area" most of the members, in connection with a discussion of cops, claimed that they knew policemen who were crooked or unfair or brutal or otherwise unsuited to be respected upholders of the law. It should be added, however, that a large proportion of these youngsters also said that they knew other cops who were "okay."

In time the child becomes aware of the symbols of social position, such as a professional man's brief case and white collar and the laborer's overalls. This kind of awareness develops somewhat slowly, according to a study by Stendler (1949). First-grade children showed little awareness of their own social class position. First-graders described their families as rich more often than fourth-graders, but even in the fourth grade some children were not as clearly aware of the economic position of their families as of other symbols of social status. At the eighth-grade level, no child in the lower economic group described his family as rich, and many of the children were reluctant to answer the question.

Children in the first grade were not only inclined to rate themselves as rich, but they also rated a large proportion of their classmates as rich. In naming children who had "lots of money" they showed little agreement with adults. At the fourth-grade level, and even more at the sixth- and eighth-grade levels, the children were much less naive and, at the two upper levels, they could rate with high accuracy (as measured against the judgment of well-informed adults) the financial status of any ten classmates named at random.

The features in his environment which a child notices are not always those which an adult would recognize as signs of socio-economic status. What is physically near the child is not necessarily psychologically near to him in the sense that he notices and comments on it (Estvan, 1952). In a study by the writer and Tasch (1949) it was found that children living under conditions of poor housing were less likely to mention housing as an unpleasant feature of their environment than children whose living quarters were comparatively good.

Children tend to describe their circumstances as being in a middle position between poverty and wealth (Stendler, 1949). Children from wealthier homes, by saying they are "in-between," tend to understate their financial circumstances, while children from poorer homes tend, at least in relative terms, to overstate their condition. Adults similarly tend to identify themselves as belonging somewhere in the middle social class (Cantril, 1946).

Many children become more distinctly aware of status differences during adolescence as they develop an interest in dating and begin to think about their vocational future. At this time the disadvantage of living on the wrong side of the tracks, and the advantage of coming from a "good" family, may be brought home to a young person quite sharply. The status of a child's family obviously has had an important effect on his ideas and attitudes concerning himself if he is ashamed of his home or lacks confidence in his manners and his ability to mingle freely with others.

Varieties of Conditions
Associated with Socio-Economic Status

Socio-economic status, or social class, is frequently treated as though it were a monolithic "independent variable." Actually, of course, it is not. It represents about as varied a conglomerate of factors as can be found in life in general.

A person may stand high or low on the socio-economic ladder because of a bit of good or bad luck. He may stand where he is because he has inherited his family name and fortune, not because of his own merit. He may be high or low because of his genetic endowment. He may have genes which give him an advantage or disadvantage in a competitive society. He may temporarily be located at a given level (as many immigrants were when they first arrived in America) and then stay there, or move on. He may be an "upward mobile" person, heading from a "blue collar" home to a "white collar" career.

The socio-economic status or social class of a family into which a child is born represents, then, a condition which has been shaped, to varying degrees, by chance, choice, tradition, heredity, inheritance of wealth, economic opportunity, educational opportunity, competition, and a host of other factors. Whatever might be the factors that have operated in shaping the class into which he is born he will, of course, be exposed to its advantages, disadvantages, and pressures. How he will react cannot be predicted simply from information about what his circumstances are. He may be born into wealth and a famous name, and go to the dogs. He may be born into a home in a "delinquency area" and rise above it. The factors that enter into the psychological dimensions of a child's life are far more complex and far less obvious than the factors that appear in the sociological dimensions of his life. Given good educational opportunities, a child born into a lowly social station has at least a sporting chance to improve his lot. But the odds are loaded against him if low socio-economic status is imposed on him and his family by prejudice.

Boy-Girl Relationships

When a young child begins to enter into social relations with other children, distinctions between boys and girls are not likely to be very noticeable. Boys and girls play together and enjoy the same activities. Even at the preschool level, however, some distinctions and differences appear. Boys tend to be more active in their play, although differences within each sex group are greater than differences between the two sexes. At the ages of three and four, boys become involved in more conflicts than do girls and are more likely to resort to hitting. In a mixed group, boy-boy and girl-girl conflicts are likely to be more frequent than boy-girl conflicts. At the preschool level, especially after the age of two years, boy-boy and girl-girl friendships are likely to be more numerous than friendships between a boy and a girl. However, even though children prefer playmates of their own sex, there is a good deal of interplay, and at this age a child is not likely to be disturbed if he is in a group in which all other members are of the opposite sex.

Social Distance between the Sexes

"Social distance" between the sexes, which appears as early as the age of two or three, becomes more conspicuous at the elementary school level (Koch, 1944). At the late preschool and early elementary school levels, boys express a greater preference for boys and girls for girls. In the past, preference for members of the same sex has tended to increase up to about the high school level and then to decrease. In recent decades it appears that active socialization between boys and girls comes at an earlier age as indicated by boy-girl friendships, dating, and heterosexual interests.[10] This acceleration of heterosexual interests is probably due in part to an acceleration in the sphere of physical development. The adolescent growth spurt comes earlier than was true a number of generations ago and the girls experience their first menstruation earlier than their mothers or grandmothers (Tanner, 1955).

Romantic Interests of Boys and Girls

It is not usually until they reach their teens that boys and girls begin to date and let it be known that they are "going steady," but many children show a romantic interest in the opposite sex long before adolescence. Many adults have tender memories of childhood "sweethearts," and recall the surges of emotion they went through, ranging from delight to jealousy and grief, during their childhood romances.[11]

A greater degree of expression of heterosexual interest at present than two decades ago was found by Kuhlen and Houlihan (1965). These investigators compared the pattern of children's and adolescents' (grades six, nine, and twelve) sociometric choices in 1942 with choices in 1963. In all six comparisons (three involving boys' choices and three involving girls' choices) a larger percentage of the youngsters chose members of the opposite sex in 1963 than in 1942. The difference at the sixth-grade level in the boys' choices was not large (45 per cent chose girls in 1942 and 48.8 per cent chose girls in 1963). The differences between the girls' choices of boys on the two dates was

---

[10] See, e.g., Hetzer (1959; Smith (1952); Jones (1960); and Broderick (1961).
[11] For a discussion of amorous sentiments in children see Grant (1948).

greater (respectively 39.2 and 52.8 per cent). The swing toward boys choosing girls was more marked at the ninth-grade level.[12]

Life with peers becomes more complicated for girls than for boys as youngsters move into later childhood and adolescence. In the early 'forties, Tryon (1944) found that the qualities that make an adolescent boy popular with other boys are also the qualities that make him a favorite with girls. On the other hand, it is less likely that the qualities which make a girl admired by other girls will also make her a favorite among the boys. A more recent study by Reese (1962) of fifth graders indicates, on the basis of sociometric choices, that girls are more favorable toward the boys who are most accepted by other boys, but a girl's acceptance by boys does not similarly mean that she will win acceptance by other girls.

Prejudice

Many children, while yet very young, are exposed to influences that produce prejudice. In a study by Ammons (1950) evidence of active prejudice was found as early as four years. The typical child in the late preschool years is more likely, if he discriminates at all, to show a preference for members of his own ethnic group than a prejudice against members of another group.

Using pictures representing Negro and white boys and girls, Abel and Sahinkaya (1962) found that boys and girls showed a preference for members of their own sex earlier than a preference for their own race. Race preference was not evident among the four-year-olds, and at the five-year level only the boys showed a definite preference for their own race. In the early preschool years children's reactions to ethnic differences are likely to be more on a perceptual than on an attitudinal or evaluative level. A child notices a difference, say, between a white or colored doll and identifies the one that most nearly resembles him before he shows any clear pattern of placing a greater value on one, and devaluating the other. White children have been found to identify themselves as white earlier than Negro children identify or acknowledge themselves as Negroes.[13]

Soon, however, the values of the adult community come into play. For reasons that are understandable, it is easier for a white child comfortably to identify himself as white than for a Negro child to recognize and accept his ethnic identity. Parents of Negro children face a difficult and poignant situa-

---

[12] An interesting additional finding was that there was a greater difference between 1942 and 1963 in percentage of persons who chose a member of the opposite sex than in percentage chosen. In other words, the proportion of boys and girls who had qualities that attract choices by the opposite sex were about the same in 1963 as in a previous generation.

[13] For discussions on the early development of discrimination and prejudice see Clark and Clark (1947); Goodman (1952); Stevenson and Stewart (1958); Clausen and Williams (1963); and Clark (1963).

tion when they feel required to communicate to their child that he is a Negro and will be discriminated against because of that fact.

Prejudice is a bias held against an individual because he is a member of a certain group. It is a form of prejudgment, a generalized attitude of disfavor. This means that a person belonging to a group against which there is a prejudice is regarded with misgiving, and perhaps with distrust or hostility, not because of his *individual* qualities but because he belongs to a *group* against which a stand has been taken.

Prejudice is a sickness within the society. It has three unhappy aspects: It is damaging to those against whom there is prejudice; it is an unhealthy condition in the person who is prejudiced; and it creates difficulties for the total social group.

Emotional Aspect of Prejudice

Persons who are conspicuously prejudiced are more likely than unprejudiced persons to be anxious, insecure, and burdened with veiled hostility.[14] Their values are more probably based on the authoritarian standards imposed by others than on personal convictions of their own. Prejudice sometimes is a form of displaced anger by which a troubled person seeks to resolve or evade his grievances by fixing blame on a scapegoat. Unfavorable attitudes toward others may be a reflection of rejecting attitudes toward oneself. As mentioned in an earlier section, it has been found that Negro children who expressed positive feelings about themselves also expressed more positive feelings toward other Negroes, and toward whites, than did children who were least positive in their attitudes toward themselves (Trent, 1953). Tabachnick (1962) found that elementary school children who expressed satisfaction with themselves tended to be less prejudiced than children who were less satisfied with themselves.

Emotional Consequences of Prejudice

When a child is treated unkindly or unfairly because he is a member of a group against which there is a prejudice he cannot help feeling hurt and angry. This is a natural response to unkindness, but it may be a seed from which he derives a set of prejudices of his own. When a person against whom there is a prejudice reacts by becoming prejudiced, the member of the minority group will have the most difficulty. Members of a minority not only have to bear the grievances of the majority group, but they also lack the strength to retaliate in kind.

A moving account of the problems and emotional difficulties faced by people because of their membership in a minority group has been offered by Goff (1949) who interviewed 150 Negro children in two cities. Among the

---

[14] For references dealing with characteristics of prejudiced persons see Adorno, *et al.* (1950); Gough, *et al.* (1950); Ammons (1950); Harris, *et al.* (1950); Frenkel-Brunswik (1951); Harding, *et al.* (1954); and Clausen and Williams (1963).

difficulties faced by the children (as seen and interpreted by them) because of their race were disparagement, ridicule, and other aggressive and hostile acts. Consider, for example, this situation:

> A Negro girl stood in line, eagerly waiting her turn to receive a doll which a storekeeper had advertised would be given free to any girl who came to the store. When she finally reached the counter she was told she could not have a doll—the dolls were only for white girls.

In Goff's study, almost half of the children said they had suffered from feelings of self-belittlement such as shame, hurt feelings, embarrassment, and the like. Girls seemed to smart more severely than boys under what they regarded as rude and humiliating treatment.

A child who is the victim of prejudice faces a tough predicament. As a member of a minority group it is dangerous for him to use against others the weapons they use against him. If he is aggressive he invites attack. If he turns the other cheek the result may be further abuse. If, as he grows older, he becomes resigned to the fact that the doors of opportunity are closed he runs the risk of being called lazy and shiftless. If he tries to assert himself through the usual channels of competition for position, wealth, or power he runs the risk of being called "pushy" or unscrupulous. In the meantime he may be denied even the solace of sharing his troubles with others. In studies of minority groups it has been noted that parents may be deeply concerned about prejudice but evade the issue when it is brought up by their children (see Goodman, 1952; and Weaver, 1955).

When a person is the victim of prejudice, one of the ironic turns of fate is that he will sometimes turn the prejudice against himself or his own group. This occurs when a member of minority group A, unable to retaliate against offending members of majority group B, "takes out" his anger against himself or his own people.

Communication of Prejudice. Children may become prejudiced because of a firsthand unpleasant experience, but prejudices are usually transmitted to them through the attitudes shown by their elders. Other things being equal, a child will tend to be favorably disposed toward other people, no matter what group they belong to. But he will be disposed against people whom his elders dislike even though he has no significant firsthand experience with them. Many children express unfavorable views toward minority groups in America even though they have had little or no contact with members of the groups (Radke, *et al.*, 1950).

Children's Games and Play Activities

Games and play activities are important factors in the "socialization" process. Moreover, a child's choice of games, and the roles he plays in them, reveal a great deal about his personality.

Games are self-chosen activities (or at least chosen by leaders within the group) and they have their own built-in rules. These are handed down, with minor adaptations, from one generation of children to the next. Although games are played for fun, they also represent a form of self-chosen discipline. The rules are sometimes relaxed by the participants (for example, by giving a younger child a chance to take part), but when children play or compete as equals the rules take on an iron-clad quality and any child who violates them is likely to meet with scorn and rejection.

Some children who rebel against adult authority will submit to rules imposed by their peers. Redl and Wineman (1952) in their work with disturbed children ("children who hate") state that in almost every neighborhood ". . . there are certain activities, behavioral customs, and games, the 'rules' for which, though unwritten, are well known and automatically accepted by everyone." They go on to say that ". . . even our very disturbed youngsters commanded a halt to their total rule rejection when it came to such well-ingrained 'neighborhood codes'."

Although the rules for a particular game are rather rigid, the variety of games and the variety of governing rules are so great that they offer even a rather timid and ineffective child a chance somewhere to fit into some games.

Through games a child has a chance to try his powers, to venture, to compete in peer-made as distinguished from adult-controlled situations, to lose without too much loss of face (unless his failure is habitual), to accept defeat "like a good sport." Some children when first introduced to rules of the game find it difficult to accept them, and the derision they receive from other players may be a bit rough, until they learn to fall in line.

A series of studies by Sutton-Smith (1955, 1962, 1964) gives a provocative insight into children's games and the characteristics of children who choose certain games and not others. Sutton-Smith has classified games into various categories (see Table 13): games of pure physical skill, games of physical skill combined with strategy, games depending primarily on strategy, and games of chance. The various games provide a "buffered" experience introduction to and experience with competition.

Sutton-Smith has also described characteristic types of participation in games. There are the "fortunists" who are players in games of chance and try to succeed by relying on luck. There are "potents" who try to succeed by physical power. There are "strategists" who try to succeed by making wise decisions, and "potent strategists."

Children from eight to twelve years who took part in a study by Sutton-Smith showed a good deal of consensus in their views regarding the characteristic types of play preferred by their peers, as well as in their naming of some children as failures.

The "strategists" and "potent strategists" were higher than chance-takers or failures in socio-economic status and in intelligence. They were also described by peers as being quieter, "not getting mad," and better sports. "Potent" boys were characterized as being more restless, bossy, more easily angered, better sports, and more inclined to take a chance.

According to Sutton-Smith, a child's play style is related to the kind of upbringing he has received. A child who has had "high obedience" training is likely to become a strategist in his play; a potent physical skill type of preference is more closely related to early "achievement training"; the "fortunists" represent largely children of low socio-economic status who have not been reared to prize achievement but to believe that success depends on lucky breaks.

In a sensitive discussion of the psychological significance of games, Sutton-Smith points out ways in which children might be encouraged to participate in play that is suited to their needs and might help them to cope with their difficulties. For example, a disturbed child who has difficulty in following rule games because of his social immaturity might succeed in "cheating games" in which the major and acceptable challenge is to fool an opponent and get away with behavior he ordinarily is supposed to guard against. The card game *I Doubt It*, for example, permits a player to "declare" the cards he has in his hand without showing them. If unchallenged, he receives the score he has declared. But if challenged after a false declaration, he loses the points he has

Table 13 Number of Games Differentiating Between the Sexes at p = .05 or Better

Game Classes	Nonsignificant	Favoring Girls	Favoring Boys
Strategy	Beast, Birds & Fish, Dominoes, Chess, Parcheesi, Scrabble, Tic Tac Toe, Clue, Monopoly (8)	I've Got a Secret, Name That Tune, Checkers, Twenty Questions, I Spy (5)	(0)
Chance	Coin-Matching, Forfeits, Cards, Seven-Up (4)	Bingo, Spin the Bottle, Post Office, Musical Chairs, Letters, Colors, Initials (7)	Dice (1)
Pure Physical Skill	Quoits (1)	Hopscotch, Jump Rope, Jacks, Tiddleywinks (4)	Bowling, Horseshoes, Racing, Tug of War, Darts, Shuffleboard, Bows & Arrows, Throwing Snowballs, Shooting (9)
Physical Skill and Strategy	Handball, Tennis, Volleyball, Prisoner's Base, Fox & Hounds, Ping Pong (5)	Pick up Sticks (1)	Marbles, Wrestling, Boxing, Basketball, Football, Capture the Flag, Punt Back, Pool, Billiards, Baseball, Soccer (11)

Reprinted, by permission, from Brian Sutton-Smith, "Child Training and Game Involvement." *Ethnology*, April, 1962, 1, 2, pp. 167–185.

declared. Suspicion and legitimate cheating are central features of this game. Some disturbed children seem to respond more enthusiastically and with less frustration to this type of game than to some other types. Sutton-Smith gives other examples of how a game with a certain structure may be more gratifying and manageable than others for a child who is hesitant or insecure. In simple Tag, for instance, the person who is It has more command of the situation than in Cross Tag. The person who is It in simple Tag can chase any player he wishes to tag; this gives him more chance to succeed. In Cross Tag, on the other hand, the person who is It does not have this choice. He must tag the player who passes between him and someone he is chasing. A child with limited confidence, who is effective in simple Tag, may become baffled, and drop out, when the game is changed to Cross Tag.

A child who is diffident and who has a low status within the group has more opportunity to be a leader if the leader is chosen by chance (such as by means of a count-out rhyme) instead of on the basis of popularity.

Usually, of course, adults do not intervene in children's games. But as Sutton-Smith points out, an adult is better able to be helpful if he is aware of some of the psychological meanings of the roles children play in games and is aware also of the power and prestige status which makes it very difficult for some children to encounter anything but neglect and failure.

Recommended Readings

Roger C. Barker and Herbert F. Wright in *Midwest and Its Children* (1954) present a very interesting, detailed picture of the many avenues through which children move as they enter the social world. A. I. Rabin's *Growing Up in the Kibbutz* (1965) gives one of the more recent accounts of children reared in a group setting. Celia B. Stendler's *Readings in Child Behavior and Development* (1964) contains several papers on the subject of social development.

PART FOUR

Emotional Development

15

The Meaning

of Emotion

AFFECTION, JOY, SEXUALITY

The day-to-day experiences of a growing child commonly include a blend of cognitive (intellectual) and affective (emotional) elements. These two aspects of mental activity are interrelated, but it is useful to consider them separately.

It is in the sphere of feeling—the qualitative aspect of an emotional experience—that a growing child is most intimately aware of his existence as a separate self.

In the course of development, a child's emotional experiences, and their after-effects, profoundly influence his "mental health." The label, "mental health," as commonly used, is practically equivalent to emotional health, just as impaired mental health consists, to an important degree, of some kind of emotional disorder.

Differences between Thoughts and Feelings

Although cognition and emotion cannot systematically be set apart in an all-or-none fashion, they have distinctive features that are important from a developmental point of view. Both are grounded in physiological functions, but they differ physiologically. Cognitive experiences, including sensation, perception, imagining and thinking, are localized primarily in the cerebral cortex. Emotional experiences not only involve the higher brain centers, but also the "lower" or phylogenetically "older" portions of the brain stem, and the autonomic nervous system.[1]

Generally speaking, cognitive behavior can be judged by a standard of truth. On a continuum ranging from relatively elementary sensory impressions to abstract thinking, cognition can, by and large, be assessed in terms of how faithfully it reflects objective reality, and in terms of its correctness from the standpoint of verifiable fact. An emotional experience, on the other hand, is neither true nor false. An emotional reaction can, of course, as regarded by others, or in terms of objective criteria, be judged as appropriate or inappropriate. But when a child is angry he is angry, and that is that. He may, as an afterthought, view a particular display of anger as justified or foolish; but in the realm of emotions there is no verification process equivalent to the formula $3 + 2 = 5$ in the sphere of thinking.

While cognitive experiences may vary in veracity, affective experiences vary in quality and intensity. The qualities embrace all the fairly well-defined feeling states occurring in everyday life, such as pleasure or fear, and a vast range of nuances of feeling.

The intensity of an affective experience has three interrelated aspects: (a) the degree to which the individual feels "moved" by the emotion—which may range, say, from mild pleasure to ecstacy; (b) the extent of the mobilization of the physiological machinery underlying emotional behavior and, (c) the degree to which, along with it all, the aroused individual involuntarily responds with mild or violent expressive reactions, and has a weak or uncontrollable impulse to action (to seize what is pleasant, to flee in fear, to fight in anger).

In the cognitive sphere, there is continuity in the progression from concrete elementary sensory experiences to abstract thinking. There is not a corresponding phenomenon in the emotional sphere. A person's emotions may, it is true, be aroused by an increasingly wide range of subtle stimuli; but there is nothing in the emotional experience of fear, for example, that corresponds, in the cognitive sphere, to the difference between knowledge of fear as a concrete experience and as an abstract concept.

In the cognitive sphere, it is possible to reconstruct, more or less accurately,

[1] In Chapter 5 there is some discussion of the functioning of the autonomic division of the nervous system and its activation in newborn children.

the steps in thinking leading from recognition of a problem to its future solution. While still staying in the cognitive milieu, a person can re-think his thoughts. It is not as readily possible, at will, to re-feel a feeling. Unless an emotion is triggered anew by a concrete happening, it is only by the intervention of cognitive processes that a person can reconstruct the circumstances in which he experienced a fear, and even then it is unlikely that he can reinstate the full impact of the fear itself, although individuals differ in this regard, and it seems that some persons, through a process of thought, can re-establish a feeling of anger more readily than a feeling of fear.

Another distinction between cognition and emotional behavior is that cognition is inherently more susceptible to self-correction. In "pure" cognition, with a minimum of emotional involvement, a person can revise his thoughts with little difficulty. He needs eight blocks to make a little walled-off enclosure, but when he goes to the pool of blocks he brings only seven. All right, back for another, and next time bring eight. No trouble.

A fervent belief may, of course, have the force of a strongly entrenched habit, but even such thinking can be changed when it bumps into realities that contradict it (unless, as a form of rationalization, it is used unwittingly to serve needs in the emotional sphere). In the sphere of emotion the process of review is not so simple. Once angered, a child must cool off before it would be possible for him even to begin to think about his anger. If he should reflect on his anger (which is extremely unlikely in a small child) there is nothing similar to a gap in the wall to remind him where he made a mistake with his building blocks. For him, through his own devices, to re-examine an emotional reaction would require quite a feat of reflection.

According to the foregoing line of thought, cognition and emotion differ in what might be called "reproductability" of the elements involved. When a child has reached the stage where he can marshall images to represent reality he can, within the limits of his intellectual ability, resurrect a great deal of a recent past experience. When he tells his father about a visit he and his mother made to grandmother, he can reconstruct mental pictures of the trip, of his grandmother's appearance, of the cookies he ate, of an oncoming car on the road, and the screech of the brakes which signified a near accident. But his reconstruction of his pleasure, and of the fear engendered by the near-accident, is usually a pale thing compared with the original experience. He can re-live the perceptual content of his day's experience—and perhaps a year or two later, he can bring it back into the stream of his consciousness. But emotional elements are much harder to recall. He can perhaps remember their structural dimensions, but in his waking moments it is unlikely that he can reinstate the feeling of fear unless it is triggered anew say, by the sound of screeching brakes.

Since the perceptual image, and not the spasm of fear, can be revived, even a child's cognitive recollection of the near accident may fade and disappear. But the fear has left a mark, if this child later, for reasons he has forgotten, is unaccountably frightened by the sound of brakes.

It is easier for a child to set up a one-man board of review in the cognitive sphere than in the sphere of feeling, since it is easier for a child to bring the cognitive than to bring the emotional into his flow of thought. Along with this, it is easier for a child to be "rational" in dealing with the intellectual elements of his on-going experience than to be similarly rational in dealing with his emotional experiences. The fact that emotional experiences may leave a mark even though they can not be recollected at the cognitive level helps to account for much of what is "irrational" in human behavior.

Freud and others have proposed the concepts of suppression and repression to explain the fact that emotional aftereffects may linger even though the cognitive aspects have waned. The "repressed" affects, presumably, are pushed into the unconscious. The concept of repression implies an active process through which, in effect, the apparatus of the mind eliminates an experience from conscious awareness. The idea of repression is controversial. Psychologists do not generally agree as to how tenable or useful the idea might be, and, if tenable, just how the process of repression occurs. However, there is quite general agreement that the aftereffects of past emotional experiences may influence present experience in ways a person cannot account for. The influence may be unconscious in the sense that an individual is not cognitively aware of how earlier experiences affect his present behavior; he is, as it were, blind to events in his own history that underlie his present tendency to react in a certain way.

The phenomenon of "transference" illustrates this point. We see the transference of the effects of earlier emotional experiences when one child fondly views his teacher as a loving person, unwittingly reacting to her as though she were his own loving mother, while another child, similarly treated by the same teacher, views her as a punitive person, without knowing or asking why. An example of such an "unconscious" reaction is offered in a study by Franco (1965). Many school beginners in this study, who perceived their mothers as using physical punishment also insisted that their teachers would strike a child. They persisted in this view even after having been with the teacher several months, with ample opportunity to learn that she actually did not strike children.

The role of unconscious processes is especially significant in areas that involve a child's emotions. A child, jealous of a younger sibling, who carefully "feeds" the larger of her two dolls and sends the other to bed without a crumb, is unlikely to be consciously aware that she is "acting out" her jealousy.

Early Emotional Reactions

In Chapter 5, we noted that at the time of birth emotional behavior is not well differentiated. A child exhibits generalized excitement, in which it is not possible to detect the distinguishing marks of discomfort, fear, or anger that will appear in time. Even a seemingly healthy, well-fed child may be so wrought up that similar behavior in an adult could only mean that a catastrophe had befallen him. A sympathetic but puzzled adult might view the child's agitation as a sign of discomfort, or as anger, or as unaccountable fear.

With the passing weeks, a child's affective behavior shows increasing differentiation. With apparent interest he explores his environment with his eyes. He fixes his eyes on a human face, sometimes with flattering intensity. The advent of this selective attention to a human face is sometimes dramatic, illustrating the principle of "wholeheartedness and gradation" mentioned in an earlier chapter. Some babies, when they reach this stage, will cry in apparent hunger and then, when the precious nipple is presented to their lips, will ignore it, gazing into the face of the one who feeds them, as though, for the moment, this were "Paradise enow," before they proceed to take the milk.

As a child grows older his expressions of emotion become more clearly distinguishable. For example, when adult judges were asked to identify pictures taken of a ten-month-old child when he was exposed to conditions that usually arouse fear, astonishment, satisfaction, anger, and the like, their identifications were more accurate than could be expected by chance. The sounds an infant uses to express emotion also become more definite after a time.

The Role of Needs, Drives, Motives, Goals

As a child matures, whether or not he will be aroused emotionally by a happening depends on what he has at stake. Emotion can be aroused by anything that furthers or threatens the gratification of his desires, his motives and plans, anything that blocks or promotes activities he desires to carry out, or anything that helps or hinders his hopes and aspirations. As a result, the same external event can produce varied effects. A child who is poised for action will be angered when someone holds him tightly, but if he is in a mood to be cuddled he will enjoy being held.

To list all the drives that make a person subject to emotion would be an impossible undertaking, for while some are "original," common to all persons, and quite obvious (such as the drive to obtain food when hungry), others have been influenced by learning and past experience and may be unique (such as a certain child's desire to collect the stubs of theater tickets). Yet it is possible to specify groups of motives that come into play.

Some drives are associated with *primary needs* of the organism, such as the need for food, for drink, for air, for rest and sleep. Connected with many of these needs are cravings of varying intensity, such as a thirsty person's craving for water. In addition, human beings, in common with other creatures, have a drive to use their energies. Another category of motives includes those involved in a child's relations with other people: his desire for company, his need to belong, to be accepted, to have a place, and to enjoy status with his own age group. These desires vary with different children, and are of course very much influenced by learning and experience. In addition, there are almost countless varieties of motives of a more optional character that are described by such everyday terms as interests, wishes and desires, wants, and hopes.

Among the most prominent concerns underlying emotion as a child grows older are those connected with his desire to maintain his self-esteem and to protect and assert the ideas and attitudes he has formed regarding himself.

Interweaving of Emotion
and Other Aspects of Development

The development of emotions during infancy and childhood is interwoven with other aspects of development. As a child's senses become more acute, as his capacities for discrimination and perception mature, the range of events which arouse emotion becomes wider and wider. As a child's capacity for understanding and imagination increase, the things that affect him emotionally become increasingly involved with symbols and fancies, with abstract plans and values.

One consequence of the interweaving of emotional and other aspects of growth is that the same external stimulus may induce quite different emotional reactions as a child moves from one phase of development to the next. At one phase, an infant smiles when spoken to, even though the voice is "angry"; but a similar angry voice can later produce fear, and, still later, annoyance. Similarly, an infant who at one point smiled at strangers may later show fear and, still later, view strangers with interest and curiosity. The youngster who merrily grabs and bangs a toy at eight months may, at about twelve months, slam it down in anger if he fails to figure out how it works, or if he tries to take it apart and does not succeed. During the next phase, he may show signs of pleasure when he discovers how the toy works. Later, when the toy is no longer a challenge to his hands or his wits, it neither attracts nor offends him. Still later, when he is aware of what is "mine" and "thine," he may angrily snatch it away if another child tries to take it, as though the toy, although no longer alluring in itself, is still valued as a piece of property.

Concealment and Suppression of Feeling

In early infancy a child's expression of emotion is rather aimless and not very precise, and then as he grows older he is able to reveal his emotions in more clearly defined ways. But from early childhood forces are at work that induce him to moderate or blunt his expressions of emotion and to conceal his feelings. The discipline most children receive from others figures importantly in inducing them to restrain their show of emotion and to conceal their "true" feelings.

We might ask, however, if the curbing of outbursts of emotion is to some degree a *developmental* as well as a cultural phenomenon. Some animals (dogs, for example) are less given to yelping, whining, or crying when they are older than when they were younger. (It may be, of course, that the older dog is not more stoical but simply has less to whine about.) More directly to the point, it has been observed that children, while yet very young, show an ability to muffle or modify their show of emotion. Meili (1957) observed, for example, that between the middle of the first and the second year of life, some children would "swallow" their crying, seemingly fighting back their tears, when a toy was taken away from them. Also about this time he noted seemingly forced or affected laughter, and laughing or smiling that seemed to express embarrassment rather than pleasure. When a child who is frustrated comes forth with an "artificial" laugh instead of a show of temper, he may be trying to be polite, as a result of the training he has received. But something within the child's own development probably also has intervened. With added mental growth he might now perceive the frustration as a challenge to his wits and not just as something that provokes his anger by thwarting his wishes.

Pressures from Others Leading to Concealment of Emotion. At first by his parents and brothers and sisters, and later by others, a child is reminded to calm down, not get angry, not be afraid. He is told, in effect, not only to conceal his emotion but even to avoid having emotion: There is "nothing to be afraid of"; "You better not get sore at me"; "There is nothing to cry about or to laugh at." There are many pressures on children to drive their emotions underground. Children learn to disguise their feelings, to hide them, to express them in devious ways.

"Don't Cry!"

Pressure on children to play false with their feelings, and thus in time to play false with themselves, appears noticeably in connection with feelings springing from grief, sorrow, pain, or anxiety so acute that the individual is helpless and feels like breaking into tears.

It is natural for a child to cry when hurt, to sob when in distress, to weep when lonely, to shriek with fright, and to scream in anger if he is helpless in his rage and there is nothing else he can do in his helplessness.

But many adults and many older children recoil when they see another person cry. Some become anxious at the sight of tears and the sound of weeping. So from an early age, quite apart from their own natural course of development (which leads to changes in the use of crying), children are constrained not to let their feelings show by crying. They also are under pressure to conceal feelings that might cause them to cry, and to guard against such feelings.

The writer recalls a newspaper story about a baby who fell out of a window several stories high and when the mother rushed out to pick up the child, mercifully alive and crying lustily, she said: "Don't cry." As though a child should fall from a skyscraper to earn the right to cry! Actually, when the mother said, "Don't cry," she was not giving a command but expressing her own agitation, yet it is noteworthy that it took this form. From the child's point of view such an admonition might sound as though there is something bad about crying.

When people say to children, "Don't cry," the reason may be that crying arouses in them buried recollections and banished impulses, going back to the time when they would like to have cried in anger, or screamed with fear, or wept out of a feeling of hurt or loneliness and helplessness. It is hard for an older person to endure a reminder of these old and buried hurts, and the harder it is the more distressed he will be when another cries.

When a child is asked to keep from crying he is being asked to bury something of himself, to conceal rather than to express and to face his impulses and his feelings at the moment they occur. And thereby we encourage him to go astray in his development. If an older person wishes to understand a child's emotions and to help him cope with the conditions that arouse emotion, it is necessary to encourage the child to face feelings rather than to falsify them or run away from them. But to do this requires courage on the adult's part, the courage to permit a child to allow his feelings to show and the courage to face feelings that are aroused within himself when the emotions of someone else appear in raw form.

It is necessary, of course, for a child as he grows older to learn to set limits on his emotional outbursts. He shouldn't laugh in church and he had better not laugh at his teacher. For his own good and the safety of others he must learn not to rend and destroy when he is angry. Children are required to curb their impulses (especially their anger) even in a therapy situation where the aim is to encourage them to reveal their feelings. However, (so the writer believes) the pressures placed on children to conceal their feelings go far beyond what is necessary for a child's own good or the welfare of others.

Hidden Currents of Feeling

As a consequence of the suppression of an outward display of emotion, there usually is a wide disparity between an older child's actions and his inner state. Even among nursery school children there is a marked difference between the person who appears in public and the hidden person who harbors feelings quite different from those he puts on display. At the adolescent level, most children have become so adept in acting the role they are supposed to play that there is a sharp difference between the "outer" and "inner" dimensions of their lives. There is the visible scholar who goes through the academic motions; and there is the invisible scholar, preoccupied with personal concerns that are a world removed from the "academic" man (or woman) who appears in the classroom or the "organization" man (or woman) who goes through the social rituals prescribed by the group.

At the adult level, the difference between what is revealed and what is concealed is likely to be even more marked, so marked, according to a study by the writer and Lazar (1962), that persons who are long-time "friends" and professional colleagues actually are strangers to one another.

One reason for this strangeness is that in the natural course of development a growing person wants to protect his privacy. But another reason is that in our culture we usually try to promote all kinds of learning except knowledge of our own feelings and the feelings of others. As a consequence, when we try to understand the emotional life of a child we seek a kind of knowledge which most of us, at home and at school, have been trained assiduously not to acquire. Therefore, it is difficult for us to fathom a child's feelings. But two circumstances come to our aid. One is that many children, if properly approached, are not only willing but pathetically eager to reveal feelings they usually keep hidden. The writer has frequently found that youngsters will disclose to a friendly inquirer joys and fears which they have not mentioned to their parents or teachers or playmates. In doing so, they usually are better able to tell what they are afraid of than to tell why they are afraid; but the information is revealing as far as it goes. The other is that many adults, uneasily troubled by their hidden problems, seek help in coming to grips with them.

Affection

Affection has been discussed in several earlier parts of this book so we will touch on only a few aspects of the subject in this section.

In his relations with his parents a child craves affection and, in time, he seeks to bestow it. As was pointed out in Chapters 6 and 13, friendly responses far outnumber unfriendly ones in a normal infant's relationships with adults and later in his dealings with other children outside the home. At the elementary school level, children show their need for affection in their intense desire to be accepted by their peers and in the emphasis they give to the qualities of kindness when they describe teachers whom they like best.

Origins of Affection

According to one theory, affection is something a child acquires; according to another, affection is inherent in a human being's "original nature."

According to the first view, love is learned. A youngster becomes attached to persons or things by virtue of the satisfaction they bring him, the role they play in gratifying his elemental needs. Briefly put, he loves his mother because he likes her milk, and then his fondness for the milk spreads to his mother. According to the second view, love is not a by-product or after-thought but is as basic a feature of human nature as legs are an original part of the body. This view is stated by Ashley-Montagu (1953) who says: "The most important thing to realize about the nature of human nature is that the most significant ingredient in its structure is love."

In his well-known studies of "The Nature of Love" Harlow (1958) went into the milk angle—the role of being nursed—in determining infant mon-key's attachments to their mothers. Baby monkeys were reared by surrogate "mothers," one constructed of wire, the other made of cloth. When both "mothers" were available, the monkeys preferred the cloth mother even though they were fed by the wire mother, equipped with a well-supplied artificial breast. Except when feeding on the wire mother, the monkeys would cling to the cloth mother, run to her as a refuge when frightened, and use her as their home base. Harlow concluded that the "contact comfort" an infant derives from a mother is more important than the mother's milk in the de-velopment of affectional attachments.

In one sense, the question we have raised is academic, for whether the need for receiving and giving affection is original or acquired it eventually plays a powerful role in a child's life. In another sense, however, it is not academic, for it touches on a basic issue in the philosophy of human growth. Our view of human potentialities is quite different if, for example, we assume that love is an acquired by-product of self-interest, or assume that it is at least as "nat-ural" for a child to love as to hate.

Varieties of Affectional Attachments

While discussions of love should, presumably, be conducted in a spirit of charity, this has not always been the case. There has been controversy, some-times a bit heated, about the role of love in the life of a young child and the conditions essential for its development.

One theoretical position, is largely an outgrowth of Freud's work. Some aspects of this position have been discussed in earlier chapters, but it is in-structive to review them in the present context: to develop in a healthy way, (1) an infant needs a primary love object; (2) this should be a single adult, preferably the mother or mother surrogate; (3) anything which might dilute the love attachment, such as the presence of "multiple" mothers is detri-mental; (4) a loving touch is an essential element not only for a child's emo-tional development but also for intellectual growth and physical well-being.

Also, in keeping with this view, it has been claimed (5) that separating a child from his mother, once he has formed a primary attachment to her, is traumatic and may even lead to death. Furthermore, according to this position, when institutional children show retarded or impaired development the primary reason is (6) that they are emotionally starved—their "affect hunger" is not satisfied. It is this lack of emotional nurture that (7) depresses their alertness and enterprise, impairs their learning of motor skills, their intellectual development and capacity for establishing wholesome social relationships.

These views express or imply that if things go badly for a child, lack of love is the main cause and, conversely, when things go well, it is mainly because he has had the right kind of love, from the right person, in the right amount.

This line of thought has been questioned. This may seem odd, for no right-minded citizen would vote against love. However, findings in numerous studies referred to in earlier chapters indicate that the statements listed above oversimplify the developmental context in which affectional attachments develop, that they do not adequately acknowledge children's flexibility and adaptability nor the role played by a child himself in promoting affectionate relationships with others. It appears from a study, and a review of the literature, by Schaffer and Emerson (1964) that the ability to form an attachment to a specific individual, which arises, in the majority of cases, in the third quarter of the first year, is one expression of "a more general development." This includes changes in a child's cognitive structure—in the manner in which a child's perceptions are organized and related to each other and to external objects. (It is at about this time, according to Piaget, that children are capable of "object conservation"—awareness that objects have a permanence of their own and continue to exist even though they are out of sight).

Many of the children in the Schaffer-Emerson study did not single out the most available person (the mother) as their favorite object of affection. Several selected the father, even though he spent less time with them. Some children formed multiple attachments, indicating that focusing affection on one person is not a necessary or inherent feature of affectional development. Schaffer and Emerson point out that a child should not simply be regarded as a passive recipient of friendly attention. He takes an active part in seeking interaction with his social environment, and frequently it is he, not an adult, who initiates contact. Children differ in the intensity of their attachments. These differences apparently are linked with a more pervasive tendency—namely, general social responsiveness.

Schaffer and Emerson express the view that further study of individual differences in the intensity of a child's attachments should not be confined to inquiry into environmental factors but must also take account of children's inherent characteristics.

The study just cited, along with many others mentioned in various sections of the book, emphasize the importance of stimulation in a child's early life and a child's own initiative in seeking stimulation. Human beings obviously are potentially the best sources of stimulation, and the authors conjecture that a child's need for having persons near him and attentive to him may arise from his need for stimulation in general.

The account given by Freud and Dann (1951) of orphaned children (reviewed in Chapter 13) indicates how versatile children can be in asserting their capacity to give and bestow affection. This study concerns six children, orphaned and uprooted during World War II. These children had formed strong attachments to one another; they found their love objects within their own group, and exhibited a degree of warmth, loyalty, and identification with one another's needs such as is rarely found among siblings. In a sense, each child was a "mother" for each of the others. For a time they manifested a number of problems, such as hypersensitivity, aggressiveness, restlessness, and autoeroticism, yet they survived, and eventually formed attachments to adults, without having had anything approaching a primary love object during the first two or three years of their lives.

Pleasures, Joys and Satisfactions

This section substantially repeats material from the preceding edition of this book. The writer, while not too satisfied with his own earlier inquiries into what makes children happy, regrets that the joys of childhood have continued over the years to receive relatively little attention in research.

The joys of childhood are as many and varied as the scope of children's activities. Most obvious as a source of pleasure is anything that gratifies an appetite or desire. Also quite apparent are the joys children derive from free and unimpeded activity.

Activity Pleasure

An infant appears to be having a pleasant time as he coos and gurgles, exercises his voice, kicks, manipulates convenient objects with his hands, and ventures to creep, crawl, and walk. We cannot tell for sure whether a child gets as much pleasure from his activities as his shouts, laughter, and eagerness seem to indicate. But it is apparent that, like a healthy puppy that frisks playfully, a child draws satisfaction from being active of his own accord.

Zestful Ventures. From infancy onward a child ventures into new activities, he stumbles into difficult situations, and he often welcomes excitement. He sometimes seems to get a thrill out of "play" with emotions which, in themselves, are not pleasant. He "plays" with anger as he tests the patience of his parents and the forebearance of his peers. He "plays" with fear, returning of his own accord to situations that are somewhat frightening to him, but not completely overwhelming. In many ways a child "asks for trouble." If he feels secure, he is likely to take chances and taste the pleasure of getting out of a tight spot.

"Pleasures of the Mind." Among the pleasures a child experiences as he grows older are those that occur when he satisfies his curiosity and applies his mind to intellectual tasks. Many children are extremely happy when they first discover that they are able to read. And even arithmetic has charms. One seven-year-old child described the happiest day of her life as the day "I learned to take away!" (the day she learned to subtract).

Joy in Self-Discovery. Prominent among the joy-producing experiences in a child's life are those that give him a new perception of himself, a new glimpse of his ability, a broadened view of his capacity to "take it," to stand up to a difficulty, to handle a troublesome problem. Many children discover such satisfactions in the process of overcoming their fears, a process by which they gain freedom from a threat and also a greater realization of their strength. In one of his studies the author had the good fortune over a stretch of several days to watch a child (aged about three) who was trying to overcome a fear of high places. The youngster had made an inclined plane with a board, one end resting on the ground, the other on a high box. Again and again he started to walk up the board, at first venturing only a few steps, then a few more. When finally he succeeded in going the whole way he stood on top of the box and let forth a shout of triumph such as Beowulf might have made after slaying a dragon.

Table 14 summarizes some of the joys of childhood as expressed in the terms children themselves use, or broad categories based on such terms. Younger children expressed their joys frequently in the language of gifts, holidays and festivities, games and sports, and visits or special contacts with people. This language reveals more concerning the objective nature of the enjoyable event than concerning its subjective meaning, for often it appeared (but was not literally stated) that the joy stemmed not from the gift alone (or the visit, and the like), but had a deeper meaning. For example, in many of these accounts of "one of my happiest days" children mentioned gifts which in themselves were not particularly valuable (when a teacher reverses the usual order of things and gives an apple to a pupil, the apple has a value far beyond that of the fruit itself). To many children, a gift is far more than just another material possession. It is a symbol of acceptance, a token of good will. It may be a gesture of forgiveness, an expression of confidence. A thoughtful person gives not simply the gift he bears in his hand but something of himself.

In view of this, many of the happy circumstances listed in Table 14 should be regarded as having a symbolic meaning.

Table 14 **Frequency of Responses in Various Categories when Children Described "One of the Happiest Days of My Life"**

Description	Grades 1-3 Ages 6-9		Grades 4-6 Ages 9-12		Grades 7-9 Ages 12-15		Grades 10-12 Ages 15-18	
	363 Boys	331 Girls	309 Boys	343 Girls	282 Boys	290 Girls	159 Boys	171 Girls
Receiving or having or otherwise enjoying material things, gifts, toys, money, living quarters	8.7	8.1	10.4	7.2	10.1	4.5	5.6	3.1
Holidays, festive occasions, birthdays, Christmas, etc.	39.1	40.5	32.4	38.9	6.3	10.1	0.6	6.5
Sports, games, hiking, hunting, bicycling, etc.	10.2	6.4	9.1	5.5	12.4	5.8	13.0	7.3
Going to miscellaneous places of recreation, going to camps, traveling, going to resorts, to parks	9.6	9.0	10.1	11.4	9.7	13.9	30.2	6.9
Self-improvement, success in school, educational opportunity, evidence of vocational competence, getting a job	2.4	2.3	2.9	1.9	4.8	4.1	13.6	15.9
Happenings connected with school, including last day, end of school, going to a certain school	3.6	3.4	5.4	4.3	14.0	11.1	7.0	5.4
Relationship with people (explicitly described), companionship, being with certain friend, return home of relatives, etc.	7.7	15.9	8.0	15.8	10.5	22.0	8.7	19.9
Residing in, moving to, a certain city or community	1.3	1.0	0.8	2.9	0.9	2.9	1.4	5.0
Benefits befalling others, or mankind in general, including end of war	0.6	0.8	3.2	2.8	2.2	2.6	7.9	9.7

Reproduced, by permission, from A. T. Jersild and R. J. Tasch, *Children's Interests*. Bureau of Publications, Teachers College, Columbia University, 1949. The table omits several categories, including hobbies, movies and radio programs, art activities, and so forth, mentioned by only small percentages of children.

Boredom

The term "boredom" covers a variety of "negative" experiences in which the individual is marking time with nothing stimulating or challenging to absorb his attention. Boredom involves an absence of "activity pleasure." Although boredom is very common, it has received scant attention in psychological research. In everyday speech it is revealed by such expressions as "nothing ever happens around here" and "feeling fed up." Being "tired" often denotes boredom rather than fatigue, and even "pain" often has this connotation, especially if the pain is located, euphemistically, in the neck.

A study of boredom would no doubt reveal that much of the mischievousness and misbehavior of children springs from a desire for action. Children will court danger or even severe punishment in order to stir up some "excitement." Similarly, mishaps and minor tragedies may be welcomed as a break in the monotony of life, as when a child dances with delight when the family car is stuck in the snow, when he learns there is a bat in Grandma's bedroom, or that Auntie has a beetle down her back.

Boredom at School

Children's boredom frequently centers in the school. The bored ones include children who are not challenged by what is taught, either because it is too easy or because it has little or no meaning for them. Even children who do well at school usually welcome a holiday to relieve the monotony. In the study from which Table 14 is taken, it was found that the children seldom expressed any great liking for school but, on the contrary, more often expressed dislike. More children mentioned the last day of a closing school year, than the opening of school when describing the happiest day of their lives. Of course, a child's pleasure or boredom with school will vary greatly from child to child and from school to school, and it probably would be impossible to make everything that goes on in school stimulating. But it is understandable that pupils will be bored when a teacher also is bored, as often she or he is, and properly might be. According to reports by teachers in one of the writer's studies (1955), a frequent "problem" in a teacher's life is the meaninglessness, from a personal point of view, of much of what a teacher has to teach.

Chronic and pervasive boredom of the sort sometimes experienced by adults is not likely to occur in a normal child, because so much still lies ahead of him and he is constantly encountering new experiences. The frontiers of his world are still open. But a child and his activities have a definite bearing on the adult problem, because the resources for satisfaction through activity which an adult possesses in his thirties and beyond are influenced considerably by his childhood training and experiences. Many adult hobbies and avocations first began to flower early in childhood; then, perhaps, they may have been dormant for a time through adolescence and youth, only to bloom again in later years. Indeed, activities and skills which a child at first enjoyed and then exercised only because he had to may, in later years, be revived with enthusiasm; this happens, for example, when a person who worked in the garden reluctantly as a child, later, as an adult, picks up a spade and hoe and goes joyfully to work.

Boredom with Self

An important aspect of boredom which shows at the adult level but which is likely to be an outgrowth, at least in part, of an individual's childhood and youth is the boredom a person feels with reference to himself. He does not like to be alone with himself. He becomes restless when left with his own thoughts. He seeks distraction, excitement, work, play, anything in preference to his own company. He feels "the itch," a constant urge to "go places and do things." When a person is thus bored, it is a sign that he is not at ease with himself. He is probably anxious and unsure, not simply bored.

Emotional Ramifications
of Sexual Development

Experiences that might influence a person's emotional reactions to sex begin in infancy. Some of Freud's theories (1930, 1933, 1938a, 1938b) relating to sexuality in infancy and various phases of sexual development in early childhood have been discussed in earlier chapters.

In a typical male infant, the penis sometimes is erect, sometimes flaccid, and both boys and girls sooner or later in infancy display sensitivity in the genital area and stimulate themselves more or less.

According to Kinsey and his associates (1953) there are children, both male and female, who are ". . . quite capable of true sexual response . . ." well before the onset of puberty. Some writers take issue with the theory of infantile sexuality, claiming that erotic behavior does not have the same quality in a child as in an adult. In one sense, this claim is correct, for clearly a six-month-old infant or a four-year-old child is "immature" both sexually and emotionally as compared with an adult. However, regardless of whether a child's sexuality is similar to that of a mature person from a *biological* point of view, it is obvious that the sexuality of a child is important from a *psychological* point of view. When children reveal sensitivity in the genital area, or show an interest in sex play and become aware of attitudes of other children or of adults relating to sex, they are undergoing experiences which can have a significant bearing on their own attitudes and behavior.

As they move into the preschool years and beyond, many children conceal their interest in sex from the eyes and ears of adults, but a large proportion of children, if not all, are actively interested in one way or another. All normal children eventually become curious about reproduction and the form of their curiosity or the kind of information they seek is likely to vary as they mature.

Tables 15 and 16 show the results of a study by Hattendorf (1932) in which parents were interviewed on what questions their children asked about sex.

Sex Experiences and Practices. During elementary school years a large proportion of children have experiences relating to sex, such as observing the sex behavior of animals or people, or being exposed to the advances of older children or adults, undertaking sex play in private, or entering into sex play with their peers. In a study of boys by Ramsey (1943) it was found that 72.6 per cent of the boys who were questioned had had experience with masturbation by the age of twelve. No physical damage was reported in connection with these experiences but boys did report many fears and considerable worry. In this same study, about a third of the boys reported that they had attempted heterosexual intercourse before adolescence. In their studies of female sex behavior, Kinsey and his associates (1953) found that about 14 per cent of the females in their sample recalled that they had reached orgasm prior to adolescence through masturbation or sexual contacts with other children or with adults. They surmise that, in addition, there might be many others who had had the experience without recognizing its nature. In a study

Table 15   Classification of Questions with Respect to Sex Asked by 1797 Boys and Girls Aged Two to Thirteen Years as Reported by Parents

Question	Number	Percentage
Origin of babies	722	40.9
Coming of another baby	256	14.5
Intra-uterine growth	42	2.4
Process of birth	183	10.4
Organs and functions of the body	209	11.9
Physical sex differences	226	12.7
Relation of the father to reproduction	92	5.2
Marriage	36	2.0

From K. W. Hattendorf: "A Study of the Questions of Young Children Concerning Sex: A Phase of an Experimental Approach to Parent Education," *Journal of Social Psychology* (1932), 3:37–65.

by Landis, Landis, and Bolles (1940) over half of a group of normal single women aged fifteen to thirty years and almost half of a group of normal married women aged twenty-two to thirty-five years reported that their first experience with sex aggressions had occurred prior to puberty, ranging from exploration of their bodies by a boy of their own age to sexual advances by an older boy or adult.

Such findings as the foregoing should not be regarded as typical for all communities or for different sections of the population. There are wide variations in sex behavior as in all other matters. The study by Kinsey and his associates (1948) of sexual behavior in males shows, for example, that persons from various socio-economic groups and from families with differing educational backgrounds vary decidedly in their sex practices, particularly before marriage. Yet, such findings as these, while dealing with only a very limited aspect of sex behavior, impressively show that a large proportion of preadolescent children have experiences with physical aspects of sex which go beyond a passive, academic interest in the subject.

The Concept of the "Latency Period"

In discussions of sexual development, writers who follow Freud's lead speak of a "latency period," which extends roughly from about the age of five to the beginning of adolescence. According to the theory of latency, a child faces certain hurdles in his early sexual development—the "oral" and "anal" phases, the need to resolve the Oedipus situation, and another hurdle when

Table 16 Rank of Interest for 856 Questions of Children Two to Five, 707 Questions of Children Six to Nine, and 191 Questions of Children Ten to Thirteen Years Classified in Eight Groups

Classification	Age in Years		
	2 to 5	6 to 9	10 to 13
Origin of babies	1	1	2
Coming of another baby	4	2	1
Intra-uterine growth	7	7	8
Process of birth	5	3	5
Organs and functions	3	4	3
Physical sex differences	2	4	6
Relation of father to reproduction	6	6	4
Marriage	8	8	7

From Hattendorf, *op. cit.*

sex takes on a new urgency at the time of puberty. The intervening time is referred to as a period of latency because during this period, according to Freudian theory, there is no new decisive stage or phase of sexual development.

When viewed in the context of this theory, "latency" has a special meaning. But when viewed in the light of empirical studies of children's interests and actions during this period, "latency" cannot be taken literally. For many children, interest in sex during this period is not latent or inactive or held in abeyance but is distinctly manifest and active. In normal development, sex never takes a holiday.

Many children, according to their own accounts, have impressions or experiences relating to sex and have discussed the topic with other children before they have received much information from their parents or from other responsible sources (Goudy, 1957). This is not surprising, since adults differ greatly in their ability or willingness to "face the facts of life." However, even when parents (or teachers) are free to discuss sex with children in their care, a youngster is likely to want to discuss sex with his peers. In the normal course of things, sex eventually is an aspect of life which people share most intimately with peers rather than with the older generation. Even after a child receives sex instruction from an adult, he is interested in exploring the subject with his peers. There will probably be matters of interest connected with sex which a ten-year-old does not especially care to discuss with Dad, just as Dad has interests he does not discuss with Grandpa.

Observations based on twenty-five years of work in the area of sex education with twelve-year-old boys (Goudy, 1957) indicate that there are aspects of a boy's sex education and of his search for understanding which cannot be met solely by academic instruction from adults. Boys from good homes, who are destined to be excellent fathers some day, go through a phase during which they are eager to take part in "bull sessions." While such sessions may not add anything important to the knowledge a boy already has acquired about the facts of reproduction, apparently they help him to explore his role as a young male. Even when a bull session deals with topics that have been covered before, it may also provide some vicarious sexual experience.

Laughter and Humor

Among the many appealing human qualities of an infant are his smiles and his laughter. The first appearance of laughter was noted in one experimental study at twelve weeks when the experimenter bent over the child and made a chirruping sound (Washburn, 1929). Most effective in producing laughter was the "threatening-head" stimulus. While holding the child's hands, the experimenter shook her head playfully from side to side and then ducked rapidly, until her head was in contact with the center of the child's body, whence it was immediately withdrawn again. Laughter in response to this act appeared at sixteen weeks.

As the months go by, most children laugh eagerly in response to a bit of horseplay. Frequently, too, a baby's laughter is aroused by an anticipated pleasure, as when he is being dressed to go out in his carriage or for a ride in a car. Many babies before the age of one year laugh at the banter of others, even though they cannot directly take part in it. Laughter also occurs in connection with the baby's own self-initiated activities.

At the preschool level laughter often occurs in connection with some form of physical activity (Ding, *et al.*, 1932), but it also appears in many other contexts.

The Young Comic

Just when a typical child acquires a "sense of humor" is hard to tell, but it is apparent that some babies have what might be called a sense of the comic well in advance of the time when they are able to express their humor through language. An illustration of the comic touch is given in Chapter 18 in the account of an eleven-month-old baby who made several false starts toward a forbidden garbage pail (while the mother was looking on), laughing at what seemed to be a merry game of "Let's Pretend."

Theories of Laughter

When the laughter of runabout children is examined in light of some of the theories that have been proposed to explain laughter of adults, several interesting observations have emerged (see Justin, 1932; Ding, *et al.*, 1932; Kenderdine, 1931, and Wolfenstein, 1954). Among the situations found to produce laughter at the preschool level are surprise, defeated expectations, incongruity, another's smile, sudden relief from strain, playful give and take, and sudden feelings of superiority or degradation. In a large collection of records of young children's laughter while at play, laughter seldom occurred as a form of derision or an expression of superiority because of another's coming to grief, or of vindictiveness (Ding, *et al.*, 1932). As children grow older, however, their laughter or "favorite jokes" often express what seem to be underlying aggressive impulses. Children's laughter or humor is frequently associated with forbidden things, such as references to sex or elimination.

Developmental Aspects of Humor

The development of humor is interrelated with other aspects of development (Laing, 1939; Omwake, 1939). When a child is able to appreciate relationships in size and space, he is able to laugh at incongruities which he did not notice before, such as Junior's small cap on Papa's big head. When he has attained command of language, he may find it humorous when a younger child makes mistakes similar to his own mistakes at an earlier age (like singing "Me muvver and fahver were Irish").

At the elementary school level and beyond, a great proportion of children's humor, at least as represented by "favorite jokes," deals with topics that are slightly if not entirely taboo. Many of these jokes support Freud's view (1938) that jokes express motives or impulses which have been suppressed and would be condemned if expressed in a more direct way. Some jokes, however, do not so clearly illustrate this view. While jokes have a comic flavor, they often deal with themes that are not basically comical. An undertone of seriousness appears when children, through jokes, express envy, or give a ridiculous turn to a common human predicament, or play with desires under the guise of foolishness. In joking about the foibles of others, or about his own, a child may be trying to make light of his own difficulties. In this respect, joking, as described by Wolfenstein, is ". . . a bit of humble heroism, which for the moment that it succeeds provides elation, but only for the moment."

Older children, like adults, frequently use humor in a hostile way by making someone the butt of a joke. But they also use humor in a friendly way to share their feelings with others. A joke may have a hidden bite, based upon something significant to the joker, but it will, of course, fall flat if it does not also touch upon something significant to the one who hears or reads it. When the other person enjoys the joke and laughs he is, in effect, saying: "I feel that way, too." Accordingly, while humor sometimes expresses malice, it also often voices a form of compassion.

Humor as Related to Self-Appraisal

Most children eventually like to think of themselves as having a sense of humor, and a number of them will take great pains to discover what they can do to make people laugh and how to gauge timing and emphasis to bring out the comic in what they have to say. In a study by the writer, in which youngsters wrote little essays on what they liked and disliked about themselves, there were many who said they were pleased about having a sense of humor, but no child admitted or expressed regret about being without a sense of humor. In this respect children resemble older persons. In a study by Allport (1937) college students were asked to estimate their sense of humor. Ninety-four per cent replied that it was as good or better than the average.

Recommended Readings

The author's chapter on "Emotional Development" in the *Manual of Child Psychology* (1954), edited by Leonard Carmichael, explores historical and theoretical issues that are still of timely concern. Martha Wolfenstein's *Children's Humor: A Psychological Analysis* (1954) gives an interpretation of motives underlying humor. The volumes on *Sexual Behavior in the Human Male* and *Sexual Behavior in the Human Female* by A. C. Kinsey and his associates (1948, 1953) include a considerable amount of information about children. These volumes perhaps need to be updated in view of recent sparsely documented pronouncements regarding changes in sex mores. Earlier and more recent writings pertaining to the role of affection are cited in Chapters 6 and 11.

16 *Fear and Anxiety*

Fear exists so generally in contemporary life that our time has been called the "age of anxiety." Actually, the present age is probably no more fear-ridden than earlier periods in history. In the folklore of many countries, one mark of a hero was that he was without fear. Such a hero probably never existed. No such hero exists today, certainly not among children, for most children, from an early age, are hosts to many fears.

Fear is both an inevitable and an essential emotion. Fear combined with vigilance helps keep lower animals alive. Fear was essential for the survival of primitive man. It is essential also in modern life, for it augments energies in times of danger and it provides an impetus to caution and prudence. But in a child of today, fear frequently outstays its usefulness. It frequently is misplaced so that a child, in effect, flees when there is no pursuer. Instead of aiding, it often curtails a child's efforts to adapt to the stresses of life. Instead of mobilizing a child's resources, it may immobilize them. Such fear not only impairs a child's freedom and spontaneity but also imposes a burden of distress. Fear also frequently represents an area of loneliness in a child's life, for many of his fears are unshared and unsuspected by those who, presumably, should be most kind to him.

In the writer's judgment, no aspect of a child's experience is more poignant and more deserving of compassionate attention than fear. Also, no aspect is more baffling, either to a child himself or to those who would like to help to relieve or to shoulder his burden.

In this chapter we will first review age trends in children's fears and worries as revealed by information obtained from parents and teachers and from children themselves. As we will see more particularly at a later point, the term "fear" is used in everyday speech to denote a variety of apprehensions, ranging from acute fear of obvious dangers (such as a snarling dog) to a more complicated kind of uneasiness (such as worry about reciting in class or fear of being caught in a tornado, even though at the moment the weather is calm).

During infancy, a child's fears arise in response to occurrences in his immediate environment. As he grows older, the range of his fears grows wider. As he acquires the ability to dwell upon his past and to anticipate his future, many fears will pertain to distant dangers, forebodings of what the future may bring, and apprehensions concerning his own impulses and what he has done or might do.

Anxiety is added to fear when a child is apprehensive not only about external dangers but is troubled by "dangers" that arise within himself.

Beginnings of Fear

In an earlier day, there were theories that many of our fears were instinctive, such as fear of animals, of the occult, of death, of large bodies of water. Later a theory was advanced that there are only two original "natural" fear stimuli —namely, loud noises and sudden displacement or loss of support (Watson, 1924a, 1924b). This account was quite simple and quite inadequate. The circumstances that give rise to so-called "unlearned" fears in an infant include not only noises and loss of support, but any intense, sudden, unexpected, or novel stimulus, or any condition which demands some kind of adaptation for which the organism is unprepared. Moreover, whether or not a certain stimulus will evoke fear depends not only on the nature of the stimulus but also on the condition of the individual who is responding and the total setting in which the stimulus occurs. A jolt or loud noise, for example, may arouse fear when a child is with an unfamiliar person but not when a familiar person is near.[1]

---

[1] English (1929) and Valentine (1930, 1946) give illustrations of the difficulty of predicting when a child will be afraid.

The Role of Maturation

An infant is unaffected by many happenings that will frighten him when he is older, when his capacities for perception and discrimination have matured. An example of this was given in the discussion of fear of strangers in Chapter 6. It has been suggested that a child's first fear of strangers, from about the fifth to the tenth month, corresponds in its origin to the flight reactions sooner or later exhibited by lower animals after birth (Freedman, D. G., 1961). That this response is influenced by genetically determined maturational factors, and not by the social environment alone, is suggested by the finding that identical twins showed a higher resemblance than fraternal twins in the pattern and timing of the fear (Freedman 1966).

Gesell's (1929) account of the response of infants at different ages to confinement in a small pen provides a further illustration of the role of maturation. At ten weeks, a child may be completely complacent in this situation; at twenty weeks, he may exhibit mild apprehension, and at thirty weeks, his response to the same situation ". . . may be so vigorously expressed by crying that we describe the reaction as fear or fright." As the child matures, new things affect him by virtue of his keener perceptions, and fear is likely to arise when an individual knows enough to recognize the potential danger in a situation but has not "advanced to the point of a complete comprehension and control of the changing situation" (Jones and Jones, 1928).

Fear responses associated with changes in age appeared impressively in a study in which a large, active, harmless snake was set free in an enclosure with persons of various ages. Children up to the age of two years showed no fear of the snake; children aged three and four tended to be cautious and hesitated to approach or touch the snake; definite signs of fear were displayed more often after the age of four and were more pronounced in adults than in children (Jones and Jones, 1928).

The important role played by maturation in children's fear is brought out by findings that a child who is precocious or advanced in his development may be afraid of things that do not disturb other children until they are older (Holmes, 1935).

Changing susceptibility to fear is interwoven with many other aspects of a child's development. As a child's imaginative abilities develop, his fears become increasingly concerned with imaginary dangers. With the development of competitiveness and awareness of status come fears of ridicule or loss of prestige. The wider the scope and range of a child's understanding, the more he is able to recognize possible disasters, and the more versatile he also becomes in fitting his apprehension into varied images and lines of thought. This does not mean, necessarily, that a child becomes more and more afraid, for as he gains in strength and understanding he is better able to handle and to "lay by" some of the situations that once frightened him.

The Role of Learning

Fears are also influenced by learning. As the result of a painful experience, or of having been startled or overwhelmed, a child may "learn" to fear something that did not disturb him previously. One of the classical experiments in child psychology, by Watson and Raynor (1920) illustrates this tendency. The subject of the experiment, a boy named Albert, was conditioned to fear a previously unfeared white rat when a loud, startle-producing noise was sounded a few times while the rat was present. After this fear had become established, Albert also showed fear of other furry or white things—a rabbit, a fur coat, a wad of cotton.

This kind of learning may be quite direct, specific, and restricted. A child is bowled over by a dog and later fears that dog. Again, the effects may be more general. The child may fear not only the dog that injured him but all dogs and, perhaps, he may be on guard, as never before, whenever he sees any four-footed animal.

The process by which fear is acquired may involve indirect or intermediate steps. For example, a child who had been knocked down but not seriously injured by an automobile was still quite wrought up when he went to bed, and then he had a bad dream. Thereafter he was afraid of going into his bedroom when it was dark. Through the dream, the accident and its emotional effects had been placed, so to speak, in the setting of darkness. Once a child is frightened, his fear may thus "spread" to many other things and conditions.

The essential element when such a "spread" occurs is the fact that something left him in a state of apprehension or fear. The conditioning process provides an object or circumstance (other than the one that frightened him in the first instance) with which his fright becomes associated.

Age Changes and Individual Differences in the Expression of Fear

As children grow older, the number of occasions per day or week when they exhibit overt signs of fear, such as crying, trembling, or clinging to an adult, decrease. However, this does not mean that there is a corresponding decline in the role fear plays in a child's everyday life. The decline in overt expression of fear is linked with a child's general tendency to display emotion less openly as he grows older. It is partly associated also with changes in the character of the dangers which a child fears. Fears formulated in terms of imaginary dangers, or apprehension concerning misfortunes that might occur, seldom express themselves in sudden starts, cries, or fleeing. Imaginary fears leave nothing to flee from, for a child who does both the fearing and the imagining cannot physically run away from himself.

Individual Variations in the Display and Acknowledgment of Fear. Because of individual differences in children's overt expression of fear, it is difficult to tell whether a child is afraid or to judge how deeply disturbed he is when he openly manifests fear. Youngsters who most freely express apprehension may be the ones who are best able to cope with their fear. In a study of children who were attending nursery school for the first time, Slater (1939) found that most children showed a marked decline in apprehension after the first day, but a child's ease in adapting to the new situation could not be judged by the intensity of his first reactions. Children who cried loudest during the first morning ". . . might often be the happiest later on." Some who were tearless on their first visit ". . . continued for days to be rather solemn and none too happy."

In a study of kindergarten children, Kraus (1956) likewise found that beginners who most openly displayed distress made, if anything, a better subsequent adjustment in school than those who seemed outwardly calm. Some interesting reports were made by children from this kindergarten group when they were asked later on how they felt on entering kindergarten. In the second grade, few children said they had been distressed. When questioned in the fifth grade, many of these same children (including youngsters who had shown fear and others who had not) admitted they had been "scared." Apparently fifth graders could look back tolerantly on themselves and acknowledge difficulties they had as "little kids," but which they did not reveal at the time and still denied at the second-grade level.

Disguises of Fear

Fear may be expressed in innumerable forms and occur in countless disguises, ranging from an obvious show of fear to a show of complete confidence, and from extremely good and compliant conduct to stubbornness, resistance, unwillingness to "see the point," and outright rebellion and defiance that resemble anger more than fear.

Because of the premium society places on apparent fearlessness a child may be driven to the point where one of his fears is the fear of showing fear. The following paragraphs illustrate how children conceal their fears.

> A girl of three-and-a-half years asked her mother to fetch a doll that had been left in a room separated by a hallway from the rest of the house, and she kept insisting violently after the mother had suggested that she get it herself. The mother then suspected what the matter was and said, "I'll hold the door while you get it." At this the girl ran happily to the room and got the doll. The mother remembered that the child had been frightened previously by the slamming of a door in this hallway, and now, instead of admitting that she was afraid, she was trying to commandeer her mother. An adult who did not know what had happened might have thought the girl was an unreasonable child, not a frightened child.
>
> A girl of seven, two nights in succession, after having been put to bed, insisted that she had to go downstairs because she had forgotten to bring

a blanket for her doll and asked her mother to go with her since she did not like to go alone. On the second night her mother, thinking that the girl was merely trying to delay her bedtime, refused to accompany her, so finally she had to go by herself. She hurriedly went all the way to the basement where she got the blanket; then she went on another quick errand on the first floor, and then returned to bed. A few minutes later she revealed that her reason for going downstairs was to make sure that the front door was locked. On some previous nights she had anxiously asked whether the front door was locked. She was using the "forgotten" doll blanket as a device for making sure that the door was locked. This fear apparently was precipitated, at least in part, by the agitation shown by a baby sitter some time before. The baby sitter was frightened by a human voice coming from outside the house. She frantically ran about, testing to see whether all doors were locked. Actually, a man's voice was audible, but it came, unknown to the baby-sitter, from a loud-speaker at a bazaar about half a mile away.

The disguise a child uses to mask his fears becomes especially troublesome if, instead of getting him out of trouble, it gets him into more trouble. A child may be so frightened at the thought of being laughed at in class that he will act dumb rather than recite and risk making a mistake. As a result, he may get a scolding from a teacher who would be willing to help him if she suspected he was afraid. To understand a child who is afraid, we must be alert to such disguises, although no adult can expect to be all-knowing.

Open and Hidden Aspects of Fear

When we try to understand a child's fear, we must recognize that there is usually more than appears on the surface. There may be both a manifest and a hidden content. Two children say they are afraid of dogs, but to one the "dogs" may be two real dogs on his street that are an actual menace, while to another child "dogs" is almost a manner of speech, for he is uneasy in the presence of any dog, or at the thought of meeting a dog, even when repeated experiences tell him that this or that dog is perfectly harmless. When he says he is afraid of dogs, he tells the truth and yet not the whole truth, for it is what the dog symbolizes rather than the external danger which the dog actually represents that bothers him. The fear named by the child may represent both an external threat and an internal disturbance—this is especially noticeable when children mention fears that have little or no basis in reality, such as when a child says he is afraid of ghosts, or when a child with an excellent record at school says he is afraid he will fail.

Age Trends in "Fears"

Figure 2, which is based on information obtained from parents, shows trends in children's openly expressed fears between birth and six years of age.[2] As a

---

[2] The data are based on "fear" records kept by parents, fears they actually observed in their childrens' daily lives and which they set down in an anecdotal report, immediately or

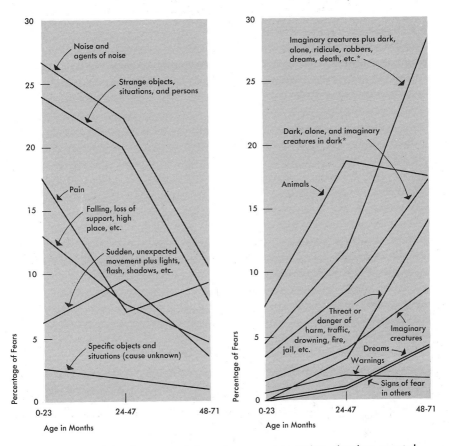

Figure 2 Relative frequency of fears in response to various situations reported by children or observed in children by parents or teachers. The data include 146 records of observation of children for periods of 21 days (31, 91, and 24 at the respective bi-yearly levels), combined with occasional records of 117 additional children (27, 67, and 23 at the respective levels). Adapted from *Children's Fears* by A. T. Jersild and F. B. Holmes, Child Development Monographs, 1935, No. 20, by permission of the publishers. Starred items represent a cumulative tally of two or more categories that also are depicted separately.

youngster grows older, his fear of certain tangible and immediate situations, such as specific objects, noises, falling and danger of falling, strange objects and persons, decreases; his fear of imaginary creatures, the dark, and being alone or abandoned increases. Figure 2 shows the results obtained when a

as soon as convenient. Information based on "live" observed episodes is probably more authentic than information gained from interviews, which call upon mothers to report in terms of their recollections of past incidents of fear. Children, however, even when quite young, may have fears that are not noticed.

Table 17 Fears Shown by Children at Yearly Age Levels from 24 to 71 Months in Various Experimental Situations

Situation	Percentage of Children Showing Fear			
	24-35 months	36-47 months	48-59 months	60-71 months
1. Being left alone	12.1	15.6	7.0	0
2. Falling boards	24.2	8.9	0	0
3. Dark room	46.9	51.1	35.7	0
4. Strange person	31.3	22.2	7.1	0
5. High boards	35.5	35.6	7.1	0
6. Loud sound	22.6	20.0	14.3	0
7. Snake	34.8	55.6	42.9	30.8
8. Large dog	61.9	42.9	42.9	. . .
Total	32.0	30.2	18.1	4.5

From F. B. Holmes, "An Experimental Study of the Fears of Young Children," in A. T. Jersild, and F. B. Holmes, *Children's Fears*, Child Development Monographs (New York: Teachers College, Columbia University, 1935), No. 20, Pt. III, pp. 167–296. Reproduced by permission.

tally of 1 was registered in the case of each child who exhibited *one* or *several* fears of a given category. The relative frequency of various fear categories would be different if each additional item in a given category received a new tally, such as three tallies under "Animals" if a child mentions lions, tigers, and wolves (Pratt, 1945).

Table 17 shows findings obtained in a study by Holmes (1935) in which the following semi-experimental situations were used to investigate children's fears:

1. *Being left alone.* A concealed observer watches the child as he is left alone in the experimental room when the experimenter leaves with the excuse that she has to get her handkerchief in another part of the building.

2. *Falling boards.* The child is asked to walk across two inclined boards so arranged that, as the child steps from one to the other, one board suddenly tilts and gives way a distance of two inches.

3. *A dark room.* The child is asked to retrieve a ball seemingly inadvertently thrown by the experimenter into a long, narrow, dark passageway.

4. *A strange person.* Standing in the child's path as he seeks to reach a box of toys is a woman rakishly dressed in a long gray coat, large black hat, and black veil that obscures the features of her face.

5. *High boards.* The child is asked to walk across a plank raised by degrees to elevations of from about two to six feet from the floor.

6. *A loud sound.* While the child is playing a sound is suddenly produced by sharply striking an iron pipe with a hammer.

7. *A snake.* The child is asked to pick a toy out of box which contains a live snake, two feet long.

8. *A large dog.* The child is asked to go and pat a dog that is brought in on a leash.

The experimental situations were not designed to frighten the child (except that he might be startled by the noise and the inclined board), but rather to confront the child with a situation into which he could choose to enter and participate or from which he was free to withdraw and retreat. Observers recorded the children's behavior, and the presence or absence of "fear" was determined according to carefully formulated criteria. The number of children at each yearly age level ranged from twelve to forty-five, the fewest being at sixty to seventy-one months.

The results shown in Table 17 indicate a trend toward a decrease with age in fear of the situations employed in the study. At the five-year level only the snake aroused signs of fear. Even the dark room did not produce overt symptoms of fear in five-year-olds. (Undoubtedly the presence of an adult accounted for this; for, according to their own reports, many children of this age are afraid of dark places, especially when they are alone.) Considerably more younger children were afraid of the dark room in the experiment than were reported by their parents as being afraid of the dark.

Age Trends in Fears of Older Children. Childrens' fears change as they move through middle childhood and into their teens (Jersild, *et al.*, 1933; Winker, 1949; Angelino, *et al.*, 1956; Maurer, 1965).

There tends to be, on the whole, a *decline* in fears relating to personal safety (including attacks from others, accidents, storms). There is also, in general, a decline in fear of animals, although findings have varied here. On the other hand, fears pertaining to school (including worries about grades, fears of teachers, stage fright) in general *increase* from age nine to about age twelve and a slight but uneven decline sets in thereafter. There is also, on the whole, an increase in fears pertaining to social relationships and in fears classified as "economic and political" (including worries about money, allowances, getting jobs). Many older children also entertain vague "fears" about their own identity. In two studies it was found that a rather large proportion of children (large as compared with what parents would surmise) feared that they had been adopted (Lapouse and Monk, 1958; Lazar, 1963).

Fears Associated with Guilt,
Remorse, and Underlying Insecurity

Many children fear punishment or harbor feelings of guilt or remorse for past misdeeds. In a study of fifth- and sixth-grade children presented with a list of "worries," a large proportion of the children checked items having to do with punishment, being scolded, "making parents sad," telling lies, and doing wrong (Jersild, *et al.*, 1941).

A tendency to be apprehensive, even though no specific fear can be named or identified, often exists in shy and withdrawn children. Pritchard and

Ojemann (1941) found that children who were rated "insecure" by their teachers exhibited a greater tendency to be apprehensive than did children rated as emotionally "secure."

"Fears" Compared with Worst Happenings. A large proportion of the fears children report are expressed in terms that are different from prosaic day-to-day injuries and threats. This is illustrated in Table 18 by a comparison between accounts given by school-age children of their fears and of the "worst thing that ever happened" to them. This table includes results obtained from two studies, one conducted in the early 1930's in New York City and another conducted in 1960 in public elementary schools in a southern state. Less than

Table 18   **Comparison of Children's Descriptions of Their Fears and of the Worst Thing that Ever Happened to Them**

Event Described	Percentage of "Worst Happenings"		Percentage of First-Named Fears	
	N.Y.C.*	South†	N.Y.C.*	South †
Bodily injury, falling, illness, traffic accident, operations, hurts and pains, etc.	72.7	54.0	12.8	7.0
Attack or danger of attack by animals	1.8	3.0	13.7	32.0
Being alone, in dark, in strange place, being lost, and dangers associated with being alone, darkness, etc.	2.3	0	14.6	10.0
Death, loss, removal of relatives, being abandoned by relatives	5.0	21.0	1.4	1.0
Contacts with, or activities of, or dangers from supernatural agents, ghosts, witches, corpses, mysterious agents or events	0	0	19.2	11.0
Scolding, embarrassment, being teased, ridiculed, etc.	5.5	9.0	3.4	1.0
Contacts with, or activities of, criminals, kidnappers, burglars, bad characters, etc.	1.3	—	8.0	—
Nightmares, visions	—	0	—	6.0
Other categories	12.4	13.0	26.9	32.0

* New York City, 1933, abridged results, based upon interviews with 398 children aged 5 to 12 years. From A. T. Jersild, F. V. Markey, and C. L. Jersild, *Children's Fears, Dreams, Wishes, Daydreams, Likes, Dislikes, Pleasant and Unpleasant Memories*, Child Development Monographs (New York: Teachers College, Columbia University, 1933), No. 12, 172 pp.

† Southern United States, urban, 1960 results, based on interviews with 240 children, aged 5 to 12, equally divided between Negro and White. Percentages are based on first-named worst happenings. From E. J. Webster, *Fears and Worst Happenings as Reported by Southern Children* (New York: Teachers College, Columbia University, 1961), Ph.D. dissertation.

2 or 3 per cent of the "worst happenings" involved dangerous experiences with animals, for example, but animals were named as the object of fear far more frequently than this.

The fears of children (and of adults) usually go far beyond the statistical probabilities of disaster. In a study by the writer and associates (1941), it was found that in a school system in which the percentage of failure or non-promotion was less than two, the percentage of children who said they "worried" about the possibility of not being promoted was about fifty. We will have more to say about "fears" of this sort in the discussion of anxiety later in this chapter.

Fears that Persist

Although many fears wane and seem to disappear, a large proportion of childhood fears persist in one form or another into adult years. In a study of childhood fears as recalled by young adults (Jersild and Holmes, 1935), it was found that of 804 fears reported, over 40 per cent still persisted into adult life. This percentage cannot, of course, be accepted without reservation, since an adult's recall of childhood fears probably will be influenced by his present apprehensions, and he would be likely to forget many passing fears that had waned. Yet, according to the testimony of adults, there is a considerable carry-over of childhood fear into later years. Of the fears described as "still persisting," about 27 per cent were also described as being the "most intense" fears recalled from childhood, and 28 per cent were described as being the "earliest recalled" fears.

Among the fears that are most often carried over into later years are fears of animals; of bodily harm through such dangers as fire, illness, and drowning; and of dangers associated with the supernatural, with the dark, and with being alone. Many of these persistent fears probably reflect anxieties such as are discussed later in this chapter.

Some Special Conditions of Fear

Fear of Noise

Noise represents a prepotent fear stimulus in infancy and early childhood, loses some of its effect as children grow older, but remains one of the most common causes of "startle reactions" throughout life. It is not the intensity of noise, as such, that usually produces fear; noise is most fear-producing when sudden, unexpected, strange and, at the instant, not clearly localized or explainable. Throughout life even a rather mild completely strange and "mysterious" noise is arresting and often fear-inducing.

Among creatures capable of vocalization, the noise of a warning cry by birds and beasts is one of the commonest signals of danger. A sudden, sharp human call of "Watch out" has about as electric an effect on a runabout child as the screech of a blue-jay has on other blue-jays.

Although noise is, sooner or later, a very effective fear stimulus, there are changes in the course of development in what constitutes a fear-provoking noise. Sharp noises will produce a startle reaction early in life, as in later years. But noises which later produce fear may have no effect on a young infant. The infant will start in response to the sharp bark of a dog, but not at a low growl, which puts an older child on guard. The influence of learning obviously is apparent here. Similarly, it is through the influence of learning that an older infant or young child reacts with fear to "strange" noises that are not strange but simply undifferentiated sounds to a young infant.

As we mentioned briefly in an earlier chapter, the strangeness of a noise may not lie in the fact that it has not occurred often before but that it has become ignored through a process of habituation. In an ordinary dwelling there are countless noises that come to be ignored but which, in the quiet and darkness of the night, may assume sinister qualities—not just for children but for adults as well. Following is an example. A sleeping, and then half-awake, adult heard sounds on a stairway leading upward outside his room. It sounded as though an animal were moving from step to step on the stair. He rushed out to investigate and then was able to detect a further movement of the "animal." The heat was coming on in a furnace immediately under the stairway, causing expansion, accompanied by creaking noises, first in the lower steps and then "moving" upward along the stairway, simulating the step-by-step progress of a creature "climbing" the stairs. The adult, quickly comprehending what was happening, was amused. But it is likely that a child, disturbed by the first sounds, and not daring to investigate, would be seriously frightened. However, if the youngster had reported in the morning that he had heard "a huge rat on the stairs," his parents probably would be completely mystified. Yet there actually was an element of "reality" in the fear, at least in the fact that the youngster did hear an unaccountable noise.

Fear of the Strange and Unfamiliar

Many children respond with fear to the strange—to strange noises, as we have seen, and to strange sights as well. What is "strange" depends, of course, on a departure from what is recognized, in a child's perceptual development, as familiar.

A new discovery in a child's life may be exhilarating, or frightening, or both. Many commonplace things that adults take for granted may suddenly "dawn" on a child as something new and possibly sinister. An example of this was shown by a two-and-a-half-year-old child who exclaimed excitedly one evening after dark, "Man out there!" The man out there was a reflection in the glass in an outside door of her grandfather sitting in the living room. Such reflections must have appeared before the child's eyes many times before without attracting her attention. This time she seemed both fascinated and disturbed. When her grandfather picked her up and showed her a number of reflections—in a mirror, in a window, in the glass of a book-case door, she responded with great interest. But some apprehension seemed to remain for a time. Before seeing the "man," she had not hesitated to go alone in the semi-darkness to a porch outside the door where he had appeared, but for a time she would go only if an adult held her hand.

In the normal process of growth, a child frequently stands at the threshold of the unknown; this may give him pause or may induce fear, but when all goes well, the strange recedes into the realm of the familiar. But sometimes a child (or an adult) stands at the threshold of something new and is unable to cross it.

The new is particularly frightening if it calls not simply for a bit of inspection and study but threatens to confront a person with a discovery concerning himself (such as the discovery that some of his judgments are prejudices).

Fear of the Dark

This fear is frequently reported by children and by adults. There is something dangerous about the dark, both in what it represents in reality and in what it symbolizes. In the dark we usually are less powerful than when we can see; we might stumble or lose our way. Darkness also signifies that we are out of sight, and that others are out of sight, so it means psychologically that we are cut off from others. Darkness is an added menace when a child is already frightened, for his imagination can supply what he cannot see, and he can project, onto the screen of darkness, dangers that reside within himself.

Fear of Solitude, Abandonment, Loneliness, Death

Many children (perhaps all) have been abandoned momentarily. The mother may be in another room, out of sight and out of earshot; on a walk the parent may have moved out of view; in a crowd the child may have found himself completely surrounded by strangers. Such an experience, even if brief and unintended, may be very frightening, but the child is likely soon to recover from his fright when his parents reappear.

Fear of abandonment does not arise solely from the physical fact of being abandoned. A child can be abandoned, psychologically, if threats and punishments are held over him in a manner that indicates he cannot count on his elders to protect him. In the studies by the writer and his associates referred to in this chapter, many children reported cruel instances of having been threatened in this way. In some children, a fear of separation or abandonment seems to be the psychological precursor of a later fear of death (Natterson and Knudson, 1960).

When the writer was a child, one form of abandonment some children had to face (and probably still do today) was the threat of death and hell fire connected with religious instruction. When the threat of hell is held over a child as a punishment for his sins, it is as though he were being consigned to outer darkness. The picture of a hell from which there is no escape, a hell beyond reach of his parents (who probably are going to heaven anyway, and between the two there is a vast gulf) presents about as bleak a prospect of abandonment as any child can imagine. Such a frightful place is not wholly imaginary from the child's point of view if his elders have told him that there is such a place.

For children who have thus been frightened, death may become a symbol of their unworthiness and of the means by which the threat of abandonment is achieved. According to this view, death is the ultimate in loneliness and isolation. This is the way a six-year-old told about his fear of being abandoned:

> His mother had told him that because he had been bad (he had quarreled with his sister) a time would come when he would not be able to move the hand that struck his sister. The mother then described what happened to a neighbor's child. This child died, the mother said, and he was placed in a coffin. But his hand remained outside the coffin, and no one could put it inside. The lid of the coffin could not be closed until a priest had struck the hand and then it slipped into the coffin. Meanwhile, his mother said, everyone talked about this child, and laughed and laughed, *and this may also happen to you."*

If a child feels abandoned he has a tendency, through his imagination, to fill the empty space. Unfriendly characters move in and appear in his fears. When a child is in the dark, isolated, separated, and alone (in a psychological sense), the characters who invade his fears often are evil ones: threatening ghosts, dead people, walking corpses, "bad guys," kidnappers, and so on. These companions are, to him, pregnant with potential harm. The pathetic thing about a child who is afraid in his solitude, alone with his troubled emotions, is that he will people his world with these cadavers and spectral creatures as though it were better to have a corpse for company than to have no companionship at all.

Fear of Animals

One of the fears most frequently named by children in the age range from about three to eight years is fear of animals. A high incidence of fear of animals in the age range from about three to eight has been found in a number of studies (from the 1930's into the 60's) of urban and rural children in various areas of the United States. (Jersild and Holmes, 1935; Pratt, 1945; Winker, 1949; Webster, 1961; Maurer, 1965.) Fear of animals usually declines at about the middle elementary school years, although one of the fears reported as persisting most frequently from childhood into early adult years is fear of animals.

Fear of animals represents a wide variety of subjective conditions ranging from apprehensions based on actual encounters with threatening animals and warnings (with a degree of realism) about the dangers animals actually represent to phobic fears in which there is a mixture of realistic apprehension and anxiety that is symbolized by the feared creature. A large proportion of animals "feared" by urban children are creatures they never will encounter in the flesh, such as lions and wolves.

Factors Contributing
to Susceptibility to Fear

Weakness and Physical Disability

Actual weakness in the face of the demands of every day life is an obvious condition underlying fear. Anything that weakens a child, such as illness or physical disability, makes him more defenseless.

When children are ill, or have an accident, or suffer from a physical disability there often is a subtle interweaving of guilt and fear. It has been observed, for example, that children who are hospitalized after an accident or to undergo an operation not only are likely to be apprehensive about what might happen to them but also, very frequently, feel it is their fault they are sick (Gips, 1956). Likewise, physically disabled children see themselves as having more fears and feelings of guilt than able-bodied children (Cruickshank, 1951).

It is not difficult to understand why such an intermingling of guilt and fear should occur. After a child has repeatedly been warned to be careful, it is not surprising that he should feel it is his own fault if he breaks a limb (he was not careful enough). Similarly, if he must have a tonsillectomy or appendectomy, it requires only a little stretch of the imagination to believe that he might have avoided an operation if he had lived right.

Even more drastic afflictions, such as polio or cerebral palsy, are likely to arouse feelings of fear tinged with guilt in parents or in children, or both (Roe, 1952). When even some adults view physical impairments as a punishment for something for which they are to blame, it is not surprising that children suffering from a physical disability sooner or later also adopt the attitude that someone is at fault—and *that someone* may be themselves.

Disparagement

Anything that lowers a child's confidence in himself, or involves him in situations where he is insecure, or threatens him with failure, conflict, remorse, self-disparagement, or temptations that disturb his own view of himself or his self-demands and self-expectations, will increase his susceptibility to fear.

The disparagement that leads a child to distrust himself may be fed in many ways. He may be given impossible standards to attain. Reminders of his unworthiness are constantly before a child if almost everything he does is wrong. He meets a steady stream of disparagement at school if he happens to be one of the millions of children who are daily reminded that they fall short.

The effects of disparagement, whether real or imagined, are likely to contain a mixture of fear, distrust, and anger. In one experimental study, Feshback and Feshback (1963) found that frightened boys are likely to attribute malice to adult males (while attributing fear to other boys). When a frightened child sees adults as full of ill will, he has all the more reason to feel alone and to be on guard.

Vicarious Dangers

At the present time children are being exposed more than ever before to vicarious fear stimulation in the form of sensational newspaper stories, the speedy communication of catastrophe, exciting movies, and hair-raising television programs. Although children's fears may be activated by these factors, the fears of children today, as they report them, do not differ substantially from the fears of children of a generation ago, as recalled by adults. More important than any specific form of excitement is the undertow of factors leading to insecurity and the threats that prevail from one generation to the next.

Influence of Example

Adults may have a distinct influence on a child's fears through the example set by their own fears. By obvious or subtle manifestations of their fears, adults may not only suggest to a child the presence of danger but also weaken a child's conviction of security in their protection. In a study by Hagman (1932), a high correlation was found between the gross number of childrens' fears and the gross number of mothers' fears, as reported by the mothers. A study by John (1941) of children's reactions to wartime events, such as an air raid, likewise emphasizes the influence of adult example. However, there is far from a one-to-one relationship between parents' reported worries and fears and their childrens' worries and fears (Lapouse and Monk, 1959).

There probably is no way to spare children from the example of fear set by others as long as fear prevails in the society in which they live. In some situations it is possible, however, to bring fear out into the open, to acknowledge it and share it. If an adult and child, during a storm, are frightened by the lightning, thunder, and the roaring wind, even so simple a statement as "Gee, that scared us both, I guess" may help to relieve the tension. According to statements made to the author by teachers who supervised air-raid drills during tense times in World War II, many children were noticeably less disturbed if a teacher was able openly to acknowledge that she and everyone else was startled by the shriek of the sirens. In many situations it appears that the courage to admit fear helps to strip away some of the sinister qualities of terror.

A show of fear in others, instead of augmenting fear, may give it a shared quality and give the frightened person assurance that he is not unusual or cowardly. A study by Sarnoff and Zimbardo (1961) suggested the theory that as fear increases there is an increased need to compare one's reaction with that of others. (This tendency was not formed in connection with anxiety, in which the contributing factors reside more in the person himself than in the external danger.)

Children's Fears as Perceived by Others

There is more of a common understanding regarding fear between children and their peers than between children and adults. In a study by Lazar (1963), children were asked to report about their own fears in response to a list of twenty-four "fears" and "worries" and then were questioned about how they thought another specified child would respond to the same questions. Mothers were also asked to indicate whether or not their children exhibited the fears on the list. There was more correspondence between the fears the children themselves reported and the fears attributed to them by other children than between the fears reported by the children themselves and the fears attributed to them by their mothers.

In an earlier investigation, Lapouse and Monk (1958) similarly found that mothers frequently reported a child having fewer fears and worries than the child himself reported.

It is interesting to note the nature of the fears which mothers do or do not detect in their children (as reported by the children themselves). On the whole, parents are more likely to agree with their children's accounts of their fears in connection with objective or practical conditions, such as thunder and lightning, going to the doctor or dentist, tests and examinations, being abused by rough children, being scolded by the teacher. Parents are likely to underestimate or not to notice children's fears of a more subjective nature.

One of the fears or worries mentioned by children but which, in a substantial number of instances, is not perceived or reported by their mothers is the fear of being an adopted child. In the study by Lazar (1963), 35 per cent of the children reported this fear but mothers attributed the fear to only 9 per cent. This means that in 26 per cent of the instances the mother either did not detect or acknowledge this fear or worry. In a study by Lapouse and Monk (1958) 28 per cent of children aged eight to twelve said they worried about being adopted, but their mothers described them as free from this worry. (In six per cent of the instances, the mothers said the children did worry about being adopted but the children denied it.) The similarity of the incidence of a discrepancy between children's affirming and mothers denying worry about adoption in the two studies is interesting (26 per cent in one study and 28 per cent in the other). This similarity may be a coincidence, yet the fact that so many children in both studies reported seemingly unsuspected worry about being adopted is very impressive.

In connection with several other fears or worries, both studies similarly cite a substantial proportion of instances in which children answered "yes" (they had the fear or worry in question) and mothers answered "no": fear of strange people (46 per cent in the Lazar study, 51 per cent in the Lapouse and Monk study); being kidnapped (respectively 42 and 57 per cent); germs (35 and 47 per cent); death, injury, or sickness phrased as "dying or being killed," in the first-named study and "getting sick, having an accident or dying," in the second (43 and 52 per cent).

A discrepancy between mothers' and children's reports also appeared in a study by Davidson, *et al.* (1958), which included interviews with the mothers (and some of the fathers) of children who had responded to a set of questions designed to measure "general" anxiety and anxiety centered on taking tests at school.[3]

Mothers described children in a "High Anxious" group as being "unanxious" about as frequently as mothers in a "Low Anxious" group described their children as unanxious. Fathers seemed to be more realistic in their appraisal of the children who themselves admitted having many anxieties, worries, and fears.

These findings support the statement, made earlier in this chapter, that children frequently face the menace of fear alone, their fears unknown. This isolation is partly compensated by the fact that a child's age-mates seem to suspect he has more fear than his parents suspect. But there is slight comfort in this, for the fears a child is most likely to confide and share with his age-mates are those relating to objective conditions rather than anxieties that have emerged in the unique stresses of his private personal life.

Helping Children to Deal with Fear

If a child is acutely frightened a kindly adult will, of course, try to comfort and protect the youngster. In dealing with lingering fears, however, it is important for an adult to bide his time, to study the child, the nature of the

---

[3] These two instruments will be discussed later in this chapter.

fear, and the context in which it occurs.[4] The first principle in dealing with fear is that we should not look simply at the specific symptoms but try to discover the conditions underlying the fear. This is essential especially in coping with fears that are rooted in a state of insecurity and conflict. When such a condition prevails, the elimination of one "fear" may quickly be followed by other fears.

Practical Steps for Dealing with Fear

Among the methods parents employ in dealing with children's fears (as reported to interviewers in a study by the writer and Holmes, 1935b), the following were regarded as probably doing more harm than good:

1. Consistently ignoring fear.
2. Ridiculing or punishing the child for being afraid.
3. Forcing the child into the feared situation.

Parents sometimes were able to help children to cope with fear when they used the following methods:

1. Explaining the situation, trying to convince the child there is nothing to be afraid of. This method sometimes helps if the explanation actually touches on the reason for the child's fear, but it probably does more harm than good if the "explanation" means, in effect, that it is foolish for the child to be afraid.

2. Setting an example of fearlessness. Such an example, among other things, may bolster a child's assurance that others will protect him and help him realize that his fear is groundless. In many situations the example of fearlessness set by other children is helpful. A child will frequently follow other children into activities he would be afraid to undertake if he were alone, such as entering a "haunted" barn, or jumping into a stream. The presence of others can not only provide an example but also a measure of reassurance which enables a child to venture into a feared situation and to discover for himself that it is harmless. The example set by others is not likely to be effective if it is merely a demonstration, with the child passively looking on.

3. Trying to effect "positive reconditioning" by presenting the feared stimulus in combination with an attractive or benign stimulus. This method is likely to work best if the feared event can be incorporated into a larger setting that is reassuring.

4. Helping a child to gain confidence in his ability to face a feared situation by bringing him, by degrees, into active dealings with it. This method, according to parents, frequently is helpful. It was tested in experimental studies by Holmes (1936). Fourteen children who showed fear in a dark room, as described earlier in this chapter, took part in this project. The children were

---

[4] For studies dealing with overcoming fear manisfested in everyday life see Hagman (1932), Holmes (1936), Jersild and Holmes (1935b), and Jones (1924).

gradually made familiar with the place, in the company of the experimenter, and they were shown how to find their way to an electric light and to turn it on. After relatively few sessions, thirteen of the fourteen children went into the dark room without hesitation and looked for and recovered a ball that had been thrown into the room. To what extent these children, now freely entering a dark place they previously feared, might also be less afraid of other dark places would require further study.

Another series of experiments by Holmes dealt with two children who were afraid to walk the length of a plank that was raised above the ground. After eight brief sessions, over a period of about a month, one child, who at first had clung to the experimenter and had whined and protested that she would fall and get hurt, cheerfully walked back and forth the length of a board raised six feet above the ground as though enjoying her victory over fear. She performed the same feat when the apparatus was moved from the laboratory to the playground. Another child also made progress, but less rapidly and then he relapsed. This occurred at a time when his nurse left the household and his mother was in the hospital having a baby. The whining and infantile responses which he showed in the fear experiment were similar to behavior he showed at home. The procedure of simply helping the child to deal directly with a specific feared situation did not suffice to overcome a fear that apparently was interwoven with other emotional difficulties.

An active approach aimed at improving a child's confidence in himself may be helpful even in dealing with fears of imaginary dangers. One child was afraid of an imaginary dog, which hounded him, troubled him when he was alone, and hunted him in dark places. His mother, aiming to help him, first watched the child in his make-believe play, and then gradually joined the child in games of "Let's Pretend." Gradually, also, she began to introduce the imaginary dog into the make-believe play. In time, the child took the dog with him into closets and elsewhere, all as part of the play pattern, and eventually he no longer appeared to be bothered by the dog.

The value of the technique of helping a child to cope directly with his fears no doubt comes more from companionship with an adult than from the specific methods used by the adult. The child's burden of fear is being shared. He is being told, in effect, that he need not be ashamed of being afraid and that he is not, at least for the time being, defenseless and alone.

Another value of helping a child to cope in an active way with a feared situation is that through it the youngster may get a changed conception of his own abilities. When a child, for example, has become able to go by himself to a remote part of the house he once feared, he has not just overcome an external danger but an internal weakness. If he now goes confidently to a place he once feared he is, to that degree, a changed person.

Encouraging Children's Efforts to Overcome Fear

Adults can sometimes help a child by encouraging him in his own self-initiated efforts to cope with his fears. Children frequently make such an effort, sometimes by facing a feared situation directly, sometimes by bringing it into their make-believe play. (Examples of this use of make-believe are given in Chapter 18. An illustration of a child's triumph over fear of a high place is given in the preceding chapter.)

Inquiry into Underlying Causes

The idea that we should try to look into the conditions underlying fear obviously is more easily said than done. Even highly trained professional psychotherapists often find it a baffling, difficult, and time-consuming job. An adult will find it especially difficult to deal with a child's fears which are related to his own. Moreover, as we have seen, a "fear" may be a child's way of giving a name or tangible reference point to a disturbance that is much more complicated than the fear appearing on the surface. Besides, even if a child's fear is a burden, he is likely to resist facing it if the fear is a screen for attitudes pertaining to himself which are even more disturbing than the particular fear which he reports. (This would be the case if, for instance, a child's fear of robbers is rooted in a conflict about his own impulse to steal.) With fear, we deal not merely with one segment of emotion but with the whole network of emotions and strivings that permeate human experience.

Even though there are very real limits to what a parent or teacher or friend can do to understand or to help a frightened child, any humane thing that one can do is well worth the effort. A child who has severe persisting fears is a tortured child. He deserves at least as much compassion as a child who is physically ill. Moreover, there are many elements in this kind of situation that make the endeavor to help such a youngster hopeful and potentially rewarding.

Since fear thrives on unresolved anger, on rejection, failure, and weakness, these conditions must be looked into. There is an affinity, too, between fear and loneliness, for a child who keeps his fears concealed keeps a lonely vigil. It is remarkable to observe, in working with children and adults, how great a relief a frightened or anxious person can derive simply from discovering that others, too, are anxious and afraid and that he is not alone.

When an adult seeks to help a child cope with fear, he needs above all to have an accepting attitude, the kind of attitude that enables him to watch, to listen, and to wait. This means he will avoid breezy assurances such as, "There really is nothing to be afraid of." Such a statement is false: A child isn't afraid just for the sport of it. An accepting attitude is essential to give the child the freedom to reveal his fears, especially those that he has learned to disguise or those he is ashamed to disclose.

To help a child, an adult needs to maintain, as well as he can, an accepting attitude toward the child and also toward himself. Such acceptance means he will try not to expect too much of himself, or to blame himself for being slow and obtuse, or for not finding a quick solution. He will be on guard against the guilt and self-reproach aroused in him by the theories of fear and anxiety which accuse him of being the source and author of his child's fears. The idea of acceptance has a homiletic sound, but it is very practical, and it is especially needed in order to combat the aura of condemnation with which the subject of fear is so often surrounded. An adult is likely to be handicapped in helping his child if he feels that he is to blame for his child's fears.

Even though children often are very defensive about revealing their fears, many are eager to share the burden of their fear with someone else whom they trust. A child who has unburdened himself already has, to that extent, done something to cope with fear. He has surmounted some of the guilt, shame, and self-reproach with which fears are often enmeshed. He has surmounted the cruel notion that it is shameful to be afraid.

Even when children feel free to confide in others, they will still have difficulty in bringing fears out into the open and in coming to grips with the conditions underlying them. Certainly no child or adult could be expected, by sheer dint of thought, to relive conditions under which fear arose and to illuminate the unconscious or unrecognized forces that might underlie fear. However, even this situation is not as hopeless as it might seem, for three reasons: (1) Dealing with the conscious elements of fear is helpful as far as it goes. (2) In exploring the conscious elements of a child's fear, an adult may get an inkling of the unconscious elements, such as the relationship between fear and punishment, fear and guilt, fear and the expectations that a person puts upon himself when he is trying to live up to a picture of what he cannot be. (3) In tracing and trying to understand a fear rooted in the past, it is impossible to go back and relive the past, but to the extent that a child's present fears are linked to experiences of the past (and most of them are) the past still lives in the present.

Anxiety

Anxiety has been defined in many ways. Some speak of fear and anxiety as though they meant the same thing, while others make a distinction between the two. There is general agreement that both fear and anxiety represent unpleasant states of mind, that both are a response to a danger or threat (which may or may not be perceived for what it is) and that both, at least when occurring to a rather intense degree, include physiological reactions. These reactions involve the sympathetic division of the autonomic nervous system; they include an activation of the adrenal glands and produce effects such as increased heart rate, lowered activity in the digestive tract, sweating of the palms of the hands, and other changes which will be noted later in this section.

The labels "fear" and "anxiety" are useful in distinguishing between two broad, although overlapping, categories of danger from which a person recoils.

Objectivity-Subjectivity

A major distinction commonly made between fear and anxiety is in the objectivity-subjectivity dimension. According to this distinction, fear is a response to an objective, tangible threat or danger, or a tangible event regarded as threatening or dangerous in its own right. An example is the fear induced by an attack by a dog, or, from past experience or warning, fear of an advancing, snarling dog. The danger may be external, such as a dog, or internal, such as frightening pains. Actually, the snarling dog may not be bent on biting, and the frightening pains may not signify anything serious, but at any rate, the response is focused upon something tangible and has a demonstrable origin. Anxiety, on the other hand, according to this common definition, lies distinctly on the subjective end of the objectivity-subjectivity continuum.

Among the conditions labeled as anxiety with a predominantly subjective element is the distress connected with "inner" conflict. Inner conflict prevails when a person is troubled by unresolved, competing, or incompatible impulses.

Sources of Conflicting Impulses

As a child progresses from early infancy, there arise inescapable conflicts between his own impulses and the restraints and demands imposed upon him. He faces delays in gratifying his desires. In time, he wants to do things that are forbidden. Even his curiosity and impulse to explore is curtailed to protect him from harm and to preserve order and property. He faces many forms of discipline, including the imposition of rules and standards. Such discipline is essential for a child's own well-being within the social order. In time, if he develops normally, he internalizes rules and restraints, much as in his early cognitive development he internalizes reality by way of images that represent phenomena in the world about him. Now conflicts which at first arose between him and the external world have turned inward.

Whenever there is a clash between an impulse and an inner restraint a child is, in effect, in conflict with himself. Such a conflict prevails, for example, when a child, whose sex play was earlier disapproved by others, incorporates the disapproval within himself, feeling (probably without being able to explain why) that sex play is wrong. But his impulse to engage in such play may be as strong as ever, even though he regards it as wrong. It is as though a part of him pushed in one direction and another part of him held him back. Furthermore, if he secretly yields to the impulse, and his inner tendency to forbid it is strong, he will feel guilty even when there is no danger of detection or external reproof. Now the initial conflict is further compounded, for, in addition to struggling against a self-forbidden desire, he now blames himself for having yielded to the desire. But in spite of internalized disapproval, in spite of the discomfort of guilt, the impulse still comes upon him. It threatens him; it is, in effect, a danger. But the danger is subjective—it resides within him.

Take another example. Early in life a normal child becomes affectionately attached to certain persons—it may be his mother or father or both. But those whom he loves are bound to arouse his anger. They cannot, and obviously should not, yield to his every demand or leave his every desire unthwarted. If a youngster is "possessive" he will become angry when his loved parents also show love for his siblings. The impulse in anger is to retaliate. This impulse clashes with the impulse to love. That means conflict. As a child grows older, he can waver uneasily between affection and anger, but he is likely to feel guilty when he yields to anger, and he may feel guilty even though he does not overtly show anger but merely entertains anger in his thoughts and fantasies.

With the addition of a few details, the foregoing account offers illustrations of the difference between states which, at the objective end of the continuum represent what in this discussion we call fear, and the subjective end of the continuum where lies the basis of anxiety. If, in the first illustration, a child remained completely amoral, with no qualms whatsoever about sex play and hurting his parent's feelings, he would be guarded in his behavior only because of the risk of punishment. This represents a realistic, objective danger, especially if the parents punish severely. This child's behavior would be governed by fear. But when he suffers distress and guilt, arising out of his own scruples, he would be confronting a subjective danger, which provides the inception of anxiety.

There are many other conditions of inner conflict that may produce anxiety. There may be a conflict between a child's need to depend on others and his desire for independence; his impulse to obey and to disobey; his impulse to gain approval (or to avoid disapproval) by being compliant and his impulse to assert himself; his desire to be regarded as a good achiever and his resentment of the effort it costs. As he grows older, clashes may arise between his desire to cooperate spontaneously with others and his competitive desire to win, between his own home-grown values and the standards urged upon him by others, his desire for the comforts of conformity and his wish to go his own way. There is hardly any area of experience in life that is free from competing inner inclinations or standards.

The subjective setting for anxiety is not only inevitable but its absence should probably be construed as a flaw in a child's development. It is healthy for a child gradually to internalize moral standards (at least those that are realistic and well-grounded). But when he does so he faces conflict, which is the soil from which anxiety springs. It is healthy for him to be able to have strong affectional ties, but also to be able to be angry; to seek approval, but also to risk disapproval by asserting himself; and so on through the whole roster of the wholesome but potentially incompatible currents of impulse and feeling in a child's inner life.

Perceptual, Feeling, and Impulse Components in Anxiety and Fear

As experienced by the individual himself, an emotional state in response to a tangible happening usually has three more or less clearly defined properties: (1) a cognitive (sensory and/or perceptual) reaction to the precipitating event; (2) feeling; and (3) impulse. A person may be aware of these only as an afterthought if he tries to untangle his experience after the wave of emotion has passed, and a young child would be unable to sort them out. But in a fear reaction a person usually can, if he tries to reconstruct the event, recognize elements such as these.

In a state of anxiety, on the other hand, these features either are not clearly discernible, or, if discernible, they do not add up to a plausible account.

Perceptual Components

On the cognitive level, fear as a response to objective situations perceived as dangerous is rational, or, at least, can be supported on rational grounds. Anxiety, on the other hand, is irrational when tested in terms of the objective or practical situation. A bright pupil who always fears he will fail on tests when his whole record is one of success is showing an irrational fear which should be regarded as a sign of anxiety. The conflict underlying his anxiety about tests may involve a variety of factors. He may feel guilty (deserving to fail) because he had played when he thinks he should have studied; his reaction to school work may be enmeshed in competitive pressures, standards set so high that he actually always is vulnerable; there may be unrecognized hostility toward the teacher or toward parents whose pressures stir up rebellion; he may even struggle against an unrecognized impulse to fail as a means of taking revenge against adults.

Fear comes as a response to a "real" danger, in the sense that the feared condition could do harm, while in anxiety there is a "hidden" danger that cannot be "explained" in terms of the practical situation.

The above-noted differences between fear and anxiety can be illustrated by an emotional state known as a phobia. A phobia, on the objective level, seems to represent a fear. On the subjective level, it represents an anxiety.

To illustrate fear, take the case of a person walking across a deep stream on a plank. Midway, there is a cracking noise and the plank begins to give way. The walker, unable to swim, is terrified; his terror represents a "rational" fear. Another person, walking across a stream on a well-constructed bridge, also becomes terrified midway. His footing is solid, the bridge is perfectly safe, but he is frightened. He may "objectify" his fear by saying he is afraid the bridge will collapse and that he will fall into the water. But this does not afford a rational explanation of his fright. The fright represents anxiety. If he has no better explanation of the danger from which he recoils, it means that the underlying condition is hidden.

This introduces a further distinction between fear and anxiety: they are on opposite sides of a conscious-unconscious dimension. Unconscious factors seem obviously to be at work when a person feels apprehensive but doesn't know why and when his distress is disproportionate, and, according to all objective standards, is inappropriate to the occasion. There are unconscious elements present when, unknown to him, the situation that now arouses anxiety triggers and reactivates feelings or impulses or attitudes embedded in his past experience. More will be said about this later.

A further difference related to the cognitive distinction between objectively focused fear and subjectively rooted anxiety lies in their response to counter-influences. Generally speaking, but not in all instances, fears recede as a child grows in competence and gains a better understanding of events that initially frightened him. A fear that represents an objectively defined danger tends to yield to experience, and it declines or disappears when the danger no longer exists. This still, of course, leaves some children with persisting fears. A child's fear of "bad people" is likely to persist, and for his own well-being it probably had better persist, if he continues to live in a neighborhood where there is considerable crime, or where other children might attack him. Adults who have been terrorized by a mugger or intruders are also likely to retain a fear of violence, although usually the fear recedes as more and more time passes with no further assault.

The "danger" involved in anxiety does not yield so readily to a child's experience in coping with the situations that activate his anxiety. The anxiety is likely to be tenacious in spite of added knowledge and practical experience unless such experience provides him insight into the nature of the "inner" danger and unless he gains confidence in his power to handle it.

Feelings of Fear and Anxiety

The feeling of fear, as experienced in everyday life, may have quite complex affective elements, but the one who is frightened definitely "feels afraid." In anxiety the feelings are not so clear or specific. One prominent feeling in a state of anxiety is fear—as in the illustration above. But anxiety may not be "felt" as fear. It may be experienced in a variety of ways: as anger, resentment, depression, vague and nameless feelings of uneasiness, being on edge, vague forebodings, irritability, unaccountable feelings of fatigue, a feeling of being under pressure, jittery; or it may be experienced as boredom or apathy. When more acute, anxiety may manifest itself as intense dread and foreboding, fear of imminent disaster, rage, crushing guilt, extreme excitement.

Anger is prominent among the feelings connected with anxiety. When a child flares with anger in response to a mild correction or criticism—in a manner that seems quite unsuited to the situation—we may suspect that his anger betokens anxiety.

Impulse and Anxiety

In a relatively uncomplicated emotional response to an objective happening, the impulse usually is quite direct and clear. In joy there is an impulse to encompass, to savor and to prolong the joyful event; in anger, an impulse to attack; in fear, an impulse to flee. In a more complicated situation, the impulses may be more complex. An angry child's impulse to strike back may not be carried out because of fear of retaliation. But, unless anger has been repressed, the impulse to "get back at" the offending person or object remains. In anxiety, on the other hand, a variety of impulses come into play. Since anxiety is an unpleasant state, the anxious person is impelled to try as best he can to protect and defend himself in an anxiety-producing situation, to ward off buried reaction tendencies which the anxiety threatens to dislodge, to avoid practical situations that touch off his anxieties, and to build defenses within himself against his anxiety.

The immediate reaction to an anxiety-producing situation may involve an "acting out" of a variety of feelings, such as those described above: efforts to escape, as in fear; belligerence; restless activity; excitable behavior; subdued behavior. The direct reaction to an anxiety situation may include inconsistent responses, such as when a child who is fond of his parents but resents them because they show affection for his sibling may become very "good" or rebellious or vascillate between the two.

The reactions of a child troubled by anxiety may add to his troubles. This happens when an anxious child at school invites failure, annoys other children by his restlessness, and does things that offends his teacher. Some of the measures taken as defenses against anxiety will be discussed after a brief consideration of some theories regarding anxiety.

Theories of Anxiety

Theories of anxiety range from those which stress age-old predicaments that confront all human beings to those which give especial emphasis to particular problems or areas of stress.[5] Kierkegaard over a century ago anticipated many of the concepts that recently have received much attention in psychological

---

[5] For discussions of anxiety, see Freud (1936); Horney (1937, 1939, 1945, 1950); Sullivan (1947, 1948); Hoch and Zubin (1950); Tillich (1952); May (1950); May, Angel, and Ellenberger (1958); W. Lowrie's translations of Kierkegaard's *Sickness Unto Death* (1951), and Sarason and his associates (1960).

thought, notably in discussions of anxiety in relation to the concept of the self. One of Kierkegaard's themes dealt with the decisions, possibilities, and alternatives which (according to him) man faces in choosing to be or not to be himself (". . . even what one might call the poorest personality is everything when he has chosen himself; for the great thing is not to be this or that but to be oneself.") (Kierkegaard, 1949).

Implicit in Kierkegaard's account is the concept of inner conflict. The concept of conflict as a source of emotional turmoil goes back into ancient secular and religious literature. The Bible (which in English translations stresses fear rather than anxiety) provides many such illustrations, notably King David and St. Paul ("For the good that I would do I do not, but the evil which I would not, that I do." "O wretched man!" Romans 7: 19, 24).

In more recent times, Freud has offered a widely accepted theory of anxiety. Orthodox psychoanalysts of the Freudian school have followed Freud's theory quite faithfully. "Neo-Freudian" psychoanalysts have, in the main, adopted certain concepts set forth by Freud (a child's initial helplessness, his need for security, his susceptibility to conflicting impulses, repression, the role of unconscious factors, the concept of defenses against anxiety) but have varied in their interpretation of the motives that come into play.

Freud's accounts of anxiety draw attention especially to two conditions. First a young child's helpless dependence on the love and care of his parents makes him vulnerable to "separation anxiety." Freud speaks of anxiety as arising in a child in a situation of being left alone, being in the dark (and thus separated), or finding himself with a stranger instead of the person to whom he clings (the mother). These situations, according to Freud, are reducible to one—namely, the loss of the loved person.

Second, according to Freud, anxiety will arise when a child, without being conscious of the nature of his predicament, is beset by an unresolved conflict between his need for "instinctual" gratification and the conditions in his environment that forbid such gratification. In his book, *The Problem of Anxiety*, Freud gives an account of little Hans, who has become a classical character. Hans was anxious—he had a phobia of horses, which arose, according to Freud's account, from the fact that Hans had an unresolved Oedipus complex. Hans had a desire to possess his mother and to replace his father. He felt jealousy toward his father, but he also loved him; he felt hostile toward his father but he also feared retaliation. To escape from this painful situation, Hans' hostility was "detoured" from his father to horses. The phobia of horses was painful, but it was less painful than to center his hostility and fear on his father. Hans was not consciously aware of the process by which he had substituted fear of a horse for fear of his father. But the fixation of his anxiety on horses was not completely fortuitous. Hans had actually witnessed a scene of a horse being injured, which probably had frightened him.

According to Horney, a chronic condition of anxiety develops when a child has to build a defense against an environment that is unreliable, unjust, and harsh, an environment he does not have the power to change, which undermines his ability to place trust in himself. He is not simply frightened in this or that particular of his life, but the environment as a whole is a menace, threatening his individuality and interfering with his opportunity to develop his potentialities as a person. Such a forbidding environment exists when a child is unloved and is treated without consideration. According to Horney's account, a child tries to find "solutions" to such predicaments, but these "solutions" may only lead to further trouble. Harsh treatment provokes hostility, but it is dangerous for a child to express hostility against the people on whom his life and everyday care depend. While he feels hostile toward them he also needs their help, and so conflicting influences are at work. Instead of fighting and freely expressing his anger he must, for his own safety, resort to other measures. His solutions take the form of defenses and stratagems. But these stratagems, although developed out of necessity, may take a turn that leaves the child at odds with himself.

Sullivan's theory of anxiety emphasizes the concept of interpersonal relationships, which has been mentioned in several earlier sections of this book. The child's self, according to Sullivan, is at first made up of "reflected appraisals." His feelings and attitudes pertaining to himself are determined by the feelings and attitudes others have toward him (and these are an expression of the feelings and attitudes others have toward themselves). Accordingly, the offspring of an anxiously self-rejecting parent faces the danger of becoming an anxiously self-rejecting child. Sullivan's theory of empathy as a means of communication between a parent and a child, and as a vehicle through which the young child of an anxious mother becomes anxious, is discussed in Chapter Four.

All three of the theories discussed above emphasize anxiety-producing conditions that arise in a child's life, but they do not touch on one important question. Is there something in the nature of children that makes some of them more susceptible to anxiety than others? As noted elsewhere in this book, children with the same home, begotten and reared by the same parents, differ greatly from birth onward in their emotional response.[6]

In extreme instances, one child moves into adolescence and adulthood so beset by anxiety that he becomes mentally ill, while his brothers and sisters remain untroubled. The findings reported by Kallman and others (cited in Chapter 3) are pertinent here, for they deal with a form of mental illness (schizophrenia) which has been regarded as representing or being a means of

---

[6] While Freud places his main emphasis on the environment—the interplay between a child and his parents—he acknowledges the role of inborn or constitutional factors. (For a review of statements by Freud regarding the interaction between inborn and environmental factors, see Frank, 1965).

escaping from extreme anxiety. As we have seen, the chances that this illness will afflict both members of a pair of identical (one-egg) twins are many times greater than the chances that it will afflict both members of a pair of fraternal (two-egg) twins, or both members of a pair of siblings. Does this mean that an anxious mother who (according to Sullivan's theory communicates her anxiety to her children) usually conveys an equally destructive amount of anxiety to them when she is rearing identical twins, but in most instances conveys an *unequal* amount of her anxiety to her children when they are fraternal twins or siblings? The answer may be "yes." But a more plausible answer is that to explain the great variations in anxiety among human beings it is necessary not only to consider a mother's anxiety, and other conditions in a child's environment that are anxiety-producing, but also genetic predispositions that make an individual vulnerable or immune to the stresses of life.

Defenses against Anxiety

Anxiety, whatever its origin, is a painful state, and when it prevails a person is likely to use various ways of coping with it as best he can. In doing so, he faces the possibility of worsening his problem.

The classical "ego defenses" described by Freud and others may be regarded, in the main, as defenses against anxiety. Through them an individual tries to minimize, blunt, explain away, or sidestep the impact of his inner conflicts. He may *rationalize*—build up a rationale for irrational tendencies. He may try to disavow what is internal within him by *projection* or *externalization*—it is not he but the other fellow who is hostile. He may try to *compensate*, trying through preoccupation with assets in one area of experience to cancel troublesome shortcomings in other areas. He can try the "sour-grapes" solution, convincing himself that the desirable things he once avidly wanted are not really sweet. He can try to *sublimate*, feeding his (to him forbidden) elementary passions in less forbidden ways. He can try to establish a systematic *denial* of the motives that press him. Other defenses against anxiety include efforts to evade or blunt it by restless activity and, among older persons, by taking flight into hard work. On the scholarly level, one way of seeking to evade the impact of anxiety is to escape to an academic ivory tower.

These and other defenses can most readily be illustrated by the behavior of older children and adults, although they can be seen also in the often-times pathetic behavior of young children. All of them represent, in military terms, a retreat from an offensive to a defensive strategy. All of them represent, in effect, a way of living with defeat rather than victory. All of them represent the best a child, or adult, seemed at the time to be able to contrive when faced with the vicissitudes of life.

Horney (1945–1950) has given an account of ways of dealing with anxiety which leaves many questions unanswered, yet it describes ways of behaving that can be observed in everyday life. Horney describes three major "strategies" which an anxious person can adopt in dealing with a threatening world. He can move *with* people by being meek, compliant, and self-effacing. He can move *against* others by being aggressive, competitive, and seeking to control others. Or he can move *away* from others by being withdrawn, detached, and aloof.

These "strategies" may not appear in "pure" form. In describing them, Horney does not assume that these represent three distinct personality types, nor does she assume that any of these forms of behavior is, in itself, a sign of anxiety. In the normal course of events there are times when a person spontaneously competes or complies or remains aloof. However, according to Horney, when used as "strategies" in dealing with anxiety these ways of behaving are not spontaneous; instead, they become a compulsive means of self-defense.

When a person resorts to such ways as these he plays a role to play safe. But any such stratagem he adopts and any role or combination of roles he assumes, other than acting "natural," so to speak, is likely to involve conflict. Instead of being spontaneous, he adopts a "front," and it is burdensome to maintain a front. If he uses compliance as a solution, there are times when, according to his spontaneous tendencies, he would like to rebel. If he seeks to relieve his anxiety by playing a competitive role there are times when this role becomes burdensome. If his front is detachment, it will be threatened whenever he has an impulse to enter into a close relationship. Such conflict is unpleasant, and so, according to Horney, the person who has gotten into this fix adopts tactics to support, defend, and rationalize the measures he has taken, and this further complicates things. What emerges is a distortion of the self through which the individual achieves a precarious unity in his style of life. He may even succeed in arriving at an uneasy conviction that his stratagems are the ideal thing. He may be able to convince himself that his compliance is not a weakness but a fine streak of gentleness and generosity; that his aggressiveness and competitiveness are not a defense against weakness but a mark of strength; or that his tendency to withdraw from close relationships with others and to remain detached is not a way of playing safe but a sign of a rugged ability to "go it alone." If he does this, he is, in Horney's account, building an "idealized self" which is false—a "pseudo-self"—but which he strives to preserve and defend.

He is likely to become anxious when anything threatens to undermine or expose the front he has assumed. Anxiety which at first arose in the child's relationships with others now arises from tendencies within himself. According to this line of thought, anxiety arises when anything threatens this "neurotic solution," represented by the superstructure of ideas, concepts, habits, and attitudes built around early attempts at protecting the self from harm (Gershman, 1950).

Empirical Measures of Anxiety

The concept of anxiety has its roots in philosophy, religion, and psychoanalysis. From time to time in the past, individuals who have known anxiety as a personal experience have tried to explore and expose it. However, through historical time into the present considerably more intellectual effort has been expended in rationalizing and side-stepping anxiety than in trying to unmask it. Although there has been a rash of studies of symptoms of anxiety in recent years, the prevailing procedure in the educational program and in the training of teachers is to ignore it, except perhaps, in its most superficial aspects.

There is an autobiographical undercurrent in the pioneer writings about anxiety, stretching from St. Augustine, and his predecessors, into modern times. One cannot read Kierkegaard without sensing that here is a man with the courage to go beyond the dialectics of philosophy into the personal meaning of philosophy. One cannot read Freud without sensing that this great man was intrepid enough to try to fathom hitherto unreached depths in man's experience. The writings of Horney and Sullivan reflect the efforts of pioneers who were dealing with deep-lying currents in human experience and, in the process, were revealing themselves.

The master works on anxiety are especially meaningful to a person who has lived uncomfortably with his own anxiety, suspecting that he is in the grip of forces which he cannot comprehend but wishes to fathom. Again and again such a person will be moved to say, "This author is not just revealing *himself*, he is not just speaking about *others*, he is speaking about *me*."

Anxiety, as a personal experience, has certain universal qualities. In the life of the individual these are uniquely imbedded in his own particular life history. But it also has certain symptoms and manifestations. This has led psychologists in recent years to try to measure anxiety in terms of what are regarded as some of its specific manifestations. In deference to the web of hidden forces that underlie the history and impact of anxiety in the life of a particular individual, the instrument most widely used for obtaining a quantitative measure of symptoms of anxiety in children is modestly called a scale for measuring "manifest" anxiety.

An instrument known as the *Children's Manifest Anxiety Scale* (often referred to as CMAS) was devised by Castaneda, McCandless, and Palermo (1953) as an adaptation, for use with children, of an earlier scale for measuring manifest anxiety in adults (Taylor, 1953). It contains 42 items, such as: It is hard for me to keep my mind on anything; I get nervous when someone watches me work; I am secretly afraid of a lot of things; my hands feel sweaty; I have trouble swallowing; my feelings get hurt easily; I blush easily; often I feel sick to my stomach. These illustrative items, it can be seen, take note of the generally held view that the anxiety syndrome, in addition to its psychological and behavioral components, also has physiological components. Blushing and sweating of the hands, for example, are controlled by the autonomic division of the nervous system.

The index of level of anxiety is obtained by the number of *yes* responses to the 42 items. In the original publication of this scale, Castaneda, *et al.*, secured results from tests of fourth- fifth- and sixth-grade children. The average number of answered items (within a total of 42) with a yes response ranged, in the several grades, from about 15 to 17 in the boys' reports and fell within the narrow range of about 18 to 19 in the girls' reports.

Several studies have confirmed that girls score somewhat higher than boys on a scale such as this. This might variously be interpreted to mean that girls are more disturbed, or that they more readily admit symptoms of distress, or that the items are not equally appropriate for boys and girls.

Two other scales for measuring anxiety have been prepared by Sarason (1960) and his associates. One of these is *The General Anxiety Scale for Children* (often referred to as GASC). The other is called *The Test Anxiety Scale for Children*. This, as its name denotes, touches specifically on children's reactions to tests, reactions to teachers questions, and other test-like conditions at school. It contains 30 items. The General Scale deals with fears and worries in a variety of situations (e.g., fear of snakes, high places, going home alone at night, worrying while trying to go to sleep, worry about what is going to happen, etc.). It contains 34 items.

The rationale underlying the Sarason Text Anxiety Scale includes a theory of anxiety quite similar to that set forth earlier in this chapter, except that, in keeping with a long-prevailing vogue, the authors center their view concerning the origins of anxiety too narrowly (in this writer's opinion) on parents, particularly the mother.

Sarason and his associates postulate that the reaction of the "test anxious" child to test or test-like evaluative situations in the classroom ". . . reflects his experiences in psychologically or interpersonally similar situations in his home both before and after the beginning of formal schooling" (1960, p. 13). They maintain that the test-anxious child is one who in the preschool period has experienced a parent-child relationship in which his adequacy had been questioned (1960, p. 13). Furthermore, they postulate that the anxiety reaction to the test situation contains, in addition to its conscious significance, ". . . a concurrent unconscious significance which primarily relates to what has been experienced by the child in the family situation" (p. 13). They further regard anxiety as a danger signal, indicating that the test situation has increased the strength of ideas, wishes, and fantasies which, if they came freely into conscious awareness and were expressed, would endanger a child's well-being. Anxiety thus viewed activates processes which help in ". . . keeping the unconscious unconscious."

According to Sarason's view, one of the components in the "matrix of unconscious factors" that operate in test anxiety is strong hostility toward parents and surrogate parents. In their evaluation of the child these persons have aroused hostility which the child could not satisfactorily express. If he showed hostility openly, he could be punished; if he vented his hostility in fantasy, it would conflict with his positive feelings toward these persons. Connected with the child's hostility it is likely that there are feelings of guilt, a tendency toward self-belittlement and buried fantasies of retaliation by parents. Sarason also postulates that the anxiety experienced by a test-anxious child is a signal that certain unconscious fantasies about bodily injury (mutilation) are dangerously near the threshold of awareness.

From the standpoint of one who has delved into the personal meaning of anxiety, the prospect of getting a realistic view of a particular child's condition by counting his yes responses to a conglomerate of specific questions seems, offhand, to be rather unpromising. Such a person would say that the measure of anxiety in an anxious individual is not the number of items in a list of symptoms he happens to have. He might have many; he might have few; he might not even have any of those on the list. This may especially be the case with a test anxiety scale if we can trust autobiographical data offered by persons who claim that they have used "flight into the intellect" as a defense against anxiety (Jersild, *et al.*, 1962). A bright anxious youngster may develop so effective a strategy of academic achievement that tests at school leave him quite undisturbed. He can so far outguess and outwit his teachers, and out-perform his rivals, that something more personal and threatening than a test is needed to activate his anxiety.

To misgivings such as these must be added the weaknesses inherent in a test that asks a person to reveal himself. He might be forthright or deny his frailties; he might wish to cooperate, or not to (theoretically one might expect a test-anxious person to be especially anxious when taking a test of anxious-ness, with a response that might range from consistent defensive falsification to abject acquiescence).

It seems that the anxiety as measured by a test of manifest anxiety is not equivalent to "clinical" anxiety—anxiety as it is encountered in children who are referred to psychological or psychiatric clinics for diagnosis and treatment of emotional disturbances. Such children are referred for a variety of reasons, and display a variety of problems, but it is usually assumed that anxiety is a significant element in the total clinical picture. Tests of manifest anxiety were administered, in separate studies by Wist and Broen (1956) and by Stone, *et al.* (1965), to children who had been referred, respectively, to a clinic under the auspices of a public school system, and to a child psychiatric service. The scores of these children were compared with those of children in the general school population. In general, the clinic patients did not score higher on the anxiety scale than the non-clinic children. The findings indicate that anxiety as defined by the anxiety scale seems to represent something different than is denoted by the clinical concept of anxiety.

In spite of these and other misgivings, it seems that tests of manifest anxiety, and "test anxiety" represent more than a superficial penetration of a child's inner life.

Relationship between Tests of Anxiety and Other Variables

Sarason and his associates found a positive correlation between children's scores on the "test anxiety" and "general anxiety" scales.

The correlation between the two tests was higher in results obtained from American children than from a sampling of children in England. In grades 1–6, the correlation between American boys' scores on the two scales ranged from .47 up to .69; the corresponding English correlations ranged from .15 to .47. This difference between American and British children apparently reflects the fact that test performance has a less crucial bearing on a pupil's future in the United States than in England, where there is a more systematic grouping of children according to ability. The British child, with more at stake than his American counterpart, is presumably under more pressure to do well on tests. As a result, a British child with only a moderate degree of "general anxiety" might be more subject to "test anxiety" than his American counterpart.

Correlations between teachers' ratings of their pupils' anxiety and the scores on the test anxiety scale were positive but low (only .20 for the total population of several grades in two American schools). Various interpretations of this are offered by the authors. This finding as related to teachers is interesting when viewed in connection with findings pertaining to parents noted earlier in this chapter (indicating that there are substantial discrepancies between the fears children say they have and the fears parents say the children have).

At all grade levels the coefficients were negative in correlations between test anxiety scores (the higher the score, the greater the assumed anxiety) and school achievement. These coefficients were, in the main, rather low, none of them exceeding −.30, although several of them were significant from a statistical point of view, notably in grades 4 and 5. Low correlations might be expected in view of findings in other studies which indicate that the relation between anxiety (as measured by tests) and intellectual performance is varied and complex.

Anxiety and Intelligence

Findings concerning the relationship between intelligence and anxiety or fear are rather conflicting and many of them are unsatisfactory. The most plausible findings are those which not only show differences in the fear or anxiety reactions of bright and less bright children, but also provide some sort of rationale for the difference.

Theoretically, from one point of view, bright young children should be more susceptible at an early age to certain fears that normally occur in the course of development. They presumably are more advanced in their perceptiveness and therefore would perceive "dangers" that are not perceived by children of lower intelligence until they are older. On the other hand, we might theorize that a bright child is less subject to certain fears as he grows older. He should presumably be less subject to fears centering around failure at school and more clever in meeting fear situations that lend themselves to a practical solution.

Findings in the Holmes (1935) laboratory study of fear, cited in the first section of this chapter, are in accord with the first assumption. Brighter children tended to manifest some fears at an earlier age.

There was a positive correlation between intelligence and number of fears manifested in the experimental situations, but this correlation declined with age (from .53 at age two to .10 at age five). A study by Boston (1939) likewise suggests that children with superior intelligence might be more sensitive to danger.

An interview study of "fears" by the writer and his associates (1933) yields comparisons between the frequency of various fears reported by children in three IQ groups: 120 or above, 100-119, and 80-99. Children in the highest group, as compared with those in the lowest group, were quite similar with respect to a number of fear categories (animals, the dark and being alone, frightening gestures and noises). A larger proportion of children of lower IQ reported fear of supernatural and mysterious events (on the basis of first-mentioned fears, 24 per cent in the lower group as compared with 15 per cent in the upper group). This difference could not be attributed to intelligence alone, for most of the children in the lower IQ group were also lower in socio-economic status.

In the studies by Sarason and his associates, cited above, there was an overall negative correlation of .20 between test-anxiety scores and scores on a test of Primary Mental Abilities (Thurstone). While this coefficient was statistically significant, it represents a rather meager relationship. Moreover, if the correlation represents a causal relationship, do children tend to do less well on mental tests because they are anxious or are they anxious because they do not do well on mental tests? Sarason and his associates sought to throw some light on this question. According to their analysis, test-anxious children are likely to do more poorly on a test that is pointedly "test-like" than on a test that is more informal and more like a game. The former, with its formal, academic, impersonal, and clearly evaluative characteristics, should, theoretically, more than the latter, trigger buried attitudes of hostility and self-derogation. They cite findings in which children's scores on a game-like test (the Davis-Eells, 1953) were compared with their scores on two more conventional tests (the Otis Alpha and Otis Beta). The game-like test deals with "real life" problems, is semihumorous, has no rigid time limits, and offers provision for praise and reassurance (which, presumably should help put an anxiously dependent child at his ease). The correlations between test-anxiety scores and the game-like test was —.14; the correlation between the test-anxiety scores and the more formal tests were, respectively —.28 and —.24. These correlations suggest that test anxiety is not quite so likely to interfere with performances in a game-like situation as in a test-like situation.

Values of Fear and Anxiety

In assessing the value of fear, it is necessary first to recognize that fear is important for self-preservation. Fear may take many foolish turns, but a creature totally without fear would probably not live very long. A rabbit who is frightened and runs away has a chance to run another day, and even the rabbit who frightens nine times out of ten when there is really no danger will be better off than a rabbit who happened not to be frightened the one time in ten when there *was* something to be afraid of. In the lives of children and adults, as in the lives of rabbits, there are many false alarms, but nature has endowed her creatures with fear to alert them to alarms that might not be false.

Any condition that mobilizes an individual's energies and puts him on the alert in the face of danger is obviously of tremendous value as a protection.

According to physiological findings, during acute emotional stress, glandular products are released into the blood stream, resulting in an increase in heart rate and blood pressure, a larger supply of available sugar, quicker coagulation of the blood and, in general, greater physical efficiency for meeting an emergency by fighting or fleeing (Cannon, 1929). However, often in modern life an issue which one fears cannot be solved by fighting or fleeing. A worried student cannot pass a hard examination by outrunning his instructor or by throwing him out the window. Most of the emergencies in modern life call for quick wits rather than for strong fists. And many of the apprehensions a child has concerning himself and his relations with others are not based on conditions which an extra spurt of physical energy can solve.

Several years ago the writer and an associate undertook an experiment which dealt with the psychological effects of physiological changes such as occur in intense emotional excitement. Through injections of adrenalin most of the physiological reactions described above were artificially induced. At the height of the physiological effects, various tests were administered. The tests showed that in the state of excitement there was an increase in physical strength and in speed of movement, but there was little or no gain in performing simple mental tasks, and, if anything, there was a loss in performing somewhat more complex intellectual tasks (Jersild and Thomas, 1931).

Findings in studies of children and adults who, according to their own self-ratings, have a high or low degree of "manifest anxiety" appear, on the whole, to be in accord with the results obtained in the study just cited. In one such study (Castaneda, McCandless, and Palermo, 1956b), an apparatus containing a series of electrical push buttons which activated a series of lights was used, and children were instructed to learn which button turned off which light. Simple as well as complex button-light combinations were used. In this study (as in earlier studies of adults) it was found that children who were in the "high-anxious" group performed better than "low-anxious" children on simple learning tasks but did more poorly on more complex tasks. In another study, manifest anxiety scores of children in the fourth, fifth, and sixth grades were correlated with academic achievement as measured by standardized tests (McCandless, *et al.*, 1956). The correlations ranged from zero to —.74, and in thirteen of the correlations there was a statistically significant *negative* correlation between manifest anxiety and performance. Children with more anxiety tended to show the poorest performance in the more complicated academic skills.

In a study by Phillips and others (1959) tests differing in difficulty and complexity were administered to children who also were given the Manifest Anxiety Scale and a test of intelligence. The tests ranged from one in which children simply had to put three pencil dots in each one of a series of circles as quickly as possible to tests of vocabulary requiring more complex forms of verbal ability. Children with higher manifest anxiety did not consistently perform more poorly on the complex than on the simple tests, but in connection with practically all the measurements there was a negative correlation between scores on manifest anxiety and performance. On the other hand, in all instances there was a positive correlation between intelligence and performance on the tests.

Several later studies have, in the main, confirmed a negative relationship between level of anxiety and intellectual performance. Stevenson and his associates (1965) conclude that anxiety has the most disruptive effect on performance in tasks involving verbal processes.

There are several factors that complicate the relationship between anxiety level and performance. Katahn (1966) found that high anxiety combined with high aptitude facilitated performance in a complex learning situation. Katahn also reports that high anxiety may facilitate academic achievement, when combined with high overall scholastic aptitude, but not when combined with low overall scholastic aptitude.

Schmeidler, *et al.* (1965), report that subjects who had a high need for achievement did better on a difficult verbal learning task if the anxiety and the stress surrounding the task were high; those with a low need for achievement performed better if the anxiety and stress were low.

These (and numerous other findings at the childhood and college-age level) indicate that the emotional disposition underlying the symptoms disclosed in response to tests of manifest anxiety is embedded within a network of forces within the personality as a whole. To unravel the origins and the cause-and-effect relationships within this network will probably require a more penetrating approach than is provided simply by manifest anxiety scales.

Recommended Readings

Several studies of anxiety as manifested by children's responses to empirical tests are cited in the text (see references in the Bibliography at the end of this book to Palermo, McCandless, Castaneda and Sarason, *et al.*). The concept of anxiety as a condition stemming from universal human conflicts and predicaments has been set forth by three outstanding psychoanalytic writers: Sigmund Freud, *The Problem of Anxiety* (1936); Karen Horney, *Our Inner Conflicts* (1945); and Harry Stack Sullivan, *The Meaning of Anxiety in Psychiatry and in Life* (1948). The theme of anxiety has also been discussed by writers with a background in philosophy and religion, notably by Sören Kierkegaard in *The Sickness Unto Death* (1951), and Paul Tillich, *The Courage To Be* (1952). Rollo May's *The Meaning of Anxiety* (1950) reviews findings regarding children's fears and theories of anxiety and then, wisely, discusses issues that are in need of further investigation. *Anxiety*, edited by Paul H. Hoch and Joseph Zubin (1950), contains contributions by a number of distinguished writers.

17　Anger and Hostility

Through anger a child asserts himself, gives a sharp edge to his demands, and retaliates against those who thwart or hurt him. Anger, like fear, is an instrument for dealing with a threatening environment. In anger a child takes action against the threat, whereas in fear he retreats from it.

A child's capacity for anger is essential for his well-being, but to get along comfortably with others he must also acquire a prudent degree of control of it. One of the most difficult tasks a child faces in his development is maintaining his ability to become angry while managing his anger so that it does not cause more trouble than it relieves.

An angry child is usually an unpleasant child. Even when he is too weak to cause harm his anger is likely to be viewed as an affront. Consequently, children are reared as though the eleventh and greatest commandment were "Thou shalt not show anger, nor even feel it." Yet to understand children it is necessary, as far as possible, to understand what prompts their anger. To do this, an adult must take stock of his own anger, including his tendency to counter a child's anger with anger, or to blame himself for the anger a child displays.

Sooner or later a child's anger is likely to involve him in conflict of a two-fold nature: conflict *with others* who object to his anger, or are threatened by it; and conflict *within himself* by reason of the fact that a healthy child's impulse to feel and express anger runs counter to other strong impulses, such as those connected with affection and fear. Partly as a consequence of this two-fold conflict, there is a complicated interplay between anger that is fully experienced and overtly expressed, and covert anger that ranges through a child's fantasies. Furthermore, partly because of this conflict, a child who at first directed his anger against other persons and things may, in time, become the object of his own rage. This happens when he becomes excessively self-reproachful and, as we say, "kicks himself."

Sources and Expressions of Anger

Anger can be aroused in young children by forcible restraint, interference with movement, blocking activities that are in progress, or anything that thwarts a child's wishes. The younger the child, the more his anger will turn upon interference with his physical needs and activities. As he grows older, the conditions that cause anger include anything that interferes with his possessions, or thwarts his plans, purposes, expectations, and his rights as he sees them, and by criticisms or fault-finding that attack ideas he has concerning himself.

Anger, like fear, is influenced by factors both of learning and maturation. During the first few days of life, such restrictions as having his arms pinned momentarily to his sides or compressing his nostrils do not especially arouse the ire of an infant. When an infant does protest, his movements are likely to be uncoordinated and display no clear pattern of rage. As he grows older, such treatment is likely to anger him.

After the child's capacities expand, learning plays an increasingly important role in determining how he will express his rage and what conditions will excite him.

Throughout childhood, however, there are great individual differences in the irascibility and violence of children. Even in early infancy, children differ in the intensity of their demands for food or attention, and in the severity of their anger when demands are not met. Children differ not only in their response to thwarting from others but also in their tendency to become angry in connection with activities of their own. One child, for example, becomes angry if he cannot put a spoon in his mouth; another child may take his failure very calmly.

Changes with Age in the Expression of Anger

As an infant grows older his outbursts of anger become less random and more directly aimed at something or someone. Before the age of one year, a child's tantrums are ineffective in removing obstacles or attacking an enemy. The most frequent single expression of anger in early childhood is crying, but crying diminishes with age. By the age of four almost half of a child's outbursts are likely to be aimed at the object of his wrath (Goodenough, 1931). Accompanying this change is an increase in retaliative behavior apparently aimed at securing revenge for an injury. Threats make their appearance between the ages of two and three and increase in frequency thereafter.

Indirect forms of retaliation and attack include such activities as overturning furniture and engaging in acts previously forbidden. One child of three, when angry, sucked his thumb conspicuously, although thumbsucking was not his usual habit. Other indirect forms of aggression are raucous laughter and refusal to speak. One child voiced resentment toward her mother by remarking, "I wish I had a mother like Mary's." In some cases, children express their anger by attacking themselves; for example, one child under study bit himself when angry. Aftereffects of anger are more frequent and prolonged in children over the age of four than in children under four (Goodenough, 1931).

In showing anger children sometimes go to extreme lengths such as holding their breath or vomiting or banging their heads against a hard surface. At about four some children resort to such threats as running away, chopping off the offender's head, or chopping his house to pieces. Many youngsters go through a period of threatening to kill when angered. In expressing anger, a child will frequently vary the nature of his outburst under different circumstances. He is more likely, for example, to cry in anger at home than at school (Ricketts, 1934) and to hit and kick when angered by another child than when angered by an adult.

Anger Directed against Self

Even when quite young, children direct anger against themselves. In addition to the physical self-punishment mentioned above (biting self, headbanging) children sometimes express anger against themselves in words, such as "I hate myself" or "I feel like killing myself," or use milder terms, such as "That's just like me" (when they make a mistake or have an accident).

The concept of self-hate is not pleasant, but it is useful in understanding adults, and it is essential in understanding children. This concept is illustrated by different forms of self-disparagement such as "running oneself down," variations of the phenomenon of masochism, by proneness to accidents, and by a compulsive tendency to get into trouble.

Factors Contributing
to Susceptibility to Anger

Many circumstances that increase a child's susceptibility to anger have been described by Goodenough (1931), who made a study of anger with the co-operation of a number of parents.[1] Children are more disposed to anger after a restless night, or when recovering from an illness, or when tired or hungry. Many adults likewise are more cranky before breakfast or when hungry. A good rule is not to start an argument before mealtime. A softboiled egg may do more to divert anger than the best logic emanating from an empty stomach.

Outbursts of anger are likely to increase when there are visitors, especially when they overstay their welcome. Also there is likely to be more anger if there are more than two adults in the household.

The fact that anger occurs more often in children in homes where there are several adults has considerable significance from a psychological and social point of view. The families in Goodenough's study lived in a Midwestern community where crowded households were rarer than in the poorer areas of large cities. Greater opportunity for annoyance when several people occupy the same space must be considered along with the fact that poor and crowded living quarters also produce many additional frustrations. The writer and his associates (1949) found that parents living in poor circumstances reported more problems connected with physical inconveniences than did more affluent parents. Slum dwellers are especially exposed to conditions that aggravate anger. They obviously live in crowded quarters; their sleep is likely to be less restful, especially on hot summer nights; the mother is more likely to suffer from fatigue; the family as a whole, although not suffering from lack of food, may hunger for a better diet. In addition, children and adults of low socio-economic status are, on the average, more openly aggressive than persons in a more favorable socio-economic situation. They are also subject to more physical punishment from adults. If, in addition to these harassments, the families are victims of prejudice, and the children do poorly at school and resent school (which occurs more often at the lower socio-economic levels), anger will abound.

Parents whose children were particularly prone to anger in Goodenough's study tried to calm them by coaxing and soothing more frequently than parents whose children were more placid. This difference provides a clue to the reason for many angry outbursts. When an angry child gets what he wants, his anger has been successful; but if he fails to get what he wants, his anger

---

[1] The writer has not been able to find any study later than Goodenough's (1931), which is based on extensive observational records of the anger of young children in their home surroundings.

has been abortive; he will have less reason to resort to anger as a means of solving a problem another time.

Boys tend to exhibit anger more openly than girls in the home. This is in keeping with other findings indicating that boys also are more openly aggressive outside the home. Mothers seem to be more at a loss in dealing with an angry boy than in dealing with an angry girl.

Anger is more likely to occur in homes where parents are over-anxious and concerned with whether a child's behavior is "good" or "bad" than in homes where parents are tolerant and capable of looking upon a child objectively. Anger is often provoked by parents who nag and recriminate instead of viewing each anger episode as a thing of the past when it is over. Consistency in methods of discipline appears to be a more important factor than the strictness or lenience of the disciplinary procedures used. Some methods, such as bribery and letting the child have his own way, may bring an outburst to an end but may also encourage future outbursts (Goodenough, 1931).

The level of a child's abilities and, in time, his ideas of what to expect of himself, will have an important bearing on whether or not a situation is potentially frustrating. When he is able, or thinks he is able, to walk by himself on rough ground, he may be angry if someone tries to take his hand, whereas earlier, when this feat was beyond what he expected of himself, he was glad to take a hand or to be carried (and even later, when the rough terrain is no longer a challenge, he again may be quite glad to hold a hand or to be given a lift).

Anger Outbursts as a "Problem"

A long-term study of over two hundred children in California by Macfarlane and her associates (1954) showed that children's temper tantrums constitute one of the most common problems reported by parents. At the age of twenty-one months (the earliest period covered by the investigation) 59 per cent of the boys and 43 per cent of the girls displayed tantrums which parents regarded as problems. The peak incidence was at three years (69 per cent of the boys, 63 per cent of the girls), but the incidence remained high throughout the pre-teen years, particularly among boys (ranging downward from 69 per cent in boys at age twenty-one months to 39 per cent at age twelve; the incidence for girls varied somewhat from year to year, ranging from a high of 63 per cent to a low of 28 per cent). The decline in overt anger with age is in keeping with a general tendency in children to moderate their open displays of emotion as they grow older.

These percentages clearly indicate that the parents of a large proportion of children are disturbed and probably also very puzzled by their children's show of anger. Perhaps they would be even more disturbed if they could detect the incidents when older children are angry but conceal their feelings.

The fact that parents of as many as two-thirds of a large sampling of children at a given age regard anger outbursts as a problem suggests that the parents are perhaps judging their youngsters by a standard that is far too perfectionistic. Indeed, since anger is so normal and common, one might ask: What is happening with the minority of youngsters whose anger is not regarded as a problem? Are they as angry as the rest, but viewed more complacently by their parents? Are some of them perhaps too lethargic to be riled? Are some of them perhaps suppressing overt signs of anger? If so, the children who do not give vent to anger should perhaps be regarded as presenting a more severe problem than those who do.

At any rate, that so many parents of children at all ages, but preponderantly of young children, regard their children's anger as a problem (and only one of many problems) underlines the fact that a parent's lot is not an easy one. But it also underscores the fact that it is not easy to be a child. Children cannot develop normally without becoming angry; but their anger is deplored by their parents and eventually most children learn to deplore it themselves. In a study by the writer and his associates (1952), a substantial percentage of children and adolescents singled out their temper as one of their major faults when asked in general terms to tell "What I dislike about myself." (The percentages at various age levels from the fourth grade through college ranged as high as 30. Probably a great many more would have mentioned their temper if they had specifically been asked about it.)

Devious Manifestations of Anger

Frequently a person will resort to sneers, innuendoes, gossip, and the like, instead of displaying his anger physically. An angry person can also resort to indirect methods of vanquishing the object of his rage, such as belittling his opponent, overcoming him in competition, rejoicing in his misfortunes, plotting against him, or imagining situations that will bring sorrow to him. Children sometimes imagine themselves as dead, secretly relishing the tears that wet the cheeks of the sorrowing persons who have abused them.

Finding a Scapegoat. When a person is not free to direct his aggressive impulses toward the person or circumstances that provoked him, he may succeed in directing them toward someone or something else. A child who has been angered by his parents, but who does not dare to strike back at his parents, may, for example, "take out" his anger on a brother or sister.

Change in Quality of Performance. Anger is sometimes expressed by a change in the quality of a child's performance.[2] One response may be restless and aimless behavior. Another response may be to withdraw—to walk away from a situation if it is possible to do so. Even when confined, in the flesh, to

---

[2] For accounts of loss of constructiveness, regression, and other forms of lowered quality of performance in frustrating situations see Barker, Dembo, and Lewin (1941); Keister (1937); and Updegraff and Keister (1937).

the annoying situation he may try to absent himself psychologically, as when he finds the arithmetic too difficult and sits through the class period without paying attention to what is going on. Instances of withdrawal from an irritating situation appeared in a study of frustration by Seashore and Bavelas (1942). One at a time the children were asked to draw a man, but as soon as a child had completed a drawing the experimenter, without taking further notice of it, gave the child another piece of paper and asked him to draw another man, and so on, one drawing after the other. As one trial followed another, many of the children gave less and less time to the drawing. A child who devoted seven or eight minutes to his first drawing or two might, several trials later, dash off a drawing in a few seconds. As one trial followed the next, the childrens' drawings deteriorated.

The change in quality of performance in response to frustration may also take the form of regression—the child backslides and behaves in a more childish or infantile manner.

Losing Touch with Anger

Anger that is expressed openly may be punished by others, but anger that is repressed is likely to produce self-punishment. The process of repression is easier to define in theory than to describe or demonstrate empirically. Yet it is possible to identify some of the ways in which anger is, so to speak, disavowed as though it did not exist.

One way of renouncing anger is not to show it. If a person still feels anger, he has not, of course, disowned it or lost touch with it. But if he curbs his anger because he fears retaliation or shrinks from hurting someone else's feelings he has, at least, surrendered his right to display anger. A tendency to curb any clear display of anger may become almost automatic.

School children are constantly suppressing anger impulses. Most children, when questioned, will talk about things they resent at school, such as what they regard as arbitrary behavior by teachers or troublesome classmates. But an outburst of anger by children in the classroom is very rare. There are, to be sure, some pupils whose anger grows to a white heat and explodes; but this does not often occur even among children who are "school problems." There are many devious ways of venting anger, such as whispering, insolent stares, not paying attention, yawning, "accidentally" making a book clatter to the floor, and so on. But however successful they may be in annoying the teacher, these recourses are rather pallid forms of revenge.

For the sake of discipline and good order it is, of course, well that school children check their anger. But this does not change the fact that anger exists. Nor does it, in many classrooms, prevent teachers from giving a tongue-lashing to a pupil who would be expelled if he lashed back in kind.

"Stored-up" Anger. One frequent result of an habitual tendency to block an anger impulse is that anger is "stored up." (A large proportion of adults, when questioned, report that they have a tendency to "store up" anger.) Anger that was withheld at the time of provocation may flare up later, as when a person afterward recalls someone's offensive remark and thinks up a sarcastic retort—a "snappy comeback"—when it is too late. (Wit is often most biting when the person who deserves to be bitten is no longer there.)

Blocking Anger through Affection, Fear and Guilt. A person has only partially renounced his anger if he blocks it at the time of provocation but then permits it to recur. He is still "in touch." A more complete disavowal of anger occurs when a person gives up not only his impulse to anger but also blunts his ability to feel it. Such blunting may come about through the intervention of fear, affection, or guilt. Fear enters the picture when a child has learned to fear retaliation. For such a child, anger is dangerous, and when he is angered the arousal of fear may be so swift that it snuffs out his anger. Guilt enters the picture if a child's tendency to blame himself for outbursts of anger is activated along with his anger. Affection also works against anger, for early in life it is the persons who love a child most, and whom he loves, that are most likely to arouse his anger. A child's feelings of affection, loyalty, and his tendency to obey and not to question his parents acts or intentions may so color his response to them that it does not even occur to him to become angry, when well he might.[3]

The above account of ways in which conflicting feelings and impulses blunt the impact of anger must be taken pretty much on faith, for it cannot be explained precisely in neurological terms (neither can any other psychological phenomenon, for that matter), and a child would not be able to identify the process and trace it step by step. It is possible, however, to note some of the explicit ways in which older persons disavow anger. One way is to minimize the offense by excusing the offender: he really didn't mean it; he must be cranky (a nice word for nasty) because he's tired; he may be gauche but he's really good at heart; he would not take on so if he really didn't care; after all, everyone has a right to be cross now and then; and so on. Another way is to shift responsibility for the offense: I had it coming; I got what I deserved; if I weren't so touchy (tired, irritable, etc.), this wouldn't make me so mad.

---

[3] An account in the writer's records of adult recollections from childhood offers what the writer believes to be an authentic illustration. The adult in this account, who was reflecting on his childhood one evening, felt a surge of long-delayed anger. Somehow he had revived a childhood scene in which he and his father carried a large rocking chair some distance to a repair shop. When carried horizontally, one end consisted of a light wooden back rest of the chair while the other contained the rocking apparatus—two steel coils. The father took the light end while the boy struggled with the heavy end. The adult reported that he had a vivid and angry recollection of this scene but no recollection at all of having resented his father's action at the time.

Anger Concealed by Friendliness. Unsolved anger toward self or others, attributed to childhood experiences, may reside under a cloak of friendliness and gentleness. This was brought out in a personal way by adults who took part in a study by the writer and his associates (1962) of the effects of undergoing intensive psychoanalytically oriented psychotherapy. Whatever may be the judgment (ranging from favorable to adverse) regarding the benefits of therapy, one thing cannot be denied. For better or for worse, the patient again and again ploughs and reploughs his past. He traverses his earlier history from one angle and then from another, through reports of his dreams and his waking reactions, through recollections of his past and reflections on his present, through coherent reminiscences and seemingly disconnected free associations.

The persons in this study were, on the whole, rather gentle in their ways. If rated on aggressiveness by colleagues and acquaintances, most of them probably would be placed somewhere below the middle of the scale.

One thing mentioned prominently in the reports of the persons in this study was anger. One of the greatest single "benefits" claimed by those who had accepted help in understanding themselves lay in what they perceived as a greater insight into the role of unsuspected anger in their lives.

The Sway of Unresolved Anger

All of the ways through which anger is demoted would work for the good if they really worked. But the trouble is, it is easier to push anger down than to push it out. As Sullivan has said, ". . . it is easier to swallow anger than to digest it."

To speak of "stored" anger smacks of mysticism. Just how, and where, are the grapes of wrath stored? But mystical or not, the concept that anger leaves its aftereffects is one of the truest and most profound concepts in the lore of human psychology. The residues of past rage appear in children who have a chip on their shoulder. We see it in children who nurture grievances. The dregs of wrath appear in those who chronically feel abused and in children who are suspicious and defensive, as though on guard against the worst.

Stored up anger appears in the hostility we encounter in people in everyday life, and in ourselves. Without the concept of residual anger in the form of hostile attitudes and impulses, we cannot account for man's cruelty to man; the ease with which slaughter is justified in "righteous" wars; the punitive policies prevailing in our educational system where millions of children are needlessly subjected to the sting of failure. And, of course, anger comes forth in all forms of delinquency and crime.

There probably is no person who leaves childhood without a measure of unrelieved, unrequited anger. The anger emerges most tragically when a mild-mannered adult, previously known as "one of the nicest boys in town" commits a senseless murder. Fortunately, suppressed anger is usually not that explosive. But unresolved anger, along with unresolved fear, is one of the sad legacies of childhood. The blame for this cannot be laid at the door of this or that stupid and perverse adult. Rather, the blame (if blame must be assigned) can be traced to two factors. One is the inevitability, in the nature of things, that children will be frightened and angered. The other is a massive tendency, in the culture at large and in education in particular, to neglect and to leave uncultivated the resources children possess for gaining some understanding of themselves.

An unfortunate aspect of hostility generated in childhood is that the hostile person does not usually perceive himself as hostile. An equally unfortunate thing is that a child who has "undigested" anger may turn it against himself.

One outstanding finding in the above-mentioned study of the effects of self-inquiry concerned the outcomes that emerged after the subjects, as they saw it, dredged up, confronted and "worked through" their anger. The result most often reported was increased amiability—less anger and more tenderness in their relations with others, and greater acceptance of themselves.

Testimony from adults about their past may be quite faulty. But such testimony, for what it may be worth, suggests one thing: When the residues of childhood anger have been examined through painful self-scrutiny, the anger is likely to lose much of its racking and irrational potency.

Resentment of Authority

As we have observed in an earlier context, the discipline children receive from those in authority—at first from their parents and later from their teachers and other adults—often produces anger. This, as we have maintained, is inevitable. A child may feel abused even when discipline is most essential and administered in the most reasonable manner.

A child's resentment of authority in the home or school leaves a lasting mark on his behavior if he continues during adult years to "take out" his anger against authority figures.

We can see evidences of reactions to the father figure (using him now as our main symbol of authority) in many reactions of older persons in everyday life. When a teacher is extremely sensitive to mild criticism from his supervisor—reacting to a helpful suggestion as though it were an affront—it is likely that he is carrying-over resentments from an earlier period in his life. The fact that reactions against an evaluating authority figure may be aroused by tests and test-like situations in school provided the impetus for studies of "test anxiety" which were reviewed in the preceding chapter.

A continuing revolt against authority figures also explains an adult's chronic opposition to anyone who stands as a symbol of authority, be he the boss, an elected official, the congenial dean of a college, the head of a department.

When adults attach resentments and loyalties carried over from childhood to authority figures, they vary considerably in their views concerning who is the good father and who is the bad one. In a political campaign, for example, a "father figure" who is regarded as a villain by one person may be a hero to another (who happens to fix his resentment on the opposing candidate). As a result, any well-known public character (particularly in the political field) who has a host of admirers is also likely to have many detractors. Long-standing resentments also are attached to causes and symbols that carry labels reminiscent of parent-child relationships.

Dealing with Children's Anger

A child's anger, like an adult's, usually means that there is an aggravation immediately at hand, and this may call attention to a condition that can be remedied. In addition, since anger is not only a response to what is present but also usually has roots in the past, the grownup faces not simply an immediate problem but also a greater opportunity and challenge when a child becomes angry.

When overtly showing anger, a child, like an adult, draws aside the curtain behind which he normally conceals himself. A child's anger can provide a significant clue to his motives and to currents in his emotional life which otherwise would go unnoticed.

Anger may be a sign of strength as well as weakness. A child's anger may be genuine, healthy, and noble. It is healthy for a child to become angry or at least to feel anger when someone abuses him, takes advantage of him, or violates his integrity. It is healthy for him to react with anger when people whom he loves are under attack, or when someone tries to demean his loyalties, or when someone tries to abuse a weaker person for whom he feels responsible. We should be more concerned about a child who seems to have lost his capacity for anger than about the one who seems too often to lose his temper.

A child's anger, like the anger of an adult, is a sign of weakness when it is not suited to the occasion, when it it is not directed against the real source of difficulty, or when it creates more difficulty for him. When a minor setback provokes rage that is kept mostly under control but betrays itself by little signs, we may suspect that a child is not only struggling with the problems that beset him in his day-to-day life but is also involved in a larger struggle. If an adult can understand a child's anger, he has gone a long way toward understanding the child and toward understanding himself.

It is difficult to deal wisely with an angry child because a display of anger is likely to arouse anger in the person against whom it is directed. Few parents or teachers are immune to this tendency, and it is helpful for everyone concerned to recognize this and not feel guilty about it. However, when the anger has passed and feelings have calmed down, it is possible for an adult to try to look at a child's anger from a larger point of view: What can be learned from it? Why was the child so angry? What touched him off? Why are his feelings so raw and sensitive on the issue that aroused him? Was he perhaps striving anxiously to protect his pride? What weakness might the anger-provoking circumstance threaten to expose? What might this flare-up of anger reveal concerning the expectations he has of himself or of others? What long-standing grievance might he be harboring?

Jealousy

Complex feelings and impulses are usually involved in jealousy. In introspective accounts of jealousy offered by adults (Gesell, 1906), anger was most frequently mentioned, including feelings of hatred and revenge. Self-pity, as well as dejection, mortification, fear, and anxiety, were also mentioned by many persons. The most frequent combination was anger, self-pity, and grief.[4]

Jealousy prevails when a child is resentful or feels threatened when attention and affection he desires for himself are bestowed on someone else. Jealousy may be centered on a parent, but it usually is more openly shown in relations between siblings within the family and, in older persons, in relationships between lovers. One characteristic of a particularly jealous older person is a desire for exclusive possession of another's affection; he responds as though the other person's acceptance of someone else is tantamount to rejection of him. In children, signs of a desire for exclusive possession can also be observed, but there are other factors present.

The birth of a younger sibling frequently evokes signs of jealousy. The jealousy is likely to be more intense in a first-born child who, for a time, has been an *only* child. Although we need not assume, as some have assumed, that the coming of a new baby is a catastrophic experience for an older sibling, it is quite understandable that he will be a bit confused and perplexed. His parents' attention has been centered on him. Even if he has not been over-indulged he has been something of a little king. Although the new baby does not lessen his parent's affection for him, there are many changes he must adapt to in the day's practical routine. And, in addition, occurrences which are not meant invidiously may upset him. For example, a four-year-old boy who at first seemed well disposed toward his baby sister was incensed when his blanket was used to cover her. This might seem like an over-reaction to a trivial offense, but when we consider how strongly attached some children often are to certain possessions (blankets among them), the taking of a child's blanket may mean far more to him than merely the loss of a bed-cover.

Jealousy toward a younger sibling is frequently expressed in aggressive ways,

---

[4] For studies of jealousy in children see Sewall (1930), Foster (1927), Neisser (1951). Thomas, *et al.* (1961).

such as biting, compressing the child's nostrils, removing his covers, or making noise when he is asleep. Jealousy is sometimes "acted out" in make-believe.

A jealous child sometimes reverts to earlier infantile habits. For example, when a new baby arrives, an older child who for some time has achieved bladder control at night may revert to bed-wetting or frequently call his parents at night to take him to the toilet. He may seek extra help and attention in connection with eating, dressing, and other activities. Apparently as a bid for attention, he may exhibit fears that were never before displayed and that, in effect, represent a plea for sympathy and attention (although such pleas can easily be misinterpreted). Again, he may become more affectionate than was his wont, or meek and submissive and very obedient.

Among 110 children whose development had been followed since early infancy by Thomas and his associates (1961) there were eighteen who had acquired a younger sibling. Over half of the children seemed to be disturbed by this event, but in several cases the reactions were mild and transient. Children's reactions to a new sibling seemed to be influenced by a number of circumstances—whether they were first-born children, their age when the new baby came (children under 18 months seemed less disturbed when a baby was born than older children), and prior relationships existing between them and their parents.

The older child's own individual characteristics also played an important role. In their reactions to a new baby, children manifested a style of behavior and temperamental characteristics which they had first manifested in early infancy before the coming of the new baby and continued to manifest in their everyday behavior. Youngsters who, from an early age on, showed mild, positive, regular responses, with quick adaptability in meeting new situations, showed a similar pattern of behavior with the new baby. They appeared only mildly disturbed or not disturbed at all. On the other hand, a group of children who, from infancy onward, had been intense and negative in their reactions, and irregular in the daily rhythm of their lives, showed more intense and prolonged reactions to the birth of a sibling.

The link between jealousy in early childhood and a jealous disposition in later years has not been traced adequately in scientific studies. Children normally lose their more obvious symptoms of jealousy as they grow older and become absorbed in interests outside the family. On the other hand, some children carry a jealous attitude into their mature years, not only toward members of their own family, but sometimes even more toward their associates in daily life.

Among adults, the degree of jealousy a person exhibits frequently bears little relationship to his relative status or power as compared with others. A person who has "arrived" and has achieved the outward semblance of success will sometimes begrudge the recognition bestowed upon an underling, much as a big hound bristles when his master pets a forlorn poodle. A person who was intensely jealous of a younger sibling may, as far as he can see, have outgrown this jealousy, but traces of these earlier bitter experiences may remain, even though jealousy is no longer overtly shown toward the brother or sister. An attitude of jealousy persists in an adult, for example, if he feels hurt when another receives recognition or wins good fortune. His feelings may also express themselves in the way he takes sides against some people in his environment who represent, psychologically, objects of jealousy similar to what his brother or sister represented when he was younger.

Recommended Readings

In recent years, writings specifically dealing with *anger* have been rather sparse. Florence Goodenough's *Anger in Young Children* (1931) contains a wealth of information about children's anger as perceived and reported by their parents. *Children Who Hate* by Fritz Redl and David Wineman (1951) gives a vivid and revealing account of children who had difficulty in managing their aggressive impulses. Although this book deals with an exceptional group of children, it contains many insightful glimpses into the working of hostility in the lives of normal children and adults. The relationship between hostility and anxiety is discussed by Freud and Horney in books cited in preceding chapters. The interplay between love and hostility is discussed in books listed at the end of Chapter 15. Elton B. McNeil's "Psychology and Aggression" (1959) is a richly documented and thought-provoking account of the sources and ramifications of aggressive impulses and the dangers inherent in unresolved hostility. The ramifications of anger, generated earlier in life, have been discussed by the author in *When Teachers Face Themselves* (1955) and *The Meaning of Psycotherapy in the Teachers Life and Work* (1962).

PART FIVE

The Growth of Understanding

18   *Fantasy and Dreams*

A large and fascinating world opens up to a child when he is able to imagine. He now begins to deal with the image of things instead of being bound to what is tangibly before him.

A child's imagination plays an important role in all aspects of his development. In the intellectual sphere, he is able through his imagination to experiment and explore, to work with ideas without being restrained by the rules of logic. In the emotional sphere, he can give play to desires, fears, hopes, and aggressive impulses. Imagination is useful in his social development, for much of his play with other youngsters occurs in make-believe settings. And there is interaction also between a child's imaginative activity and his motor development. Many important motor skills are acquired or are practiced in play activities that have a high imaginative content, such as doll play and housekeeping. Make-believe also often supplies the plot or purpose when a child practices such motor activities as climbing, swinging, or riding a bicycle.

Early Manifestations

A child's ability to imagine appears at least as early as his ability to talk, and some children enter into complicated imaginative ventures before they are able to speak. A child of eleven months, who was observed by the author, provides an example of imaginative behavior preceding the ability to talk.

> In the course of her creepings about the house this child discovered the garbage pail and she also discovered that she was not supposed to pry into it. Once, as her mother was watching, she started to creep across the kitchen floor toward the pail. When her mother gave a warning sound the child stopped for a moment, then crept a short distance, then looked up at her mother, laughing heartily. Again she made a false start and again she looked up, laughing merrily. She obviously was getting great sport out of this game of pretending to go to the garbage pail while her mother looked on. This episode occurred several months before she combined two or more words in her speech.

Another early sign of imaginative activity appears when children imitate other persons or imitate the actions of animals, even though the model for such imitation is not present. At ten months, for example, one child went through the motions of "telephoning" with a toy phone. Similarly, a child about a year old went through the motion of putting on his father's hat while dragging his briefcase toward the door, as though going off to work.

After about the age of two, most children show an increase in imaginative activity, as revealed by their language and play behavior. In one study in which records were kept of children's language, it was found that 1.5 per cent of their remarks at twenty-four to twenty-nine months of age were imaginative in character; at forty-two to forty-seven months, the percentage of imaginative remarks was 8.7 (Burnham, 1940). In another study, in which language as well as overt behavior was recorded, there was a sixfold increase in frequency of imaginative episodes from two-and-a-half years to four years (Markey, 1935).

Changing Structure of Make-Believe

In addition to changes in the amount of make-believe activity, there are changes in the themes with which children deal. In one study (Markey, 1935) it was observed that much of the imaginative activity of children under the age of three fell into three categories: (1) personification, such as talking to inanimate objects; (2) make-believe use of materials, such as calling a slide a train, drinking out of an empty cup; and (3) participation in make-believe situations, such as putting out a fire or taking a bath. At the age of three, make-believe uses of materials were among the most typical imaginative activities. But after the age of three and a half years, longer make-believe situations were devised, including complicated dramatic play.

A young child most frequently throws himself into make-believe situations in which he himself supplies the setting, the necessary equipment, and the dramatic content. He uses and enjoys treasures which no Midas could supply, and, young as he is, he anticipates that great faculty that older persons have for building a world *as if* which differs from the world *as is*, yet sometimes comes closer to revealing a person's most pressing preoccupations than his more prosaic behavior.

As children move into and beyond the preschool period, much of their imaginative activity is pursued in the privacy of their own thoughts. Sometimes a child will afford us glimpses of these private day-dreams through what he says or does. Sometimes, however, these daydreams are unrevealed or are reported only, if at all, as recollections when a youngster is older.

Private daydreaming sometimes occurs in the form of a "continued story." The child may return again and again, for weeks, months, or even years, to add new episodes to what has gone before.

The "continued story" type of day-dream may include exploits (such as illicit sex behavior) which a child does not undertake in "real" life and which he would not reveal to anyone else. With some children, fantasies of this kind may comprise a significant part of his "secret self" which lies hidden from the view of others. This kind of make-believe behavior has been reported in fiction —fiction that no doubt is largely autobiographical but has not, as far as the author knows, been subjected to systematic study. Obviously it would be difficult to make a systematic study of such "forbidden" fantasy material. An attempted indirect approach to forbidden fantasies has been made through the use of projective techniques, which will be discussed in a later section. However, even these techniques, which permit a person to attribute actions and traits to pictured or storied characters, as though they were not his own, do not capture the essence of a child's fantasy life.

Make-Believe as a Kind of Thinking

Imagination begins when a child is capable of forming images and is able to organize these images into a structured intellectual activity. Images originally grew out of concrete experiences that have become internalized in such a way that a child can (in the field of visual imagery) see things in his "mind's eye" even though they are not visible. Imagination also involves an intellectual flow, which means that images have become mobile, and bits from here and there can be joined in a manner that is not bound to a pattern of experience with concrete things. As mentioned in an earlier chapter, Piaget, who speaks of images as interiorized imitation, regards the capacity for imagery as an essential development in a child's transition from the sensory-motor to conceptual thinking.

Through use of his imagination, a child is able to form total images out of fragments, using these fragments in a flexible way. A wagon with which he plays is now a car, now a train, now a ship, now a lunch counter in a restaurant. He can manipulate ideas which he only partly grasps. For example, he knows the names of certain cities where relatives live or through which he and his parents have recently traveled, but then, in connection with imaginary boat play, he can visit these cities, going by boat from a city on the seacoast to another city that lies far inland. A trip between two cities 500 miles apart requires less time than a trip between adjacent towns. And even though the voyage is by water, there is nothing to prevent him from stepping off and making little side trips on foot, for when he steps off, the water becomes dry land. Such ventures seem quite illogical and may even seem to be a retreat from reality, yet it is important to recognize that the child has made a journey of the mind, an ambitious one at that; and he has made it in the only way that would be possible for him.

Through make-believe a child is able to experiment and explore without being bound by a pre-determined logic. Examples of this appear when children are in the beginning stages of drawing. If certain lines and colors that have been put together resemble a flower, it is easy to give the product a logical structure by calling it a flower.

Through make-believe a youngster can substitute one rationale for another. A five-year-old girl who had visited her grandmother in the city was inspired to make a colored drawing of her grandmother's apartment house. She first made a good representation of an eight-story apartment building. Then, in the process of putting a street into the drawing, she happened to run the lines of the street through the fourth floor so that the lower floors were buried below ground level. This apparently was not in keeping with the original theory of the drawing and so, it being impossible to erase the crayoned street, the youngster changed the theory of her drawing. She shaded the entire portion below the fourth-floor level. She added little insect-like creatures, both in the floors under the ground and above the ground. Then she triumphantly displayed the drawing as the "home of the ant-killers." (The insect-like creatures were ants.) In experimenting with lines and relationships, she had produced a striking drawing. From the point of view of a literally-minded architect, the drawing would be regarded as a failure, but the youngster, by supplying a new name and rationale, converted it into an artistic success.

Motives Underlying Imaginative Activity

Make-believe is impelled by all the motives that underlie human activity. In his earliest imaginative activities a child uses make-believe as a form of play in connection with his own self-initiated impulse to use his growing powers. Make-believe also serves as a means of dealing with problems.

Make-Believe
as a Means of Coping with Fear

A two-and-a-half-year-old child who was frightened whenever she saw a dog on the street often at home went through a game in which she would get down on all fours, bark, growl, and head toward her mother saying, "I'm going to bite you." When she came close to her mother, she would say in a comforting tone, "I'm a good dog. I'm not going to bite you, Mama, I will kiss you." Then she would proceed to lick her mother's stockings with a great show of affection. It was as though she were transforming a threatening dog (or mother!) into a friendly creature and "proving" to herself that there was nothing to fear. After several episodes in which the child had played the part of a dangerous dog, suddenly turned friendly, the youngster took to using similar words on the street. While holding her mother's hand, she would say about a dog—very much in the same tone as she had used in her play— "Mama, he's a good dog. He doesn't bite me." She still stayed close to her mother, but there was now less fear in the way she clutched her mother's hand and in her tone of voice than when the fear of dogs was first observed.

Another example of the use of make-believe as a means of coping with fear appeared in the behavior of a four-year-old girl who had a fear of a bogey man. She sometimes faced this fear on an imaginary level by getting her two-year-old brother to play the role of a bogey man. She would put a white towel over his head and he would sit by as she called him a bogey man. As part of the game the four-year-old then would take to her heels to escape from the bogey man. The youngster's intention, it seemed, was to confront her fear within the safety of a make-believe situation. This was not at first an easy task. Several times the fleeing which began in fancy ended in earnest—she seemed to become genuinely afraid of the bogey man she had created. But as time went on, the bogey man became less menacing. Here is one example of how development is accomplished through play.

A further illustration of make-believe as a means of facing fear is supplied by a boy who was afraid of crossing streets for fear he might be run over by a car (Griffiths, 1935). He played incessantly with toy cars, pushing them around and causing "accidents" to occur. In this harmless way he gradually overcame his fear and "gained a sense of power" over the object he had feared (Griffiths, 1935). According to Griffiths, "It can often be observed that children who are afraid of some object, like that very object more than any other as a miniature toy." In this instance, the boy's passion for toy cars was no mere accident. Through his make-believe play with them he was attending to some very serious personal business.[1]

---

[1] An example such as this probably provides the key for explaining many of the toys children choose (including instances when a child who has received many presents concentrates on a toy which, from an adult's point of view, is not the most attractive one).

Make-Believe
as an Outlet for Aggression

Aggressive impulses are prominent in the imaginings of young children. This was brought out impressively in a study by Griffiths (1935) of five-year-old children, mentioned in Chapter 11. These children were observed at play and their imaginings were also studied through a variety of other techniques, including an "imagery test" (the child was asked to cover his eyes with his hands and then was asked to tell what he could see). The subjects included children from middle- and lower-class homes. In both groups children expressed fantasies containing violence and brutality.

Children often use make-believe to deal with irritations, to take action against conditions that annoy and thwart them in real life. The way they dispose of such problems is sometimes rather drastic. If children were suddenly to translate their fantasies into action, widespread carnage would result. In the study by Markey, cited above, children were provided with small pieces of kitchen equipment and a "family" in the form of dolls and were encouraged to play a housekeeping game. One boy proceeded to lay hands on the dolls. He called them bad babies, put them on the toy stove, and said, "You've got to be dead. You've got to stay on there for three weeks." Then he proceeded to tear the house down and to beat the dolls, talking while he did so about burning the bad babies in the imaginary fire. The school records of this child revealed that he was very jealous of a baby brother and, at home, had been delighted when the baby squirmed and cried while his nose was being cleaned. Now, in the imaginary situation, he seemed to relish the thought of watching the baby burn. Although the records in this case were not complete, it seems reasonable to conjecture that the boy came closer to grips with his antagonism to his brother by showing his hostility in a make-believe setting than he would have come if he had not dared to express this hostility even in his fantasies.

Aggression in imaginative situations sometimes not only seems exaggerated but also misplaced. Griffiths (1935), noted a preferred parent, rather than the one less preferred, may be the victim of the child's aggressive fantasies.

Removal of the Unpleasant. Some children through make-believe convert a disagreeable reality situation into something more to their taste. One child, about three years old, began to "make supper for the little girls." She opened the icebox and said, "Dolly dear, we *always* leave the icebox door open." The child's mother explained that, to keep the youngster from raiding the icebox at home, it had become necessary to tie a wire around it. One night the mother had discovered the child trying unsuccessfully, while muttering angrily to herself, to open the icebox. In her doll play the child not only solved the problem of the icebox but seemed also to express anger toward her mother.

Escape by way of the imagination from an unpleasant situation appeared also in the case of a child of four-and-a-half years who announced to her mother: "I'm inventing a new paint for the bathtub. It will take twelve years to dry, and you can't use the bathtub for twelve years."

Make-Believe Undercurrents in Seemingly Unreasonable Behavior

The fact that a child is able through his imagination to endow the happenings of everyday life with a drama of his own making sometimes adds undercurrents to his behavior that are difficult for others to understand. If a child seems to be unduly unreasonable, or takes offense at a minor frustration, the reason may be that in his fancy he has built vivid expectations which now are thwarted. So, for example, a five-year-old who has looked forward to going on a shopping trip with his mother may become extremely angry and disappointed when the mother is unable at the moment to make the trip. In his fancy he not only has made the trip several times but he may also have built elaborate plans and experiences around what he expected his mother to buy. The fact that the trip simply had to be postponed does not minimize the child's disappointment.

Imaginative Activity and "Waiting Ability"

According to a theory suggested by Freud and discussed by Rappaport (1951, 1960), daydreaming comes into play early in life when there is a delay between a child's experience of a need or desire and gratification of the need. A child "fills" the gratification, for the time being, through his imagination. Taking off from this theory, Singer (1961) raised the question whether highly imaginative children would better be able to bide their time—to wait—without protesting or becoming restless than less imaginative children. He divided forty children aged six to nine into high- and low-fantasy groups on the basis of questions designed to elicit imaginative answers. The children were then asked to cooperate in a situation which called upon them to remain quietly in one spot as long as possible. Children with high imaginative ability, as measured by the methods employed in the study, "waited" for a significantly longer period of time than those rated as having lower imaginative ability.

*Facing the Future
through Fantasy*

Imaginative activity enables a child to anticipate the future. This ability to borrow what is yet to be augments a child's powers but also exposes him to difficulties. Just as he can savor future pleasure and success he also, in anticipation, can taste fear and trouble. A toddler may feel delight at the prospect of taking a walk when he sees his mother bring his wraps from the closet, but his delight is diminished when, similarly in anticipation, he dreads a ride on the elevator he fears. When he is in the park he may feel depressed when he sees that his mother is preparing to take him home, for now, still eager to taste the excitement of the outside world, he can anticipate the unwelcome prospect of having to leave.

As a child becomes older, this ability to anticipate both the good and the ill appears in more complicated forms. An older child lives with much reference to the future. The expectation that the work of the present will pay off in the future can give meaning to a chore which in itself is rather unrewarding. The image of future fulfillment will, for example, sustain some children through long periods when they practice a musical instrument, or laboriously assemble materials to build a raft.

The capacity to work for deferred goals, based in part on a dream of what is yet to be, is prominent in the later high-school years and at the college level. Students spend years preparing for a profession and accept the academic chores that are assigned them even though many of these assignments at the time have little or no meaning in themselves.

To entertain expectations about the future, a person must be able to imagine. Unless a child can imagine, he cannot know what it is to hope. As children grow older and approach adolescence, their ability to build their labors on a hoped-for future gives substance to the present. Through such imagining an older child is able to endure more easily the hurt and unpleasantness he finds in the real world in which he resides. For example, a boy who is nearing his teens and feels that his lot is not favorable may, in his imagination, picture the time when he will be able to move out of his present environment and into a better world.

Make-Believe
in Social Relationships

Often when two or more young children play with one another they are bound together by a make-believe activity. Make-believe can also supply the basis for play between children who are several years apart in age. Thus two sisters or brothers, an eight-year-old and a three-year-old, might play at a game of being parent and child, doctor and patient, captain and engineer on a boat, although there are few activities of a more prosaic character that would keep the two together (unless an adult entered into the activity with them). Make-believe is thus one of mother's greatest helpers.

Make-believe activities provide a setting in which children are better able to tolerate and enjoy one another than in a realistic setting. A six-year-old may be annoyed when in real life her two-year-old sister cries easily, or needs help with her clothes, or spills her food. Now, in a make-believe setting, in which she is the mother and the two-year-old is the baby, the same six-year-old not only accepts but may even encourage babyish behavior of this sort. Likewise, a younger child who resents the bossing of an older sibling may, in a make-believe role as a pupil or a baby, cheerfully obey orders and even accept punishment from the older sibling. In a make-believe setting with other children, a child often will accept restraints and deprivations which he would resent if they were imposed by a well-liked adult. Thus, when told by an older child who is the "teacher" that he must sit very still, a young child may remain quiet for a relatively long time; and when at a "birthday party" he may wait Spartanlike until all imaginary guests are served before he begins to eat.

Often, of course, reality intrudes upon such idyllic scenes, especially if the demands within the imaginary setting become too taxing. For example, a four- or five-year-old in a cops-and-robbers game with an older child will rebel if required to be "dead" for an unendurable period of time. Even so, it appears that it is often in a make-believe setting, in play with other children, that youngsters for the first time achieve feats of self-restraint, patience, perseverance at a task, good manners, and the like, which adults constantly are trying to promote.

Daydreams and Fantasies

Toward the end of the preschool period and throughout later years, much of a child's imaginary activity takes the form of private fantasies and daydreams as distinguished from the acting out which appears in make-believe play. These fantasies variously serve as a means of wish-fulfillment, riddance, escape, compensation, revenge, vicarious adventure, and excitement, and they may provide a means for the exercise of many interests and ideas. In many of these daydreams, a child plays dramatic and heroic roles that are more remote from everyday happenings than the make-believe activities of an earlier age.

Daydreams continue throughout life. The themes involved and the extent to which the individual indulges vary as different life situations arise, and at times the daydreams may range from the abandonment of sheer fancy to an ordered procession of ideas. Such enterprises are related to an individual's everyday problems and desires.

Even though the imaginings of an older child are not bound by the facts of experience, some of his make-believe is likely to have more logical coherence than it had when he was young. In the process of achieving a semblance of plausibility, an undertaking that begins as a fanciful daydream may end as a form of businesslike problem-solving. Thus, an eight-year-old boy rides, in his fancies, jauntily over the western range on a fine horse, ready for combat with horse thieves, coyotes, or Indians. As the plot unfolds, his activities become increasingly complex. He has a trusty rifle and a belt of ammunition at the start; but when he stops to camp, he needs materials for making a fire, cooking utensils, and what not, so he finds it necessary to pretend that he had an extra pack horse with him from the beginning. As the drama goes on, he may find himself so burdened with equipment, horses, and other paraphernalia that the job of planning and ordering things in the daydream becomes somewhat arduous. This tendency for a daydream to bog down under its own weight as it calls for more and more ingenuity and "thinking" frequently happens to adults, spoiling what might otherwise have been a fine time.

Imaginary Companions

An especially interesting form of imagery in childhood is the "imaginary companion." [2] This phenomenon, if it appears at all, is likely to occur some time between the ages of three and ten years, more probably during the earlier than during the later years within this range.

It is difficult precisely to define an imaginary companion. The label imaginary companion is commonly applied to an imagined creature (person or animal) or thing that is unusually vivid (it has a vitality of its own as experienced by the one who has the companion); it is quite stable in its characteristics (while it lasts); it appears for varying lengths of time during childhood and then "disappears," in the sense that it loses its vitality, although it may remain as a memory.

Actually, to speak of an imaginary companion as "it," as though all companions had a common definable identity is misleading, for "it" is the unique product of a particular child's imagination.

The difficulty of defining and describing this phenomenon is increased by the fact that it typically occurs during a period when children are not very articulate or precise in expressing what goes on in their minds. Adult recollections of imaginary childhood playmates may be very vivid—as vivid as most of their recollections of "real" childhood events—but these recollections are likely to be colored by afterthoughts.

In spite of these difficulties, it is possible to describe some of the varied characteristics of imaginary playmates, as described by children and recalled by adults.

One way of visualizing some imaginary companions is to regard the child who maintains them as a host and the companions as a viable and more or less tractable guests, with an independent reality of their own.

The imagined characters are more likely to be persons than animals. The companionship may consist of one character or several (one child, known to the author, had four companions: a married couple with two children). The companions usually occupy space and can be played with and talked to. When

---

[2] For studies of imaginary companions, see Hurlock and Burnstein (1932), Svendsen (1934), Ames and Learned (1946).

talked to they may communicate as equals or serve as a captive audience. They may display a variety of admirable qualities or human foibles. They may be obedient or stubborn; always hale and hearty or subject to various ailments; they may be docile or belligerent. A companion is likely to be amicable, but some youngsters describe playmates who seem to be rather nasty, at least at times (one boy, in describing a companion he once had—but had no longer—spoke of him in the past tense as a "fake boy" who was always fighting).

Imaginary companions are (to their hosts) far more "real" than the characters in a typical daydream, but children vary in the degree to which they regard their companions as solid substances. Following is an example of vivid objectification of a companion. A girl of four screamed a warning to her father as he was in the act of sitting down on a sofa. When questioned she said that her playmate (an imaginary monkey) was having a sick spell and had just soiled the cushion on which her father was about to sit.

When a child conjures up creatures which, to him, have the substance of reality, it might seem that he is subject to hallucinations. But experience with an imaginary companion differs from a hallucination. A child with a companion is not beset by demons such as those which terrorize a youngster, who, in a delirious fever, screams that he is being attacked by snakes or villains with knives. When he "talks" to his companion he is not, like a person having hallucinations, "hearing voices." It is true, as we will see below, that imaginary companions, are, in a sense, visited upon a child, but they behave as companions and not as over-mastering intruders.

Needs Served by Imaginary Companions

Imaginary companions are a versatile lot. Taken at face value they serve a child in a variety of ways, such as the following:

Companionship. An imaginary playmate or companion (true to the magic inherent in a name!) provides friendship and companionship. As such, the companion may be more agreeable, more available, amenable, handy, manipulable and generally satisfactory than an actual playmate.

Self-Aggrandizement. Some companions (but not all, it depends on the child), in company with their host do daring and stunning deeds; dress in stunning outfits; win approval such as can be won, in real life, only by a home-run with the bases loaded.

Collaboration in Practice. The imaginary companion may be used as a faithful partner in a child's endeavor to practice his skills and to test himself. A companion is especially useful in the early years when a child, in practicing his skill of speech, is trying out his ability to hold the ear of an audience. The steadfast companion never gets impatient, nor does he nod drowsily as the speech goes on.

Offering Release for Forbidden Impulses. Some children "use" their companions to act out impulses that ordinarily are decried. The boy in one of the illustrations above was able to fight without let or hindrance with a "fake boy" whose only passion was to fight.

The Coming and Going
of Imaginary Companions

As a rule, children are unable to give any clear account of how they acquired an imaginary companion. More likely than not he "just came." There must, of course, be some link between the companion and a child's past experience, but the question why a child should hit upon one imaginary creation from among the innumerable ones he might have chosen is largely a mystery. Although a child can seldom remember why or just when his companion appeared, he usually is glad he did appear. Although the character seemed to materialize spontaneously, children usually have a good deal of freedom to summon him or dismiss him once he has arrived.

A companion's disappearance seems usually to be as unaccountable as his coming. The conditions underlying the sudden or gradual relinquishment of a companion has not been adequately explored. Some children probably still keep a secret companion after they have discontinued overt play or open conversation with him.

The disappearance of a companion does not necessarily coincide with a decline in a child's ability to construct and to lose himself in vivid imagery. A youngster may, for example, continue to have vivid fantasies, such as making the figures in the wall paper come alive, after he has abandoned his imaginary playmate.

In some instances it is likely that the motive for relinquishing the imaginary character is that the child desires more range and freedom in his imaginative ventures. When a child, in his fancy, rides out upon the untamed western prairie, his companion may be an encumbrance. He would require an extra horse or take saddle-bag space needed for ammunition and provender.

The age at which an imaginary companion is "lost" has been placed at various times by various writers. A rough estimate would put the waning of the vividness of the imaginary figure at about six years, but many children apparently retain their companions until they are older. And even when a companion no longer exists as a quasi-"real" figure, a child may still retain a clear recollection of it, more often than not rather tender.

Incidence of Imaginary Companions. Several studies have shown that a rather large proportion of young children have imaginary companions, but it is difficult to determine the exact number, for several reasons. One difficulty is that children differ in the extent to which they reveal their "companions." When a youngster openly "plays" with a companion, and clearly, over a period of time, is dealing with a creature that has stable characteristics and a definite name, there is little doubt that he has an imaginary companion. However, the situation is not so clear if a child only refers in passing to what might be a companion. One four-year-old boy, for example, frequently mentioned a character named "John Trot," but never openly went through the motions of playing with him and never described "John Trot" in clear terms. In this instance, there was something resembling an imaginary playmate, but the boy's parents could not be sure.

When an older child brings certain characters into his daydreams again and again—as happens when he has fantasies of a "continued story" type, stretching over a period of months or even years—it is difficult to tell whether these qualify as imaginary companions. On the one hand, he may not tell anyone else about them. On the other hand, even if he does tell about them it is not easy to determine whether these imaginary creatures have a quality of seeming "real" or are just convenient characters which he can round up and then lay aside, much as a writer of fiction constructs characters to suit the purpose of his story.

Estimates of the proportion of persons who have (or have had) imaginary playmates have ranged from about 15 to close to 30 per cent. In one investigation (Ames and Learned, 1946) of 210 children who had been studied at the Yale Clinic of Child Development (including over a hundred who had been enrolled in a guidance nursery), 21 per cent of the children exhibited ". . . imaginary companions and other imaginative phenomena." The authors add: "Probably the incidence is higher than this. Frequently, we believe, parents are not aware of these phenomena." In another group of children (Svendsen, 1934), 13 per cent appeared to have imaginary companions. In a study in which adults described their childhood experiences (Hurlock and Burnstein, 1932), 31 per cent of the women and 23 per cent of the men reported that they remembered having imaginary playmates. In a study by the writer and associates (1933) in which several hundred children were interviewed, almost a third of the youngsters described imaginary creations that seemed to have "fairly definite and stable characteristics," but more direct and intimate observations would be needed to establish an exact figure. Ames and Learned state that imaginary companions and related phenomena appear in many, although not in all, children ". . . as a natural developmental phenomenon characteristic of the age period from 2½ to 4½ years, and perhaps persisting secretly considerably beyond that age."

Personality Traits of Children with Imaginary Companions. Imaginary companions, in common with other imaginative constructions, appear in children with a wide range of personality traits. We cannot assume that having an imaginary playmate is, of itself, a sign of either a healthy or an unhealthy trend in a child's development. This goes counter to the opinion of some adults who seem to view imaginative behavior as a sign of maladjustment. A child who has an imaginary companion may be timid and withdrawn, or just the opposite. He may have obvious emotional difficulties or he may be managing his emotions very well. According to Ames and Learned, "We definitely do not find imaginary companions only in timid or lonely children or in those exhibiting personality difficulties" (1946). Similarly, Hurlock and Burnstein (1932) did not find marked general or unique differences between adults who had had companions and those who had not. About the only thing of a general nature that can be said is that a bright child is more likely to have imaginary companions (or at least to disclose them) than a child below average in intelligence. Each child employs his companions in his own way to satisfy his own particular needs, and there are youngsters who, in time of need, use their companions in a constructive way and then give them up when the need no longer exists.

Girls seem to have imaginary companions more often than boys, but this may reflect a cultural rather than a genuine developmental difference. According to a study by the writer and associates (1933), there is reason to believe that boys have as much need for make-believe outlets as girls. However, boys are not so openly encouraged to reveal their fantasies. We encourage girls to give play to their fancies in doll play, but boys do not have a similar imaginative outlet to which they can freely and unashamedly turn. Boys are, it is true, permitted, as miniature he-men, to play cops-and-robbers and to commit carnage with their toy guns. When a boy mows down Indians and outlaws he does have a chance to act out his aggressive impulses; but the girl, in her doll play, can project a far greater flow of feelings, including anger at the child who is being "spanked," worry over the one who is "sick," sympathy for the baby who is "crying," concern for the baby who is "tired."

The Imaginary Companion as a Prophet

One of the many ramifications of the meaning of imaginary companionships in particular, and childhood make-believe in general, is the light they might throw on what the child's "style of life" portends regarding his future. Repeatedly in this book, beginning with the discussion of behavior before birth, we have raised this question about what in the child's way of life today foreshadows his life in a distant tomorrow. Do the interests a child displays with his companion, or in his daydreams, reveal budding interests that will flower later in life? Do the sentiments he shows provide a foretaste of sentiments that will characterize his later years?

Studies by Symonds and Jensen (Symonds, 1942; Symonds and Jensen,

1961) have explored the relation between fantasies at the adolescent level and behavior in adult life. The fantasies were elicited by a picture-projective technique. According to the interpretation they give to their findings, many of the fantasies of the adolescent will be converted into reality later in life. There is a hitch in this interpretation, however, for simply by the law of averages, rather than as a unique individual phenomenon, many fantasies of adolescents are bound to be translated into reality. (Practically all adolescents have aggressive fantasies and practically all adults are aggressive in one way or another.)

The prophetic implication of early behavior tendencies becomes more meaningful when specific patterns of childhood behavior seem to culminate in what seem to be rather closely related outcomes in adult years. In the author's opinion, imaginary playmates, as well as distinctively individual and pervasive themes in the daydreams of children before ten, are likely to be prophetic of their later way of life. This conjecture obviously needs to be tested by empirical research.

Other Forms of Vivid Imagery and Association of Images

In addition to ordinary make-believe, special forms of imagery can be observed in some children. People differ in the vividness of their images; at one extreme are those who seem to have difficulty in forming a clear image of an absent event, while at the other are individuals who report images almost as vivid as the event itself.

A phenomenon known as *synaesthesia* also occurs in some children of school age (and perhaps at an earlier time), as well as among adults.[3] A sensation from one sense modality has associated with it images from another modality. In "colored hearing," an individual reports, for example, that bass tones look blue and high soprano tones look pink. Or the synaesthesia may take the form of colors associated with certain names, as when a child of six reports that Mildred, her friend, is blue and Margaret is yellow, the number "17" is pink, and the word "rush" is gray. Tones likewise may accompany words, according to the testimony of those who report this phenomenon; thus, "paper" brings an association of soprano tones, "piazza" carries a tinkling sound, and so on.

Projective Methods

Projective methods include a variety of procedures that enable a child (or adult) to reveal his perception of things, his fantasies, thoughts and feelings, without speaking directly about himself. The assumption underlying these

---

[3] For an interesting account of a case of synaesthesia persisting over a period of years, see Hollingworth and Weischer (1939).

procedures is that a person's interpretation of what he hears or sees is determined not only by the objective nature of the stimulus situation but by subjective factors within himself. For example, when asked to tell what he sees in a somewhat blurred picture of two children facing an adult one child might say, "There is a father and two boys and they are planning a trip"; another might say, "There are two boys and the father is scolding them." We cannot conclude from these responses alone just what the attitudes of these two boys toward their fathers might be. But we can assume that it is not solely the picture itself but something within the children that led one to see a friendly father and another an angry father.

The following brief account describes some projective methods that have been widely used. The descriptions are sufficient to enable a reader to experiment with the methods in an informal way, but for a full account of ways of using the methods and precautions that are necessary in interpreting the responses, the reader is referred to writings mentioned in the footnotes.[4]

Play Techniques. The use of play situations in the study of children is illustrated by the doll family referred to earlier in this chapter. In devising a play situation, it is possible to use a great variety of materials: dolls that might be interpreted as representing parents, siblings, or playmates; toys and equipment that might be used in make-believe play; fragile things that might be handled carefully or destroyed; household scenes (such as a kitchen, bedroom, or bathroom).[5]

Drawing and Painting. Drawing or painting under free or quasi-controlled conditions provides a child with an opportunity to express fantasies and moods (Alschuler and Hattwick, 1943). A child's choice of a theme for his drawing may reveal something about his concerns, and in many studies it has also been assumed that various themes and particular aspects of a drawing symbolize particular desires and conflicts of various kinds. One variation of this procedure is finger painting, which has been described by Shaw (1934), and another is an analysis of drawing of the human figure (Machover, 1949). Claims concerning the extent to which a child (or an adult) unknowingly reveals himself are difficult to confirm, but a study of children's art seems most promising as a means of studying children. Sometimes, also, a drawing that the child has made can serve as a point of departure for discussion of what he is concerned about.

Response to Pictures. The way in which a child describes, interprets, or tells a story about pictures that he sees may provide a good deal of information about him. In the use of this procedure it is assumed that what a child

---

[4] For earlier discussions of techniques that involve an interpretation of imaginative productions, see Frank (1939); Lerner, *et al.* (1941); White (1945); Abt and Bellak (1950); Anderson and Anderson (1951); and Harris (1963).

[5] See, for example, the Driscoll Playkit (1952); also Bach (1945); Erikson (1940); and Axline (1947).

sees in a picture or reads into it might reveal something about his own attitudes, his desires, his hopes, and his fears. Among the most widely used sets of pictures are those contained in the *Thematic Apperception Test* (Murray, 1937) and in the *Children's Apperception Test* (Bellak and Bellak, 1949–1950).

Story Completion. Here again the assumption is that the way in which a child (or adult) completes a story might reveal something about his inner life. Unfinished stories have been used to study children's punitive attitudes (offering them an opportunity, for example, to end a story about a child who has committed a misdeed by punishing him, or excusing him). They have been used to study children's attitudes toward their parents (for example, the story tells that a child has just heard that one of his parents and one of his friends have been in an accident; the story might be completed by having the child go to help his father or to help his friend).

The Rorschach Test. The Rorschach test material consists of a set of cards each one of which contains an enlarged "ink blot"; the ink blots vary in contour and include some that are in black and white and others that are multicolored. On being shown each ink blot the person is asked to tell what it might be or what it looks like. There are standard directions for administering the test and very elaborate directions for interpreting the results.[6]

Interpretation
of Projected Responses

Many questions arise when we try to interpret children's responses to projective situations. Frequently there is a marked difference between a child's responses to a projective situation, his overt behavior and what he tells about himself.[7] For example, in doll play a youngster may treat a "baby" violently, suggesting that he is fiercely jealous of a younger sibling; in his actual conduct, however, he treats his sibling quite gently; and if we question him, he may say that he likes his younger sibling. Similarly, one youngster may be very aggressive in a projective situation but say, when questioned, that a child should not hit another child; still another youngster who gives an aggressive projective

---

[6] For discussions of the Rorschach test see Beck (1937); Klopfer (1956); Klopfer and Kelley (1946); Krugman (1940); Rorschach (1937); Ames, *et al.* (1952); Blum, *et al.* (1954); and Halpern (1953). Ames (1965) has described constant and changing characteristics of Rorschach during large sections of the life span by comparing responses of children and adults who have been tested and retested over varying intervals of time. For reviews of studies using doll-play techniques see Corn (1962) and Levin and Wardwell (1962). (An ink-blot resembling one of the Rorschach cards can be made as follows: fold a piece of paper down the middle, making a sharp crease; open the paper and place a drop of ink at the center of the crease, then close the fold again, as before. Place the paper on a hard surface and stroke from the crease outward until the ink has spread as far as it will go.)

[7] McElvaney (1958) has reviewed findings dealing with the similarities and discrepancies between children's projective responses and observations or ratings of their overt behavior.

response may say that all children hit one another and that it is quite all right for him to hit.

When such discrepancies occur we face the question: Which is the truest measure of a child's state of mind: his overt action, his verbal report, or his projected response? This question cannot be answered categorically in the abstract. A projective technique should provide the most revealing information if it is so designed that it enables a child to react spontaneously, to let down his guard, and to "act out" thoughts and feelings he ordinarily would not talk about or openly express in his behavior. But without further evidence we cannot assume in advance that a certain projective method will give a truer picture of a child than is revealed by his overt conduct or by a series of skillfully conducted interviews.

A child's projected reaction may furnish a clue to an attitude which can be confirmed by closer observation of his behavior and by questioning. For example, we may discover that a youngster who treats a baby sibling violently in a doll-play situation also in his everyday conduct betrays resentment toward his sibling, not by openly hitting him but in more subtle ways (such as excluding him from his play or by tattling or by luring him into misbehavior).

Children's Dreams

Children's dreams, like their waking fancies, draw upon the materials of actual experience, but often the events and emotional elements in a dream are so diverse that it is impossible to trace them to their source.

Early Signs of Dreaming

It is likely that many children dream before they are able to remember or describe their dreams. Stern (1926), who made an intensive study of the development of a child, states that dreaming possibly begins as far back as a child's first year. The first sign of dreaming may occur when a child screams in his sleep, or awakens in apparent fright, or makes sucking movements, or throws out his arms, or smiles while asleep. The age at which the first signs of dreaming appear, as reported by parents, varies considerably with different children.

Some children when they first begin to dream seem to confuse the dream with reality not only while still asleep and dreaming, but also, at least momentarily, on awakening. Thus, as a child emerges from sleep he may look around searchingly and say, "There was a pony here; where did he go?"

Some evidence suggests that younger persons dream more than older ones (Ramsey, 1953), but if this is the case it may reflect the fact that children sleep longer than older persons and thus have more "dream time" available. It is likely that the dreams of children are more forthright and less camouflaged than those of older persons. Dreams containing an element of violence or fear are more likely to cause a young child than an older child to awaken. Similarly, wishes and desires seem to appear more openly in the dreams of young children. In dreams, as in waking life, the emotions of a younger child are likely to "show through" more than those of an older person. It probably would be a great help in understanding children (and adults) if somehow it were possible for an adult student of dreams to revive his childhood dreams.

Terror Dreams. The extent to which unpleasant dreams occur and some of the symptoms and conditions associated with them have been described in a study (Foster and Anderson, 1936), conducted in cooperation with a large number of parents who kept records of their children's dreams for a seven-day period. The parents and children in this study represented all socio-economic levels but included more persons of high socio-economic status than would be found in a normal sampling of the population. Some of the findings revealed by a classification of the parents' reports are summarized in Table 19.

Table 19 Evidences and Frequencies of Unpleasant Dreams Exhibited by 519 Children, as Reported by Parents Who Kept Records for a Seven-Day Period

Age in Years	1-4	5-8	9-12
Number of Children	81	215	223
Average Frequency per Week of Various Evidences of Unpleasant Dreams:			
Moans during the night	.81	.57	.17
Comes to adult	.18	.16	.05
Reports bad dream in the morning	.21	.42	.26
Any evidence of bad dreaming	.93	.71	.39
Percentage of Children Having Some Unpleasant Dreams During the Week	43.0	39.2	22.2
Subject Matter of Bad Dreams (Percentages):			
Personal difficulties	26.7	33.3	54.5
Difficulties of friends, pets	13.3	6.3	18.2
Animals (probably strange or fearful)	40.0	15.9	9.1
Strange or bad people	6.7	20.6	13.6
The unknown, dark, etc.	6.7	7.9	.0
Loss of property	.0	4.6	.0
Impersonal dangers	6.7	9.5	.0
Miscellaneous	.0	1.6	4.5

Adapted from J. C. Foster and J. E. Anderson, "Unpleasant Dreams in Childhood," *Child Development* (1936), 7:77–84. Reproduced by permission.

While some dreams almost seem to be carbon copies of everyday experiences, many seem to be quite unreal. Yet no matter how foreign and bizarre a dream may seem, it is something that originated within the dreamer. Every image in the dream, however strange—every emotion, however gratifying or horrible—every impulse, however noble or savage—every sensation of pleasure and of joy, however sweet or colored with guilt—arises out of the reservoir of the dreamer's own thoughts and feelings. The frightful monster that threatens to devour the child, leaving him screaming and in a state of panic, was not thrust upon him by someone else; it is his own creation. The angry creatures who threaten to attack him and the terrifying beasts that pursue him are his creatures. The desires that are gratified in his dreams are his own desires. The high place to which he ascends and the pit to which he descends are heights and depths within himself. The good deeds he performs, the struggles he undertakes, the fortune he finds, the tenderness he shows, and the love he receives in his dreams embody something within him. The events that occur in a dream may be unreal in the sense that happenings are combined which have never been so combined during waking moments. But the substance of the dream is not unreal; it arises out of the substance of the dreamer's life.

Each dream contains a message that might reveal something about the experiences of life from which it springs. For this reason a study of dreams can be very instructive in connection with a person's efforts to understand himself and in his efforts to understand a child. The view that dreams have meanings, although the meanings are disguised and difficult to untangle, stems largely from the pioneer work of Freud.[8] Freud's theories about the manifest and the latent or disguised elements of the dream, the symbolism of the dream, the relationship between dream and desire and between the dream and currents in a person's life which he does not consciously recognize or admit in his waking thoughts, have given a powerful impetus to those who are seeking to uncover the hidden reaches of man's mental life.

Laboratory Studies of Dreams and Dreaming

During recent years a spectacular "breakthrough" has been made in the study of dreams and dreaming. Dement and Kleitman and their associates [9] found that it is possible to detect when a sleeping person is in the act of dreaming by means of a device that records the sleeper's eye movements. When sleeping

---

[8] See Freud's *The Interpretation of Dreams* (1950; originally published in 1900). A number of earlier studies of dreaming have been reviewed by Ramsey (1953) and De-Martino (1955). Additional studies are cited later in this chapter.

[9] Aserinsky and Kleitman, 1953; Dement and Kleitman, 1957a, 1957b; Dement and Wolpert, 1958a, 1958b; Dement, 1960; Kleitman, 1960.

persons are awakened at a time when rapid eye movements (REM) are occurring, they will in a large proportion of instances be able to report a dream that was in progress.

The discovery that eye movements can serve as an objective sign that dreaming is in progress was made by accident during a study of cyclic variations in the sleep of infants (Aserinsky and Kleitman, 1953, 1955; Kleitman, 1960). It was noted that, when falling asleep, an infant's eyes continued to move under the closed lids even though bodily movements had ceased. The eye movements would stop and begin again from time to time and were the first movements that signaled an infant's awakening. Eye movements provided a more reliable means of distinguishing between active and quiescent phases of sleep than did gross bodily movements.

In subsequent work with adults, Kleitman and his associates obtained recordings of eye movements (through leads connected with electrodes taped to the skin in the region of the eye) combined with brain wave or electroencephalographic recordings (EEG), recordings of pulse and respiration rates and of gross bodily movements.

Tracings from the eyes not only revealed eye movements such as had been observed earlier in studies of infants, but also showed that rapid eye movements occurred in clusters, and these were associated with a brain-wave pattern. Pulse and respiration rates also increased. These observations suggested that "an emotionally charged cerebral activity" was in progress, such as might occur in dreaming. When this surmise was tested by arousing sleepers while a succession of rapid eye movements was occuring, the sleepers, when questioned, usually (in about 80 per cent of the instances) reported they had been dreaming. According to Dement (1957), a person's brain-wave pattern and his eye-movement pattern together signalize dreaming more effectively than either of the two indicators taken alone.

Typical Sleep Patterns

During sleep there are cycles of changes in brain-wave patterns, as shown by electroencephalographic recordings. Each cycle lasts about 60 to 90 minutes and it includes four stages. The cycles recur from four to six times during a night's sleep. Rapid eye movements in older persons (but not in a newborn child) typically appear after the first 60 to 90 minutes of sleep, in the first stage of the second EEG cycle, and then recur in the first stage of each succeeding cycle. Dreaming has been reported in about 80 per cent of instances when laboratory subjects have been awakened from REM (rapid eye movement) sleep. This phase in the sleep cycle has been called the REM or dream stage of sleep. The three other phases are known as NREM (non-REM) stages. The number and length of the sleep cycles reveal individual variations, and they also may vary in length as sleep progresses. As sleep proceeds, REM periods tend to become longer and NREM periods become shorter. In young adults the recurring REM periods (following the first complete cycle) comprise about 20 to 25 per cent of an ordinary night's sleep (Roffwarg, *et al.*, 1966).

During the REM stage there is a much greater activation of the central nervous system than during the non-REM periods. There are irregular changes in heart-rate, blood pressure, and breathing; there is an increase in muscle tone, and gross bodily movements may appear from time to time. As shown by studies of animals (which, like human beings manifest the REM phenomenon) the areas of the brain that receive sensory stimuli are activated. It is as though the cortex were in a state of far greater excitation and alertness than during NREM sleep. Laboratory studies of young men also show that there is almost always an erection of the penis during REM sleep.[10]

The excitation occurring in REM sleep appears to be due to endogenous stimulation (generated from within) as distinguished from the exogenous stimulation (coming from the external environment) that impinges on the sense organs during the waking hours.

While dreaming typically occurs during REM sleep periods, some mental activity also occurs during NREM sleep. This activity does not, however, correspond to a full-scale hallucinatory REM dream. The NREM "dreamlets," as they have been called, tend to include thought-like snatches, images, and memories resembling day time mental processes. (More will be said about this type of mental activity—referred to as "mentation" by some writers—later in this chapter.)

During REM sleep there is excitation in the phylogenetically older part of the brain, commonly known as the "limbic system." This section of the brain has been called the "old mammalian brain" as distinguished from the "new mammalian brain," sometimes also referred to as the "higher centers" in the cortex that have developed in the process of evolution. Fisher (1965) has pointed out that the areas of the brain which regulate REM sleep appear to be closely related to the areas that activate primitive impulses essential for survival. It is possible that the neural excitation in REM sleep may spread to these centers, activating sexual and aggressive impulses and bodily hungers which, in effect, belong to a simpler level of existence. It is possible that these in turn are converted or translated in the higher nerve centers into the concrete imagery which constitutes the content of dreams.

Sleep Patterns, REM Periods, and Age

Infants display the REM phase of the sleep cycle from the time of birth. Newborn children may go almost directly from a waking state to REM sleep (Roffwarg, *et al.*, 1966). In this they differ from adults, who usually do not make the transition until after a 50- to 70-minute period of NREM sleep.

---

[10] For descriptions and reviews of phenomenon that accompany REM sleep see Fisher (1965), Roffwarg, *et al.* (1966), and Ephron and Carrington (1967).

Newborn children exhibit wide variations in the length of their sleep cycles and in the duration of REM sleep. But the fact that REMS are present at birth indicates, according to Roffwarg and his associates, that the ". . . neurophysiological setting for hallucinatory repetition of accumulated experience . . ." such as occurs in the dreams of older persons apparently is available at birth or before birth. These investigators state that we can only speculate whether newborn children dream and, if they do, what might be the nature of their dreams. They point out that dreaming need not be confined to visual imagery. Prior to the time when the infant has acquired visual perception and visual memory, ". . . rudimentary hallucinations might be expressed in sensory modalities in which intra-uterine experience had occurred" (1966, p. 612). These writers go on to say, "Speculations aside, however, whether or not 'dreaming' understood as subjective sensation exists in the newborn, 'dreaming' understood as physiological process certainly does."

Roffwarg, *et al.* (1966) report data indicating that newborns spend about one-third of their day and about one-half of their sleep in the REM state. This high ratio declines as children mature. This finding, according to Roffwarg, *et al.*, suggests that REM sleep plays an important role in the maturation of the nervous system. According to their theory, the REM mechanism provides an endogenous (internally generated) source of stimulation, ". . . furnishing great quantities of excitation to higher centers (p. 617)." Such stimulation, they believe, may have great value before birth and shortly after birth in furthering structural maturation and differentiating key sensory and motor areas within the central nervous system, ". . . partially preparing them to handle the enormous rush of stimulation provided by the postnatal milieu, as well as contributing to their further growth after birth" (p. 617).

Exactly when a typical child begins to have dreams similar to those of older children and adults is a question that perhaps will never be answered. Children at age three or four who are awakened during rapid eye-movement periods give reports of visual dreams, although less often than adults, but adult-like dreaming undoubtedly occurs before that age.

Characteristics of REMS

In young adults the recurring REM periods (following the first complete cycle) comprise 20 to 25 per cent of an ordinary night's sleep (Roffwarg, *et al.*, 1966).

REMS in Persons Who Say They Never Dream. Rapid eye-movement (REM) periods are displayed by all normal persons, including those who say they never dream ("non-recallers"), or who say they seldom dream. When such "non-recallers" participate in laboratory studies and are awakened when the instruments have recorded rapid eye movements, they report dreams such as are reported by persons who say they habitually dream a great deal, although their ability to recall dreams at the moment of awakening may be weaker than that of persons who say they dream frequently (Goodenough, *et al.*, 1959).

Amount and Direction of Rapid Eye Movement. During a dream episode most of the rapid eye movements are horizontal. As described by Kleitman, ". . . these movements represent a busy scanning of the scene of dream action" (Kleitman, 1960, p. 6). Rapid vertical eye movements occur less frequently. When they appear, an awakened sleeper is likely to report a dream that involved the upward or downward motion of objects or persons.

Sometimes the recorded brain-wave pattern and the eye-movement recordings seem inconsistent. The EEG pattern may indicate that a subject must be dreaming although the record shows no or few rapid eye movements. In such instances the dreamers, on being awakened, may report that in a dream they were watching a distant point or that the dream action required little eye movement, such as when the dream involved watching television (Rothwarg, *et al.*, 1962b). As stated by Kleitman, the amount and direction of the eye movements correspond to what the dreamer is looking at or following with his eyes (such as the shifting of the eyes in watching a tennis match), and rapid eye movements ordinarily seem to indicate the degree to which the dreamer participates in the events of the dream. A dream in which the dreamer is greatly involved is more likely to be accompanied by rapid eye movements than a more "passive" dream.[11]

Laboratory Findings Regarding Dreams and Dreaming

Frequency. Usually a person has from three to five or six dreams during the night. Dreams are likely to become longer and occur after shorter intervals of dreamless sleep as the night progresses (Trosman, 1963).

Speedy Decline in Recall of Dreams. A person's ability to recall details of a dream drops sharply when he awakens, so when a dreamer tries to give the full story or plot of his dream by telling how the dream began he may, in the process, forget later portions of the dream that was occurring at the time he was awakened. For this reason, when investigators are studying the dream

---

[11] Gross bodily movements sometimes occur during dreams, but frequently not, especially in older children and adults. However, when bodily movements do appear, they seem to have a significance analogous to the movements of the eyes. In one situation, for example, a record obtained through electrodes attached to the limbs of a sleeping subject showed a sequence of activity first in the right hand and then in the left and finally in one leg. When aroused immediately thereafter, the sleeper reported a dream in which he had lifted a bucket with his right hand, transferred it to his left, and then started to walk (for an account of sequential dream episodes, see Wolpert and Trosman, 1958).

action in relation to the simultaneous pattern of eye movements, they have asked the awakened subject first to tell what was happening during the last scenes that were visualized in the dream (Roffwarg, *et al.*, 1962a) before trying to give a full acount of the dream.[12]

Duration of Dreams. Some writers have believed that a dream which extends over a period of time actually erupts and ends within moments. Laboratory studies do not support this view. A dreamer's impression of the period of time covered by a dream actually tends to coincide with its duration, as indicated by brain-wave and rapid eye-movement recordings.

Effects of Dream Deprivation

The idea that dreams serve an important function has been set forth by Freud, among others. Freud regarded the dream as the guardian of sleep and as a means of protecting a dreamer from the full explosive impact of buried emotional conflicts.

The work of Dement and others has strongly underscored the idea that dreams not only serve an important but even an indispensable function in the life of the dreamer. This fact has been established by "dream deprivation" studies in which a sleeper is awakened each time laboratory instruments indicate that he might be dreaming. A person whose dreams are thus interrupted is likely to show an increase in "dream attempts" as the night goes on, as though he were trying to make up for lost dreams. If the deprivation is continued, an individual may become irritable, anxious, and unable to concentrate during the day (Fisher and Dement, 1963). If deprivation is protracted, the person, while awake, may have dream-like hallucinations.

These reactions cannot be explained by loss of sleep, for persons awakened during moments of non-dreaming do not exhibit such symptoms. The need for dreaming seems to be so strong that instead of saying that we dream so we may continue to sleep, we might almost say that we sleep so that we may dream.

Recent empirical findings regarding the importance of dreams are interesting in relation to a finding obtained by the writer and his associates many years ago (1933), in a study in which 400 children were questioned about their dreams, daydreams, and other matters. Dreams reported by the children were classified as "pleasant" or "unpleasant" or "uncertain" according to two criteria: the children's own designations whether a dream was "good" or "bad," and their answers when questioned specifically about good and bad dreams or "dreams you like" and "dreams you don't like." According to one classification, 557 dreams in a total of 1,124 were unpleasant, 407 were pleas-

---

[12] Experiments designed to explore the manner in which dreams might be influenced by variables, such as sounds, tactual stimulation, alcohol, drugs, and hypnosis, have been reviewed by Tart (1965).

ant, and the rest were judged uncertain. According to another classification scheme, 54.5 per cent of the dreams were unpleasant and 45.5 per cent pleasant. Even though there was a preponderance of "unpleasant" dreams in their actual dream narratives, the children expressed a more favorable view of dreaming than might have been expected. When asked, "Do you wish you would never dream?" 168 of those who were questioned and who gave unequivocal answers said they would prefer to continue having dreams, as compared with 128 who said they wished not to dream. More information is needed than these bare figures provide, but it is possible that children who described more unpleasant than pleasant dreams, and yet said they still wanted to go on dreaming, unwittingly sensed that it was well for them to dream.

Differences between Sleeping and Waking Thought

According to Freud's theory, dreams emanate from the unconscious; they spring from impulses (particularly sexual drives and hostility) that have been repressed and banished from waking consciousness but press for some kind of expression during sleep when a person's censorship is less vigilant. A dream offers a means of giving play to forbidden impulses that would not "get by" during waking moments. Even when freed from the inhibitions of waking life, however, the impulses do not usually appear in a bold, unexpurgated manner. They parade in many disguises. An erotic desire or hostile impulse may appear in symbolic form; events of the past are condensed, transformed, and displaced from their actual moorings in such a way that the dreamer, even though his inhibitions are somewhat relaxed, is not confronted with the full impact of his repressed desires. According to this view, the dream offers a compromise—it "releases" explosive forces, but not completely, and in a manner that does not afford the dreamer a coherent portrayal of what these forces might be. In Freud's terms, dreams have a manifest content—that which, so to speak, meets the dreamer's eye—and a latent content—meanings that are symbolized or disguised by the manifest content.

According to Freud's theories, the thought processes of the dream and the thought processes of waking life are quite different, and impulses that come to the fore in dreams are alien to the motives that a person acknowledges when awake. According to other theories, especially those advanced by Adler in 1931 (republished in 1958) and others who have adopted his views in whole or in part, there is not as sharp a dichotomy between a person's mental activities while awake and while dreaming, as Freud's treatise on *The Interpretation of Dreams* implies. If these views are correct, or even partially correct, they might, when combined with recently discovered methods for catching dreams on the wing, reduce to some degree the inscrutability of dreams. If this were achieved, dreams could not only provide "a royal road to the unconscious" but might supply a way of illuminating many facets of a person's everyday mental life that now are enveloped in darkness.

Laboratory studies of mental activities that occur during sleep lend support to the view that there is some continuity in a person's mental state while he is awake and while asleep. These findings rest, in part, on the discovery that the mental activities of a sleeping person are not confined to periods of dreaming (when the recordings show that a person is in the Stage 1, REM "dream stage," of the sleeping cycle).

Foulkes (1962) and Rechtschaffen, *et al.* (1963a, 1963b) and others have found that subjects when awakened during non-REM periods of sleep report a variety of mental states. These range from dream-like states (although usually not with the bizarre and distorted and emotional character of the typical dream) to memories that provide an undistorted recall of occurrences in a dreamer's life and "thoughts" resembling the plausible kind of thinking that occurs when a person is awake. Apparently, a great deal of mentation occurs while we sleep. As described by Foulkes (1964), the periods of sleep in which no dreams occur cannot be regarded as periods of unconsciousness. "The typical bizarre and elaborate REM-period dream does not burst like a sudden firework against a background of complete darkness; it develops in a context of already on-going mental activity" (p. 242).

When a sleeping person shifts from a non-REM into a REM stage of sleep, there is a shift from the more daytime-like type of mental activity to the bizarre, more emotional and dramatic events appearing in dreams. But the dream is not wholly separate from the general flow of mental activity. In his account of dreams, Freud speaks of "day residues" in dreams—a revival of daytime impressions, and experiences that appear in dreams, often quite briefly; but in Freud's interpretation, this carry-over is not particularly helpful in the interpretation of a dream. Foulkes, however, sees a possibility that these experiences might help in dream interpretation for there is, he reports, a strong resemblance between the content embodied in mental states preceding the onset of a dream period and the "day residues" described by Freud.

There is an additional characteristic of the mentation that occurs during the non-dreaming state that might provide a clue to the interpretation of dreams. As described by Rechtschaffen, *et al.* (1963), the content of such thinking, while it resembles waking thought much more than dream thought, also has a quality that differs from the usual flow of consciously directed waking thought. In this kind of thinking, a person usually fixes his attention on a central line of thought and does not give heed to other eddies that flow in his stream of consciousness. The mentation that occurs during non-dreaming periods of sleep is more likely to incorporate incidental or marginal accompaniments of thought which, in the waking state, are, so to speak, pushed aside by the main preoccupation. With an effort, it is true, a waking person can school himself to capture some of these currents—appearing as stray images, vagrant thoughts, fleeting associations that are aroused by the main sweep of his thought and then cast aside. Sometimes, in a state of reverie or "wool-gathering," when the brain is idling, so to speak, elusive currents such as these may take full possession of the mind. If a person, as he snaps out of his reverie, is able to capture and tries to examine these oddments, he may find that they are very revealing. The fact that the thought of non-dream sleep actually seems to capture such material opens a further channel for exploring dreams.

Motivation
and Emotional Content of Dreams

The foregoing observations suggest that dreams are not completely set apart from the general flow of daytime mental activity. To what extent might there also be continuity in the underlying motivation and emotional content of dream experiences and waking experiences? In Freud's account, the motives underlying dreams are derived primarily from repressed sexual and hostile impulses which are incompatible with the motives a person consciously entertains in his waking thoughts. On the other hand, Adler (in common with many others who do not basically question Freudian theories of dreams) believes that the motives that influence dreams are as many and as varied as the motives that prevail when a person is awake.

As far as manifest content is concerned, it seems that dreams as experienced and reported by the dreamer himself cover the whole spectrum of human motivation and emotion, but, as noted below, aggression appears far more frequently in dreams than friendliness, and there seems to be an intimate connection between dreaming and sexual excitation.

When children and adults report their dreams, they are far more likely, as one would expect, to identify the emotional content or feeling than to name or speculate about the underlying motive. In the study by the writer and his associates referred to above, a large number of children reported dreams definitely designated as pleasant, such as: getting or finding things; enjoying food; taking part in amusements, games and sports; enjoying visits, companionship, return of relatives, etc.; achievement, adventure, prestige. Other categories containing dreams preponderantly described as "bad" included: being powerless; re-living the action in movies or in stories portraying crime or violence; being involved in strange, unfamiliar, baffling situations; being involved in fights; falling; being chased; activities of wicked characters; and activities of supernatural beings such as ghosts and devils.

The children in this study did not explicitly describe erotic dreams, but this probably was due, at least in part, to reticence about sex, for the oldest children in the study, aged twelve, were at an age when boys begin to have "wet dreams." Apart from the absence of erotic dreams, the feelings reported ranged from intense pleasure to extreme terror. The action described in the dreams ranged from friendly interchanges to extreme violence, but dreams involving aggression (fighting, "bad guys," being chased) and dreams with a sinister flavor (such as "spooky" dreams) far outnumbered dreams involving a friendly interchange.

The fact that aggression occurs frequently in dreams has been documented by Hall and Domhoff (1962a, 1962b, 1962c) through an examination of dream narratives obtained from persons in the age range from two to eighty years. In 3,049 dream narratives, 1,490 included acts of aggression and 711, acts of friendliness. Not only did dreams of aggression outnumber dreams of friendliness but the friendly acts were, on the whole, rather mild, such as extending greetings or doing a small favor. The aggressive acts were on the whole, far more intense, with a large proportion consisting of gross actions ranging from stealing or destroying and physical attack to outright murder.

Aggressiveness exceeded friendliness at all age levels. In the age range consisting of children aged two through twelve, there were 217 dream narratives from boys; of these, 169 were dreams of aggression and 37 were dreams of friendliness. The corresponding values in 274 girls' dreams were 207 and 48.

As summarized by Hall and Domhoff, "Love, altruism, humanitarianism, benevolence, generosity, and unselfishness, on any large scale, are not characteristic of the dream world. Hate and violence are (1962c, p. 1)." In speculating about the fact that the "situation in dreams" consists of "a lot of hate, a little love," (1962b, p. 6), Hall and Dumhoff raise the question whether the abundance of hate in dreams means that there is less hate in waking life. It might be hypothesized that a fight in a dream discharged aggressive energy that a person could otherwise discharge by fighting while awake. If so, aggressive dreams would provide a handy and harmless way for human beings to deal with their aggressive impulses. Hall and Dumhoff do not, however, think that experimental tests would confirm this hypothesis.

When ordinarily mild-mannered persons have dreams of aggression, we might ask: Who is the *real* person, the one who is peaceable during the day or the one who (directly or by proxy) fights in his dreams? Hall and Dumhoff point out that not enough is known about the relation between dream aggression and aggression during waking hours to answer this question.

The question just raised is probably somewhat over-simplified. Aggressive action in a dream is not necessarily equivalent to aggressive acts committed when a person is awake. We cannot take actions in a dream at face value, for the manifest action is often exaggerated or even falsified (as happens, for example, when a dreamer walks on air, falls from a great height, performs monumental feats of strength, and so on). As against this we might ask, if exaggeration is at work in dreams of aggression why are not friendly acts equally exaggerated? The dream itself does not provide an answer.

On a different tack, we might conjecture that aggressiveness in dreams is symbolic; it may not denote hostility but a manner of representing less belligerent experiences, such as effort or struggle or the kind of contention that occurs when children, when awake, wrestle, vie with one another or chase one another, more in a spirit of fun than in a mood of anger. The idea that fighting in dreams should be viewed symbolically is, of course, completely conjectural, but it is no more conjectural than the view that practically everything else in dreams is symbolic.

If manifest aggression in dreams is to be taken as signifying aggressiveness in the dreamer then, by the same token, the manifest emotional quality should also be considered. Here we meet the curious fact that many persons initiate aggression or are victims of aggression in their dreams without having any experience of anger in these dreams. Persons who seldom if ever feel a surge of anger in dreams of aggression report that in dreams not involving aggression they have a wide array of emotional experiences, such as mild pleasure, intense erotic pleasure, and apprehensions ranging from fear to terror and horror. The fact that erotic pleasure appears in dreams more than anger suggests that anger is even more strongly suppressed than sex.

Sex in Dreams

Laboratory studies of the physiological processes accompanying dreams have given rather dramatic support to Freud's view that sex plays a prominent role in dreams. As noted earlier in this chapter, Fisher and his associates (1965), working with young adult males, report that REM periods of sleep were almost always accompanied by an erection. Some degree of erection, ranging from full to partial tumescence, occurred in 95 per cent of the REM periods. According to their findings, there is approximately as much erection during a night as there is dreaming, which means, according to their measurements, that from one-fifth to one-quarter of sleep in the young adult male is spent in a state of full erection.[13]

In a later study with Gross and Byrne, Fisher (1965) studied dream content in relationship to REM erections. The manifest content of dreams occurring during REM erection periods included a marked amount of aggressive action (such as being bitten by or threatened by an animal).

When the male dreamers were awakened after the instruments showed tumescence had occurred, the dream content frequently included overt sexual activity or manifest erotic elements such as kissing, having felt sexually aroused, hand-holding, and other physical (but not overtly sexual) contacts, such as watching a girl undress. The dream content also contained symbolism that seemed erotic in character, such as dreaming about going up and down in an elevator with several girls.

The manifest dream content reported after a dream period including a

---

[13] Erections were recorded by means of genitograms, comparable to cardiograms. The apparatus included an elastic silicon plastic tube about the size of a small rubber band attached to the penis.

cycle of tumescence and detumescence frequently included anxiety associated with aggression. It appears that aggression followed by anxiety inhibits the erection.

From his own and other findings, Fisher (1965) concludes that dreaming in the male is accompanied, on a psychological level, by massive, sustained genital excitation.

Although Fisher's studies were conducted with young adults, they probably would be confirmed by studies of children. Fisher indicates, as is documented elsewhere in this book, that an erection cycle occurs in infants, and he also notes that the erection cycle persists into extreme old age. As mentioned earlier, REM periods also appear in early infancy. According to Fisher, ". . . the REM cycle is built into the organism and appears to be regulated by one of the biological clocks that are under intensive investigation these days. Because it is so closely linked with massive sexual excitation one is left with the impression that we are dealing with Eros or the life force itself" (p. 25).[14]

---

[14] In a review of other studies, Fisher notes that one response of cats and monkeys to prolonged deprivation of REM sleep is to become hyperactive sexually when awake, with a seemingly compulsive and indiscriminate drive to establish sexual contacts. Another response shown by some animals is markedly disturbed oral behavior expressed by putting objects into their mouths, biting, chewing, licking, and touching with their lips. This affinity between sex behavior and oral behavior lends support to Freud's theory that the region of the mouth, like the genitals, is an erogenous zone and a source of "organ pleasure."

Recommended Readings

Ruth Griffiths' *Imagination in Early Childhood* (1935) continues to be one of the richest sources of information concerning the fantasy life of young children. Two publications based on studies of adolescents that have important implications for understanding the fantasy life of persons at all age levels are Percival M. Symonds' *Adolescent Fantasy* (1949) and a monograph by Lawrence K. Frank and his associates, *Personality Development in Adolescent Girls* (1953). Books dealing with the content of dreams and efforts to interpret their meaning include Sigmund Freud's classic work, *The Interpretation of Dreams* (1950 translation), and a paperback volume by J. A. Hadfield, *Dreams and Nightmares* (1954). Calvin S. Hall presents an account of dreams in a paperback book entitled *The Meaning of Dreams* (1959).

Nathaniel Kleitman's "Patterns of Dreaming" (1960), published in the *Scientific American* Reprint Series, gives an account of the discovery of rapid eye movements as a signal of dreaming. For more recent studies in this burgeoning field, the reader should consult *Psychological Abstracts*. References to some of the pioneer studies with projective techniques are cited in the text.

19   *Language Development,*

Perceptual Development

This chapter and the one that follows resume the discussion of intellectual development begun in Chapter 7. In that chapter we considered the sensory-motor phase of development as described by Piaget. The present chapter will first offer a brief recapitulation of some of the strides a child makes during the first two years. This will be followed by a discussion of language and perceptual development.

As we noted in Chapter 7, the child at first responds only to the tangible properties of the world about him, as they act upon him through his sense organs and as he acts upon them. Throughout the sensory-motor period (and beyond) as described by Piaget, the child's orientation is still egocentric. He is unable to view things from any standpoint but his own. But he has, in important ways, disengaged himself from reliance solely on a direct sensory and motor encounter with the world. He has begun to make distinctions between the separateness of his own experience and events in the world about him. All being well, he has grasped the idea that objects remain permanent, they have an existence of their own even though out of view. He has begun to grasp the idea that the spatial environment remains constant. He can begin, within the sphere of his own understanding, to reproduce a past event through imitation. He can formulate intentions, act upon them and anticipate the outcome of a sequence of actions. He can begin to deal with problems by devising a mental solution, then trying it out. He has begun to establish order in the world about him through rudimentary classification of things, such as things that will roll, or clatter when dropped, or bounce, and things that won't. He has begun to use symbols—the mental images of things and, through language, the words for things.

The Development of Language

The language a child will use increasingly is composed of a common set of symbols shared by those who speak the same tongue. Language represents what might be called a socialized set of symbols. Within a given frame of reference, the same symbol has the same general meaning for all who employ it, although it may, in addition, have shades and nuances of meaning that vary from person to person.

Language is a unique accomplishment of human beings and it represents perhaps the highest form of behavioral development. It is also interlinked with bodily functions necessary to survival: the organs of speech are also involved in breathing, eating, and food-getting. There are parallels, too, between language development and motor development. A child begins to babble at about the time he is able to sit alone; he speaks his first word at about the time he becomes able to stand alone. And a child's early progress in speech formation is related to emotional factors, particularly the affection and attention he receives from adults.

Early Vocalizations

During the first two or three weeks of life a child's vocalizations include cries of varying pitch, quality, and loudness. He produces also a number of other sounds, such as grunts, yawns, sighs, an "inspirational crow," and of course, sounds connected with coughing, sneezing, and belching. During his very first days of life the aspirate *h* is the most recurrent sound an infant utters (Irwin, 1947a, 1947b). McCarthy (1952a) regards these sounds as possibly linked to a young child's gasping for breath.

Missing from a child's earliest vocalizations are numerous sounds he will make later on in life. Vowel sounds predominate, accompanied by certain consonant sounds.

In recent years, studies of language development have injected into the field of child psychology a number of terms from descriptive linguistics. Unfortunately, writers have not defined some of these terms very clearly, and the reason seems to be that even those who specialize in linguistics have difficulty with definitions. The "most basic elements" in the expression system (spoken language) are known as *phonemes*. Gleason in his *Introduction to Descriptive Linguistics* (2nd edition, 1961) speaks of the phoneme as ". . . one of those basic concepts, such as may be found in all sciences, which defy exact definition."

Phonemes are the minimum or elemental sound features of a particular language, out of which all speech sounds are constructed. As described by Gleason, these sound elements may be regarded as roughly analogous to the chemical elements out of which all substances are constructed. There are 46 phonemes in spoken English.

The sound basic unit is the *morpheme*. Morphemes are the smallest individually meaningful elements in a language. They cannot be divided without destroying or altering meaning. Gleason uses as an example the word strange (s t r e y n j), consisting of one vowel and several consonant phonemes. If broken, it either yields meaningless fragments, such as *str* and *ange*, or an altered meaning, such as *stray*.

A child uses many utterances in communicating with others long before he acquires the ability to articulate precise words. The median child in one study (Shirley, 1933a) was credited by the examiner with his "first word" at about sixty weeks. But the babies babbled to the examiner at twenty-five weeks, and many of the mothers reported babbling at considerably earlier ages. Inflections and intonations similar to those in adult speech were also noted in advance of the "first word." Among these expressive utterances were ". . . squeals of delight, strong grunts of pain or disgust, grunts with the rising inflection of a question, guttural barking growls that reminded the examiner of a dog worrying a bone, shouting and calling to attract attention, and calling in scolding or warning tones." A child usually understands many words and inflections before he himself can use words. Gesture language, such as pointing, reaching, and movements indicating rejection, aversion, or acceptance, frequently serves as a means of communication long before a child can express himself verbally.

A child's early vocalizations, prior to his so-called "first word," are charming but also quite baffling from a psychological point of view. To a listener a child's babbling may not have any particular meaning. Although intense, it may seem to be merely a succession of sounds and not a series of meaningful utterances. Yet anyone who has listened to the fervent utterances of a babbling child cannot help being convinced that these represent something very different from the sounds emitted by an off-track phonograph needle.

Long before a child can "speak," in the sense of communicating ideas, many of his utterances are a response to someone, and if there is someone to respond to, the babbling is likely to be more profuse. Brodbeck and Irwin (1946) found that during the first six months, children reared within their own family vocalized more than children reared in an institution where they had fewer contacts with adults.

From Vocalization to Vocabulary

A newborn child starts life with only a limited inchoate supply of vocalizations (at least so it seems to adults). Then new sounds emerge. Soon there are different ones for hunger, pain, and discomfort (Gesell, 1928), along with the coos and gurgles expressive of a more serene state. Then a child's own initiative takes over. He catches new intonations of his own and repeats them. He cries and then hears bustling sounds—sounds which again and again herald the coming of someone to his side. These sounds soon signify to him that help is near. So he ceases his crying—he waits in apparent expectation of what is to be. Such waiting is what Mowrer (1958) has called the beginning of *hope*. It might also be described, in Erikson's (1950) terms, as a sign of *trust*.

A parent who brings comfort to a child usually also speaks to him playfully, soothingly, coaxingly, and sometimes interrogatively, as though the child might answer, and usually, all being well, with an affectionate tone of voice. Soon after birth an infant can be soothed by sound and, within a short time, the sound of a human voice becomes especially effective. As time passes, a child not only imitates the sounds he makes himself but also echoes the sounds made by others. He copies sounds that fall within the repertoire of the utterances he already is able to produce, and then goes further to experiment with sounds that resemble the utterances of others. He reproduces intonations of his mother tongue [1] long before he can formulate sounds to convey meaning by way of words.

A child is by nature a vocal creature. He produces sounds and then, as Piaget would describe it, he makes interesting sounds last. He is, to a large extent, his own professor of linguistics. But the sounds made by others serve him well. According to Mowrer (1958), a child makes sounds like his mother's because they are reassuring and, when alone, such sounds make it seem that the mother is there. So viewed, a child's utterances have an emotional significance before they become significant from a cognitive standpoint.

The "First Word"

Eventually comes the "first word." It may be *a* first word as perceived by others, and not actually the child's first word—a word used discriminatingly, selectively, and with reference to a definite thing. Such seemed to be the character of one twelve-month-old child's "first word." Looking out of a

---

[1] This expression gives a touch of intimacy to language development. A child is born into the land of his fathers but the language he acquires is his "mother tongue."

window while held in her father's arms she heard the bark of a dog and exclaimed, "Bru!" The dog, Brutus, was there, visible to the eye and audible to the ear. The word "Bru" was used again but not applied to any other creature or thing. (It might have been applied to other dogs for a time but there was no opportunity to observe this.) [2]

Children frequently use a certain sound to convey a definite meaning even though that sound cannot be found in any dictionary. For example, one child used the expression "oi-yoi" to ask for water and for no other purpose. The expression functioned as a word even though a stranger would not know what it meant. On the other hand, a child might use an utterance that sounds like a word without apparently intending to use it as a word. Because of ambiguities of this sort, one mother may credit her child with a "first word" where another would not. In the study by Shirley, cited above (in which children were somewhat above the average of children in the general population), the first comprehensible word was spoken in the examiner's presence at a median age of sixty weeks, but most of the mothers reported that the babies had a vocabulary of two or three words at fifty-two weeks. Twenty-five per cent of the children spoke their first comprehensible words in the presence of the examiner by the age of forty-seven weeks, and 25 per cent had not yet reached this stage by the age of sixty-six weeks. The age at which the first word was spoken varied from eight months or less to well over two years.

Although a child's first word is quite an event (at least as viewed by his parents), it should be regarded more as an outcropping than a turning point in an on-going developmental process. It does not, like the first little chick that breaks through the shell, mean that quickly a whole brood will be hatched. A child proceeds, pretty much as before, to advance in his ability to discriminate sounds, to articulate, to recognize the meanings of sounds and words which he is not yet able to use. He advances in his perception of the distinctive features of speech sounds, and in his awareness that certain sounds have a constant meaning even though they vary in their acoustic properties. McCarthy (1961) notes how a child's mastery of the perceptual properties of speech overrides many acoustic variations. As his language development proceeds, a child learns to understand a word whether it is whispered, or shouted, or spoken by a man, woman, or child.

A child's early vocabulary is dominated by short words. Up to the age of two years, one-syllable words constituted about 70 per cent of all the comprehensible words spoken by all the babies in the study by Shirley, cited earlier. For several years many youngsters continue to shorten words by dropping a syllable or two so that "inspect" is " 'spect," "conductor" is " 'ductor," a neighboring "Missus" with four children is a maiden "Miss."

Some of the children in Shirley's study began to use phrases and sentences

---

[2] A visiting investigator, not knowing Brutus, would not have recognized "Bru" as a first word. And the father himself might have missed many words equivalent to "Bru" previously spoken by his child.

shortly before the age of fourteen months, but such combinations of words were relatively infrequent before the age of two years. When the children began to form sentences, they frequently repeated a sentence over and over. One child, for example, repeated "Wha's dat?" seventeen times during an examination and used only two other sentences.

The increase in number of words per remark with age has been measured with considerable care in several studies. The averages in different studies agree quite closely when based upon a substantially normal or representative selection of children. The average length per remark is considerably higher, however, in the case of bright children (McCarthy, 1930).

Content of Early Vocabulary
and Expressions

Nouns are likely to be most numerous among children's "first words," but there is also a sprinkling of verbs, adverbs, and adjectives. Pronouns usually appear later.

In a study of the range of vocabularies at different ages, Smith (1941) found an average vocabulary of three words at twelve months, nineteen words at fifteen months, and twenty-two words at eighteen months. At two years the average number of words spoken by children in the study was 272. Such vocabulary counts as these are instructive even though they cannot be regarded as establishing a norm for children in general.

Young children (in common with persons at all age levels) comprehend many words they do not themselves use. Children also comprehend many grammatical constructions—the plural as distinguished from the singular, and the possessive, before they use these forms. The typical adult likewise understands many more spoken words than he ordinarily can call to mind, and his reading vocabulary is greater than his speaking vocabulary. The difference between what is understood and what is usable is commonly very wide in reading and speaking a second, or foreign, language.

The fact that children can understand meanings which they are not yet able themselves to express is reflected in the expression, "Children have big ears." Adults are sometimes mortified when they discover that a child understands more than they suspected and "takes in" things not intended for him to grasp.

The Development
of Rudimentary Sentence Structures

When once a child has begun to "talk" he can make a few words go a long way. He can express a great deal with a limited vocabulary. A single word can serve as a sentence, and not just one sentence but several sentence forms. The word that is used to serve as a sentence may not be recorded in any dictionary.

It may resemble a nonsense syllable. The child mentioned above whose first word was "Bru" soon was using other words, some of them similarly abbreviated. One word was "ap" for "apple." She used this word as a request, "Ap!" meaning "Give me an apple!" She used it simply as a way of calling attention, saying "Ap," and pointing when she discovered some windfall apples lying on the ground. Soon she combined "ap" with "mo" to ask for more apples. In time, "ap" was combined with "all gone" and still later with "no mo ap." Later still she combined "no mo ap" with "ap all gone," spoken in what sounded like a tone of regret. She was not heard using "no mo ap" with a rising inflection, as though asking a question, "Are there more apples?" but other children have been observed using an equivalent version of the question form.

First words and first-word combinations vary from child to child. So do the words used in children's first ventures into grammatical forms and primitive sentences. Miller and Ervin (1964) point out that even though children differ in the details of their early language and in their language style, they still are likely to exhibit certain common characteristics. Miller and Ervin kept records of the language of a number of children, beginning at about age two or earlier. In their earlier grammatical constructions the children quite characteristically used certain words that occurred frequently in their speech as anchor words when they first began to form sentences. One child, for example, frequently used the words "on" and "off." When shown a Santa Clause whose head came off she said, "Hat off, hat off." When the investigator reminded her that more than the hat, actually the whole head, came off, she said, "Santa head off." Then she added, "Head on. Fix on, fix on." Among her other early usages of *off* and *on* were "White sweater on." "This dress off." "Put that on," and so forth. Another child used *this* and *that* (and variations such as "thisa" and "thatsa") to begin many of his first sentences. Miller and Ervin designate pivotal words such as these as "operators."

Learning Syntax

Syntax pertains to sentence structure—the proper arrangement of word forms to show their mutual relationships within a sentence, in keeping with established grammatical usage. It is a rather remarkable achievement when children eventually are able to deliver, on request, well-formed sentences. In everyday life they probably have heard many more poorly-formed than well-formed sentences. Speech within a family is often quite elliptical, with grammatically incomplete sentences, mixed clauses, and unmatched singulars and plurals. Even a veteran lecturer is likely to wince at recordings of his extemporaneous remarks. They often resemble the transcripts of White House press conferences during the days of Eisenhower and Kennedy. Nonetheless, children somehow learn to draw order from confusion.

Children's language achievement is even more remarkable when one considers how early in life they begin to apply rules of grammar. They apply rules to word constructions and sentence constructions that have not specifically been taught to them. When a child says "goed" for *went* he is using the *ed*, as in *waited*, to express the past tense. He does the same when he says, "seed" and "bringed" for *saw* and *brought*. He is applying an *ed* systematically to express the past tense. From a grammatical point of view he is in error; from a psychological point of view these are "good" errors. He has applied the rule that to express something in the past tense one adds an *ed*. He does this long before he would be able to express this rule explicitly in answer to the question, "How do you usually change a verb from the present to the past tense?"[3]

Children's acquisition of grammar has been explored in interesting studies by Brown and Berko. These investigators used a "word game" technique, with pictures and nonsense syllables, with children at the preschool level and in the early elementary school grades. Nonsense syllables were used to rule out grammatical constructions the children might have learned by rote. In a study by Berko (1958) a child was shown, for example, a picture of a nondescript animal called a "wug." Then he was shown a picture of two of these creatures and told, "Now there are two of them," and was asked to complete the sentence: "There are two ——." If the child implicitly knew that adding an *s* denotes the plural he would say "two wugs." The procedures Berko used cover the English inflectional system: plural and possessive endings of nouns, the simple past, the third person present indicative, the progressive usage of verbs, and comparative and superlative adjectives.

Children tended to use regular forms when confronted with nonsense syllables resembling an actual word with an irregular declension. One test, used with adults as well as children, showed a man swinging something about his head and the subject was told: "This is a man who knows how to *gling*. He *glings* every day. Today he *glings*; yesterday he ——." Adults responded with *gling, glang, glung,* and even *glaught,* but the children mostly came up with *glinged.* In one test item, the children were explicitly given the correct irregular form of the plural. "Here is a goose and here are two geese. There are two ——." Even with the reminder of *geese,* most of the children said there were two *gooses.* Here, as in an earlier example, children apply a rule to new expression without specifically having been taught. This tendency to apply a rule is so strong in young children that it will prevail over a reminder that a word has an irregular plural form, such as *geese.*

In their language development children, as we have seen, apply constructions which they have learned to new terms and even to nonsense syllables. They generalize "rules" from familiar to unfamiliar terms even though they

---

[3] Adults make similar "good" errors. A Japanese student, bent on learning English, said to one of the writer's colleagues in Tokyo, "I backed from Radio Tokyo to the Dai Ichi." He was saying that he first went to Radio Tokyo in trying to locate a person and then went back to the hotel.

Table 20   Word Associations by Adults and Children

Stimulus	Response	1,000 Children	1,000 Men and Women
Table	Eat	358	63
	Chair	24	274
Dark	Night	421	221
	Light	38	427
Man	Work	168	17
	Woman	8	394
Deep	Hole	257	32
	Shallow	6	180
Soft	Pillow	138	53
	Hard	27	365
Mountain	High	390	246
	Hill	91	184

are unable to express the rule in words. But as children grow older, they increasingly learn irregular forms, such as *went* instead of *goed*.

They also become more aware of the logic of parts of speech, as shown in a study by Brown and Berko (1960). In the English language there are nouns that represent things that can be *counted* (a table, a house, and, in the plural, tables and houses) as distinct, separable structures; there are nouns representing amount or mass (such as milk; the usage does not allow speaking of *a* milk and there are not *many* milks, but there is much or little milk); adjectives; transitive verbs which require an object (I sent something); intransitive verbs without an object (I shouted, I lived); and adverbs.

Brown and Berko employed a free-association procedure with children and adults. The subject was asked, when given a word, to respond with the first word that came into his mind.

It is possible to respond in various ways. A person might offer what has been called a "clang" association, such as responding to the stimulus word "food" with the word "mood." Or he might respond with an evaluative association "food—good." Or he might offer a noun response that is of the same grammatical form as the stimulus, "food—meat." Older persons tend to respond with associations that are of the same part of speech as the stimulus word, such as in the last example.

Table 20, taken from an adaptation by Woodworth (1938) from earlier studies, compares the free-association responses of children with those of adults.

As the table indicates, there is a strong tendency in adult responses to follow the logic of grammatical forms; "chair" in response to "table," for instance, is far more frequent in the adults' than in the children's list.

In their study of children's and adults' usage of parts of speech by a free-association technique, Berko and Brown (1960) used 36 stimulus words selected to provide six words for each of six parts of speech. The responses were scored as homogenous-by-part-of-speech (table-chair, happy-glad) and heterogeneous-by-part-of-speech (table-eat, happy-boy).

In a second test, Brown and Berko (1960) asked their subjects to build sentences around nonsense syllables. A picture was displayed with each problem sentence. For example, a picture of a girl was shown along with the statement: "Do you know what a *wug* is? This is a picture of a girl thinking about a *wug*." This sentence, using the form, *a wug*, identified *wug* as a count noun. The subject then was asked to make up sentences of his own. These were scored homogenous-by-part-of-speech if the new word, *wug*, was used as a part of speech implied by the introductory sentences (e.g., "She is thinking *a wug* is funny," or "She is thinking about a *bug*").

When *wug* was to be identified as a transitive verb, the investigator said (showing a picture): "This girl wants to *wug* something." To produce an intransitive verb the same sentence was used with the omission of *something*. *Wug* also was used as an adjective, *wuggy*, and as an adverb, *wuggily*.

The two tests were administered to adults and to third-, second-, and first-grade children. Results obtained with the word association test and the sentence usage test are shown in Table 21.

Table 21   Average Number of Homologous-by-Part-of-Speech Responses to a Free Association Test Representing Each of Six Parts of Speech, and Average Number of Homologous-by-Part-of-Speech Sentence Usage*

Free Association (Maximum Score: 6)

Group	Count Nouns	Adjectives	Intransitive Verbs	Transitive Verbs	Adverbs	Mass Nouns	Total
Adult	5.10	5.00	4.80	4.45	4.95	2.35	4.44
3rd Grade	4.65	3.65	3.40	2.95	1.95	2.40	3.17
2nd Grade	4.55	3.90	2.75	2.40	2.25	1.90	2.96
1st Grade	3.95	1.25	1.60	1.40	.80	1.20	1.70
Total	4.56	3.45	3.14	2.80	2.49	1.96	3.07

Usage (Maximum Score: 2)

Group	Count Nouns	Adjectives	Intransitive Verbs	Transitive Verbs	Adverbs	Mass Nouns	Total
Adult	1.85	1.75	1.70	1.60	.95	1.20	1.51
3rd Grade	1.45	1.65	1.65	1.75	.55	.55	1.27
2nd Grade	1.55	1.50	1.20	1.10	.70	.45	1.08
1st Grade	1.20	.75	.90	.90	.45	.10	.72
Total	1.51	1.41	1.36	1.34	.66	.58	1.15

*See text for further information. Adapted by permission from R. W. Brown and J. Berko, "Word Association and the Acquisition of Grammar," *Child Development*, 1960, 31, 1–14.

As can be seen from Table 21, all parts of speech appeared at all age levels, although some parts of speech were more correctly employed than others.

Increased Understanding of Word Meanings

A child's progress in language includes not only the addition of "new" words but also in an increased understanding of the connotations of "old" words. Many terms that a child uses have relatively little meaning to him, as compared with the meaning intended by the writer or the teacher. Quite a few words have several meanings (for example, the word *run*). A person's vocabulary as measured by the number of words for which he knows at least one meaning is likely to differ considerably from his vocabulary as measured by the number of words for which he knows all or several meanings (Thevaos, 1951).

Vague meanings. In their schoolwork, children in the elementary grades come across and use many words without having a clear notion of their meaning. In an unpublished study by the writer, children were asked, among other things, to tell what is meant by a strike. To some children, the term was associated only with the verb *to hit*. In the fourth through the sixth grades many children associated other meanings with the term. Some of them answered little more than: "It's when people break windows and throw stones;" or "It's when people walk outside a shop with signs on their backs with words like 'unfair' on them." These answers indicated that these children had a notion that a strike meant conflict of some sort. Still more comprehension was revealed in an answer such as "It's when the workers and the bosses have an argument and the workers stop working." At a higher level of understanding, some children not only mentioned the fact of a dispute, and parties in the dispute, but also described the issues involved, such as demands for more pay or shorter hours. At a still higher level of comprehension, a few children not only described what happened in a strike and the issues that might be involved but also discussed steps that might be taken to terminate a strike and the possible effects on the employer's business or on the cost to the consumer if the strikers won.

Language and Mental and Social Orientation

Once a child has begun to talk, his language development reflects his mental processes, his interests, and his orientation to the material and social world in which he lives.

"I" and "You." When pronouns appear, various forms of "I" predominate. In a study by Smith (1931) of children aged two to five years, "I" had a frequency of 2,543, as compared with a score of 955 for "you." "I" is especially frequent as compared with other pronouns at the earlier age levels, and it continues to show a high frequency of use throughout the preschool period (and from that point onward, too); but as children advance in age during preschool years, there also is an increase in other forms, such as "we," "you," "she," and "it." Table 22 summarizes the number of times various pronouns were used at half-yearly age levels in the spontaneous speech of two- and three-year-old children (above average in IQ), as recorded during observation of the children on a nursery school playground.

The high frequency of the first-person pronoun in the speech of young children is not difficult to understand. A child's own impulses and desires, activities, pleasures, and pains are more vivid and closer to him than is his comprehension of the personalities and concerns of other people. The prime position held by his own concerns is evident in the child's language—not only through his frequent use of "I" but also through the content and tone of his remarks, questions, and demands. However, from the time he begins to talk, the very fact that he expresses himself at all bespeaks a certain degree of sociability and adaptation to other persons. This point has been emphasized in a study by Fisher (1934) of the content of children's spontaneous speech on the playground. When comprehensible remarks were analyzed according to three categories—self as subject: "I want to be first"; other person as subject: "Mary is coming along"; and thing as subject: "The carriage goes there"—it was found that slightly over one-third of the remarks were of the first-named type. However, while a child's remarks are heavily studded with "I's," there is also a vein of sociability running through them, for they are usually addressed to another person.

Jean Piaget (1932), working with French-speaking children in Europe, distinguished between "egocentric" and "socialized" speech. In "egocentric"

Table 22 Frequency of Various Pronouns in Children's Conversations

	24-29	30-35	36-41	42-47
Age in Months				
Number of Children	11	11	11	11
Total Words Spoken During Period of Recording	13,124	22,016	46,624	64,352
Pronouns Used:				
I (my, me, etc.)	1,442	2,991	5,692	5,753
you (your, -self)	94	468	1,770	2,372
we (our, us, etc.)	28	177	406	881
he, she (him, her, etc.)	33	187	437	698
it (it's, -self, etc.)	155	567	1,206	1,485
they (their, them, etc.)	24	58	139	266

Adapted from A. T. Jersild and R. Ritzman, "Aspects of Language Development: The Growth of Loquacity and Vocabulary," *Child Development* (1938), 9:243-259. Reproduced by permission.

speech there is no endeavor to interchange ideas, to consider the other person's point of view; rather, it is a form of "collective monologue" or "pseudo-conversation." In "socialized" speech, on the other hand, a talker really addresses a listener, considers the other person's viewpoint, and tries to communicate ideas and to share meanings. One conclusion in Piaget's earlier work was that there is little in the nature of a meeting of minds and of ability to take account of another person's point of view until about the age of seven or eight years. Many other investigators, however, have noted that children are capable of "socialized speech" well before the age of seven or eight (Mc-Carthy, 1946). "Socialized" language in children as young as three or four has been noted by many observers. In general, however, the less mature a child the more limited he will be in understanding or taking another's point of view.

"Nominal Realism"

In early childhood it appears that the name of a thing is not just a symbol or representation of a thing but an inherent part of the thing itself. "Horse" is not simply a convenient label but is one of the attributes of a horse. It would not be possible, by common consent, according to this view, to call a horse a cow or to call a cow a horse. To do so would be to violate nature. A boy in one of Piaget's studies acknowledged that God might have called the moon "sun," but if God did so it would be a mistake. This view that a name is part of the nature of the thing has been called "word realism" by Werner (1964) and "nominal realism" by Piaget (1932a).

The idea that a name is part of the essence of what the name stands for appears also in primitive thought. Among some primitive people, a curse or a blessing pronounced on a person's name is regarded as equivalent to bestowing a curse or a blessing on the person himself.

The notion that a name is an essential element of the thing that is named declines with age, but it still persists among many children well into the elementary school grades. In a study by Brook (1967) children in the first, third and fifth grades were asked questions to elicit their views with regard to the origin of names. One series of questions dealt with the name of the sun. For example: How did the name of the sun begin? How did we know the name of the sun? Why is the sun called the sun? The children's answers were analyzed according to categories representing three stages as described by Piaget. The first stage is that of unreserved nominal realism: The sun is called the sun because it is the sun and it's sunny. The second stage is that of a modified nominal realism: God (or the first men) named the sun; they could have named it light because the sun has light. In the third stage, nominal realism is abandoned; a name is described as having been invented; it is arbitrary and could be changed.

As can be seen in Table 23, most of the children in the first grade and about half of the children in the fifth grade answered predominantly in terms of nominal realism: a name is indivisible from the thing that is named. Even at the fifth grade, only about half of the children most frequently gave answers indicating that names are arbitrary labels and have no inherent relationship to what is named.

According to Piaget, a child's tendency to regard the name of a thing as an essential part of the thing is linked with his egocentricity, his inability to "decenter" himself from things in the surrounding world and to regard them as having an independent existence apart from his own. A convinced nominal realist with an egocentric turn of mind would regard as faulty any name for an object other than the name it has in his own language. When "soleil" is, from the French child's point of view, an integral part of *le soleil*, an Englishman is obviously mistaken when he calls it "sun." but it seems that young children are not as adamant in their nominal realism as Piaget's theory implies. Bilingual children, for example, seem to be quite content to use different names for the same thing.

*Factors Related
to Language Development*

Learning and Growth. Changes associated with maturation, as distinguished from practice, play an important role in early language development, as we have seen in Chapter Two. It is obviously through a process of learning, however, that a child becomes proficient in his use of language.

Table 23. Type of Answer Predominating in Responses of First-, Third-, and Fifth-Grade Children (50 at Each Level) in Answer to Eight Questions Dealing with the Origin and Nature of Names

Type of Answer	Grade Level		
	1st	3rd	5th
Type 1. Nominal realism: Name inherent in thing named. Sun is called sun because it is the sun and it is sunny.	46	29	21
Type 2. Intermediate: God (or first men) named the sun, but could have called it light because the sun has light.	2	9	5
Type 3. Nominal relativism: Name is invented, arbitrary: You could call the sun any name you want to.	2	12	24

Adapted by permission from Judith S. Brook. *Children's Conception of Language.* In press, *Journal of Genetic Psychology,* 1967. The values in the table represent the number of children whose modal (most frequent) responses fell in each of the three categories. If a child answered two questions with a Type 1 response, two with a Type 2, and four with a Type 3 response, his modal position would be Type 3.

A great amount of a child's language learning is self-initiated. Some children, for periods of time, show a voracious appetite for words. A three-year-old might, for example, repeat or try to repeat, every word spoken in his hearing, day after day. All he needs is a model, and he will spontaneously copy it.

Language as Related to Socio-Economic Status and Age of Associates. Various studies have shown that children of higher socio-economic status surpass those of lower status in such matters as length of sentences used, frequency of questions, and vocabulary. This difference may be due in part to a higher level of intelligence, but it seems reasonable to assume that children living in homes at a higher socio-economic level (which usually means a higher educational level) would have advantages even if the factor of intelligence were equalized. There is evidence that children who associate primarily with adults are more precocious in their language development than children who associate mainly with children.

Language of Twins and "Singletons." Twins have been found to progress less rapidly in their language development from two to five years of age than "singletons" (Day, 1932a, 1932b, and Davis, 1937). Apart from hereditary or congenital factors that might account for this, the phenomenon is probably due largely to environmental factors. Twins seem to be able to communicate with each other by using fewer words than would be required to communicate the same meanings to someone else. Facial expressions, gestures, single words, cryptic murmurings, and the like, which each has learned to understand through close companionship with the other, take the place of conventional words and sentences.

Sex Differences. In several investigations girls have been found to surpass boys in many aspects of early language development, such as amount of talking, number of different words used, and use of sentences. The extent of the difference between boys and girls has varied in different studies, and exceptions to a tendency toward superiority of girls have been noted. McCarthy (1953) has discussed the ways in which a girl may have an advantage in language development because she has more access to common interests with the mother than a boy has. At the elementary school level there usually are far more boys than girls with reading difficulties, but factors in addition to language development as such are involved here.

Language and Intelligence. A positive relationship usually exists between language ability and mental ability, as measured by standard intelligence tests. Since the understanding and use of words play so large a role in many intelligence tests it is difficult to determine just what this relationship means. Does a child earn a high score on a verbal intelligence test because he has a good command of a language or does he have a good command of language because he is highly intelligent? Probably it works both ways. The relationship is not so high that early language development can be used to predict later intelligence, except within broad limits.

Bilingualism. Many children in this country and throughout the world are called upon to adjust to two different languages. Bilingualism poses a problem, both for children whose parents commonly use a foreign language in the home, and—to a lesser extent—for educators who must determine when foreign languages should be introduced into the school curriculum.

As communication between the various peoples of the world continues to expand, it seems likely that learning two or more languages will, for many persons, become commonplace and not merely the fulfillment of a formal academic requirement (as it so often has been in the past).

The ways in which children are called upon to acquire two different languages vary decidedly. A child who lives in a home or community where two languages are spoken is likely, through practical necessity, to become familiar with both, even though he is also likely to become more fluent in one than in the other. There are many interesting combinations of bilinguality: a child may be able to understand and use both languages; he may be able to speak both, but able to write only one; he may be able to understand both, but able to speak only one.

A youngster who has to acquire two different languages will probably, during early childhood, make slower progress in each than he would make if he were acquiring only one language (Smith, 1931, 1935, 1949).

In a study of matched children at the preschool level, Darcy (1946) found that bilingual children did relatively much better on a "performance" test of intelligence (Adkins Object-Fitting Test) than on a test which involves greater use of language (the Stanford-Binet).

Anastasi and Cordova (1953) found that Puerto Rican children who had suddenly been required to cope with an all-English school situation "insulated" themselves by becoming rather passive and apathetic in their attitudes.

A child from a foreign-language background is likely, in some situations, to be teased and cut off from the group. Even when he is not singled out by his peers, the child himself may be self-conscious about his background and language, and may be timid (or sometimes overassertive) when called upon to express himself, especially if he is in the process of transition from one tongue to another, still uses accents and speech forms from the foreign language, or still "thinks" in a foreign language.

The problems faced by children who come from one language background and then are forced at school to learn another are different from those faced by youngsters whose mother tongue is the prevailing language but who take up a foreign language as a school subject. Observers report that children of elementary school age show a remarkable facility for learning a new **language** if it is introduced in a "functional" way (such as combining the learning of the French names for common plants with a trip to the fields or combining the learning of the words on a French menu with a meal in a French restaurant). If a youngster is going to be required some time in school to learn a foreign language, he probably will have an advantage (especially in learning the correct accent) if he is introduced to the language *before* rather than after he reaches the teens.

In commenting on studies pertinent to this topic, McCarthy (1961) notes that young children appear to be more attuned to the sound and feeling tone of language, while those in the early teens appear to be more concerned with the cognitive and semantic aspects.

Through several years of observation of children in bilingual homes the writer has the impression that young children, to a greater extent than older persons, learn a second language in much the same way they learn a first language. The young English-Danish speaking child speaks, in English, about "a piece of bread" without deriving the meaning from the meaning of the separate words. "Et stykke bröd" in Danish likewise is a unit of expression, not requiring a separate piecing together of "et" plus "stykke" plus "bröd." Indeed if you asked the child, in Danish, whether "stykke" should be preceded with an "en" (masculine-feminine) or an "et" (neuter) he would probably be thrown off stride and say he wasn't sure. But when this child, studying French in the conventional manner in high school, is learning to name the same object in French, he must apply terms that he has learned separately, *un,* the masculine article, *morceau* for piece, the preposition *de,* of, and *pain* for bread.[4]

Children's Thinking
as Expressed by Their Questions

Once a child has learned to talk he begins to ask a vast number of questions. He asks questions mainly to satisfy his curiosity, but many other motives come into play such as a desire to establish social contact, or to receive attention, or to gain reassurance, solace, or help. Children also use persistent questioning as a form of resistance or as a means of expressing resentment. And questioning sometimes occurs as a general outflow of language spoken for its own sake without apparent expectation of an answer. One of the means a child uses to practice his language is to raise questions.

An increase with age in the proportion of questions in children's language in their play with one another has been noted in observations of nursery school children (from 2 to 15 per cent in a study by Fisher, 1934). One ob-

---

[4] A study by Huttenlocher (1964) shows that children have difficulty in breaking a meaningful combination of words into separate elements. For example, they made considerably more errors when asked to say I-do in reverse than to render 5-2 into 2-5.

server, who recorded a child's language at home, noted that questions occurred at the rate of thirty-one per hour at thirty-eight months (Brandenburg, 1915), and another observer noted that questions comprised 2 per cent of a child's language at two years and about a fourth to a fifth at ages three to eight years. It is clear that a youngster, if given the chance, will raise a staggering number of questions during a week or month.

Questions raised by children vary according to their language abilities and interests. When a child is in the "naming stage" in his language development he is likely to ask many "what" questions. Youngsters likewise go through a "Who is that?" period. Such questions usually precede "why" questions which deal with causal relations in everyday happenings or with reasons for another's behavior.

In an analysis of 3,650 questions asked by seventy-three children aged three to twelve years, as recorded by parents, 87.8 per cent of the questions seemed to arise from something in the immediate situation, as distinguished from questions about remembered or remote events (which constituted 10.8 per cent; 1.4 per cent could not be accounted for). A novel occurrence was more likely to provoke a long series of logically related questions than an ordinary situation, but the latter also frequently provoked such a series of questions. Boys asked more questions involving causal explanations while girls exceeded boys in questions regarding social relations (Davis, 1932).

The following questions, asked by preschool children (above average in intelligence) are from data collected by Rust in a study of the growth of children's concepts.[5] The first questions dealing with time were asked by a four-and-a-half-year-old girl who had just been told a story about a six-year-old girl:

CHILD: I'm four, aren't I?
MOTHER: Yes, four years.
CHILD: What's a year?
MOTHER: (*Explains.*)
CHILD: Is that a long time?
MOTHER: Quite a long time.
CHILD: How long?
MOTHER: It's hard to explain, but it is a lot of days, 365, and that's many.
CHILD: Well, but how long?
MOTHER: Well, well, you know when it was Christmas.
CHILD: Oh, yes, and I had a tree, and once I had a tree in the corner and once I had it on the table.
MOTHER: Well, that was twice, and it takes a year to have a Christmas. You see we have Christmas, then the time between that Christmas and the time between the next is a year.
CHILD: Well, that's a very long, long time. When I was very small we had a Christmas. Is a year a birthday?
MOTHER: Well, you have one birthday, then the time between is called a year, then you have the next birthday.

_____

[5] M. M. Rust, *The Growth of Children's Concepts of Time, Space, and Magnitude*, unpublished (Teachers College, Columbia University). Reproduced by permission.

CHILD: Yes, three then four—then five— Say, how old are you?
MOTHER: Thirty.
CHILD: How did you stretch up?

This turn in the conversation appeared to suggest another line of questions. She continued:

CHILD: When I'm thirty will I be a mother?
MOTHER: If you have a baby you will.
CHILD: Do all womans have babies?
MOTHER: No.
CHILD: Why?
MOTHER: Some are not strong enough, some are too busy doing other things —some . . .
CHILD: Well, in three or six weeks when I'm thirty, I shall have a baby— Where do babies come from?
MOTHER: Seeds.
CHILD: Where do the seeds come from?
MOTHER: The father and the mother.
CHILD: Where does the father keep his?
MOTHER: They're in his body.
CHILD: Oh, is he keeping them warm same as the mother does the baby?
MOTHER: He doesn't have them there to keep them warm, but because they belong there.
CHILD: Well, when I'm six weeks I'll marry you because you're so cute.
CHILD: Hello, Daddy. Did you buy me something? (*No further questioning.*)

The following questions and comments of another four-year-old child deal in part with concepts of time:

CHILD: Is this today?
TEACHER: Yes, why?
CHILD: Well, is tomorrow tomorrow?
TEACHER: Yes.
CHILD: Well, Sunday is my birthday.
TEACHER: Do you know what date that is?
CHILD: Yes, it's March 5 and I will be four years old. That's this many (*counts down four buttons on his coat*).
TEACHER: That is right, Frank.
CHILD: Some day I will be this old (*stretches out his arms at full length*).

The problem of time was the subject of the questions of another child, aged four and a half.

CHILD: What time is it?
MOTHER: 6:30.
CHILD: What means that?
MOTHER: What do you mean?
CHILD: What means 6:30?

MOTHER: Well, when it's evening it means time for you to think of bed and time for me to get dinner.
CHILD: How long is 6:30?
MOTHER: Just one minute, then it is 6:31.
CHILD: Is a minute big?
MOTHER: No, very short.
CHILD: Just a little bit like this? (*Demonstrates with finger and thumb and a tiny pinch.*)
MOTHER: I'll show you with my watch.
CHILD: (*Watches watch for a minute or two, then speaks.*) Do you like me, Mummy? (*Dismisses subject of time.*)

The same child, on another occasion, ended a series of questions concerning the days of the week with the query, "Where does time go?"

Many of the questions raised by young children are difficult if not impossible to answer. Sometimes an adequate answer would go beyond the child's comprehension or willingness to listen (for example, an answer to this question by a three-year-old: "Where is the people in the TV set?" or "What makes the subway run?"). Sometimes the adult is at a loss how to put his answer (for example, if the question asked is: "Who made God?").

Children's questions may spring from motives more pressing than intellectual curiosity. There may be fear, worry, or uneasiness. A child who has been frightened by an animal may ask about any new thing that he sees, "Has it got a mouf? Does it bite?" The child of a mother who works away from home a good deal may ask, repeatedly, on seeing an unaccompanied adult or a child, "Where is his mamma?" A three-year-old boy raised many questions after the slaughter of two pigs that had been reared by his father since they were little. "Why did you butcher Blackie and Whitie?" (the pigs). When told (as he had been told repeatedly beforehand) that pigs are butchered for meat when they are big and fat, he asked, "Will me and— (naming his sister) be butchered when we are big?" On later days he asked such questions as, "Do people close their eyes when they are dead?" After one such question, he asserted firmly, "When I be dead I won't close my eyes and I'm going to run around." (In this remark he seems to show resistance to the idea of death). Apparently it was the idea of death rather than the demise of the two particular pigs that bothered him, for he later identified parts of the pigs at the table and ate with great relish.

The following (also from Rust) is another example of a child who was puzzled about death:

CHILD (*four and a half years old*): Mummy, what means a dead mother?
MOTHER: A woman that has died and does not walk or talk any more.
CHILD: But what will the children do?
MOTHER: Well, if a mother should die, the father would take care of them and maybe an aunt.
CHILD: Will you be a dead mother some day?
MOTHER: Why yes, though I don't expect to be for a long time.

CHILD: A *very* long time?
MOTHER: Yes.
CHILD: But I don't want you to die; I want you here like this.
MOTHER: Well, you will probably be quite grown-up before that happens.
CHILD: A *long* time?
MOTHER: Yes.
CHILD: But what means dead, mummy?
MOTHER: Well, your heart stops beating and you lie still without breathing.
CHILD: And what do you do with the talking part—you know, the inside talk?
MOTHER: I'm not sure, but some people think you live in another world and, of course, some don't.
CHILD: I guess we do (*excitedly*). Yes! And then you die in a *long*, long time—a *very* long time, and then I die and we both hug each other and then you won't have any wrinkles—Oh, look at that cute pussy? Isn't she darling? (*Runs off.*)

Often a child will continue to repeat a question after an adult has given an answer. Such repetition may be aimed at getting attention, but it may also mean the child is still troubled. Sometimes the meaning of the question is hidden. For example, a child might ask again and again during an afternoon, "Are you going to put the car in the garage?" This repetition becomes more understandable if the parent realizes that the question really means, "Are you going to stay home or are you going out this evening?"

In trying to fathom the meaning of a child's question it is well, on the other hand, not to read too much into his inquiry. An example of this occurred in a home in which a bright two-and-a-half-year-old girl had just received a new rubber doll. She held it up for both her father and mother to see, saying, "See my baby?" Then she asked, "Where baby come from?" The father thought the child was asking her first question about the origin of babies, but before he could gather his wits to give an answer worthy of this great occasion the mother simply said, "Woolworth's." This answer suited the child perfectly.

Language and Thought

In the cognitive sphere, language serves manifold functions. Through words a child can deal, on a symbolic level, with things and their meanings. Words provide the child with a vicarious source of experience. They enable him to extend his knowledge concerning matters that lie outside the field of his perception but within the range of his understanding.

Language also serves as a way of communicating thoughts to others and in serving this desire it provides a child with a medium for formulating his thoughts. He cannot make a thought clear to others unless it is clear to him. This clarification depends to a large degree on formulation in terms of language. To tell an idea to another he must, in effect, be able to tell it to himself.

Students of language differ in the relative emphasis they place on language as a vehicle of thought and as a molder of thought. Language is, of course, a fabricated set of symbols. The word used to name a thing is not inherent in what is named. Although an Englishman spoke of a pig as "properly so called," implying that anything as piggish as a pig should be called a pig, there is nothing in the animal that decrees it should be called a pig in English and *schwein* in German.

However, words, whatever their origin, become tools of thought. They aid in the formulation of concepts; they serve as embodiments of meanings which a person can add to, reflect on, and refine in the course of further experience. Moreover, the expressions used in a given language may produce a turn of thought different from the counterpart expressions in another language. A French child who reads in the Bible that God was "tres irrité" probably forms a milder impression of the Lord's mood than the English child who reads that God was "sore wroth."

The view that language is not merely a tool for formulating and expressing thought but also regulates thought has been set forth by Luria (1959). Through words, a person is able to abstract and isolate meanings, to generalize and relate what he perceives into categories of thought. It is this systematization of direct experience that makes the role of the word in the formulation of mental processes so exceptionally important, according to Luria and Yudovich (1959).

Words that originally were constructed to signalize and describe something perceived in the physical world may, in turn, shape the perceptions of those to whom they are taught. Words and expressions such as "sunset," "the half moon," "the rising moon," "the stars come out," and even "the wide, wide world" (implying flatness), give a child a picturesque but inaccurate image of the earth and its surrounding planets. A child also encounters many expressions which encourage him to think in terms of what Piaget describes as animism—endowing inanimate things with life and motives—i.e., a "live" wire, a "stubborn" motor, a "wild" wind, an "angry" sea.

Perceptual Development

As a child matures he is increasingly able to add what he knows to what he sees and to add what he sees to what he knows. More and more of what he meets acquires meaning by virtue of his past experience. He needs less obvious cues to recognize an object for what it is, to discriminate between the properties of things and what can be done with them, to recognize another person's mood or intention.

Just what might be a child's first impressions of the world about him no one is likely ever to tell. It is impossible for an older person to denude his perception of the overlay of past experience and to go back to his original state. Does the world at first strike a child as a huge, heaping mass of things? —"And the earth was without form, and void; and darkness was on the face of the deep." [6] Perhaps not, for even from the start there seems to be some degree of discrimination; and somewhere along the line a child's world increasingly assumes an orderly shape. Sounds that once, perhaps, struck a child as part of a confused medley are singled out as distinct. The gentle voice of the one who cares for him soon has a quality that makes it unique among other sounds that reach his ears. It is fascinating to observe how even after the first few days of life a child no longer behaves as one who is lost in a wilderness of sights and sounds.

A growing child gains familiarity with things about him through all channels of sensing experience. He can touch them, explore their contours with his tongue and lips, heft them (through the kinesthetic sense), watch them, and via his sense of hearing, tell whether an object that he strikes is solid or hollow.

Sensory Channels

There has been some conjecture about what, at the beginning, might be the primary channel of experience. Might touch, for example, be regarded as the "mother of the senses?" And does "haptic" perception—perception by way of what we commonly call the sense of touch (which embraces touch, pressure, and temperature) have priority over other forms of perception? Actually, a child is exposed to touch and pressure stimulation and apparently is able to respond to vibrations that produce auditory sensation before birth. Visual stimulation and visual perception do not come into the picture until after birth.[7]

The most obvious overtly "activist" approach to the perception of form is by way of touch and movement. A child encloses things that come in contact with the palm of his hands, and he brings them into contact with his lips. Here, as in other aspects of a child's experience, it is difficult for an adult to tell what are the cues, what are the messages through which a child recognizes and distinguishes.

Even though touch may be a more primitive avenue of sensory experience

---

[6] Genesis I, 2. King James Version.

[7] Whether or not touch should be regarded as the mother of the senses, it might properly be regarded as the most "motherly" of all the senses. The infants in Harlow's (1958) well known studies of monkeys sought "contact comfort" from their artificial mothers. Among human beings, "mothering" is established largely by way of touch and pressure as the child is held and cuddled and motherly "warmth" literally at first is conveyed by way of temperature.

than vision, it appears that vision gains priority, early in life, over touch and other sense modalities as a major source of a child's growing awareness of the world about him.

Visual Perception of Pattern and Depth

One question concerning visual perception involves whether a child can perceive spatial patterns directly through vision alone or whether such perception requires prior experience through movement and action, such as exploring contours of a figure with his hands and surveying its contours, width, and breadth with his eyes, and, so to speak, giving it a manual and visual workover.

The reader may recall from an earlier chapter that the world that meets the eye of a child soon after birth apparently is not completely a blurred, undifferentiated mass. Fantz (1961) found that infants fixed their gaze longer and more often on some visual displays than on others: a bull's-eye pattern was preferred over a striped surface, a checker-pattern was preferred over a plain surface. When shown solid objects and a flat surface together, they paid more attention to the solid shape. Fantz concluded that when infants thus prefer one object or pattern over another they must be sensitive to a difference between them.

The visual aspect of things becomes so prominent it sometimes prevails even when belied by the sense of touch. This was noted in infants' responses to the Gibson "visual cliff" apparatus, described in Chapter 6. Children would avoid what seemed to the eyes to be a cliff or drop-off even when they took the opportunity to discover that the surface was flat by patting it, rubbing it, and putting their faces to it. Apparently the surface had to look safe to be safe.

Recognition of Pictured Objects

One test of the potency of visual cues is a child's reaction to pictures. Can he, with a minimum of previous experience, identify an object from a *picture* of the object, or does he need prior experience in associating the pictured object with the actual object? This question was raised in a study by Hochberg and Brooks (1962). They brought up a child with a minimum of contact with pictures (TV, movies, magazines, etc.). He was taught the names of objects entirely through the presence of the objects themselves. This phase of the experiment was ended at nineteen months. Then they continued the experiment by showing the child twenty-one pictures. These included photographs and outline drawings of toys, utensils, wearing apparel, common objects such as keys and a car, and persons. The child's responses showed that he apparently recognized the photographic or line drawing representations of common things without having previously connected these with the things portrayed and without having been taught to connect a verbal or naming response to the things portrayed.

Gibson (1963) cites other findings which indicate that persons in primitive cultures can identify things from pictures—a picture of a thing as standing for a thing—without previously having actively associated the two.

Visual and Haptic Perception

A young child makes many fine visual distinctions between objects and forms while he is still unable to do so through haptic perception alone (touching and handling an unseen object or form). According to Piaget and Inhelder (1956) it is not until about the age of six that a child, by touch and handling, can distinguish between complex forms such as stars, crosses, and crystal-like shapes. Visual discrimination between such forms is possible considerably earlier (Page, 1959).

Page repeated experiments reported by Piaget and Inhelder in 1956 under the title "Haptic Perception." Into the child's hands, extended through holes in a screen, various objects or forms were placed, unseen, for him to hold, touch, feel, or explore tactually as he chose. If the figure was a common object, he was asked to name it; if it was a form, he was asked to point it out in a collection of pictured forms, or to draw it.

The figures included common objects such as a spoon, comb, pencil, small hard ball and key; simple geometrical shapes; more complicated asymetrical geometrical shapes; and a group of irregular "topological" shapes (e.g., a ⊃ and a ⊖ shape somewhat resembling a pretzel).[8]

Page's results correspond generally to observations reported by Piaget and Inhelder. Up to age three and one half or four years, most of the children, through touch and handling, identified unseen familiar common objects, but in only 16 of 98 presentations could the children correctly identify simple geometrical shapes such as circles, squares, oblongs, and triangles. Beyond four or five years the children improved in their ability to differentiate shapes according to their angles and according to their dimensions. At about five and a half years, children began to differentiate cross and star forms, the rhombus (an equilateral parallelogram with oblique angles) and the trapezium (a figure formed by four lines, no two of which are parallel); but they made many mistakes. After the age of about six and a half years children increasingly searched for symmetry and balance, with less haphazard handling and with some evidence of anticipating what the handling might reveal.

---

[8] "Topological" here refers to space relationships that can be described qualitatively, for example, as open or closed, inside or outside, side by side, separated or edge to edge, and so on.

Children's drawings of the figures tended to improve with age in a manner paralleling their ability to identify shapes by tactual exploration.

The children in Page's study, as in the observations by Piaget and Inhelder, were better able to recognize non-geometric topological forms even though, to adults, these forms seem more complicated than the simple geometrically shaped spheres, triangles, and squares.[9] It seems that such forms represent more primitive and naturalistic phenomena in a child's perceptual world than the abstractions represented by Euclidean geometric forms, with their lines and angles, precise curves and circles, and the complicated forms that can be derived from these. In his natural habitat, a child has more experience with irregular borders and contours, broken surfaces, open and closed surfaces, and discontinuous projections (like the tines of a fork).

Some of the younger children in Page's study made no exploratory movements at all, but simply grasped the object. After age four, the children explored more actively, such as turning the model slightly. Still later there was apparently a deliberate plan to discover features, coupled with controlled tracing of the outline with the fingers.

With few exceptions, the children in Page's study tried to find some meaningful association with the object they had felt, and to name it—e.g., a half-moon, egg, and so on. One child described a shape (resembling a patriarchal or archepiscopal cross) ". . . like one of those things you dig in the ground and put your chest on and it goes brrp-brrp." Apparently the child meant a pneumatic drill.

Perception of Graphic Symbols

The development of perception demonstrates that the human mind is capable of a vast amount of shorthand. Judging from the above-noted study by Hochberg and Brooks, it can capture a thing through a representation of the thing (as in pictures) without having to go through the steps of fixing its attention now on the concrete object, now on a picture of it, in order to decide that one represents the other.

With all this facility of the human mind to embrace the real through symbolic representation there still remains, for many children, a roadblock along the way. This roadblock arises when children, for one reason or another, fail to distinguish between details that are important in what they are expected to learn, notably the graphic symbols (letters of the alphabet) of written language. These are harder to come by than many other things the child

[9] This is in keeping with Piaget's view that a child's discovery of spatial relationships—his "spontaneous geometry"—reverses the historical order of the development of geometry, in which the Euclidean system, concerned with figures, angles, and the like, preceded topological geometry. The child can, for example, draw a circle within a circle, or a circle edge to edge, "before he can draw a rectangle or express the Euclidean characteristics (number of sides, angles, etc., of a figure," 1953, p. 3).

perceives, for in much of his perceptual learning a child has several sources of information. When he eventually distinguishes his mother from other persons, he has had many opportunities to see her, to hear her voice and the sound of her footsteps, to finger her hair, and so on. Perhaps he does not need all these multiple sources ("redundancy" of impressions, it has been called); perhaps he could learn to recognize her just as speedily by sight alone. However this may be, in his day-to-day experience a child can learn in a naturalistic setting that hard things can't be dented, heavy things are hard to lift, and so on. Such perceptions can be learned by a process of self correction. If a child applies a light "heft" to a heavy object it simply does not budge.

Graphic symbols, on the other hand, do not possess natural properties that convey their own message. There is nothing inherent in *b* that demands correction if it is confused with *d*. A child must learn to discriminate what is unique about *b* that makes it different from *d*.

A series of studies by Gibson and her associates (reviewed by Gibson, 1963) offers interesting information about the development of discrimination of letter-like forms. Gibson and her associates devised forms that were designed to represent features that make letters unique and then presented variations in these forms by changing, for example, one of the lines in a figure from straight to curved (simulating the difference between V and U); by a 180-degree rotation (simulating the difference between d and b); by changing an open to a closed form (simulating the difference between c and o); and by changing the perspective, such as might be obtained by changing the position of a book so that the print is seen from different angles.

The standard "letters" and their transformed shapes were mounted on cards, and children aged four to eight were asked to choose from a display of cards those that were like the standard form.[10] The closed and open forms were most accurately discriminated (representing, figuratively, the distinction between an O and C). The greatest number of errors, throughout the age range, occurred with transformations that changed the perspective.

In interpreting their results, Gibson and her associates conjectured that correct detection in the recognition of letter-like forms is related to the type of perceptual learning that occurs in daily life. A "topological" difference, such as an open or closed figure, is detected quite readily, even at four years ("topological" perception was discussed earlier in this section). According to Gibson, *et al.*, children learn to perceive by noting an object's *distinctive features*. When a C-shape is changed to an O-shape, it is as though there were a new or different object. But rotating an object, even to the extent of 180 degrees, changes its *position* but does not change the object itself. An upside-down dog is still the same dog. But in the written alphabet, an upside-down d becomes a p. A change in perspective likewise changes the position

---

[10] There was a high correlation between errors in the tests with letter-like forms and errors made by children with real letters.

but not the object. A face remains a face whether it is seen frontally or in profile. It seems that to learn some of the letters of the alphabet a child must learn to single out features which he has learned to overlook in his actual experience.

Perceptual Development and Learning

Progress in perception is influenced both by maturation and learning. Writers differ both in the emphasis they give to maturation and in their accounts of what is involved in the learning process.

Perception builds, in part, on increased ability to recognize likenesses and to discriminate differences. When a person perceives something new as *identical* to something he already is familiar with, he is applying what he knows to what he sees. When he perceives it as *different*, he is also applying what he knows. The new event does not fit into any established thought structure, and he now must accommodate himself to that fact. As time passes, as we have seen before, he becomes able to respond to "reduced cues." The hair of the dog that bit him stands for the dog. But why the hair? According to Gibson (1963), the process by which a certain cue becomes potent does not merely involve the way *any* element in a past stimulus situation becomes effective in reintegrating (re-establishing, standing for) the whole, but involves the way certain cues become *distinctively* effective. Given an assortment of houseware, it is the handle of a cup that distinguishes it from a bowl; the spout in the tea-kettle and coffee-urn that distinguishes these from other utensils.

Effect of Desires and Motives on Perception

The role of personal feelings and motives has been demonstrated in interesting fashion in studies of children's perceptions. A child's likes, dislikes, expectations and fears may, for example, influence his judgment of the relative size of things. Dukes and Bevan (1952) give an interesting illustration of the influence of children's liking for candy on their judgment of weight. When shown jars of candy and jars containing sand and asked which weighed more they over-estimated the weight of the candy jars. This is quite a misjudgment for even the most delicious fudge usually weighs less, jar for jar, than sand.

Recommended Readings

Several studies dealing with the language development and the functions of language are reproduced by Celia B. Stendler in her *Readings in Child Behavior and Development* (1964). The section on developmental psychology in the *Annual Review of Psychology*, edited by P. R. Farnsworth, regularly reports recent studies of language development. Piaget's *The Language and Thought of the Child* (1932) is a classic. For accounts of perception, see Aline H. Kidd and Jeanne L. Rivoire's *Perceptual Development in Children* (1966); Eleanor J. Gibson, "Perceptual Development," in *Child Psychology* (1963), edited by Harold W. Stevenson; and the *Annual Review of Psychology*.

20   *Conceptual Development*

The first section of this chapter will deal with the development of reasoning and concept formation, centering mainly on children as they move from the preschool to the adolescent level.

Much of contemporary research on children's thinking has been influenced by the writings of Jean Piaget. There is widespread interest in what his work means for developmental psychology and in what it might imply for schools that aim to "teach children to think."

According to Piaget, as was noted in Chapter 7, a child in the first phase of his intellectual development incorporates objects into sensory-motor "schemata"[1] (sucking, seeing, hearing, handling, and so on). Through a process of assimilation he fits more and more new things into an already

---

[1] Some English translators use "schemata," others "schemas" as the plural of "schema."

established scheme (e.g., things that can be sucked, things that can be banged to make a noise). Through a process of accommodation he modifies his approach to things, or his views of things, that will not fit into an established pattern (he must, for example, accommodate himself to the fact that salt, although it looks like sugar, does not taste like sugar).

The early sensory-motor schemata, according to Piaget, ". . . constitute the functional equivalent of concepts and of the logical relationships of later development" (1962, p. 161). The young child's accommodation to concrete reality through direct action (e.g., maneuvering a doll into position for pushing it through the bars of his crib, and repeating the same approach in retrieving the doll) is the precursor of the thinking of a scientist who tests an abstract hypothesis in a laboratory experiment. The young child's assimilation of reality into a sensory-motor schema (e.g., applying the approach he learned with the doll to other objects, such as a yardstick or a long spoon) is the precursor of the deductive reasoning of a mature thinker.

According to Piaget's account, a child makes a transition from the sensory-motor intelligence phase into the beginning phase of conceptual intelligence at about the age of two. He first embarks on what Piaget calls the "preoperational" stage, extending from about two to seven years. Then he moves into a stage of "concrete operations," extending to about age eleven, followed by the phase of "formal operations." As we mentioned before, the chronological ages assigned to the levels of cognitive development are roughly approximate.

"Operational" Thought

The terms "operations" and "operational," as used by Piaget, have several interrelated connotations. In a mathematical sense, an operation is "some transformation indicated by rules or symbols." From a psychological standpoint, an operation is an "interiorized action" by means of which a child, as a consequence of previous interaction with his environment, mentally transforms things by imposing upon them a structure of his own. According to one definition (as translated) operations are "active schemas constructed by the mind" (1962, p. 161).

A child is performing an operation when he knowingly orders things by putting them into a series, or classifies them in a consistent manner according to a principle he understands. When, for example, a child arranges a scattering of pebbles from smallest to largest, he has transformed the pebbles into an orderly array. He gives evidence of understanding the rule underlying this transformation if he then leaves half of the pebbles ordered as they are and arranges the other half in the reverse order, from largest to smallest.

A child has likewise made a transformation according to a consistent principle when he groups a disarray of blocks according to color, disregarding other attributes such as shape or composition, or regroups them according to composition (wood and plastic) and disregards their color and shape.

A child in an advanced stage of intellectual development—the stage of "formal operations"—can apply rules of thought not only in dealing with concrete things, as in the examples above, but also in the abstract, as when he formulates a theory or hypothesis.

An operation, according to Piaget, is the essence of knowledge. The "interiorized action" of which it consists ". . . modifies the object of knowledge." In Piaget's view, knowledge is not a copy of reality, for to know an object is to act upon it; to know is to modify, to transform the object and to understand the process of this transformation (1964, p. 8).

The Pre-operational Stage

When a child enters the pre-operational stage at about age two he has begun, as we have seen, to use images and words to represent actions and things which earlier came into his ken only through sensation, concrete perceptual cues, and direct action. But in the pre-operational stage he does not yet apply a general principle that might lend order to a diversity of phenomena, or grasp a general principle that might explain diversity, such as explaining why a large cork floats in water while a small nail sinks. He does not feel it necessary to resolve the contradiction in his answers when he says, for example, that the cork *floats* because it is big and that a large lump of putty *sinks* because it is big. He can deal concretely with a relevant detail (such as size) but does not grasp the relationship between this and another relevant detail (such as weight in relation to size).

During the later part of the pre-operational period (about four to seven years), a child continues to be governed by the appearance of things, although he may be able to form rudimentary generalizations about some of them. When, for example, he sees two beakers of equal size containing water up to the same level, he correctly states that the amount of water in the two beakers is "the same." He does not, however, cling to this conclusion if the perceptual properties of the containers are changed. He is not sure, for example, that the amount of water remains the same if the contents of one of the beakers are poured into a shallow dish.

The Stage of Concrete Operations

As he enters the stage of *concrete operations* (approximately 7 to 11 years) a child begins to use elementary logic and to reason about size, space, weight, volume, number, and time. As he progresses he becomes able to apply conceptual systems to concrete things. He can order objects according to a given attribute, such as color, while recognizing also that they can be regrouped according to another property (such as size). He can order things into a series (seriation) from larger to smaller, darker to paler, heavier to lighter, and so on.

Conservation

During this stage he becomes increasingly able to apply the principle of *conservation:* the principle that certain properties remain constant and invariant regardless of changes in their appearance. When he has grasped this principle, he understands that the water from the tall beaker remains the same when poured into a shallow dish. And the process is reversible—the water remains the same if it is poured back into the beaker. Weight is conserved—remains constant, whether clay is in the form of a ball, or rolled into a sausage form, or broken into pieces, or again rolled into a ball. Likewise, the number of blocks remains the same whether they are bunched or scattered about.

When a child has grasped the principle of conservation as applied to a given attribute such as number or amount, he is governed by a conceptual as distinguished from a perceptual view of things. He has faith in what he knows and is not misled by what he sees. (The concept of conservation will be considered further in later pages.)

During this period a child also begins to reason deductively in concrete situations. If a picture shows John to be taller than Sam and another picture shows Sam to be taller than Harry, then John must be taller than Harry.

Also, during this period, a child begins to grasp the idea that it is possible to retrace a process of thought and to reverse it. If $3 + 2 = 5$; then $5 - 3 = 2$; if John is taller than Harry, then Harry is shorter than John.

A child in the concrete operations stage is capable of a wide range of logical thinking but he is still bound to concrete realities. He does not think in terms of abstract propositions. He deals with what is actual rather than speculating about where a train of thought might lead him.

Formal Operations

A child in the stage of *formal operations* can deal abstractly with the logic of things without having to deal with them concretely. He becomes increasingly able to retrace and correct his thinking, to conjecture, reflect, and to devise hypotheses and theories.

From Reflex Action to Reflective Thought

The foregoing sketch, combined with the discussion of the sensory-motor period discussed in Chapter 7, reviews some features of cognitive development as described by Piaget. At first a child's experience is limited to a few primitive reflex actions and stimulus-response reactions. Then, in keeping with his biological endowment, a child becomes increasingly a cognitive creature. His neurological organization enables him, as he matures, to incorporate the structures of reality more and more into "mental structures" or "active schemas constructed by the mind" (1962, p. 161).

He has a further potential. When he reaches the stage of "formal operations" he is able to disengage himself from his thought and examine it.

This exalted potential ability of the human mind—the ability to treat its own content and conclusions as an objective of inquiry—is not, of course, recognized only in Piaget's system. The ability of the mind "to think on thought" is recognized in the philosophy of the ancients. It was implied when Socrates invoked the Delphic admonition, *Know thyself*. Yet it is highlighted anew when we follow Piaget's account of how a child is transformed from a bundle of reflexes to a creature capable of reflection.

Concepts of Number and Quantity

Piaget's studies of conceptual development cover so wide a range that an adequate account of them would require several lengthy books.[2]

It is instructive, however, to examine his treatment of selected conceptual systems: first, the concept of number and quantity.

To grasp the concept of number, according to Piaget, it is essential for a child to grasp the concept of conservation. This means more than just the ability to count. A child may be able to count correctly the units in a group of objects without having grasped the ". . . essential idea of number: namely, that the number of objects in a group remains the same, is 'conserved' no matter how they are shuffled or arranged" (Piaget, 1953).

A child may be able to count correctly eight red chips in a row and eight blue chips in a similar row and declare that each row contains the same number of chips. But if he has not progressed beyond counting, he will not remain convinced that the number still is the same if the red ones stay as before while the blue chips are set farther apart, making a wider row, or if the blue chips are scattered. Likewise, he may be able to say that two boxes into which he has placed blue and red beads, one by one simultaneously with his right and left hands, contain the same number of beads. But now let the child pour the blue beads into an elongated receptacle. If he has not grasped the concept of conservation he may hesitate about saying that the number of beads remains the same, for there must be more blue beads in the new container if they fill it almost to the top. To one who is able to "conserve," the fact that the number of beads remains the same, no matter what the container might be, is so obvious that it seems foolish even to raise the question.

---

2 John H. Flavell's *The Developmental Psychology of Jean Piaget* (1963) offers a systematic account of Piaget's work. Millie Almy and her associates in *Young Children's Thinking* (1966) present findings and review earlier studies dealing primarily with the concept of quantity and number. The Flavell and the Almy volumes both have an imprimatur in the form of a Foreword by Piaget.

According to Piaget, "children must grasp the principle of the conservation of quantity before they can develop the concept of number." And . . . "conservation of quantity is not in itself a numerical notion; rather, it is a logical concept" (1953, p. 3). The logical concept of number develops along with the understanding of other logical concepts. To grasp the concept of number a child must understand that cardinal numbers represent units that are invariant regardless of other factors. The number 1 remains 1, whether the 1 refers to a horse, or a rabbit. If there are 10 beads, the number remains inviolate, whether they are scattered or bunched. If there are 10 pieces of fruit in a bowl, this number remains larger than the constituent parts, such as 6 bananas and 4 oranges.[3]

To understand the concept of number, a child must be able to classify objects according to similarities—such as placing round beads into one collection and square beads into another. He must also be able to order objects according to differences, such as ordering beads from larger to smaller, regardless of their shape.

When a child has formed the concept of a cardinal number (1, 2, 3, etc.), it means that he has grasped the idea of the "sameness" of 1 and 1 and the difference between 1 and 2. When he has grasped the idea of an ordinal number (first, second, third, etc.), he can apply a system of order according to any factor, such as length or weight. Moreover, he can reverse this order. When these abilities are fully developed, a child can classify things according to a number system regardless of how else the things might be ordered. He can sort all the pictures showing one object into one pile even though the objects pictured are different (e.g., one apple, one horse, one person). He can likewise put all the pictures showing two objects into another pile even though this means separating things that seemingly should go together: e.g., a picture showing both a box and a ball goes into a collection different from pictures showing a single box or a single ball. He can also place things systematically into an ordinal position (first, second, third, etc.) according to their differences, to produce, for example, a staircase effect with blocks of differing size.

According to Piaget, it is not until about the age of six and a half or seven that a typical child can utilize the concept of number. He may then acquire this concept "spontaneously" even though he may not yet have been taught to count. Moreover, Piaget maintains that "It is a great mistake to suppose that a child acquires the notion of number and other mathematical concepts just from teaching. . . . When adults try to impose mathematical concepts on a child prematurely, his learning is merely verbal; true understanding of them comes only with his own mental growth" (1953, p. 2).

---

[3] If a reader thinks this is too obvious to deserve mention he is invited to make a test. Present five- or six-year-old children with ten pieces of fruit, 6 apples and 4 oranges. Let the child count them and also make certain that he understands that apples and oranges both are called "fruit." Then ask, "Which are more, the apples or the fruit?" The child, more likely than not, will say "apples."

Tests of Piaget's Theories

Piaget's ideas concerning the development of thinking as applied to number and quantity and as applied to other phenomena such as weight, volume, space, floating objects, and the like, have inspired considerable research. Many investigators have sought to test Piaget's theories that there are orderly, sequential stages in children's thinking.

Findings have varied, but the weight of evidence has supported the position that there are qualitative changes in the nature of children's thinking during their course of growth. The changes in a child's understanding of things do not come about simply by a process of adding more of the same to what he knew before. Nor does it come about, according to Piaget, simply by associative learning. The findings have also indicated that there are wide individual variations among children in the timing (age level) of their transition from one stage to the next.

The studies aimed to test Piaget's conclusions are so numerous that only an example can be offered here. One such example is provided by a recently completed series of investigations by Almy and her associates (1966). These studies center primarily on children's ability to "conserve" number in a "discontinuous" array (separate objects) and quantity in a "continuous" state (such as an amount of liquid).

As the reader will recall, a child who *conserves* applies the principle that a given quantity remains invariant regardless of how it may be fractionated or transformed in appearance. He also applies the principle that the number of units in an aggregation remains constant no matter how these units are arranged.

Almy and her associates used both a cross-sectional and a longitudinal approach, but the present discussion will center on the most distinctive of Almy's investigations. Here she used a longitudinal approach. Children were first studied at the kindergarten level and then later in the first and second grades. The children who were tested and retested included one group of low socio-economic status and another of middle socio-economic status.

Almy and her associates used sets of blocks to test a child's ability to "conserve" number. They used containers of water to test conservation of quantity. The children were first given sample materials to make sure they understood the meaning of the terms "more than," "the same," and "just as many."

Two tasks involving number were employed. In one (Task A) a child was presented with two rows of blocks, one red the other yellow, exact in number (eleven) and recognized as such by the child. The blocks in the red row were then bunched together irregularly and the child was asked, "What about now." If he did not respond to this question, he was asked, "Are there more red blocks, or more yellow blocks, or are they the same?" A child who "conserved" would say that the number remained the same: change in the appearance did not change the number. This test was repeated by increasing the distance between the blocks in the yellow row (widening it) and changing the scatter pattern of the red blocks.

In Task B, the child was shown a row of eleven yellow blocks and asked to count them. The blocks were separated more widely, making a wider row. He was asked, "So how many blocks are there; can you tell without counting?" Then the blocks were bunched together and the child was asked, "How many now?" After each answer the child was asked, "Why do you think so?"

There were eight tasks involving conservation of an amount of liquid. In preliminary work the investigators made sure that the child understood the terms "more" and "the same" in judging the amounts of water in two identical glass tumblers. After several comparisons with varying amounts of water and with answers of "same" or "more," the child poured water into the two tumblers to make the amounts equal. Then a shallow glass bowl was brought in and water from one tumbler was poured into the bowl and the child was asked, "What about now?" [4]

Findings from the above-described parts of the study by Almy and her associates are set forth in Table 24.

_____

[4] Almy and her associates also used other tasks not discussed here.

Table 24 **Number of Children Showing Conservation Ability in Three Tasks, Two (B and A) Involving Number and One (C) Involving Quantity of Liquid, When Tested at the Kindergarten Level and Again at the First- and Second-Grade Levels.**

	Kindergarten		First Grade		Second Grade
	Fall 1961	Spring 1962	Fall 1962	Spring 1963	Fall 1963
Middle-Class Children. N=41 C. A. at last interview: 88.07 months					
No conservation	12	10	3	3	1
Conservation only on Task B	15	7	10	10	3
Conservation on both B and A	9	14	11	7	6
Conservation on B, A, C	5	10	17	21	31
Lower Class Children. N=24 C. A. at last interview: 89.71 months					
No conservation	14	11	7	3	1
Conservation only on Task B	10	9	11	11	14
Conservation on both B and A	0	2	5	4	2
Conservation on B, A, C	0	2	1	6	7

See text for description of tasks. Reproduced, by permission, from M. Almy, E. Chittenden, and P. Miller. *Young Children's Thinking: Studies of Some Aspects of Piaget's Theory.* (New York: Teachers College Press, Teachers College, Columbia University, 1966), p. 91.

As Table 24 indicates, there is a progressive increase within the middle-class group in Almy's study in the number of children who "conserved" on all three tasks, rising from about 13 per cent at the kindergarten level to about 76 per cent at the beginning of the second grade, when the average age of the children was 7 years, 4 months. The findings in this group correspond with Piaget's report that 75 per cent of the children he has studied at Geneva understood conservation at age seven.

The fact that age alone is not the determining condition stands out sharply, however, in comparisons between the middle-class and lower-class groups of children in Almy's study. At the *second grade level*, only about a third of the lower-class children "conserved" on all three tasks. Well over a third of the middle-class children had reached this level at the beginning of the *first grade*. The lower-class group also was less "mature" in a number of other respects as indicated by an intelligence test, a test of reading readiness, and other measures.

Other studies have also shown that there are wide individual variations in the age at which children reach a given level of thinking as described by Piaget. Such findings, however, have not negated Piaget's idea that a child's thinking changes, as he matures. Those who are more precocious and those who move more slowly do not differ in the basic thinking process but go from one phase to the next at a different pace.

Decline in Egocentrism. As a child advances in his ability to think conceptually, he is also moving away from a predominantly egocentric type of thinking. In the egocentric stage he does not recognize that there are realities and relationships that exist independent of his own point of view. If he is French, a German is a foreigner; but he does not realize that to a German, a Frenchman is a foreigner. He forsakes the egocentric stance (in this context) when he recognizes that the status of being a foreigner is independent of his own identity—a German is a foreigner in France and a Frenchman is a foreigner in Germany.

When he achieves the ability to "decenter," a child can, at least to some degree, contemplate another's thoughts and beliefs, even if these differ from his own. He can, to some degree, view himself objectively.

One aspect of egocentrism can be observed in a child's notions about left and right. According to Piaget (1928) it is not until about the age of eight that a child is able to place himself in the position of another person in his view of what is left and right. Before that time, he is likely to use his own egocentric locus as a reference point, rather than to think of right and left in relativistic terms.

Picture techniques were used by Gellert (1967) to study the development of ability to view right and left in relativistic terms. In two separate approaches a child faced drawings, one made by himself and another showing an adult, and he was asked either to designate the pictured hand he himself used in drawing (whether right or left) or the right and left hand of the photographed figure. The child could respond by pointing to the directly opposite pictured hand, or to point diagonally, thereby correctly indicating the right or left hand in the picture. The subjects were about 400 boys and girls aged five to about thirteen years of age. There was a high degree of correspondence between responses to drawings of one's self and photographs of another. Twenty-three per cent of the five-year-olds (boys and girls combined) designated the appropriate hand by pointing diagonally; the percentage rose to 51 at six years, and remained near that point until age nine, when 73 per cent responded correctly.[5] The percentage at age twelve was 88.

The drift away from egocentrism is likely to be quite uneven, and so is the sway of egocentrism at a given juncture of a child's life. According to Piaget, children become increasingly capable of an exchange of ideas through socialized as distinguished from egocentric speech at about the age of seven or eight. However, some children are capable of such an exchange considerably earlier. Moreover, what seems to be an ability to perceive things from someone else's standpoint appears quite strikingly in the emotional sphere when children of preschool age are able to recognize signs of distress in others and show solicitous sympathy for the one who is in distress. Furthermore, some children at four years, or even younger, are able to speak quite objectively about their own feelings—as in an earlier example of a child who warned his parents: "Don't bother me, I'm in a bad mood." (Children's ability to recognize their own and others' feelings is discussed in Chapters 10 and 14.)

The unevenness of the egocentric orientation can be seen when a person—child or adult—views himself quite objectively under some conditions but reverts to egocentric thinking when his prejudices take command of his thoughts.

Other Aspects of Children's Thinking

Inductive Reasoning

In a study by Burt (1919) tests were made of the ability of English children at various age levels to reason inductively—that is, from the particular to the general—and their ability to handle arguments that proceed by eliminating in succession each of a number of alternative hypotheses except the right one.

At seven years, for example, children could solve this problem:

---

[5] When Piaget names an age for the appearance of a given response, he usually means that about three-fourths of the children at that age exhibit it. As can be seen, it was not until age nine that about three-fourths of the children in Gellert's study made the correct response.

Tom runs faster than Jim; Jack runs slower than Jim: Who is the slowest, Jim or Jack or Tom?

At eight years, the children solved a problem, such as this, which likewise called for elimination of untenable hypotheses:

I don't like sea voyages, and I don't like the seaside. I must spend Easter either in France, or among the Scottish Hills, or on the South Coast. Which shall it be?

It was not until a later age, near the end of the elementary-school period, however, that the children were able to solve a problem calling for the discovery of a general rule from a number of particular instances, such as:

One pound of meat should roast for half an hour; two pounds, three-quarters of an hour; three pounds, one hour; eight pounds, two-and-a-quarter hours; nine pounds, two-and-a-half hours. From this, can you discover a simple rule by which you can tell from the weight of a joint how long it should roast?

Reasoning from an Abstract Proposition

In time, most children are able not only to apply a general proposition which they know or believe to be true but also are able to reason in terms of a hypothesis which for the time being is supposed to be true. Eventually, a large proportion of people are able also to reason from the standpoint of a proposition that assumes what is contrary to what they regard as fact ("If Columbus had not discovered America, it is likely that. . . .").

Some persons eventually achieve, with varying degrees of success, the ability to reason in terms of a proposition that goes contrary to their wishes, although this is not an easy task. The writer observed an example of this in a fifth-grade discussion of current events prior to World War II. A boy reported his current event in the form of a question: "There will be no war if the president of what country gives in to Hitler's demands?" At the time, Hitler was making demands on Czechoslovakia, and the idea behind the boy's question was that if the Czechoslovakian government yielded, Hitler would not start a war. When no one else ventured an answer, the boy himself answered that if the president of Czechoslovakia yielded to Hitler there would be no war. But many children protested that this answer was wrong. When the teacher let the children debate the issue, it was apparent that most members of the class were arguing the merits of Hitler's demands and not the substance of the boy's question. The class argument was: What right has Hitler to ask for this territory? How would you like it if you were a Czechoslovakian? and so on. The boy who first raised the issue maintained that he was not arguing the merits of the demands, he was simply arguing that *if* the Czechoslovakians yielded there would be no war between Czechoslovakia and Germany. When a vote was taken, almost every pupil in the class voted that the boy who had presented the proposition had lost the debate.

Other Differences in the Reasoning of Older and Younger Persons

Various studies have shown that when older and younger persons are confronted with a similar problem the older ones usually are more deliberate in their procedure, turning the matter over in their minds, whereas children are more likely to forge ahead in overt trial and error. Also, as we might expect, adults are likely to reach a conclusion or correct answer more quickly and to see the point more readily. On all these points there are, of course, wide individual differences both among children and adults. The more mature person also is better able to perceive the inevitable and to accept objective facts. The older person is also better able to understand ideas which a child can apply in a practical way without being able to formulate the underlying principle. A youngster applies many scientific principles in his everyday actions. He uses a stick to pry a stone out of the ground or props up a plank so that he can push his wagon from the ground onto the porch. He can do this without having abstract knowledge of the principle of the lever or of the principle of the inclined plane.

Young children's explanations of natural phenomena often are naive and self-contradictory and when pressed, they may resort to animistic or magical answers. A child is giving an animistic explanation, when, for example, he is asked, "Why does an icicle fall to the ground?" and answers, "Because it wants to." He seems to endow the icicle with a life and will of its own. However, reasoning that seems to be animistic may be more a manner of speaking than a manner of thinking. When a child speaks of an object as being alive, he does not necessarily mean that it is able to see or think or have a will of its own (Klingensmith, 1953). He may be using the term "alive" or an equivalent term to denote activity rather than life: e.g., a clock is alive in the sense that it ticks. In everyday speech children hear many animistic expressions: the motor that was dead has "come to life"; this is a "live wire"; the wind is "sighing"; this is a "stubborn knot." Moreover, when adults are called upon to deal with wholly unfamiliar material they also frequently give answers that are animistic or even mystical. In one study (Oakes, 1947), thirty-five college faculty members were faced with a number of experiments which demonstrated certain principles of physics and were asked to predict what would happen and to give an explanation of what did happen. The answers ranged from precise explanations to what have been regarded as typically "childish" answers. Twenty-three comments made by eighteen different adults bordered on the mystical and magical: "It's a long time since I studied any science. Maybe nature has changed a little," or "It seems a bit unfair that the iron doesn't get there first."

Awareness of People

One form of expansion in the child's world appears in the child's awareness of people in the world at large. An example of this change appears when children name the persons whom they admire. In one study, in the age range from six to eight, 58 per cent of the characters named by the children as heroes and ideals belonged to the immediate everyday environment of the children. At the age of twelve about a third belonged in this category. Only about one-third of the persons named by the younger children were historical or public characters—people not in the child's immediate environment; at the age of twelve almost two-thirds of the characters were in this category (Hill, 1930).

Widened Response to the World at Large

A child's intellectual life expands also through an increased interest in happenings in the world outside his own immediate day-to-day existence. Table 25, based on a study of what children said during free discussion periods in the classroom, illustrates this.

Table 25 Subject Matter, Content, and Source of Experiences Represented in Topics Contributed During Class Discussion in Grades 2, 4 and 6

Subject and Source	62 Second-graders	54 Fourth-graders	45 Sixth-graders
Subject Matter Content:			
Personal activity	61%	41%	18%
Animals	10	7	8
Books, radio, movies	7	13	6
Current happenings in world at large	18	29	60
Miscellaneous	4	10	9
Medium of Acquisition:			
Personal presence	83	52	25
Reflection	1	15	18
Other media (books, magazines, radio, theater, personal conversation)	16	31	56
Unknown	0	2	1

* Adapted from H. V. Baker, *Children's Contributions in Elementary School General Discussion*, Child Development Monographs (New York: Teachers College, Columbia University, 1942), No. 29, pp. 32-33.

One conspicuous change, as we can see, is a decided drop from the second to the sixth grade in discussion of topics relating to a child's own personal activities and experiences. At the second grade, 61 per cent of all contributions dealt with personal activities and experiences as contrasted with 18 per cent at the sixth grade.

There was a corresponding increase from the second to the sixth grade in contributions dealing with world and domestic news, and with activities of people other than the child himself. A change also appeared in the extent to which children were preoccupied with events they had directly witnessed, whether or not they themselves were the main actors in an event. At the second grade, most of the topics or items of information discussed by the children dealt with matters that had actually happened in their lives or in their presence (83 per cent of contributions fell in this category). At the sixth grade, however, only about one-fourth of the contributions dealt with matters that the children had become aware of through personal experience or direct contact.

When older children deal more than the younger ones with world affairs and with events unrelated to their day-to-day experience, many of them probably are simply conforming to what is expected in school. It is likely that most of these youngsters in their out-of-school conversations concentrate more on topics that are of immediate practical and personal concern than on the problems of the Middle East or on the natural resources of Alaska (the same probably also holds true for their teachers). The findings do not indicate how much meaning the news items pertaining to world affairs have for the children but they do indicate that the youngsters are at least able to handle the formal academic aspects of such topics.

Table 26   **Percentage of Children in the Age Range from Five to Twelve Whose First Wish was for Specific Things or for More General Benefits**

Other categories not reproduced bring the total at each level to 100 per cent

Type of Wish	Age Groups				IQ Groups		
	5-6	7-8	9-10	11-12	120 and above	100-119	80-99
Specific material objects and possessions	55.	48.	26.	14.	23.3	38.3	47.9
General benefits for self and others	8.	14.	22.	27.	25.6	17.1	8.3

Adapted from A. T. Jersild, F. V. Markey, and C. L. Jersild, *Children's Fears, Dreams, Wishes, Daydreams, Likes, Dislikes, Pleasant and Unpleasant Memories,* Child Development Monographs (New York: Teachers College, Columbia University, 1933), No. 12, 172 pp. Reproduced by permission. This version omits comparisons between boys and girls and between school groups that are included in the original table.

Increased Capacity for Generalizing

During the elementary school years and beyond, a child acquires increased ability to use general and inclusive categories of thought. This ability to think in terms of the more inclusive concepts is illustrated when children express their wishes. A younger child might wish, for example, for a football, a football helmet, a football suit, while an older child, instead of devoting three wishes to different objects, might wish for money to buy a football outfit and still have two wishes left. In one such study, in which children aged five to twelve were asked to name three wishes, the responses were tabulated under a number of headings including one that represented wishes for specific material objects and another that included wishes for general benefits for self and others. The percentages are shown in Table 26.

Children's Information

Inquiries into the "content of children's minds" give an interesting picture of what children know and do not know. Almost all children are informed on some topics while only a few possess items of information which most educated adults take for granted. Tables 27 and 28 give illustrative findings. The first of these tables is based in part on carefully conducted studies of kindergarten children in Minneapolis, Minnesota, in 1928 and again, with some modifications, in 1954-1955.

The influence of television was especially noteworthy in the 1954-1955 results. Two prominent television personalities (Howdy Doody and Arthur Godfrey) were identified by considerably more children than the president of the United States or the former president (who also made television appearances, but not so frequently). In the 1954-1955 results, differences between boys and girls and between children of higher and lower socio-economic status were not as great as in 1928.

The answers children give when their information is tested often yield many clues to the flow of a child's thoughts, as illustrated by the following replies in the study cited above: A carpenter fixes carpet sweepers or repairs cars; the Great Northern (railroad) is the North star; butter is made from buttermilk or butterflies make it; plants, seeds, and flowers are manufactured in the Ford plant; a plumber plumbs, pulls out plums, or sells plumbers; beans grow in gardens but bees make them. The source of incorrect answers may be obscure, as when a child asserts that a man who raises corn or wheat is called a "bachelor" (Probst, 1931).

A further brief sampling of children's information concerning certain topics is shown in Table 28. This table is based on results obtained by the

Table 27 Selected Results of Information Test Administered to 100 Children, Aged 5 Years and 4 Months to 6 Years

The values show the percentage of children who answered each question correctly. Some of the items and questions have been abbreviated in the present table.

Test Items	Percentage Answering Correctly
Local Points of Interest: *	
Tell me the name of a Minneapolis newspaper	85
What is the name of a lake in Minneapolis?	27
What is the Mississippi?	78
What is the Great Northern?	39
Time and Number:	
How many pennies in a dime?	22
What time of year do flowers grow outdoors?	99
How many eggs in a half a dozen?	12
What time or what o'clock is it at noon?	30
How many pennies in a nickel?	37
Animals, Birds, and Insects:	
How many legs has a horse?	100
From what are little chickens hatched?	63
What do bees make that we eat?	59
A baby dog is called a puppy; what is a baby cow called?	26
Plants and Flowers:	
What do apples grow on?	97
What color is wheat when it is ripe?	35
What do we call the part of the plant underground?	32
What do we eat that grows on vines?	29
Occupations and Industries:	
Who makes money by cutting hair?	96
What does a plumber do?	60
What is butter made from?	40
Where does coal come from?	32
Simple Mechanics:	
What do you see on the ground that trains run on?	98
What is the brake on an automobile for?	55
How are trees made into boards?	19
What is a thermometer for?	50
Current Topics and Miscellaneous: †	
What is a helicopter?	47
Who is Dwight D. Eisenhower?	51
Who is Harry Truman?	12
Who is Howdy Doody?	96
Who is Arthur Godfrey?	83

* The first six sections of this table are adapted from C. A. Probst, "A General Information Test for Kindergarten Children," *Child Development*, 1931, 2:81-95.
† The last section of this table is adapted from M. C. Templin, "General Information of Kindergarten Children: A Comparison with the Probst Study After 26 Years," *Child Development*, 1958, 29:87-96. The original tables report separate scores for boys and girls and for different occupational groups. For an earlier study of children's informations, see Hall (1891).

Table 28 Percentage of Children in Greater New York Choosing Correct Alternative Answer or Supplying Correct Answer to Various Items of an Information Test

Abridged and adapted from an unpublished study by the writer

Test Item	Percentage of Children Giving Correct Answer				
	Age 8	Age 9	Age 10	Age 11	Age 12*
The sun rises in the: (a) east; (b) north; (c) west; (d) south	54	51	63	66	71
The moon sets in the: (a) east; (b) north; (c) west; (d) south	29	40	35	50	49
Up the Hudson River is: (a) east; (b) north; (c) west; (d) south	29	50	59	54	65
To the Rocky Mountains is: (a) east; (b) north; (c) west; (d) south	10	34	53	59	70
A boy walks a mile in about: (a) 1 hour; (b) 2 hours; (c) 25 minutes; (d) 5 minutes	27	44	58	52	47
Which is bigger, a corn plant or a wheat plant?	54	58	66	77	77
Which is bigger, a duck or a goose?	92	84	91	89	79
Which of the following is known as: (a) a President; (b) an actor; (c) a prizefighter:					
Hoover?	45	66	76	84	95
Roosevelt?	93	97	96	99	100
Joe Louis?	79	92	96	98	95
Clark Gable?	87	96	98	98	100
From what animal do we get:					
Bacon?	41	51	67	63	65
Beef?	48	48	62	74	78
Pork?	32	65	84	92	91
Does a mother .... have milk for her baby? †					
Elephant?	18	16	23	18	20
Wolf?	19	19	28	32	20
Goat?	69	81	90	91	93
Do the following grow: (a) on vines; (b) in the ground; (c) on trees; (d) on bushes:					
Watermelons?	10	17	45	48	45
Carrots?	65	80	73	91	93
Apples?	98	96	99	99	98
Which of the following comes from: (a) an animal; (b) a mine; (c) a plant; (d) the air:					
Linen?	29	50	69	68	83
Salt?	30	44	74	82	85
Sugar?	44	58	75	82	80
Cotton?	42	75	87	90	92
Leather?	63	68	82	92	80
Coal?	64	82	94	96	92
Wool?	89	93	95	93	94
Meat?	92	100	91	99	100

* The twelve-year-olds were not as representative as the younger children, since they included no pupil above the sixth grade.

† Introductory item: A mother cow has milk for her baby, but a mother hen does not. Does a mother .... have milk for her baby?

writer during the 1940's in a study of about 500 children, aged eight to twelve years, most of whom were pupils in public schools in New York City. The younger children were interviewed; the older ones wrote their answers on individual test blanks. The percentages shown in this table might be different if a similar study were made today or if rural rather than urban children were questioned.

On many of the items in Table 28 the percentage of children who answered correctly would no doubt be considerably lower if guesses were eliminated. On some items, the percentage of correct answers is not much larger than could be expected by chance.

Certain comparisons, not reproduced in the table, revealed considerable differences between brighter and duller children. In one public school, the children in two bright classes were correct on 67 per cent of the questions concerning directions (e.g., If you go *up* the Hudson River do you go north? south? east? west?) as compared with a score of only 28 per cent in the case of older children in four classes of less intelligent children. The difference between the bright and dull children was not so wide, however, in answers to questions which they could answer on the basis of everyday observation (such as the question about where apples grow).

Erroneous Beliefs and Misconceptions

From their own childhood practically all adults can recall harboring many erroneous impressions and false beliefs and misinterpreting words and phrases. These misconceptions throw some light on the difficulties children have in incorporating the ideas presented to them by others.

Mistaken beliefs frequently arise by chance or through the solemn testimony of a playmate. Unless a child, through somewhat bitter experience, has learned to distrust others, he is prone to accept as true anything told to him that is not contradicted by his own experience or by some higher authority. Here are some of the things believed by one child. A swallowed hair will turn into a worm; a swallowed apple seed may sprout in the stomach; a withered spot on the lawn or in the pasture means that the ground is hollow underneath and, if one lands on such a spot hard enough, he may sink all the way to China; the devil comes when people whistle.

Misconceptions may likewise arise through malicious remarks made by adults concerning individuals against whom they are prejudiced. Such remarks are often elaborated by children and passed along to others. Thus, a boy of nine believed that members of a certain small religious denomination could spit blood whenever they wanted to and that children would catch a bad disease by using a toilet that was used by members of another denomination.

Faulty perception of a word may lead to confusion. At the dinner table a boy devoutly closed his eyes and folded his hands when his mother said, "Now we are to have pears" ("pears" at the time, was his pronunciation of the word "prayers"). A boy, after finishing his bedtime prayer said, "Mama, I want to say the wort prayer." After some questioning it became clear: He wanted the prayer used by his older sister, "Our Father Who'rt in heaven." A boy in a geography class, hearing his teacher discuss "the earth as a whole," was so lost in thought trying to picture the earth as a hole that he failed a few moments later to answer a question put to him by his teacher and got a sharp rebuke.

Many of the more obvious misconceptions involve misinterpretation or lack of understanding of words and phrases. Thus a child was overheard giving this version of the pledge of allegiance to the flag: "I pledge a legion to the flag of the Republic of Richard Sands; one nation and a vegetable with liberty and justice to all." Another sang: "Long train run over us" ("Long to reign over us"); and another patriotically intoned: "I love thy rots and chills" ("rocks and rills"). After a moment's hesitation on a line in "The Night Before Christmas," a child came forth with: "I rushed to the window and vomited (threw up) the sash." One youngster for several years patriotically sang, "the grandpas we watched were so gallantly screaming."

Children may be able to deliver the right answers without actually knowing the meanings of the words they are using. For instance, a girl came home from school and excitedly announced that she now knew where hens lay their eggs: "They lay their eggs on the average." Her teacher had told the class that hens, in the laying season, lay one egg a day, *on the average*.

Understanding Academic Terms and Concepts

In their school work, children are often called upon to use ideas when they have little understanding of the underlying meanings of the individual terms and ideas. This was first demonstrated in a study by Scott and Meyers in 1923. The chances are that a similar study today would reveal as much or perhaps even more misunderstanding. A child may correctly give the name of a colony, of an explorer, and so on, and yet have only a hazy notion of just what an explorer or a colony *is*. On a test, a child may be able correctly to identify Benjamin Franklin as a *minister* to France, but still wonder why we sent a *clergyman*, with a big wig and tight breeches over to preach to the Frenchmen. A child may fail for a long time to see any relationship between the taxes he reads about in his history class and the extra pennies he pays as sales tax in making a small purchase.

Vague Concepts of Time

Through concrete experience in the day's routine, a child has opportunities gradually to formulate notions of what is meant by a minute or a day, although much confusion often prevails, partly because of vagueness in adult usage (such as "Just a minute" which sometimes stretches to an hour).

Young children refer to the present before they refer to the future, and deal with the future before they seem to have clear ideas about the past (Ames, 1946). The word "today" was used by children in one study at about twenty-four months, "tomorrow" at thirty months, and "yesterday" at thirty-six months (Ames, 1946).

Children's ideas of historical time, in terms of decades, centuries, or epochs are likely to be quite hazy until they are well along in school. Even in high school some youngsters have difficulty in grasping concepts of duration and sequence in connection with historical events and movements.

Much that a child is exposed to in history lessons, or in units on Ancient Egypt, or on the Early American Indian (not to mention units in geology dealing with the age of the earth!) is lost upon him as far as time relations are concerned. In one fifth-grade class, the children were discussing the Appalachian Mountains, and the teacher took the opportunity to question them on what they had retained from previous discussions of the age of the earth. The question, "How old do you think those mountains are?" stumped the group, until a hardy youngster answered, "I think those mountains came here at about the same time as the Pilgrim Fathers."

Findings indicate that children's ability to grasp subject matter in the areas commonly known as the "social studies" depends in part upon a process of maturing and upon experiences associated with the fact of growing older. Children's knowledge in these areas does not increase in proportion to the length of time devoted to them (Eaton, 1944). We have no assurance, for example, that a child who has studied history in school since he entered fourth grade will have a significantly more profound grasp of historical concepts at the end of the sixth grade than a child of similar mental ability who first began to study history when he entered the sixth grade.

Factors Facilitating Conceptual Development

It has long been held that schools should teach children "how to think." The foregoing discussion suggests, however, that there often is a discrepancy between the ideas teachers (and textbooks) are trying to teach and what children actually comprehend.

The school curriculum has, to a large extent, grown out of pedagogical and scholarly traditions, with relatively little attention to adapting the ideas that are taught to a child's thought processes, scaling and pacing what is taught according to a child's growing intellectual capacities, or testing to find whether a child has learned to think or just to memorize.

One essential issue in "teaching children to think" is the relative role of maturation and experience in the development of children's thinking. Through the years, this issue has received some attention, but not nearly as much as it deserves. The role of maturation has been considered in connection with children's readiness for reading, although studies in this area dealt more with measures of "reading readiness" than with an inquiry into how children happen to have reached, or have failed to reach, a given level of "reading readiness."

Studies with older children indicate that the timing of what is taught in terms of maturity level makes a difference. A relatively short period of training at a more mature level may produce as much progress in the mastery of some ideas and intellectual skills as a longer period of training begun earlier. In an experiment by Benezet (1935) many of the formal steps in arithmetic were postponed beyond the early grade levels when they customarily had been introduced. When these exercises in arithmetic were taught at the sixth- and seventh-grade levels children rapidly mastered them. Pupils in classes involved in the experiment were able within a relatively short period to do as well as agemates who had been in regular classes and who had had several previous years of instruction. Those whose formal training in arithmetic had been postponed not only were spared a good deal of time and effort but had the additional advantage of learning other things in the time so saved. A study by Pistor (1940) deals with the role of maturity level in the development of time concepts. A time-concept test was given to two groups of sixth-grade pupils, aged ten, eleven, and twelve years. One group had previously, in the fourth and fifth grades, received systematic training in both history and geography and during the sixth grade the concept of historical time was taught to them quite intensively. The children of the other group had received training primarily in geography alone, with only incidental attention to historical matters. In the seventh grade the average scores of the two groups of children were practically equal. Special emphasis on time concepts in one case, and absence of special attention to such concepts in the other, had not produced any significant differences.

These limited studies, conducted many years ago, suggest that it might be a good idea to examine the whole teaching program from the standpoint of the role of maturation.

Interest in the relative roles of experience and maturation has been revived by Piaget's studies of cognitive development. Investigators are asking, can a child's transition from one stage of thinking to the next be expedited by special training?

According to Piaget, the adaptation process underlying the development of thinking is facilitated by four main factors. One is *maturation*. This involves an increasing capacity, through growth of the nervous system, to absorb, to discriminate, to register, and to manipulate data. Another factor is *experience*, which feeds the mind from empirical sources of information. Another is *social facilitation*, which presses a child to formulate his thoughts to himself so he can express them to others. The fourth is *equilibration* or self-regulation. Equilibration involves the two processes of adaptation described in an earlier chapter: assimilation and accommodation. Through "equilibration" a child reorganizes his view of things when he is aware of contradictions within his thinking. It also leads him to re-organize his ideas when, within his level of awareness, his thinking is contradicted by observable facts. The modifier "within his level of awareness" is an important one, for at a given stage a child is not troubled by contradictions which he himself will remedy later on.

Two of these factors have attracted particular attention. One is the role of maturation and the other, even more emphatically, the role of experience. There seems to be a compulsion among psychologists and educators to assume that if something gradually comes about through growth and experience it should be possible to hasten it by piling on more experience. If a child ordinarily is able to "conserve" at the age of six or seven or eight, why not saturate him with experience so he can "conserve" at four or five? [6]

The Influence of Training on Conceptual Development

A number of efforts have been made to find whether the transition from one level of thinking to another can be hastened by extra instruction or special training. In the main, the findings have indicated that a child's pace cannot be altered materially. But the issue is still in doubt. Piaget himself, in many contexts, has taken a rather skeptical view of what can be done to accelerate the development of a child's cognitive capacities. He constantly emphasizes that turning points in a child's cognitive development emerge from the child's own spontaneous discoveries. This does not, of course, mean that thinking develops without experience. Rather, it means that the factor of maturation is an essential but not a sufficient condition for cognitive development. Likewise, experience is an essential but not a sufficient factor. Available evidence indicates that special training is more likely to have an effect if the child is teetering on the brink of moving into a new phase of thought. He may be helped over the hump, so to speak.

In an interesting experiment, Smedslund (1961) worked with two groups of children. Children in one group were able to "conserve" and children in another group were not able to "conserve" weight. Children who initially were unable to conserve were shown, by means of a balance scale, that two objects weighed the same even after the shape of one had been changed. After some instruction these children correctly said that objects shown to weigh the same when first presented continued to weigh the same when the shape of one of them had been altered. Smedslund then presented these chil-

---

[6] The writer is indebted to a student-colleague, Miss Judith Spitler (1966) for a thoughtful paper on this subject, "Educational Implications of the Theories of Jean Piaget." Miss Spitler contrasts the go-getter "more-sooner-faster" approach to learning by American psychologists and educators with the more somber view that a child learns what he is ready to learn, regardless of what is heaped upon him.

dren, and children who already were conserving when the experiment began, with a new set of conditions. They were shown, for example, two plasticene balls and were told that they weighed the same. Then one of the balls was changed into a sausage shape. Unknown to the children, a piece was removed from the sausage. The children were then asked to tell whether they would weigh the same, or whether one would weigh more, and, if so, which one, when weighed on the balance. When the balance showed that the ball actually weighed more, all the children who had learned to conserve during the experiment reverted to non-conservation. They exhibited little surprise but switched to their previous answers based on the perceptual appearance of the objects (e.g., the ball weighs more because it is rounder and fatter). On the other hand, children who were able to conserve when the experiment began were not so readily converted. Six of them (in a group of thirteen) refused to yield to the notion that a change in shape could produce a change in weight. They said, for example, "I think you have taken away some of the clay," or "We must have lost some of the clay on the floor." Apparently, these children who had learned to conserve in their own way had confidence in what they knew rather than in what they saw.

The effects of instruction on children's ability to solve "class inclusion" problems was investigated by Miller (1966) in an experiment involving ninety kindergarten and ninety second-grade children. Miller used a variety of sets of materials, such as blue and red metal toy cars. These materials gave the children an opportunity (1) to classify according to given attributes, such as the color *blue and red*; and (2) to classify according to a more inclusive category, which would comprise all *metal* cars, whether blue or red; and to show (3) whether they grasped the idea that class based on an attribute common to all objects in a collection (metal, in this example) is more inclusive (larger; has "more" cars) than either of its two sub-classes.

Given eight blue cars and four red ones, all metal, a child capable of classification can sort them according to color and correctly state that there are more blues than reds. But if he does not understand class inclusion, he is likely again to say "blue" when asked "Are there more blue cars, or more metal cars, or are they the same?"

The children at each grade level were divided into three groups. One served as a control group, tested initially and then retested at the end of the experiment. The two other groups received instruction during six individual training sessions (following pre-tests and followed by post-tests), lasting from ten to fifteen minutes each and spaced approximately a week apart.

One of these two groups received training only in related classification activities (without formal and explicit instruction in "class inclusion logic"). The other group, at the sixth session, received direct instruction.

Instruction in "related" classification activities included work with a wide range of objects and materials which the children were told to sort in various ways, manually, or by drawing a circle around the appropriate items, or putting them into sections of interlocking rings. The activities involved classification of objects that could be classed in many different ways, such as according to color, then according to use; simultaneous sorting according to two common attributes such as being similar in both color and form; classification by subtraction and addition to produce sub-classes and superordinate classes. Through these activities the children had repeated opportunities to classify in various ways and to notice, for example, whether a grouping which included all the metal cars contained more cars, and whether a grouping including only the red (metal) or the blue (also metal) contained fewer cars.

The instruction in "class inclusion logic" given to one of the two trained groups in the sixth training session was direct and explicit. If a child gave the wrong answer (to any or each in a series of classification tasks involving a variety of materials) the experimenter repeatedly questioned him until he found the right answer such as, "You need a bigger circle to hold the metal cars because there are more of them." The experimenter would confirm this by continuing to impress on the child that there were metal cars and turning them over so only the metal (and not the coloring) was visible.

As interpreted by Miller, the results in Table 29 (and in other divisions of her study) demonstrate both the effectiveness of training and the importance of maturation. A number of children at both the kindergarten and second-grade levels benefited from training. But gains were greatest at the more mature level. Almost twice as many second-graders as kindergarten children benefited (according to the criteria used in the study) when they received direct instruction in the logic of class inclusion. A bit over four times as many of the older children, as compared with the younger ones, benefited from instruction in related activities only.

In a review of findings from a number of studies, Almy (1966) points out that the question of what is involved in the transition from one stage of thinking to the next, and what might be done to expedite this transition, is far from settled.[7]

According to Piaget, if a child is exposed to an "inexhaustible stock of concepts" he "begins by borrowing from this collection only as much as suits him, remaining disdainfully ignorant of everything that exceeds his mental level, and again, that which is borrowed is assimilated in accordance with his intellectual structure." (Piaget, 1950, p. 159.)

The case for disciplined instruction in concept formation as against self-directed discovery has been pressed vigorously by the Russian psychologist, Vygotsky (English translation, 1962). According to Vygotsky, the concepts a child forms spontaneously through his own experience differ from, and do not adequately realize, the concepts he can acquire through instruction.

---

[7] The educational implications of cognitive development have been explored by Bruner (1960) and Almy (1966) among others. A three-year research program by Almy, still in progress (1967), deals with the effects of planned instructional programs on cognitive development in the early grades.

Table 29 Percentage of Children who Learned the Logic of Class Inclusion after Receiving a Given Type of Instruction Compared with a Control Group

The criterion for having learned the logic was correct solution of 8 out of 10 class inclusion problems

	Instructional Groups		Control Group
Grade and performance	Five sessions of instruction in related classification activities plus one session of direct instruction in class inclusion logic	Six sessions with instruction in related classification activities only	Pre-tests and post-tests but no instruction
Kindergarten	N=30	N=30	N=30
Number of children who learned the inclusion logic	14	3	0
Percentage of children who learned the inclusion logic	46.66%	10.00%	0
95% confidence intervals for percent who learned	28%-66%	2%-27%	0
Second Grade	N=30	N=30	N=30
Number of children who learned the inclusion logic	25	13	0
Percentage of children who learned the inclusion logic	83.33%	43.33%	0
95% confidence intervals for percentage who learned	65%-94%	25%-65%	0

Reproduced by permission from Paula Miller, *The Effects of Age and Training on Children's Ability to Understand Certain Basic Concepts.* Unpublished Ph.D. Dissertation (New York: Teachers College, Columbia University, 1966.)

Actually, as he concedes, Piaget judiciously takes account not only of ideas formed mainly through a child's own spontaneous efforts but also those deliberately promoted by the influence of adults. But he believes that Piaget relies too much on a child's spontaneously arrived at concepts.

In keeping with his general emphasis on the need for intellectual discipline, Vygotsky, in dealing specifically with language points out that there is a great difference between spoken speech, largely acquired spontaneously, and written speech (largely acquired through instruction). According to Vygotsky, the grammar of thought is not the same as the grammar of speech. Written speech requires a deliberate structure such as is not demanded in spoken speech. Anyone who has tried to transform what seemed to be lucid oral lectures into a comprehensibly written book must ruefully agree with Vygotsky.

"Cognitive Style"

The development of perception, imagination, and thinking is not confined to changes in the functioning of the intellect. It is embedded in a larger matrix of developments in the motor, social, and emotional spheres. There are some modes of perceiving and thinking that reflect currents within the personality as a whole rather than simply a cognitive process.

Concrete and Abstract
Cognitive Orientation

An interesting account of the interplay between cognitive development and aspects of personality development has been offered by Goldfarb (1955). As the reader may recall from Chapter 11, Goldfarb found a defect in the thinking abilities of many of the children in his study who had been committed to institutional care, and who were retained under institutional care while other children were being placed for adoption. These children, when older, showed impaired conceptual ability. They did poorly, for example, when presented with material that can be sorted or grouped according to a conceptual classification scheme. (One such test consists of twelve pieces of cardboard in four colors and three shapes; a child is asked to put together those pieces that belong together.)

According to Goldfarb, difficulty in conceptual thinking in children who have suffered from deprivation is linked with other difficulties. They tend to be impulsive, restless, unable to concentrate. They have difficulty in delaying the execution of an impulse and in anticipating an outcome. Their lack of inhibition is a lack of planfulness and foresight which, according to Goldfarb, are essential to conceptual thought.

Intellectual Development
as Related to Drive Level

A child's level of intellectual functioning may be associated with traits of temperament or personality that are manifested in his general behavior. Studies by Sontag and his associates (1958) suggest that children's gains or losses in IQ with the passage of time are related to such factors as dependence and independence, and motivation to master and achieve, or lack of such motivation.

Analytic vs. Thematic Approaches

Children have been found to differ in their tendency to view things analytically, noting distinctive details in a complex stimulus, as distinguished from responding to a complex field in a more global fashion, drawing inferences, or giving attention to relationships within the field (Kagan, *et al.*, 1963; Kagan, 1964).

One series of tests used by Kagan consists of thirty cards, each presenting line drawings of three familiar objects. In responding to each set of three drawings, a child is asked to select two things that are alike or go together in some way.

When presented, for example, with pictures of line drawings of a man, a watch, and a ruler, a person with an analytic turn of mind might pick out the watch and the ruler, saying, "The watch and ruler have numbers."

In a non-analytic response a child might select the man and the watch, saying, "The man needs to know the time" (an inference that does not follow from what is objectively portrayed) or "The man wears a watch" (assuming a relationship that is not actually portrayed).

Youngsters tended to show a considerable degree of consistency in giving analytic or non-analytic responses. Moreover, Kagan and his associates found interesting characteristics associated with the tendency to be analytic or non-analytic. The youngsters who came forth with many analytic concepts were less distractible in the classroom and less likely to show restless activity on the playground or when confined to a restricting laboratory setting. They were less likely impulsively to give incorrect solutions. They were more likely to become involved in tasks requiring long periods of concentration and they expressed preference for intellectual vocations that required little motor activity. When asked to make drawings, their drawings were more complete.

"Analytical-Global Field Approach"

Two "styles" of perception have been identified by Witkin and his associates (1962), one originally called "field-independent" and the other "field-dependent." A person who is field-independent is able to pursue a perceptual objective—to concentrate on one element in the context in which it is contained—in spite of confusing features in the perceptual field. One situation used to study this characteristic is known as the body-adjustment test. A person sits in a chair which can be tilted clockwise or counter-clockwise. This chair is located in a small room which can also be tilted clockwise or counterclockwise, independent of the chair. The subject is instructed to keep his body upright. Some persons (field independent) keep their bodies close to the true upright, regardless of the tilt of the surrounding field. Others, to perceive their bodies as upright, align themselves with the surrounding field.

Another test is a rod-and-frame test. Here again the objective is to maintain an upright position, this time of the rod. Stable cues that a person usually employs to maintain something in a vertical position are eliminated. The rod is pivoted in a luminous frame which can be tilted clockwise or counterclockwise. Only the rod and luminous frame are visible in the darkened room. The subject is asked to move the tilted rod to an upright position while the frame remains tilted. Some persons adjust the rod to the axes of the tilted frame. Others adjust it independently of this context.

Another test, quite different in structure, is an "embedded-figure" test. The subject is asked to locate figures embedded in complex designs (a simple version of this would be to locate the X in a series of figures which includes ⬭).

Field-dependent persons have more difficulty with this test than field-independent persons. Performance in these situations (and in others Witkin and his associates have used) tends to be consistent from test to test. Moreover, although the two groups do not differ materially in general intelligence, those who are independent in their perceptions do better in mental tests requiring analytical ability. For this reason, Witkin and his associates changed the designation of the cognitive style they at first studied on a perceptual level to "analytical-global field approach." This approach involves a tendency, at the analytical extreme, to experience items as discrete from an organized context, and at the global extreme "a tendency to experience items as fused with context" (p. 180). Persons who are "analytic" or "global" in their approach to the tasks noted above tend to show corresponding behavior in various other intellectual tasks.

Reflectiveness and Impulsiveness

In almost any classroom there are children who immediately speak out or wave their hands when the teacher asks a question, while others seem to stop and think. Interesting studies by Kagan (1964) have indicated that some children quite characteristically are intellectually *impulsive* while others are characteristically *reflective*. The impulsive children as described by Kagan "have a fast conceptual tempo." They come forth with the first answer they can think of. The reflective ones, on the other hand, take time to think before they speak, as though weighing the problem and evaluating alternative answers. The impulsive child seems more concerned about delivering a quick response. The reflective child acts as though he would rather give a correct response than a quick one.

One of the tests used by Kagan and his associates required a child to identify geometrical forms or familiar objects hidden behind a screen by exploring them with his hands and fingers. Having finished his exploring and withdrawing his hands, the child was shown five forms or objects and asked to designate the one which corresponded to the one he had explored by touch.

It was possible to derive three scores from these tests: the amount of time the child spent in tactual exploration, his response time when shown the five forms from which he had to choose, and his errors. Other tests in the experiment called for matching, delayed recall, and visual analysis.

Kagan and his associates found that children tended to show a high degree of consistency in the manner in which they responded to a variety of tasks. If a youngster reacted impulsively, responding quickly in one situation, he tended to do so in response to other situations. Moreover, since children who responded impulsively tended to make more errors, there was also a considerable degree of consistency in the number of errors they made as they moved from test to test.

There are several strands of evidence which indicate that a tendency to react impulsively to intellectual tasks at the elementary school level is linked with factors that have appeared earlier in the child's life. The restlessness of some extremely impulsive boys suggests the possibility that they may have suffered a certain amount of brain damage. It is possible also that genetic factors are at work.

The fact that children display "styles" in their intellectual approach to things, and that these may be linked with pervasive personality traits, has ramifications which investigators have begun to explore.

It seems that a tendency toward physical impulsiveness early in life as shown by restless activity may be a sign that a child will not be inclined to settle down to quiet intellectual work later on. Children who are highly active at one year tend not to be interested in intellectual problems at five or six (Shaefer and Bayley, 1963). Children who are hyperkinetic (overactive) at ages three to six tend to have lower ratings on involvement in intellectual activity during adolescence and adulthood (Kagan and Moss, 1962) than children who exhibit a more normal pace of activity when young. Kagan cites preliminary findings in another study which suggest that there is an inverse relationship between amount of motor activity and ability to give sustained attention to external stimuli early in life.

Several writers have suggested that impulsiveness (whether manifested by "cognitive impulsivity" as described above, or by a more generalized lack of "impulse control"), often seems to be associated with under-achievement at school. The under-achiever does not, as a rule, work in a steady methodical, even-paced manner. He does not show the quiet involvement in an intellectual task that one sees in a reflective child, as described by Kagan and his associates.

Moreover, impulsivity may impair a child's performance in specific ways. Kagan (1965) found that children in the first and second grades who have a tendency to make fast decisions and to commit many errors on tests of impulsivity-reflectiveness make more errors in reading than children who are more deliberate. Kagan and his associates (1966) also found that impulsive first grade children make more errors on a test of inductive reasoning. They tend to respond quickly where inferences are required, giving forth the first reasonable answer that occurs to them, without taking time to evaluate it.

Childhood Memories

During the first few years of life, children remember a vast number of happenings from day to day which they are unable to recall later.

No aspect of child psychology is potentially more revealing than the study of childhood memories. (Before proceeding, the reader is invited to write down his earliest recollections.) The reason is not that memories give a faithful story of one's life. Indeed, memories, may be scanty, fragmentary, and distorted. Their significance from a personal point of view outweighs their authenticity from an historical point of view. Early memories can be used, if one wishes, as a starting point for a chain of associations that can lead to unexpected discoveries.[8]

Bartlett, in his classic book on *Remembering* (1932), speaks of memory as a construction, not a reproduction. Memories of the past are clearly not like a sound videotape recording of what happened. They have a strong subjective slant. They represent events of the past as *perceived* at the time and as edited in the light of later experience. Moreover, they may not even reflect a real experience but a fantasy. Early in his work in psychoanalysis, Freud recognized that childhood experiences narrated by his patients could not be taken at face value. But this did not destroy their significance as a glimpse of the patient's present view of himself.

Timing and Number
of Early Recollections

There have been claims that individual persons have recollected happenings that occurred early during the first year of life, even extending as far back as the day of birth. Before such claims could be accepted, however, further verification would be required.

In one study (Dudycha and Dudycha, 1933), reports were obtained from college students concerning the earliest experiences they could remember, and then an effort was made through the help of parents and others to verify memories and the age at which the remembered incidents occurred. The average age referred to in these earliest memories was three years and seven months. Four per cent of the earliest memories dated back to the first year

---

[8] For reviews of studies of early memories see Thompson and Witryol (1948), and Charry (1959).

of life, 19 per cent to the second, 37 per cent to the third, 38 per cent to the fourth, and 2 per cent to the fifth.

Seventh-, ninth-, and eleventh-grade children gave written reports about their earliest memories in a study by Cameron (1966). About half of the youngsters (144 of 300 boys; 145 of 300 girls), attributed their first memories to the third year of life, or earlier.

College students in a study by Waldfogel (1948) were asked to record ". . . all the experiences of which they had any knowledge or recollection up to the time of their eighth birthday . . ." and to state as accurately as possible, within the nearest year, the age at which the remembered experience occurred. They were given eighty-five minutes to write their reports and later another eighty-five minute period. At one extreme was a person who reported only 10 memories and at the other extreme one who reported 137; the average number of memories was about 50. Relatively few of the experiences that were recalled extended back to the third year or earlier. There was an increase in memories attributed to the fourth year and a still larger number assigned to the fifth year.

Developmental Factors
Limiting Recall of Early Experiences

There are many conditions that make it difficult for a young child to formulate his experiences in such a way that he could recall them in later years.

What an adult remembers is often, to a large degree, an abstraction—an image or *idea* of what happened. A young child tends to think in concrete terms. He does not possess what has been called "the abstract faculty" to the same degree as an older person, and this circumstance limits his recall of early experiences.

In the mental operations of older children and adults *language* is a very important tool, but a young child lacks the ability to formulate his experiences by way of "inner speech" or by way of the kind of language that is used when a person communicates something to others. There is an interesting parallel between the course of language development and the number of experiences recalled from early childhood (Waldfogel, 1948).

Content of Early Memories

Regardless of intellectual factors that limit later recall of early experiences we still face another question. Why, in view of the thousands of things a child might remember, does he recall some events and not others. This question may be approached from two angles: first, what in actual experience, as far as it can be verified, is most likely and least likely to be recalled? What is there on the subjective side that influences recall and forgetting?

In an illuminating account, Madorah E. Smith (1952) compared the reported childhood memories of a number of persons with independent documentation of what had occurred, by means such as diaries that had been put away, a mother's records, school records, photographs of homes where her subjects lived, and verifiable dates when recalled events occurred, such as moving to one locale from another.

In Smith's study, memories of childhood experiences contained somewhat more unpleasant than pleasant items. A recent study by Cameron (1966) reports a similar finding. Fear was the most conspicuous single emotional experience. Dudycha and Dudycha (1933a, 1933b) also report fear as the most frequent remembered emotion. Findings have varied, however, with respect to the relative prominence of pleasant and unpleasant states in early memories.

An investigator of early memories faces a problem of interpretation when he undertakes to judge the emotional tone of a recalled experience. The issue is clear if the recaller specifically labels a remembered event as an experience of anger, joy, fear, or the like. But unless so labeled, it cannot be taken for granted, for example, that a remembered birthday party was pleasant, or even that an illness that is recalled was unpleasant.

According to Smith's findings, experiences that occur repeatedly—and thus constitute a large element in a person's day-to-day life—tend to be merged or fused and not to stand out in memory in proportion to their occurrence. Something out of the ordinary is more likely to be remembered. Gifts, however much they may be treasured, are less likely to be recalled than completely unexpected gifts of a lesser nature. More unfulfilled than fulfilled wishes are likely to be remembered.

Smith provides interesting information concerning what was remembered and what was forgotten by one of her subjects. This subject, later in life, over an extended period of time, recorded reminiscences from various periods of her childhood. She then compared her memories with records of happenings in her childhood as set down in a diary kept by her mother.

As an older person she remembered all of the accidents that befell her in the age range from about four to seven (as recorded by her mother). She had forgotten seven of ten illnesses, somewhat over half of her medical and dental treatments, two or three worries that had troubled her, and three of four punishments. "Accidents, operations, and illnesses, if severe enough, often make good stories but punishments, accompanied usually by shame or guilt rarely do," Smith states (1952, p. 171).

Errors in memory may represent an attempt to lessen guilt, according to Smith. An episode involving "immodest" exposure by a girl and her brother was later remembered by the girl as involving herself and her sister. In another episode the subject had provoked her sister by refusing to let her join in a game of croquet. When the players momentarily left the game, the sister pulled up all the wickets and scattered the balls. The subject later remem-

bered nothing about her refusal to let her sister play, only her sister's mean-
ness, her own wrath, and the satisfaction she felt when the sister was punished.

Childhood Characteristics Recalled
by the Self and Viewed by Others

Fifty adults reported recollections from childhood in a study by Jayaswal
(1955). When these adults were children, they had been rated on an Ascendance-Submission scale on the basis of systematic observation of their behavior
in nursery school and other settings. Now, as adults, they were asked to rate
themselves on an adaptation of that scale, checking those items on the scale
which they recalled as descriptive of them when they were children not more
than six years old. These self-ratings revealed that in 52 per cent of the cases
the recall of childhood behavior (as seen by others) was inaccurate and unreliable; in 32 per cent of the cases the recall was partially inaccurate; and in
18 per cent of the cases the older persons' recall of their childhood corresponded to their behavior as observed at the time.

Why, we might ask, did these adults do so poorly in recalling childhood
characteristics which, according to observers at the time, were clearly evident? Part of the answer is that this behavior occurred at a time of life which
adults ordinarily do not remember very well. But other factors were probably
at work, too. These adults, as children, probably did not perceive their behavior in the same light as it was perceived by adult observers. An "ascendant" child who barges into things, asserts himself, demands to be seen and
heard, may not see himself as being particularly pushy. (Even an "ascendant"
adult who charges into a group meeting, monopolizing the discussion, is not
likely to see himself as he appears to others.) When older persons do not
remember some aspects of their childhood behavior, the reason may be that,
from their view of things, there wasn't anything particular to remember.
Findings similar to these would quite likely appear in connection with adult
recall of many other aspects of childhood. But the findings probably underestimate the extent to which an adult can recapture his childhood.

Conditions that Influence
Forgetting and Facilitate Recall

In considering the memory fragments an adult recalls from childhood as
compared with all that he might conceivably recall, Freud (1938a) says "we
can only ask ourselves in amazement" why just this or that particular detail
should escape oblivion.

According to Freud (1938b), during the first years of life there is a kind of
blotting out of memory, ". . . a peculiar amnesia which veils from most people
(not from all) the first years of their childhood, usually the first six or eight

years." While the particular detail that is recalled might not be important in itself, it represents something significant. Freud speaks of early memories as "screen memories" in the sense that the particular event recalled is a disguise behind which lies something more important. The important latent or hidden meaning may be represented "in the memory by something that seems quite trivial." Freud implies that most people (although not all) need the help of an analyst to uncover memories and the meaning of the memories hidden behind the screen.

Whether we agree or disagree with Freud's views in this matter, it seems that the usual person does not commonly try to penetrate very deeply into the meanings of his or her early memories. A moderately intelligent person with an interest in exploring his own mind (or in exploring another's) can probably go considerably farther than people usually go. By a process of free association, "letting the mind go," it is possible to start with a fragment of memory and then to bring forth many other memories and many additional thoughts and feelings connected with the fragment. In the process, a person may discover that a particular early memory takes on a different meaning, or takes on several added meanings. Here are some examples, from an informal study by the writer, of additional ideas that emerged when persons were asked to make only a brief and limited effort to go beyond the details they gave at first in reporting an early memory. (The interviewer's questions are given in parentheses.)

I remember a very happy time I once had with my grandfather when I was about four years old. I polished his shoes and he was very pleased with me. (*Anything else?*) When I think back to that time I also remember that I was vying with my brother with a feeling that I could never match him. He got a lot of praise from my grandfather and maybe that made grandfather's praise for me mean so much. (*Anything else?*) As I think of it now, I was getting praise for being a very good girl, not for being a bright and witty person like my brother, and I guess the praise I got was like triumph in the midst of defeat. At any rate, I do know that it has been hard for me to feel the confidence in myself that I really have a right to feel. (*Any further thoughts?*) Yes, a memory of something I don't remember except in a sketchy way. When I was four I was able to read; I definitely know this because my family moved to another place when I was four and I was able to read before we moved. I don't remember how or when I learned—just the fact that I was able to do it.

I remember being terribly afraid of a steam threshing rig, especially the engine, the clanking noise, the big wheels with iron treads, the deep marks the wheels made in the road, and the whistle and the smoke. (*Any other thoughts or feelings about it?*) Yes, this fear is connected in my mind with a fear of death and punishment. The smoke and noise remind me of the first idea I had about hell, full of flames and horrible sounds. And the man who ran the rig, he was called "The Thresher"; when I think of that I think of a thrashing, getting a beating from my father for being bad. (*Anything else?*) Yes, the great joy I felt several years later on a farm at threshing time when I was able to walk right up to the machine and touch it without being afraid.

(There was a sequel to this. The association between "thresher" and "father" later led to a further stream of associations regarding the recaller's fears and relations with his father. These, from the recaller's point of view, were very revealing and, although the subject was painful, offered gratifying results.)

> I remember being terribly embarrassed at a wedding when I had a bowel movement in my pants. I had on a new white suit. I stayed out behind a grove of trees. I don't remember how it ended. (*Any other thoughts or feelings?*) Now, as I look back, I wonder how this happened. I couldn't manage the buttons but I guess I was ashamed to go and ask my mother for help.

In these examples, further thought not only led to additional material, but even the emotional quality of the early memory as first formulated, underwent a change. One of the "pleasant" memories brought back a recollection of sibling rivalry and a feeling of inadequacy, which was somewhat painful; this led to another memory (being able to read at an early age), which somehow had little feeling attached to it—though ordinarily we might expect this to be a pleasant recollection. The memory of fear of a threshing rig was interwoven with a kind of foreboding and guilt and was topped off with a recollection of a feeling of triumph. A memory of shame was left dangling with a note of reproach against the mother.

In connection with each of these memories, further exploration might uncover additional meanings.

Smith (1952) gives an interesting account of how one of the adult participants in her study (identified as Subject A) reached a significant insight by way of a childhood memory combined with a reminder (from her mother's diary) of a childhood happening:

> A [tried] to discover the meaning of the disturbing memory of her one-armed great aunt seen only once at 3:5 [three years, five months] when she found it always appearing when she tried to trace the origin of a phobia for mutilated persons. One night in a hypnogogic state when she had been pondering upon it, it suddenly flashed across her that the memory was connected with an incident that took place at 2:10 and was recorded thus by her mother, "When we reached the question (in a child's catechism) 'How did God make Adam and Eve?' she said, 'Beloie don't want God to take one of Beloie's bones and make a woman.'" Her mother had explained "bone" by having the child feel the bone in her arm so when A later saw her great aunt with that "bone" missing the child's former fear was aroused. Although the earlier incident was never really remembered by A, upon discovery of its connection with her phobia, the phobia began to disappear.

Influence of Present Situation on Recall of the Past

What we remember from the past is influenced not only by what actually happened but also by the manner in which a past event was in keeping with a person's mood at the time or with his present mood and outlook on life

(Adler, 1937; Kadis, 1957). According to this theory, the one who has a cheerful view of life would be more likely to remember happy experiences, and the one who feels that life has treated him unjustly would remember grievances, and so on.

In one study of college students it was found that those who rated themselves as "insecure," reporting feelings of isolation or rejection or uniqueness, reported more unpleasant childhood memories than did "secure" persons who, as college students had a tendency toward optimism, happiness, and self-acceptance (Purcell, 1952). Insecure persons described significantly more of their memories as being unpleasant than did the secure persons. Low but positive correlations have also been found between the percentage of unfavorable childhood memories reported by older children and the extent to which they rate themselves unfavorably on a test of personal adjustment (Pattie and Cornett, 1952).

The relationship between a person's present view of himself (as measured by his response to a personality test) and his tendency to take a somewhat similar view of his past (as indicated by his childhood memories) is not so close that a record of a person's early memories can be used as a reliable measure of his personality in the present. Yet the fact that there is some correspondence between present characteristics and recollections of the past suggests that the particular events which a person recalls from an earlier period of his life may be biased in keeping with his present frame of mind. For example, a parent who feels guilty about his performance as a parent may remember, with a twinge of self-accusation, episodes in his dealings with his children which another parent would neither regret nor remember.

There are two further considerations concerning the nature of what people remember from the past. One is that what a person selects to report may be influenced by the views of the person to whom he is reporting. A person telling about his past to a psychologist who emphasizes the importance of sex in personality development may come forth with a good deal of material about sex, while a person recounting his past to one who emphasizes the importance of sibling relationships may come forth with a good deal of material pertaining to that topic (Bach, 1952).

Residual Effects
of Early Experiences

Another consideration is that though a person may not recall a childhood experience, it may still leave a residue. This may happen not only with experiences that are definitely traumatic but also with experiences that are rather mild, as shown in an interesting study by Burtt (1932, 1937, 1941). Passages from Sophocles in the original Greek were read to a child (who had no other contact with Greek) when he was no more than fifteen months old; twenty lines were read to him daily for a period of three months, and at the end of each period a new selection was read. This reading was continued until the child was three years old. When he was eight and a half years old, the same passages, as well as new ones, were read to him; but he was now required to memorize the lines. To commit to memory new passages that never before had been read to him required an average of 435 repetitions, while an average of only 317 repetitions was needed for passages that had been read to him when he was a baby.

Again, when this child was fourteen years old, he undertook to memorize Greek passages, some of which had been read to him before the age of three and some of which were new. This time, the difference between the effort required to learn "old" and "new" material was appreciable but much decreased. A final check was then made when the child was eighteen years old. At this age no difference was apparent in the number of repetitions required to master new and old passages.

Recommended Readings

Stendler's *Readings* (referred to in Chapter 19) contain several contributions on the subject of cognitive development. All the books by Jean Piaget listed in the Bibliography are recommended. J. H. Flavell's, *The Developmental Psychology of Jean Piaget* (1963) gives a comprehensive presentation of Piaget's works. *Young Children's Thinking* by Millie Almy, Edward Chittenden, and Paula Miller (1966) presents findings from a longitudinal study of children's thinking and contains a thought-provoking chapter on the educational implications of Piaget's work. Educational implications of cognitive development are discussed in Jerome S. Bruner's well-known book *The Process of Education* (1960). Also recommended is *Basic Cognitive Processes in Children*, edited by John C. Wright and Jerome Kagan (1963). For references to recent and forthcoming studies of cognitive development see *The Annual Review of Psychology.*

21

Measuring

and Predicting

Intellectual Ability

In this chapter we will consider mental ability as measured by intelligence tests and types of ability that fall under the heading of general intelligence.

E. L. Thorndike's account of the nature of intelligence in 1927 named a variety of operations including attention, retention, recall, recognition, selective and relational thinking, abstraction, generalization, and inductive and deductive reasoning. Definitions have varied, but "general intelligence" generally denotes abstract intelligence—"the ability to see relations in, make generalizations from, and relate and organize ideas represented in symbolic form" (Thorndike and Hagen, 1961).

One definition is that intelligence is that which is measured by intelligence tests. This seems a bit sardonic. Yet it is not, for historically efforts to measure intelligence grew out of practical, humanitarian considerations. Early efforts were inspired by a desire to ascertain the potentialities and limitations of retarded children.

Intelligence Tests

The typical comprehensive intelligence test consists of a number of concrete tasks yielding, in the aggregate, a total score. Tests designed for children are scaled to children's capacities at various maturity levels. Thus a young child may be asked to fit blocks of varying shapes (round, square, triangular) into corresponding depressions in a board, to repeat numbers that are spoken to him, to name objects or to identify pictures of objects. An inventory of mental growth in infancy and early childhood developed by Bayley in 1933 and revised in 1958 includes such items as response to sounds, giving sustained attention to an object, and securing a ring by pulling a string to which it is attached. Tests of older children include measures of vocabulary, ability to solve problems of various kinds, immediate memory, speed of learning, ability to understand and interpret the meanings of written passages, to make deductions or inductions from observed facts, and so forth.

The Stanford-Binet Scale

The best-known individual intelligence test is the Stanford-Binet scale, an instrument originated by Binet and subsequently revised and improved by Terman, later by Terman and Merrill (1937), and revised again in 1960 (Terman and Merrill, 1960). This scale consists of test items graded in difficulty from the age of two upward. Each item can be scored as passed or failed. There are six test items at each half-yearly level from two years through four years, and six test items at each yearly age level thereafter up through age fourteen. After these follow tests for the "average adult" and "superior adult" levels.[1] The items at any age level represent tasks that the normal child of that age has been able to perform successfully.

A child's performance on the scale can be scored in terms of *mental age*. Thus, if he passes all the tests up to and including the third year and fails all tests beyond that point, he has a mental age of three years. If he succeeds on tests beyond the three-year level, he receives credit for each such success. Each of the twelve tests at the two-, three-, and four-year levels counts as one month of mental age; and each of the six tests at later yearly levels counts as two months of mental age. Thus, if a child passes all tests up to and including three years, plus four of the twelve tests at four years, he is credited with a mental age of three years, four months, which means that his mentality is equal to that of the average child of three years and four months.

---

[1] This statement refers to the 1937 revision. An earlier revision included tests from the age of three upward, with six tests at each age level. For a discussion of intelligence tests, steps involved in constructing tests and in determining their effectiveness, see Thorndike and Hagen (1961).

The Intelligence Quotient. To obtain an index of a child's brightness, when the Stanford-Binet scale is used, the *mental age* is divided by the *chronological age* and the result multiplied by 100 to yield a value known as the *intelligence quotient.* Thus a normal or average three-year-old child will have a mental age of three, a chronological age of three, and an IQ of 100. If the same child earns a mental-age score of four years, his IQ is 133; if he does no better than the normal two-year-old, his IQ is only 67.[2]

Other Types of Intelligence Tests

The Sanford-Binet test is administered to one child at a time. There are other individual tests and also tests applicable to older children and adults that can be administered to several persons in a group simultaneously. Among the intelligence tests widely used with children is the WISC—Wechsler Intelligence Scale for Children (Wechsler, 1949, 1950a, 1950b, 1951).

The most commonly used tests are administered verbally. For young children and children with a language handicap there are performance tests. An example of a performance item is a picture arrangement test. the pictures when placed in the right order tell a story—such as a sequence of pictures showing the building of a snow man. One group test that uses verbal instructions but requires no verbal response is the *Lorge-Thorndike Intelligence Test, Non-Verbal Series.*

The Goodenough Draw-A-Man test, recently revised and improved by Harris (1963), can be used with persons of varied language backgrounds.

Consistency and Reliability
of Intelligence Ratings

Bayley (1933b) and others have shown that intelligence scales designed for children below the age of three are less reliable than scales designed for older children. Many difficulties arise in testing a child before he has learned to talk and to understand spoken language. With young children it is more difficult than at later levels to segregate the more strictly mental from the motor, social, and emotional forms of response. The young child's response is also likely to be more variable than the older child's.

Infant tests, in their present form, do not give an accurate prediction of a child's intelligence. The younger the child, the less certain we are that his score gives an indication of his probable IQ in later years, although even in early infancy a markedly subnormal or a markedly superior rating is likely to have significance for the future.

---

[2] When the test is used with adults, the value representing chronological age does not become higher as the person becomes older; instead, an upper limit of eighteen years is set. Thus, a man of thirty-six with a mental age of eighteen has an IQ of 100.

A young child's ratings on *consecutive* tests, near in time, are likely to show a good deal of resemblance, but the longer the interval between two tests, the lower the resemblance is likely to be. Bayley found, for example, a positive correlation [3] of .57 between average scores at one to three months

---

[3] Two examples of a correlation coefficient are given below. The first shows the correlation between IQ ratings based on two separate tests; the second, the correlation between IQ and strength of grip. In these examples, one of the simplest methods of correlation, known as the "rank-difference method," is used. It can be applied when there are only a small number of cases. Only seven cases are included here; this number is large enough for illustrative purposes but too small for ordinary statistical work.

The rank difference correlation coefficient is expressed by the symbol ρ. The formula used in the present case is:

$$\rho = 1 - \frac{6 \times \text{sum of } D^2}{N(N^2 - 1)}$$

The illustrations show that the subjects' scores must first be ranked. D represents the difference between the same subject's rank in the two tests; N, the number of cases.

Individuals Tested	IQ Test I	Rank	IQ Test II	Rank	D	D²	IQ Test I Rank	Strength of Grip in Kgm.	Rank	D	D²
Albert	80	7	79	7	0	0	7	22	6	1	1
Henry	90	6	95	4	2	4	6	28	3	3	9
John	104	3	110	3	0	0	3	20	7	4	16
Peter	95	5	92	6	1	1	5	30	2	3	9
Palmer	140	1	135	1	0	0	1	26	4	3	9
Robert	120	2	125	2	0	0	2	34	1	1	1
Walter	100	4	94	5	1	1	4	24	5	1	1

$N = 7$ Sum of $D^2 = 6$ Sum of $D^2 = 46$
$N^2 - 1 = 48$ $6 \times$ sum of $D^2 = 36$ $6 \times$ sum of $D^2 = 276$
$N(N^2 - 1) = 336$

$$\rho = 1 - \frac{6 \times \text{sum of } D^2}{N(N^2 - 1)}$$

$= 1 - 36/336$

$= + .89$ (between the first and second test of IQ)

$\rho = 1 - 276/336$

$= + .18$ (between first IQ test and strength of grip)

In the first example, there is a high degree of correspondence between the children's IQ's on Tests I and II. Each child maintains about the same rank on both tests. If each child kept exactly the same rank on both tests, there would be a perfect correlation of $+1.00$. If there were no consistency at all between scores on the first and second tests, the correlation would be 0. If there were a complete reversal of ranks, the correlation would be -1.00. For practical purposes, we would be able to make a fairly accurate estimate of what a child's rating on Test II would be if we knew his relative standing on Test I.

In the second example, we find a positive but low correlation between IQ and strength of grip. On the basis of the figures in this example, there is a likelihood that a child with a high IQ will also tend to be above rather than below average in strength of grip. But the correspondence is so small that, if we tried to estimate his score in one test on the basis of our knowledge of his score on the other, our estimate would be little more than a guess.

and at four to six months, and a correlation of .42 between scores at one to three and seven to nine months. As the interval increased, the correlations decreased, so that there was practically a zero correlation between scores at one to three months and scores beyond the age of twelve months. As children grow older, the scores usually become more stable.

Many factors contribute to the lack of consistency in young children's ratings on consecutive tests: different rates of growth; irregularities in rate of growth; changes in adjustment to the test situation; and the likelihood that the various functions measured by the test mature at different rates.

According to Bayley's findings, differences between children become greater with advancing age, and there is also a greater spread in the performance of individual children on a given examination (as when a child of eighteen months performs at a level of a two-year-old on some parts of the scale and no better than the average child of eighteen months on other parts).

Theoretically, we might expect less consistency in rate of mental growth during the earlier years. The young child is progressing rapidly; new abilities are emerging at different rates and are being consolidated. At six or seven years the child is still maturing rapidly, but his gains from year to year consist more of added competence in using his existing capacities than in the emergence of new abilities.

The lower predictive value of tests at the preschool than at the school-age level is not due entirely to irregularities in the growth pattern or to imperfections in the measuring instruments. As in infancy, so to a lesser but important degree at the preschool level, the reliability of test results depends upon the tester's success in winning the child's cooperation. Resistance or fear on the child's part may interfere with the test. The young child is less likely to recognize the importance (from the adult's point of view) of doing things according to the letter of the tester's instructions, and his interest may

Table 30   Composite of Test-Retest Correlations from Several Studies of Infant and Preschool Groups

Age at Earlier Test	Interval between Test and Retest (in Months)							
	Less than 4	4-9	10-15	16-21	22-29	30-41	42-53	Over 53
Under 4 months	.57	.33	.10	—.03	—.09			
4- 9 months	.77	.53	.49	.23	.16	.46	.00	
10-15 months	.78	.66	.50	.45	.33			.55
16-21 months	.76	.68	.51	.44	.38	.41	.25	.33
22-29 months	.82	.74	.68					.43
30-41 months	.87	.68	.66	.49	.57	.57	.56	.66
42-53 months	.81	.65	.72	.71	.66	.63	.63	.41
54-65 months			.76		.73			

From R. L. Thorndike, " 'Constancy' of the I.Q.," *Psychological Bulletin* (1940), 37, p. 173. Reproduced by permission of the American Psychological Association.

turn to features of the test that don't count. Also, a child who has learned to conform to directions will have an advantage over a child who has not learned to do so.[4]

Constancy of Mental Test Scores Beyond the Preschool Level. As we have noted above, there is a relatively high degree of consistency in intelligence-test ratings from year to year at the school age and beyond. Children have approximately similar IQ's on successive tests if no significant changes in their circumstances have intervened (such as illness, emotional maladjustment, or transfer to a different environment).

It should be emphasized that when psychologists speak of the "constancy" of the IQ they do not at all imply that the IQ will remain precisely the same from year to year. Rather the concept implies a high degree of probability (not certainty) that fluctuations will be relatively small in a majority of cases. Indeed, because of the variables involved in measuring the complex operations that constitute intelligence, it is improbable that a child would obtain precisely the same score on two equivalent forms of the same test, even if they were administered on successive days. In discussing results obtained with the best known of all individual tests for children (the Stanford-Binet scale), Terman some years ago pointed out that the chances were one in two that the IQ might increase as much as six points or decrease as much as four points; the chances of an increase of twelve points or a decrease of eight points were one in five; the chances of shifts larger than twelve points were considerably smaller but still impressive.

Goodenough in 1940 estimated that in tests of a group of 500 children under the best conditions, at least 100 may be expected, on retests, to show changes in IQ of as much as ten points; changes of as much as fifteen points may be expected in about twenty-five instances, and four or five children may shift as much as twenty points.

Honzik, *et al.* (1948) show that fluctuations as high as 50 points may occur and changes as great as 15 points are likely to appear in somewhat over 50 per cent of the cases.

Extreme changes are rare. It is unlikely that a child will shift from a below-average to a "superior" rating (IQ of 120 or 125 or more). But during the elementary school years, shifts from an "average" to a "superior" rating and vice versa are relatively frequent.

In the study by Honzik, *et al.*, it was noted that irregularities in intellectual growth tended to be associated with life histories in which there were unusual variation and disturbing factors.

When children show irregularities in their intellectual growth patterns the fluctuations may be up or down. Some children, however, show a trend toward lower or descending scores while some show a trend toward higher or ascending scores.

---

[4] For a review of literature on infant and preschool tests see Stott and Ball (1965).

Sontag, *et al.* (1958) found that there were more "ascending" boys than girls. According to Sontag, *et al.*, and Kagan, *et al.* (1958) children showing an ascending trend rated somewhat higher than others in traits such as independence, aggressiveness, initiative, and competitiveness.

A child's score on an intelligence test will be inaccurate if the child, by reason of unique circumstances in his environment, is at a disadvantage on certain test items. Thus, a child who seldom has a chance to use money is at a disadvantage on test items dealing with the names and values of coins. Similarly, the score earned by a bilingual child may not represent his true ability. If a test involves questions that are better suited to the experience of one group than another (as, for example, urban as compared with rural, or isolated mountaineer, or Indian reservation groups), it will yield misleading results.

Limits of Intellectual Growth

The abilities measured by intelligence tests increase on the average from year to year during childhood and the yearly increase continues, but at a lower rate, during the late teens; and an increase in intelligence test performance continues into the twenties and beyond (notably among those who continue their schooling or are engaged in intellectual work). Continued gains in IQ from adolescence into adulthood were found by Bradway and Thompson (1962) who made a 25-year followup study of children who had first been tested at the preschool level. These gains were not evenly distributed, however. Boys showed somewhat higher increases than girls after reaching adolescence. The gains after adolescence were greater in abstract reasoning and vocabulary than in rote memory and practical reasoning.

Components of Intelligence

A child's measured intelligence is commonly represented by an IQ ranging upward or downward from 100. So represented, it seems that two children with an IQ, say, of 115 have the "same" intelligence. Actually, they may differ considerably in the make-up of their intelligence. As Guilford (1959) has pointed out, there are many ways of being intelligent. A comprehensive mental test taps a variety of abilities or operations. These abilities are interrelated—a person is not likely to make a top score in one and a bottom score in another. But a given person may show quite an uneven pattern of abilities. In a test which includes problems expressed in numbers, and problems requiring ability to detect meanings or solve logical problems expressed in words, one person may do better on items that tap numerical ability, another on items that test verbal ability. But both might have the same total composite score.

Numerous investigators have studied what might be called the anatomy of intelligence. Spearman in 1927 described intelligence as consisting of a general factor (g) representing the total mental energy at an individual's command and operating through the channel of specific abilities. Thurstone (1938) identified seven "primary abilities" including vizualization of figures in space; perceptual speed; quickness in dealing with numerical computations; grasp of ideas and meanings of words; word fluency; rote memory; and the ability through induction to extract a rule common to the materials of a problem or test.

Guilford (1959) identifies five major groups of intellectual abilities or operations: (1) *cognition*—"discovery or rediscovery or recognition"; (2) *memory* —"retention of what is cognized"; (3) *convergent thinking*—using information in a way that "leads to one right answer or to a recognized best or conventional answer"; (4) *divergent thinking*—thinking "in different directions, sometimes searching, sometimes seeking variety"; and (5) *evaluation*—through which we "reach decisions as to the goodness, correctness, suitability or adequacy of what we know, what we remember, and what we produce in productive thinking." Guilford's distinction between convergent and divergent thinking has been particularly meaningful, both as a stimulus to further research and from the standpoint of its educational implications.

Intelligence and School Achievement

Work at school is predominantly a verbal occupation; even in classes in cookery and mechanics a pupil must know the right words and how to spell them. So we might expect that there would be a high correspondence between a child's verbal intelligence and his achievement at school. Actually, the correlation between intelligence test scores and school marks is not high —it is generally in the range from .40 to .60. The correlations are higher for some school subjects than for others. They are higher, for example, between IQ and marks in science in high school than between IQ and marks in literature. Moreover, the correlations are higher between IQ and standardized, objective, academic achievement tests than between IQ and the marks children receive from their teachers. The marks teachers give, quite understandably, will be influenced by personal factors. They will also be governed, to a greater degree than objective tests devised by outsiders, by the specific content covered in a given classroom.

When performance at school and IQ are less in accord than might theoretically be expected, why is this? The answer in part is that we can expect less than complete correspondence between two scores obtained by means of fallible instruments. There are discrepancies between scores even when children are measured by two independent forms of the same intelligence test. But this still leaves much to be accounted for.

Tests of intelligence tell more about what a person *can* do, under the challenge of a test situation, than what he *will* do in his day-to-day performance. The tests do not measure the effort, patience, perseverance, drive, and ambition a person will bring to bear on his work at school. They do not measure a child's self-assurance regarding his own competence which, as indicated in an earlier chapter, may influence his approach to school work even in the first grade.

Achievement tests, presumably, come closer to measuring not just what a person has the ability to do but also how effectively he has applied this ability. But both tests fail to tap important individual resources.

A further factor that contributes to discrepancies between performance on an intelligence test and an achievement test is that one test may measure a composite of mental operations that is unevenly matched by the mental operations required by the other. For example, in learning a language, a person can go a long way by depending on rote memory. Presumably, to predict achievement in language usage (as distinguished from the rules and logic of grammar) an intelligence test should be loaded heavily with memory items. Memory likewise is important, up to a point, in arithmetic (a person can memorize the multiplication table) but sooner or later effective achievement in arithmetic requires a grasp of concepts of quantity and number.

An intelligence test which covers a variety of operations, with only a small loading of items pertinent to numerical ability, probably should not be expected to predict adequately achievement in advanced arithmetic. In geometry, a bright student can memorize the easy exercises early in the text, but sooner or later he will bog down if he has not grasped the underlying theory. Presumably an intelligence test substantially loaded with items dealing with spatial relationships would be needed to distinguish between achievement in geometry based on memory and achievement based on conceptual grasp of the subject.

The examples given above do not imply that intelligence tests should imitate tests of academic achievement. That would be redundant. The intelligence test should, ideally, measure basic mental processes rather than test a pupil's mastery of the contents of a particular school subject.

The relationship between intelligence and school achievement could probably be shown more clearly if the teaching of academic subjects were based to a greater degree on an assessment of the psychological operations required by this or that subject. An adaptation of an approach such as Piaget's might provide a fruitful lead.

As we have seen in earlier chapters, Piaget has described the varying levels or stages in the development of children's thinking. A child may, for example, be able to go through the motions of counting to a hundred without having grasped the concept of number. Moreover, Piaget's account stresses that the processes of assimilation and accommodation at one stage of cognitive development provide an essential foundation for the next stage. Generally speaking (at least until quite recently), the subject matter taught at school has been roughly scaled on the basis of academic tradition as to what is elementary and what is advanced rather than on an analysis of the thought processes that are involved.

Nature, Nurture, and Intellectual Ability

This section on the role of heredity and environment in intellectual development will add some further material to the discussion of this subject in Chapter 3.

Resemblances between
Parents and Children and between Siblings

In a study in 1903, Pearson compared certain physical characteristics of parents and children and found correlations of about .50. When he compared certain of their mental characteristics, he found about the same correlations. Pearson made a historic conclusion that physical and mental characteristics in man are inherited within broad lines in the same manner and with the same intensity. Later investigations have, in the main, supported this generalization, although it is generally easier to demonstrate the role of genetic factors in the physical sphere.

In a large number of studies during the past decades correlations of about .50 have been found in comparisons between the intelligence of fathers and their children, between mothers and their children, and between children and their siblings living in the same environment.

In measurements of sibling resemblances in intelligence it is prudent to take account of irregularities in rate of intellectual growth, as described earlier in this chapter. And, as was pointed out in Chapter 3, a correlation between the present scores of a sampling of twelve-year-old boys and their ten-year-old brothers may mask certain underlying resemblances. A more accurate procedure would be to correlate the scores of ten-year-olds with the scores of their brothers when they were ten years old.

While a correlation of +.50 is very respectable, it falls far short of a "perfect" correlation of +1.00. Actually, even if heredity, or the environment, were the one and only factor in determining intelligence, a correlation of +1.00 between fathers or mothers and their children could not be obtained unless fathers and mothers had exactly the same intelligence level or had an identical influence on their children's environment. It is, of course, very unlikely that fathers and mothers would be identical in intelligence or in the nature of their relationships with their children, and whatever either parent contributes to the heredity of a child reflects not only what is measurable in the parent's own make-up, but also hereditary influences that are latent and not apparent.

When we study parent-child resemblances in intelligence it is important to take account of the age level of the children at the time when the intelligence tests are administered. In long-term studies it has been found that resemblances between parents and children are quite low when based on measurements of children before the age of three, and then become higher as the children approach adolescence (see, e.g., Honzik, 1957; Bayley 1954).[5]

In the large-scale, long-term follow-up study of foster children by Skodak and Skeels, cited in Chapter 3, the children were tested at the age of about 2, 4, 7 and again at an average age of 13.5. The correlations between the children's IQ's at these age levels and their "true" mothers' IQ's were respectively 0, .28, .35, and .38 (based on the 1916 version of the Stanford-Binet Scale and .44 based on the 1937 edition).[6]

Effect of Schooling
on Intellectual Development

Many studies have raised the question whether attending nursery school is likely to raise a child's IQ above the level it would reach had he not gone to nursery school. The findings here have varied. When gains have been reported they have not, on the average, been large compared with the differences between the IQ's of children in the population at large.[7]

Children from privileged backgrounds who attend nursery school are not likely to differ from non-nursery school children of similar backgrounds (Olson and Hughes, 1940). Nursery school experience is likely to have a more conspicuous effect on children from a sub-standard environment.

In studies of older children, gains in intelligence have been noted in children after they have been transferred from institutions to foster homes or after they have moved from one community to another offering better educational opportunities. O. Klineberg (1935, 1938) found that Negro children who had come to New York from the South with their families and who had lived longer periods in the North earned higher average scores than those who had arrived more recently. A Philadelphia study reports results that are, in the main, in keeping with those reported by Klineberg (Lee, 1951).

---

[5] Resemblances between identical and non-identical twins reared together and reared apart are discussed in Chapter 3.

[6] The initiation of a further follow-up study of the adopted children in the Skeels-Skodak study was reported by Skeels in 1965.

[7] A number of studies of the effects of schooling on IQ were reported in the Thirty-Ninth Yearbook of the N.S.S.E. (1940).

Another study which indicates that problems associated with a child's cultural background may adversely affect his response to an intelligence test has been reported by Anastasi and Cordova (1953), who gave intelligence tests to Puerto Rican children, most of whom had learned to speak Spanish and then had to learn English. The test performance of the children was below the norm. They appeared to have little or no desire to excel in a competitive intellectual situation, and they showed a lack of interest in the relatively abstract and intellectual content of the test. This reaction to the testing situation was apparently related to a rather passive and unresponsive attitude toward school, brought about in part, so it seemed, by the fact that the children had been thrust into an exclusively English-speaking environment at a time when they knew little English.

It does not appear that considerable changes in IQ can be expected simply by sending children who already have reasonably good educational opportunities to relatively superior elementary schools (Thorndike *et al.*, 1940) or by transferring children from regular classes to special "opportunity" classes (Pritchard, Horan, and Hollingworth, 1940).

Would dropping out of school entirely make a difference? Findings in a study by Lorge (1945) bear on this question. A number of boys who were first tested in 1921-1922 when they were in the eighth grade were retested, twenty years later, in 1941. During the intervening twenty years some of the young people had gone no further than eighth grade while others had gone beyond high school. In a large number of comparisons, higher scores were earned by those who had gone on to complete higher grades in school. The further persons went in their schooling (as measured by *highest grade completed*, not the number of years of school attended) the higher their scores tended to be as compared with their original ratings in 1921.

These findings do not mean that intelligence rises in proportion to amount of schooling or that people with equal schooling will have equal intelligence. In spite of gains in scores of many (but not all) individuals who continued their schooling in Lorge's study, there was a high degree of correspondence between scores obtained twenty years apart (correlations of .62 and .64 respectively on the two instruments that were used at the time of the final test). Gains were relative to initial scores. Some children whose scores were among the highest on the first test and who went no further than the eighth grade earned decidedly higher scores twenty years later than did children initially in lower brackets who successfully completed two, three, or four grades in high school.

The value of schooling cannot, of course, be measured simply by "before-and-after" mental tests. There may be gains also in a child's "functioning intelligence," in the effectiveness and the ways in which he puts his intelligence to everyday use, even if there are no demonstrable gains in his intelligence quotient as measured by mental tests.

Family and Socio-Economic Status and Intelligence

In general, children of higher socio-economic status have been found to have a higher average level of intelligence than children of lower status. These differences are not so apparent while children are still quite young, and needless to say, individual differences within each occupational group are a good deal greater than the differences between the average scores of different groups.

To what extent is the higher average intelligence of children in the "upper" occupational levels due to a better environment? To what extent is it due to heredity? To what extent is the difference only an apparent one because of faults in the testing instruments? A precise answer cannot be given to these questions. A child's environment obviously has an important influence on his performance on an intelligence test. When a child responds to an intelligence test, he draws on what he has learned and learning obviously requires an appropriate environment. It is also possible that the native abilities of a child's parents played a part in determining their occupational status. Other things being equal, we might expect, in a competitive society, that the hereditary endowment of a child's parents will have an important bearing on the vocation they choose and on their ability to "get ahead." However, the "other things" are far from "equal" if, for example, a child is reared in circumstances which do not foster his potentialities, or do not encourage the kind of learning and verbal ability that is measured by intelligence tests.

Parents of low socio-economic status usually also are of low educational status—as measured by the highest grade level they completed in school. Children of such parents are likely to have less by way of a model that would provide stimulation and incentive toward the kind of intellectual proficiency valued at school and the kind of ability measured by intelligence tests. However, it has been found that low socio-economic status is less of a deterrent to children who happen to be bright.

Exceptional Children

The label "exceptional" is commonly applied to children who differ notably from the average. Among them the outstandingly bright ones are referred to as *gifted* children. Those who possess outstanding aptitudes in music, the arts, mechanics, and other areas are usually referred to as *talented*. The exceptional ones who are distinctly below average in mental ability are labeled *mentally retarded* or *deficient*. Those who suffer from special disabilities, such as brain damage, blindness, or other impairments, are referred to as *handicapped* children.

The exceptional child clearly stands out as different from others, yet he is still a child. To understand him, we must appreciate the humanity he shares with ordinary human beings, and also assess the qualities that set him apart.

Gifted Children

Children with IQ's of 120 or 125 or above are described as "superior." They represent from 5 to 10 per cent of the population. Among the superior ones are the "gifted" with IQ's of 135 or 140 and above; and the "extremely gifted" with IQ's of 170 or 180 or above. The "gifted" group constitutes approximately 1 to 3 per cent of the total population.

Personal Characteristics

Children with high intelligence are usually above rather than below average in many other characteristics, but it is in the intellectual field that their qualities are especially outstanding. A gifted child is likely to be curious and to ask many questions when he is young and to push into many areas of knowledge as he grows older. He is likely to be adept in the use of language, and many gifted children at an early age acquire a large vocabulary and an awareness of subtle shades of word meanings.

Gifted children frequently excel in reading. Many learn to read before entering school, and shortly thereafter plunge into materials designed for older children and adults. Many of the anecdotes about gifted youngsters deal with their appetite for reading, and barriers they encounter in trying to satisfy this appetite. One fourth-grade child in a small school had read and re-read everything in sight, including a set of encyclopedias and the books used by children in upper grades. When the school acquired a huge, unabridged dictionary, he proceeded to devour it, standing as he read—for he was not allowed to bring it to his desk. Judy, a second-grader (described by Dunlap, 1958), came home from school one day with seven library books recommended by her teacher. When the teacher telephoned in the evening to explain that she was trying to encourage Judy to get a taste for the normal interests of her age-group, the mother exclaimed, "Oh, Judy read all seven books for you this afternoon so she could finish *Green Pastures* before bedtime." The fact that gifted children are able readers does not, however, mean that all of them are ávid readers, or that all have sophisticated tastes (Strang, 1956).

The proportion of gifted children who come from middle-class or upper-class homes is higher than would be expected from the number of such homes in the total population. However, there are gifted children in all segments of the population. Recent studies suggest that there is a larger proportion of gifted children at the lower socio-economic levels than would appear from the number of such children included in Terman's classical study.[8]

Brightness and Astuteness in Responding to Tests. A person who is able to earn a high score on an intelligence test is also likely to be more clever than the average person in responding to other forms of tests. Some gifted persons have a knack of anticipating the questions a teacher will ask on an examination and the kinds of answers he expects. This knack is especially handy at the high school and college level. One bright student earned a mark of 99 on the first examination he took in a college course, and a glowing public tribute from the instructor. This student had deftly slanted all the answers on his examination to support the bias of the instructor, even though he disagreed with the instructor's point of view. (He was practicing what Hollingworth, in her classic work on the gifted, described as the art of "benign chicanery.")

The knack for figuring out the right or expected answer has undoubtedly colored the findings obtained in studies of the moral attitudes and emotional adjustment of gifted persons. A person who "knows the score" can, for example, give a "mature" answer on a test of moral judgment, and the "correct" answer on a test of politeness, social intelligence, civic responsibility, or neuroticism whether or not the answer expresses his personal attitudes or convictions. Even with this reservation, however, the weight of evidence indicates that gifted persons are more likely to be above than below average in character, responsibility, respectability, and conformity to what society regards as proper ways of behaving.

Discrepancies between Brightness and Academic Achievement. While bright children, on the average, do superior work at school, there are many individual exceptions to this rule.

From a review of the literature by Goldberg, Gotkin, and Tannenbaum (1962) and a later review by Goldberg (1965), it is evident that many bright children do not use their superior ability to earn high grades. There probably are several reasons for this. Some children undoubtedly are bored; some have poor work habits; some are deterred by emotional problems; probably also (although this has not been explored adequately) many of them feel that much of what is prescribed in the academic program is rather meaningless from a personal point of view. Some youngsters do not earn high marks for fear of disapproval by their peers. This is more likely to occur at the high school than at the elementary school level (Goldberg, 1960). A deliberate policy of not aiming for the highest marks seems to prevail especially among high school girls. Colemen (1963) reports that the brightest girls frequently

---

[8] Findings on this score and on other aspects of giftedness have been summarized in an excellent review by Goldberg, 1965.

do not try to qualify for the high school Honor Roll on the ground that this might make them unpopular. A study by Tannenbaum (1962) offers interesting findings about the values children assign to studiousness at the high school level. Tannenbaum asked 615 eleventh-graders (305 boys and 310 girls) to record their attitudes toward hypothetical high school students with various combinations of the following characteristics: brilliance, studiousness, and participation in athletics. The ratings are shown in Table 31.

As can be seen in Table 31, the student described as athletic consistently received a much higher rating than the one who was nonathletic. Brightness alone did not seem to be a decisive factor, for although the lowest rank was given to the student described as brilliant-studious-nonathletic, the highest rank was given to the one described as brilliant-non-studious-athletic. The brilliant or average *nonstudious*-athletic person was regarded more favorably than the brilliant or average *studious* person. In this study, higher ratings were given to the athletic than to the non-athletic person by boys and by girls, by young people in a number of different communities, by students of higher as well as lower intelligence, and by students whose parents were in the upper as well as the lower educational brackets. Preliminary results in a study of younger children by Tannenbaum and his associates indicate that the studious pupil is likely to be viewed with more favor by his classmates at the elementary school level than at the high school level, yet the findings in Table 31 suggest that he cannot count on continued favor in the eyes of his classmates as he moves into the high school grades.

According to the findings in Table 31, the stereotype of the studious high school student is, comparatively, not a favorable one. Brightness, as such, is valued more than studiousness. Actually, as a group, gifted children are likely

Table 31   **Average Ratings Made by 615 Eleventh-Graders of the Social Acceptability of Eight Hypothetical Students**

Hypothetical Student	Average Rating	Rank in Acceptability
Brilliant—Nonstudious—Athletic	28.35	1
Average—Nonstudious—Athletic	26.11	2
Average—Studious—Athletic	24.20	3
Brilliant—Studious—Athletic	23.75	4
Brilliant—Nonstudious—Nonathletic	11.78	5
Average—Nonstudious—Nonathletic	10.65	6
Average—Studious—Nonathletic	8.44	7
Brilliant—Studious—Nonathletic	2.20	8

From A. J. Tannenbaum, 1962, *Adolescent Attitudes toward Academic Brilliance.* New York: Bureau of Publications, Teachers College, Columbia University.

to be named as the preferred companions of their classmates more often than children of average or below average intelligence (Miller, 1956; Gallagher and Crowder, 1957). However, Gallagher and Crowder (1957) found that a "sizable minority" had difficulties in their social relationships.

Tannenbaum's study raises many questions. Are high school students perhaps envious of a classmate who works hard? Are they reflecting attitudes prevailing in the adult population? When they give such a relatively low rating to the student who takes his work seriously are they perhaps expressing disenchantment with school and even a growing rebellion against what the school claims to offer them? Further research would be required to answer these questions. Whatever the reasons underlying the results shown in Table 31 may be, these findings are consistent with trends in other studies which show that many children become less enthusiastic about the academic program as they move from elementary school into high school. It seems that the elementary school offers a more favorable environment for the bright child than does the high school. Even the effects of low socio-economic status do not seem to deter the intellectually able child from doing good work in the elementary school, although they may have an adverse effect on pupils of average or low ability (Curry 1962; Svensson 1962).

Brightness and Undisclosed Personal Problems. Partly because of their higher intelligence, gifted children may be able to conceal personal problems from the eyes of their teachers. Many of them come from middle or high socio-economic backgrounds in which there is less openly expressed emotional reaction than is found among children of lower socio-economic status. In a study of 100 children with IQ's ranging from 150 to over 180, Gallagher and Crowder (1957) report that 20 per cent of the youngsters had emotional problems sufficient to cause personal difficulties; but usually the children managed not to bring these to the surface in a manner that was irritating to their teachers or so obvious that the teachers would rate them as emotionally maladjusted.

Giftedness
and Attitudes toward Self

Since brains are a great asset, the gifted child has a great potentiality for developing a realistic conception of himself and a favorable attitude regarding his worth. He is more likely than the average child to win success and praise at school. He has a better than even chance in competition with others. His family is more likely to be of middle or high than low socio-economic status and thus he avoids the stigma of being born on the wrong side of the tracks (there are, of course, many exceptions to this). He is potentially better able than those who are less richly endowed to take a thoughtful view of things, to plan, and to avoid the penalties of foolish actions. Theoretically, also, he should be able to use his superior intelligence in dealing with predicaments which lead to fear, anger, or unresolved grievances. In addition, his greater ability to deal with moral questions (at least on an intellectual level) should help him to take a reasonable view of his conduct and to avoid a burden of irrational guilt.

Actually, however, high intelligence does not guarantee insight or healthy self-esteem. While gifted children generally rate higher than below-average children in tests of emotional adjustment, it has not been found that they uniformly rate themselves high.

In an ordinary school situation, with pupils possessing a wide range of intellectual abilities, a bright child is bound sooner or later to come upon reminders that he is bright, or at least brighter than some of the other pupils. This discovery may come slowly. And one of the ironies of life is that some bright children regard themselves as rather stupid. Such a view of self may arise if a bright child has measured himself (or has been measured) unfavorably against an even brighter sibling. It may also occur if he measures himself primarily against the brightest pupils at school.

Bright children differ greatly in ratings of their abilities and in their attitudes toward themselves. In several studies it has been found that bright "underachievers" at the junior high school level and beyond have more negative feelings about themselves (or others) than equally bright high-achieving pupils. Negative self-assessment appears particularly in underachieving boys. (Studies in this area have been reviewed by Goldberg, 1965.)

"The Promise of Youth"

In a classic study by Terman and his associates, the careers of a thousand gifted persons who first had been studied as children were followed into adult years (Terman and Oden, 1940, 1959). Almost 90 per cent of the boys and 85 per cent of the girls had attended college, and although these gifted children were, on the average, nearly two years younger than their classmates, about three times as many of them graduated with honors. About two-fifths of the boys and one-fifth of the girls had earned half or more than half of their expenses as undergraduates.

Of those who had completed their training and could be classed as employable, less than 1 per cent were unemployed in 1936, even though this was a period of widespread unemployment. The moral record of the group was found to be "well above that of the generality." At least half of the boys were launched upon promising careers in 1936, and several of them were already nationally or internationally known. While a large majority of these young people made superior records in college, some did not.

An interesting conclusion in Terman's study was that an IQ in excess of 140 or 150 added little to achievement in early adult years. Above this level, adult success seemed to be determined by social adjustment, emotional stability, and the drive to accomplish. This does not mean, the investigators state, that the potentiality for achievement is the same for individuals with an IQ of 150 as for persons with even higher IQ's. Rather, the more probable interpretation, according to Terman and Oden, is that we have not learned how to bring the highest gifts to fruition and how best to guide the personality development of those who are extremely bright.

The fact that a person's achievement and excellence as a person does not depend on intelligence alone appears in an account by Hollingworth of exceedingly bright persons with IQ's of 180 or more (1942). A person with such towering intelligence may perform spectacular feats and yet, for lack of well-balanced personal qualities, his achievements as an individual or his contribution to society may be mediocre.

The gifted persons in the Terman group were studied again (Terman and Oden, 1959) in "mid-life" (between the ages of forty and fifty). With few exceptions they were superior adults. They excelled the average to the greatest extent in intellectual ability, scholastic accomplishment, and vocational achievement. Although many of them had achieved distinction, the number who had made outstanding contributions to arts and letters or who had reached the highest standings in the fields of science was not large (Goldberg, 1965). The adults in the Terman group excelled the average in physical health, and their mortality rate was below average. A smaller proportion of these persons than in the general population had been delinquents or alcoholics. Apart from this, however, they did not differ greatly from the general population in the extent to which they had encountered personal difficulties.

On the basis of information concerning their personal adjustment, supplied by the gifted persons themselves and by others, they were classified according to three categories, as follows:

1. *"Satisfactory adjustment."* Essentially normal; not necessarily perfectly contented or without difficulties but able to cope adequately with life's problems as they arose and possessing desires, emotions, and interests that were compatible with the social standards and pressures of this group; 68.8 per cent of the men and 65.9 per cent of the women were classed in this category.

2. *"Some maladjustment."* In this category were persons with "excessive feelings of inadequacy or inferiority, nervous fatigue, mild anxiety neurosis, and the like." These were persons who definitely had problems but were able to handle them without "marked interference with social or personal life or achievement." Persons whose behavior was noticeably odd or freakish, but without evidence of serious neurotic tendencies, were also included in this group. Over a fifth of the gifted persons were in this "Some maladjustment" category (22.3 per cent of the men and 25.1 per cent of the women).

3. *"Serious maladjustment."* These people were judged to have "serious maladjustment": (a) persons who had shown "marked symptoms of anxiety, mental depression, personality maladjustment, or psychopathic personality" and "nervous breakdown," but whose condition was not so severe that they

went to hospitals for the mentally ill; and (b) those who at some time had had "a complete mental breakdown requiring hospitalization." Eight and nine-tenths per cent of the gifted men and 9 per cent of the women at middle age were in this "serious maladjustment" group (about two-thirds were in category 3a and about one-third in 3b).

The findings in this study of gifted persons indicate that unusually high intellectual ability is more likely to insure that a person will make important achievements and win success in the eyes of the world than to protect him from misfortunes in the more intimate and personal dimensions of his private life.

The story of gifted children told by Terman and his associates is dramatic but it leaves many questions unanswered. The measurement of the intellectual abilities of these bright persons when young were based primarily on the conventional types of tests and scholastic records. There are qualities of the human intellect that are not measured by the typical IQ test. Moreover, if from the beginning this research had given careful attention to the ideas and attitudes these gifted children held regarding themselves as they moved from childhood into adulthood it could have added greatly to our understanding of human development.

Education of the Gifted

Although gifted children are very resourceful in finding ways of putting their abilities to work, they cannot themselves create an environment that will bring out their full potentialities. Hollingworth estimated that in the ordinary elementary school situation children of 140 IQ waste half of their time and those above 170 IQ waste practically all their time!

In one case described by Hollingworth (1939), the most tangible results of a girl's brightness was an increase in the amount of laundering her mother had to do because the teacher, to keep her occupied, asked her to clean the blackboards and erasers while the other children were working at their lessons.

Hollingworth also described a ten-year-old boy with an IQ of 165 who was referred to as a problem: "Not interested in schoolwork. Very impudent. A liar." His trouble was by no means lack of interest. The teacher had resented the boy's superior knowledge and had given him a "raking-over" before the whole class. A friendly counselor to whom the boy was telling his troubles suggested that he should learn to be more tolerant. But the child was so filled with resentment that when told "One of the first things to learn in the world is to suffer fools *gladly*," he heard only the word "suffer" and replied, "Yes, that's it. That's what *I* say! Make 'em suffer. Roll a rock on 'em." As the conversation proceeded, however, this boy was "straightened out on the subject of who was to do the suffering. He agreed to do it himself." In another instance, the epithet, "Perfesser," was thrown at a ten-year-old child, of IQ 175, when he tried to discuss events of medieval history.

The children in Hollingworth's experiment were able to cover the regular elementary school course requirements in less than half their time and were able to push far ahead into projects with which the average child, and even the average adult, usually does not become familiar. Hollingworth has emphasized that a program of intellectual training represents only a part of the bright child's needs. He needs adequate opportunities to develop wholesome attitudes toward himself and toward others and to achieve competence as a social being.

Creativity

According to a statement by Guilford, cited earlier, there are many ways of being intelligent. One of many ways is to employ what Guilford calls "convergent" thinking; another is to use "divergent" thinking. The convergent thinker follows conventional paths. He uses the information at hand to arrive at conclusions leading to one right answer. This is also the answer another would reach, if he used straight thinking. It is the answer that someone, who already has traversed the ground, knows in advance.

The divergent thinker does not move in such an ordered way from given premises to foregone conclusions. He makes excursions from the beaten track. He seeks variety. He goes beyond what is obvious and apparent. He seeks not the *one* correct solution, but considers several possible answers. He is not sure where his thoughts will lead; perhaps nowhere, and perhaps into a new way of looking at things.

Divergent thinking, as compared with convergent thinking, is more flexible and fluid; it is not confined to the information at hand; it permits a richer flow of ideas, and thus opens a way toward solutions that are novel and "creative."

Creativity is a rather elusive talent, but much effort has been directed in recent years toward developing tests that measure creativity (or at least some aspects of creative thinking).

In tests of creativity, the aim has not been to measure a person's ability to give a predetermined correct answer to a test item (as in the usual intelligence test), but rather to measure the number, variety, or novelty of ideas that are evoked by a given problem or task. In giving the meaning of the word "bolt," for example, a person might confine himself to one category (to fasten down; to secure; bolt a door; bolt a hatch on a ship); another with a more prolific and varied set of associations, will use a number of categories, such as to fasten down, to run away quickly; to eat food rapidly; a horse bolts; a bolt of cloth; a bolt of lightning.[9]

Among the achievements used to identify persons with creative talent are: having made an invention; having won a prize for creative writing; having

---

[9] This example is from a study by Getzels and Jackson (1960).

won an award in art competition (see, e.g., Torrance, 1962). Ratings have also been used to distinguish between youngsters judged by their teachers to be creative and non-creative. In a study by Rivlin (1959) teachers judged pupils on the basis of a number of criteria of creativeness, such as giving work a "personal touch"; imaginative and original solutions to problems; ventures into unfamiliar or new areas.

Findings regarding the personalities and school performance of children with varying creativity—IQ patterns have varied somewhat, but some characteristics seem to stand out in distinguishing the highly creative from the less creative. The highly creative tend to be playful, to appreciate humor, to formulate ideas outside the "beaten track," to be venturesome, to pursue or express self-chosen interests. Highly creative children, notably the boys, frequently have "wild" or "silly" ideas as judged by their teachers and peers.

High creativity is less of an asset than high IQ in meeting demands at school, and a child with high creativity coupled with a substantially lower level of IQ may be at odds with the school.

In a thoughtful critique of earlier studies of creativity, Thorndike (1962) has called attention to problems connected with the identification of creative acts and creative persons. When we speak of creative persons we imply that however much they may differ in the medium they employ (art, music, poetry, science, etc.) they have a common quality and that this quality can be differentiated from qualities designated by other labels.

From an analysis of several studies, Thorndike concludes that ". . . there is some reality to a broad domain, distinct from the domain of the conventional intelligence test, to which the designation divergent thinking or creative thinking might legitimately be applied." However, his analyses suggest that this is a ". . . rather more nebulous and loosely formed domain than that of conventional intellect."

In an effort to differentiate creative thinking from the thinking measured in the usual type of intelligence test, Wallach and Kogan (1965) devised procedures that departed in important respects from the usual standardized test. The procedures were designed to tap the ability to generate a flow of associations in response to verbal and visual stimuli. Sample verbal test items included: "Name all the round things you can think of." "Tell me all the ways in which a potato and a carrot are alike." The visual items included pattern drawings and line drawings. The child was told to respond to these by using his imagination in relating all the things each pattern might mean or what each line made him think of. Each of the testing instruments produced two measures: the number of associations produced and the uniqueness of the associations that were produced. This was in keeping with the concept that creativity rests on "associative freedom and uniqueness: the ". . . ability to give birth to associative content that is abundant and original, yet relevant to the task at hand rather than bizarre" (p. 289). No time limit was placed on the tests.

The extent to which Wallach and Kogan were able to produce measures of what they regard as creativity, as distinguished from general intelligence, is indicated by the following. The average correlation among ten tests of creativity was about .40, and the average correlation among ten intelligence measures that were used was about .50, but the average correlation between the creativity and general intelligence indicators was only about .10. This means that the subtests of creativity, to a significant degree, measured abilities that had a common quality; likewise that the intelligence subtests measured abilities with a common quality; while the two tests, in their totality, had very little in common.

The children in the Wallach-Kogan study were classified according to four categories. The four categories, and additional characteristics shown by children in each group, as determined by other measures, follow:

> *High creativity-high intelligence.* These children, to a greater extent than children in other groups, combined self-control with freedom; they were capable of both adultlike and childlike forms of behavior.
>
> *High creativity-low intelligence.* These children, while able to function well at times on a cognitive level, tended to be in conflict with themselves and with their school environment and to manifest feelings of inadequacy.
>
> *Low creativity-high intelligence.* These youngsters were "addicted" to school achievement. Academic failure they regarded as "catastrophic."
>
> *Low creativity-low intelligence.* These children were bewildered, used defensive strategies ranging from ". . . useful adaptations such as intensive social activity to regressions such as passivity or psychosomatic symptoms" (p. 303).

Systematic inquiry into creative talent in children is more recent than investigation of general intelligence as measured by conventional tests. Nothing equivalent to Terman's long-term study of gifted children is available in the field of creativity. What might be the results if persons judged to be highly creative as children and adolescents were compared in "mid-life," with the high IQ persons in the Terman studies? There undoubtedly would be some similarity between the findings because the groups would overlap: a large number of persons in the Terman group would no doubt have scored high in creativity, and a large number of a hypothetical group of highly creative children would have high IQ's. The chances are, however, that a "high-creativity" group of persons might not, on the whole, confirm "the promise of youth" as well as did the Terman group. The odds favor the child with a high IQ as measured by conventional tests. As Torrance (1962) has pointed out, schools encourage and reward convergent thinking more than potentially creative divergent thinking. The creative child must come up against an adverse wind when teachers and peers regard his ideas as wild or silly. He must struggle, often single-handedly, to assert and maintain the integrity of his individual talents. As he moves into adult life, the person with a high IQ usually can find a ready-made market for his abilities. He can through his energies single-mindedly win his way into his vocation. The creative person is less sure of a market. He may have to pursue his creative interests through an avocation.

Recent emphases in psychology and trends in education do not promise to make it easier for the child who has a capacity for divergent thinking. If anything, they promise to make it harder. In many schools—even at the kindergarten level—there now is a move underway to push children as expeditiously as possible into mastering the principles underlying the mathematics and science on which modern technology rests. From another quarter comes an emphasis on training children to master the operations involved in logical thinking, as expounded by Piaget. These pressures are directed primarily toward getting the young to grapple with answers scientists already know and to master time-worn steps in logic.

As usually presented, Piaget's principle of conservation is a prime example of convergent thinking: everything is given; all that remains is for a child to grasp ideas that already are obvious to logicians. But to deal with problems confronting an uneasy nuclear-age world it probably is necessary to go beyond obvious, time-worn methods of solution—to go beyond say, the extension of knowledge from missiles to anti-missiles to anti-anti-missiles. The solutions probably lie more in the psychological sphere—where so much still remains unknown—and in the moral sphere where ancient precepts need to be reinterpreted in terms of modern life. Pioneering in these areas requires creative thinking. The divergent thinking of one creative mind might perhaps achieve more, for better or for worse, than the collective minds of millions.

Children with Below Average IQ's

Children whose mental ability is below average range from those who are able to gain some benefit from regular school attendance (although they are likely to have difficulties) to those whose handicap is so severe that they are classed as mentally deficient.

The youngsters who stand highest in the mentally backward group are frequently referred to as "slow learners." According to a survey by Johnson (1958), the slow learners include the 15 to 17 per cent of school children who cannot quite "keep up" and who usually do the poorest work in the regular classroom. Among the youngsters in the lowest segment of the mentally retarded group are those who in the past have been classed as "feeble-minded." According to one definition, the "feeble-minded" or mentally deficient category includes youngsters with an IQ below 70.

A child who suffers from severe mental deficiency presents a special problem both to society and—more especially—to his family. If such a child is born into a family in which there are other children with normal intelligence, as sometimes occurs, the whole family faces a heavy burden. By reason of guilt or compassion or a combination of both, parents may go to great expense and trouble to get medical aid for the youngster when he is young and to protect him as he grows older. If urged, for the good of the total family situation, to place him in an institution, they face an agonizing conflict. When the child is young his parents go through an anxious period when they begin to sense, but perhaps refuse to admit, that their child is defective. As the youngster grows older many parents have forebodings about the future and about what might happen to the helpless child if they should die. In the meantime the child's brothers and sisters, even if they are basically goodhearted, may feel that their family is under a cloud, or feel that *their* rights are being sacrificed in favor of the unfortunate sibling. The label "mental deficiency" or "feeble-mindedness" covers a great amount of human tragedy.

Slow Learners

Slow learners usually have difficulty in meeting ordinary school requirements, but many of them have potentialities for "essentially normal" emotional, social, physical, and motor development (Johnson, 1958). Sooner or later, however, many of these youngsters encounter emotional difficulties. A large proportion of "trouble makers" in school are youngsters with low intelligence. But their troublesomeness does not arise primarily because of a special bent for getting into difficulty; the trouble springs largely from the kinds of demands placed on them. If pressure is put on slow learners to keep pace with others in the conventional curriculum, to learn faster than their ability permits, or to learn in a setting in which they soon realize that others are much better than they, it is difficult for them to avoid feeling that they are not much good. They especially face difficulties if they are taunted by other children, referred to as "dopes," or are lashed by the sarcasm of impatient teachers. Yet within the limits of their ability they have the capacity to enjoy the thrill of achievement. Unless they have acquired deep grievances, they are as eager for acceptance and affection as anyone else. In common with all other human beings, they know the meaning of fear and taste the bitterness of anger. Many of them also are likely to be rather lonely people, for when other children in a regular classroom pick out their companions, they are unlikely to pick the slow learners. The slow learners did not choose the poor heredity or poor environment underlying their inability to do well at school. Yet they are likely to feel that from the point of view of the school, and from their point of view, it is their own fault when they fail to make the grade.

The main goals in an educational program for slow learners are much the same as those that should prevail in an educational program for all children —namely, to help the youngsters as far as possible to develop their potentialities, to use their resources, to develop skills and the attitudes that will enable them to achieve a healthy regard for themselves and to live productive lives.

Recommended Readings

Measurement and Evaluation in Psychology and Education, by Robert L. Thorndike and Elizabeth Hagen (1961), is recommended to those who are interested in studying the nature and results of tests of mental ability and achievement. *Education of Exceptional Children and Youth,* edited by William M. Cruickshank and G. Orville Johnson (1967), and *The Exceptional Individual* (1967), by Charles W. Telford and James M. Sawrey, contain excellent chapters dealing with the characteristics of children with exceptional abilities or handicaps and educational programs that have been established to meet the needs of these children. Factors influencing the reliability of tests of young infants have been analyzed by Werner and Bayley (1966).

22

Moral Development

and Religion

A child's moral code eventually consists of his ideas of right and wrong, his convictions about his responsibilities and about what he should or should not do or be, and the values and standards by which he judges the worthiness or unworthiness of his thoughts and actions.

Trends and Directions in Moral Development

The work of Piaget (1932) has greatly influenced the study of children's moral development. He has described certain qualities of children's moral judgments during various periods of childhood.

Among the important developments, as described by Piaget, that mark a change from what is less mature to more mature moral judgment are the following:

>A shift from morals based on specific rules to more general conceptions of what is right and wrong.
>
>A shift from a "morality of constraint" to a "morality of cooperation."
>
>A shift away from belief in "immanent justice," the view that punishment for wrong-doing flows automatically from the child's acts, without the intervention of a punishing person (e.g., if a child stumbles and hurts himself after stealing apples from an orchard, he was hurt because he stole).
>
>A shift from moral conduct that is primarily a response to external demands toward a moral code that is based on internal standards which the child has adopted as his own.
>
>An increased ability to perceive rules of the game as rules based on mutual respect and mutual consent rather than on arbitrary edicts.
>
>An increased ability and willingness, in judging the acts of others, to take account of the circumstances in which these acts occur and of the motives and intentions underlying them, instead of judging them according to inflexible standards. For example, a young child may voice the opinion that to steal is to steal and all stealing is bad. When he is a bit older he will view the stealing of an apple by a hungry child as a less serious offense than the stealing of an apple by a well-fed adult.

In his account of the development of moral judgment, Piaget makes a distinction between moral "realism" and "relativism." The moral "realist" is literal in his interpretation of rules. He applies the letter rather than the spirit of the law (as when he equally condemns the two apple-stealers mentioned above). He judges the seriousness of an act according to its practical consequences (for example, the *accidental* spilling of a pitcher full of milk is a more serious offense than the *intentional* spilling of a cupful).

Further, according to the concept of moral realism, duty is a strict matter of obedience. What is right is *heteronomous* (subject to laws imposed by others) as distinguished from being *autonomous* (subject to the individual's own judgment and his right to make decisions and allowances). Moral realism also prevails if a person not only judges the seriousness of an act according to the arbitrary letter of the law but also according to the severity of the punishment that is applied. (A "moral realist" might, for example, regard a child who is slapped for whispering in class as a more serious offender than a youngster who is mildly reprimanded for smashing a window.)

With changes in the child's moral judgment according to Piaget, there also are changes in his views regarding justice and punishment.

At first, justice requires that a person who has committed a wrong should suffer for it—the justice of expiation. There also is the justice of retribution: if he breaks your toy, you (or someone) should break his. At a later stage, justice rests on the idea of reciprocation and restitution. Let the wrongdoer make up for what he has done, for example, by giving up a toy of his own, or supplying the money for mending the toy he has broken.

Piaget regards the less mature types of moral judgment as lasting into the age of about seven or eight, followed in the ensuing years by the emergence of a more mature moral outlook.

Shifts in moral orientation, such as those described, seem quite convincing from a logical point of view; and the changes might be expected if a child, as he matures, views justice less from a punitive and more and more from a philosophical point of view.

According to Piaget, the changes in children's ideas about morality and justice come about through maturation and environmental influences. There are ideas regarding morality, just as there are ideas about natural phenomena, that a younger child does not have the intellectual power to grasp.

Although children are uneven in their moral development, and many do not seem to acquire an autonomous system of morality, some of the sequences Piaget describes have been confirmed by other investigators.

Children aged nine to thirteen, as compared with children aged six or seven, are likely to show more "mature" responses in judging the seriousness of an act in terms of the underlying intention rather than in terms of what objectively happened, in applying rules more flexibly, in viewing right and wrong in relative rather than absolute terms, in not judging that the greater the punishment an act evokes the more seriously wrong it must be, in accepting the idea of achieving justice through making amends rather than through punishment, and in abandoning the concept of "immanent justice." [1] However, the findings do not generally show that children near their teens have formulated an internal set of moral standards of their own to the extent that Piaget's statements would indicate.

Actually, children seem to be rather perverse when their moral development is judged in terms of what it theoretically might be and what, perhaps, it morally should be. It seems that a child's morals do not "grow" as his body and intellect grow. Some children, even in their teens, appear to be childishly amoral (Peck, *et al.*, 1960). Some practice a morality of expediency (it's o.k. if I can get away with it). Some follow a morality of conformity (others do it, so it must be right, so I guess I'd better do it, too). Some, in their teens, exhibit a "rational conscientious" type of morality. This, in the classification scheme used by Peck, *et al.*, goes well beyond an amoral stance, or a morality of expediency or conformity. The "rational conscientious" person has his own internal standard of what is right and wrong. But he regards an act as good or bad because he rationally defines it as such and not primarily out of consideration for the good or ill effects his behavior might have on others. Only a minority of the adolescents in the Peck, *et al.*, study reached what they regarded as ". . . the highest level of moral maturity." This they describe as the "rational altruistic type." A person with this moral orientation has a stable set of moral principles of his own; he applies it with an eye both to his own good and the good of others.

---

[1] Findings bearing on this have been reviewed by Kohlberg (1963) and Grinder (1964).

**Moral Judgment
as Related to Family Background**

Children of low IQ and socio-economic status tend to lag behind in developing ideas of morality. This is illustrated in a study by Harrower (1934) who questioned children about cheating.

Children from homes of relatively high educational and socio-economic status most frequently answered to this effect: "It doesn't do any good," or "One can't learn that way." Children from a poorer environment more frequently gave such answers as "Cheating is forbidden. It is naughty. It is a lie. It is unfair."

Harrower also questioned children concerning their ideas of punishment. They were told a tale about two boys, Peter and Tommy, who were playing together. Peter had a lovely new engine and Tommy had a boat. Naughty Tommy suddenly kicked Peter's engine and smashed it. Now, what should be done with naughty Tommy? Should he be "smacked" (appeal to authority and a *retaliatory* concept of punishment), should his own boat be broken up (the idea of *reciprocation*—an eye for an eye), or should he be made to save up his pocket money until he can buy Peter a new engine (the idea of equity, *restitution*, or making amends)? In response to these questions, a majority of the poorer children, in the age range from six to eight years, gave the authoritarian answer: "Smack him." At eight to eleven years a majority of the poorer children gave the third type of answer: "He should make up for the damage." A large majority of children from more privileged homes, both at the age range from six to eight and from eight to eleven, answered that Tommy should replace the toy that he had broken. In both groups and at both age ranges, the "eye-for-an-eye" (break his toy) type of answer occurred relatively infrequently.

Children of low socio-economic status are, on the average, more authoritarian in their judgments. They recommend more severe punishment for misconduct (Dolger and Ginandes, 1946). But while recommending more severe punishment, they also commit offenses which get them into trouble relatively more often (as seen from the high delinquency rate in some low socio-economic groups).

When children of low socio-economic status have a poorer moral record than children of higher socio-economic status many influences are at work, including such factors as the effects of poverty and neglect, lower average level of intelligence, differences in the standards or examples that are set before them, and a tendency among persons of lower status to lay down rules of conduct in an arbitrary way rather than to discuss the pro's and con's of what constitutes good moral behavior.

There are many interesting paradoxes in the relationship between socio-economic status and moral attitudes and conduct. On the one hand, in some lower socio-economic groups the standards seem, if anything, to be more severe than those prevailing in upper socio-economic groups. Standards of modesty and obedience to authority, for example, are especially strict among some lower groups, and, as noted above, members of lower socio-economic groups tend to prescribe more severe punishment for misconduct. On the other hand, many forms of conduct that are generally disapproved in the higher socio-economic groups prevail relatively more frequently in the lower groups, including truancy, fighting, sexual misconduct, stealing, and vandalism. From this we might infer that a child who is subjected to rigid rules and the threat of punishment is likely, if anything, to be less morally upright than a youngster for whom the rules of conduct and threats of punishment are not so severe. However, we are dealing here with a very complicated psychological situation that cannot be explored simply by a statistical comparison between groups. We face enigmas which have confronted us elsewhere in this book. One child who is brought up strictly turns out to be a fine moral character, while another does not. A youngster who has been reared in a very permissive moral atmosphere turns out to be a splendid character, while another runs into trouble. Two youngsters—one from the slums and the other from the best section of the community—acquire fine moral characters. Even within the same home much the same kind of moral training may lead to a high degree of conformity in one child and a considerable amount of rebellion in another.

An interesting comparison of the moral judgments of children differing in social origins was made in a study by Liu (1950) of fifty-two New York City Chinese-American children and fifty-two children of American-born parents. Both groups were of relatively low socio-economic status. The Chinese children had been brought up in the so-called tradition of "ancestor worship." This might, theoretically, mean that they should show greater respect than others for adult authority. According to Liu they did. But, paradoxically, they also appeared to display more maturity in their moral judgments. According to Liu, the Chinese-American children's greater respect for authority does not necessarily mean that they are subservient and unable to form autonomous moral concepts. Respect for age and seniority, according to Liu, is not just a one-way affair. An older person who wins respect from younger persons also, along with this, has a responsibility for them. The twelve-year-old who is entitled to respect from the six-year-old also has obligations toward the six-year-old to understand, defend, and protect him. According to Liu, the well-defined roles of Chinese-American children give them more freedom to assess responsibility and to judge an act from the point of view of the motive or intention underlying it. More children in the Chinese-American group than in the other said, for example, that a girl who accidentally cut a *little* hole in her dress while playing with scissors, after she had been forbidden to use the scissors, was committing a more serious moral offense than a girl who accidentally cut a *large* hole in a dress while cutting out a picture which she thought her mother would especially like.

Relationship between Cognitive Ability and Moral Judgment

Piaget (1962) has set forth the hypothesis that moral sentiments rest on a conservation of values, analogous to the way in which the principle of conservation is an essential attribute of logical thinking (see discussion of the concept of conservation in Chapter 20). This is an attractive theory since, if verified, it would be valuable both from the standpoint of providing an important lead to research in moral development and also from the practical standpoint of moral instruction. It obviously requires conceptual ability of some sort to conceptualize moral principles, as distinguished from simply repeating them by rote.

Findings regarding the relationship between moral reasoning and conceptual ability, as indicated by ability to conserve and to deal with problems of class-inclusion, have been reported in a study of 142 first grade children by Hardeman (1967). The test of moral reasoning consisted of brief stories, offering a child opportunities to evaluate the goodness or badness or seriousness of acts and happenings under a variety of circumstances (e.g., making a distinction between an accidental mishap or an intentional misdeed). The measures of cognitive ability included those used by Almy and her associates and by Miller, as described in Chapter 20.

There was a positive relation between "conservation" scores and total moral reasoning scores. There were sixty-three "total conservers" (earning a perfect score); five of these earned a maximum score (11) on moral reasoning and about half of this group had moral reasoning scores of five or more. By contrast, in the totally "non-conserving" group of twenty-two children about half the number earned moral reasoning scores of two or less. There was no clear relation between scores on moral reasoning and scores on class-inclusion.

The findings suggest that conservation ability is ". . . a necessary but not sufficient condition" for ensuring a mature level of moral reasoning.

The Moral Conscience

Sooner or later, all being well, a child will acquire a conscience: a system of ideas, attitudes, and inner controls that decree what is right and wrong and what are his duties and responsibilities. The conscience has been described as a super-ego or internalized set of values and controls that originally were prescribed by others but eventually are administered by the child himself.

From a psychological point of view, the conscience is a rather nebulous thing. From a pragmatic point of view, it is a very handy thing, unless it is "too severe." The person who has a clear set of internalized principles does not have to go through a long debate with himself each time he confronts a moral issue. The conscience contains scruples against what he should not do (a guardian against errors of commission) and ideas concerning what he ought or should do (a guardian against errors of omission).

The conscience usually does not represent a unitary, internally consistent set of principles or sanctions. It has many facets. It may be the voice of expedience (better not, someone might be looking). It may be rigorous in some matters, not in others. It may prevail over temptation. Or it may be a sort of gadfly, which does not prevent a person from doing what he thinks he ought not to do, but only prevents him from enjoying it.

There are many views regarding the origin of the individual conscience, in particular, and the origin of morality and ethics in general. Broadly speaking, these views range at one extreme from the position that a human being's ability to become morally responsible is inherent within the structure of his personality. At the other end is the view that morality and ethics are superimposed (the superego) on a human creature who is essentially self-centered, pleasure-seeking, amoral, and unprincipled.

Parents as Models of Morality

According to one theory, a child's conscience is based on his *identification* with his parents. A more exact expression would be *identifications*. The ways in which individual children, consciously or unconsciously, use their parents as models and incorporate the ways of their parents into their own style of life are about as varied as life itself. Given a thousand children and their parents, there most likely will be a thousand distinct ways in which the children "identify."

Since parents offer instruction both by precept and example, we might expect children, eventually, to adopt their parent's moral standards and values. But any parent is likely to testify, with a mixture of satisfaction, regret, and perplexity, that this model works in unpredictable ways. The model may, of course, be so complicated that no child could adopt it. Parents may differ considerably in their moral outlook, in the importance they attach to various virtues and faults, in the degree to which they practice what they preach, in the internal consistency of their moral standards, in the extent to which their morality rests on values to which they are committed as distinguished from hidden currents of anxiety, guilt, and resentment of authority.

Generally speaking, we may expect a child of parents with reasonably good moral characters to have a chance to develop a good moral character of his own. However, children usually are rather selective in the virtues and foibles they choose to emulate.

A number of reasons have been advanced to explain why a child might identify with his parents.[2] He adopts their ways (or the ways of one of his parents) for reasons of love and security to keep them near him even when they are absent. He may identify out of fear, to avoid their wrath. He may identify with the most loving, or the most powerful, or the one most representing the sources of the things he desires. Views (and findings) with regard to identification vary greatly, and most of them fail adequately to consider the fact that a child who does the "identifying" has his own individual bent.

On the whole, it seems that a child is likely to be swayed by his parents' example if they use "psychological" rather than arbitrary methods. In the long run, reasoning or disapproval, through seeming withholding of affection, are likely to have more effect on a child's character than peremptory physical punishment. Physical punishment is more likely to induce a morality based on fear than on commitment. A child who is physically assaulted cannot help but be resentful, although, consciously, at the moment, he may think the punishment was deserved, and that it atones for his wrong-doing.

Many investigators have attempted to study the relation between parents' child-rearing procedures and the development of the conscience in children. Most of the data regarding child-rearing practices have been obtained from interviews with mothers. (The reader may recall, from studies reviewed in Chapter 12, that parents' reports are quite unreliable, especially when parents have to draw on their recollections.) The results, on the whole, are rather inconsistent and inconclusive. When relationships have been found, they usually rest on low statistical values.

Resistance to Temptation

Burton, *et al.* (1961) used an experimental procedure (a bean-bag game) with four-year-old children to measure resistance to temptation to cheat. They also obtained information from the children's mothers about certain child-rearing practices and aspects of the children's behavior at home. They devised an "evidence of conscience" measure, based on mothers' reports of how the children behaved when they had done something wrong and before the mother knew about it. One interesting finding was that children who rated high on the measure of conscience or evidence of guilt on the basis of mothers' reports cheated more in the bean-bag game than those who, according to the mothers' reports, were less conscientious or inclined to express guilt. The negative relationship between conscience ratings and resistance to temptation suggests that conditions underlying guilt and the ability to resist temptation are not the same. This is in keeping with other findings that moral development is a rather complex affair, a multiple rather than a single process, as indicated in an earlier writing by Allinsmith (1960). It appears

---

[2] For a thoughtful discussion of the concept of identification see Bronfenbrenner (1960).

that resistance to temptation and guilt cannot be regarded as alternative or equivalent measures of moral standards but must be regarded as distinct phenomena.

Relationship between "Maturity" of Moral Concepts and Behavior

As we have seen, a child's tendency to be conscientious in the sense of blaming and condemning himself for wrongdoing apparently does not indicate how well he can resist the next temptation that comes along. Furthermore, the "maturity" of a child's ideas about morality and justice does not give a clear indication of how moral his behavior will be. Knowledge of moral principles does not mean that the principles will be scrupulously applied.

An interesting study by Grinder (1964) deals with the relation between resistance to temptation and certain aspects of maturity of moral judgment. Grinder used an apparatus to assess resistance to temptation (see Grinder, 1961), consisting of a realistic "ray-gun" shooting gallery so contrived that any cheating by a child could be detected and recorded, unknown to the subject. To measure children's ideas regarding morality Grinder used familiar story situations. One story sequence told about a child who accidentally broke a number of cups and about a child who broke one cup as a consequence of an intentional act. The immature "moral realist" would regard the accidental act as more serious because more damage was done. Grinder also tested for the presence of the idea of "immanent justice" by means of an uncompleted story (such as, what happens to a child who, knowing it is against the rules when no adult is near, has climbed halfway up a jungle gym). The children in the study ranged from seven to twelve years.

In keeping with Piaget's theory, the results showed that there was a rather sharp drift, from age 7-8 to 11-12, in children's cognitive moral maturity as measured by the tests of "moral realism" and "immanent justice." There was not, however, a corresponding change in conforming to the rules in the shooting game, as shown by yielding to or resisting the temptation to cheat. There was little support for the conjecture (tentatively advanced by Piaget) that as children advance toward mature moral judgment their behavior will change. From this study it appears that the process of maturation and learning that underlies changes in children's understanding of moral concepts as they grow older is relatively independent of the processes by which they are conditioned to apply concepts of morality to their own behavior.

The findings in this study by Grinder are pretty much in line with what we can observe in everyday life. Added knowledge about rules and standards and their underlying logic does not, in itself, seem to produce conformity to these rules.

Children's ideas regarding morality and their resistance to temptation as measured by the Grinder technique were further studied by Medinnus (1966). Sixth-grade children were questioned regarding their reaction to a news account about cheating. Cadets who had subscribed to an honor code had stolen examination papers and offered them for sale. The children's replies were classed as representing an "externalized" standard of morality (e.g., cheating is forbidden, you might get caught) or an "internalized" standard (cheating is not honorable; it is not fair; it takes an unfair advantage of others).

According to Piaget's account, children at this age have "internalized" standards. In the Medinnus study, however, about twice as many children expressed "externalized standards." Moreover, the study showed, as several other studies have indicated, that there is no firm relationship between moral behavior (in this case, refraining from cheating) and understanding of moral rules. The proportion of children who yielded to the temptation to cheat was practically the same in the group with "internalized" moral rules as in the group with externalized ideas about cheating.

Some readers perhaps will raise questions about the experimental studies reviewed above, and others to be described later. Studies of children's resistance to temptation should perhaps be regarded as studies of their resistance to devious ways of seduction. A child is tempted by rewards of various kinds. He is deceived into thinking that he is quite safe in breaking the rules. If he were capable of mature after-thoughts, he might even claim that if the experimenter can be devious, why not I? Moreover, many studies of cheating do not involve anything more than an academic moral principle. Children who cheat to get a star of approval or some candy or a toy are not harming anyone. They are not taking candy from a hungry mouth. Indeed a "mature" philosophical "moral relativist" might even say that children who refrain from cheating in contrived experimental situations are not so much practicing the virtue of honesty as the somewhat dubious virtue of scrupulosity.

Virtues Children Regard as Important

Younger children as well as adolescents quite consistently give a high rating to certain virtues or values. They usually ascribe greater importance to scruples of the more conventional sort than to moral attitudes which reflect loyalty and feeling for others. It has been found, for example, that children are likely to rate honesty and politeness as being more praiseworthy than kindness and generosity (Thompson, 1949, 1952). Even at the senior high school level such virtues as honesty and sportsmanship receive a higher rating than kindness and charity (Mitchell, 1943). It appears that many children and adolescents in expressing their moral beliefs accept familiar cultural stereotypes without inquiring very deeply into what these stereotypes might mean to them in a personal way (Taba, 1953). It has also been found that children may profess a certain social value, such as the idea that a person should be considerate, and yet apply it unequally in their relationships with others. Foshay and Wann (1954) found that children who stood high in social acceptance in the group to which they belonged were more likely to be considerate toward children who also stood high in acceptance than toward children who did not. ". . . considerateness tended to be directed toward social equals, and to be withheld from social inferiors."

Honesty

In view of the fact that many children claim that honesty is the most important moral virtue, it is instructive to examine some of the findings in a classical study of children's honesty and deceit conducted about forty years ago (Hartshorne and May, 1928). A number of tests were applied, so devised that it was possible to detect whether children had cheated or had given truthful or deceptive answers. It was found that older children were slightly more deceptive than younger ones. This is interesting since several studies have shown that older youngsters are quite as likely as younger ones to regard honesty as being especially praiseworthy. In general, there was no outstanding difference in the deceptiveness of boys and girls. Brighter children were, on the whole, more honest than duller children. Children who showed symptoms of emotional instability (as measured independently by a standard test) showed a greater tendency to be deceptive than those who were better adjusted emotionally. When children were classified into four occupational levels, according to socio-economic status of their parents, those at the highest level deceived the least; those at the second and third highest levels, progressively more; and those at the lowest level, the most.

Children belonging to the same family resembled each other more in honesty and deceptiveness than children matched at random. But the authors of the study believe it is possible that children would vary in deceptiveness even if all were brought up under similar conditions.

There was a positive relationship between cheating and low marks in school deportment.

Children who were friends, even though not members of the same class, showed more than a chance resemblance in the amount of cheating. Children who cheated less tended to be less suggestible. Children in the care of a teacher who was able to stimulate cooperation and good will cheated less than those who were taught under a more conventional and rigid routine. Children who were members of organizations purporting, as one of their aims, to teach honesty, cheated about as much as nonmembers.

The findings in this study indicate that there seems to be no generalized, uniform trait that can be labeled "honesty" which characterizes the child's behavior in all situations. The child who lies, steals, or cheats in one situation may be quite without guile in another; he may be a brazen cheater when given a chance to copy in a test and be completely honorable in an athletic contest.

But the fact that cheating is quite specific does not mean it occurs by chance. When a child cheats there is a motive underlying his behavior— he has something at stake, a desire or purpose. One situation may be seen as an important challenge to win or to succeed by hook or by crook, and another may not. A child may undertake one activity with a desire to learn and to correct his mistakes (and in keeping with this, let his errors be known so that he can get help in learning), whereas, in another situation in which he desires only to "get by," he may cheat if that shortens or eases the task. Accordingly, a child may seem inconsistent in his tendency to cheat when his behavior is viewed from the standpoint of the external situation, and yet his tendency to cheat or to be honest may be consistent when viewed in the light of his own motives.

Children's Ideas
Regarding What Is Wrong or Wicked

There is a change in the course of development both in what children regard as admirable and in what they regard as evil. This change, according to Pringle and Gooch (1966), follows a developmental pattern. A pioneer study in this area was conducted with over 2,000 subjects, aged 8 to 19 years, by Macauley and Watkins (1926). They asked the subjects to ". . . make a list of the most wicked things anyone could do." Up to about nine years of age, the wicked deeds reported consisted of small, individual acts which the children had been taught to regard as wrong. There was very little generalization regarding categories of wrong acts. Generalizations began to appear at around nine or ten years, but it was not until about fourteen years that the children broke away from "conventional, uncritical morality" to a more personal morality. Offences were qualified, with regard for mitigating circumstances. Sensational crimes gave way to crimes involving personal responsibility and "sins of the spirit (selfishness, hypocrisy) and sexual offenses came to the fore."

Pringle and Gooch (1966) made a study in 1964 of fifteen-year-old children who four years earlier had given their versions of wicked deeds. They found that brighter children mentioned certain categories of deeds, such as murder, stealing, and lying, at an earlier age than children of average or below average intelligence. When the latter, at a later age, mentioned these deeds, the brighter children had begun to qualify their ideas of what was most wicked.

Interesting differences between children's ideas regarding misconduct as related to school and as related to the home were found in a study by Gump and Kounin (1961). Children in the first and third grades were asked, "What is the worst thing a child could do at school? Why is that so bad? What is the worst thing a child could do at home? Why is that so bad?" In the two grades combined, misconduct in the category of violations of rules was by far the most frequently mentioned. These violations were, on the whole, rather mild, such as (in the home situation) going out without asking permission and, in the school, "talking when you are supposed to study." Other categories included assaults on children (the examples given by the authors are also rather mild and hardly deserve to be called assaults); breaking or damaging property; disregard for authority (not minding mother; not doing what the teacher says); and miscellaneous. Violation of rules was mentioned more in connection with school than in connection with the home. When asked why the various types of school behavior were bad, a large proportion of the children could give no cogent reason (many gave answers such as, "it's bad because it's bad"). Gump and Kounin point out that children seem to have difficulty in seeing any sound justification for some of the rules at school. "Apparently, at school, one simply takes some prohibitions on faith, . . ." leaving the teacher in a ". . . relatively unassailable role."

The findings in this study take on added interest when viewed in relation to studies of developmental changes in moral judgment. Durkin (1959), for example, tested Piaget's claim that older children, more than younger ones, regard reciprocity ("an eye for an eye") as a principle of justice among peers. Older children regard it as fair, according to Piaget, to return the blows one has received when asked what should be done "if someone punches you?" Younger children are more likely, according to Piaget, to appeal to authority to remedy a wrong. Durkin used brief stories to test this theory. She found, contrary to Piaget, that older children in grades five and eight offered fewer rather than more reciprocity solutions than children in grade two. So it seems Piaget was mistaken. However, the evidence is ambiguous. All the stories Durkin used centered on school. In one of them, a boy named Keith took a ruler off Russell's desk and broke it in two. What should Russell do? According to theory, Russell should have broken Keith's ruler. But only 3, 4, and 0 children, respectively, in grades 2, 5, and 8, prescribed this solution. The others (25, 34, and 35, respectively) said that an authority person (the teacher) should handle it. This seems to refute Piaget. But in this situation it might be conjectured that the older youngsters were not morally immature, nor refuting Piaget; they were simply being realistic. Russell might feel that the thing to do was to break Keith's ruler (and maybe ram it down his throat), but for Russell to break Keith's ruler would be a "violation of rules" and the teacher would give Russell a hard time. (What happened to Keith does not come into the story.)

Moral Orientation as Revealed
by Choices of "Heroes" and "Ideals"

One approach to the study of moral development has been to find who are the characters children admire most or regard as "ideal." In an early study, Macauley and Watkins (1926) asked over two thousand children of varying ages to write accounts under the heading: "What person of whom you have ever heard or read would you most wish to resemble? Give reasons." Since then, numerous other investigators have studied children's heroes and ideals.

One team of investigators, Pringle and Gooch (1965), made a followup study of youngsters' "chosen ideal person" over a four-year period. The first reports were obtained when the children were eleven and the later reports when they were fifteen years old.

In a review of earlier studies and in discussing their own findings, these investigators note that certain age trends are discernible in children's accounts of whom they regard as ideal characters. Up to about eight years, children are likely to name a parent or a parent-figure. Then follows a period up to approximately thirteen years when the choice is more likely to be a glamorous figure, expressing fantasy and wish fulfillment. Later, at about age thirteen and on, the "ideal" person is more likely to be one who represents, or combines, realistic attributes.

These differences do not represent distinct and inevitable stages, but a general trend. Some additional trends can be noted. Girls seem to arrive sooner than boys at a rather realistic assessment of attributes that commonly are regarded as worthy. Children of high socio-economic status tend to be more "realistic" than children below them on the socio-economic ladder. Children who are achieving well at school seem also to accept as their ideals persons with solid attainments rather than persons of transient and evanescent fame (such as those who imitate the Beatles).

Religion

Religion plays a large part in the lives of most people in one way or another. All children in such a culture as ours are influenced by religious practices, ideas, and beliefs, whether or not they receive formal religious instruction. Moreover, in some circles it seems that religion is especially designed for children. Children are dutifully sent to Sunday school even if their parents seldom if ever attend church.

Whether or not a child or his family are actively "religious," they commonly identify themselves with a certain religious background. In the United

States such identification usually is in terms of being Jewish, Catholic, or Protestant. In a series of studies, Elkind (1961, 1962, 1963) has explored the more formal aspects of a child's conception of what this religious identification means. He found that a child moves through certain phases of conceptualization. At first up to about age six, children have only an undifferentiated impression of their religious community: a Jew (Catholic, Protestant) is a person. They cannot tell how a Catholic, Jew, or Protestant differ from one another. Later on, religious identification is described in concrete terms: a Jew goes to the Synagogue; a Catholic goes to Mass; a Protestant goes to church. In a still later phase, at about ten or eleven, more abstract ideas enter the picture: "a Jew is a person who believes in one God"; "a Catholic is one who believes in the truths of the Roman Catholic Church"; "a Protestant believes in God and Christ." Such abstract conceptualization of the meaning of religious affiliation obviously deals more with the institutional than with the personal meaning of being "religious."

Factors Influencing the Meaning of Religious Teachings. A child's religious ideas and images will, of necessity, be influenced by his experiences in everyday life. This fact presents a practical issue to parents and teachers who endeavor to give religious instruction. If the instruction is to be genuine, it must not merely come by way of verbal precepts but must be interpreted also by the practical example set by the child's elders. A child's image of God the Father may include a blend of details from pictures he has seen and Bible stories he has heard. The image may vary from time to time, including now a kindly expression, now a wrathful countenance. His conception of the attributes of a fatherly God will be influenced, perhaps imperceptibly, by his experience of the attributes of his own father or of others in a paternal role. His ideas of sin will be influenced by his experiences of grief or remorse through having caused distress to other persons, and by experiences of regret flowing from hostility or fear aroused by the treatment he has received as a consequence of having disobeyed someone in authority. His ideas of forgiveness will be influenced by his own experience of being forgiven by his elders. The idea of forgiveness will be a difficult one for him to grasp if in his relations with others he finds it impossible to confide or confess his troubles and must bottle up his feelings of guilt and fears of retribution.

The younger the child, the more his ideas in matters of religion, and in other matters, will be built upon his own concrete experiences. These are likely to be elaborated by fantasies. His ideas may be influenced by a multitude of conditions, such as the physical appearance, atmosphere, furnishings, the odors and echoes of the church or synagogue; the confinement of movement imposed upon him if he must sit quietly longer than is agreeable to his limited attention span; the kindliness or austerity of those who give him religious instruction.

From early childhood through the elementary school years, numerous religious concepts will have relatively little meaning to a child in the abstract, and a problem in religious education is how to translate religious concepts into terms that are meaningful. Misconceptions through failure to understand the terms that are used can be seen when a child, for example, comes home and tells his mother about Jesus' twelve bicycles (disciples), or is puzzled by "the consecrated cross-eyed bear" (the consecrated Cross, I'd bear). Children also are confused at times by denominational differences, and frequently they have difficulty in distinguishing between the form and intended substance of religious observances.

In a brief passage, Murphy (1937) has tried to construct a picture, from the child's point of view, of the way Jesus is sometimes presented. Children are likely to learn of Jesus, ". . . not as an ideal grown-up who helped people, but as a little baby whose mother put him in a straw thing in a barn instead of a crib, and to whom queer-looking men in striped gowns brought presents no baby could use. They learn, too, that there was a bad king, with a ferocious face, of whom the baby's mother was afraid, so that she had to take him a long way from home, riding on an animal that is not seen in the city, nor even in the zoo."

Interest in the Bible. Children's interest in Biblical characters and scenes and in different portions of the Bible have been studied in an investigation conducted many years ago in a New England community (Dawson, 1900). Since results of such a study are likely to be influenced by the religious background and affiliations of the children, and might also vary over a period of time, the findings cannot be regarded as typical for all children who have had religious training, but the general trends are noteworthy.

Up to eight or nine years, children with a Christian background expressed most interest in accounts of the birth and childhood of Jesus and in stories concerning the childhood of such characters as Moses, Samuel, Joseph, and David. From nine to thirteen or fourteen years, portions of the Old Testament, especially the historical books, had greatest appeal. At about the age of fourteen, and from then until twenty years (the upper age level in the study), interest in the historical sections receded and there was an increased interest in the Gospels. Dawson also shows "age curves" for other portions of the Bible. From the age of about ten through adolescence, poetic sections of the Bible appeal to numerous children, although the number who chose these sections was considerably smaller than the number who selected the historical books and the Gospels. Books of prophecy received a few votes from the age of twelve and onward. The Proverbs and doctrinal sections received relatively little mention until about the adolescent period and then were preferred by relatively few children. At all ages, children expressed more interest in persons than in other elements of the Bible.

Children's Prayers. One of the many aspects of childhood religion that adults have difficulty in understanding from the child's point of view is prayer. In teaching a child to pray, parents may become involved in many pitfalls, as when they teach a child to approach God as though He were an absent-minded magician, given to granting any thoughtless petition. The idea of praying to a higher power is usually accepted quite readily by children, who, in their experiences, frequently have occasion to be reminded of their own limitations and unfulfilled desires. The desires that lie back of the child's frequent "I wish" or "If only I had" and which he realizes vicariously in his own make-believe can readily be translated into the petition: "Please give." It is considerably easier, of course, to lead a child to petition that his passing desires be granted than to petition that he be helped to have desires and aspirations of the kind that should be granted and the determination to carry out these aspirations. The same, to be sure, also holds true of adults.

Effects of Religious Training. The influence of religious training on children has not been studied systematically. In the general literature of psychology there are miscellaneous findings dealing, for example, with such points as the honesty of children who have attended Sunday school and of children who have not (as measured by tests that give the children an opportunity to cheat), the generosity of such children (again as measured by limited test situations), the degree of "liberal-mindedness" (as defined by the investigator) of members of various religious denominations and of nonmembers, the religious affiliations of delinquents, and so forth. Such studies, do not, on the whole, show that youngsters who regularly receive religious instruction are signficantly more honest or humane than those who don't. The available studies in this area, however, have dealt with the problem in a limited and inconclusive manner.

This problem is difficult to explore in a scientific way, especially since many ends sought by religious instruction reside in the subjective realm of faith, hope, and charity and since the objective good works of religion are supposed to be done with a minimum of fanfare. It is very difficult to measure the "inward" aspects of religious convictions and commitments, the attitude of religious devotion, and the attitudes of humility and compassion which many religions stress.

Even if measurement of outward and visible signs of an inward religious orientation were possible, it would be difficult to find a control group with which to compare the religiously trained individual. Religious influences are deeply imbedded in the culture and there is considerable overlapping between the morals and virtues that are promoted under religious and nonreligious auspices. Because of this distinct overlap between the kind of training and influence brought to bear upon technically religious and nonreligious individuals, it is difficult adequately to measure the effects of religious training even on the more commonplace expressions of moral conduct.

Apart from this overlap on many points between those who have formal religious affiliations and those who do not, there also are wide variations in the religious influences brought to bear upon children who technically receive religious instruction. One child may be required to attend religious services by parents who never themselves attended; another attends with his entire family. In one case, the religious practices of the child's elders may be quite perfunctory, while in another case they occupy an important place in the family's everyday activities. One child's attention may be centered only upon some of the formalities and externals of religion while another may be impressed by the feeling and concern his elders invest in their religion. There are differences also in the extent to which youngsters participate in religious practices as though they were responsible members of the religious community to which they belong. The Jewish boy, after Bar-Mitzvah, can join his elders in prayers for the dead. The Mormon boy and girl assume a succession of titles and responsibilities. In many other denominations the growing child is, so to speak, more of a spectator than a participant.

Religion and Self-Realization

There are many parallels between the psychology of self-realization and psychological features of a religious view of life. In the process of realizing himself, a person will draw upon his capacity for entering into relationships with other people; the religious person will draw on similar capacities as he joins with others in his devotions. In realizing himself, a person will draw upon his capacity for love; the idea of love is also central to most religious faiths. He will draw upon his capacity for realizing the joys and hurts, fears and hopes, struggles and disappointments, pains and gratifications associated with a compassionate way of life; most religions adjure their followers to be compassionate.

In the religious sphere as in the moral sphere, there is a vast discrepancy between what is publicly subscribed to and what is privately embraced, between what is professed and what is realized as a matter of genuine conviction and commitment. Ross (1950), in a study of the religious attitudes of young people, estimates that while about three-fourths of those who were questioned assented to various orthodox religious beliefs and doctrines, only about 16 per cent seemed to show the kind of firmness of belief, zest, and security of conviction which might be expected in a genuinely religious person. In a Foreword comment on Ross' findings, Allport (1950) speaks of the same paradox: Belief in God is almost universal; prayer is widely used; and there is a friendly estimate of the church, and a widely expressed conviction that man needs religion. Yet there is at the same time, in Allport's words, a "ghostly quality" about these attitudes. Many religious teachings are unclear to those who profess them, and their bearing on people's everyday lives is vague.

These observations, in the writer's opinion, touch upon a condition of confusion which faces children in our society. Whether or not the proportions mentioned in this study between those who give lip service and those who speak from genuine conviction are precise is not so important. The fact that there are dislocations of this sort is the important consideration, and it is not in the religious sphere alone that these exist, for we can find large gaps between what is assented to and what is realized as a genuine kind of personal involvement also in politics, in the teaching profession, in scientific bodies, and in all spheres and walks of life.

Such divisiveness, such a schism between the official pose and the personal life that is lived, is, of course, a commonplace. However, this does not free a child from the confusion and inconsistency he faces in connection with his upbringing.

Recommended Readings

Jean Piaget's *The Moral Judgment of the Child* (1932) is an important book which has stimulated a large number of studies of moral development. For an excellent statement of issues in the study of moral development, and a review of findings, see Lawrence Kohlberg's "Moral Development and Identification" (1963), and *The Development of Motives and Values in the Child* by Leonard Berkowitz (1964). Dilemmas in the adult world which directly or indirectly influence the moral climate in which children are reared have been discussed by Karen Horney in *The Neurotic Personality of Our Time* (1937), by Erich Fromm in *The Sane Society* (1955), and in Part I of *Existence*, edited by Rollo May (1958).

PART SIX

Personality Development

23 *Personality*

NORMAL, DEVIANT,

CONSTANT, CHANGING

Personality means the sum-total of an individual's characteristics as a distinct and unique human being. The outer dimensions of personality include an individual's measurable characteristics, his physique, talents, and abilities and the qualities of temperament and disposition that are observable in his public conduct. The inner dimensions comprise an individual's drives and emotional tendencies; the total system of ideas and attitudes that constitute his awareness of himself; and unrecognized or unconscious tendencies that affect his impulses, feelings, and actions.

Heredity, Environment, and Personality Development

When, in everyday life, we speak of a child's "personality" we usually refer to his characteristic ways of behaving. He may be cheerful or moody, impulsive or deliberate, quick-tempered or slow to take offense, dependent or independent, shy or brash, and so on through an almost interminable list of labels used in daily speech and in psychological writings.

Characteristics such as these, and a child's manner of expressing them, become established through his interaction with his environment. Children at birth, it is true, may manifest certain consistent tendencies. One child, for example, shows a high and another a low level of excitability. This suggests that youngsters perhaps differ, genetically, in their predisposition to be excitable under stress. But whatever a child's predisposition might be, the traits he manifests with the passage of time are not directly inherited. They become established in the process of experience and learning. For this reason, it would be difficult, and perhaps impossible, ever to make any precise assessment of the relative roles of heredity and environment on the general course of personality development.

It is possible, however, to demonstrate the effects of genetic factors even though these cannot be weighed precisely.

As noted in earlier chapters, in an environment that provides adequate nutrition and stimulation heredity plays a prominent part in determining how a child will compare with others in bodily size, rate of physical growth, motor ability, "general intelligence" and certain specific mental abilities. Genetic factors are also responsible for several types of mental deficiency, and in determining a person's susceptibility to some forms of mental disorder, although the environment, in the protection it affords or the stresses it imposes, may play an important role in deciding whether or not a person will display a mental disorder. Any genetically determined physical or intellectual characteristic is likely, of course, in one way or another, to influence a child's response to his environment and the way the environment responds to him.

The ramifications of hereditary physical characteristics in the psychological sphere have never fully been explored, although everyday observation and several strands of research evidence indicate that these may be significant. A person with a robust physical constitution obviously has many advantages which indirectly may influence his self-reliance. In a culture that places a high value on physical prowess, physically early-maturing boys may have advantages that are reflected in their personality traits not only during adolescence but also when they are adults (P. H. Mussen and M. C. Jones, 1957; M. C. Jones, 1957; and H. E. Jones, 1949). Young adults who had matured early received higher ratings than late-maturers in characteristics such as social participation, making a good impression and ability to take responsibility.

In earlier chapters we have noted other evidence of an interplay between the physical and behavioral characteristics. For example babies with a high level of physical activity (which apparently is determined at least in part by genetic factors) surmounted the effects of hospitalization more successfully than babies with a low activity level (Schaffer, 1966).

Genetic studies of laboratory animals, cited in Chapter 3, have dealt, to a degree, with "personality" manifestations that have their counterparts in human beings. As we noted, these studies have demonstrated the influence of genetic factors on characteristics such as aggressiveness, timidity, strength of sexual drive, "emotionality," and response to stimulation or deprivation in infancy.

In human beings studies of identical twins and other kinfolk by Eysenck (1956), Cattell (1963), Gottesman (1963), Shields (1962), and Scarr (1966), indicate that some traits seem to be more strongly influenced than others by genetic factors. Statistical problems and problems of methodology in the study of behavior genetics have been discussed by Cattell (1963) and in several papers included in a symposium edited by Vandenberg (1965a).

It appears that among the human characteristics that manifest the influence of heredity are a tendency toward introversion or extroversion; the relative presence or absence of tendencies to be anxious, or depressed; a tendency to manifest temperamental qualities which, in their exaggerated form, are found in persons diagnosed as schizophrenic. The fact that investigators in this area vary in the terms they use and the trait clusters they describe makes it difficult to compare their findings.

The resemblances between twins and blood relatives (within the normal range) in various personality traits, as measured by personality tests, have generally been found to be lower than corresponding resemblances in intelligence. This may reflect the fact that personality tests are not generally as reliable as well established tests of intelligence. But it also appears that characteristics measured by personality tests are more susceptible to environmental variations.

In the study by Shields (1962) described in Chapter 3, there was a lower correlation between twins' scores on two personality tests than between their scores on intelligence. There also was a greater difference between monozygotic twins reared together and reared apart. The correlations between intelligence scores in the groups were almost identical (.76 and .77). The correlations between scores on an introversion-extroversion test were .42 and .61, and on a test of "neuroticism," covering characteristics such as depression, emotionality, and nervousness, the correlations were .38 and .53.[1]

Most of the information about genetic factors in personality development comes from studies of persons at an age when personal characteristics have

---

[1] The somewhat curious finding was that the correlations on both personality tests were higher in the group of twins reared apart than in the group of twins reared together. Paradoxically, the explanation may be that twins reared apart have a more equivalent environment than twins reared together. One-egg twins presumably have an identical heredity, but they do not share an identical environment, even though reared together. Shields describes how, in a twinship, one twin may be the "leader." Other observers likewise have shown that one member of a twinship may clearly be the dominant one. This condition of leader-follower, and dominating or being dominated, is broken when the twins are reared apart. Each one then, to a greater extent than if bound to the other, has an opportunity single-handed to adapt himself to his environment in his own fashion.

been influenced by several years of experience. It is likely that this limitation will be corrected if the current upsurge in interest in behavior genetics is combined with the current upsurge of interest in behavior at birth and in early infancy.

In Chapter 6 and elsewhere, we examined studies showing that newborn children differ in ways that apparently cannot be explained by known environmental factors prior to or during birth. Large differences are displayed in overt physical behavior before infants have come under the varying influences of their home environment. Differences also appear in the pattern of children's physiological responses as shown by functions controlled by the autonomic division of the nervous system. When such differences appear, it seems reasonable to assume that genetic factors might be responsible, but rigorously controlled long-term research would be necessary to confirm this assumption.

Studies of identical and non-identical twins during the first year of life, when new patterns of response are emerging, probably will also throw light on the role of genetic factors. In one such study Friedman (1965) found that there is more concordance between identical than fraternal twins in the emergence of early social responses, including smiling, and in the onset of fear of strangers.

The factors influencing the course of a child's development are so intricate that two children are likely to differ even if both seem to have the "same" heredity and, while they are babies, seem to share the "same" environment. A study by Blatz and Millichamp (1937) of the Dionne quintuplets from the time they were twelve to thirty-six months old illustrates the complexity of early personality development. The physical characteristics of the five sisters led authorities to conclude that they were "identicals"—derived from a single fertilized egg. Some doubt with regard to this conclusion has since been expressed, but at any rate, as babies the quintuplets were so much alike that a casual observer could not tell them apart. Closer examination revealed small variations in form of the face, ears, teeth, and other physical characteristics; and when their behavior was closely observed it was also noted that they differed in their social behavior—in the number of social contacts they initiated and received, in aggressiveness, in their skill in manipulating material, in their efforts to gain attention. The differences between them made a difference in the response they elicited from one another. It appeared, for example, that one of the girls in seeking to attract attention, stimulated one of her sisters to become aggressive in *her* efforts to satisfy a "need for an audience."

On the basis of their observations of the Dionne quintuplets, Blatz and Millichamp make this interesting statement: "The environmental characteristics most influential in moulding an individual are those which result from the individual's own response to his social environment."

Continuity and Change
in Various Facets of Development

Following is a review of representative findings regarding continuity and change in children's characteristics. We will begin first with attributes that can be measured quantitatively.

Physical Traits

Nature has kindly decreed that there is relatively little correspondence between the size of a child at birth and his size later on. The child of a large father might otherwise cause difficult labor for a small mother. But when a child is about two-and-a-half years old, it is possible to predict what his mature height will be with a high degree of certainty.

Intelligence

Children's IQ's begin to stabilize at about the age of four, and the correlation between IQ's at about age six and age eighteen are in the order of about .70 to .80, a rather high degree of constancy. As we noted in Chapter 21, considerable individual fluctuations may occur, although it is unlikely that a child will move from a "below average" to a "superior" rating, or from "superior" to "below average."

School Achievement

A child's pattern of school achievement tends to be strongly established at about the third grade (Kraus, 1956), and there is likely to be considerable similarity between achievement in the first and third grades. Moreover, as we noted in Chapter 10, a child's performance in the first grade may be predicted, to a considerable degree, by evidences of his confidence in his competence and ability to achieve before he enters the first grade.

The further one moves from characteristics that can be assessed quite reliably on a continuous scale (such as intelligence), the more difficult it obviously becomes to obtain reliable measurements. There are many personal and social characteristics that cannot be measured by the same yardstick as a child grows older.

A thoughtful study by Meili (1956, 1957) underscores the idea that to discover whether individual characteristics remain consistent with the passage of time requires more than simply repeated measurements of the same behavior manifestations. A fearful or irascible child at three may seem to have no fears and to be quite even-tempered at ten—but this can be misleading. There may be a shift in the way he openly displays fear or anger, and an even greater shift from overt to covert behavior.

To conduct a longitudinal study of personality development, it is essential therefore to try to find what, at an early age, might be psychologically equivalent to reaction tendencies displayed at a later age.

Early Display of Unique Personality Traits

When babies show distinct marks of individuality at a very early age it is difficult to tell whether they were "born that way" or whether, at a very early age, they have acquired certain ways of responding because of the way they are handled by their mothers. It is clear, however, that babies in the care of the same person frequently differ greatly in their reactions to this person, and continue to differ as time passes. This was noted by Berezin (1959) in a study of babies cared for by twenty-two boarding mothers while awaiting adoption. Through direct observation, information supplied by a psychologist, and records kept by the adoption agency, Berezin obtained ratings of the temperamental qualities of the boarding mothers and of the infants. The mothers perceived distinct individual characteristics in the babies in their care. Five of the mothers studied were each caring for three infants. These five mothers saw each of the three babies in their care as having his own unique characteristics. Such differences were noted regardless of the personalities of the mothers as appraised by the adoption agency. One mother, for example, who rated high in expression of affection, in responsiveness, and in sensitivity, was observed while caring for three infants almost identical in age (aged ten and eleven weeks). According to her perception, these infants differed in their disposition, their needs and demands and, as a consequence, her child-care practices varied with each one.

In observations of twenty-five babies during the first two years of life Shirley (1933b) found that the children showed a high degree of consistency in the general pattern of their behavior from month to month. Their behavior changed as they matured but there were always "identifying earmarks." A given form of behavior "waned and lapsed, only to be supplanted by another that apparently was its consistent outgrowth." For example, one baby was distinctive at an early age for his "timorous crying"; this crying waned, but then he exhibited "apprehensive watching" and, at a later age, showed a similarly timorous trend by hiding behind his mother and by reluctance to play and talk in the presence of a visitor. Shirley (1933b) gives a further example of two infants, one of whom remained consistently the most irritable and the other the least irritable among the youngsters in her group even though, during the course of the study, both of the children showed a decrease in irritability, in common with children in the group as a whole.

In a later study, Shirley (1941) gives a detailed description of two boys who were reared quite differently by their mothers and yet retained their individuality. The mother of one of the boys seemingly tried to keep him a baby, sought to prolong his attachment to her, and appeared anxious about practical details of his everyday care. Yet by the age of six this boy, according to Shirley, had grown into "an independent, objective little boy . . . a person in his own right." His mother, through her lack of firmness and her inability to pursue a consistent course of action, had left her baby "to grow up on the shifting sands of insecurity," and the boy "therefore had to build his own foundation of security." He did this by means of different techniques at different times. He gained attention at first by crying, later by refusing to eat. He used what seemed at the time to be "problem behavior" as a means of asserting himself. (Other writers have also noted that what seems, on the surface, to be a behavior problem may, in the context of a particular child's life, serve constructive ends.) As time passed this boy's methods took a more constructive form. At six he appeared to be a well-adjusted and quite self-sufficient person.

It would, of course, require more than one case study to establish how far a child can go in building "his own foundations of security." The boy might not have been able to assert himself so effectively if his mother, instead of being over-zealous, had neglected him or actively rejected him. However, this boy, in common with many children who have been studied less intensively, gives some support to Shirley's theory that each child has a "tough core" of temperamental qualities.

Constancy and Change
in Early and Middle Childhood

Among other earlier studies (ante-dating more recent investigations which will be noted at a later point) which underscore Shirley's notion of an underlying "core" is one by McKinnon (1942) of children first observed in a nursery school and then followed through the first two elementary grades. At the nursery school age the youngsters were classified into four groups on the basis of the most prominent characteristics of their social behavior: "conforming," "invasive," "withdrawn," and "cautious." Ten of the sixteen children continued from the age of three to the age of eight or nine to remain in the same classification. The changes that occurred were in the direction of "conforming." Changes consisted in building upon characteristics that previously were manifested rather than in an about-face or in the tacking on of something strange or new. One child, for example, changed from predominantly "invasive" behavior at three to "conforming" behavior at eight, but the underlying direction of his behavior remained the same: at both ages he was very eager to be noticed by other children. At three his techniques were crude and produced many conflicts, but at eight he had acquired more effective techniques.

A high degree of persistence in "ascendance-submission" was found in an investigation by Stott (1957), who studied over a hundred youngsters during a period of approximately twelve years. The first assessment was made while the children were in nursery school, and later the children were observed in recreational clubs which they attended. The children were rated on a scale of ascendance-submission ranging from extreme bossiness to "dependent ineffective submissiveness."

Stott found that "persistence of pattern was far more frequent than change during the period covered." Eighty-two per cent of the children ". . . showed no consistent direction of change." When changes did occur, they were temporary in most instances, with a subsequent return to the earlier pattern. Some children continued, in later years, to display the characteristics they had shown at the beginning of their nursery-school experience even though considerable effort had been made by teachers and other members of the staff to change them. Many aspects of each child's personality did change in the sense of becoming more mature, and marked changes in overall social behavior occurred. But even with these changes in capacity to function and modifications of patterns of functioning, the distinctive qualities of his person and of his functioning remained to give him uniqueness and individuality among his play peers.

A study by Martin (1964) revealed a high degree of constancy in social behavior patterns of nursery school children. On the basis of observational records. children were scored in terms of several response categories including aggression; "nurturance" (offering attention and reassurance to others); social participation; efforts to affiliate with others in friendly and sharing ways; avoidance or withdrawal from situations arising in the nursery school; and autonomous achievement (initiative, self-help, effective goal-directed behavior). Each of these behavior groupings included several sub-categories. Behavior in all categories increased in frequency during the two-year period covered by the study. This increase was quite marked in several types of behavior; for example, the incidence of "autonomous achievement" behavior more than doubled. But the pattern of increased frequency was such that an individual child tended to maintain his rank order position in the group.

A high degree of stability, with the passage of time, also appeared in the individual profiles, depicting the relative frequency of behavior in each of the seven categories. Such a profile might show, for example, that child A has a higher score in "aggression" than in "achievement control," while in child B's case the order is reversed. Only nine of fifty-three children showed a significant change in their behavior profiles from about two to about five years of age. All told, ". . . a pattern of individual social behavior that is strikingly unchanged emerged. It is as if each child has his own *behavior economy* which persists through time" (p. 464). Martin points out that a later study will be required to tell to what extent stability of patterns persists into later years. Moreover, he also expresses special interest in what a follow-up study might show regarding the children who were relatively "unstable."

Long-Term Reaction Tendencies

Several studies have dealt with stability and change in personality development from early childhood into adolescent or adult years. It is not possible to compress the main findings of these studies into a neat summary. Some characteristics apparently are quite persistent from early childhood onward; others seem stable for a time, then fluctuate and then, later on, become stabilized again; some seem to be rather transient. There are several differences in the patterns manifested by boys and girls. A further problem in summarizing the findings is that investigators differ in the terminology they use.

Honzik (1964) speaks of ". . . the unbelievably complicated equation of predicting personality development in the human organism with its prolonged period of growth and its extraordinary capacity for change. There are just too many unknowns for most of us" (p. 141). Bayley (1964) comments in a somewhat similar vein: "A study of children's behaviors over time, when one compares specific variables, presents a confusing array of changing patterns. However, there are some indications of persistence over time of characteristic reaction-tendencies. These reactions appear to be classifiable into consistent broad categories" (p. 93).

In reviewing the main findings in a study by Schaefer and Bayley (1963) of consistency and change in personality development from birth to eighteen years, Bayley states: "The children are most generally consistent in behaviors which may be characterized as active or passive or as extraverted outgoing and impulsive, as contrasted with introverted and controlled." Girls tend to be more consistent than boys in this dimension of behavior. Honzik (1964) reports findings that are in keeping with this from an unpublished study by Macfarlane of children from the age of twenty-one months to sixteen years: ". . . the most consistent dimensions . . . (were) . . . styles of behavior, namely, reactive-expressive or retractive-inhibitive." Among the higher correlations in re-assessment from age four to sixteen were those dealing with the dimension of introversion-extroversion. Kagan and Moss (1962) found considerable consistency through time in "passive-dependent" behavior (in girls) and aggressiveness in boys.

In a later account of the children in the long-term study directed by Macfarlane, Bronson (1966) reports detailed results of repeated ratings in the age span of five to sixteen years. The three groupings or dimensions of behavior found to be the most stable and predictive were: *withdrawal-expressiveness*, including at one end of the continuum such characteristics as being reserved, somber or shy, or, at the opposite end, being expressive, gay or "socially easy;" *reactivity-placidity*, including at one end of the continuum such characteristics as being reactive, explosive or resistive, and, at the other extreme, being phlegmatic, calm and compliant; and *passivity-dominance*. Although these dimensions of behavior tended to be relatively stable in both sexes, boys and girls differed in the ways they manifested various traits and in both sexes there were changes also in the manner and extent to which a given characteristic was expressed from time to time during the course of development.

Murphy (1964), in a longitudinal study of thirty-two children, found that among the tendencies more likely to persist were "tempo, vigor, alertness, motor coordination and skill, and capacities for delay and for control" (p. 111).

Another dimension that has shown a rather high degree of consistency through time is "task-oriented" behavior as described by Bayley and "achievement behavior" (mainly in the intellectual sphere) as described by Kagan and Moss (1962).

Kagan and Moss (1962) found a considerable degree of continuity of aggressive behavior in the age period of three to six and similar behavior at the adult levels in men, but not in women. They found continuity of passive-dependent behavior from childhood into adult life in women but not in men. They interpret these findings, along with their findings regarding achievement behavior (noted above), as indicating that cultural forces have a strong influence in determining continuity and change in personal characteristics. According to their interpretation, aggressiveness is tolerated in males, not in females, so females stop being aggressive; passive-dependency is deplored in males, but not in females, so males modify their behavior accordingly.[2] Achievement-oriented behavior is encouraged in everyone, so it persists in both sexes.

The Kagan and Moss study (1962) offers findings regarding stability and change in a number of additional characteristics. They found that a competitive attitude toward peers, appearing at the preschool level, is prognostic of competitive behavior during the elementary and high school period, and competitiveness at age six to ten was significantly correlated with adult competi-

---

[2] This interpretation might be questioned. Data at the adult level were obtained through interviews, in which the men and women might try to paint an appropriately masculine or feminine picture of themselves. Moreover, to measure continuity it would be necessary to take account of what is the "psychological equivalent" in a woman in her twenties of aggressive tendencies shown at age three, and similarly for passive-dependency in a young man. From a different angle, Honzik (1964) suggests that if the culture succeeds in pressing boys to be aggressive and girls to be passively dependent, that should have the effect of making all boys aggressive and all girls dependent and this would lower the correlations between childhood and later behavior. Honzik believes that when boys maintain their position on a high-to-low aggressive continuum while girls maintain their relative degree of passive-dependency, these findings might better be explained on genetic than on cultural grounds.

tive behavior. There was a considerable degree of consistency in a tendency to view people as threatening. "A child's labeling of people as cruel or kind, rejecting or accepting, resists change to a remarkable degree . . . ," and apprehension in social relations with peers in early school years was positively related to "social anxiety" at the adult level.

Investigators who have made long-term studies of personality development have succeeded better (as one might expect) in telling whether given traits remain stable or change with time than in explaining why some traits seem to be more persistent than others, and why some children show more consistency than others. Murphy (1964) and her associates have examined a number of factors that come into play. It appears that the most consistent pattern of development is likely to appear in characteristics that are to a large degree (1) genetically determined and which contain a degree of (2) harmony or balance (between, say, a child's social responsiveness and his ability to adapt himself to the demands of his environment), and which (3) are allowed to develop and flourish in an environment that is relatively stable, permitting a child to proceed at his own pace.

The fact that genetically determined factors may have varying effects at different maturity levels appears from a finding reported by Macfarlane (1964). There may be more apparent similarity in an early maturing girl's personality at age nine compared with age fourteen than between age eleven and twelve.

Although, under ordinary circumstances, a child's environment is quite stable, changes may occur even under relatively stable circumstances. Schaefer and Bayley (1963) found that as time passes parents become more variable in some respects than in others. As they grow older, and their children grow older, parents in their study changed their tactics in controlling their children. Those who at first had exerted rather tight controls granted children more self-direction or autonomy as they grew older. On the other hand, there was not a corresponding change in the degree to which they showed affection and displeasure or rejection in dealing with their children.

Constancy and Resiliency

One of the most striking—and gratifying—features of studies of constancy and change in personality development is the evidence that has been unearthed regarding the tremendous adaptability of human beings. As expressed by Murphy (1964) "We found one or another surprise in the development of over half of our children" (p. 97). An account by Macfarlane (1964) tells a similar story.

Macfarlane speaks of the ". . . almost incredible capacity" of the individual to process the ". . . welter of inner-outer stimulation." Many of the most outstandingly mature adults in the group she and her associates studied had by-passed or overcome difficult situations, even though ". . . their characteristic responses during childhood or adolescence seemed to us to compound their problems (p. 121)." Among these were chronic rebels who were expelled from school, persons who had combined hostility with dependency on others, and withdrawn schizoids. Macfarlane states that she and her associates had not previously appreciated the maturing utility of many painful, strain-producing and confusing experiences. On the other hand, many subjects who ". . . early had had easy and confidence-inducing lives," who had been free from severe strains and had exhibited very promising abilities and talents were ". . . brittle, discontented and puzzled adults (p. 122)." Macfarlane's findings indicate that theories and generalizations based primarily

Table 32 Percentage of Boys and Girls Who Mentioned Items in Various Categories of Self-Description in Reporting "What I Like about Myself"

		Elementary Grades						Junior High School					
	Grade	IV		V		VI		VII		VIII		IX	
	Sex	B	G	B	G	B	G	B	G	B	G	B	G
Category	Number	220	206	147	142	171	172	96	77	134	151	170	204
1. Physical characteristics and appearance		15	19	22	30	12	30	14	13	29	42	23	35
2. Clothing and grooming		16	27	12	26	12	28	14	12	13	25	13	23
3. Health and physical soundness		6	2	8	8	7	5	8	0	8	5	4	3
3x. Bodily pleasures		3	3	1	1	1	1	2	1	2	2	2	0
4. Material possessions		3	4	3	1	1	2	1	0	1	1	0	0
5. Animals and pets		4	2	1	1	4	6	5	1	1	1	5	1
6-7. Home and family		18	24	7	13	14	16	11	9	13	11	7	7
8. Recreation: enjoyment of		15	10	7	4	18	10	13	5	15	5	7	3
9. Ability in sports, play		13	9	20	6	24	9	13	4	16	7	10	5
10. School: ability in school; attitudes toward, etc.		21	33	13	17	23	21	19	29	21	27	15	12
11. Intellectual abilities		5	3	6	6	8	3	4	4	7	7	8	6
12. Special talents (music, arts)		14	11	14	17	16	20	8	23	16	18	8	11
13. Just me, myself		11	6	7	5	15	9	9	8	14	13	11	10
13x. Personality, character, inner resources, emotional tendencies		23	19	20	13	24	28	37	35	35	36	29	39
14. Social relationships and attitudes		20	22	22	29	22	38	38	51	37	50	34	52
15. Religion		4	2	1	0	4	2	0	1	1	5	1	1
16. Independence, self-help		5	2	3	2	1	2	2	0	4	2	6	1
16x. Privacy		1	0	3	1	1	2	1	0	1	0	2	0
17. Attitude toward world		1	0	1	1	1	1	3	1	2	1	2	1
18. No response		2	4	4	3	4	4	6	3	1	3	7	6

Reproduced, in abridged form, with permission from A. T. Jersild, *In Search of Self*, Bureau of Publications, Teachers College, Columbia University, 1952. Approximately forty subcategories in the original table are not reproduced.

on an effort to reconstruct the childhood and adolescent experiences of abnormal adults are likely to give a very inadequate portrayal of personality development.

Children's Assets as Viewed by Themselves

Table 32 gives a summary of the kinds of ideas children express when they are asked to describe the qualities they admire in themselves. It is based on compositions written by young people of elementary, high school, and col-

High School						College			
						Fresh. & Soph.		Jr. & Sr.	
X		XI		XII					
B	G	B	G	B	G	B	G	B	G
151	157	112	124	137	122	50	50	50	50
25	37	17	19	15	20	40	28	20	38
17	11	10	15	9	6	10	34	24	20
5	5	8	2	4	2	4	0	6	0
1	0	3	1	1	2	0	0	2	0
0	1	1	0	2	0	0	0	2	0
1	2	1	2	0	1	0	0	2	4
5	6	4	10	4	5	0	8	4	4
8	5	8	6	4	3	0	2	6	6
17	5	11	6	8	2	28	2	8	8
11	8	12	6	9	9	14	18	16	18
6	11	14	9	12	9	26	22	34	36
12	11	14	14	13	12	14	26	22	28
21	27	19	9	17	11	24	16	12	8
36	38	31	30	35	45	78	72	78	94
42	43	51	46	42	61	74	82	76	86
1	3	2	2	1	4	4	2	0	2
5	0	8	7	6	2	6	8	12	2
0	0	2	1	1	1	6	2	0	4
2	4	0	2	4	2	0	2	16	4
5	10	5	12	16	3	0	2	0	0

lege age on the theme, "What I Like About Myself." Compositions of this sort touch only lightly on children's views about themselves (a thorough investigation would require more intensive study), yet they bring out some matters of considerable interest.

At all ages, for example, a large proportion of young people, without any leading questions, evaluated themselves in terms belonging to the category of "personality traits, character, inner resources, and emotional tendencies." Likewise, a large proportion at all ages appraised themselves in terms falling under the category "social relationships and attitudes." This last-named category included mention of their attitudes toward others as well as the attitudes of others toward them. Children of elementary school age pointed with pride to their homes and family life more often than did the older subjects.

Table 33 **Percentage of Boys and Girls Who Mentioned Items in Various Categories in Reporting "What I Dislike about Myself"**

		Elementary Grades						Junior High School					
	Grade	IV		V		VI		VII		VIII		IX	
	Sex	B	G	B	G	B	G	B	G	B	G	B	G
Category	Number	220	206	147	142	171	172	96	77	134	151	170	204
1. Physical characteristics and appearance		11	16	17	30	17	41	17	26	24	48	32	53
2. Clothing and grooming		4	10	7	5	4	9	2	8	4	7	3	10
3. Health and physical soundness		2	3	3	4	5	2	4	1	4	1	6	2
3x. Bodily pleasures		4	4	4	1	2	2	4	1	3	1	4	3
4. Material possessions		0	0	1	1	1	1	0	0	1	1	0	0
5. Animals and pets		2	1	0	1	0	1	2	0	0	0	1	0
6-7. Home and family		17	19	9	22	11	21	8	10	7	14	11	11
8. Recreation: enjoyment of		5	1	1	1	4	2	3	0	2	0	2	0
9. Ability in sports, play		4	4	7	1	10	6	3	1	7	5	7	3
10. School: ability in school; attitudes toward, etc.		22	22	18	23	32	27	31	27	26	34	36	24
11. Intellectual abilities		1	1	3	2	6	4	5	8	7	4	5	4
12. Special talents (music, arts)		9	10	5	4	9	15	4	10	7	11	2	6
13. Just me, myself		1	2	4	3	5	5	0	1	1	6	4	9
13x. Personality, character, inner resources, emotional tendencies		37	38	37	32	44	43	53	43	51	57	55	65
14. Social relationships and attitudes		16	14	15	18	15	20	13	22	22	28	16	26
15. Religion		0	0	3	0	1	0	1	0	1	1	1	0
16. Independence, self-help		0	0	1	0	1	1	2	1	4	1	5	3
16x. Privacy		0	0	0	0	1	0	1	0	0	0	0	0
17. Attitude toward world		0	0	0	0	1	0	0	4	0	0	0	0
18. No response		10	5	5	3	3	5	5	1	4	1	11	1

Reproduced, in abridged form, with permission, from A. T. Jersild, *In Search of Self,* Bureau of Publications, Teachers College, Columbia University, 1952.

According to the results in this study, many of the criteria young people use in judging themselves at any level tend to stand out prominently at all levels. The standards by which young people judge themselves are not distinctly scaled according to age or developmental stages, or in the manner of subjects taught at school.

Children's Shortcomings as Viewed by Themselves

Table 33 shows results obtained when young people from the fourth grade through college wrote compositions on the subject, "What I Dislike About Myself." Again it appears that certain categories of self-evaluation, notably

High School						College			
X		XI		XII		Fresh. & Soph.		Jr. & Sr.	
B	G	B	G	B	G	B	G	B	G
151	157	112	124	137	122	50	50	50	50
27	44	13	32	10	30	12	20	8	12
1	3	3	2	4	2	0	0	2	0
3	3	0	6	1	2	6	2	0	2
1	3	2	1	3	3	0	2	6	0
0	0	1	0	1	0	0	0	0	0
0	0	0	0	0	0	0	0	0	0
7	8	4	15	6	6	6	6	2	6
2	1	2	1	1	0	0	0	2	0
5	2	7	0	5	0	0	2	0	4
25	17	27	15	15	23	36	10	14	16
7	4	11	10	8	9	8	2	4	4
5	7	5	10	5	6	12	8	6	8
4	6	2	9	6	8	0	0	0	0
44	55	51	67	58	72	84	90	72	94
25	25	18	30	24	25	52	58	50	48
1	2	2	1	0	1	4	0	6	0
3	2	8	2	9	4	12	12	18	10
0	0	0	0	0	0	2	2	0	0
0	0	0	0	1	1	0	0	0	2
11	12	14	4	16	4	0	0	8	0

those referring to personality, character, and emotional tendencies, and those pertaining to social attitudes and relationships with other people, are mentioned quite frequently at all levels.

However, there are some differences between the details mentioned in the "Like" and "Dislike" descriptions. For example, from 6 to 30 per cent of the young people deplored their tendency to become angry or to lose their temper at something they disliked about themselves (the subcategory covering this is not reproduced in Table 33). On the other hand, the percentage of young people in the various groups who spoke favorably of their ability to manage their anger ranged from zero to six. The young people mentioned inability to control anger as a fault more often than they mentioned control of anger as an asset. In a similar manner, upwards of 18 per cent of the young people in some groups deplored their tendency to be afraid when they described their unfavorable characteristics, but no more than 3 per cent of the young people in any of the groups described their ability to cope with their fears as a favorable trait. These findings are in keeping with what we noted in earlier chapters concerning the influences at home and at school that induce growing children to reproach themselves for being angry or afraid.

*Experiences at School
as Related to Self-Evaluation*

Experiences at school and attitudes toward school figure prominently in children's evaluations of themselves. Roughly about one-fourth of the children in the study cited above made reference to the school in telling about what they liked or did not like about themselves. (The proportion would have been larger, of course, if they had been asked specific questions about their experiences at school instead of being asked to write on the general theme of what they liked or disliked about themselves.) At practically all levels (except college), experiences at school were mentioned more often as a source of self-disparagement than as a source of self-esteem. According to the children's own accounts, life at school does more to weaken than to strengthen their assurance of personal worth.

Why is this? To answer this question would require a more intensive inquiry than the one just cited. Such an inquiry would probably show in many instances that experiences at school are mentioned as a source of self-disparagement even though the school is not the primary source. A youngster who is not living up to his *own* expectations may, for example, phrase his self-reproach by saying he is not living up to the *school's* expectations. However, a more intensive inquiry would also reveal, so the writer believes, conditions at school that hinder children from acquiring healthy attitudes of self-regard.

One condition is that schools constantly impress upon large numbers of children the idea that they are not much good. Children who are lacking in the intellectual aptitudes that are praised in most schools meet failure and rejection on a vast scale. Schools expose some children endlessly to situations in which the teacher and the school administration know in advance that they will fail.

Children's Problems
as Viewed by Themselves and Others

A large proportion of children, according to their own accounts, have "problems" and according to the judgment of others, many youngsters move from childhood into adolescence and adult years with severe personality disorders.

Behavior problems or disorders appear in many forms. A child may be regarded as a "problem" because he lags behind others in his development: for example, a youngster at age five still has not achieved bladder control. His problem may be a form of regression; he reverts to bed-wetting at five at a time of stress after having had the dry habit for some time. He may have weaknesses that hamper the general course of development, such as a reading disability. His problem may be extreme manifestations of behavior that most children normally show to some degree at some time or other, such as temper tantrums, aggressiveness, negativism, fears, shyness, preoccupation with fantasies, dependency, and the like. Problems may occur at either end of a given continuum of behavior, such as lethargy at one extreme and over-excitability at the other; rigidity as against extreme distractibility; apathy as against emotionalism and lack of impulse control; volatile shifts of mood as against extreme perseveration of mood.

Extent of Personality Disorders

When we ask, "What is the proportion of children who suffer from personality disorders?" the answer depends on the standards we apply. According to a perfectionist standard, we could label children as "maladjusted" if they have persisting fears, grievances, or guilt feelings or if (as they grow older) they feel that there is a discrepancy between what they are and what they ought to be. By this criterion, practically all children would be regarded as being somewhat maladjusted. At the other extreme, we might class as maladjusted only those so seriously disturbed that they have to be placed in an institution for the mentally ill. Under conditions now prevailing, it has been estimated that one child in every ten who lives to be seventy-five years old will be hospitalized for mental illness (Goldhamer and Marshall, 1953). This is a somber statistic. It would be smaller if we did not count those whose illness is associated with other evidences of deterioration in old age. But the percentage would be larger if we included not only those who are hospitalized but also the unhospitalized persons who are so disturbed that they withdraw from life through invalidism and complete dependence on others.

An even more somber picture of mental health in the adult population, which a child rather soon will enter, is offered by Srole, *et al.* (1962) in their "Midtown Manhattan Study." According to the judgments of a team of psychiatrists, 18.5 per cent of the persons in the sample could be rated as mentally "well." Over a third of the persons were rated as having "mild" symptoms from a psychiatric point of view, and another 21.8 per cent were classed as having "moderate symptoms." Persons with "marked" and "severe" symptoms and those diagnosed as "incapacitated" were all regarded as having impaired mental health. The impaired group included 23.4 per cent, or almost a fourth of the sampling.[3]

Estimates of the percentage of children who suffer from personality disorders have varied, depending on the criteria of adjustment that have been applied and the nature of the information that has been gathered. In a survey by Ullman (1952) of ninth graders, the teachers identified 8 per cent of the children as likely sooner or later to have serious problems of adjustment. This percentage is smaller than that obtained when ratings by teachers are supplemented by other sources of information. Many youngsters who have serious emotional difficulties manage to do good work at school and are not regarded by their teachers as "problem" children (Pilzer, 1952; Harris, 1952). In a study by Rogers (1942a) of over 1,500 elementary-school children, several criteria of maladjustment were applied: truancy; distinctly unfavorable ratings by classmates; unfavorable ratings by teachers and visiting observers or on an adjustment inventory; non-promotion; information that labeled a youngster as a "misfit" by virtue of differing from the group in reading ability, mental ability, or age. A child was regarded as "seriously maladjusted" if he was in the "maladjusted" category according to four or more of the criteria that were applied. By this standard, 12 per cent of the pupils were seriously maladjusted, and 30 per cent gave evidence of being poorly adjusted, but not to a degree that would place them in the seriously maladjusted group.

A large proportion of young people at the adolescent and late adolescent level have personal problems, and many of these are very serious (Frank, *et al.*, 1953). Heath and Gregory (1946) found that 92 per cent in a group of 259 male college sophomores had personal problems. These young men were selected to represent a "normal" and "healthy" sampling of Harvard College sophomores; they did not include boys who sought help of their own accord. Seventeen per cent of the college boys had "urgent or acute" problems as judged by a research staff consisting of a physician, several psychiatrists, a psychologist, and a social case-worker (who interviewed practically all of the families of the young men as well as the young men themselves).

---

[3] Srole and his associates review findings in other large surveys, including a survey in Baltimore and an Army study, and conclude that their findings are not exceptional.

Personality Problems
as Revealed by Self-Ratings

When children describe or rate themselves on personality tests, or on scales dealing with specific facets of their emotional lives, it commonly is found that the "normal" or typical child has many problems. In a section of one test (California Test of Personality Adjustment, Thorpe, *et al.*, 1942, 1953) dealing with "personal adjustment," a child, in rating himself, might obtain a score ranging from 90 (best possible adjustment) to 0 (poorest adjustment). When several thousand children from the kindergarten through the tenth grade rated themselves on this test, their median score was about 67. This means that half of the children described themselves as having either symptoms or as leaning toward the maladjusted side in marking approximately one-fourth of the items.

In a test of "manifest anxiety" adapted to children (Castaneda, *et al.*, 1956), 50 per cent of the children marked 16 of 42 items as problems which prevailed in their own lives.

It appears from a study by Sutton-Smith, *et al.* (1961) that in recent years children report more problems than they reported about thirty years ago. When a personality test (the Brown Personality Inventory), first standardized in 1934, was applied in 1959, the 1959 population showed considerably higher "neuroticism" scores. Sutton-Smith and his associates interpret this to mean that children now may be under more tension or it might mean that they are more free to profess their problems.

Factors Underlying Problem Behavior

Behavioral problems, particularly those in the emotional sphere, have been explained by a variety of theories. One theory, not generally advanced as a sufficient explanation, is that a child suffers from a genetic weakness or defect that makes him vulnerable to stress. According to psychoanalytic theory, a child's problems stem mainly from an insupportable conflict between his basic drives and a forbidding environment which demands that he inhibit the expression of his drives. According to a more eclectic learning theory, problem behavior comes about through learned or conditioned ways of behaving that impair a child's adaptations to his environment. According to a cultural theory, some problems arise as a consequence of inability or failure to meet cultural demands, such as failure to meet standards set at school.

These theories need not be regarded as mutually exclusive. But each of these theories, as commonly applied, attributes causation to what the environment imposes on a child. An adequate theory must take account of the fact that, whether a child is a problem or a model of excellence, his personal characteristics emerge through interaction between his environment and what he himself brings to this environment. As we observed in earlier chapters, children may respond quite differently to similar circumstances.

Antecedents of Behavior Problems

The most common procedure in studying the presumed causes of behavior disorders has been to inquire into these after a child has become a problem. A search is then made into his background. His past history commonly is reconstructed on the basis of what he or his parents or others can tell about it in retrospect. Such an approach has the benefit of hindsight, which, it has been said, has 20-20 vision. Things in retrospect are likely to seem especially clear if one looks through the lenses of a preconceived theory and is able to seize upon this or that circumstance in the past to explain what is happening in the present. But hindsight provides only a frail basis for an explanation. A more substantial basis for uncovering factors that might be salient in a child's development is to build on uncolored information that has been recorded before rather than after this or that good or ill fortune in his life has come to a head.

The longitudinal study of children by Thomas, Chess, and Birch, referred to in earlier chapters, throws interesting light on the conditions that antecede the outcropping of behavior problems. In this study begun in 1956, 39 of 156 children had displayed behavior disturbances of varying severity as of 1965 (Chess, *et al.*, 1967). Information about these children was gathered before these children were regarded by their parents or by psychiatrists as problems.

An analysis of the data does not support the simple notion that if a child is troubled it is his parents who made him so. Neither does it support the notion that a child's individual temperament is, alone, decisive in determining the outcome. Nor does it show that the role of persons outside the home environment is decisive in itself. Rather the outcome, for better or for worse, grows out of interaction between a child with his individual temperamental characteristics and his elders and associates (in the home, school, and social environment at large).

According to the findings by Chess, *et al.*, young children who are most likely later to display behavior problems are those with a temperamental pattern that includes: (a) irregularity in biological functions (notably sleeping and feeding); (b) a predominant tendency to show a negative response to new conditions (new foods, new faces, new routines, etc.) when these are first introduced; (c) slow adaptation or non-adaptation to such conditions with the passage of time; (d) frequent negative mood; and (e) a tendency toward intense reaction (violent tantrums, loud crying, loud laughter, etc.). A significantly larger proportion of children in the behavior problem group than in the sampling at large showed these characteristics in infancy. The children who developed problems had difficulty in meeting the demands of socialization which require that a child must modify his own patterns when these are at variance with the rules of living within the family, the school, the peer group, and so on.

Chess and her associates ". . . found no evidence that parents of difficult infants are essentially different from the other parents." They do, however, face a more difficult child-rearing task than parents of a youngster with a more favorable pattern of temperamental qualities. Difficulties mount if a parent does not have the patience, serenity, and astuteness required to manage this task. As a consequence, a parent who is relaxed and consistent in dealing with an "easy" child may become anxious or feel guilty when another child who happens to be difficult comes along.

Life is not guaranteed to be smooth, however, for an enterprising child who makes a fine adjustment in his home life in early childhood. His resourcefulness in adjusting readily to reasonable requirements is likely to encourage his parents to have considerable confidence in him and to build in him a trusting attitude toward them. But now, if he moves into a school situation, or a peer group, that has standards differing from those in the home, he may run into difficulties. It is ironic that the very attitudes of a child and his parents that should, and do, help to create a healthy and reasonably harmonious pace within the home can expose a child to difficulties, at least temporarily, outside the home.

Implications of Findings
Relating to Personality Problems

One thing is clear from the foregoing studies (and many others that could be named): The normal or typical child, according to his own account, or according to the judgment of others, is beset by many problems. These findings raise challenging questions. Is a person in a "normal" state of mental health a troubled person? Actually, there is little agreement among psychiatrists or psychologists as to how mental health should be defined, although most would probably agree that children rated as severely maladjusted do not possess it.

In the present scheme of things, it is inevitable that some children will have difficulties. Among these are children with poor heredity; children with congenital defects; children with low intelligence who are destined to be "misfits" in our present school systems; youngsters who face an uphill struggle due to a variety of conditions such as poverty, broken homes, neglect, harsh home conditions. But many individuals eventually suffer from personal difficulties even though the odds seem to be in their favor, as shown by findings (reviewed in Chapter 21) concerning the lives and careers of gifted children. Most of these gifted children came from environments that were above average, and their native abilities gave them a great advantage in school and in competition for jobs after they left school. Yet, according to the information they and others supplied, over a fifth of them in their forties (22.3 per cent of the men and 25.1 per cent of the women) suffered from "some maladjustment," including such difficulties as "excessive feelings of inadequacy or inferiority, nervous fatigue, mild anxiety neurosis and the like." And almost one in ten (8.9 per cent of the men and 9 per cent of the women) suffered from "serious maladjustment."

According to these results, it is not just the disinherited or underprivileged who bear a heavy burden of distress. Mild or acute personality disorders run through all segments of society.

When we face the fact that large numbers of children (and adults) struggle with problems ranging from worries, anxiety, and hostile attitudes to severe personality disorders, we face these questions: Is so much distress inevitable? Are we *tapping* or *blocking* the resources for health that human beings possess?

A point of view bearing on these questions is discussed in the section that follows.

Knowledge of Self, Acceptance of Self, and Mental Health

There is no way of ridding life of adversity, but in the writer's judgment more could be done than is being done to help children face the rigors of life in a more realistic and effective way. A growing child strives to make use of his powers. He possesses a large capacity for self-repair. Most children who have "problems" possess an impulse to grow, and this impulse, and the potential of health behind it, is far more important than the disorders that appear. But if children are to use this impulse and to realize this potential, it is necessary to help them rather than to put barriers in their way.

According to the view here set forth, human beings, from an early age, have a greater capacity for taking a thoughtful and realistic view of the affairs of their inner lives than we have commonly assumed in our psychological theories and our educational practices.

Each child is deeply immersed in the psychological issues that influence his way of life. Each, in his way, is a psychologist. From early infancy, without being deliberate about it, he acquires ideas and attitudes about himself and others. These are woven into the pattern of his life. They may be true or false, healthy or unhealthy. With most children the development of these ideas and attitudes is left largely to chance, but it is not necessary that this should be so.

Children's potentialities for self-understanding are usually neglected while other aspects of their training are being pushed. Past generations of school children learned about Mother Goose, the dates of bygone wars and the amendments to the Constitution. Present-day children are being introduced to physics, economics and the logic of mathematics. But human motives and the inner life of man are largely ignored in education from nursery school through college.

A policy of encouraging children to evade rather than to face their personal concerns is deeply imbedded in our culture and strongly entrenched in our educational system. Even in schools that claim to deal with the "whole child," and with children's "basic needs and concerns," a wide gulf often exists between a child's most pressing preoccupations and the things emphasized in the course of study. An example of this appeared in an informal offshoot of a study of children's interests conducted by the writer and his colleagues. When children were asked in the usual manner to tell about their "interests," what they would "like to know more about," they mentioned the conventional things, ranging from games, arts, crafts and athletics to the subject matter of literature, arithmetic, history, and the like. In a small section of the study we questioned children a bit more deeply and found that practically all of them were troubled with fear. Yet it did not occur to a single child to express the idea that the subject of fear was one that the school might be concerned about. Other studies, notably at the adolescent level, have shown that nearly all children harbor grievances and attitudes of hostility. But the barriers against self-scrutiny are usually so high that it would require an exceptionally bold youngster to bring up the subject of the *personal* meanings of hostility even when the class is studying evidences of human hostility as revealed by the cruelty, warfare, and bloodshed recorded in history books.

When elementary school children (as well as high school and college students) avoid an inquiry into the personal dimensions of their existence, they are conforming to a standard set for them by others. They have learned to take for granted that the educational program does not subscribe to the principle that "the proper study of mankind is man." Yet many youngsters who studiously conform to impersonal academic expectations are pathetically eager, if given a little encouragement, to explore their personal concerns.

A person's search for knowledge of self has many facets: a willingness to examine the experiences through which he perceives the objective dimensions of his personality; a willingness to explore the bases of his conception of his properties as a person—his conception of who and what he is; and an inquiry into the standards according to which he evaluates his worth.

Self-understanding means *knowing*, as in Socrates' "Know thyself"; it means being conscious of one's own being, such as is implied in Macmurray's (1935) statement that "Until we know ourselves we cannot be ourselves."

Self-acceptance and understanding of self are closely associated. To accept himself, a growing person must be aware of himself. To accept his limitations he must be able to recognize them. Self-acceptance, in other words, requires awareness and perception. But a child's ability to become aware of himself will be influenced by the way he feels about himself, and the way he feels about himself will depend, in part, on the way others feel about him and encourage him in the process of self-discovery.

According to this conception of self-acceptance, a child is "successful" in his development if he is making constructive use of his capacities whether he happens to be the brightest child in the community or one of the dullest, the handsomest or one of the ugliest, the tallest and best built or the puniest and most ungainly. By the same token, there is defeat in the process of development if a child, whether he is talented or humbly endowed, draws only to a small extent upon his intellectual and emotional resources even though he is quite successful by external standards and seems to meet most of the common standards of "adjustment."

Emotion, Self-Acceptance, and Mental Health

If children are to acquire emotional health, it is necessary for parents and teachers to allow children to show and examine their emotions. Only through such a policy is it possible to understand the child and to help him to understand and accept himself in a realistic way. It is essential, of course, both at home and at school to set limits beyond which a child must not go in expressing his emotions, especially his anger. But schools go far beyond this need for setting limits when they emphasize academic learning and the outward forms of social conformity to such an extent that children's emotional development is ignored.

An emotional outburst *as such* probably has little or no value for a child, but something significant can take place when feelings are shown or "released" in an atmosphere where learning is encouraged. When a child, in a setting in which self-discovery is encouraged, has a chance to express his feelings he not only may be able to get a clearer view of them but he also may make the discovery (surprising to some children) that he can have pretty intense feelings without being rebuked.

A classroom teacher who has been trained in the usual fashion is not a psychotherapist and should not pretend to be, but the school situation offers teachers many opportunities for exploring and applying many of the concepts underlying psychotherapy and mental hygiene. The procedures used in group therapy as described, for example, by Slavson (1943, 1947), and by Hinckley and Herman (1951), and in therapeutic relationships as described by Rogers (1942b, 1951), and Allen (1942) have many implications for teachers. Snygg and Combs (1949) and Combs and Snygg (1959) have discussed implications of the concept of the self for education. The writer and his associates, in cooperation with several hundred teachers, have explored the emotional currents within themselves which teachers must face whenever they seek to understand children's emotions or help children to understand their emotions, and the resources within the teaching situation for mutual self-help in group situations (1952, 1953, 1955, 1960, 1965). A provocative team approach to the study of school health, with an emphasis on emotional health and self-understanding, has been described by Hull, Krippene and Porter (1966). The influence of teachers, and of the total school situation, on elementary school children's self-esteem has been explored in a series of enlightening case studies by Sears and Sherman (1964).

An important consequence of freedom to express feeling may be that children are relieved from some of the burden of secrecy which many of them bear. Children live in an isolated and lonely world when they must struggle to keep their emotional difficulties hidden from others. A child is afraid of corpses, for example, but he harbors this fear within the privacy of his life as a guilty secret. When he is free to tell of this fear, he has, in a sense, not only confessed but thrown himself on the mercy of others. When the confession does not bring shame and ridicule upon him, he can relax a bit, and perhaps not feel so strong a need to hide within himself. Moreover, when a child has the courage to reveal something about his feelings, under the eye of a watchful and considerate teacher, other children may find that they have the courage to do so, too. When this happens, all may discover that they are not alone in their troubles: They are not queer, for others have exactly the same troubles, or worse ones. Fears and anxieties and grievances are not banished simply by realizing that others also are anxious and angry. But when a frightened child feels free to express his fright and is struck by the fact that others also are afraid, at least a small dent has been made in the vicious chain of fear and blame through which a child becomes alienated from others and from himself.

The same line of thought applies also to hostility and the consequences of hostility. It is in an interpersonal setting that most of the resentments a child harbors arise, and if he can bring them out into an interpersonal setting there is a chance that they might be relieved.

To have access to his feelings it is necessary for a child to experience the actual feelings rather than just talk about them. To talk about joy, fear, or hate in intellectual terms is similar to talking about a steak instead of tasting and chewing it. This fact stands out when one observes that children often feel guilty (as adults often do) even though they have openly confessed and made a clean breast of some transgression or other. The confession, which represents what they can grasp intellectually and express verbally, may not represent the real psychological issue or the real emotional content. So a child may continue to feel badly, even though he has been assured that God has forgiven him and that no human being will hold his faults against him. Jimmy confesses, for example, that he stole a dime from Johnny's desk, and then Johnny forgives him, and his teacher and parents and pastor forgive him, but he still feels guilty. He feels guilty because the act of confession and the gift of forgiveness did not touch upon his real problem. He stole, it is true, but his real trouble is not that he is a thief. Perhaps he stole because he feels envious of Johnny who always has spending money—but it was theft, not envy, that he confessed, and by being absolved of theft he did not learn to cope with envy.

Or he stole the dime, let us say, to buy candy to bribe a big boy next door into liking him; so he stole because he was lonely, not because he was a thief. But after the theft has been forgotten and forgiven he may still be as lonely as ever.

Perhaps he stole to buy candy for another boy who might tell on him because Jimmy had been involved in sex play with him. In that event it was a sexual conflict that made him so frightened he became involved in theft.

After the theft had been forgiven by others Jimmy might be no nearer than before in solving his fear or his loneliness or his conflicts regarding sex. But if a situation were provided in which an adult, for the time being at least, was not interested in getting Jimmy to inform on himself, or to promise to live a new life, or to put his trouble into one nice verbal package, but was interested in letting Jimmy reveal some of the drama of his feelings, something very significant might take place. Both Jimmy and the teacher, in their common search, might come to a clearer grasp of Jimmy's struggle.

There are ramifications of this kind of exploration that go far beyond the province of this book, and so we leave the topic with only a few summary statements.

To grow in understanding of what is important in his life and in the life about him, a child must be encouraged to make the most important discovery of all: himself. To discover himself and his resources, and to grow in knowledge of himself, it is essential for him to have a chance to test the reaches and limits of his abilities and to draw upon his feelings and face their impact and meaning. To face his feelings, he needs freedom to experience them and he needs freedom to reveal them, if not to others, then at least to himself. To help a child to maintain his freedom to feel, and to regain it if he has lost it, is not an easy task. Teachers who try to promote children's understanding of their feelings are rather humble about their efforts. But these efforts, however humble, can have a health-promoting effect when they spring from compassion.

Compassion

This final section does not deal specifically with children, nor is it documented with empirical findings. But the writer wishes to include it for, in his judgment, compassion is an essential feature of mental health, emotional maturity, and acceptance of self and others.

To be compassionate a person must draw, as far as he is able, upon all his resources, his ability to have a feeling of fellowship with all that is glorious and sordid in the human situation, the noble things, the comic, the tragic, the wells of sorrow and the currents of joy. To do this, a person must endeavor to realize the meaning and quality of his own emotions in such a manner that he can be compassionate with himself.

Often we think of compassion as a kind of pity, a sort of readiness to commiserate with another who is in serious trouble. But compassion means more than to grieve with those who weep. It means more than to rejoice with those who are happy. It means an ability to enter into the meaning of any of a vast range of emotions. To be compassionate with one who is angry we must draw upon our own capacity for anger, and what we can learn from our own rage—the rack and grind of it; the bitter gall of it; the spite and vindictiveness that often go with it.

To be compassionate with one who is frightened, we must be able to draw upon our own experiences of fear. These go back to our early childhood and extend through the entire span of our lives. To be compassionate with those who are afraid, we must be willing, in effect, to say: Fear was a companion of my childhood and it has been my companion ever since. Fear has been at my side at times when I have cried and trembled, at times when I showed anger instead of apprehension, at times when I chose not to do what I might have done, saying to myself, "I am not afraid—I just don't care."

To be compassionate with one who is happy, we must draw upon our own experiences of happiness—the joy of being accepted, the pleasure of achievement, the triumphant feeling of having overcome a weakness, the ecstasy of loving and being loved or anticipating what it might mean to be loved, and the uprush of gladness that comes with the giving or receiving of kindness. Unless a person has realized some of his potentialities for happiness he will have nothing on which to base his appreciation of another's gladness. For this reason, some persons find it harder to be compassionate with those who are joyful than with those who are in distress.

Compassion for self means compassion for children, for the major concerns of childhood continue into adult life. So when we seek, as described in Chapter 1, to enter a child's world, we do not come as strangers. We are homeward bound.

Recommended Readings

From Birth to Maturity (1962) by Jerome Kagan and Howard A. Moss, Benjamin Bloom's *Stability and Change in Human Characteristics* and Mary M. Shirley's classic *The First Two Years, Vol. III. Personality Manifestations* (1933b) are recommended. *Vita Humana,* 1964, Volume 7, Number 2, contains excellent articles under the title "Symposium on Personality Consistency and Change: Perspectives from Longitudinal Research."

Bibliography

Abel, H., and R. Sahinkaya, 1962, "Emergence of Sex and Race Friendship Preferences," *Child Development*, 33, 939–943.

Abt, L. E., and L. Bellak, 1950, *Projective Psychology*. N. Y.: Knopf.

Adler, A.
1931, *What Life Should Mean to You*. N. Y.: Blue Ribbon Books, Inc.
1937, "The Significance of Early Childhood Recollections," *International Journal of Individual Psychology*, 6, 484–493.

Adler, R., 1957, "Effects of Early Experience on Emotionality," *American Psychologist*, 12, 410.

Adorno, T. W., E. Frenkel-Brunswik, D. J. Levinson, and R. N. Sanford, 1950, *The Authoritarian Personality*. N. Y.: Harper.

Albee, G. W., 1950, "Patterns of Aggression in Psychopathology," *Journal of Consulting Psychology*, 14, 465–468.

Allen, F., 1942, *Psychotherapy with Children*. N. Y.: Norton.

Allinsmith, W., 1960, "The Learning of Moral Standards," in *Inner Conflict and Defense*, edited by D. R. Miller and G. E. Swanson, pp. 141–176. N. Y.: Holt.

Allport, G. W.
1937, *Personality*. N. Y.: Holt.
1950, "Foreword," in M. G. Ross, *Religious Beliefs of Youth*. N. Y.: Association Press.

Almy, M. C., 1967, *Ways of Studying Children*. N. Y.: Teachers College, Columbia University.

Almy, M. C., E. Chittenden, and P. Miller, 1966, *Young Children's Thinking*, N. Y.: Teachers College, Columbia University.

Alschuler, R. H., and L. A. Hattwick, 1943, "Easel Painting as an index of Personality in Preschool Children," *American Journal of Orthopsychiatry*, 13, 616–626.

Amatora, M., 1954, "Similarity in Teacher and Pupil Personality," *Journal of Psychology*, 37, 45–50.

Ames, L. B.
  1940, "The Constancy of Psycho-Motor Tempo in Individual Infants," *Journal of Genetic Psychology*, 57, 445–450.
  1946, "The Development of the Sense of Time in the Young Child," *Journal of Genetic Psychology*, 68, 97–125.
  1952, "The Sense of Self of Nursery School Children as Manifested by Their Verbal Behavior," *Journal of Genetic Psychology*, 81, 193–232.
  1965, "Changes in the Experience-Balance Score on the Rorschach at Different Ages in the Life Span," *Journal of Genetic Psychology*, 106, 279–286.

Ames, L. B., and J. Learned, 1946, "Imaginary Companions and Related Phenomena," *Journal of Genetic Psychology*, 69, 147–167.

Ames, L. B., J. Learned, R. W. Metraux, and R. N. Walker, 1952, *Child Rorschach Responses, Developmental Trends from Two to Ten Years*. N. Y.: Hoeber.

Ammons, R. B., 1950, "Reactions in a Projective Doll-Play Interview of White Males Two to Six Years of Age to Differences in Skin Color and Facial Features," *Journal of Genetic Psychology*, 76, 323–341.

Anastasi, A., and F. A. Cordova, 1953, "Some Effects of Bilingualism upon the Intelligence Test Performance of Puerto Rican Children in New York City," *Journal of Educational Psychology*, 44, 1–19.

Anderson, H. H.
  1937a, "Domination and Integration in the Social Behavior of Young Children in an Experimental Play Situation," *Genetic Psychology Monographs*, 19, 343–408.
  1937b, "An Experimental Study of Dominative and Integrative Behavior in Children of Preschool Age," *Journal of Social Psychology*, 8, 335–345.

Anderson, H. H., and G. L. Anderson.
  1951, eds., *An Introduction to Projective Techniques and Other Devices for Understanding the Dynamics of Human Behavior*. N. Y.: Prentice-Hall.
  1954, "Social Development," in *Manual of Child Psychology*, 2nd ed., edited by L. Carmichael, pp. 1162–1215. N. Y.: Wiley.

Anderson, H. H., G. L. Anderson, A. I. Rabin, A. S. Elonen, T. M. Abel, and R. Diaz-Guerrero, 1960, "Culture Components as a Significant Factor in Child Development: Symposium," *American Journal of Orthopsychiatry*, 31, 481–520.

Anderson, H. H., and H. M. Brewer, 1945, *Studies of Teachers' Classroom Personalities: I. Dominative and Socially Integrative Behavior of Kindergarten Teachers*. Applied Psychology Monographs, No. 6. Stanford, California: Stanford University Press.

Anderson, H. H., J. E. Brewer, and M. F. Reed, 1946, *Studies of Teachers' Classroom Personalities: III. Follow-up Studies of the Effects of Dominative and Integrative Contacts on Children's Behavior*. Applied Psychology Monographs, No. 11. Stanford, California: Stanford University Press.

Angelino, H., J. Dollins, and E. V. Mech, 1956, "Trends in the Fears and Worries of School Children as Related to Socio-economic Status and Age," *Journal of Genetic Psychology*, 89, 263–276.

Appel, M. H., 1942, "Aggressive Behavior of Nursery School Children and Adult Procedures in Dealing with Such Behavior," *Journal of Experimental Education*, 11, 185–199.

Arnon, Y., 1961, "Hahorim vehayeladim begil haneurim bakibuts," (Parents and Adolescent Children in the Kibbutz) *Ofakim*, 15, 28–36.

Aserinsky, E., and N. Kleitman.
  1953, "Regularly Occurring Periods of Eye Motility, and Concomitant Phenomena, During Sleep," *Science*, 118, 273–274.
  1955, "A Motility Cycle in Sleeping Infants as Manifested by Ocular and Gross Body Activity," *Journal of Applied Physiology*, 8, 11–18.

Ashley-Montagu, M. F.
  1953, ed., *The Meaning of Love*. N. Y.: Julian Press.
  1962, *Prenatal Influences*. Springfield, Illinois: Charles C Thomas.
Ausubel, D. P., 1958, *Theory and Problems of Child Development*. N. Y.: Grune and Stratton.
Ausubel, D. P., E. E. Balthazar, I. Rosenthal, L. S. Blackman, S. H. Schpoont, and J. Welkowitz, 1954, "Perceived Parent Attitudes as Determinants of Children's Ego Structure," *Child Development*, 25, 173–183.
Axline, V. M., 1947, *Play Therapy: The Inner Dynamics of Childhood*. Boston: Houghton Mifflin.
Bach, G. R.
  1945, *Young Children's Play Fantasies*. Psychological Monographs, 59, No. 2. Evanston, Ill.: American Psychological Association.
  1952, "Some Diadic Functions of Childhood Memories," *Journal of Psychology*, 33, 87–88.
Baker, H. V., 1942, *Children's Contributions in Elementary School General Discussion*. Child Development Monographs, No. 29. N. Y.: Teachers College, Columbia University.
Baldwin, A. L., 1967, *Theories of Child Development*. N. Y.: Wiley.
Baldwin, A. L., J. Kalhorn, and F. H. Breese
  1945, *Patterns of Parent Behavior*. Psychological Monographs, 58, No. 3. Evanston, Ill.: American Psychological Association.
  1949, *The Appraisal of Parent Behavior*, Psychological Monographs, 63, No. 4.
Baldwin, J. M., 1925, *Mental Development in the Child and the Race*. London: Macmillan.
Bandura, A., and R. H. Walters, 1963, "Aggression," *Child Psychology, The 62nd Yearbook of the National Society for the Study of Education*. Chicago: The University of Chicago Press, 364–415.
Barker, B., 1961, "Social Class Differences in Educational Life Chances," *Teachers College Record*, Columbia University, 102–113.
Barker, R. G., and H. F. Wright, 1954, *Midwest and Its Children*. Evanston, Illinois: Row Peterson.
Barker, R., T. Dembo, and K. Lewin, 1941, *Studies in Topological and Vector Psychology: II. Frustration and Regression*. University of Iowa Studies in Child Welfare, 18, No. 1. Iowa City: University of Iowa Press.
Bartlett, F. C., 1932, *Remembering: A Study in Experimental and Social Psychology*. N. Y.: Macmillan.
Bayley, N.
  1933a, *The California First Year Mental Scale*. University of California Syllabus Series, No. 243. Berkeley: University of California Press.
  1933b, "Mental Growth During the First Three Years," *Genetic Psychology Monographs*, 14, 7–92.
  1935, *The Development of Motor Abilities During the First Three Years*. Monographs of the Society for Research in Child Development, No. 1. Washington, D. C.: National Research Council.
  1954, "Some Increasing Parent-Child Similarities During the Growth of Children," *Journal of Educational Psychology*, 45, 1–21.
  1958, *An Infant Scale of Mental Development*. Revised mimeographed form. Laboratory of Psychology, National Institute of Mental Health.
  1964, "Consistency of Maternal and Child Behaviors in the Berkeley Growth Study," *Vita Humana*, 7, 73–95.
Beadle, G. W., 1964, "The New Genetics: The Thread of Life," in *Britannica Book of the Year*, 1964. Chicago: Encyclopedia Britannica, 44–72.
Beasley, W. C., 1933, "Visual Pursuit in 109 White and 142 Negro Newborn Infants," *Child Development*, 4, 106–120.
Beck, S. J., 1937, *Introduction to the Rorschach Method: A Manual of Personality Study*. Research Monograph of the American Orthopsychiatric Association, No. 1, Menasha, Wisconsin: American Orthopsychiatric Association.
Behrens, M. L., 1954, "Child Rearing and the Character Structure of the Mother," *Child Development*, 25, 225–238.

Bellak, L., and S. S. Bellak, 1949–   , *Children's Apperception Test*, rev. ed., ages 3–10. C.P.S. Co., P. O. Box 42, Gracie Station, N. Y. C.

Benezet, L. P., 1935, "The Story of An Experiment," *Journal of the National Association*, 24, 241–244; 301–303.

Berezin, D., 1959, "An Inquiry Into the Temperamental Differences of Infants Noted by Their Boarding Mothers in Adoption Studies," unpublished Doctor of Education dissertation, Teachers College, Columbia University.

Berger, E., 1952, "Relation Between Expressed Acceptance of Self and Others," *Journal of Abnormal and Social Psychology*, 47, 778–782.

Berko, J., 1958, "The Child's Learning of English Morphology," *Word*, 4, 150–177.

Berko, J., and R. Brown, 1960, "Psycholinguistic Research Methods," *Handbook of Research Methods in Child Development*, edited by P. H. Mussen, 517–557. N. Y.: Wiley.

Berkowitz, L., 1964, *The Development of Motives and Values in the Child*. N. Y.: Basic Books.

Berlyne, D. E., 1958, "The Influence of the Albedo and Complexity of Stimuli on Visual Fixation in the Human Infant," *British Journal of Psychology*, 49, 315–318.

Bernard, J., 1964, "Prediction From Fetal Measures," *Child Development*, 35, 1243–1248.

Bernstein, B., 1959, "A Public Language: Some Sociological Implications of a Linguistic Form," *British Journal of Sociology*, December, 311–327.

Bibring, G. L., T. F. Dwyer, D. S. Huntington, and A. F. Valenstein, 1961, "A Study of the Psychological Processes in Pregnancy and of the Earliest Mother-Child Relationship," *Psychoanalytic Study of the Child*, 16. N. Y.: International Universities Press, 9–72.

Biehler, R. F., 1954, "Companion Choice Behavior in the Kindergarten," *Child Development*, 25, 45–51.

Bills, R. E., E. L. Vance, and O. S. McLean, 1951, "An Index of Adjustment and Values," *Journal of Consulting Psychology*, 15, 257–261.

Birns, B. M., 1965, "Individual Differences in Human Neonates' Responses to Stimulation," *Child Development*, 30 (1), 249–256.

Birns, B. M., M. Blank, and W. H. Bridger, 1965, "The Effectiveness of Various Soothing Techniques on Human Neonates," N. Y.: Department of Psychiatry, Albert Einstein College of Medicine, Yeshiva University. Paper presented in part at the meeting of the Society for Research in Child Development in Minneapolis, Minnesota.
1965, "The Effectiveness of Various Soothing Techniques on Human Neonates," *Psychosomatic Medicine* (in press).

Birns, B. M., M. Blank, W. H. Bridger, and S. K. Escalona, 1965, "Behavioral Inhibition in Neonates Produced by Auditory Stimuli," *Child Development*, 36 (3), 639–645.

Birns, B. M., and W. H. Bridger
1963, "Neonates' Behavioral and Autonomic Responses to Stress During Soothing," *Recent Advances in Biological Psychiatry*, 5, Plenum Press.
1965, "Experiences and Temperament in Human Neonates," *Early Experience and Behavior* (in press).

Blatz, W. E., and D. A. Millichamp, 1937, "The Mental Growth of the Dionne Quintuplets," University of Toronto Studies, Child Development Series, No. 12, in Blatz, W. C., et al., *Collected Studies of the Dionne Quintuplets*. Toronto: University of Toronto Press.

Blatz, W. E., D. A. Millichamp, and M. W. Charles, 1937, "The Early Social Development of the Dionne Quintuplets," University of Toronto Studies, Child Development Series, No. 13, in Blatz, W. C., et al., *Collected Studies of the Dionne Quintuplets*. Toronto: University of Toronto Press, 52, 441–442.

Blau, T. H., and L. R. Blau, 1955, "The Sucking Reflex: The Effects of Long Feeding vs. Short Feeding on the Behavior of a Human Infant," *Journal of Abnormal and Social Psychology*, 51, 123–125.

Blauvelt, Helen H., 1962, "Capacity of a Human Neonate Reflex to Signal Future Response by Present Action," *Child Development*, 33, 21–28.

Bloom, B., 1964, *Stability and Change in Human Characteristics*. N. Y.: John Wiley.

Blum, L. H., 1950, "Some Psychological and Educational Aspects of Pediatric Practice: A Study of Well-Baby Clinics," *Genetic Psychology Monographs*, 41, 3–97.

Blum, L. H., H. H. Davidson, and N. D. Fieldsteel, 1954, *A Rorschach Workbook*. N. Y.: International Universities Press.

Bonney, M. E., and E. L. Nicholson, 1958, "Comparative School Adjustments of Elementary School Pupils With and Without Preschool Training," *Child Development,* 29, 125–133.

Bossard, J. H. S., and E. S. Boll, 1957, "Child Behavior and the Empathic Complex," *Child Development,* 28, 37–42.

Bowerman, C. E., and D. P. Irish, 1962, "Some Relationships of Stepchildren to Their Parents," *Marriage And Family Living,* 24 (2), 113–121.

Bradway, K. P., and C. W. Thompson, 1962, "Intelligence at Adulthood: A Twenty-Five Year Follow-up," *Journal of Educational Psychology,* 53, 1–14.

Brandenburg, G. C., 1915, "The Language of a Three Year Old Child," *Journal of Genetic Psychology,* 22, 89–120.

Brandt, R. M., 1958, "The Accuracy of Self Estimate: A Measure of Self-Concept Reality," *Genetic Psychology Monographs,* 58, 55–100.

Bridger, W. H., 1961, "Sensory Habituation and Discrimination in the Human Neonate," *American Journal of Psychiatry,* 991–996.

Bridger, W. H., and B. M. Birns, 1963, "Neonate's Behavioral Autonomic Responses to Stress During Soothing," *Recent Advances in Biological Psychiatry,* 5, 1–6.

Bridger, W. H., B. M. Birns, and M. Blank, 1965, "A Comparison of Behavioral Ratings and Heart Rate Measurements in Human Neonates," *Psychosomatic Medicine,* XXVII (2), 123–134.

Brodbeck, A. J., and O. C. Irwin, 1946, "The Speech Behavior of Infants without Families," *Child Development,* 17, 145–156.

Broderick, C. B., and S. E. Fowler, 1961, "New Patterns of Relationships Between the Sexes among Preadolescents," *Marriage And Family Living,* 23, 27–30.

Bronfenbrenner, U.
1960, Freudian Theories of Identification and Their Derivatives," *Child Development,* 31, 15–40.
1961, "The Changing American Child: A Speculative Analysis," *Journal of Social Issues,* 17 (1), 6–17.
1963, "Developmental Theory in Transition," in H. W. Stevenson, ed., *Child Phychology,* NSSE Yearbook. Chicago: University of Chicago Press.
1964, "Freudian Theories of Identification and Their Derivatives," in C. B. Stendler, *Readings in Child Behavior and Development,* 2nd edition, pp. 102–121. N. Y.: Harcourt, Brace & World.

Bronson, W., "Central Orientation: A Study of Behavior Organization from Childhood to Adolescence," *Child Development,* 37, 125–155.

Brook, J., 1967, "Children's Conception of Language," in press, *Journal of Genetic Psychology.*

Brown, A. W., and R. G. Hunt, 1961, "Relations Between Nursery School Attendance and Teachers' Ratings of Some Aspects of Children's Adjustment in Kindergarten," *Child Development,* 32, 585–596.

Brown, D. G.
1956, *The IT Scale for Children.* Missoula, Montana: Psychological Test Specialists.
1957, "Masculinity-Femininity Development in Children," *Journal of Consulting Psychology,* 21, 197–202.

Brown, R., and J. Berko, 1960, "Word Association and the Acquisition of Grammar," *Child Development,* 31, 1–14.

Bruch, H.
1947, "Psychological Aspects of Obesity," *Psychiatry,* 10, 373–381.
1952, *Don't Be Afraid of Your Child.* N. Y.: Farrar, Straus & Young.

Bruck, M., 1957, "A Study of Age Differences and Sex Differences in the Relationship Between Self-Concept and Grade-Point Average," unpublished doctoral dissertation, Michigan State University.

Bruner, J. S., 1960, *The Process of Education.* Cambridge: Harvard University Press.

Bühler, C.
1930, *The First Year of Life.* N. Y.: John Day.
1933, "The Social Behavior of Children," in *A Handbook of Child Psychology,* 2nd revised edition, edited by C. Murchison, pp. 374–416. Worcester, Massachusetts: Clark University Press.
1952, "The Diagnostic Problem in Childhood Schizophrenia," *Nervous Child,* 10, 60–62.

Bühler, C., and H. Hester, 1928, "Das erste Verständnis von Ausdruck im ersten Lebensjahr, *Zsch. f. Psychol.*, 107, 50–61.

Bühler, K., 1924, *Kie geistige Entwicklung des Kindes*, 4th edition. Jena: Gustav Fischer.

Burchinal, L. G., 1964, "Characteristics of Adolescents From Unbroken, and Reconstituted Families," *Journal of Marriage and the Family*, 26 (1), 44–51.

Burchinal, L. G., and J. E. Rossman, 1961, "Relations among Maternal Employment Indices and Developmental Characteristics of Children," *Marriage and Family Living*, 23, 334–340.

Burlingham, D.
1952, *Twins: A Study of Three Pairs of Identical Twins*. N. Y.: International Universities Press.

Burnham, M. P., 1940, "Imaginative Behavior of Young Children as Revealed in Their Language," unpublished Doctor of Philosophy dissertation, Teachers College, Columbia University.

Burt, C.
1919, "The Development of Reasoning in Children," *Journal of Experimental Pedagogy*, 5, 68–77; 121–127.
1940, "The Incidence of Neurotic Symptoms among Evacuated School Children," *British Journal of Educational Psychology*, 10, 8–15.
1966, "The Human Perspective," *Perspectives in Biology and Medicine*, 9 (3), 317–332.

Burton, R. V., E. E. Maccoby, and W. Allinsmith, 1961, "Antecedents of Resistance to Temptation in Four-Year-Old Children," *Child Development*, 32, 689–710.

Burtt, H. E.
1932, "An Experimental Study of Early Childhood Memory," *Journal of Genetic Psychology*, 40, 287–295.
1937, "A Further Study of Early Childhood Memory," *Journal of Genetic Psychology*, 50, 187–192.
1941, "An Experimental Study of Early Childhood Memory: Final Report," *Journal of Genetic Psychology*, 58, 435–439.

Caille, R. K., 1933, *Resistant Behavior of Preschool Children*. Child Development Monographs, No. 11. N. Y.: Teachers College, Columbia University.

Caldwell, B. M., 1962, "The Usefullness of the Critical Period Hypothesis in the Study of Filiative Behavior," *Merrill-Palmer Quarterly of Behavior and Development*, 8, 4, 229–242.

Cameron, C. L., 1966, *Early Memories as Recorded by Seventh, Ninth and Eleventh Grade Boys and Girls*. N. Y.: Teachers College, Columbia University, Doctor of Education Project Report.

Cannon, W. B., 1929, *Bodily Changes in Pain, Hunger, Fear, and Rage*, 2nd edition. N. Y.: Appleton-Century.

Cantril, H., 1946, "Identification with Social and Economic Class," in *Twentieth Century Psychology*, edited by P. L. Harriman, pp. 146–152. N. Y.: Philosophical Library.

Caplan, H., R. Bibace, and M. S. Rabinovitch, 1963, "Paranatal Stress, Cognitive Organization and Ego Function. A Controlled Follow-Up Study of Children Born Prematurely," *Journal of Child Psychiatry*, 2, 434–450.

Carlson, R., 1963, "Identification and Personality Structure in Preadolescents," *Journal of Abnormal and Social Psychology*, 67, 566–573.

Carmichael, L., 1954, "The Onset and Early Development of Behavior," in *Manual of Child Phychology*, 2nd edition, pp. 60–185. N. Y.: Wiley.

Casler, L., 1961, "Maternal Deprivation: A Critical Review of the Literature," *Monographs of the Society for Research in Child Development*, 26 (2), 3–64.

Castaneda, A., B. R. McCandless, and D. S. Palermo
1956a, "The Children's Form of the Manifest Anxiety Scale," *Child Development*, 27, 317–326.
1956b, "Complex Learning and Performance as a Function of Anxiety in Children and Task Difficulty," *Child Development*, 27, 327–332.

Cattell, R. B.
1963, "The Interaction of Hereditary and Environmental Influences," *The British Journal of Statistical Psychology*, XVI (2), 191–210.
1965, "Methodological and Conceptual Advances in Evaluating Hereditary and Environ-

mental Influences and their Interaction," in *Methods and Goals in Human Behavior Genetics*, edited by S. G. Vandenberg, p. 95. N. Y.: Academic Press.

Champney, H., 1941, "The Measurement of Parent Behavior," *Child Development*, 12, 131–166.

Charry, J. B., 1959, "Childhood and Teen-Age Memories in Mentally Ill and Normal Groups," unpublished Doctor of Philosophy dissertation, Teachers College, Columbia University.

Chess, S., A. Thomas, and H. G. Birch
1966, *Your Child Is A Person*. N. Y.: Viking Press.
1967, "Behavior Problems Revisited: Findings of an Anterospective Study," *Journal American Academy Child Psychiatry*, 6, 321–331.

Chittenden, G. E., 1942, *An Experimental Study in Measuring and Modifying Assertive Behavior in Young Children*. Monograph of Society for Research in Child Development, 7, No. 1. Washington, D. C.: National Research Council.

Clark, K. B., 1963, *Prejudice and Your Child*. Boston: Beacon Press.

Clark, K. B., and M. K. Clark
1940, "Skin Color as a Factor in Racial Identification of Negro Preschool Children," *Journal of Social Psychology*, 11, 159–169.
1947, "Racial Identification and Preference in Negro Children," in *Readings in Social Psychology*, edited by G. Swanson, T. Newcomb, and E. Hartley, pp. 169–78. N. Y.: Holt.

Clausen, J. A., and J. R. Williams, 1963, "Sociological Correlates of Child Behavior," *Child Psychology: The 62nd Yearbook of the National Society for the Study of Education*. Chicago, Illinois: University of Chicago Press, 62–107.

Clements, E. M. B., 1953, "Changes in the Mean Stature and Weight of British Children over the Past Seventy Years," *British Medical Journal*, No. 4841, Oct. 17, 892–902.

Clifford, E., 1962, "Expressed Attitudes in Pregnancy of Unwed Women and Married Primigravida and Multigravida," *Child Development*, 33 (4), 945–951.

Coghill, G. E.
1929, *Anatomy and the Problem of Behavior*. N. Y.: Macmillan
1936, "Integration and Motivation of Behavior as Problems of Growth," *Journal of Genetic Psychology*, 48, 3–19.

Cohen, A. I., 1966, "Hand Preference and Developmental Status of Babies," *Journal Genetic Psychology*, 108, 337–345.

Coleman, J. S., 1961, *The Adolescent Society; The Social Life of the Teenager and Its Impact on Education*. N. Y.: Free Press.

Coleman, R. W., E. Kris, and S. Provence, 1953, "The Study of Variations of Early Parental Attitudes," in *The Psychoanalytic Study of the Child*, Vol. 8, pp. 20–47. N. Y.: International Universities Press.

Combs, A. W., and D. Snygg, 1959, *Individual Behavior: A Perceptual Approach to Behavior*, 2nd edition. N. Y.: Harper.

Combs, A. W. *See also* Snygg, D., 1949; Taylor, C., 1952.

Conn, J. H., 1940, "Children's Reactions to the Discovery of Genital Differences," *American Journal of Orthopsychiatry*, 10, 747–755.

Connor, R. F., H. F. Greene, and J. Walters, 1958, "Agreement of Family Member Conceptions of 'Good' Parent and Child Roles," *Social Forces*, 36 (4), 353–358.

Coopersmith, S., 1959, "A Method of Determining Types of Self-Esteem," *Journal of Abnormal and Social Psychology*, 59, 87–94.

Corn, F. S., 1962, "Fantasy Aggression in Children as Studied by the Doll Play Technique," *Child Development*, 33, 235–250.

Cox, F. N., 1953, "Sociometric Status and Individual Adjustment Before and After Play Therapy," *Journal of Abnormal and Social Psychology*, 48, 354–356.

Crandall, V. J., and A. Preston, 1955, "Patterns and Levels of Maternal Behavior," *Child Development*, 26, 267–277.

Cruickshank, W. M., and G. O. Johnson, eds., 1967, *Education of Exceptional Children and Youth*. Englewood Cliffs, N. J.: Prentice-Hall.

Cunningham, R., 1947, "How to Construct a Sociogram," Horace Mann-Lincoln Institute of School Experimentation, Bureau of Publications, Teachers College, Columbia University.

Cunningham, R., A. Elzi, J. A. Hall, M. Farrell, and M. Roberts, 1951, *Understanding*

Group Behavior of Boys and Girls. N. Y.: Bureau of Publications, Teachers College, Columbia University.

Curry, R. L., 1962, "Effect of Socioeconomic Status on the Scholastic Achievement of Sixth Grade Children," *British Journal of Educational Psychology*, 32, 46–49.

Damann, V. T., 1941, "Developmental Changes in Attitudes as One Factor Determining Energy Output in a Motor Performance," *Child Development*, 12, 241–246.

Darcy, N. T., 1946, "The Effect of Bilingualism upon the Measurement of the Intelligence of Children of Preschool Age," *Journal of Educational Psychology*, 37, 21–44.

Davidson, K. S., 1959, "Interviews of Parents of High Anxious and Low Anxious Children," *Child Development*, 30, 341–351.

Davidson, K. S., S. B. Sarason, F. Lighthall, R. R. Waite, and I. Saranoff, 1958, "Differences Between Mothers' and Fathers' Ratings of Low Anxious and High Anxious Children," *Child Development*, 29, 155–160.

Davis, A.
1944, "Socialization and Adolescent Personality," National Society for the Study of Education, *Adolescence*, Forty-third Yearbook, Part I, pp. 198–216. Chicago: University of Chicago Press.

Davis, A., and K. Eells, 1953, *Manual for the Davis-Eells Test of General Intelligence or Problem-Solving Ability.* Yonkers, N. Y.: World Book Co.

Davis, C. M.
1928, "Self-Selection of Diet by Newly Weaned Infants," *American Journal of Diseases of Children*, 46, 743–750.
1931, "Self-Selection of Diets: An Experiment with Infants," *The Trained Nurse and Hospital Review*, 86, 629–634.
1933, "A Practical Application of Some Lessons of the Self-Selection of Diet Study to the Feeding of Children in Hospitals," *American Journal of Diseases of Children*, 46, 743–750.
1935, "Choice of Formulas Made by Three Infants Throughout the Nursing Period," *American Journal of Diseases of Children*, 50, 385–394.

Davis, E. A.
1932, "The Form and Function of Children's Questions," *Child Development*, 3, 57–74.
1937, *The Development of Linguistic Skills in Twins, Singletons with Siblings, and Only Children from Age Five to Ten Years.* Institute of Child Welfare Monograph Series, No. 14. Minneapolis: University of Minnesota Press.

Davitz, J. R.
1952, "The Effects of Previous Training on Postfrustration Behavior," *Journal of Abnormal and Social Psychology*, XLVII, 309–315.
1958, "Contributions of Research with Children to a Theory of Maladjustment," *Child Development*, 29, 3–7.
1964, *The Communication Of Emotional Meaning.* N. Y.: McGraw-Hill.

Dawson, G. E., 1900, "Children's Interest in the Bible," *Journal of Genetic Psychology*, 7, 151–178.

Day, E. J.
1932a, "The Development of Language in Twins: I. A Comparison of Twins and Single Children," *Child Development*, 3, 179–199.
1932b, "The Development of Language in Twins: II. The Development of Twins: Their Resemblances and Differences." *Child Development*, 3, 298–316.

Debus, R. L., 1953, "Aggressive Behavior in Young Children," *Forum of Education*, 11, 95–105.

DeMartino, M. F., 1955, "A Review of the Literature on Children's Dreams," *Psychiatric Quarterly Supplement*, 29, 90–101.

Dement, W., 1960, "The Effect of Dream Deprivation," *Science*, 131 (3415), 1705–1707.

Dement, W., and N. Kleitman
1957a, "Cyclic Variations in EEG During Sleep and Their Relation to Eye Movements, Body Motility, and Dreaming," *Electroencephalography and Clinical Neurophysiology*, 9, 673–690.
1957b, "The Relation of Eye Movements During Sleep to Dream Activity: An Objective Method for the Study of Dreaming," *Journal of Experimental Psychology*, 53, 339–346.

Dement, W., and E. A. Wolpert

1958a, "Relationships to the Manifest Content of Dreams Occurring on the Same Night," *Journal of Nervous and Mental Disease*, 126 (6), 568–578.
1958b, "The Relation of Eye Movements, Body Motility, and External Stimuli to Dream Content," *Journal of Experimental Psychology*, 55 (6), 543–553.
Dennenberg, V. H., 1963, "Early Experience and Emotional Development," *Scientific American Reprints*, No. 478, 1–6. San Francisco: Freeman.
Dennis, W.
1938, "Infant Development Under Conditions of Restricted Practice and of Minimum Social Stimulation. A Preliminary Report," *Journal of Genetic Psychology*, 53, 149–157.
1942, Piaget's Questions Applied to a Child of Known Environment," *Journal of Genetic Psychology*, 60, 307–320.
1949, "Historical Beginnings of Child Psychology," *Psychological Bulletin*, 46, 224–235.
1951, ed., *Readings In Child Psychology*. N. Y.: Prentice-Hall.
1958, "Early Graphic Evidence of Dextrality in Man," *Perceptual and Motor Skills*, 8, 147–149.
1960, "Causes of Retardation Among Institutional Children: Iran," *Journal of Genetic Psychology*, 96, 47–59.
Dennis, W., and P. Najarian, 1957, *Infant Development Under Environmental Handicap*. Psychological Monographs, 71, No. 7. Washington, D. C.: American Psychological Association.
Despert, J. L.
1944, "Urinary Control and Enuresis," *Psychosomatic Medicine*, 6, 294–307.
1946, "Anxiety, Phobias and Fears in Young Children with Special Reference to Pre-natal, Natal, and Postnatal Factors," *Nervous Child*, 5, 8–24.
Deutch, M. P., 1960, *Minority Group and Class Status as Related to Social and Personality Factors in Scholastic Achievement*. Monograph No. 2, Ithaca, N. Y.: Society for Applied Anthropology.
Deutsch, H., 1944–1945, *The Psychology of Women* (2 vols.). N. Y.: Grune and Stratton.
Dimitrovsky, L., 1964, "The Ability to Identify the Emotional Meaning of Vocal Expressions at Successive Age Levels," in *The Communication of Emotional Meaning*, edited by J. R. Davitz, pp. 69–86. N. Y.: McGraw-Hill.
Ding, G. F., and A. T. Jersild, 1932, "A Study of the Laughing and Smiling of Preschool Children," *Journal of Genetic Psychology*, 40, 452–472.
Dixon, J. C., 1957, "Development of Self Recognition," *Journal of Genetic Psychology*, 91, 251–256.
Dobzhansky, T., 1962, *Mankind Evolving*. New Haven: Yale University Press.
Dolger, L., and J. Ginandes, 1946, "Children's Attitude Toward Discipline as Related to Socioeconomic Status," *Journal of Experimental Education*, 15, 161–165.
Donaldson, R. S., and S. G. Kohl, 1965, "Perinatal Mortality in Twins by Sex," *American Journal of Public Health*, 55, No. 9.
Douvan, E.
1956, "Social Status and Success Striving," *Journal of Abnormal and Social Psychology*, March, 219–223.
1960, "Sex Differences in Adolescent Character Processes," *Merrill-Palmer Quarterly*, 6, 203–211.
Driscoll, G. P., 1952, *Driscoll Playkit*. N. Y.: Psychological Corporation.
Dublin, L. I., 1965, *Factbook On Man*. N. Y.: Macmillan.
Dudycha, G. J., and M. M. Dudycha
1933a, "Some Factors and Characteristics in Childhood Memories," *Child Development*, 4, 265–278.
1933b, "Adolescents' Memories of Preschool Experiences," *Journal of Genetic Psychology*, 42, 468–480.
Dukes, W. F., and W. Bevan, 1952, "Accentuation and Response Variability in the Perception of Personally Related Objects," *Journal of Personality*, XX, 457–465.
Dunlap, J. M., 1958, "The Education of Children with High Mental Ability," in *Education of Exceptional Children and Youth*, edited by W. M. Cruickshank and G. O. Johnson, pp. 147–188. Englewood Cliffs, N. J.: Prentice-Hall.
Dunnington, M. J., 1957, "Behavioral Differences of Sociometric Status Groups in a Nursery School," *Child Development*, 28, 103–111.
Durkin, D., 1959, "Children's Acceptance of Reciprocity as a Justice-Principle," *Child Development*, 30, 289–296.

Eaton, M. T., 1944, *A Survey of the Achievement in Social Studies of 10,220 Sixth-Grade Pupils in 464 Schools in Indiana.* Bulletin 20, No. 3. Bloomington, Indiana: School of Education, University of Indiana, Bureau of Cooperative Research and Field Service.

Edwards, N., 1967, "Relationship Between Indicies of Neonatal Physical Condition at One and Five Minutes After Birth and Mental and Motor Functioning at Age Four," unpublished Doctor of Education dissertation, in press, *Genetic Psychology Monographs.*

Eells, K. W., 1951, *Intelligence and Cultural Differences: A Study of Cultural Learning and Problem-Solving.* Chicago: University of Chicago Press.

Eichorn, D. H.
1959, "Two-Generation Similarities in Weight, Height and Weight/Height During the First Five Years." Reported at the Twenty-fifth Anniversary Meeting, Society for Research in Child Development, National Institute of Health, Bethesda, Maryland, March, 1959.
1965, "Developmental Psychophysiology: Precis and Prophecy." Paper presented at Symposium on Developmental Psychophysiology, Biennial Meeting of the Society for Research in Child Development, Minneapolis, March 24, 1965. Multigraphed. Berkeley: Institute of Human Development, University of California.

Eissler, R. S., A. Freud, H. Hartmann, and M. Kris, eds., 1965, *The Psychoanalytic Study of the Child.* N. Y.: International Universities Press.

Elkind, D.
1961, "The Child's Conception of His Religious Denomination: I. The Jewish Child," *Journal of Genetic Psychology,* 99, 209–225.
1962, "The Child's Conception of His Religious Denomination: II. The Catholic Child," *Journal of Genetic Psychology,* 101, 185–193.
1963, "The Child's Conception of His Religious Denomination: III. The Protestant Child," *Journal of Genetic Psychology,* 103, 291–304.

Emmerich, W., 1961, "Family Role Concepts of Children Ages Six to Ten," *Child Development,* 32, 609–624.

Emmerich, W., 1966, "Continuity and Stability in Early Social Development: II. Teacher Ratings," *Child Development,* 37, 17–27.

Engen, T., L. P. Lipsitt, and H. Kaye, 1963, "Olfactory Responses and Adaptation in the Human Neonate," *Journal of Comparative Physiology and Psychology,* 56 (1), 73–77.

English, H. B., 1929, "Three Cases of the Conditioned Fear Response," *Journal of Abnormal and Social Psychology,* 24, 221–225.

Ephron, H. S., and P. Carrington, 1967, "Ego Functioning in Rapid Eye Movement Sleep: Implications for Dream Theory," *Science and Psychoanalysis,* XI, 75–102.

Epstein, R., 1963, "Social Class Membership and Early Childhood Memories," *Child Development,* 34, 503–508.

Erikson, E. H.
1940, "Studies in the Interpretation of Play," *Genetic Psychology Monographs,* 22, 557–671.
1950, "Eight Ages of Man," *Childhood and Society.* N. Y.: Norton, pp. 247–274.

Escalona, S.
1945, "Feeding Disturbances in Very Young Children," *American Journal of Orthopsychiatry,* 15, 76–80.
1963, "Patterns of Infantile Experience and the Developmental Process," in *The Psychoanalytic Study of the Child,* pp. 197–244, edited by R. S. Essler. N. Y.: International Universities Press.

Estvan, F. J., 1952, "The Relationship of Social Status, Intelligence, and Sex of Ten- and Eleven-Year-Old Children to an Awareness of Poverty," *Genetic Psychology Monographs,* 46, 3–60.

Eysenck, H. J., 1956, "The Inheritance of Extraversion-Introversion," *Acta Psychologika,* 12, 95–110.

Ezekiel, L. F., 1931, "Changes in Egocentricity of Nursery School Children," *Child Development,* 2, 74–75.

Falek, A., 1959, "Handedness: A Family Study," *American Journal of Human Genetics,* 11, 52–62.

Fantz, R. L.
1961, "The Origin of Form Perception," *Scientific American,* CCIV, 66–72.
1963, "Pattern Vision in Newborn Infants," *Science,* 140, 296–297.

Farnsworth, P. R., ed., 1967, *Annual Review of Psychology*. Palo Alto, California: Annual Reviews, Inc.

Fauquier, W., 1940, "The Attitudes of Aggressive and Submissive Boys Toward Athletics," *Child Development*, 11, 115–125.

Feldman, D. A., G. Pascal, and C. H. Swenson, 1954, "Direction of Aggression as a Prognostic Variable in Mental Illness," *Journal of Consulting Psychology*, 18, 167–170.

Feldman, W. M., 1920, *The Principles of Ante-Natal and Post-Natal Child Physiology, Pure and Applied*. N. Y.: Longmans, Green.

Fenichel, O., 1945, *The Psychoanalytic Theory of Neurosis*. N. Y.: Norton.

Feshback, S. and N. Feshback, 1963, "Influence of the Stimulus Object on the Complementary and Supplementary Projection of Fear," *Journal of Abnormal and Social Psychology*, 66, 498–502.

Fey, W. F., 1955, "Acceptance of Others and Its Relation to Acceptance of Self and Others: A Revaluation," *Journal of Abnormal and Social Psychology*, 274–276.

Fiedler, F. E., 1954, "Assumed Similarity Measures As Predictors of Team Effectiveness," *Journal of Abnormal and Social Psychology*, 49, 381–388.

Fiedler, F. E., W. G. Warrington, and F. G. Blaisdell, 1952, "Unconscious Attitudes as Correlates of Sociometric Choice in a Social Group," *Journal of Abnormal and Social Psychology* 47, 790–796.

Fisher, C., 1965, "Dreaming and Sexuality." Multilithed by the Institute of Psychiatry, Department of Psychology. N. Y.: Mt. Sinai Hospital.

Fisher, C., and W. C. Dement, 1963, "Studies in the Psychopathology of Sleep and Dreams," *American Journal of Psychiatric Association*, 119 (12) 1160–1163.

Fisher, C., J. Gross, and J. Zuch, 1965, "A Cycle of Penile Erection Synchronous with Dreaming (REM) Sleep," *Archives of General Psychiatry*, 12, 29–45.

Fisher, M. S., 1934, *Language Patterns of Preschool Children*. Child Development Monographs, No. 15, N. Y.: Teachers College, Columbia University.

Fite, M. D.
1940, "Aggressive Behavior in Young Children and Children's Attitudes Toward Aggression," *Genetic Psychology Monographs*, 22, 151–319.

Fitz-Simons, M. J., 1935, *Some Parent-Child Relationships As Shown in Clinical Case Studies*. Contributions to Education, No. 643. N. Y.: Bureau of Publications, Teachers College, Columbia University.

Flapan, D., 1965, "Children's Understanding of Social Interaction," unpublished Doctor of Philosophy dissertation, Columbia University.

Flavell, J. H., 1963, *The Developmental Psychology of Jean Piaget*. Princeton, N. J.: Van Nostrand.

Flory, C. D.
1936a, "Osseous Development in the Hand as an Index of Skeletal Development," *Monographs of the Society for Research in Child Development*, I, No. 3.
1936b, "The Physical Growth of Mentally Deficient Boys," *Monographs of the Society for Research in Child Development*, I, No. 6.

Forbes, H. S., and H. B. Forbes, 1927, "Fetal Sense Reaction: Hearing," *Journal of Comparative Psychology*, 7, 353–355.

Foshay, A. W., and K. D. Wann, *et al.*, 1954, *Children's Social Values: An Action Research Study*. N. Y.: Bureau of Publications, Teachers College, Columbia University.

Foster, J. C., and J. E. Anderson, 1936, "Unpleasant Dreams in Childhood," *Child Development*, 7, 77–84.

Foster, J. C., F. L. Goodenough, and J. E. Anderson
1928, "The Sleep of Young Children," *Journal of Gentic Psychology*, 35, 201–218.
1930, *The Sleep of Young Children*. Institute of Child Welfare Monograph Series, Circular No. 4. Minneapolis: University of Minnesota Press.

Foster, S., 1927, "A Study of Personality Make-Up and Social Setting of Fifty Jealous Children," *Mental Hygiene*, 11, 53–77.

Foulkes, D., 1964, "Theories of Dream Formation and Recent Studies of Sleep Consciousness," *Psychological Bulletin*, 62 (4), 236–247.

Foulkes, W. D., 1962, "Dream Reports From Different Stages of Sleep," *Journal of Abnormal and Social Psychology*, 65, 14–25.

Franco, D., 1965, "The Child's Perception of 'the Teacher' as Compared to his Perception of 'the Mother,' " *Journal of Genetic Psychology*, 107, 133–141.

Frank, G. H., 1965, "The Role of the Family in the Development of Psychopathology," *Psychological Bulletin*, 64 (3), 191–205.

Frank, L. K.
1939, "Projective Methods for the Study of Personality," *Journal of Psychology*, 8, 389–413.

Frank, L. K., R. Harrison, E. Hellersberg, K. Machover, and M. Steiner, 1953, *Personality Development in Adolescent Girls*. Monographs of the Society for Research in Child Development, 16, No. 53. New Orleans: Child Development Publications of the Society for Research in Child Development.

Freedman, D., 1965, "An Ethological Approach to the Genetical Study of Human Behavior," in *Methods and Goals in Human Behavior Genetics*, edited by S. G. Vandenberg, pp. 141–161. N. Y.: Academic Press.

Freedman, D. G.
1961, "The Infant's Fear of Strangers and the Flight Response," *Journal of Child Psychology and Psychiatry*, 2, 242–248.
1966, *Longitudinal Studies in the Social Behavior of Twins: Birth Through Five Years*. Paper presented at the American Psychological Association's 74th Annual Convention. N. Y., Sept. 2–6.

Frenkel-Brunswik, E.
1951, "Patterns of Social and Cognitive Outlook in Children and Parents," *American Journal of Orthopsychiatry*, 21, 543–558.

Freud, A., 1955, "Safeguarding the Emotional Health of our Children—An Inquiry into the Concept of the Rejecting Mother," *Child Welfare*, 34, 1–4.

Freud, A., and D. Burlingham, 1944, *Infants without Families*. N. Y.: International Universities Press.

Freud, A., and S. Dann, 1951, "An Experiment in Group Upbringing," *The Psychoanalytic Study of the Child*, Vol. 6. pp. 127–168. N. Y.: International University Press.

Freud, S.
1925a, "Character and Eroticism," in *Collected Papers*, Vol. II. London: Hogarth.
1925b, "The Relationship of the Poet to Daydreaming," in *Collected Papers*, Vol. IV. London: Hogarth.
1930, *Three Contributions to the Theory of Sex*. Nervous and Mental Diseases Monograph Series, No. 7. N. Y.: Nervous and Mental Disease Publishing Co.
1933, *New Introductory Lectures on Psycho-Analysis*, translated by W. J. H. Sprott. N. Y.: Norton.
1936, *The Problem of Anxiety*. N. Y.: Norton.
1938a, *A General Introduction to Psychoanalysis*. N. Y.: Garden City.
1938b, *The Basic Writings of Sigmund Freud*, edited by A. A. Brill. N. Y.: Modern Library.
1938c, "Wit and Its Relation to the Unconscious," in *The Basic Writings of Sigmund Freud*, translated and edited by A. A. Brill, pp. 633–803. N. Y.: Modern Library.
1950, *The Interpretation of Dreams*, translated by A. A. Brill. N. Y.: Modern Library.

Freudenberg, E., 1921, "Der Morosche Umklammerungsreflex and das Brudzinkische Nackenzeichen als Reflexe das Säuglingsalters," *Müchen med. Wchnuschr.*, 68, 1646–1647.

Fried, Y., 1960, "Hahitapthut hapsikhomotorit shel yaldey kibuts," (Psychomotor development of kibbutz children) *Ofakim*, 14, 303–312.

Friedman, P., 1964, "The Relationship Between 'Primary Reaction Patterns' in Early Infancy and Behavior in Early Childhood," unpublished Doctor of Education dissertation, Teachers College, Columbia University.

Fries, M. E., 1947, "The Child's Ego Development and the Training of Adults in His Environment," in *The Psychoanalytic Study of the Child*, Vol. 2, pp. 85–112. N. Y.: International Universities Press.

Fromm, E., 1955, *The Sane Society*. N. Y.: Rinehart.

Fuller, J. L.
1964, "From Genes to Behavioral Traits," in *Genetics Today*: Proceedings of the XI International Congress of Genetics, The Hague, The Netherlands, September, 1963. N. Y.: Pergamon Press, 789–794.
1965, Quoted in *New York Times*, Friday, August 31, p. 26.

1965, "Suggestions from Animal Studies for Human Behavior Genetics," in *Methods and Goals in Human Behavior Genetics,* edited by S. G. Vandenberg, pp. 245–253. N. Y.: Academic Press.

1966, *Genotype and Early Social Deprivation.* Paper presented at Symposium on Genetics and Social Behavior. N. Y., American Psychological Association's 74th Annual Convention.

Fuller, J. L., and W. R. Thompson, 1960, *Behavior Genetics.* N. Y.: Wiley.

Gallagher, J. J., and T. Crowder, 1957, "The Adjustment of Gifted Children in the Regular Classroom," *Exceptional Children,* 23, 306–312, 317–319.

Gardner, D. B., G. R. Hawkes, and L. G. Burchinal, 1961, "Noncontinuous Mothering in Infancy and Development in Later Childhood," *Child Development,* 32, 225–234.

Gates, A. I., 1928, "The Nature and Limit of Improvement Due to Training," National Society for the Study of Education. *Nature and Nurture.* Twenty-seventh Yearbook, Part I, pp. 441–460. Bloomington, Illinois: Public School Publishing Co.

Gates, A. I., and A. W Scott, 1931, "Characteristics and Relations of Motor Speed and Dexterity Among Young Children," *Journal of Genetic Psychology,* 39, 423–454.

Gates, G. S.

1923, "An Experimental Study of the Growth of Social Perception," *Journal of Educational Psychology,* 14, 449–462.

1925, "A Preliminary Study of a Test for Social Perception," *Journal of Educational Psychology,* 16, 452–457.

1926, "An Observational Study of Anger," *Journal of Experimental Psychology,* 9, 325–336.

Gavrin, J. B., and L. S. Sacks, 1963, "Growth Potential of Preschool Aged Children in Institutional Care: A Positive Approach to a Negative Condition," *American Journal of Orthopsychiatry,* 3 (33), 399–408.

Gellert, E., 1967, "Children's Lateralizations of Human Figures: Analysis of a Developmental Transition," *The Journal of Psychology,* 67, 107–126.

Gershman, H., 1950, "The Problem of Anxiety," *American Journal of Psychoanalysis,* 10, 89–91.

Gesell, A.

1906, "Jealousy," *American Journal of Psychology,* 17, 437–496.

1928, *Infancy and Human Growth,* N. Y.: Macmillan.

1929, "The Individual in Infancy." in *The Foundations of Experimental Psychology,* edited by C. Murchison, pp. 628–660. Worcester, Massachusetts: Clark University Press.

Gesell, A., and C. S. Amatruda, 1945, *The Embryology of Behavior.* N. Y.: Harper.

Gesell, A. L., C. S. Amatruda, B. M. Caster, and H. Thompson

1939, *Biographies of Child Development.* N. Y.: Harper.

1959, "Biographies of Child Development; the Mental Growth Career of 84 Infants and Children; a Ten Year Study," in *Longitudinal Studies of Child Personality; Abstracts with Index,* edited by A. A. Stone and O. Cochrane, p. 115. Commonwealth Fund.

Gesell, A. L., and L. B. Ames, "Early Evidence of Individuality in the Human Infant," in *Longitudinal Studies of Child Personality; Abstracts with Index,* edited by A. A. Stone and O. Cochrane, p. 116. Commonwealth Fund.

Gesell, A., and F. L. Ilg

1937, *Feeding Behavior of Infants.* Philadelphia: Lippincott.

1943, *Infant and Child in the Culture of Today.* N. Y.: Harper.

Gesell, A., and H. Tompson

1929, "Learning and Growth in Identical Infant Twins: An Experimental Study by the Method of Co-Twin Control," *Genetic Psychology Monographs,* 6, 1–124.

1934, *Infant Behavior.* N. Y.: McGraw Hill.

1941, "Twins T and C from Infancy to Adolescence: A Biogenetic Study of Individual Differences by the Method of Co-Twin Control," *Genetic Psychology Monographs,* 24, 3–122.

Getzels, J. W., and P. W. Jackson, 1960, "The Study of Giftedness: A Multidimensional Approach," *The Gifted Student,* Cooperative Research Monographs, No. 2, Washington, D. C.; U. S. Office of Education, 1–18.

Gibson, E. J., 1963, "Perceptual Development," *Child Psychology:* National Society for the Study of Education. Chicago: University of Chicago Press, 144–195.

Gibson, E. J., and R. D. Walk, 1960, "The Visual Cliff," *Scientific American*, CCII, 64–71.

Gips, C., 1956, "How Illness Experiences are Interpreted by Hospitalized Children," unpublished Doctor of Education dissertation. N. Y.: Teachers College, Columbia University.

Gleason, Jr., H. A., 1961, *An Introduction to Descriptive Linguistics*, revised edition. N. Y.: Holt, Rinehart and Winston.

Goff, R. M., 1949, *Problems and Emotional Difficulties of Negro Children*. Contributions to Education, No. 960. N. Y.: Bureau of Publications, Teachers College, Columbia University.

Golan, S., 1961, *Sugyot hakibuts* (Problems of the Kibbutz). Merhavia, Israel: Sifriyat Poalim.

Goldberg, M. L.
1960, "Studies in Underachievement Among the Academically Talented," in *Freeing the Capacity to Learn*, edited by A. Frazoer, pp. 56–73. Washington, D. C.: Association for Supervision and Curriculum Development.
1965, *Research on the Talented; Talented Youth Project*: Horace Mann-Lincoln Institute of School Experimentation. N. Y.: Bureau of Publications, Teachers College, Columbia University.

Goldberg, M. L., L. G. Gotkin, and A. J. Tannebaum, 1959, Cultural, Social and Personal Factors Influencing Talent Fruition. Mimeographed report. Horace Mann-Lincoln Institute of School Experimentation, Teachers College, Columbia University.

Goldberger, A., 1964, Follow-up notes on the children from Bulldog Bank. March.

Goldfarb, W.
1945, "Psychological Privation in Infancy and Subsequent Adjustment," *American Journal of Orthopsychiatry*, 15, 247–255.
1955, "Emotional and Intellectual Consequences of Psychologic Deprivation in Infancy: A Revaluation," in *Psychopathology of Childhood*, edited by P. Hock and J. Zubin, pp. 105–119. N. Y.: Grune and Stratton.

Goldhammer, H., and A. Marshall, 1953, *Psychosis and Civilization*. Glencoe, Illinois: Free Press.

Goldman, J. R., 1964, "The Effects of Handling and Shocking in Infancy upon Adult Behavior in the Albino Rat," *Journal of Genetic Psychology*, 104, 301–310.

Goodenough, D. R., A. Shapiro, M. Holden, and L. Steinschriber, 1959, "A Comparison of 'Dreamers' and 'Non-Dreamers': Eye Movements, Electroencyphalograms, and the Recall of Dreams," *Abnormal and Social Psychology*, 59, 295.

Goodenough, F. L.
1931, *Anger in Young Children*. Institute of Child Welfare Monograph Series, No. 9. Minneapolis: University of Minnesota Press.
1932, "Expression of the Emotions in a Blind-Deaf Child," *Journal of Abnormal and Social Psychology*, 27, 328–333.
1940, "New Evidence on Environmental Influence on Intelligence," National Society for the Study of Education. *Intelligence: Its Nature and Nurture*, Thirty-ninth Yearbook, Part I, 307–365. Bloomington, Illinois: Public School Publishing Co.

Goodenough, F. L., and D. B. Harris, 1950, "Studies in the Psychology of Children's Drawings. II, 1928–1949," *Psychological Bulletin*, 47, 369–433.

Goodman, M. E.
1952, *Race Awareness in Young Children*. Cambridge, Massachusetts: Addison-Wesley.
1964, *Race Awareness in Young Children*. N. Y.: Macmillan.

Goslin, D. A., 1962, "Accuracy of Self Perception and Social Acceptance," *Sociometry*, 25 (3), 283–296.

Gottesman, I. I., 1963, "Heritability of Personality: A Demonstration," *Psychological Monographs*, 77 (9), Whole 572, 1–21.

Goudey, E. S., 1957, "The Sex Education of Fifteen Hundred Twelve-Year-Old Boys," unpublished Doctor of Education dissertation, Teachers College, Columbia University.

Gough, H. G., D. B. Harris, W. E. Martin, and M. Edwards, 1950, "Children's Ethnic Attitudes: I. Relationship to Certain Personality Factors," *Child Development*, 21, 83–91.

Grant, V. W., 1948, "A Major Problem of Human Sexuality," *Journal of Social Psychology*, 28, 79–101.

Green, E. H.
1933a, "Friendships and Quarrels Among Preschool Children," *Child Development,* 4, 237–252.
1933b, "Group Play and Quarreling Among Preschool Children," *Child Development,* 4, 302–307.
Greenberg, P. J., 1932, "Competition in Children: An Experimental Study," *American Journal of Psychology,* 44, 221–248.
Greulich, W. W., 1951, "The Growth and Developmental Status of Guamanian School Children in 1947," *American Journal of Physical Anthropology,* N. S., 9, 55–70.
Griffiths, R.
1935, *Imagination in Early Childhood.* London: Kegan, Paul.
1954, *The Abilities of Babies.* N. Y.: McGraw-Hill.
Griffiths, W. J., and W. F. Stringer, 1952, "The Effects of Intense Stimulation Experienced During Infancy on Adult Behavior in the Rat," *Journal of Comparative and Physiological Psychology,* 45, 301–306.
Grinder, R. E.
1961, "New Techniques for Research in Children's Temptation Behavior," *Child Development,* 32, 679–683.
1964, "Relations Between Behavioral and Cognitive Dimensions of Conscience in Middle Childhood," *Child Development,* 35, 881–891.
Grossman, H., 1966, "Behavior Directed Against Others as a Prognostic Indicator of Pathology," unpublished Doctor of Philosophy dissertation, Teachers College, Columbia University.
Guilford, J. P., 1959, "Three Faces of Intellect," *American Psychologist,* 14, 469–479.
Gump, P. V., and J. S. Kounin, 1961, "Milieu Influences in Children's Concepts of Misconduct," *Child Development,* 32, 711–720.
Hadfield, J. A., 1954, *Dreams and Nightmares.* London: Penquin Books.
Haggard, E. K., 1954, "Social Status and Intelligence: An Experimental Study of Certain Cultural Determinants of Measured Intelligence," *Genetic Psychological Monographs,* 141–186.
Hagman, R. R., 1932, "A Study of Fears of Children of Preschool Age," *Journal of Experimental Education,* 1, 110–130.
Hall, C. S.
1938, "The Inheritance of Emotionality," *Sigma Xi Quarterly,* 26, 17–27.
1959, *The Meaning of Dreams.* N. Y.: Dell.
Hall, C. S., and B. Domhoff
1962a, "Aggression in Dreams," preprint, *Institute of Dream Research.* Coral Gables, Florida.
1962b, "Friendliness in Dreams," preprint, *Institute of Dream Research.* Coral Gables, Florida.
1962c, "Friends and Enemies in Dreams," preprint, *Institute of Dream Research.* Coral Gables, Florida.
Hall, C. S., and S. J. Klein, 1942, "Individual Differences in Aggressiveness in Rats," *Journal of Comparative Psychology,* 33, 371–383.
Hall, G. S., 1891, "The Contents of Children's Minds on Entering School," *Journal of Genetic Psychology,* 1, 139–173.
Haller, A. O., and S. Thomas, 1962, "Personality Correlates of the Socioeconomic Status of Adolescent Males," *Sociometry,* 25 (4), 398–404.
Hallowell, A. T., 1940, "Aggression in Saulteaux Society," *Psychiatry,* 3, 395–407.
Halpern, F. C., 1953, *A Clinical Approach to Children's Rorschachs.* N. Y.: Grune and Stratton.
Halverson, H. M.
1931, "An Experimental Study of Prehension in Infants by Means of Systematic Cinema Records," *Genetic Psychology Monographs,* 10, 107–286.
1940, "Genital and Sphincter Behavior of the Male Infant," *Journal of Genetic Psychology,* 56, 95–136.
Hamachek, D. E.
1960, "A Study of the Relationship Between Certain Measures of Growth and the Self-Images of Elementary School Children," unpublished Doctor of Philosophy dissertation, University of Michigan.

1965, editor, *The Self in Growth, Teaching, and Learning: Selected Readings.* Englewood Cliffs, N. J.: Prentice-Hall.

Hamilton, E., 1955, "Emotional Aspects of Pregnancy: An Intensive Study of Fourteen Normal Primiparae," unpublished Doctor of Philosophy dissertation, Teachers College, Columbia University.

Hamilton, W. J., J. D. Boyd, and H. W. Mossman, 1962, *Human Embryology: Prenatal Development of Form and Function.* Baltimore: Williams and Wilkins.

Hardeman, M., 1967, "Children's Moral Reasoning," in press, *Journal of Genetic Psychology.*

Hardin, G., 1962, "Biology and Individual Differences," in *Child Psychology*, NSSE Yearbook LXI: Individualizing Instruction. Chicago, Illinois: University of Chicago Press.

Harding, J., B. Kutner, H. Proshansky, and I Chein, 1954, "Prejudice and Ethnic Relations," in *Handbook of Social Psychology*, edited by G. Lindzey, Vol. 2, pp. 1021–1061. Cambridge, Massachusetts: Addison-Wesley.

Harlow, H. F., 1958, "The Nature of Love," *American Psychologist*, 13, 673–685.

Harlow, H. F., and M. K. Harlow, 1962, "Social Deprivation in Monkeys," *Scientific American*, 207 (5), 136–146.

Harlow, H. F., M. K. Harlow, and R. Meyer, 1950, "Learning Motivated by a Manipulation Drive," *Journal of Experimental Psychology*, 40, 228–234.

Harris, D. B.
1950, "How Children Learn Interests, Motives and Attitudes," National Society for the Study of Education. *Learning and Instruction*, Forty-ninth Yearbook, Part I, pp. 129–155. Chicago: National Society for the Study of Education.
1952, "Intellective Functions: Children," in *Progress in Clinical Psychology*, edited by D. Brower and L. E. Abt, Vol. I. pp. 26–45. N. Y.: Grune and Stratton.
1957, editor and contributor, *The Concept of Development.* Minneapolis: University of Minnesota Press.
1963, *Children's Drawings as Measures of Intellectual Maturity.* N. Y.: Harcourt, Brace & World.

Harris, D. B., H. G. Gough, and W. E. Martin, 1950, "Children's Ethnic Attitudes: II. Relationship to Parental Beliefs Concerning Child Training," *Child Development*, 21, 169–181.

Harris, D. B., and E. S. Harris, 1946, "A Study of Fetal Movements in Relation to Mother's Activity," *Human Biology*, 18, 221–237.

Harrison, G. A., R. J. Morton, and J. S. Weiner, 1959, "The Growth in Weight and Tail Length of Inbred and Hybrid Mice Reared at Two Different Temperatures," *Philos. Trans.* (Series B), 242, 479–516.

Harrison, G. A., J. M. Tanner, *et al.*, 1964, *Human Biology.* Oxford: Clarendon Press.

Harrower, M. R., 1934, "Social Status and the Moral Development of the Child," *British Journal of Educational Psychology*, 1, 75–95.

Hartley, R. E., 1962, "Children's Perceptions and Expressions of Sex Preference," *Child Development*, 33, 221–227.

Hartley, R. E., and R. M. Goldenson, 1963, *The Complete Book of Children's Play.* N. Y.: Crowell.

Hartley, R. E., L. K. Frank, and R. M. Goldenson
1952a, *Understanding Children's Play.* N. Y.: Columbia University Press.
1952b, *New Play Experiences for Children: Planned Play Groups, Miniature Life Toys, and Puppets.* N. Y.: Columbia University Press.

Hartshorne, H., and M. A. May, 1928, *Studies in the Nature of Character.* Vol. I: *Studies in Deceit.* N. Y.: Macmillan.

Hartup, W. W., and E. A. Zook, 1960, "Sex-Role Preference in Three- and Four-Year-Old Children," *Journal of Consulting Psychology*, 24, 420–426.

Hattenford, K. W., 1932, "A Study of the Questions of Young Children Concerning Sex: A Phase of an Experimental Approach to Parent Education," *Journal of Social Psychology*, 3, 37–65.

Hattwick, B. W., 1936, "The Influence of Nursery School Attendance upon the Behavior and Personality of the Preschool Child," *Journal of Experimental Education*, 5, 180–190.

Hattwick, L. A. *See* Alschuler, R. H., 1943.

Havighurst, R. J., and A. Davis, 1955, "A Comparison of the Chicago and Harvard Studies of Social Class Differences in Child Rearing," *American Sociological Review*, 20, 438–442.

Heath, C. W., and L. W. Gregory, 1946, "Problems of Normal College Students and Their Families," *School and Society*, 63, 355–358.

Heinstein, M. I., 1963, "Behavioral Correlates of Breast-Bottle Regimes under Varying Parent-Infant Relationships," *Monographs of the Society for Research in Child Development*, 28 (4, Whole No. 88).

Henry, A. F., 1957, "Sibling Structure and Perception of the Disciplinary Roles of Parents," *Sociometry*, 20, 67–74.

Herbert, J., and J. Swayze, 1964, *Wireless Observation*. N. Y.: Horace Mann-Lincoln Institute of School Experimentation, Bureau of Publications, Teachers College, Columbia University.

Herrick, V. E., 1945, "Teachers' Classroom Personalities," *Elementary School Journal*, 46, 126–129.

Hess, E. H., 1959, "Imprinting," *Science*, 130, 133–141.

Hetzer, H., 1959, "Der Körper in der Selbstdarstellung von Kinder im Jahre 1926 und im Jahre 1957" (The Body in Self-Descriptions of Children in 1926 and 1957), *Zeitschrift für Experimentale und Angewandte Psychology*, 6, 15–21.

Hill, D. S., 1930, "Personification of Ideals by Urban Children," *Journal of Social Psychology*, 1, 379–392.

Hinckley, R. G., and L. Hermann, 1951, *Group Treatment in Psychotherapy: A Report of Experience*. Minneapolis: University of Minnesota Press.

Hoch, P. H., and J. Zubin, eds., 1950, *Anxiety*. N. Y.: Grune and Stratton.

Hochberg, J., and V. Brooks, 1962, "Pictorial Recognition as an Unlearned Ability: A Study of One Child's Performance," *American Journal of Psychology*, 75 (4), 624–628.

Hollingshead, A., 1949, *Elmtown's Youth*. N. Y.: Wiley.

Hollingworth, H. L., 1942, *Children Above 180 IQ: Origin and Development*. Yonkers, N. Y.: World Book Co.

Hollingworth, H. L., and V. Weischer, 1939, "Persistent Alphabetical Synthesis," *American Journal of Psychology*, 52, 361–366.

Hollingworth, L. S.
 1926, *Gifted Children: Their Nature and Nurture*. N. Y.: Macmillan.
 1939, "What We Know About the Early Selection and Training of Leaders," *Teachers College Record*, 40, 575–592.

Holmes, F. B.
 1935, "An Experimental Study of the Fears of Young Children," in *Children's Fears*, edited by A. T. Jersild and F. B. Holmes, pp. 167–296. Child Development Monographs, No. 20. N. Y.: Teachers College, Columbia University.
 1936, "An Experimental Investigation of a Method of Overcoming Children's Fears," *Child Development*, 7, 6–30.

Holzinger, K. J., 1929, "The Relative Effect of Nature and Nurture Influences on Twin Differences," *Journal of Educational Psychology*, 20, 241–248.

Honzik, M. P.
 1957, "Developmental Studies of Parent-Child Resemblance in Intelligence," *Child Development*, 28, 215–228.
 1964, "Personality Consistency and Change: Some Comments on Papers by Bayley, Macfarlane, Moss and Kagan, and Murphy," *Vita Humana*, 7, 139–142.

Honzik, M. P., J. W. Macfarlane, and L. Allen, 1948, "The Stability of Mental Test Performance Between Two and 18 Years," *Journal of Experimental Education*, 17, 309–324.

Hooker, D., 1952, *The Prenatal Origin of Behavior*. Lawrence, Kansas: University of Kansas Press.

Horney, K.
 1937, *The Neurotic Personality of Our Time*. N. Y.: Norton.
 1939, *New Ways in Psychoanalysis*. N. Y.: Norton.
 1945, *Our Inner Conflicts*. N. Y.: Norton.
 1950, *Neurosis and Human Growth*. N. Y.: Norton.

Horowitz, E., 1935, "Spacial Localization of the Self," *Journal of Social Psychology*, 6, 379–387.

Horowitz, R.
   1939, "Racial Aspects of Self-Identification," *Journal of Psychology,* 7, 91–99.
Hovland, C. I., and I. L. Janis, eds., 1959, *Personality and Persuasibility.* New Haven: Yale University Press.
Hull, V., B. Krippene, and F. Porter, 1966, *Manitowoc Story: A Team Approach to a School Health Study.* Fond du Lac, Wisconsin: Wisconsin State Board of Health.
Hunt, H. F., and L. S. Otis, 1955, "Restricted Experience and 'Timidity' in the Rat," *American Psychologist,* 10, 432.
Hurlock, E. B., and M. Burstein, 1932, "The Imaginary Playmate: A Questionnaire Study," *Journal of Genetic Psychology,* 41, 380–392.
Huschka, M., 1942, "The Child's Response to Coercive Bowel Training," *Psychosomatic Medicine,* 4, 301–308.
Huttenlocher, J., 1964, "Children's Language: Word-Phrase Relationship," *Science,* 143 (3603), 264–265.
Ingraham, R. C., and R. Videbeck, 1965, *Comparison of Observed and Recall Behavior.* Group Psychology Branch Office of Naval Research. Technical Report No. 15. February.
Irwin, O. C.
   1932, "Infant Responses to Vertical Movements," *Child Development,* 3, 167–169.
   1947a, "Infant Speech: Consonantal Sounds According to Place of Articulation," *Journal of Speech Disorders,* 12, 397–401.
   1947b, "Infant Speech: Consonantal Sounds According to Place of Articulation," *Journal of Speech Disorders,* 12, 402–404.
Isaacs, S.
   1933, *Social Development in Young Children.* N. Y.: Harcourt, Brace.
   1936, *The Nursery Years.* N. Y.: Vanguard Press.
Jack, L. M., 1934, "An Experimental Study of Ascendant Behavior in Preschool Children," *Behavior of the Preschool Child,* edited by L. M. Jack, *et al.,* pp. 7–65. University of Iowa Studies in Child Welfare, 9, No. 3. Iowa City: University of Iowa Press.
Jackson, P. W., 1956, "Verbal Solutions to Parent-Child Problems," *Child Development,* 27, 339–349.
James, W., 1890, *Principles of Psychology,* 2 Vols. N. Y.: Holt.
Jameson, S. H., 1941, "Adjustment Problems of University Girls Arising from the Urge for Recognition and New Experiences," *Journal of Social Psychology,* 144, 129–144.
Jayaswal, S. R.
   1955, "Adult Recall of Early Memories," *Uttara Bharati,* July, 69–74.
   1955a, "Early Childhood and Adult Personality," *Manasi,* 1, 12–15.
   1955b, "Ascendance-Submission in the Preschool Child and in His Adult Personality," *Dissertation Abstracts,* 15.
Jenkins, L. M., 1930, *A Comparative Study of Motor Achievements of Children at Five, Six, and Seven Years of Age.* Contributions to Education, No. 414. N. Y.: Bureau of Publications, Teachers College, Columbia University.
Jensen, K., 1932, "Differential Reactions to Taste and Temperament Stimuli in Newborn Infants," *Genetic Psychology Monographs,* 12, 361–479.
Jersild, A. T.
   1932, *Training and Growth in the Development of Children.* Child Development Monographs, No. 10. N. Y.: Teachers College, Columbia University.
   1952, *In Search of Self.* N. Y.: Bureau of Publications, Teachers College, Columbia University.
   1954, "Emotional Development," in *Manual of Child Psychology,* Edited by L. Carmichael, 2nd edition. N. Y.: Wiley.
   1955, *When Teachers Face Themselves.* N. Y.: Bureau of Publications, Teachers College, Columbia University.
Jersild, A. T., and S. F. Bienstock, 1935, *Development of Rhythm in Young Children.* Child Development Monographs, No. 22. N. Y.: Teachers College, Columbia University.
Jersild, A. T., and M. D. Fite, 1939, *The Influence of Nursery School Experience on Children's Social Adjustments.* Child Development Monographs, No. 25. N. Y.: Teachers College, Columbia University.
Jersild, A. T., and K. Helfant, 1953, *Education for Self-Understanding.* N. Y.: Bureau of Publications, Teachers College, Columbia University.
Jersild, A. T., E. A. Lazar, and A. M. Brodkin, 1962, *The Meaning of Psychotherapy in*

the Teacher's Life and Work. Horace Mann-Lincoln Institute of School Experimentation. N. Y.: Teachers College, Columbia University.

Jersild, A. T., F. V. Markey, and C. L. Jersild, 1933, *Children's Fears, Dreams, Wishes, Daydreams, Likes, Dislikes, Pleasant and Unpleasant Memories.* Child Development Monographs, No. 12. N. Y.: Teachers College, Columbia University.

Jersild, A. T., and R. Ritzman, 1938, "Aspects of Language Development: I. The Growth of Loquacity and Vocabulary," *Child Development,* 9, 243–259.

Jersild, A. T., and R. J. Tasch, 1949, *Children's Interests.* N. Y.: Bureau of Publications, Teachers College, Columbia University.

Jersild, A. T., E. S. Woodyard, and C. F. del Solar, 1949, *Joys and Problems of Child Rearing.* N. Y.: Bureau of Publications, Teachers College, Columbia University.

Jersild, A. T., B. Goldman, and J. Loftus, 1941, "A Comparative Study of the Worries of Children in Two School Situations," *Journal of Experimental Education,* 9, 323–326.

Jersild, A. T., and F. B. Holmes
1935a, *Children's Fears.* Child Development Monographs, No. 20. N. Y.: Teachers College, Columbia University.
1935b, "Methods of Overcoming Children's Fears," *Journal of Psychology,* 1, 75–104.

Jersild, A. T., and F. V. Markey, 1935, *Conflicts Between Preschool Children.* Child Development Monographs, No. 21. N. Y.: Teachers College, Columbia University.

Jersild, A. T., and W. S. Thomas, 1931, "The Influence of Adrenal Extract on Behavior and Mental Efficiency," *American Journal of Psychology,* 43, 447–456.

Jervis, F. M., 1958, "The Meaning of a Positive Self-Concept," unpublished Doctor of Philosophy dissertation, Teachers College, Columbia University.

John, Enid M., 1941, "A Study of the Effects of Evacuation and Air-Raids on Children of Preschool Age," *British Journal of Educational Psychology,* 11, 173–182.

Johnson, G. O.
1958, "The Education of Mentally Handicapped Children," pp. 189–226, and "Guidance for Exceptional Children," pp. 611–647, in *Education of Exceptional Children and Youth,* edited by W. M. Cruickshank and G. O. Johnson. Englewood Cliffs, N. J.: Prentice-Hall.

Jones, H. E., 1949, *Motor Performance and Growth.* Berkeley, California: University of California Press.

Jones, H. E., and M. C. Jones, 1928, "Fear," *Childhood Education,* 5, 136–143.

Jones, M. C.
1924, "The Elimination of Children's Fears," *Journal of Experimental Psychology,* 7, 383–390.
1957, "The Later Careers of Boys Who Were Early—or Late—Maturing," *Child Development,* 28, 113–128.
1960, "A Comparison of the Attitudes and Interests of Ninth-Grade Students Over Two Decades," *Journal of Educational Psychology,* 51, 175–186.

Jones, T. D., 1939, *The Development of Certain Motor Skills and Play Activities in Young Children.* Child Development Monographs, No. 26. N. Y.: Teachers College, Columbia University.

Justin, F., 1932, "A Genetic Study of Laughter Provoking Stimuli," *Child Development,* 3, 114–136.

Kadis, A., 1957, "Early Childhood Recollections As Aids in Group Psychotherapy," *Journal of Individual Psychology,* 13, 182–187.

Kaffman, M., 1961, "Evaluation of Emotional Disturbance in 403 Israeli Kubbutz Children," *American Journal of Psychiatry,* 117, 732–738.

Kagan, J.
1956, "The Child's Perception of the Parent," *Journal of Abnormal and Social Psychology,* 53, 257–258.
1961, "Child's Symbolic Conceptualization of Parents," *Child Development,* 32, 625–636.
1964a, "American Longitudinal Research on Psychological Development," *Child Development,* 35, 1–32.
1964b, "Acquisition and Significance of Sex Typing and Sex Role Identity," in *Review of Child Development Research,* edited by M. L. Hoffman and L. W. Hoffman, pp. 137–167. N. Y.: Russell Sage Foundation.

1964c, *Developmental Studies of Reflection and Analysis.* Cambridge: Harvard University Press.

1964d, "Impulsive and Reflective Children," in *Learning and the Educational Process,* edited by J. D. Krumbolz, pp. 133–161. Chicago: Rand McNally.

Kagan, J., 1965, "Reflexion-Impulsivity and Reading Ability in Primary Grade Children," *Child Development,* 36, 609–628.

Kagan, J., and J. Lemkin, 1960, "The Child's Differential Perception of Parental Attributes," *Journal of Abnormal and Social Psychology,* 61, 440–447.

Kagan, J., and M. Lewis, 1965, "Studies of Attention in the Human Infant," *Merrill-Palmer Quarterly,* 11 (2), 95–127.

Kagan, J., and H. A. Moss, 1962, *Birth To Maturity: A Study in Psychological Development.* N. Y.: Wiley.

Kagan, J., H. A. Moss, and I. E. Sigel, 1963, "Psychological Significance of Styles of Concepualization," in *Basic Cognitive Process in Children,* edited by J. C. Wright, and J. Kagan, Monographs of the Society for Research in Child Development, 28, No. 2.

Kagan, J., L. W. Sontag, C. T. Baker, and V. L. Nelson, 1958, "Personality and IQ Change," *Journal of Abnormal and Social Psychology,* 56, 261–266.

Kagan, J., L. Pearson, and L. Welch, 1966, "Conceptual Impulsivity and Inductive Reasoning," *Child Development,* 37, 583–594.

Kallman, F. J.
1953, *Heredity in Health and Mental Disorder.* N. Y.: Norton.
1954, "Genetic Principles in Manic-Depressive Psychosis," in *Depression,* edited by P. H. Hoch and J. Zubin. N. Y.: Grune and Stratton.
1962, editor, *Expanding Goals of Genetics in Psychiatry.* N. Y.: Grune and Stratton.

Kallman, F. J., and L. F. Jarvik, 1959, "Individual Differences in Constitution and Genetic Background," in *Handbook of Aging and the Individual,* edited by J. E. Birren, pp. 216–263. Chicago: University of Chicago Press.

Kantrow, R. W., 1937, *An Investigation of Conditioned Feeding Responses and Concomitant Adaptive Behavior in Young Infants.* University of Iowa Studies in Child Welfare, 13, No. 3. Iowa City: University of Iowa Press.

Karelitz, S., V. R. Fisichelli, J. Costa, R. Karelitz, and L. Rosenfeld, 1964, "Relation of Crying Activity in Early Infancy to Speech and Intellectual Development at Age Three Years," *Child Development,* 3, 769–777.

Katahn, M., 1966, "Interaction of Anxiety and Ability in Complex Learning Situations, *Journal of Personality and Social Psychology,* 3, 475–479.

Kawi, A., and B. Pasamanick, 1959, *Prenatal and Paranatal Factors in the Development of childhood Reading Disorders.* Monographs of the Society for Research in Child Development, 24, No. 4. Lafayette, Ind.: Child Development Publications.

Kawin, E., and G. Hoefer, 1931, *A Comparative Study of Nursery School vs. a Non-Nursery School Group.* Chicago: University of Chicago Press.

Keisler, E. R., 1953, "A Distinction Between Social Acceptance and Prestige Among Adolescents," *Child Development,* 24, 275–283.

Keister, M. E.
1937, "The Behavior of Young Children in Failure: An Experimental Attempt to Discover and to Modify Undesirable Responses of Preschool Children to Failure," *Studies in Preschool Education.* University of Iowa Studies in Child Welfare, 14, No. 346. Iowa City: University of Iowa Press.

Kenderdine, M., 1931, "Laughter in the Pre-School Child," *Child Development,* 2, 228–230.

Kerlinger, F. N., 1953, "Behavior and Personality in Japan: A Critique of Three Studies of Japanese Personality," *Social Forces,* 31, 250–258.

Kessen, W., and A. M. Leutzendorff, 1963, "The Effect of Non-Nutritive Sucking on Movement in the Human Newborn," *Journal of Comparative Psysiology and Psychology,* 56 (1), 69–72.

Khon, A. R., 1961, "Self-Evaluation as Related to Evaluations by Parents and Peers at Preadolescence and Adolescence," *Dissertation Abstracts,* 22 (5), 1716–1717.

Kidd, A., and J. Rivoire, eds., 1966, *Perceptual Development in Children.* N. Y.: International Universities Press.

Kierkegaard, S.
1949, *Either/Or,* translated by W. Lowrie. Princeton, N. J.: Princeton University Press.

1951, *Sickness Unto Death,* translated by W. Lowrie. Princeton, N. J.: Princeton University Press.

Kinsey, A. C., W. B. Pomeroy, and C. E. Martin
1948, *Sexual Behavior in the Human Male.* Philadelphia: Saunders.
1953, *Sexual Behavior in the Human Female.* Philadelphia: Saunders.

Kleitman, N.
1960, "Patterns of Dreaming," *Scientific American Reprints.* San Francisco: Freeman.

Klineberg, O.
1935, *Negro Intelligence and Selective Migration.* N. Y.: Columbia University Press.
1938, "The Intelligence of Migrants," *American Sociological Review,* 3, 218–224.

Klingensmith, S. W., 1953, "Child Animism: What the Child Means by 'Alive'," *Child Development,* 24, 51–61.

Klopfer, B., 1956, *Development in the Rorschach Technique.* Yonkers, N. Y.: World Book Co.

Klopfer, B., and D. McG. Kelley, 1946, *The Rorschach Technique.* Yonkers, N. Y.: World Book Co.

Knobloch, H., and B. Pasamanick, 1966, "Prospective Studies on the Epidemiology of Reproductive Casualty: Methods, Findings, and Some Implications," *Merrill-Palmer Quarterly,* 12, 27–42.

Knop, C., 1946, "The Dynamics of Newly Born Babies," *Journal of Pediatrics,* 29, 721–728.

Koch, H. L.
1935, "An Analysis of Certain Forms of So-Called 'Nervous Habits' in Young Children," *Journal of Genetic Psychology,* 46, 139–170.
1944, "A Study of Some Factors Conditioning the Social Distance Between the Sexes," *Journal of Social Psychology,* 20, 79–107.

Kohlberg, L., 1963, "Moral Development and Identification," in *Child Psychology: The Sixty-second Yearbook of the National Society for the Study of Education,* edited by H. W. Stevenson, pp. 277–332. Chicago: University of Chicago Press.

Komarovsky, M., 1946, "Cultural Contradictions and Sex Roles," *American Journal of Sociology,* 52, 184–189.

Koppitz, E. M., 1957, "Relationships Between Some Background Factors and Children's Interpersonal Attitudes," *Journal of Genetic Psychology,* 91, 119–129.

Kraus, P. E.
1956, "A Longitudinal Study of Children." Mimeographed by the New York Board of Education.
1965, *Journey Through School.* Mimeographed by Hunter College, New York.

Krogman, W. W., 1962, "How Your Children Grow," *Saturday Evening Post,* July 14–21, 50–53.

Krugman, M., 1940, "Out of the Inkwell: The Rorschach Method," *Character and Personality,* 9, 91–110.

Kuhlen, R. G., and N. B. Houlihan, 1965, "Adolescent Heterosexual Interests in 1942 and 1963," *Child Development,* 36 (4), 1049–1052.

Kuo, Z. Y., 1960, "Studies on the Basic Factors in Animal Fighting: VII. Inter-species Coexistence in Animals," *Journal Genetic Psychology,* 97, 221–225.

Lacan, J., 1953, "Some Reflections on the Ego," *International Journal of Psychoanalysis,* 34, 11–17.

Lafore, G. G., 1945, *Practices of Parents in Dealing with Preschool Children.* Child Development Monographs, No. 31. N. Y.: Teachers College, Columbia University.

Laing, A., 1939, "The Sense of Humor in Childhood and Adolescence," *British Journal of Educational Psychology,* 9, 201.

Lakin, M., 1957, *Personality Factors in Mothers of Excessively Crying (Colicky) Infants.* Monographs of the Society for Research in Child Development, 22, No. 1. Washington, D. C.: National Research Council.

Landis, C., A. T. Landis, M. M. Bolles, *et al.,* 1940, *Sex in Development.* N. Y.: Hoeber.

Landis, J. T., 1960, "The Trauma of Children When Parents Divorce," *Marriage and Family Living,* 22, 7–13.

Lansky, L. M., V. J. Crandall, J. Kagan, and C. T. Baker, 1961, "Sex Differences in Aggression and its Correlates in Middle-Class Adolescents," *Child Development,* 32, 45–58.

Lansky, L. M., and G. McKay, 1963, "Sex Role Preferences of Kindergarten Boys and Girls: Some Contradictory Results," *Psychological Reports*, 13, 415–421.

Lapouse, R., and M. A. Monk
1958, "An Epidemologic Study of Behavior Characteristics in Children," *American Journal of Public Health*, 48, 1134–1144.
1959, "Fears and Worries in a Representative Sampling of Children," *American Journal of Orthopsychiatry*, 29, 803–818.

Lasko, J. K., 1954, "Parent Behavior Toward First and Second Children," *Genetic Psychology Monographs*, 49, 97–137.

Laughlin, F., 1954, *The Peer Status of Sixth and Seventh Grade Children*. N. Y.: Bureau of Publications, Teachers College, Columbia University.

Lazar, E. A., 1963, *Children's Perceptions of Other Children's Fears*. Doctor of Philosophy dissertation. Teachers College, Columbia University.

Lecky, P., 1945, *Self-Consistency: A Theory of Personality*. N. Y.: Island Press.

Lee, E. S., 1951, "Negro Intelligence and Selective Migration: A Philadelphia Test of the Klineberg Hypothesis," *American Sociological Review*, 16, 227–233.

Le Masters, E. E., 1957, "Parenthood as Crisis," *Marriage and Family Living*, 19, 352–355.

Lenneberg, E. H., F. G. Rebelsky, and I. A. Nichols, 1965, "The Vocalizations of Infants Born to Deaf and Hearing Parents," *Human Development*, 8, 23–37.

Lerner, E., L. B. Murphy, L. J. Stone, E. Beyer, and E. W. Brown, 1941, *Methods for the Study of Personality in Young Children*. Monographs of the Society for Research in Child Development, 6, No. 30. Washington, D. C.: National Research Council.

Leuba, C., 1933, "An Experimental Study of Rivalry in Young Children," *Journal of Comparative Psychology*, 16, 367–378.

Leventhal, A. S., and L. P. Lipsitt, 1964, "Adaptation, Pitch Discrimination and Sound Localization in the Neonate," *Child Development*, 35, 759–767.

Levin, H., and E. Wardell, 1962, "The Research Uses of Doll Play," *Psychological Bulletin*, 59, 27–56.

Lévine, J., 1964, "Progrès et problèmes de la conscience de soi chez l'enfant d'age scolaire," *Psychological Abstracts*, 38 (648).

Levine, S.
1956, "A Further Study of Infantile Handling and Adult Avoidance Learning," *Journal of Personality*, 25 (1), 70–80.
1957, "Infantile Experience and Resistance to Physiological Stress," *Science*, 126 (3,270), 405.
1960, "Stimulation in Infancy," *Scientific American*, May, 1–8.

Levine, S., M. Alpert, and G. W. Lewis, 1958, "Differential Maturation of an Adrenal Response to Cold Stress in Rats Manipulated in Infancy," *The Journal of Comparative and Physiological Psychology*, 51 (6), 774–777.

Levy, D. M.
1928, "Fingersucking and Accessory Movements in Early Infancy," *American Journal of Psychiatry*, 7, 881–918.
1937, "Thumb or Finger Sucking from the Psychiatric Angle, *Child Development*, 8, 99–101.
1940, "Control Situation Studies of Children's Responses to the Difference in Genitalia," *American Journal of Orthopsychiatry*, 10, 775–763.

Levy, J., and R. Monroe, 1938, *The Happy Family*. N. Y.: Knopf.

Lewis, M., J. Kagan, and H. Campbell, 1965, *Studies of Attention. I. The Infant*. Yellow Springs, Ohio: Fels Research Institute.

Lewis, M., J. Kagan and J. Kalafat, 1965, *Patterns of Fixation in the Infant*. Paper read at Meeting of the Society for Research in Child Development. Minneapolis, Minnesota, March 25.

Lewis, S. J., 1937, "The Effect of Thumb and Finger Sucking on the Primary Teeth and Dental Arches," *Child Development*, 8, 93–98.

Lipsitt, L. P.
1964, "Learning in the First Year of Life," in *Advances in Child Development and Behavior in First Year of Life*, edited by L. P. Lipsitt and C. C. Spiker, pp. 147–195. N. Y.: Academic Press.

1966, "Learning Processes of Newborns," *Merrill-Palmer Quarterly*, 12, 45–68.

Lipsitt, L. P., T. Engen, and H. Kaye, 1963, "Developmental Changes in the Olfactory Threshold of the Neonate," *Child Development*, 34 (2), 371–376.

Lipsitt, L. P., and H. Kaye, 1965, "Changes in Neonatal Response to Optimizing and Non-optimizing Sucking Stimulation," *Psychonomic Science*, 2, 221–222.

Lipsitt, L. P., and C. C. Spiker, editors, 1964, *Advances in Child Development and Behavior in First Year of Life*. N. Y.: Academic Press.

Liu, C. H., 1950, "The Influence of Cultural Background on the Moral Judgment of Children," unpublished Doctor of Philosophy dissertation, Teachers College, Columbia University.

Lively, E. L., S. Dinitz, and W. C. Reckless, 1962, "Self Concept as a Predictor of Juvenile Delinquency," *American Journal of Orthopsychiatry*, 32 (1), 159–168.

Lorge, I., 1945, "Schooling Makes a Difference," *Teachers College Record*, 46, 483–492.

Lorge, I, and R. L. Thorndike, 1964, *Lorge-Thorndike Intelligence Tests*. Boston: Houghton-Mifflin.

Lubchenco, L. O., F. A. Horner, L. H. Reed, I. E. Hix, Jr., D. Metcalf, R. Cohig, H. C. Elliott, and M. Bourg, 1963, "Sequelae of Premature Birth," *American Journal of Diseases of Children*, 106 (1), 101–115.

Luria, A. R., 1959, "The Directive Function of Speech in Development and Dissolution," *Word*, 15, 341–352.

Luria, A. R., and F. I. Yudovich, 1959, *Speech and the Development of Mental Processes in the Child*. Translated by O. Kovasc and J. Simon. London: Staples.

Macauley, E., and S. H. Watkins, 1926, "An Investigation Into the Development of the Moral Conceptions of Children," Parts 1 and 2. *The Forum of Education IV*, 13–33, 92–108.

Maccoby, E. E., P. K. Gibbs, *et al.*, 1954, "Methods of Child-Rearing in Two Social Classes," in *Readings in Child Development*, edited by W. E. Martin and C. B. Stendler, pp. 380–396. N. Y.: Harcourt, Brace.

Macfarlane, J. W., 1964, "Perspectives on Personality Consistency and Change from the Guidance Study," *Vita Humana*, 7, 115–126.

Macfarlane, J., L. Allen, and M. P. Honzik, 1954, *A Developmental Study of the Behavior Problems of Normal Children Between Twenty-One Months and Fourteen Years*. Berkeley: University of California Press.

Machover, K.
1949, *Personality Projection in the Drawing of the Human Figure: A Method of Personality Investigation*. Springfield, Illinois: C C Thomas.

Markey, F. V.
1935, *Imaginative Behavior in Preschool Children*. Child Development Monographs, No. 18. N. Y.: Teachers College, Columbia University.

Markley, E. R., 1958, "Social Class Differences in Mothers' Attitudes Toward Child Rearing," unpublished Doctor of Philosophy dissertation, Teachers College, Columbia University.

Marquis, D. P.
1931, "Can Conditioned Responses Be Established in the New-Born Infant?" *Journal of Genetic Psychology*, 39, 479–492.
1941, "Learning in the Neonate: The Modification of Behavior Under Three Feeding Schedules," *Journal of Experimental Psychology*, 29, 263–282.

Martin, W. E., 1964, "Singularity and Stability of Profiles of Social Behavior," in *Readings in Child Behavior and Development*, edited by C. B. Stendler, pp. 448–466. N. Y.: Harcourt, Brace.

Martin, W. E., and C. B. Stendler, 1954, *Readings in Child Development*. N. Y.: Harcourt, Brace.

Masters, W. H., and V. E. Johnson, 1966, *Human Sexual Response*. Boston: Little, Brown.

Matsumoto, M., H. T. Smith, 1961, "Japanese and American Children's Perception of Parents," *Journal of Genetic Psychology*, 98, 83–88.

Maudry, M., and M. Nekula, 1939, "Social Relations Between Children of the Same Age During the First Two Years of Life," *Journal of Genetic Psychology*, 54, 193–215.

Maurer, A., 1965, "What Children Fear," *Journal of Genetic Psychology*, 106, 265–277.

May, R., 1950, *The Meaning of Anxiety*. N. Y.: Ronald Press.

May, R., E. Angel, and H. F. Ellenberger, eds., 1958, *Existence: A New Dimension in Psychiatry and Psychology*. N. Y.: Basic Books.

McCandless, B. R., C. B. Bilous, H. L. Bennett, 1961, "Peer Popularity and Dependence on Adults in Preschool-Age Socialization," *Child Development*, 32, 511–518.

McCandless, B. R., and A. Castaneda, 1956a, "Anxiety in Children, School Achievement, and Intelligence," *Child Development*, 27, 379–382.

McCandless, B. R., A. Castaneda, and D. S. Palermo, 1956b, "Anxiety in Children and Social Status," *Child Development*, 27, 385–391.

McCarthy, D.

1930, *The Language Development of the Preschool Child*. Institute of Child Welfare Monograph Series, No. 4. Minneapolis: University of Minnesota Press.

1952, "Organismic Interpretation of Infant Vocalizations," *Child Development*, 23, 273–280.

1953, "Some Possible Explanations of Sex Differences in Language Development and Disorders," *Journal of Psychology*, 35, 155–160.

1961, *Affective Aspects of Language Learning*. Presidential address before Division of Developmental Psychology, American Psychological Association. September.

McElvaney, M. E., 1958, "Four Types of Fantasy Aggression in the Responses of 'Rebellious' and 'Submissive' Children to the Driscoll Playkit, Structured by Parental-Demand and Neutral Studious Stress," unpublished Doctor of Philosophy dissertation, Teachers College, Columbia University.

McFarland, M. B., 1938, *Relationships Between Young Sisters As Revealed in Their Overt Responses*. Child Development Monographs, No. 23. N. Y.: Teachers College, Columbia University.

McGraw, M. B.

1935, Growth: *A Study of Johnny and Jimmy*. N. Y.: Appleton-Century.

1937, "The Moro Reflex," *American Journal of Diseases of Children*, 54, 240–251.

1939, "Later Development of Children Specially Trained During Infancy: Jimmy and Johnny at School Age," *Child Development*, 10, 1–19.

1940, "Neutral Maturation as Exemplified in Achievement of Bladder Control," *Journal of Pediatrics*, 16, 580–590.

McGuire, C.

1953, "Family and Age-Mates in Personality Formation," *Marriage and Family Living*, 15, 17–23.

McKinnon, K. M., 1942, *Consistency and Change in Behavior Manifestations*. N. Y.: Bureau of Publication, Teachers College, Columbia University.

McMahon, B., and J. M. Sowa, 1959, 1961, "Physical Damage to the Fetus," in *Causes of Mental Disorders: A Review of Epidemiological Knowledge*, pp. 51–110. N. Y.: Milbank Memorial Fund.

McNeil, E. B.

1956, "Social Class And The Expression of Emotion," *Michigan Academy of Science, Arts And Letters*, 41, 341–348.

1959, "Psychology And Aggression," *Journal of Conflict Resolution*, 3, No. 3.

McNemar, Q.

1933, "Twin Resemblances in Motor Skills, and the Effect of Practice Thereon," *Pedagogical Seminary and Journal of Genetic Psychology*, 42, 70–99.

1964, "Lost: Our Intelligence? Why?" *American Psychologist*, 19, 871–882.

Mead, G. H., 1934, *Mind, Self and Society*. Chicago: University of Chicago Press.

Medinnus, G. R.

1961, "Q-Sort Descriptions of Five-Year-Old Children by Their Parents," *Child Development*, 32, 473–489.

1965, *Readings in the Psychology of Parent-Child Relations*. N. Y.: Wiley.

1966, "Behavioral and Cognitive Measures of Conscience Development," *Journal of Genetic Psychology*, 109, 147–150.

Meili, R.

1956, Longitudinal Studies of Child Development," Office of Naval Research. London: American Embassy.

1957, "Anfänge Der Karakterentwicklung," Beitrange Zur Genetische Characterologie, Hans Huber, Bern and Stuttgart.

Meissner, W. W., 1965, "Functional and Adaptive Aspects of Cellular Regulatory Mechanisms," *Psychological Bulletin*, 64 (3), 206–216.

Mengert, I. G., 1931, "A Preliminary Study of the Reactions of Two-Year-Old Children to Each Other When Paired in a Semi-Controlled Situation," *Journal of Genetic Psychology*, 39, 393–398.

Miller, P. E., 1966, "The Effects of Age and Training on Children's Ability to Understand Certain Basic Concepts," unpublished Doctor of Philosophy dissertation, Teachers College, Columbia University.

Miller, R. V., 1956, "Social Status and Socioempathic Differences Among Mentally Superior, Mentally Typical, and Mentally Retarded Children," *Exceptional Children*, 23 (3), 114–119.

Miller, W., and S. Ervin, 1964, "The Development of Grammar in Child Language," in *The Acquisition of Language*, edited by U. Bellugi and R. Brown, pp. 9–34. Monographs of the Society for Research in Child Development, Vo. 29, No. 1.

Mitchell, C., 1943, "Do Virtues and Vices Change?" *School and Society*, 57, 111–112.

Moore, S., and R. Updegraff, 1964, "Sociometric Status of Preschool Children Related to Age, Sex, Nurturance-Giving, and Dependency," *Child Development*, 35, 519–524.

Moreno, J. L.
1934, *Who Shall Survive?* Washington, D. C.: Nervous and Mental Disease Publishing Co.
1954, "Old and New Trends in Sociometry: Turning Points in Small Group Research," *International Social Science Bulletin*, 17, 179–193.

Morris, D. P., E. Soroker, and G. Buruss, 1954, "Follow-up Studies of Shy, Withdrawn Children: I. Evaluation of Later Adjustment," *American Journal of Orthopsychiatry*, 24, 743–754.

Mowrer, O. H., 1958, "Hearing and Speaking: An Analysis of Language Learning," *Journal of Speech and Hearing Disabilities*, 23, 143–151.

Moyer, K. E., and B. Von Haller Gilmer, 1955, "Attention Spans of Children for Experimentally Designed Toys," *Journal of Genetic Psychology*, 87, 187–201.

Munn, N. L., 1965, *The Evolution and Growth of Human Behavior*. Boston: Houghton Mifflin.

Murphy, G.
1945, "The Freeing of Intelligence," *Psychological Bulletin*, 42, 1–19.
1958, *Human Potentialities*. N. Y.: Basic Books.

Murphy, L. B.
1937, *Social Behavior and Child Personality*. N. Y.: Columbia University Press.
1964, "Factors in Continuity and Change in the Development of Adaptational Style in Children," *Vita Humana*, 7, 96–114.

Murphy, L. B., and R. Horowitz, 1938, "Projective Methods in the Psychological Study of Children," *Journal of Experimental Education*, 7, 133–140.

Murray, H. A., 1937, *Thematic Appreciation Test*. Cambridge, Massachusetts: Harvard Psychological Clinic.

Mussen, P. H., 1960, *Handbook of Research Methods in Child Development*, N. Y.: John Wiley.

Mussen, P. H., and M. C. Jones
1957, "Self-Conceptions, Motivations and Attitudes of Late- and Early-Maturing Boys," *Child Development*, 28, 243–256.
1958, "Self-Conceptions, Motivations, and Interpersonal Attitudes of Early- and Late-Maturing Girls," *Child Development*, 29, 491–501.

Nameche, G., M. Waring, and D. Ricks, 1964, "Early Indicators of Outcome in Schizophrenia," *Journal of Nervous and Mental Diseases*, 139, 232–240.

Natterson, J. M., and A. G. Knudson, 1960, "Observations Concerning Fear of Death in Fatally Ill Children and Their Mothers," *Psychosomatic Medicine*, 22, 456–465.

Neel, J. V., 1960, "The Genetic Potential," in *The Nation's Children*, Vol. 2, edited by E. Ginzberg, pp. 1–23. N. Y.: Columbia University Press.

Neisser, E. G., 1951, *Brothers and Sisters*. N. Y.: Harper.

Newman, H. H., F. N. Freeman, and K. J. Holzinger, 1937, *Twins: A Study of Heredity and Environment*. Chicago: University of Chicago Press.

Newton, N. R., 1951, "The Relationship Between Infant Feeding and Later Behavior, *Journal of Pediatrics*, 38, 28–40.

Nichols, R. C., 1965, "The National Merit Twin Study," in *Methods and Goals in Human Behavior Genetics*, edited by S. G. Vandenberg, pp. 231–243. N. Y.: Academic Press.

Nye, F. I., 1959, "Employment Status of Mothers and Adjustment of Adolescent Children," *Marriage and Family Living*, 21, 240–244.

Oakes, M. E., 1947, *Children's Explanations of Natural Phenomena*. Contributions to Education. No. 926. N. Y.: Bureau of Publications, Teachers College, Columbia University.

Olson, W. C., 1959, *Child Development*, second edition. Boston: Heath.

Olson, W. C., and B. O. Hughes, 1940, "Subsequent Growth of Children With and Without Nursery-School Experience." National Society for the Study of Education. *Intelligence: Its Nature and Nurture*, Thirty-ninth Yearbook, Part II, 237–244. Bloomington, Illinois: Public School Publishing Co.

Omwake, L., 1939, "Factors Influencing the Sense of Humor," *Journal of Social Psychology*, 10, 95–104.

Orlansky, H., 1949, "Infant Care and Personality," *Psychological Bulletin*, 46, 1–48.

Osler, S. F., and M. W. Fivel, 1961, "Concept Attainment: I. The Role of Age and Intelligence in Concept Attainment by Induction," *Journal of Experimental Psychology*, 62, 1–8.

Ourth, L., and K. B. Brown, 1961, "Inadequate Mothering and Disturbance in the Neonatal Period," *Child Development*, 32, 287–295.

Page, E. I., 1959, "Haptic Perception: A Consideration of One of the Investigations of Piaget and Inhelder," *Educational Review*, 11, 115–124.

Palermo, D. S., A. Castaneda, and B. R. McCandless, 1956, "The Relationship of Anxiety in Children to Performance in a Complex Learning Task," *Child Development*, 27, 333–337.

Parten, M. B., 1932, "Social Participation Among Preschool Children," *Journal of Abnormal and Social Psychology*, 27, 243–269.

Pasamanick, B., F. K. Constantinou, and A. M. Lilienfeld, 1956, "Pregnancy Experience and the Development of Childhood Speech Disorders," *American Medical Association Journal of Diseases of Children*, 91, 113–118.

Pasamanick, B., and A. Kawi, 1956, "A Study of the Association of Prenatal and Paranatal Factors with the Development of Tics in Children," *Journal of Pediatrics*, 48, 596–601.

Pasamanick, B., and H. Knobloch, 1966, "Retrospective Studies on the Epidemiology of Reproductive Casualty: Old and New," *Merrill-Palmer Quarterly*, 12, 7–23.

Pasamanick, B., and A. M. Lilienfeld
1955a, "The Association of Maternal and Fetal Factors with the Development of Cerebral Palsy and Epilepsy," *American Journal of Obstetrics and Gynecology*, 70, 93–101.
1955b, "Association of Maternal and Fetal Factors with the Development of Mental Deficiency: I. Abnormalities in the Prenatal and Paranatal Periods," *Journal of American Medical Association*, 159, 155–160.

Pasamanick, B., M. E. Rogers, and A. M. Lilienfeld, 1956, "Pregnancy Experience and the Development of Behavior Disorder in Children," *American Journal of Psychiatry*, 112, 613–618.

Pattie, F. A., and S. Cornett, 1952, "Unpleasantness of Early Memories and Maladjustment of Children," *Journal of Personality*, 20, 315–321.

Pearson, K., 1903, "On the Inheritance of the Mental and Moral Characters in Man, and Its Comparison with the Inheritance of the Physical Character," *Journal of the Anthropological Institute*, 33, 179–237.

Peck, R. F., R. J. Havighurst, R. Cooper, J. Lilienthal, and D. Moore, 1960, *The Psychology of Character Development*. N. Y.: Wiley.

Penrose, L. S., 1961, *Recent Advances in Human Genetics*. London: Churchill.

Penrose, L. S., J. R. Ellis, and J. D. A. Delhanty, 1960, "Chromosomal Translocation in Mongolism and in Normal Relatives," *Lancet*, 2, 409–410.

Perkins, H. V., 1958, "Teachers' and Peers' Perceptions of Children's Self-Concepts," *Child Development*, 29, 203–230.

Perry, D. C., 1961, "Self-Acceptance in Relation to Adjustment," *Dissertation Abstracts*, 22 (1), 317–318.

Perry, J. B., Jr., 1961, "The Mother Substitutes of Employed Mothers: An Exploratory Inquiry," *Marriage and Family Living*, 23, 362–367.

Peterson, E. T., 1961, "The Impact of Maternal Employment on the Mother-Daughter Relationship," *Marriage and Family Living*, 23, 355–361.

Phillips, B. N., 1963, "Age Changes in Accuracy of Self-Perceptions," *Child Development*, 34, 1041–1046.

Phillips, B. N., F. J. King, and C. McGuire, 1959, "Studies on Anxiety: I. Anxiety and Performance on Psychometric Tests Varying in Complexity." *Child Development*, 30, 253–259.

Phillips, E. L., 1951, "Attitudes Toward Self and Others: A Brief Questionnaire Report," *Journal of Consulting Psychology*, 15, 79–81.

Piaget, J.
1928, *Judgment and Reasoning in the Child*, translated by M. Gabain. N. Y.: Harcourt, Brace.
1929, *The Child's Conception of the World*. N. Y.: Harcourt, Brace.
1932a, *The Language and Thought of the Child*, 2nd ed., translated by M. Gabin. N. Y.: Harcourt, Brace.
1932b, *The Moral Judgment of the Child*. London: The Free Press.
1950, *The Psychology of Intelligence*. London: Routledge and Kegan Paul.
1953, "How Children Form Mathematical Concepts," *Scientific American*, 189, 74–79.
1954, *Construction of Reality in the Child*. N. Y.: Basic Books.
1959, *The Language and Thought of the Child*, 3rd ed., N. Y.: Humanities Press.
1960, *The Psychology of Intelligence*, trans. M. Piercy and D. E. Berlyne. Paterson, N. J.: Littlefield, Adams.
1962, *Play, Dreams and Imitation in Childhood*. N. Y.: Norton.

Piaget, J., 1962a, "The Relation of Affectivity to Intelligence in the Mental Development of the Child," *Bulletin Menninger Clinic*, 26, 129–137.
1963, *Origins of Intelligence in Children*. N. Y.: Norton.
1964, "Cognitive Development in Children: The Piaget Papers," in *Piaget Rediscovered: A Report of the Conference on Cognitive Studies and Curriculum Development*, edited by R. E. Ripple and V. N. Rockcastle, pp. 6–48. Ithaca: School of Education, Cornell University.

Piaget, J., and B. Inhelder, 1956, *The Child's Conception of Space*. N. Y.: Humanities Press.

Pilzer, E., 1952, "Disturbed Children Who Make a Good School Adjustment," *Smith College Studies in Social Work*, 22, 193–210.

Pinneau, S. R., 1950, "A Critique on the Articles by Margaret Ribble," *Child Development*, 21, 203–228.

Pistor, F., 1940, "How Time Concepts Are Acquired by Children," *Educational Method*, 20, 107–112.

Pratt, K. C.
1945, "A Study of the 'Fears' of Rural Children," *Journal of Genetic Psychology*, 67, 179–194.
1954, "The Neonate," in *Manual of Child Psychology*, 2nd ed., edited by L. Carmichael, pp. 215–291. N. Y.: Wiley.

Pratt, K. C., A. K. Nelson, and K. H. Sun, 1930, *The Behavior of the Newborn Infant*. Columbus: Ohio State University Press.

Prechtl, H. F. R., 1958, "The Directed Head Turning Response and Allied Movements of the Human Baby," *Behaviour*, 8, 212–242.

Preyer, W., 1888, *The Mind of the Child*. N. Y.: Appleton.

Pringle, M. L. K., and S. Gooch
1965, "Chosen Ideal Person Personality Development and Progress in School Subjects," *Human Development*, 8, 161–180.
1966, "Children's Judgment of Wickedness: A Longitudinal Pilot Study," *Human Development*, 9, 177–190.

Pritchard, E., and R. Ojemann, 1941, "An Approach to the Measurement of Insecurity," *Journal of Experimental Education*, 10, 114–118.

Pritchard, M. C., K. M. Horan, and L. S. Hollingworth, 1940, "The Course of Mental Development in Slow Learners Under an 'Experience Curriculum,'" National Society for the Study of Education. *Intelligence: Its Nature and Nurture*, Thirty-ninth Yearbook, Part II, 245–254. Bloomington, Illinois: Public School Publishing Co.

Probst, C. A., 1931, "A General Information Test for Kindergarten Children," *Child Development*, 2, 81–95.

Prout, C. T., and M. A. White, 1956, "The Schizophrenic's Sibling," *Journal of Nervous and Mental Disorders,* 123, 162–170.

Purcell, K., 1952, "Memory and Psychological Security," *Journal of Abnormal Social Psychology,* 47, 433–440.

Rabban, M., 1950, "Sex-Role Identification in Young Children in Two Diverse Social Groups," *Genetic Psychology Monographs,* 42, 81–158.

Rabin, A. I., 1965, *Growing Up in the Kibbutz.* N. Y.: Springer.

Radke, M., J. Sutherland, and P. Rosenberg, 1950, "Racial Attitudes of Children," *Sociometry,* 13, 154–171.

Radke-Yarrow, M., 1963, *The Elusive Evidence.* Presidential address to the Division of Developmental Psychology, American Psychological Association Annual Convention. Philadelphia, Pennsylvania, August 1963.

Ramsey, G. V.
1943, "The Sexual Development of Boys," *American Journal of Psychology,* 56, 217–233.
1953, "Studies of Dreaming," *Psychological Bulletin,* 50 (6), 432–455.

Rapaport, D.
1951, "States of Consciousness, A Psychopathological and Psychodynamic View," in *Problems of Consciousness: Transactions of the Second Conference,* edited by M. A. Abramson. N. Y.: Josiah Macy Foundation.
1960, "The Structure of Psychoanalytic Theory," *Psychological Issues,* 2 (2).

Rechtschaffen, A., P. Verdone, and J. Wheaton, 1963, "Reports of Mental Activity During Sleep," *Canadian Psychiatric Association Journal,* 8, 409–414.

Rechtschaffen, A., G. Vogel, and G. Shaidun, 1963, "Interrelatedness of Mental Activity During Sleep," *Archives General Psychiatry,* 9, 536–547.

Redl, F., and D. Wineman
1951, *Children Who Hate.* Glencoe, Illinois: Free Press.
1953, *Controls from Within.* Glencoe, Illinois: Free Press.

Reese, H. W., 1962, "Sociometric Choices of the Same and Opposite Sex in Late Childhood," *Merrill-Palmer Quarterly,* 8 (3), 173–174.

Reynolds, M. M., 1928, *Negativism of Preschool Children.* Contributions to Education, No. 288. N. Y.: Bureau of Publications, Teachers College, Columbia University.

Reynolds, M. M., and H. Mallay, 1933, "Sleep of Young Children," *Journal of Genetic Psychology,* 43, 322–351.

Rheingold, H. L., 1956, *The Modification of Social Responsiveness in Institutional Babies.* Monographs of the Society for Research in Child Development, 21, No. 2. Lafayette, Indiana: Child Development Publications.

Rheingold, H. L., and N. Bayley, 1959, "The Later Effects of an Experimental Modification of Mothering," *Child Development,* 30 (3), 363–372.

Ribble, M. A., 1943, *The Rights of Infants.* N. Y.: Columbia University Press.

Richards, T. W., and H. Newbery, 1938, "Studies in Fetal Behavior: III. Can Performance in Test Items at Six Months Postnatally be Predicted on the Basis of Fetal Activity," *Child Development,* 9, 79–86.

Ricketts, A. F., 1934, "A Study of the Behavior of Young Children in Anger," in Jack, *et al., Behavior of the Preschool Child,* pp. 159–171. University of Iowa Studies in Child Welfare, 9 (3). Iowa City: University of Iowa Press.

Riessman, F., 1962, *The Culturally Deprived Child.* N. Y.: Harper and Row.

Rigney, M. G., 1952, "Practices of Teachers in Dealing with Preschool Children," unpublished Doctor of Philosophy dissertation, Columbia University.

Rivlin, L. G., 1959, "Creativity and the Self-Attitudes and Sociability of High School Students," *Journal of Educational Psychology,* 50 (4), 147–152.

Robbins, L. C., 1963, "The Accuracy of Parental Recall of Aspects of Child Development and of Child Rearing Practices," *Journal of Abnormal Psychology,* 66 (3), 261–270.

Robins, L. N., and P. O'Neal, 1958, "Mortality Mobility and Crime: Problem Children Thirty Years Later," *American Social Review,* 23, 162–171.

Robinson, G. L., "Family Structure and Sex Role Preference," unpublished Doctor of Philosophy dissertation, Teachers College, Columbia University.

Roe, H., 1952, "Psychological Effects of Having a Cerebral Palsied Child in the Family," unpublished Doctor of Philosophy dissertation, Teachers College, Columbia University.

Roffwarg, H. P., W. C. Dement, and C. Fisher, 1962, *Observations on the Sleep-Dream Pattern in Neonates, Infants, Children and Adults.* Mimeographed. N. Y.: New York State Psychiatric Institute.

Roffwarg, H. P., W. C. Dement, J. N. Muzio, and C. Fisher, 1962, "Dream Imagery: Relationship to Rapid Eye Movements During Sleep," *Archives of General Psychiatry*, 7, 235–258.

Roffwarg, H. P., J. N. Muzio, and W. C. Dement, 1966, "Ontogenetic Development of the Human Sleep-Dream Cycle," *Science*, 152, 604–619.

Rogers, C. R.
1942a, "A Study of the Mental Health Problems in Three Representative Elementary Schools," *A Study of Health and Physical Education in Columbus Public Schools*. Monographs of the Bureau of Educational Research, No. 25. Columbus: Ohio State University Press.
1942b, *Counseling and Psychotherapy: Newer Concepts in Practice*. Boston: Houghton, Mifflin.
1951, *Client-Centered Therapy: Its Current Practice, Implications, and Theory*. Boston: Houghton, Mifflin.

Rogers, M. E., A. M. Lilienfeld, and B. Pasamanick, 1955, "Prenatal and Paranatal Factors in the Development of Childhood Behavior Disorders," *Acta Psychiatrica et Neurologica Scandinavica, Supplementum* 102 (Copenhagen). Baltimore: Johns Hopkins University, School of Hygiene and Public Health.

Rorschach, H., 1937, *Psychodiagnostik. Methodik und Ergebnisse eines wahrnehmungs-diagnostischen Experiments*, 3rd ed. Berlin: Huber.

Rosenzweig, M. R., 1966, "Environmental Complexity, Cerebral Change, and Behavior," *American Psychologist*, 21, 321–332.

Ross, H., 1952, *Fears of Children*, 5th ed. Chicago: Science Research Associates.

Ross, M. G., 1950, *Religious Beliefs of Youth*. N. Y.: Association Press.

Rossier, A., 1962, "The Future of the Premature Infant," *Developmental Medicine Child Neurology*, 4 (5), 483–487.

Rousselet, J., 1963, "Quelques aspects des ambitions sociales des adolescents," *Psychological Abstracts*, 37 (7897).

Salam, M. Z., and R. D. Adams, 1966, "New Horizons in the Neurology of Childhood," *Perspectives in Biology and Medicine*, 9 (3), 384–417.

Sarason, S. B., K. S. Davidson, F. F. Lighthall, R. R. Waite, and B. K. Ruebush, 1960, *Anxiety in Elementary School Children*. N. Y.: Wiley.

Sarbin, T. R., 1952, "A Preface to a Psychological Analysis of the Self," *Psychological Review*, 59, 11–22.

Sarnoff, I., and P. G. Zimbardo, 1961, "Anxiety, Fear and Social Isolation," *Journal of Abnormal and Social Psychology*, 62, 356–363.

Scammon, R. E., and I. A. Calkins, 1929, *The Development and Growth of the External Dimensions of the Human Body in the Fetal Period*. Minneapolis: University of Minnesota Press.

Scarr, S., 1966, "Genetic Factors in Activity Motivation," *Child Development*, 37, 663–673.

Schachter, J., L. Bickman, J. S. Schachter, J. Jameson, S. Lituchy, T. A. Williams, 1965, *Behavioral and Physiological Reactivity in Human Neonates*. Multigraphed. N. Y.: College of Physicians and Surgeons.

Schaefer, E. S., and N. Bayley, 1963, *Maternal Behavior, Child Behavior and their Intercorrelations from Infancy Through Adolescence*. Monographs of the Society for Research in Child Development, 28 (3), 1–127.

Schaefer, E. S., and R. Q. Bell, 1955, "Parental Attitude Research Instrument (PARI)," unpublished preliminary draft, National Institutes of Mental Health, Bethesda, Maryland.

Schaffer, H. R., 1966, "Activity Level as a Constitutional Determinant of Infantile Reaction to Deprivation," *Child Development*, 37 (3), 595–602.

Schaffer, H. R., and P. E. Emerson, 1964, *The Development of Social Attachments in Infancy*. Monographs of the Society for Research in Child Development, 29 (3).

Schaltenbrand, G., 1925, "Normale Bewegungs- und Lage-Reaktionen bei Kindern," *Deutsch Ztschr. f. Nervrnh.*, 87, 23–59.

Schmeidler, G. R., I. Bruel, S. Ginsberg, and M. Lukomnik, 1965, "Motivation, Anxiety and Stress in a Difficult Verbal Task," *Psychological Reports*, 17 (1), 247–255.

Schofield, W., S. R. Hathaway, D. W. Hastings, and D. M. Bell, 1954, "Prognostic Factors in Schizophrenia," *Journal of Consulting Psychology*, 18, 155–166.

Scott, F., and G. C. Myers, 1923, "Children's Empty and Erroneous Concepts of the Commonplace," *Journal of Educational Research*, 8, 327–335.

Scott, J. P.
  1942, "Genetic Differences in the Social Behavior of Mice," *Journal of Heredity*, 33, 11–15.
  1944, "The Magnification of Differences by a Threshold," *Science*, 100, 569–570.
  1957, "The Genetic and Environmental Differentiation of Behavior," in *The Concept of Development*, edited by D. Harris, pp. 59–77. Minneapolis: University of Minnesota Press.
Scott, J. P., and M. S. Charles
  1953, "Some Problems of Heredity and Social Behavior," *Journal of Genetic Phychology*, 48, 209–230.
  1954, "Genetic Differences in the Behavior of Dogs: A Case of Magnification by Thresholds and by Habit Formation," *Journal of Genetic Psychology*, 84, 175–188.
Searle, L. V., 1949, "The Organization of Heredity Maze-Brightness and Maze-Dullness," *Genetic Psychology Monographs*, 39, 279–325.
Sears, P. S., 1951, *Doll Play Aggression in Normal Young Children: Influence of Sex, Age, Sibling Status, Father's Absence*. Psychological Monographs, 65 (6). Washington, D. C.: American Psychological Association.
Sears, P. S., and V. S. Sherman, 1964, *In Pursuit of Self-Esteem: Case Studies of Eight Elementary School Children*. Belmont, California: Wadsworth.
Sears, R. R., E. E. Maccoby, and H. Levin, 1957, *Patterns of Child Rearing*. Evanston, Illinois: Row, Peterson.
Sears, R. R., and G. W. Wise, 1950, "Relation of Cup Feeding in Infancy to Thumb-Sucking and the Oral Drive." *American Journal of Orthopsychiatry*, 20, 123–138.
Seashore, H. G., and A. Bavelas, 1942, "A Study of Frustration in Children," *Journal of Genetic Psychology*, 61, 279–314.
Seidman, J. E., ed., 1958, *The Child: A Book of Readings*. N. Y.: Rinehart.
Sewall, M., 1930, "Two Studies in Sibling Rivalry: I. Some Causes of Jealousy in Young Children," *Smith College Studies in Social Work*, 1, 6–22.
Sewall, W. H., and P. H. Mussen, 1952, "The Effects of Feeding, Weaning, and Scheduling Procedures on Childhood Adjustment and the Formation of Oral Symptoms," *Child Development*, 23, 185–191.
Shaw, R. F., 1934, *Finger Painting*. Boston: Little, Brown.
Shaycoft, M. F., J. T. Dailey, I. B. Orr, C. A. Neyman, Jr., and S. E. Sherman, 1963, *Project Talent: Studies of a Complete Age Group Age 15*. Mimeograph Pittsburgh: University of Pittsburgh.
Sherman, M., 1930, "Afternoon Sleep of Young Children: Some Influencing Factors," *Journal of Genetic Psychology*, 38, 114–126.
Shields, J., 1962, *Monozygotic Twins Brought Up Apart and Brought Up Together*. N. Y.: Oxford University Press.
Shirley, M. M.
  1931, The First Two Years: A *Study of Twenty-Five Babies, Vol. I. Postural and Loco-motor Development*. Institute of Child Welfare Monograph Series, No. 6. Minneapolis: University of Minnesota Press.
  1933a, *The First Two Years: A Study of Twenty-Five Babies, Vol. II. Intellectual Development*. Institute of Child Welfare Monograph Series, No. 7. Minneapolis: University of Minnesota Press.
  1933b, *The First Two Years: A Study of Twenty-Five Babies, Vol. III. Personality Manifestations*. Institute of Child Welfare Monograph Series, No. 8. Minneapolis: University of Minnesota Press.
  1938, "Development of Immature Babies During the First Two Years," *Child Development*, 9, 347–360.
  1939, "A Behavior Syndrome Characterizing Prematurely-Born Children," *Child Development*, 10, 115–128.
  1941, "Impact of Mother's Personality on the Young Child," *Smith College Studies in Social Work*, 12, 15–64.
Shoben, E. J., 1949, "The Assessment of Parental Attitudes in Relation to Child Adjustment," *Genetic Psychology Monographs*, 39, 103–148.
Shumsky, A., 1964, *Social Orientation and Intellectual Approach*. Rexographed. Privately communicated.
Siegel, A. E., and M. B. Haas, 1963, "The Working Mother: A Review of Research," *Child Development*, 34 (3), 513–551.

Siller, J., 1957, "Socioeconomic Status and Conceptual Thinking," *Journal of Abnormal and Social Psychology*, November, 365–371.

Sillman, J. H., 1951, "Thumb-Sucking and the Oral Structure," *Journal of Pediatrics*, 39, 424–430.

Simpson, R. L., 1962, "Parental Influence, Anticipatory Socialization, and Social Mobility," *American Sociological Review*, 27, 517–522.

Simsarian, F. P., 1948, "Self-Demand Feeding of Infants and Young Children in Family Settings," *Mental Hygiene*, 32, 217–225.

Simsarian, F. P., and P. A. McLendon, 1942, "Feeding Behavior of an Infant During the First Twelve Weeks of Life on a Self-Demand Schedule," *Journal of Pediatrics*, 20, 93–103.

Singer, J. L., 1961, "Imagination and Waiting Ability in Young Children," *Journal of Personality*, 29, 396–413.

Skeels, H. M.
   1965, "Effects of Adoption on Children from Institutions," *Children*, U.S. Public Health Service, 12 (1), 33–34.
   1966, *Adult Status of Children with Contrasting Early Life Experiences*, Monographs of the Society for Research in Child Development, 31 (3).

Skeels, H. M., R. Updegraff, B. L. Wellman, and H. M. Williams, 1938, "A Study of Environmental Stimulation: An Orphanage Preschool Project," *University of Iowa Studies in Child Welfare*, 16 (1).

Skodak, M., and H. M. Skeels, 1949, "A Final Follow-Up of One Hundred Adopted Children," *Journal of Genetic Psychology*, 75, 85–125.

Slater, E., 1939, *II. Types, Levels, and Irregularities of Response to a Nursery School Situation of Forty Children Observed with Special Reference to the Home Environments*. Monograph of the Society for Research in Child Development, 4 (2). Washington, D. C.: National Research Council.

Slavson, S. R.
   1943, *An Introduction to Group Therapy*, N. Y.: Commonwealth Fund.
   1947, ed., *The Practice of Group Therapy*. N. Y.: International Universities Press.

Smedslund, J., 1961, "The Acquisition of Conservation of Substance and Weight in Children. III. Extinction of Conservation of Weight Acquired 'Normally' and by Means of Empirical Controls on a Balance Scale," *Scandinavian Journal of Psychology*, 2, 71–84.

Smith, M. E.
   1931, "A Study of Five Bilingual Children from the Same Family," *Child Development*, 2, 184–187.
   1935, "A Study of the Speech of Eight Bilingual Children of the Same Family," *Child Development*, 6, 19–25.
   1949, "Measurement of Vocabularies of Young Bilingual Children in Both the Languages Used," *Journal of Genetic Psychology*, 74, 305–315.
   1952, "Childhood Memories Compared with those of Adult Life," *Journal of Genetic Psychology*, 80, 151–182.

Smith, M. K., 1941, "Measurement of the Size of General English Vocabulary Through the Elementary Grades and High School," *Genetic Psychology Monographs*, 24, 311–345.

Smith, R. T., 1965, "A Comparison of Socioenvironmental Factors in Monozygotic and Dizygotic Twins, Testing an Assumption," in *Methods and Goals in Human Behavior Genetics*, edited by S. G. Vandenberg, pp. 45–61. N. Y.: Academic Press.

Smith, W. M., 1952, "Rating and Dating: A Re-Study," *Marriage and Family Living*, 14, 312–317.

Snygg, D., and A. W. Combs, 1949, *Individual Behavior*. N. Y.: Harper.

Sontag, L. W.
   1944a, "Differences in Modifiability of Fetal Behavior and Physiology," *Psychosomatic Medicine*, 6, 151–154.
   1944b, "War and the Fetal Maternal Relationship," *Marriage and Family Living*, 6, 3–4, 16.

Sontag, L. W., C. T. Baker, and V. L. Nelson, 1958, *Mental Growth and Personality Development: A Longitudinal Study*. Monographs of the Society for Research in Child Development, 23 (2). Washington, D. C.: National Research Council.

Sontag, L. W., S. I. Pyle, and J. Cape, 1935, "Prenatal Conditions and the Status of Infants at Birth," *American Journal of Diseases of Children*, 50, 337–342.

Sontag, L. W., and T. W. Richards, 1938, *Studies in Fetal Behavior: I. Fetal Heart Rate as a Behavioral Indicator*. Monographs of the Society for Research in Child Development, 3 (4). Washington, D. C.: National Research Council.

Sontag, L. W., and R. F. Wallace
1934, "Preliminary Report of the Fels Fund: Study of Fetal Activity," *American Journal of Diseases of Children*, 48, 1050–1057.
1935, "The Movement Response of the Human Fetus to Sound Stimuli," *Child Development*, 6, 253–258.

Spearman, C. E., 1927, *The Abilities of Man*. N. Y.: Macmillan.

Spitler, J., 1966, *Educational Implications of the Theories of Jean Piaget*. Unpublished paper. Teachers College, Columbia University.

Spitz, R. A.
1949, "Autoeroticism, Some Empirical Findings and Hypotheses on Three of its Manifestations in the First Year of Life," in *Psychoanalytic Study of the Child*, edited by A. Freud, *et al.*, Vol. 3/4, pp. 85–120. N. Y.: International Universities Press.
1951, "The Psychogenic Diseases in Infancy: An Attempt at Their Etiologic Classification," in *Psychoanalytic Study of the Child*, edited by A. Freud, *et al.*, Vol. 6, pp. 255–275. N. Y.: International Universities Press.

Spivack, S. S., 1956, "A Study of a Method of Appraising Self-Acceptance and Self-Rejection," *Journal of Genetic Psychology*, 88, 183–202.

Srole, L., T. S. Langner, S. T. Michael, M. K. Opler, and T. A. C. Rennie, 1962, *Mental Health in the Metropolis: The Midtown Manhattan Study*, Vol. 1. N. Y.: McGraw-Hill.

Staines, J. W., 1958, "The Self-Picture as a Factor in the Classroom," *British Journal of Educational Psychology*, June.

Starkweather, E. K., 1962, "A Comparison of Two Techniques for Measuring Sociometric Status Among Nursery School Children," *Proceedings of the Oklahoma Academy of Science*, 42, 199–205.

Stendler, C. B.
1949, *Children of Brasstown*. Urbana: University of Illinois Press.
1964, *Readings in Child Behavior and Development*. N. Y.: Harcourt, Brace & World.

Stephenson, W., 1935, "Correlating Persons Instead of Tests," *Character and Personality*, 4, 17–24.

Stern, W., 1926, *Psychology of Early Childhood*. N. Y.: Holt.

Stevenson, H. W., ed., 1963, *Child Psychology*, NSSE Yearbook. Chicago: University of Chicago Press.

Stevenson, H. W., and R. D. Odom, 1965, "The Relation of Anxiety to Children's Performance on Learning and Problem-Solving Tasks," *Child Development*, 36 (4), 1003–1012.

Stevenson, H. W., and E. C. Stewart, 1958, "A Developmental Study of Racial Awareness in Young Children," *Child Development*, 29, 399–410.

Stewart, A. H., I. H. Weiland, A. R. Leider, C. A. Mangham, T. H. Holmes, and H. S. Ripley, 1954, "Excessive Infant Crying (Colic) in Relation to Parent Behavior," *American Journal of Psychiatry*, 110, 687–694.

Stith, M., and R. Connor, 1962, "Dependency and Helpfulness in Young Children," *Child Development*, 33 (1), 15–20.

Stolz, L. M., 1960, "Effects of Maternal Employment on Children: Evidence from Research," *Child Development*, 31, 749–782.

Stone, F. B., V. N. Rowley, and E. D. Keller, 1965, "Clinical Anxiety and the Children's Manifest Anxiety Scale," *Journal of Clinical Psychology*, 21 (4), 409–412.

Stone, L. J., 1954, "A Critique of Studies of Infant Isolation," *Child Development*, 25, 9–20.

Stott, L. H., 1957, "Persisting Effects of Early Family Experiences upon Personality Development," *Merrill-Palmer School Quarterly*, Spring, 3 (3), Detroit. (Special Issue, Seminar on Child Development.)

Stott, L. H., and R. S. Ball, 1965, *Infant and Preschool Mental Tests*. Monographs of the Society for Research in Child Development, 39, No. 3.

Strang, R., 1956, "Gifted Adolescents View Growing Up," *Exceptional Child*, 23, 10–15.

Strayer, L. C., 1930, "Language and Growth: The Relative Efficacy of Early and Deferred Vocabulary Training Studied by the Method of Co-Twin Control," *Genetic Psychology Monographs*, 8, 209–319.

Sturtevant, A. H., and G. W. Beadle, 1962, *An Introduction to Genetics*. N. Y.: Dover Publications.

Sullivan, H. S.
1947, *Conceptions of Modern Psychiatry*. Washington, D. C.: William Alanson White Psychiatric Foundation.
1948, *The Meaning of Anxiety in Psychiatry and in Life*. N. Y.: William Alanson White Institute of Psychiatry.
1953, *The Interpersonal Theory of Psychiatry*. N. Y.: Norton.
Sutton-Smith, B., 1955, "The Psychology of Children's Games" (Part I), *National Education* (New Zealand), 37, 228–229, 261–263.
Sutton-Smith, B., 1962, "Child Training and Game Involvement," *Ethnology*, 1 (2), 167–185.
Sutton-Smith, B., and P. Gump, 1955, "Games and Status Experience," *Recreation*, April 15.
Sutton-Smith, B., and J. M. Roberts, 1964, "Rubrics of Competitive Behavior," *Journal of Genetic Psychology*, 105, 13–37.
Sutton-Smith, B., B. G. Rosenberg, and E. F. Elmer, Jr., 1961, "Historical Changes in the Freedom with which Children Express Themselves on Personality Inventories," *Journal of Genetic Psychology*, 99, 309–315.
Svendsen, M., 1934, "Children's Imaginary Companions," *Archives of Neurology and Psychiatry*, 32, 985–999.
Svensson, N., 1962, "Ability Grouping Scholastic Achievement," *Educational Research*, 5 (1), 53–56.
Symonds, P. M., 1949, *Adolescent Fantasy*. N. Y.: Columbia University Press.
Symonds, P. M., and A. R. Jensen, 1961, *From Adolescent to Adult*. N. Y.: Columbia University Press.
Taba, H., 1953, "The Moral Beliefs of Sixteen-Year-Olds," in *The Adolescent: A Book of Readings*, edited by J. Seidman, pp. 315–318. N. Y.: Dryden.
Tabachnick, B. R., 1962, "Some Correlates of Prejudice Towards Negroes in Elementary Age Children," *Journal of Genetic Psychology*, 100 (2), 193–203.
Tannenbaum, A. J.
1962, *Adolescent Attitudes Toward Academic Brilliance*. N. Y.: Bureau of Publications, Teachers College, Columbia University.
Tanner, J. M.
1955, *Growth At Adolescence*. Springfield, Illinois: Charles C Thomas.
1963, "The Regulation of Human Growth," *Child Development*, 34 (4), 817–847.
Tart, C. T., 1965, "Toward the Experimental Control of Dreaming: A Review of the Literature," *Psychological Bulletin*, 64 (2), 81–91.
Taylor, C., and A. W. Combs, 1952, "Self-Acceptance and Adjustment," *Journal of Consulting Psychology*, 16, 89–91.
Taylor, J. A., 1953, "A Personality Scale of Manifest Anxiety," *Journal of Abnormal and Social Psychology*, 48, 285–290.
Telford, C. W., and J. M. Sawrey, 1967, *The Exceptional Individual*. Englewood Cliffs, N. J.: Prentice-Hall.
Templin, M. C., 1958, "General Information of Kindergarten Children: A Comparison with the Probst Study After 26 Years," *Child Development*, 29, 87–96.
Terman, L. M., and M. A. Merrill
1937, *Measuring Intelligence*. Boston: Houghton Mifflin.
1960, *Revised Stanford-Binet Intelligence Scale*. 3rd ed. Boston: Houghton Mifflin.
Terman, L. M., and M. Oden
1940, "Status of the California Gifted Group at the End of Sixteen Years," National Society for the Study of Education. *Intelligence: Its Nature and Nurture*. Thirty-ninth Yearbook, Part I, pp. 67–89. Bloomington, Illinois: Public School Publishing Co.
1959, *The Gifted Group at Mid-Life: Thirty-five Years' Follow-up of the Superior Child*. Stanford University Genetic Studies of Genius, Vol. 5. Stanford: Stanford University Press.
Thevaos, D. G., 1951, "The Influence of Semantic Variation on Word Difficulty, with Consequent Effects on Vocabulary Estimates and Frequency-Difficulty Variations," unpublished Doctor of Education dissertation, Teachers College, Columbia University.
Thomas, A., 1966, *Progress Report: Primary Reactions in Childhood*. Multigraphed. N. Y.: New York University Medical School.
Thomas, A., H. G. Birch, S. Chess, and L. C. Robbins, 1961, "Individuality in Responses

of Children to Similar Environmental Situations," *American Journal of Psychiatry*, 117, 798, 803.

Thomas, A., S. Chess, H. G. Birch, M. E. Hertzig, and S. Korn, 1963, *Behavioral Individuality in Early Childhood*. N. Y.: New York University Press.

Thompson, G. G.
 1944, *The Social and Emotional Development of Preschool Children Under Two Types of Educational Programs*. Psychological Monographs, 56 (258). Evanson, Illinois: American Psychological Association.
 1949, "Age Trends in Social Values During Adolescent Years," *American Psychologist*, 4 (7).
 1952, *Child Psychology*. N. Y.: Houghton Mifflin.

Thompson, G. G., and S. L. Witryol, 1948, "Adult Recall of Unpleasant Experiences During Three Periods of Childhood," *Journal of Genetic Psychology*, 72, 111–123.

Thompson, H.
 1954, "Physical Growth," in *Manual of Child Psychology*, 2nd ed., edited by L. Carmichael, pp. 292–334. N. Y.: Wiley.

Thompson, W. R., 1953, "The Inheritance of Behavior: Behavioral Differences in Fifteen Mouse Strains," *Canadian Journal of Psychology*, 7, 145–155.

Thorndike, E. L., E. O. Bregman, M. V. Cobb, E. S. Woodyard, *et al.*, 1927, *The Measurement of Intelligence*. N. Y.: Teachers College, Columbia University.

Thorndike, R. L.
 1940, " 'Constancy' of the I.Q.," *Psychological Bulletin*, 37, 167–186.
 1962, "Some Methodological Issues in the Study of Creativity," *Proceedings of the 1962 Invitational Conference on Testing Problems*. Princeton: Educational Testing Service, 40–54.

Thorndike, R. L., and E. Hagen, 1961, *Measurement and Evaluation in Psychology and Education*. N. Y.: Wiley.

Thorndike, R. L., C. W. Flemming, G. Hildreth, and M. Stanger, 1940, "Retest Changes in the I.Q. in Certain Superior Schools." National Society for the Study of Education. *Intelligence: Its Nature and Nurture*, Thirty-ninth Yearbook, Part II, pp. 351–361. Bloomington, Illinois: Public School Publishing Co.

Thorpe, L. P., W. W. Clark, and E. W. Tiegs, 1942–53, *California Test of Personality*. Los Angeles: California Test Bureau.

Thurston, J. R., and P. H. Mussen, 1951, "Infant Feeding Gratification and Adult Personality," *Journal of Personality*, 19, 449–458.

Thurstone, L. L., 1938, *Primary Mental Abilities*. Psychometric Monographs No. 1. Chicago: University of Chicago Press.

Tillich, P., 1952, *The Courage To Be*. New Haven: Yale University Press.

Tilton, J. W., 1949, "Intelligence Test Scores as Indicative of an Ability to Learn," *Educational and Psychological Measurement*, 9, 291–296.

Torrance, E. P., 1962, *Guiding Creative Talent*. Englewood Cliffs, N. J.: Prentice Hall.

Trainham, G., G. J. Pilafian, and R. M. Kraft, 1945, "A Case History of Twins Breast-Fed on a Self-Demand Regime," *Journal of Pediatrics*, 27, 97–108.

Trent, R.
 1953, "The Correlates of Self-Acceptance Among Negro Children," unpublished Doctor of Education dissertation, Teachers College, Columbia University.
 1957, "The Relationship of Anxiety to Popularity and Rejection Among Institutionalized Delinquent Boys," *Child Development*, 28, 379–384.

Trosman, H., 1963, "Dream Research and the Psychoanalytic Theory of Dreams," *Archives of General Psychiatry*, 9 (1), 9–18.

Tryon, C. M.
 1939, *Evaluation of Adolescent Personality by Adolescents*. Monographs of the Society for Research in Child Development, 4 (4).
 1944, "The Adolescent Peer Culture," Forty-third Yearbook of the National Society for the Study of Education, Part I, pp. 217–239. Chicago: University of Chicago Press.

Tryon, R. C., 1940, "Genetic Differences in Maze Learning," *National Society for the Study of Education*, Thirty-ninth Yearbook, Part I, 111–119.

Tyler, L. E., 1965, *The Psychology of Human Differences*. N. Y.: Appleton.
 Three Methods of Screening. Public Health Monograph, No. 7. Washington, D. C.:

Ullmann, C. A., 1952, *Identification of Maladjusted School Children. A Comparison of* Government Printing Office.

Updegraff, R., and M. E. Keister, 1937, "A Study of Children's Reactions to Failure and an Experimental Attempt to Modify Them," *Child Development*, 8, 241–248.

Valentine, C. W.
   1930, "The Innate Bases of Fear," *Journal of Gentic Psychology*, 37, 394–420.
   1946, *The Psychology of Early Childhood*, 3rd cd. London: Methuen and Co.

Vandenberg, S. G.
   1965a, ed., *Methods and Goals in Human Behavior Genetics*. N. Y.: Academic Press.
   1965b, Report of paper presented at AAAJ convention. *New York Times*, Dec. 31, 1965, p. 20.

Van Krevelen, A., 1962, "Characteristics Which 'Identify' the Adolescent to His Peers," *Journal of Social Psychology*, 56, 285–289.

Vygotsky, L., 1962, "The Developments of Scientific Concepts in Childhood," in *Thought and Language*, edited and translated by E. Hanfmann and G. Vakar pp. 82–118. N. Y.: Wiley.

Waldfogel, S., 1948, "The Frequency and Affective Character of Childhood Memories," *Psychological Monographs*, 62 (291).

Walk, R. D., and E. J. Gibson, 1961, "A Comparative and Analytical Study of Visual Depth Perception," *Psychological Monographs*, 75, 44, whole No. 519.

Wallach, M. A., and N. Kogan, 1965, *Modes of Thinking in Young Children*. N. Y.: Holt.

Wallin, P., 1950, "Cultural Contradictions and Sex Roles: A Repeat Study," *American Sociological Review*, 15, 288–293.

Walsh, A. M., 1956, *Self-Concepts of Bright Boys with Learning Difficulties*. N. Y.: Bureau of Publications, Teachers College, Columbia University.

Walters, E. C., 1965, "Prediction of Postnatal Development from Fetal Activity," *Child Development*, 36 (3), 801–808.

Walters, J., D. Pearce, and L. Dahms, 1957, "Affection and Aggressive Behavior of Preschool Children," *Child Development*, 28, 15–26.

Washburn, R. W., 1929, "A Study of the Smiling and Laughing of Infants in the First Year of Life," *Genetic Psychology Monographs*, 6, 397–539.

Washburn, T. C., D. N. Medearis, and B. Childs, 1965, "Sex Differences in Susceptibility to Infections," *Pediatrics*, 35, 57–69.

Waston, J. S., 1966, "Perception of Object Orientation in Infants," *Merrill-Palmer Quarterly*, 12, 73–93.

Watson, G. B., 1957, "Some Personality Differences in Children Related to Strict or Permissive Parental Discipline," *Journal of Psychology*, 44, 227–249.

Watson, J. B., and Rayner, R., 1920, "Conditioned Emotional Reactions," *Journal of Experimental Psychology*, 3, 1–14.

Watson, J. B., and R. R. Watson, 1928, *Psychological Care of Infant and Child*. N. Y.: Norton.

Wattenberg, W. W., and C. Clifford, 1964, "Relation of Self-Concepts to Beginning Achievement in Reading," *Child Development*, 35, 461–467.

Weaver, E., 1955, "How Do Children Discover They are Negroes," *Understanding the Child*, 24, 35–41.

Webster, E. J., 1961, "Fears and Worst Happenings as Reported by Southern Children," unpublished Doctor of Philosophy dissertation, Teachers College, Columbia University. Microfilm No. 740.

Wechsler, D.
   1949, *Wechsler Intelligence Scale for Children Manual*. N. Y.: Psychological Corporation.
   1950a, "Cognitive, Conative, and Non-Intellective Intelligence," *American Psychologist*, 5, 78–83.
   1950b, "Intellectual Development and Psychological Maturity," *Child Development*, 21, 45–50.
   1951, "Equivalent Test and Mental Ages for the WISC," *Journal of Consulting Psychology*, 15, 381–384.

Weiner, P. S., 1964, "Personality Correlates of Accuracy of Self-Appraisal in Four-Year-Old Children," *Genetic Psychological Monographs*, 70, 329–365.

Wellman, B. L.
   1937, "Motor Achievements of Preschool Children," *Childhood Education*, 13, 311–316.

Wenar, C., and J. B. Coulter, 1962, "A Reliability Study of Developmental Histories," *Child Development*, 33 (2), 453–462.

Wenger, M. A., 1936, *An Investigation of Conditioned Responses in Human Infants.* University of Iowa Studies in Child Welfare, 12 (318). Iowa City: University of Iowa Press.

Wenkart, A., 1955, "Self-Acceptance," *American Journal of Psychoanalysis*, 15, 135–143.

Werner, E. E., and N. Bayley, 1966, "The Reliability of Bayley's Revised Scale of Mental and Motor Development During the First Year of Life," *Child Development*, 37, 39–50.

Werner, H., and B. Kaplan, 1964, *Symbol Formation*. N. Y.: Wiley.

Wertheimer, M., 1961, "Psychomotor Coordination of Auditory and Visual Space at Birth," *Science*, 134, 1692.

White, R. W.
1945, "Interpretation of Imaginative Productions," in *Personality and the Behavior Disorders*, edited by J. McV. Hunt, Vol. 1, pp. 214–251. N. Y.: Ronald Press.
1959, "Motivation Reconsidered: The Concept of Competence," *Psychological Review*, 66, 297–333.

Whiting, B. B., ed., 1963, *Six Cultures*. N. Y.: Wiley.

Whiting, J. W. M., and I. L. Child, 1953, *Child Training and Personality: A Cross-cultural Study*. New Haven: Yale University Press.

Wickens, D. D., and C. Wickens, 1940, "A Study of Conditioning in the Neonate," *Journal of Experimental Psychology*, 26, 94–102.

Winker, J. B., 1949, "Age Trends and Sex Differences in the Wishes, Indentifications, Activities and Fears of Children," *Child Development*, 22, 189–200.

Wist, R. D., and W. E. Broen, 1956, "The Relation of the Children's Manifest Anxiety Scale to the Concept of Anxiety as Used in the Clinic," *Journal of Consulting Psychologists*, 20, 482.

Witkin, H. A., 1962, "Origins of Cognitive Style," in *Cognition: Theory, Research, Promise*, edited by C. Sheerer, pp. 172–205. N. Y.: Harper.

Witryol, S. L., and G. G. Thompson, 1953, "A Critical Review of the Stability of Social Acceptability Scores Obtained with the Partial-rank-order and the Paired-comparison Scales," *Genetic Psychology Monographs*, 48, 221–260.

Wittenberg, R. M., and J. Berg, 1952, "The Stranger in the Group," *American Journal of Orthopsychiatry*, 22, 89–97.

Wolf, T. H., 1938, *The Effect of Praise and Competition on the Persisting Behavior of Kindergarten Children*. Institute of Child Welfare Monograph Series, No. 15. Minneapolis: University of Minnesota Press.

Wolfenstein, M.
1953, "Trends in Infant Care," *American Journal of Orthopsychiatry*, 33, 120–130.
1954, *Children's Humor: A Psychological Analysis*. Glencoe, Illinois: Free Press.

Wolpert, E. A., and H. Trosman, 1958, "Studies in Psychophysiology of Dreams. I: Experimental Evocation of Sequential Dream Episodes," *A.M.A. Archives of Neurology and Psychiatry*, 79 (4), 603–606.

Woodworth, R. S., 1938, *Experimental Psychology*. N. Y.: Holt.

Wright, H. F.
1956, "Psychological Development in Midwest," *Child Development*, 27, 265–286.
1960, "Observational Child Study," in *Handbook of Research Methods in Child Development*, edited by P. H. Mussen, pp. 71–139. N. Y.: Wiley.

Wright, J. C., and J. Kagan, eds., 1963, *Basic Cognitive Processes in Children*. Monographs of the Society for Research in Child Development, 28 (2).

Yarrow, L. J., 1961, "Maternal Deprivation: Toward an Empirical and Conceptual Reevaluation," *Psychological Bulletin*, 58 (6), 459–490.

Zazzo, R., 1948, "Images du Corps et Conscience de Soi. Matériaux pour L'Etude Expérimentale de la Conscience," *Enfance*, I, 29–43.

Author Index

A

Abel, H., 297
Abel, T. (*see* Anderson, H. H., *et al.*)
Abt, L. E., 398
Ader, R., 100
Adler, A., 410, 478
Adorno, T. W., 298
Albee, G. W., 289
Allen, F., 550
Allen, L. (*see* Honzik, M. P., and Macfarlane, J.)
Allinsmith, W., 513
Allport, G. W., 325, 523
Almy, M. C., 8, 98, 291, 447, 449–451, 466, 479, 511

Alpert, M. (*see* Levine, S.)
Alschuler, R. H., 398
Amatora, M., 240
Amatruda, C. S. (*see* Gesell, A.)
Ames, L. B., 11, 165, 395–396, 399, 462
Ammons, R. B., 297, 298
Anastasi, A., 429, 491
Anderson, G. L. (*see* Anderson, H. H.)
Anderson, H. H., 227, 240, 241, 267, 298
Anderson, J. E. (*see* Foster, J. C.)
Angel, E. (*see* May, R.)
Angelino, H., 335
Appel, M. H., 259

Arnon, Y., 215
Aserinsky, E., 402–403
Ashley-Montagu, M. F., 51, 58, 314
Ausubel, D. P., 218–219, 242
Axline, V. M., 398

B

Bach, G. R., 398, 478
Baker, C. T. (*see* Kagan, J., Lansky, L. M., Sontag, L. W.)
Baker, H. V., 271, 455–456
Baldwin, A. L., 24, 227, 229–230
Baldwin, J. M., 109
Ball, R. S. (*see* Stott, L.L.)

Balthazar, E. E. (*see* Ausubel, D.P.)
Bandura, A., 290
Barker, B., 178
Barker, R. G., 268, 302, 371
Bartlett, F. C., 472
Bavelas, A. (*see* Seashore, H.G.)
Bayley, N., 143–144, 145, 146, 150, 155, 157, 160, 207, 471, 481, 482–484, 490, 535, 536, 537 (*see also* Schaefer, E.S., Rheingold, H. L., and Werner, E. E.
Beadle, G. W., 26, 45, 46 (*see also* Sturtevant, A. H.)
Beasley, W. C., 62
Beck, S. J., 399
Behrens, M. L., 198
Beinstock, S. F. (*see* Jersild, A.T.)
Bell, D. M. (*see* Schofield, W.)
Bell, R. Q. (*see* Schaefer, E.S.)
Bellak, L., 399 (*see also* Abt, L.E.)
Bellak, S. S. (*see* Bellak, L.)
Benezet, L. P., 463
Bennett, H. L. (*see* McCandless, B. R.)
Berezin, D., 87, 532
Berg, J. (*see* Wittenberg, R. M.)
Berger, E., 174
Berko, J., 421, 423 (*see also* Brown, R. W.)
Berkowitz, H., 524
Berlyne, D. E., 16
Bernard, J., 50
Bernstein, B., 178
Bevan, W. (*see* Dukes, W. F.)
Beyer, E. (*see* Lerner, E.)
Bibace, R. (*see* Caplan, H.)
Bibring, G. L., 54
Bickman, L. (*see* Schachter, J.)
Bienstock, S. F. (*see* Jersild, A. T.)
Bills, R. E., 174
Bilous, C. B. (*see* McCandless, W. R.)
Birch, H. G. (*see* Chess, S., and Thomas, A.)
Birns, B., 64–67
Birren, J. E. (*see* Kallman, F.J.)
Blackman, L. (*see* Ausubel, D.P.)

Blaisdell, F. G. (*see* Fiedler, F.E.)
Blank, M. (*see* Birns, B., *et al.*)
Blatz, W. E., 73, 530
Blau, L. R. (*see* Blau, T.H.)
Blau, T. H., 122, 123
Blauvelt, H. H., 60
Bloom, B., 553
Blum, L. H., 129, 399
Boll, E. S. (*see* Bossard, J.H.S.)
Bolles, M. M. (*see* Landis, C.)
Bonney, M. E., 262
Bossard, J. H. S., 239
Bourg, M. (*see* Lubchenco, L.O.)
Bowerman, C. E., 216
Boyd, J. D. (*see* Hamilton, W.J.)
Bradway, K. P., 486
Brandenburg, G. C., 431
Brandt, R. M., 182–183
Breese, F. H. (*see* Baldwin, A.L.)
Bregman, E. O. (*see* Thorndike, E.L.)
Brewer, H. M. (*see* Anderson, H.H.)
Brewer, J. E. (*see* Anderson, H.H.)
Bridger, W. H., 63, 66, 67 (*see also* Birns, B.)
Brodbeck, A. J., 416
Broderick, C. B., 296
Brodkin, A. M. (*see* Jersild, A.T.)
Broen, W. E. (*see* Wist, R.D.)
Bronfenbrenner, U., 197, 513
Bronson, W., 535–536
Brook, J., 426–427
Brooks, V. (*see* Hochberg, J.)
Brown, A. W., 262–263
Brown, D. G., 191–192
Brown, E. W. (*see* Lerner, E.)
Brown, K. B. (*see* Ourth, L.)
Brown, R., 421–423
Bruch, H., 130, 197
Bruck, M., 179
Bruel, I. (*see* Schmeidler, G.R.)
Bruner, J. S., 467, 479
Bühler, C., 85, 87, 89, 244, 246, 267, 270
Bühler, K., 16
Burchinal, L. G., 216

Burlingham, D., 198, 238, 248
Burnham, M. P., 384
Burstein, M., 395, 396
Burt, C., 135, 452–453
Burton, R. V., 513
Burtt, H. E., 478–479

C

Caille, R. K., 263
Caldwell, B. M., 15
Calkins, I. A. (*see* Scannon, E.E.)
Cameron, C. L., 473
Campbell, H. (*see* Lewis, M.)
Cannon, W. B., 363
Cantril, H., 294
Cape, J. (*see* Sontag, L.W.)
Caplan, H., 74
Carlson, R., 190
Carmichael, L., 49, 58, 325
Carrington, P. (*see* Ephron, H.S.)
Casler, L., 207, 209
Castaneda, A., 358, 364, 365, 545 (*see also* McCandless, B.R., and Palermo, D. S.)
Caster, B. M. (*see* Gesell, A.)
Cattell, R. B., 529
Champney, H., 227
Charles, M. S. (*see* Scott, J. P.)
Charles, M. W. (*see* Blatz, W. E.)
Charry, J. B., 472
Chein, I. (*see* Harding, J.)
Chess, S., 87 ff., 225, 546, 547 (*see also* Thomas, A.)
Child, I. L. (*see* Whiting, J. W. M.)
Childs, B. (*see* Washburn, T. C.)
Chittenden, E., 449–451
Chittenden, G. E., 260
Clark, K. B., 171, 297
Clark, M. K. (*see* Clark, K.B.)
Clark, W. W. (*see* Thorpe, L.P.)
Clausen, J. A., 171, 297, 298
Clements, E. M. B., 19
Clifford, C. (*see* Wattenberg, W.W.)
Clifford, E., 54
Cobb, M. V. (*see* Thorndike, E.L.)
Coghill, G. E., 49

Cohen, A. I., 157–158
Cohig, R. (*see* Lubchenco, L.O.)
Coleman, J. S., 190
Coleman, R. W., 198
Combs, A. W., 183, 195, 550
Conn, J. H., 186
Connor, R., 247
Constantinou, F. K. (*see* Pasamanick, B.)
Cooper, R. (*see* Peck, R.F.)
Coopersmith, S., 179
Cordova, F. A. (*see* Anastasi, A.)
Corn, F. S., 399
Cornett, S., 478
Costa, J. (*see* Karelitz, S.)
Coulter, J. B. (*see* Wenar, C.)
Cox, F. N., 281
Crandall, V. J., 227, 233 (*see also* Lansky, L.M.)
Crowder, T. (*see* Gallagher, J.J.)
Cruickshank, W. M., 341, 501
Cunningham, R., 278
Curry, R. L., 496

D

Dahms, L. (*see* Walters, S.)
Damann, V. T., 148–149
Dann, S. (*see* Freud, A.)
Darcy, N. T., 429
Davidson, H. H. (*see* Blum, L.H.)
Davidson, K. S., 219, 344 (*see also* Sarason, S.B.)
Davis, A., 292, 293, 362 (*see also* Havinghurst, R. J.)
Davis, C. M., 127 ff.
Davis, E. A., 428, 431
Davitz, J. R., 272, 273, 276
Dawson, G. E., 521
Day, E. J., 428
Debus, R. L., 257
Delhanty, J. D. A. (*see* Penrose, L.S.)
del Solar, C. F. (*see* Jersild, A.T.)
DeMartino, M. F., 402
Dembo, T. (*see* Barker, R.G.)
Dement, W., 402–403, 407 (*see also* Fisher, C., and Roffwarg, H.P.)
Dennenberg, V. H., 99
Dennis, W., 8, 97, 147, 157, 206, 209
Despert, J. L., 68, 137
Deutch, M. P., 178

Deutsch, H., 198–199
Diaz-Guerrero, R. (*see* Anderson, H.H.)
Dimitrovsky, L., 272–273
Ding, C. F., 324
Dinitz, S. (*see* Lively, E.L.)
Dixon, J. C., 169
Dobzhansky, T., 28, 45, 46
Dolger, L., 509
Dollins, J. (*see* Angelino, H.)
Domhoff, B. (*see* Hall, C.S.)
Donaldson, R. S., 188
Douvan, E., 178, 179, 190
Driscoll, G. P., 398
Dublin, L. I., 188
Dudycha, G. J., 472
Dudycha, M. M. (*see* Dudycha, G.J.)
Dukes, W. F., 441
Dunlap, J. M., 493
Dunnington, M. J., 280
Durkin, D., 518
Dwyer, T. F. (*see* Bibring, G.L.)

E

Eaton, M. T., 462
Edwards, M. (*see* Gough, H.G.)
Edwards, N., 142
Eells, K. W., 178, 362
Eichorn, D. H., 144–145
Eissler, R. S., 8
Elkind, D., 520
Ellenberger, H. F. (*see* May, R.)
Elliott, H. C. (*see* Lubchenco, L.O.)
Ellis, J. R. (*see* Penrose, L.S.)
Elmer, E. F., Jr. (*see* Sutton-Smith, B.)
Elonen, A. S. (*see* Anderson, H.H.)
Emmerich, W., 219
Emerson, P. E. (*see* Schaffer, H.R.)
Engen, T., 63, 77
English, H. B., 328
Ephron, H. S., 404
Epstein, R., 292
Erikson, E. H., 398, 417
Ervin, S. (*see* Miller, W.)
Escalona, S., 71, 211, 234 (*see also* Birns, B.)
Estvan, F. J., 294
Eysenck, H. J., 529
Ezekiel, L. F., 263

F

Falek, A., 157
Fantz, R. L., 61, 62, 95, 437
Farnsworth, P. R., 8, 442
Farrell, M. (*see* Cunningham, R.)
Fauquier, W., 156
Feldman, D. A., 289
Feldman, W. M., 122
Fenichel, O., 124–125, 137
Feshback, N. (*see* Feshback, S.)
Feshback, S., 342
Fey, W. F., 174
Fiedler, F. E., 276
Fieldsteel, N. D. (*see* Blum, L.H.)
Fisher, C., 404, 407, 412, 413 (*see also* Roffwarg, H. P.)
Fisher, M. S., 425, 430
Fisichelli, V. R. (*see* Karelitz, S.)
Fite, M. D., 257, 264, 265 (*see also* Jersild, A. T.)
Fitz-Simons, M. J., 202
Flapan, D., 194, 273–275
Flavell, J. H., 447, 479
Flemming, C. W. (*see* Thorndike, R.L.)
Flory, C. D., 188
Forbes, H. B. (*see* Forbes, H.S.)
Forbes, H. S., 50
Foshay, A. W., 516
Foster, J. C., 131, 401
Foster, S., 377
Foulkes, D., 409
Fowler, S. E. (*see* Broderick, C.B.)
Franco, D., 308
Frank, G. H., 232, 242, 355
Frank, L. K., 398, 413
Freedman, D. G., 85, 86, 329
Freeman, F. N. (*see* Newman, H.H.)
Frenkel-Brunswik, E., 298
Freud, A., 8, 215, 247–248, 267, 316
Freud, S., 22, 68, 124, 137, 195, 314, 320, 322, 325, 353–355, 358, 365, 389, 402, 408, 410–413, 472, 475
Freudenberg, E., 60
Fried, Y., 215
Friedman, P., 235

Fries, M. E., 137
Fromm, E., 524
Fuller, J. L., 27, 29, 33, 36, 40–46, 101, 211

G

Gallagher, J. J., 496
Gardner, D. B., 214
Gates, A. I., 153
Gates, G. S., 272
Gavrin, J. B., 207
Gellert, B., 451–452
Gershman, H., 357
Gesell, A., 40, 41, 60, 73, 84, 87, 89, 122, 126, 127, 134, 140, 148, 329, 377 417
Getzels, J. W., 500
Gibbs, P. K. (*see* Maccoby, E.E.)
Gibson, E. J., 96, 97, 437, 440–441 (*see also* Walk, R. D.)
Ginandes, J., 509
Ginsberg, S. (*see* Schmeidler, G.R.)
Gleason, H. A. Jr., 416
Goff, R. M., 298–299
Golan, S., 215
Goldberg, M. L., 494, 497, 498
Goldberger, A., 248
Goldenson, R. M., 160
Goldfarb, W., 212–213, 468
Goldhammer, H., 543
Goldman, B. (*see* Jersild, A.T.)
Goldman, J. R., 100–101
Gooch, S. (*see* Pringle, M.L.K.)
Goodenough, D. R., 406
Goodenough, F. L., 91, 369 ff., 379, 482, 485
Goodman, M. E., 297, 299
Goslin, D. A., 184–185, 281
Gotkin, L. G., 494 (*see also* Goldberg, M.L.)
Gottesman, I. I., 529
Goudey, E. S., 323
Gough, H. G., 298 (*see also* Harris, D.B.)
Grant, V. W., 296
Green, E. H., 245, 257
Green, H. F. (*see* Connor, R.)
Greenberg, P. J., 255
Gregory, L. W. (*see* Heath, C.W.)
Greulich, W. W., 188

Griffiths, R., 217, 387–388, 413
Griffiths, W. J., 100
Grinder, R. E., 514, 515
Gross, J. (*see* Fisher, C.)
Grossman, H., 289
Guilford, J. P., 486, 487, 500
Gump, P. V., 518 (*see also* Sutton-Smith, B.)

H

Haas, M. B. (*see* Siegel, A.E.)
Hadfield, J. A., 413
Hagen, E. (*see* Thorndike, R.L.)
Haggard, E. K., 178
Hagman, R. R., 342, 345
Hall, C. S., 29, 411, 413
Hall, G. S., 458
Hall, J. A. (*see* Cunningham, R.)
Haller, A. O., 291
Hallowell, A. T., 241
Halpern, F. C., 399
Halverson, H. M., 138, 145
Hamachek, D. E., 179, 195
Hamilton, E., 55
Hamilton, W. J., 58
Hardeman, M., 511
Hardin, G., 30
Harding, J., 298
Harlow, H. F., 16, 100, 314, 436
Harlow, M. K. (*see* Harlow, H.F.)
Harris, D. B., 24, 51, 298, 398, 482 (*see also* Goodenough, F.L., and Gough, H.G.)
Harris, E. S. (*see* Harris, D.B.)
Harrison, G. A., 160
Harrison, R. (*see* Frank, L.K.)
Harrower, M. R., 509
Hartley, R. E., 160, 186–187
Hartman, H. (*see* Eissler, R.S.)
Hartshorne, H., 516 ff.
Hartup, W. W., 192
Hastings, D. W. (*see* Schofield, W.)
Hathaway, S. R. (*see* Schofield, W.)
Hattendorf, K. W., 321
Hattwick, B. W., 262

Hattwick, L. A. (*see* Alschuler, R.H.)
Havighurst, R. J., 293 (*see also* Peck, R.F.)
Hawkes, G. R. (*see* Gardner, D.B.)
Heath, C. W., 544
Heinstein, M. I., 125
Helfant, K. (*see* Jersild, A.T.)
Hellersberg, E. (*see* Frank, L.K.)
Henry, A. F., 219
Herbert, J., 251
Hermann, L. (*see* Hinckley, R.G.)
Herrick, V. E., 240
Hertzig, M. E. (*see* Thomas, A.)
Hess, E. H., 14, 20
Hetzer, H., 244, 296
Hildreth, G. (*see* Thorndike, R.L.)
Hill, D. S., 455, 519
Hinckley, R. G., 550
Hix, I. E., Jr. (*see* Lubchenco, L.O.)
Hoch, P. H., 353, 365
Hochberg, J., 437, 439
Hoefer, G. (*see* Kawin, E.)
Holden, M. (*see* Goodenough, D.R.)
Hollingshead, A., 293
Hollingworth, H. L., 397
Hollingworth, L. S., 44, 282, 491, 499
Holmes, F. B., 93, 324–325, 329, 341, 345, 346, 362 (*see also* Jersild, A.T.)
Holmes, T. H. (*see* Stewart, A.H.)
Holzinger, K. J., 36
Honzik, M. P., 34, 122, 485, 490, 535, 536 (*see also* Macfarlane, J. W.)
Hooker, D., 47
Horan, K. M. (*see* Pritchard, M.C.)
Horner, F. A. (*see* Lubchenco, L.O.)
Horney, K., 181, 195, 353, 355, 356 ff., 365, 524
Horowitz, E., 170
Horowitz, R., 171 (*see also* Murphy, L. B.)
Houlihan, N. B. (*see* Kuhlen, R.G.)
Hovland, C. I., 190
Hughes, B. O. (*see* Olson, W.C.)

Hull, V., 551
Hunt, H. F., 100
Hunt, R. G. (*see* Brown, A.W.)
Huntington, D. S. (*see* Bibring, G.L.)
Hurlock, E. B., 395, 396
Huschka, M., 137
Huttenlocher, J., 430

I

Ilg, F. L. (*see* Gesell, A.)
Ingraham, R. C., 236
Inhelder, B. (*see* Piaget, J.)
Irish, D. P. (*see* Bowerman, C.E.)
Irwin, O. C., 73, 415, 416 (*see also* Brodbeck, A. J.)
Isaacs, S., 68, 138, 267

J

Jack, L. M., 260–261
Jackson, P. W., 219 (*see also* Getzels, J.W.)
James, W., 195
Jameson, J., 190
Jameson, S. H. (*see* Schachter, J.)
Janis, I. L. (*see* Hovland, C.I.)
Jarvik, L. F. (*see* Kallman, F.J.)
Jayaswal, S. R., 475
Jenkins, L. M., 151–152
Jensen, A. R. (*see* Symonds, P.M.)
Jensen, K., 60
Jersild, A. T., 189, 194, 257, 259, 265, 291, 318, 324, 335, 345, 360, 364, 456, 538–540
Jersild, C. L. (*see* Jersild, A.T.)
Jervis, F. M., 174
John, E. M., 342
Johnson, G. O., 503, 505
Johnson, V. E. (*see* Masters, W.H.)
Jones, H. E., 155, 281, 329, 345, 528
Jones, M. C., 32, 296, 329, 528 (*see also* Jones, H. E., and Mussen, P. H.)
Jones, T. D., 149–150, 152
Justin, F., 324

K

Kadis, A., 478
Kaffman, M., 215
Kagan, J., 93, 94, 219, 469, 470–472, 486, 535, 536, 553 (*see also* Lansky, L. M., Lewis, M., and Wright, J. C.)
Kalafat, J. (*see* Lewis, M.)
Kalhorn, J. (*see* Baldwin, A.L.)
Kallman, F. J., 28, 42, 45–46, 355
Kantrow, R. W., 76
Karelitz, R. (*see* Karelitz, S.)
Karelitz, S., 70
Katahn, M., 364
Kawi, A., 52 (*see also* Pasamanick, B.)
Kawin, E., 262
Kaye, H. (*see* Engen, T., and Lipsitt, P.)
Keisler, E. R., 281
Keister, M. E., 371
Keller, E. D. (*see* Stone, F.B.)
Kelley, D. McG. (*see* Klopfer, B.)
Kenderdine, M., 324
Kerlinger, F. N., 241
Kessen, W., 63
Khon, A. R., 172
Kidd, A., 442
Kierkegaard, S., 353, 354, 365
King, F. J. (*see* Phillips, B.N.)
Kinsey, A. C., 188, 320, 321, 326
Klein, S. J. (*see* Hall, C.S.)
Kleitman, N., 402–403, 406, 413 (*see also* Dement, W.)
Klineberg, O., 490
Klingensmith, S. W., 454
Klopfer, B., 399
Knobloch, H., 52–54, 58, 158 (*see also* Pasamanick, B.)
Knop, C., 189
Knudson, A. G. (*see* Natterson, J.M.)
Koch, H. L., 138, 296
Kogan, N. (*see* Wallach, M.A.)
Kohl, S. G. (*see* Donaldson, R.S.)
Kohlberg, L., 508, 524
Komarovsky, M., 190
Koppitz, E. M., 232

Korn, S. (*see* Thomas, A.)
Kounin, J. S. (*see* Gump, P.V.)
Kraft, R. M. (*see* Trainham, G.)
Kraus, P. E., 233, 269, 331, 531
Krippene, B. (*see* Hull, V.)
Kris, E. (*see* Coleman, R.W.)
Kris, M. (*see* Eissler, R.S.)
Krogman, W. W., 31
Krugman, M., 299
Kuhlen, R. G., 296
Kuo, Z. Y., 14
Kutner, J. B. (*see* Harding, J.)

L

Lacan, J., 169
Lafore, G. G., 227–228, 231
Laing, A., 324
Lakin, M., 71
Landis, A. T. (*see* Landis, C.)
Landis, C., 322
Landis, J. T., 216
Langner, T. S. (*see* Srole, L.)
Lansky, L. M., 192, 287
Lapouse, R., 335, 342–344
Lasko, J. K., 200
Laughlin, F., 279–280, 281
Lazar, E. A., 126, 313, 335, 343, 344 (*see also* Jersild, A. T.)
Learned, J. (*see* Ames, L.B.)
Lecky, P., 195
Lee, E. S., 490
Leider, A. R. (*see* Stewart, A.H.)
Lemkin, J. (*see* Kagan, J.)
LeMasters, E. E., 57, 200
Lenneberg, E. H., 91
Lerner, E., 398
Leuba, C., 255
Leutzendorff, A. M. (*see* Kessen, W.)
Leventhal, A. S., 62
Levin, H., 399 (*see also* Sears, R.R.)
Lévine, J., 179
Levine, S., 98 ff.
Levinson, D. J. (*see* Adorno, T.W.)
Levy, D. M., 122–123, 138, 186
Levy, J., 225
Lewin, K. (*see* Barker, R.G.)
Lewis, G. W. (*see* Levine, S.)
Lewis, M., 93

Lewis, S. J., 112
Lighthall, F. F. (*see* Davidson, K.S., and Sarason, S.B.)
Lilienfeld, A. M. (*see* Pasamanick, B., and Rogers, M. E.)
Lilienthal, J. (*see* Peck, R.F.)
Lindzey, G. (*see* Harding, J.)
Lipsitt, L. P., 63, 77, 78 (*see also* Engen, T., and Leventhal, A.S.)
Lituchy, S. (*see* Schachter, J.)
Liu, C. H., 510
Lively, E. L., 186
Loftus, J. (*see* Jersild, A.T.)
Lorenz, K., 14
Lorge, I., 482, 491
Lubchenco, L. O., 74
Lukomnik, M. (*see* Schmeidler, G.R.)
Luria, A. R., 435

M

Macauley, E., 517, 519
Maccoby, E. E., 242, 293 (*see also* Sears, R. R.)
Macfarlane, J. W., 129–130, 132, 136, 269, 535, 537, 538
Machover, K., 398
Mallay, H. (*see* Reynolds, M.H.)
Mangham, C. A. (*see* Stewart, A.H.)
Markey, F. V., 258–260, 336, 384, 456 (*see also* Jersild, A. T.)
Markley, E. R., 228, 292, 293
Marquis, D. P., 76, 78–79
Marshall, A. (*see* Goldhammer, H.)
Martin, C. E. (*see* Kinsey, A.C.)
Martin, W. E., 534–535 (*see also* Harris, D.B., and Gough, H.G.)
Masters, W. H., 137
Matsumoto, M., 219
Maudry, M., 244
Maurer, A., 235, 241
May, M. A., 516 ff.
May, R., 353, 365, 524
McCandless, B. R., 251, 358, 364, 365 (*see also* Castenada, A., and Palermo, D.S.)

McCarthy, D., 415, 418, 419, 426, 428
McElvaney, M. E., 399
McFarland, M. B., 254, 255
McG. Kelley, D. (*see* Klopfer, B.)
McGraw, M. B., 13, 61, 134
McGuire, C., 239 (*see also* Phillips, B. N.)
McKay, G. (*see* Lansky, L.M.)
McKinnon, K. M., 533–534
McLean, O. S. (*see* Bills, R.E.)
McLendon, P. A. (*see* Simsarian, F. P.)
McMahon, B., 51, 52
McNeil, E. B., 292
McNemar, Q., 153–154
Mead, G. H., 195
Mech, E. V. (*see* Angelino, H.)
Medearis, D. N. (*see* Washburn, T.C.)
Medinnus, G. R., 176, 225, 515
Meili, R., 168, 311, 531
Meissner, W. W., 26
Mengert, I. G., 247
Merrill, M. A. (*see* Terman, L.M.)
Metcalf, D. (*see* Lubchenco, L.O.)
Metraux, R. W. (*see* Ames, L.B.)
Meyer, R. (*see* Harlow, H.F.)
Michael, S. T. (*see* Srole, L.)
Miller, D. R. (*see* Allinsmith, W.)
Miller, P. E., 450, 465–467, 479, 511
Miller, R. V., 496
Miller, W., 420
Millichamp, D. A. (*see* Blatz, W.E.)
Mitchell, C., 515
Monk, M. A. (*see* Lapouse, R.)
Monroe, R. (*see* Levy, J.)
Moore, D. (*see* Peck, R.F.)
Moore, S., 251
Moreno, J. L., 278
Morton, R. J. (*see* Harrison, G.A.)
Moss, H. A. (*see* Kagan, J.)
Mossman, H. W., 58
Mowrer, O. H., 417
Munn, N. L., 45
Murchison, C., 267

Murphy, L. B., 68, 252 ff., 262, 521, 536, 537 (*see also* Lerner, E.)
Murray, H. A., 399
Mussen, P. H., 8, 32, 125, 528 (*see also* Sewall, W. H., and Thurston, J.R.)
Muzio, J. N. (*see* Roffwarg, H.P.)
Myers, G. C. (*see* Scott, F.F.)

N

Najarian, P. (*see* Dennis, W.)
Nameche, G., 289
Natterson, J. M., 340
Neel, J. V., 30
Neisser, E. G., 377
Nekula, M. (*see* Mandry, M.)
Nelson, A. K. (*see* Pratt, K.C.)
Nelson, V. L. (*see* Kagan, J.)
Newbery, H. (*see* Richards, T.W.)
Newman, H. H., 136
Newton, N. R., 125
Nichols, I. A. (*see* Lenneberg, E.H.)
Nichols, R. C., 35–36, 37–38
Nicholson, E. L. (*see* Bonney, M.E.)
Nye, F. I., 216

O

Oakes, M. E., 454
Oden, M. (*see* Terman, L.M.)
Odom, R. D. (*see* Stevenson, H.W.)
Ojemann, R. (*see* Pritchard, E.)
Olson, W. C., 37, 490
Omwake, L., 324
O'Neal, P. (*see* Robins, L.N.)
Opler, M. K. (*see* Srole, L.)
Orlansky, H., 137
Otis, L. S. (*see* Hunt, H.F.)
Ourth, L., 210

P

Page, E. I., 438–439
Palermo, D. S., 358, 364, 365 (*see also* Castenada, A., and McCandless, B.R.)
Parten, M. B., 245
Pasamanick, B., 52–54, 58, 74, 158 (*see also* Kawi, A.A., Knobloch, H., and Rogers, M.E.)

Pascal, G. (*see* Feldman, D.A.)
Pattie, F. A., 478
Pearce, D. (*see* Walters, J.)
Pearson, K., 489
Pearson, L. (*see* Kagan, J.)
Peck, R. F., 508
Penrose, L. S., 31
Perkins, H. V., 185
Perry, D. C., 183
Perry, J. B., 216
Peterson, E. T., 216
Phillips, B. N., 183, 364
Phillips, E. L., 174
Piaget, J., 12, 98, 103, ff., 193–195, 315, 385, 414, 417, 425, 438, 443–452, 463, 479, 488, 503, 506 ff., 515, 518, 524
Pilafian, G. J. (*see* Trainham, G.)
Pilzer, E., 544
Pinneau, S. R., 125
Pistor, F., 463
Pomeroy, W. B. (*see* Kinsey, A. C.)
Porter, F. (*see* Hull, V.)
Pratt, K. C., 62, 79, 341
Prechtl, H. F. R., 60
Preston, A. (*see* Crandall, V. J.)
Preyer, W., 167
Pringle, M. L. K., 517–519
Pritchard, E., 335–336
Pritchard, M. C., 491
Probst, C. A., 457–458
Proshansky, H. (*see* Harding, J.)
Prout, C. T., 44
Provence, S., 198
Purcell, K., 478
Pyle, S. I. (*see* Sontag, L.W.)

R

Rabban, M., 192
Rabin, A. I., 215, 302
Rabinovitch, M. S. (*see* Caplin, H.)
Radke, M., 299
Radke-Yarrow, M., 216, 237
Ramsey, G. V., 188, 321, 402
Rapaport, D., 389
Rebelsky, F. G. (*see* Lenneberg, H.)
Rechtschaffen, A., 409
Reckless, W. C. (*see* Lively, E.L.)
Redl, F., 300, 379

Reed, L. H. (*see* Lubchenco, L.O.)
Reed, M. F. (*see* Anderson, H.H.)
Reese, H. W., 297
Rennie, T. A. C. (*see* Srole, L.)
Reynolds, M. M., 132, 221–223
Rheingold, H. L., 85–86, 206, 207
Ribble, M. A., 125
Richards, T. W., 50, 51 (*see also* Sontag, L. W.)
Ricketts, A. F., 368
Ricks, D. (*see* Nameche, G.)
Riessman, F., 178
Rigney, M. G., 266
Ripley, H S. (*see* Stewart, A.H.)
Ritzman, R. (*see* Jersild, A.T.)
Rivlin, L. G., 501
Rivoire, J. (*see* Kidd, A.)
Robbins, L. C., 238
Roberts, J. M. (*see* Sutton-Smith, B.)
Roberts, M. (*see* Cunningham, R.)
Robins, L. N., 289
Robinson, G. L., 191
Roe, H., 341
Roffwarg, H. P., 404–405, 407
Rogers, C. R., 195, 544, 550
Rogers, M. E., 74
Rorschach, H., 399
Rosenberg, B. G. (*see* Sutton-Smith, B.)
Rosenberg, P. (*see* Radke, M.)
Rosenfeld, L. (*see* Karelitz, S.)
Rosenthal, I. (*see* Ausubel, D.P.)
Rosenzweig, M. R., 99
Ross, M. G., 523
Rossier, A., 74
Rossman, J. E. (*see* Burchinal, L.G.)
Rousselet, J., 179
Rowley, V. N. (*see* Stone, F.B.)
Ruebush, B. R. (*see* Sarason, S.B.)
Rust, M. M., 431–433

S

Sacks, L. S. (*see* Gavrin, J.B.)
Sahinkaya, R. (*see* Abel, H.)

Sanford, R. N. (*see* Adorno, T.W.)
Sarason, S. B., 553, 559 ff., 565
Sarbin, T. R., 164
Sarnoff, I., 343
Sawrey, J. M. (*see* Telford, C.W.)
Scammon, R. E., 48, 73
Scarr, S., 529
Schachter, J., 67
Schachter, J. S. (*see* Schachter, J.)
Schaefer, E. S., 228, 471, 535, 537
Schaffer, H. R., 212, 315, 528
Schaltenbrand, G., 61
Schmeidler, G. R., 364
Schofield, W., 289
Schpoont, S. H. (*see* Ausubel, D. P.)
Scott, A .W. (*see* Gates, A.I.)
Scott, F., 431
Scott, J. P., 14, 20, 29
Searle, L. V., 39
Sears, P. S., 551
Sears, R. R., 125, 236, 228, 242, 259, 292, 293
Seashore, H. G., 290, 372
Seidman, J. E., 160
Sewall, M., 377
Sewell, W. H., 125
Shaidun, G. (*see* Rechtschaffen, A.)
Shapiro, A. (*see* Goodenough, D.R.)
Shaw, R. F., 398
Sherman, M., 132
Sherman, V. S. (*see* Sears, P.S.)
Shields, J., 36, 529
Shirley, M. M., 40, 41, 75, 83, 87, 89, 146, 160, 197, 246, 418, 532–533, 553
Shoben, E. J., 228
Shumsky, A., 178
Siegel, A. E., 216
Sigel, I. E. (*see* Kagan, J.)
Siller, J., 178
Sillman, J. H., 122
Simsarian, F. P., 123, 126, 127
Singer, J. L., 389
Skeels, H. M., 34–35, 208, 213, 490
Skodak, M., 34–35, 490
Slater, E., 331
Slavson, S. R., 550
Smedslund, J., 464–465

Smith, H. T. (*see* Matsumoto, M.)
Smith, M. E., 429, 474–475, 477
Smith, R. T., 35
Smith, W. M., 296
Snygg, D., 195, 550
Sontag, L. W., 51, 468, 486 (*see also* Kagan, J.)
Sowa, J. M. (*see* McMahon, B.)
Spearman, C. E., 487
Spiker, C. C. (*see* Lipsitt, L.P.)
Spitler, J., 464
Spitz, R. A., 138, 205
Spivack, S. S., 174
Spock, B., 140, 237
Srole, L., 544
Staines, J. W., 184–185
Stanger, M. (*see* Thorndike, R.L.)
Starkweather, E. K., 251
Steiner, M. (*see* Frank, L.K.)
Stendler, C. B., 171, 267, 294, 302, 441, 479
Steinschriber, L. (*see* Goodenough, D.R.)
Stephenson, W., 174
Stern, W., 400
Stevenson, H. W., 297, 364, 442
Stewart, A. H., 70, 71
Stewart, E. A. (*see* Stevenson, H.W.)
Stith, M., 247
Stolz, L. M., 216
Stone, F. B., 360
Stone, L. J., 125 (*see also* Lerner, E.)
Stott, L. H., 485, 534
Strang, R., 493
Strayer, L. C., 12
Stringer, W. F. (*see* Griffiths, W.J.)
Sturtevant, A. H., 45
Sullivan, H. S., 120–121, 124, 172, 195, 198, 353, 355, 365, 374
Sun, K. H. (*see* Pratt, K.C.)
Sutherland, J. (*see* Radke, M.)
Sutton-Smith, B., 300–302, 545
Svendsen, M., 395
Svensson, N., 496
Swanson, G. E. (*see* Allinsmith, W.)
Swayze, J. (*see* Herbert, J.)

Swensen, C. H. (*see* Feldman, D.A.)
Symonds, P. M., 396–397, 413

T

Taba, H., 515
Tabachnick, B. R., 276, 298
Tannenbaum, A. J., 494–495 (*see also* Goldberg, M.L.)
Tanner, J. M., 31, 32, 142, 160, 188, 296 (*see also* Harrison, G. A.)
Tart, C. T., 407
Tasch, R. J., 189, 318
Taylor, C., 183
Taylor, J. A., 358
Telford, C. W., 505
Templin, M. C., 458
Terman, L. M., 481, 485, 497 ff., 502
Thevaos, D. G., 424
Thomas, A., 87 ff., 216, 225, 234–235, 237, 377, 378, 546
Thomas, S. (*see* Haller, A.O.)
Thomas, W. S. (*see* Jersild, A.T.)
Thompson, C. W. (*see* Bradway, K.P.)
Thompson, G. G., 262, 266, 279, 472, 515 (*see also* Witryol, S.L.)
Thompson, H., 148, 160
Thompson, W. R., 27, 29 (*see also* Fuller, J.L.)
Thorndike, E. L., 480
Thorndike, R. L., 480, 481, 482, 484, 491, 501, 505
Thorpe, L. P., 545
Thurston, J. R., 125
Thurstone, L. L., 487
Tiegs, E. W. (*see* Thorpe, L.P.)
Tillich, P., 353, 365
Torrance, E. P., 501, 502
Trainham, G., 127
Trent, R., 276, 280, 298
Trosman, H., 406 (*see also* Wolpert, E.A.)
Tryon, C. M., 189, 297
Tryon, R. C., 29, 38, 39

U

Ullmann, C. A., 544
Updegraff, R., 208, 251, 371 (*see also* Skeels, H.M., and Moore, S.)

V

Valenstein, A. F. (*see* Bibring, G.L.)
Valentine, C. W., 328
Vance, E. L., 174
Vandenberg, S. G., 38, 46, 529
Van Krevelen, A., 280
Verdone, P. (*see* Rechtschaffen, A.)
Videbeck, R. (*see* Ingraham, R.C.)
Vogel, G. (*see* Rechtschaffen, A.)
Vygotsky, L., 466–467

W

Waite, R. (*see* Davidson, K.S., and Sarason, S.B.)
Waldfogel, S., 473
Walk, R. D., 96 ff. (*see also* Gibson, E.J.)
Walker, R. N. (*see* Ames, L.B.)
Wallace, R. F. (*see* Sontag, L.W.)
Wallach, M. A., 501–502
Wallin, P., 190
Walters, E. C., 50
Walters, J. (*see* Connor, R.)
Walters, R. H. (*see* Bandura, A.)
Wann, K. D. (*see* Foshay, A.W.)
Wardwell, E. (*see* Levin, H.)
Waring, M. (*see* Nameche, G.)
Warrington, W. G. (*see* Fiedler, F.E.)
Watkins, S. H., 517
Washburn, R. W., 323
Washburn, T. C., 188
Watson, G. B., 229, 230
Watson, J. B., 87, 240, 328, 330
Watson, R. R. (*see* Watson, J.B.)
Wattenberg, W. W., 174, 179
Weaver, E., 299
Webster, E. J., 336, 341
Wechsler, D., 482
Weiland, I. H. (*see* Stewart, A.H.)
Weiner, J. S. (*see* Harrison, G.A.)
Weiner, P. S., 183

Weischer, V. (*see* Hollingworth, H.L.)
Welch, L. (*see* Kagan, J.)
Welkowitz, J. (*see* Ausubel, D. P.)
Wellman, B. L., 153 (*see also* Skeels, H. M.)
Wenar, C., 237
Wenger, M. A., 77
Werner, E. E., 505
Werner, H., 426
Wertheimer, M., 62, 63
Wheaton, J. (*see* Rechtschaffen, A.)
White, M. A. (*see* Prout, C.T.)
White, R. W., 16, 399
Whiting, B. B., 241, 242
Whiting, J. W. M., 241–242
Wickens, C. (*see* Wickens, D.D.)

Wickens, D. D., 76, 77
Williams, H. M. (*see* Skeels, H.M.)
Williams, J. R. (*see* Clausen, J.A.)
Williams, T. A. (*see* Schachter, J.)
Wineman, D. (*see* Redl, F.)
Winker, J. B., 335, 341
Wise, G. W. (*see* Sears, R.R.)
Wist, R. D., 360
Witkin, H. A., 469, 470
Witryol, S. L., 279 (*see also* Thompson, G.G.)
Wittenberg, R. M., 282
Wolf, T. H., 255
Wolfenstein, M., 197, 324, 325
Wolpert, E. A., 406
Woodworth, R. S., 422
Woodyard, E. S. (*see* Jersild, A.T.)

Wright, H. F., 251, 268–269 (*see also* Barker, R.G.)
Wright, J. C., 479

Y

Yarrow, L. J., 207
Yudovich, F. I., 435

Z

Zazzo, R., 169
Zimbardo, P. G. (*see* Sarnoff, I.)
Zook, E. A. (*see* Hartup, W.W.)
Zubin, J. (*see* Hoch, P.H.)
Zuch, J. (*see* Fisher, C.)

Subject Index

A

Abandonment, fear of, 339
Abnormalities, prenatal and paranatal, 52–54
Abstract thinking (*see* Conceptual development
Acceptance by peers, 277 ff.
"Accepting parent," the, 200
Accident proneness, as related to brain damage, 53
Accommodation:
in cognitive development, 105 ff., 444, 463–464
in imitative behavior, 113 ff.

Achievement, view of self as capable of, 177–178
Activity-passivity patterns, 88
Activity pleasure, 116, 316
Activity level:
as related to styles of thinking, 471
as self-initiated source of stimulation, 212
in infancy, 88
in the neonate, 64 ff.
Adaptability as related to:
temperamental style, 88;
ease of child rearing, 235;
susceptability to problem behavior, 546

Adaptation, role of in development of intelligence, 104 ff. (*see also* Accommodation, Assimilation)
Adopted child, worries of, 344
Adopted children, intelligence of, 33–34
Adrenalin, effects of injection of, 363–364
Affection:
as a factor in suppression of anger, 373
conflicting with anger as a source of anxiety, 350
development of, 86, 313 ff.

Affective components of the self, 164

Aggression:
in children's fantasies about parents, 217
in dreams, 411 ff.
in older children, 287 ff.
parental attitudes toward, 228–229

Aggressive behavior, age changes in, 259

Aggressiveness, 256 ff.
adult reactions to, 260
as related to recovery from mental illness, 289–290
as related to socio-economic status, 292
covert, 241
frequency of as related to sympathetic behavior, 257
genetic aspects of, 41, 488
in dreams, 289
stability of, 536

Aggressiveness (*see also* Anger)

Alcohol, genetic differences in tolerance of, 31, 41

Alphabet, discrimination of elements in, 439–440

Altruism, as a feature of moral maturity, 508

Ambivalence, in relations between parents and children, 217 ff.

Anal eroticism, 137

Analytic as compared with thematic thinking, 469–470

Analytical as compared with global thinking styles, 469–470

Androgen, genetic differences in concentration of, 38

Anger, 366–379
as an aspect of jealousy, 377
as a source of anxiety-producing conflict, 350
as the feeling experienced in anxiety, 353
in the neonate, 72
recognition of expressions of, 273

Anger (*see also* Aggressiveness)

Animal "intelligence":
genetic factors in, 38–39
specific aspects of, 38–39

Animals, fear of, 333, 340

Animism, 435, 454

Animistic thought, 454

Anoxia, 53

Anxiety, 328, 348–365
as a consequence of inner conflict, 349 ff.
as distinguished from fear, 348 ff.
definitions of, 348 ff.
genetic aspects of, 529
theories of, 353 ff.

Apgar Scale, 64

Apgar scores at birth as related to later development, 142

Appetitional conditioned responses, 76

Approach-withdrawal patterns, 88

Archaic reation patterns, 23–24

Arithmetic, influence of maturation and training in mastery of, 463

Assets, personal, as viewed by children, 528–529

Assimilation, role of:
in cognitive development, 105 ff., 444, 463–464
in play, 115 ff.

Athletic ability, high evaluation of, 495

Attachment, emotional, development of, 86, 313

Attention span, 88

Attentional behavior, 92–93

Attitudes (*see also* Emotion; Parent-child relations; Sex; Moral development):
parental, instruments for measurement of, 228
toward self, 164 ff.
with respect to elimination, 135

Audiogenic seizures, 44

Auditory aspects of early cognitive development, 107 ff.

Auditory stimuli, varying neonatal response to, 64

Authority, resentment of, 375

Autism, 53

Autonomic division of nervous system:
functioning of in neonate, 66–67
role of, in emotion, 66, 306
significance of for study of early personality manifestations, 45, 66–67

Aversive conditioned responses, 76

Awareness of own and others' feelings, 194

B

Babbling, 417 ff.

"Baby-party" technique, 244

Bar Mitzvah, 523

Bayley Mental and Motor Development Scales, 157

Bedtime, significance of, 133

Behavior problems (*see* Problem behavior)

Beliefs:
erroneous, 460
religious, 519–540

Bible, children's interest in various parts of, 521

Bilingualism, 429–430

Biochemical understructure of development, 10–11

Biographical studies of development, 89

Biological roots of intelligence, 104–105

Birth injury, 53

"Birth ordeal," 56

Birth order and sibling roles, 238–239

Birth rate, 188

Birth trauma, 57

Bladder control (*see also* Elimination):
loss of, as form of regression, 135, 378

Boredom, 319–320

Bowel control (*see* Elimination)

Boy-girl relationships, 295 ff.

Brain damage, 52–54

Breast feeding, 125

British compared with American children's scores on general and "test" anxiety, 361

C

Candor, as related to authenticity of self-ratings, 174

Cardinal numbers, development of concept of, 448

Cephalocaudal direction of development, 48

Cerebral palsy, 52

Cheating:
as related to maturity of moral judgment, 514
studies of, 514, 515, 516 ff.

Chewing, 126

Child rearing practices:
  as related to socio-economic status, 292
  changing fashions in, 197
  parental recollection of, 236–237 (*see also* Parent-child relationships)
Children as parent substitutes, 247–248
Choice, as aspect of development of the self, 167–168
Chromosomes, 25 ff.
  faulty disjunction of, 40
Circular reactions, 109 ff.
Class inclusion (*see also* Classification):
  understanding of, 448
  as related to maturity of moral judgment, 511
  influence of special training on, 465–466
Classification, understanding of, 109, 445–446, 448, 465 ff.
Climbing, 148–149
Cognition, role of in emotional development, 310
Cognitive and emotional processes, distinction between, 306 ff.
Cognitive components of the self, 164
Cognitive development (*see* Intelligence, origins of; Conceptual development; Language development; Perception; Moral development)
Cognitive styles, 468 ff.
Colic, 70–71
Companionship, imaginary, 392 ff.
Compassion, 553
Competence, drive toward, 16
Competition:
  developmental aspects of, 253 ff., 283 ff.
  relation of, to development of self, 170
  unwholesome aspects of, 285
  values of, 285
Competitiveness:
  as defense against anxiety, 357
  role of, in fear, 329
  stability of, 536
Comprehension of language, 419

Concepts (*see also* Conceptual development):
  historical, understanding of, 462
  pertaining to religious affiliation and teachings, 520 ff.
Conceptual development, 443–479 (*see also* Language development; Moral development; Origins of intelligence; Perception)
Conceptual thinking, impairment of, in institutionalized children, 213
Concrete operations, stages of, in thinking, 445–446
Conditioned response, 12, 91
  in establishment of fears, 320
  in the neonate, 76 ff.
Conflict, emotional, as a source of anxiety, 349 ff.
Conformity, sex differences in, 189–190
Congenital differences between boys and girls, 187–188
Congenital disorders, 52–54
Conscience, development of, 511 ff.
Conservation, understanding of concept of, 446, 448
  as related to moral judgment, 571
  influence of special training on, 464–465
  longitudinal study of, 449 ff.
Constancies in external environment, development of awareness of, 110 ff.
Constancy and change in personality development (*see* Stability and change)
Constancy of intelligence ratings, 482–486
Contact comfort, 314
"Continued story" type of daydream, 385
Convergent thinking, 487, 500
Cooperation, morality of, 507
Cooperative behavior, 248 ff., 283 ff.
Correlation coefficient, illustration of computation, 483
Cortex, influence of stimulation on, 99
Creative children, characteristics of, 501–502
Creativity, 500–503

Creeping, 146
Critical phase, 13–15, 20
Crying:
  adult response to, 71
  as prediction of later development, 70
  in the neonate, 69 ff.
  suppression of, 311–312
Cue reduction, 96
Cultural influences on child-rearing practices, 240–242
Curiosity, 16 (*see also* Questions asked by children):
  as related to attainment of pleasure, 317

D

Darkness, fear of, 333, 339
Daydreams (*see* Fantasy)
Day residues in dreams, 409
Death:
  children's questions regarding, 433–434
  fear of, 339
Delinquency:
  as expression of anger, 374
  as related to socio-economic status, 293
  continuation of, as related to prior aggressiveness, 289
Delinquents, self-concepts of, 186
Deoxyribonucleic acid, 26
Dependency, 199
  as a source of emotional conflict, 350
  as related to social acceptance, 251
  stability of, 536
Deprivation, effects of (*see also* Institutionalization):
  in infancy, 97 ff.
  in later childhood, 212
  on conceptual thinking, 468
Deprivation of dreams, effects of, 407 ff.
Depth, perception of, 96–97, 437
Desires, effects of, on what is perceived, 441
Detachment, as defense against anxiety, 357
Developmental quotient of institutionalized babies, 206–207
Developmental revision of habits, 17–18

Deviations from normal parent-child relationships, 201 ff.

Dextrality (see Hand preference)

Diet:
during pregnancy as related to brain damage, 53
self-selection of, 127 ff.

"Difficult child," rearing, 234–235

Dionne quintuplets, resemblances and differences in, 530

Direct observation, 250–251

Discipline, 138–140
as related to susceptibility to anger, 370

Discrepancies between "real" and "ideal" self, 177

Discrimination between strange and familiar persons, 86

Distractibility, 88

Divergent thinking, 487, 500

Divorce, children's reactions to, 216

Dizygotic twins, 33 (see also Twins)

DNA, 26

Doll play (see Fantasy and Make-believe):
as a projective technique, 399

Dominant genes, 28, 43

Dominative behavior, 227

Drawing and painting as projective techniques, 398

Dreams and dreaming, 132, 400–413

Drive level and intellectual development, 468

Drives (see Motives, Motivation)

E

Early memories, 472 ff.
as related to socio-economic status, 291

Early physical maturing, effects of, 32

"Easy child," rearing, 234–235

Eating (see Feeding behavior)

Educational level and intelligence, 34

Effectance, 16

EEG sleep cycles, 403–404

Egocentric speech, 425–426

Egocentricity:
decline with age in, 451–452

Egocentricity (cont.):
in infancy, 117–118
relation of, to capacity for self-understanding, 193–194

Electroencephalographic recordings, patterns of in sleep, 403 ff.

Elimination, 134 ff.

Embryo (see Prenatal development)

Emotion (see also Emotional development; Parent-child relationships; Dreams; and references to emotional states, such as, anger, fear, affection):
communication of, from mother to child, 120
general characteristics of, 305–310
recognition of expressions of, 272 ff.

Emotional development, 67 ff., 305–379

Emotional aspects of prejudice, 298

Emotional aspects of self-awareness, 169–170

Emotional behavior:
in laboratory animals, influence of infancy stimulation on, 99–100
of institutionalized children, 205 ff.

Emotional content of early memories, 474–475

Emotional stability as related to honesty, 516

Emotionality and heredity, 41

Endocrine glands, 42 (see also Autonomic division of nervous system)
role of, in emotion, 363

Enuresis, 135

Environment, as affected by child's response, 530

Environment, influence of, on physical growth, 145

Environment, influence of (see Deprivation; Stimulation; Institutionalization; Heredity; Learning; Cultural influences; Socio-economic status)

Environment, prenatal, 51

Environmental stress, effects of, in relation to genetic susceptibilities, 42, 44

Epilepsy, 52

Equilibration as a factor in development of thinking, 463

Erection:
in infant boys, 138
during dreams, 412–413

Erogenous zones, 124

Ethnic origins, awareness of, 171, 297

Euclidean forms, recognition of, 438–439

Exceptional children, 492 ff.

Excitability:
at neonatal level, 65
genetic factors in, 41

Expediency, morality of, 508

Expressive reactions (see also Emotional development):
development of recognition of, 272–275
of blind-deaf children, 93

Extroversion, studies of genetic factors in, 529

F

Family size, as related to socio-economic status, 291

Fantasies pertaining to parents, 217

Fantasy, 383–400

Fat deposits, 19

Fear, 327–365
as a factor in suppression of anger, 373
as related to pregnancy, 55
compared with anger, 366
in the neonate, 72
irrational, 93
of strangers, beginning of, 86
pleasure in overcoming, 317
prevalence in early memories, 474
regarding child's safety, 148

Feeding behavior, 121 ff.

Feeding problems, 129

Feeding schedule, adaptation to, 78–79

Feeling (see also Emotional development):
as component of emotional reaction, 306
awareness of, 194
in fear as distinguished from anxiety, 352
of efficacy, 16
regarding self, 164

Female chromosomes, 26

Femininity (see Sex role identification)

Fetal activity as related to later development, 50

Fetus:
development and behavior of, 45 ff.
effects of postnatal simulation on condition of, 210–211

Fights and quarrels, 256 ff.

First-born child as a "crisis event," 57

First words, 417 ff.

Food demands, spontaneous, 121 ff.

Foster children, intelligence of, 33–34

Fraternal twins (*see* Twins)

Free Association:
age changes in, 422–424
as a facilitator of early memories, 476
as a measure of creativity, 501

Friendliness, 85 ff., 247
as a cloak for anger, 374
in dreams, 411

Friendships among young children, 249–250 (*see also* Peer relationships)

Frustration, response to, 290

"Function pleasure," 16

Future, as incorporated in fantasy, 389–390

Future role, projection of self into, 177–178

G

Galvanic skin reflex, 67

Games, nature and meaning of, 299

Gamete, 26

General Anxiety Scale, 359

Generalized movement, 59–60

Generalization (*see also* Conceptual development):
age changes in capacity for, 456–457
of use of grammatical forms, 421–422

Generosity, as related to religious instruction, 522

Genes (*see* Heredity, physical basis of)

Genetic code, 26

Genetic factors:
general treatment of, 25 ff.
and susceptibility to imprinting, 20

Genetic factors (*cont.*):
in development of social discrimination, 86
in hand preference, 157
in mental illness, 355–356
in motor ability, 153–154
in personality development, 527 ff.
in physical development, 143–144
in response to stimulation and isolation, 101–102

Genetic variations, range of, 30

Genotype, 29–30

Geometric forms, recognition of, 438–439

Gesell Developmental Schedule, 50

Gifted children, 493 ff.

Gifts, symbolic significance of, 317

Goals (*see also* Intentional behavior):
envisioning of, through fantasy, 390
role of in arousal of emotion, 309

Goodenough-Harris Draw-a-Man Test, 482

Gossip, as expression of hostility, 241

Grammar, learning rules of, 420–424

Graphic symbols, discrimination of, 439–440

Grasp reflex, 61

Grievances, as a form of suppressed anger, 374

Group behavior, beginnings of, 245

Group formation, 269 ff.

Guilt:
as a factor in suppressing anger, 373
as reaction to illness in infancy, 341
as related to early memories, 474
as related to temptation resistance, 513–514
as related to test anxiety, 360
associated with fear, 335–336
role of, in pregnancy, 55

H

Habit formation:
as distinguished from self-initiated innovations, 113

Habit formation (*cont.*):
as related to eating, sleeping, elimination, and other routines, 119–140

Habits, developmental revision of, 17–18

Habituation:
as an aspect of learning, 92
evidence of, in the neonate, 77

Hand-preference, 157 ff.

"Happiest day," 318

Haptic perception, 438–439

"Head Start" Program, 267

Hearing:
in the neonate, 62
role of, in early cognitive development, 108

Heart rate, variations in, in neonate, 66

Height, development of, 142 ff.

Heredity (*see* Genetic factors)

Heterosexual interests, 295–297

Heterozygous genes, 27, 28

Home care, compared with institutional, 206–207

Homozygous genes, 27

Honesty, as related to religious instruction, 522

Honesty, rating of, as a virtue, 515

Honesty, studies of, 516 ff.

Hope:
beginnings of, 417
role of imagination in, 390

Hospitalization, effects of, 53

Hostility:
and anger, general treatment of, 366–379
role of, in test anxiety, 360

Human face, attention-getting value of, 94

Humor, 323 ff.

Hyperkinetic tendency, as related to interest in intellectual achievement, 471

I

Ideal child, as assessed by parents, 176

"Ideal self," 175

Idealized parent, 220–221

Idealized self, 181, 357

Ideals and heroes, age changes in choices of, 455, 519

Identical twins (*see also* Twins):
controlled study of, 210
differences between, 83, 238

Identical twins (*cont.*):
mental illness in, 42
Identification:
as a factor in moral development, 511–512
as related to proception of others, 276
theoretical explanations of, 512–513
Imagery, role of, in cognitive development, 115 ff.
Imaginary companions, 392–397
Imagination (*see also* Fantasy): role of, in fear, 329 ff.
Imitation, role of, in early cognitive development, 113 ff.
Immanent justice, 507
Imprinting, 14, 20
Impulse:
as component of emotional reaction, 306
nature of, in anxitey, 351 ff.
Impulsiveness, as compared with reflectiveness in style of thinking, 470–472
Indigenous motivation, 16–17
Individuality:
early manifestations of, 21
in infancy, 87 ff.
influence of, on parent-child interaction, 198, 234
Inductive reasoning, development of, 452–453
Infancy, 83 ff.
Inflectional system, learning of, 421–422
Information, children's, at various age levels, 457–460
Insight, as related to authenticity of self-assessment, 174
Institutional care, nature and consequences of, 204 ff.
Institutionalized children, 97, 204 ff.
Integration of behavior, 48–49
Intellectual ability (*see* Intelligence)
Intellectual development, as related to motor performance, 151–152
Intellectual growth, limits of, 486
Intellectual performance, as related to anxiety, 364–365
Intellectual teamwork, development of, 271

Intellectualism, as defense against anxiety, 360
Intelligence:
definitions and theories pertaining to, 480, 486–487
family resemblances in, 489–490
general and specific factors in, 38
influence of genetic factors on, 31–38
measurement and prediction of, 480–505
origins of in infancy, 103 ff.
Intelligence, related to:
language development, 428
moral judgment, 509
motor ability, 155
onset of fears, 362
popularity, 281
scores on anxiety tests, 361–362
socio-economic status, 291
Intelligent behavior in the neonate, 77
Intensity of reaction:
in infancy, 88
in neonates, 64–65
Intention, consideration of, in moral judgment, 507 ff.
Intentional behavior, 110
Interests, sex differences in, 189
Interpersonal relationships, 120 (*see also* Individuality)
Interpersonal theory of anxiety, 355
Introversion, studies of genetic factors in, 529
IQ:
derivation of, 482
gains in, as related to personality factors, 468
of institutional children, 208
Isolation in infancy:
effects of on animal sexual response, 41
genetic differences in reaction to, 101
influence of, on later behavior, 100
IT Scale, 191–192

J

Jealousy, 377 ff.
Jokes, 325
Joy, 316 ff.
Judgment, moral, 507 ff.
Jumping, 149–150

K

Kibbutz, children of the, 215
Knowledge (*see* Cognitive development)
Knowledge as "interiorized action," 445 (*see also* Conceptual development)
Knowledge of self, 194–195

L

Language:
as related to early memories, 472
development and characteristics of, 415–435
imaginative content of, 384
relation of, to thinking, 434–435
Latency period, 322–333
Laughter, 323 ff.
Leadership, 249–250
Learning (*see also* Conditioning; Cultural influences; Habit formation; Self-initiated activities, Maturation; Parent-child relationships; Socio-economic status):
and perception, 95
as related to maturity level, 12–14
as related to overcoming of fear, 345 ff.
definition of, 12
experimental controls in studies of, 92
in early infancy, 90 ff.
in the neonate, 76 ff.
of socially approved practices, 260
self-initiated, 92 (*see also* Self-initiated activities)
Localization of self, 170
Locomotion, 146 ff.
Logical concepts, development of (*see* Conceptual development)
Love:
characteristics of, 199
recognition of expression of, 273
theories regarding nature of, 313–314
Love (*see* Affection; Acceptance; Compassion; Boy-girl relationships, mothering, Parent-child relationships)

M

Major genes, 27
Make-believe (*see also* Fantasy):
as a means of coping with fear, 347, 387
Maladjustment, emotional, 498, 543 ff.
Male chromosome, 26
Malnutrition, 31
Manic-depressive psychosis, genetic factors in, 42
Manifest anxiety, measurement and ramifications of, 358 ff.
Marasmus, 205
Masculinity (*see* Sex role identification)
Masturbation, 321
and the process of development, 11 ff.
Maturation, role in:
bladder control, 134
development of understanding 462–467
locomotion, 148
onset of certain fears, 329
social discrimination, 86
Maze learning, as related to genetic factors, 38–39
Means-end combinations, 110
Meiosis, 26, 40
Memory, 94 ff. (*see also* Early memories, Learning)
Memory:
dependability of, in parents' reports of child-rearing histories, 235 ff.
early childhood characteristics, 472–473
residual effects of childhood experience on, 478–479
Mental deficiency:
as consequence of brain damage, 52
forms of, 503–504
genetic factors in, 39–40
Mental disorders (*see* Mental illness)
Mental health, potential role of school in promotion of, 550 ff.
Mental illness:
genetic factors in, 28
in children, as related to parental child-rearing practices, 232
prevalence of, in general population, 543–544

Mential illness (*cont.*):
prevalence of, in gifted adults, 498, 499
Mentation during sleep, 407–409
Methods of studying social interaction, 250–251
"Midwest, U. S. A.," 268
Mirror image, development of recognition of, 168–169
Misconceptions, 460–461
Mitosis, 26
Mongolism, 40
Monozygotic twins, 33 (*see also* Twins)
Mood, as an aspect of temperamental predisposition, 86
Moral development, 506–519
Moro reflex, 60–61
Morpheme, 416
Mother, role of, 69, 120 ff. (*see also* Parent-child relationships)
Mothering, multiple, 214
Motivation as related to:
creeping and climbing, 148
dreaming, 410 ff.
fantasy, 386 ff.
imitation, 114
intellectual development, 112 ff.
Motivation, nature of, 15–16 (*see also* Emotion)
Motives:
effect of, on what is perceived, 441
role of, in emotion, 309–310
Motor ability and skills:
genetic factors in, 153–154
influence of maturation and learning on, 13
specificity of, 152
Motor activity, interplay of, with sensory, 84
Motor development, 145 ff.
sex differences in, 189
Multifactor type of inheritance, 27–28
Multiple word meanings, aquisition of, 424

N

Naps, 132
Native, as distinguished from acquired forms of behavior, 61–62, 90–91, 96–97, 313–314, 328
Needs (*see* Motivation)

Negativism, 221
Neonate, the, 59 ff.
physical dimensions of, 31
rapid eye-movement (REM), sleep patterns of, 403 ff.
Neurotic defenses against anxiety, 357
Neuroticism, genetic factors in, 529
Neuroticism (*see* Personality disorders)
Newborn child, (*see* Neonate)
Noises, fear of, 33, 338
Nominal realism, 426–427
Non-rapid eye movement sleep (*see* Dreams)
Non-recalled dreaming, 405–406
Novelty, as a stimulus to asking questions, 431
NREM sleep (*see* Dreams)
Number, concept of:
development of, 447–448
longitudinal study of, 449 ff.
Nursery School:
effects of, on institutionalized children, 208–209
effects of on IQ, 490
effects of variation in program of, 265–266
evaluations of, 261 ff.
practices in, 260
Nutrition:
and brain damage, 53
physical development, 19, 145

O

Objectification of external environment, 109–110
Observational procedures in study of parent-child relationships, 227 ff.
Oedipus situation, 215, 322, 354
Olfactory reactions in the neonate, 63
"Open field" tests, 96
Operant learning, 91
Operational thinking, 444 ff.
Oral activity, 121 ff. (*see also* Sucking)
Oral behavior, following dream deprivation, 413
Oral drive, 122 ff.
Oral region as an erotogenic zone, 124
Oral satisfaction, effects of deprivation of 124 ff.

Ordinal number, development of concept of, 448
Organization:
biological role in cognitive development, 104–105
of behavior in fetus, 48–49
Orgasm:
age of onset of, 321
rectal sphincter contractions during, 137
Originality (*see* Divergent thinking, Creativity)
Over-indulgence, 202
Ovum (*see* physical basis of heredity)

P

Pain reactions in the neonate, 64
Parent-child interactions as affected by:
consequences of brain damage in child, 53
child's individual characteristics, 65–66, 88–89
prematurity, 75
Parent-child relationships as related to:
anxiety in children, 354 ff.
children's fantasies, 388
children's fears, 342 ff.
child's self-evaluation, 172
development of affection, 313 ff.
everyday practical aspects of, 119 ff., 196–242
moral development, 509, 512–513
Parent-child resemblances:
in height, 144
in intelligence, 489 ff.
Parental behavior, patterns of, 226 ff.
Parental evaluation of child as forerunner of test anxiety, 359
Parents' reaction to subject of prejudice, 299
Parents' reports, dependability of, 235 ff.
Parents' self-perceptions of, 233
Participant observer, 6–7
Parts of speech, learning of, 421–423
Pattern vision in the neonate, 61

Peer preferences, 249 (*see also* Sociometric findings)
Peer relationships:
beginnings of, 243 ff.
influence of, 240
in later childhood, 268 ff.
role, in sex education, 323
Perception, 95 ff., 435–442
field-dependent vs. field-independent styles of, 469–470
influence of language usage on, 435
of children's fears by parents, 343–344
of depth, 96–97
of graphic symbols, 439–440
of other persons' feelings and intentions, 272–275, 276
of parents by child, 173, 218 ff.
of properties of speech, 418
of self, 21, 164, 182–183
Perceptual as contrasted with conceptual thinking, 44–445
Perceptual components of fear and anxiety, 351
Perceptual development, interweaving of, with social and emotional, 86, 315
Performance, change in, as affected by anger, 371
Performance tests, 209
Permanence of objects, awareness of, 95, 110, 315
Permissiveness:
as related to socio-economic status, 292
findings regarding effects of, 228–230
Persistence, 88
Personal contact, significance of, in the neonate, 68–69
Personality development, genetic factors in, 40–45
Personality, general treatment of, 527–553
Personality:
as manifested in motor activities, 156
as related to choice of games, 300 ff.
as related to oral drives and anal eroticism, 124 ff., 137
"germinal layers" of, 89
manifestations of, in the neonate, 63 ff.
prediction of trends in, 88 ff.

Personality (*cont.*):
subjective dimensions of, 5–6
Personality problems and disorders, 543 ff.
Personality problems of intellectually gifted persons, 496, 498
Personality traits (*see also* Self):
admired or lamented by children in themselves, 538–541
as related to content of early memories, 477–478
as related to styles of thinking, 471–472
associated with peer acceptance and rejection, 280–281
of children with imaginary companions, 395–396
of creative children, 501–502
of gifted children, 493
Phenotype, 29–30
Phenylketonuria, 38–39
Phobia, 351–352, 354
Phoneme, 416
Physical care, psychological meanings of, 119 ff.
Physical development, 141 ff.
genetic factors in, 19, 31–32
Physical disability, as related to fear, 341
Physical punishment, as related to moral development, 513
Physiological changes in emotional arousal, 363
Physiological components of emotion, 306
Physiological reactions in the neonate, 66–67, 141–142
Piaget's theories, tests of, 449 ff.
Pictures, recognition of, 437–438
Play:
as related to pleasurable emotion, 316
role of, in early cognitive development, 115 ff.
Play (*see* Fantasy, Games)
Play techniques, 398
Polygenic inheritance, 27, 33, 43
Popularity, 251
accuracy of self-appraisal, 184–185
girls' self-regard, 190

Positive response to human contact, 85–86

"Practice games," 115, 116

Predictive significance of:
amount of fetal activity, 50
Apgar Scale scores at birth, 142
"cry scores" of new-born children, 70

Pregnancy:
abnormalities of, 52–54
psychology of, 54–56

Prehension:
development of, 145
role of, in early cognitive development, 107 ff.

Prejudice, 297 ff.
effects of, 172

Prematurity, 52 ff., 73 ff.

Prenatal conditions harmful to fetus, 52 ff.

Prenatal development, 45 ff.

Prenatal influences, 50 ff.

Preoperational thought, 445–446

Primary mental abilities, 487

"Primary reaction patterns," 87 ff.

Principles of development, 9–24

Privacy, desire for, 313

Problem behavior, 129 ff.
as related to elimination, 136
as related to sleep, 132
associated with anger, 370
temperamental antecedents of, 546

Problems, personal, as viewed by children themselves and/or by others, 543 ff.

Projective methods, 397 ff.

Pronouns, use of in early language development, 424–425

Proximodistal direction of development, 48

Psychological habitat, 268

"Psychological parent," the, 198–199

Psychophysiological approach to personality study in neonates, 45, 66–67

Punishment, ideas concerning, 507

Q

Q-Sort, 174

Quantity:
concept of, 446–448

Quantity (*cont.*):
longitudinal study of development of concept of, 449 ff.

Quarrels and fights, 256 ff.

Questions asked by children, extent and content of, 430–431

R

Rapid eye movement (REM):
as indication of dreaming, 402 ff.
phase of sleep cycle, 124

Reading disability, as consequence of brain damage, 52

Reading, effects of impulsivity on progress in, 472

Reading (*see* Graphic symbols, discrimination of)

Realism vs. relativism:
moral, 507 ff.
nominal, 426–427

Reasoning, moral, 507 ff.

Reasoning (*see* Conceptual development)

Recessive genes, 28, 43

Reciprocity, as a moral principle, 508, 518

Recognition of pictured objects, 437–438

Recognition (*see* Perception)

Rectal sphincter contractions, 137

Reduced cues, 95–96

"Reflected appraisals," 172

Reflection, capacity for, 193 ff.

Reflective thinking, 446

Reflectiveness as compared with impulsiveness in style of thinking, 470–472

Reflex activity, 59–61

Reflex stage of development, 109–110

Regression to earlier behavior, 135, 378

Regressive behavior as a response in anger, 372

Reinforcement, 15, 91

"Rejecting parent," the, 202

Rejection:
by parents, consequences of, 203
by peers, 277 ff.
parental toleration of, 199

Religion in childhood, 519–524

Religious instruction as related to fear, 340

REM (*see* Rapid eye-movement phase of sleep)

Representative thought, 111 ff.

Resiliency, in recovering from stress and misfortune, 537–538

Resistant behavior, 222–223

Respect for authority, as related to moral maturity, 510

Restitution, as a principle of moral justice, 509

Restrictions on learning, effects of, 207

Retaliatory concept of punishment, 509

Retardation in institutionalized children, 206

Retrolental fibroplasia, 74

Retrospective reports by parents, credibility of, 235 ff.

Reversibility of thought processes, 446

Rhythmicity:
as a primary reaction pattern, 88
as related to ease of child-rearing, 234–235

Right and left, comprehension of relative nature of, 451–452

Rivalry, 253, 283 ff.

Roles in children's games, 301–302

Romantic interests, 296–297

Rooting reflex, 60

Rorschach Test, 399

Rules, observance of, 270, 300

Running ability, 149–150

S

Sadness, recognition of expression of, 273

Saulteaux Indians, 241

Scapegoat, use of, 371

Schemata, cognitive, 106 ff., 443–444

Schizophrenia:
genetic factors in, 42–43
recovery from, as related to prior aggressiveness, 289

School achievement or performance as related to:
anxiety scores, 361
intelligence, 487–489
self-assessment, 179

School (*see also* Nursery school):

School (*cont.*):
boredom in, 319
children's understanding of rules in, 518
deportment in, and performance on tests of honesty, 516
effects of, on self evaluation, 542
emotional reactions to first days of, 269, 331
provision in, for exceptional children, 499–500, 504
suppression of anger in, 372
Schooling:
attitudes toward, as related to socio-economic status, 293
effects of, on intelligence test scores, 490–492
Screen memories, 476
Selective attention, 93–94
Self:
accuracy of perception of, as related to other factors, 182–183
assessment of, as related to early memories, 477–478
attitudes toward, as related to intelligence, 496
attitudes toward, as related to training in bladder control, 136
boredom with, 320
conflict within, as source of anxiety, 349 ff.
knowledge and acceptance of, as related to mental health, 548 ff.
liked and disliked aspects of, 538–541
role of, in maturation, 21
Self-acceptance:
as related to mental health, 548 ff.
as related to prejudice, 298
Self-assertion, 170, 221 ff.
Self-awareness, beginnings of, 165
Self-blame as a factor in suppression of anger, 374
Self-concept of kindergarten children as related to later school achievement, 179
Self-consciousness, 168
"Self-demand" feeding schedule, 126 ff.
Self, development, assessment, and ramifications of, 163–195

Self-discipline, 140
Self-discovery, as source of joy, 317
Self-effacement, as defense against anxiety, 357
Self-esteem, as related to timing of sexual maturity, 32
Self-evaluation, as related to control of anger, 371
Self-help in eating, 129
Self-initiated activity, 16, 211, 316
Self-initiated aspects of children's thinking, 466
Self-initiated behavior as a medium for early intellectual development, 112–113
Self-pity as expression of jealousy, 377
Self-regard and regard for others, 181–182
Self-repair, 23
Self-selection of food, 127
Self-understanding:
capacity for, 193–195
implications of, for education, 550 ff.
influence of teaching on, 184–185
Sensory-motor intelligence, 443–444
Sensory-motor phase of intellectual development, 106 ff.
Sentence formation, development of, 419 ff.
Sentient self, the, 166
Separation anxiety, 354
Separation from parents, 204
Seriation, 445, 448
Sex, awareness of anatomical aspects of, 186
Sex, developmental aspects of, 123 ff., 137–138, 320 ff.
Sex differences in:
aggressiveness, 259
chromosome structure, 26, 54
game preferences, 301
incidence of imaginary companions, 396
infants' reactions to humanlike representations, 94
intellectual performance, 189
language development, 428
open display of anger, 370
prenatal and paranatal abnormalities, 53–54
social interests, 189

Sex differences in (*cont.*):
standards of self-appraisal, 190
susceptibility to brain damage, 53–54
various aspects of development, 187 ff.
Sex experiences prior to puberty, 321–322
Sex organs, tumescence of, in infant boys, 138
Sex-role identification, 186–192
Sexual activity:
in dreams, 412
influence of dream deprivation on, 413
Sexual behavior:
in Kibbutz children, 215
recollections of, 291
Sexual maturity:
early or late onset of, as related to other traits, 32
sex differences in onset of, 188
Sexuality:
as related to the elimination processes, 137
genetic aspects, 41
infantile, 138
Shyness, 246
Siblings:
intelligence of, 36–37
relationships, 239
resemblances in intelligence, 489
rivalry, 254 (*see also* Jealousy)
Singing, influence of training on, 13
Sinistrality (*see* Hand preference)
Size:
at birth and later, 31
development of concept of, 445–446
Skills, influence of, on social competence, 260–261 (*see also* Motor development)
Sleep:
brain-wave patterns in, 402 ff.
daily aspects of, 130–133
rapid eye-movement phases of, 402 ff. (*see also* Dreaming)
"Slow learner," 503–504
Smiling, 85, 244, 246

Social acceptance, measurement of, 278
Social behavior, development of, 84 ff., 243 ff.
Social class (*see* Socio-economic status)
Social development:
  as related to motor development, 151–152
  interweaving of, with perceptual and emotional development, 86
"Social distance" between sexes, 296
Social facilitation, as a factor in development of thinking ability, 463
Social orientation in self-appraisal, 190–191
Social perception, 244
Social pressures against expression of emotion, 311–312
Social relations, role of make-believe in, 390–391
Socialized speech, 425–426
Socio-economic status as related to:
  abnormalities of pregnancy and childbirth, 53
  aggressive behavior, 259–260
  attitudes regarding schooling, 178–179
  complex ramifications of, 291 ff.
  conceptual development, 450–451
  delinquency, 293
  exposure to anger, 369
  expression of emotion, 292
  game preferences, 300
  intelligence, 492
  language development, 428
  maturity of moral judgment, 509
  motor ability, 155–156
  projection of self into future roles, 178
  self-assessment, 178–179
  sex-role identification, 192
  social development and behavior, 290 ff.
Sociometric procedures, nature of, and resulting findings, 251, 278 ff.
Soothability, variations of, in neonates, 65
Space, perception of (*see* Perception of depth, Geometric forms)
Spectator observer, 6–7

Speech, difference between spoken and written forms of, 467
Speech sounds in infancy, 416–417
Speech (*see* Language)
Speed of movement, developmental changes in, 151–152
Spermatozoa (*see* Physical basis of heredity)
Spontaneous acquisition of concept of number 448
Stability and change in:
  dominance and submissiveness, 534
  intelligence, 531
  patterns of social behavior, 533 ff.
  physical characteristics, 531
  school achievement, 531
  sociometric ratings, 280
  temperamental characteristics, 89, 532
  various trait clusters, 535–537
Stability of self-ratings, 185–186
Stanford-Binet Scale, 481
Step-parents, reaction to, 216
Stimulation and deprivation in infancy, influence of, on later development, 97–101, 207, 209–211
Stimulation, need for, 315–316
Stimulation (*see* Environment)
"Stored-up anger," 373
Story completion as projective technique, 399
Strabismus, 53
Strangeness, fear of, 333, 338
Strangers, fear of, 329, 333–338
Strength, developmental changes in, 151–152
Strictness, parental, 229
Stuttering, as related to shift in hand preference, 159
Styles of thinking, 468 ff.
Subjective and objective dimensions of a child's world, 5–6, 21
Sucking, 60, 121 ff.
Sucking:
  as related to cognitive development, 106 ff.
  as related to sexuality, 123 ff.
Sucking response, conditioning of, 76–77

"Sucking schema," 106 ff.
Suppression:
  of anger, 372 ff.
  of feeling, 310–313
Symbolic meaning of gifts, 317
Symbols:
  graphic, recognition of, 439–440
  of social class, awareness of, 294
Sympathy, development and manifestations of, 252 ff.
Synaesthesia, 397
Syntax, learning of, 420 ff.

T

"Target-seeking" tendency in physical growth, 31
Taste reactions in the neonate, 62
Taylor Manifest Anxiety Scale, 358
Teacher, potential role of, in promotion of mental health, 550 ff.
Teacher ratings of children's anxiety, 361
Teamwork, 269 ff.
Temper, loss of (*see* Anger)
Temperamental characteristics in early childhood:
  and later behavior problems, 546–547
  and parent-child interactions, 234
  and susceptibility to jealousy, 378
Temperament, style or distinctive characteristics of, 87 ff.
Temptation, resistance to, 513–515
Tenderness, as related to parenthood, 198
Terror dreams, 401
Test anxiety, 359 ff.
Test Anxiety Scale for Children, 359 ff.
Tests of creativity, 500–502
Thematic Apperception Test, 125
Thematic as compared with analytic thinking, 469
Thinking:
  as revealed by children's questions, 431–433
  by means of make-believe, 385–386

Thinking (*cont.*):
development of (*see* Cognitive development)
training of, 462–467

Thought:
as related to language development, 434–435
processes during sleep, 408–409

Threshold of responsiveness, 88

Time and age, children's questions concerning nature of, 431–433, 461–462

Topological shapes, recognition of, 438–439; 440

Touch, as "mother of the senses," 436 (*see also* Haptic perception)

Toxemia of pregnancy, 52

Transformation, as related to logical thinking, 444

Trisomism, 40

Trust, beginnings of, 417

Tumescence in infant boys, 138

Twin resemblances in:
intelligence, 33 ff.
motor ability, 153–154
personality, 529–530

Twins:
genetic characteristics of, 35
language development in, 428

U

Unconscious processes, 22
in anxiety, 349 ff.

Unconscious processes (*cont.*):
in dreams (*see* Dreaming)
in self-evaluation, 180 ff.

Underachievement, 494

Undernourishment and hazards of pregnancy, 53

Understanding, growth of, 414 ff.

Unpleasant dreams, 407–408

Upward mobility, 295
as related to self-assessment, 179

V

Verbal learning (*see* Language)

Virtues, regarded as important, 515–516

Vision:
early refinement of, 83–84
in the newborn, 61–62
predominance over other sensory modalities, 436 (*see also* Perception)

Visual aspects of early cognitive development, 107 ff.

Vocabulary, growth of, 419 ff.

Vocalizations:
of infants of deaf parents, 91
nature of in infancy, 415

W

Waiting ability, as related to imaginativeness, 389

Walking, 146 ff.

Weaning (*see* Sucking)

Wechsler Intelligence Scale for Children, 482

Weight at birth, 142

Wheel toys, developmental changes in use of, 149–151

Wholeheartedness and gradation, 17

Wickedness, ideas concerning, 517–518

Wishes, age changes in specific and general content of, 456

Wit as a response in anger, 373

Word realism, 425

Working mothers, 216

Worries, 337 (*see also* Fear)

"Worst happenings," as compared with fears, 326

X

XX and XY chromosomes, 26, 188

Y

"You," frequency of use in early language development, 424–425

Z

Zygote, 26